FULFILMENT
AND BETRAYAL
1975-1995

Women
Singular Encounters
Of a Certain Age
More of a Certain Age
Speaking for the Oldie
Asking Questions
In Conversation with
Insights
Dialogues
The Old Ladies of Nazareth
The Boy in England
In Touch with His Roots

FULFILMENT AND BETRAYAL
1975–1995

NAIM ATTALLAH

QUARTET BOOKS

First published in 2007 by
Quartet Books Limited
A member of the Namara Group
27 Goodge Street
London WIT 2LD

A catalogue record for this book
is available from the British Library

ISBN 978 07043 7121 7

Typeset by Antony Gray
Printed and bound in Great Britain by
T J International, Padstow, Cornwall

For My Four Beautiful Goddaughters

PHOEBE FORD

NADIA ABDUL MASSIH

JOSEPHINE PIELE

MARIELLA RYECART

It is notorious that the memory strengthens
as you lay burdens upon it, and becomes
trustworthy as you trust it.

THOMAS DE QUINCEY
Confessions of an English Opium Eater

Preface

For this volume of memoirs, covering the years 1975 to 1995, I have chosen to write in the first person. 'The boy' in my first effort in autobiography, *The Boy in England*, grew into maturity to become the banker in the succeeding volume, *In Touch with His Roots*. Now in *Fulfilment and Betrayal*, the banker completes his transformation into a man in charge of his own destiny. I become myself, as it were – writing as 'I' because no other narrative device could give events the same degree of authenticity.

Many things happen over a period of twenty years. Some are joyous, others turn your life upside down and threaten to undermine all that you have worked tirelessly to achieve. The good and the bad need to be looked at with the same detachment. The former should never be allowed to lull you into feeling too secure and the latter should not in any circumstances force you into abandoning your principles. To be complacent is to be vulnerable.

I have endeavoured throughout the complex twists and turns of these memoirs to relate events as they happened, without sanitizing any aspects for fear of causing controversy. It is a project I would never have embarked upon if I had had to exercise restraint for the sake of avoiding disquiet in certain quarters. I realize that my own perception of things will not necessarily coincide with the views of others, but most of the incidents described are substantiated by documentary evidence. Any resulting debate can only help to shed additional light on the chronicle.

During these years I was equally active in two parallel worlds: that of the arts through the Namara Group and its main publishing wing, Quartet Books; and that of the luxury-goods trade as chief executive of the Asprey group. It was not always the case that these two worlds sat well together, for each had its own quite distinct ethos. These memoirs frankly describe the internal conflict that beset some of my plans for moving forward, especially when the constraints of high corporate office made the going pretty hard, as when I was at Asprey. My loyalties there were in constant turmoil. And my health suffered as a result.

If, in the course of emphasizing a point, I draw on relevant background information, then this is in order to give a fuller picture of the subject and not as a means of settling scores. Any criticism levelled is without rancour or malice. I have tried to be as objective as possible, hoping to avoid any accusation of tunnel-vision. My detractors may not agree with some of my judgements, but I suspect the instinct of self-preservation lies behind the tendency of some to refuse to accept the facts and to rely on the principle: If something goes wrong, blame it on others. It takes a steely character to admit a failure but a weak one to absolve himself from any responsibility.

However, it is not all gloom in the pages that follow. Life had its lighter moments, its lunatic escapades and its determined efforts to uphold the rights of any repressed or dispossessed minority. And above all, in both my spheres of operation, I tried to provide a forum for the young, for future achievers, for the disgruntled and for those seeking a better environment with less conventional boundaries in which to realize their full potential.

Do I have any regrets? Not on the whole. Perhaps I could have been more alert for signs of impending danger; more prudent over decisions made in haste; less combative in fraught situations. But again these were processes through which much wisdom was gained and a measure of humility gratefully accepted.

NAIM ATTALLAH

Acknowledgements

So many people helped me in the compilation of this large volume of memoirs. Some jogged my memory about particular events, others graciously contributed their own recollections, written in their own words and faithfully reproduced within the book. To all of these I convey my heartfelt thanks for their generosity of spirit and for their friendship.

A particular mention goes to my editor, Peter Ford, who had to put up with my constant nagging and my manic obsession with deadlines. Now, with the task completed, he has no doubt suffered from withdrawal symptoms as his life has reverted to a structured normality that perhaps eluded him during the fifteen months it took to finish the work. The resulting peace is certainly well earned and he deserves all the accolades possible for having stayed the course without a murmur of complaint. My gratitude to him is boundless. My grateful thanks go as well to my copy editor, Rosemary Gray (formerly Graham), who has laboured meticulously over checking and correcting the final text and proofs for this volume of my memoirs, as she did for the first two.

And last but not least I pay tribute to my wife for her encouragement throughout the ordeal of writing this volume, when she, too, reminded me of things I had clearly forgotten and gave a boost to a slightly fading memory.

The moving finger writes; and, having writ,
Moves on: nor all thy piety nor wit
Shall lure it back to cancel half a line,
Nor all thy tears wash out a word of it.

from *The Rubáiyát of Omar Khayyám*
translated by Edward Fitzgerald

One

There is a nineteenth-century saying: 'What the fool does in the end the wise man does at the beginning.' I was never sure in which category I belonged. There were times when I was an odd mixture of the two. Sometimes I faltered at the start and redeemed myself at the end; on other occasions the reverse was true. But I always learnt the lesson, even if I forgot it soon after. That, in brief, was the essence of my life – a long hazardous journey, punctuated by great moments of triumph and short periods of disenchantment.

My business career in banking and commerce followed a somewhat unconventional pattern, and 1975, a year of major diversification, proved true to form. Opportunities opened up and my agenda began to brim with new enterprises. Show business was one of them. John Asprey and I had become directors of Paradine Co-Productions Ltd, a company formed with David Frost to produce a new film adaptation of the story of Cinderella. The script, based on the French version of the folk tale written by Charles Perrault in the late seventeenth century, was to be a collaboration between Bryan Forbes and the song-writer brothers Richard and Robert Sherman. Bryan was an experienced actor, scriptwriter and director who had worked on many successful films, among those he directed being *Whistle Down the Wind* and *The L-Shaped Room*. The brothers Sherman, whose previous credits included such hits as *Mary Poppins* and *Chitty Chitty Bang Bang*, were to write the score, which would include twelve original songs. Bryan would direct. It was an ambitious project requiring a budget of two million pounds and John and I secured this from an overseas source.

In May we announced the film was going into production. Richard Chamberlain, famous for his role as Dr Kildare in the television series, was to play the charming prince, with a relatively unknown young actress, Gemma Craven, as his Cinderella. Others in the cast included Margaret Lockwood and Kenneth More, Michael Hordern and Dame Edith Evans. An unusual amount of press coverage followed the announcement, focusing on my involvement. The journalist George Hutchinson, who had been a friend since my early days in England, featured me in his weekly column in *The Times* as 'the one who intends to save the British film industry from eclipse . . . for which', he added, 'we would have cause to thank him'. Others took a more political approach, the show-business journal *Variety* heading its report, 'Palestinian Financier Invades Showbiz with Shangri-La Coin', while the *Jewish Chronicle* asserted that there were 'No Strings to Arab Film Money'. The film's profile received a further boost when the Queen Mother, accompanied by Princess Margaret, visited the set at Pinewood Studios to watch Bryan Forbes directing his illustrious cast.

Since several scenes for the film were shot on location in Austria, I went with my wife Maria and son Ramsay, then aged eleven, to stay five days with the crew. It was a novel and exciting experience that left us with some vivid memories. Richard Chamberlain pranced around, looking rather effete in his costume and keeping to himself most of the time, whereas the rest of the cast were more sociable and warm. Kenneth More in particular displayed an affable humour and entertained us with some amusing stories. He had an immediate rapport with Ramsay, taking him under his wing throughout our stay to explain all the intricacies of film-making. Kenneth closely resembled in real life the characters he had portrayed on screen in films like *A Night to Remember*, *Genevieve* and *Northwest Frontier*. He was a British actor of the old tradition, possessing a special quality of poise and charm all but extinct today. In his memoirs, *Kenneth More or Less*, he recollected the scene we shot in Southwark Cathedral by special dispensation of the bishop, Dr Mervyn Stockwood, when the aged Dame Edith Evans, who had only one line in the scene, 'That girl ought to go', kept nodding off. Every time Kenneth nudged her awake she immediately delivered her line, 'That girl ought to go', with impeccable professionalism.

All the signs for the film, given the title of *The Slipper and the Rose*, looked promising. This was in wide contrast with my first theatrical venture, where the outcome had been less than happy, despite the project being a new presentation of *Happy End*, the musical play by Berthold Brecht and Kurt Weill set in a Chicago dancehall. Although its song numbers, such as 'Surabaya Johnny' and 'The Bilbao Song', were in vogue and the critical reception was respectable, the public failed to turn up in sufficient numbers. After a short run it folded. The *Sunday Times* wrote of its demise under the heading, 'Naim Attallah: not upset'.

I had no time to brood. Earlier that year I had been producing a unique musical documentary on Bahrain, with Herbert Chappell of the BBC as director. This came about through a brief association with Yorkshire Television when I acted as a consultant on their series *The Arab Experience* by Anthony Thomas, a follow-up to his universally acclaimed trilogy *The Japanese Experience*. The atmospheric music for the soundtrack to *The Arab Experience* had been provided by a group of local street musicians in Cairo, and the result had a fascinating sound. It occurred to me that it might be given a Western flavour to make it more appealing to listeners worldwide. The appreciation of ethnic forms was far more limited then than it is today. The music industry had yet to introduce 'world music' as a whole new genre. What I had in mind for the Bahrain film was a score which would give rise to an album capable of capturing a small corner of the record market.

When the publisher Alexander Macmillan, now Viscount Stockton, came to have lunch with me one day in my office at Wellington Court, I mentioned the idea *en passant*. His immediate reaction was more positive than I expected, and he suggested approaching the composer David Fanshawe, whose album *African Sanctus* had recently been released and attracted a lot of attention. In this Fanshawe had treated the sounds of Africa in much the mode I was describing. And so it came to pass: I commissioned Fanshawe, who readily accepted the challenge. EMI produced the record, *Arabian Fantasy*, in association with Namara Music, and it hit the shops at the same time as the documentary film, under the same title, was screened by BBC 2. The success of this project put me in a state of euphoria which fuelled a moment of utter folly. I had a sudden grandiose vision of how *Arabian Fantasy* might be staged in the Royal Albert Hall as an extravaganza featuring Arabian music and dancing, with all the exotic sights and sounds of the Middle East, from harem girls to real camels. No sooner did the thought occur to me than I went into action. A lead dancer, Ludmilla Nova, was engaged, the hall was hired and a performance date was set for 2 April 1976.

Only a few days before the performance, on 24 March, *The Slipper and the Rose* received its première at the Odeon, Leicester Square, having been selected as the Royal Command Performance film for the year. As I stood waiting to be presented to the royal patrons, the Queen Mother and Princess Margaret, the press-camera lights flashing all around, I felt I had entered a new world. What a journey I had travelled since the early days of my marriage, when we lived in a small flat in Holland Park that did not even have its own bathroom. There, in sheer frustration, with my life still going nowhere, I once wrote a fan letter to my hero of the time, Marlon Brando – hoping to find a way into the film industry. Of course, I received no reply. But here I was now in this select line-up, among stars and show-business celebrities. The Sherman brothers, being American, were every bit as elated as I was to be waiting to meet the Queen Mother and Princess Margaret. The Queen Mother took everything in her stride. One of the brothers had a girlfriend in tow – a stunning blonde, dressed to kill and exhibiting a most impressive cleavage. The Queen Mother didn't bat an eyelid.

Afterwards, along with David Frost, Bryan Forbes and Stuart Lyons, we partied till well beyond midnight and sent out for the morning papers to read the press notices and comments. Critics hailed *The Slipper and the Rose* as a shining example of what the British film industry was capable of achieving if given the chance. The *Evening Standard* emphasized the fact that it was a British musical with British stars and a British director, which had provided four months of much-needed work for Pinewood Studios. All the excitement and acclaim was probably the reason why, in my eagerness to keep the impetus going for the *Arabian Fantasy* production, I never paused to reflect on the possibility that I was attempting to transform the Royal Albert Hall into a bizarre circus that the music itself could never sustain. I was convinced that the enterprise was going to make a star of our lead dancer, Ludmilla Nova. Baroness Ludmilla von Faiz-Fein of Lichtenstein was a twenty-four-year-old beauty who was quite entrancing and came with impeccable credentials. We had developed a close friendship since I had first got to know her many months before. She was often to be seen cycling to my office at Wellington Court for afternoon tea. Ludmilla introduced me to her mother, and to her stepfather, the novelist Paul Gallico, who worshipped Ludmilla and dedicated several of his books to her. He even inscribed some to me, writing on the title page of one, 'To Naim, the character I wish I had invented.'

The mistake I made with the *Arabian Fantasy* extravaganza was that I depended too much on the leading professionals I had hired to oversee the entire production and did not allow enough time for proper rehearsals. The focus of my efforts was to fill the Royal Albert Hall through the show's promotion, and I very nearly brought it off; but the result was an audience that was probably out of its depth with such a production. There were many there from the City alongside those from the world of show business, and a large number of celebrities whose presence was merely cosmetic. From the very start the night was destined to be the most embarrassing of my entire career. It was obvious that everything about the show was a shambles. It lacked coherence and was badly choreographed. Both David Fanshawe and Ludmilla gave it their best shot, but they were defeated by the sheer implausibility of the exercise. The whole concept was wrong and its execution amateurish. I felt too ashamed to emerge from my box in the interval as I saw members of the audience leaving by the score. The critics had a field-day panning the show. A scathing piece in the *Guardian* concluded, 'Naim Attallah, the entertainment financier who commissioned this expensive joke, is also a director of Asprey. I enjoyed his associates moaning in the bar that they didn't dare leave before the end.'

Never again, I promised myself, would I embark on such an undertaking without assuming full responsibility for the proceedings. Sadly I failed in my ambition to make a star of Ludmilla – it was not possible on the basis of one night's performance. It was not her fault; it was mine. She was just a victim of the fiasco.

Meanwhile the drift of events was taking me steadily closer to the mainstream of publishing, subsequent to the collaboration of Namara Publications, a subsidiary of my company Namara Ltd, with Quartet Books in publishing three coffee-table volumes. One of these was based on the Yorkshire Television series of documentaries *The Arab Experience*, with a text by Michael Deakin written jointly with the director Anthony Thomas, and Robin Constable as photographer. The second was based on an independently commissioned documentary on Oman entitled *The Last Corner of Arabia*. Michael Darlow was the director, and he and Richard Fawkes collaborated on producing the text. The photographs were by Robin Constable and Peter Middleton. Then a third volume followed, a book on Ras al-Khaimeh written by Michael Deakin and again illustrated with Robin Constable's photographs. With that venture behind me, I was poised to take the plunge into the world of serious publishing.

Another significant development was set in motion in late 1975 by George Hutchinson's arrival at my office in Wellington Court with a proposition. He wanted me to accompany him to Pakistan, having received an invitation to visit the country from President Zulfikar Ali Bhutto through his secretary of information Nassim Ahmed. Some years before, Mr Ahmed had been a political correspondent for a Pakistani newspaper reporting on the British House of Commons at the same time as George was fulfilling a similar role for the *Evening Standard*. It was a trip George very much wanted to undertake, but his fear of flying held him back. If I agreed to travel with him, he said, it would go a long way towards helping him overcome his phobia, adding that there would be no problem with securing an additional invitation for me.

It was a proposal hard to turn down. Two weeks later the journey began. We were accorded full VIP treatment and taken on a grand tour of the country as far up the Khyber Pass as the Afghan border. We met President Bhutto twice and were impressed by the breadth of his intellect and his shrewd analysis of world affairs. He dressed immaculately and oozed charm. His presidential environment was as finely tuned as his wardrobe, with opulence much in evidence wherever he went. A banquet was held in our honour to mark the occasion, and as his fêted guests we enjoyed every aspect of his generous hospitality. Bhutto was without doubt a man of outstanding charisma. I soon warmed to him as formalities were pushed gently aside and a natural rapport seemed to develop between us.

A few weeks after my return to London I was pleasantly surprised to receive a telephone call from Bhutto. He spoke about a manuscript he had just completed which summed-up his political philosophy, and he said he would like to see it appear in book form. Would I be prepared to pass it on to Quartet Books? Overwhelmed by his telephone call, I said of course I would. Bhutto then added that his friend, Professor Hugh Trevor-Roper, later Lord Dacre, had encouraged him to take that route and would be willing to help if needed. The manuscript arrived by way of the diplomatic bag. I read it closely, and it seemed worth publishing for two specific reasons, even though it might have a limited appeal in the United Kingdom. First, the sale of the book in Pakistan would be substantial – the Pakistani authorities would ensure it. They would distribute copies to visiting heads of state and other notables, which would have a knock-on effect in promoting Quartet Books. Secondly, it would give the imprint a foothold in a country whose cultured élite would recognize the list as being both trendy and readable. In the wake of *The Arab Experience*, *The Last Corner of Arabia* and the book on Ras al-Khaimeh, the Bhutto book fell into place and was published in January 1977 under the title *The Third World: New Directions*.

A few months later I returned to Pakistan with Michael Deakin of Yorkshire Television. We were again the guests of President Bhutto, who, having heard of my association with David Frost, wished to sound me out on the possibility of an interview to be conducted by David and produced for television by Paradine Co-Productions Ltd, our joint company. David was then at the zenith of his career and an interview with him was likely to be given international coverage. Michael, who had to his credit the hugely successful trilogy on Japan and the Arab world, came along as both adviser and friend. We flew to Karachi and were taken on a tour of Pakistan that included such highlights as lunch with the Khyber Rifles in their mess, with all the regimental silver on display, and an excursion to Lahore to visit the famous Red Mosque.

As soon as I was back in London the filming arrangements were put in place. A camera and sound crew were dispatched to Pakistan, with David Frost in his customary role of interviewer and John Birt, the future director-general of the BBC, heading the outfit as producer. The programme had been completed as planned without a hiccup when the unfortunate fact emerged that not a single network would be willing to show it. Their grounds for turning it down were that because the finance for it came from the Pakistani government it would look suspiciously like a promotional exercise. Barely two years later, Bhutto was unceremoniously deposed by a coup led by the army chief of staff he had himself appointed, General Zia ul-Haq, and suffered the indignity of being incarcerated like a common criminal in the worst possible conditions. He was accused of having conspired to murder one of his political opponents by an ambush in which the opponent's father died. Many commentators insisted that the charge was a frame-up and remained convinced that after his trial his eventual execution by hanging was a shameful and cruel act of expediency and revenge. Bhutto had been in many ways ahead of his time, and I felt sure that at his death Pakistan lost a leader of exceptional ability and flair. There can be no limits to the savagery meted out to fallen leaders in the often dirty game of politics. In 1980, a year after Bhutto's judicial murder, Quartet reissued his book *The Third World* with a foreword by Hugh Trevor-Roper.

Trevor-Roper was clear in his opinion that Bhutto, the first civilian to rule Pakistan, had been in his day 'the ablest statesman in Asia' next to Chou En-lai, but that he had also harboured 'vast ambition, acute personal sensitivity, great pride, even vanity', and herein lay the seeds of his downfall. 'My vision,' Bhutto had stated, 'is that of a Pakistan whose social standards are comparable with those in parts of Europe. This means a war against illiteracy and ignorance. It means fighting prejudice and obscurantism. It involves the equality of men and women.' Better education, better health, a better environment and the restoration of human dignity were all part of his programme. He founded the instantly popular Pakistan People's Party to realize these goals and foster his concept of a 'middle way', called bilateralism, for the unaligned nations, to enable them to work towards economic independence in the context of world trade and development.

Professor Trevor-Roper saw Bhutto as a tragic figure in the classical sense, brought down by hubris, and his death as a disaster for his country, which, after his repudiation, 'stood in greater need than ever of his political ability'.

From the moment of General Zia's usurpation, it was clear that the new regime would never take root as long as Bhutto was alive. If elections were held, the People's Party would undoubtedly win them, for Bhutto was still the hero of the people. If elections were not held, Bhutto would be a formidable opponent who would never leave the usurper in peace.

Therein lay the reasons for his death. The spirit of the martyrs may live on, commented Trevor-Roper, but unfortunately 'the intelligence . . . is buried with their bones'.

Two

In June 1976, barely ten years after the crash of Intra Bank, chronicled in my book *In Touch with His Roots* (published by Quartet in 2006), and only two months after the *Arabian Fantasy* débâcle at the Royal Albert Hall, I achieved my most cherished dream: to become a publisher and to be able to call myself a man of letters. This was the ambition I had conceived long ago when, as a boy aged eleven in Palestine, I had produced my first publication – a daily stencilled handwritten broadsheet. At last my dream came true through the association of Namara Publishing with Quartet over the publishing of *The Arab Experience*, *The Last Corner of Arabia* and the book on Ras al-Khaimeh. These three titles spearheaded my entry into serious publishing under the Quartet banner in my new role as proprietor of Quartet Books.

The Quartet Books imprint had its origins in the autumn of 1970 when four executives with Granada Publishing began talking about setting up their own company. Within Granada they had contributed to making the Panther Books subsidiary into probably the most strongly individualistic paperback fiction list at the time after Penguin. Having concluded their plans in the utmost secrecy, they handed in their resignations to Granada on 1 May 1972, a date that was highly significant. On the same day they launched their share-offer document on to the financial market. By choosing May Day they were nailing their colours to the mast and declaring their intention of becoming a radical publisher, broadly left of centre, championing the underdog while pursuing a boldly adventurous programme. The four Granada executives were Ken Banerji (sales director), John Boothe (editorial director), William Miller (editorial director) and Brian Thompson (sales director). With Quartet their aim was to form a collective executive, with John Boothe and William Miller maintaining their ideals for a non-hierarchical structure. The financial background to the project had been carefully explored and it had been agreed that backing would best be raised via loan-stock financing. William Camp, a bestselling author and former head of information at British Steel, was also invited to join the board to advise on public relations and share his valuable City and media contacts. They had calculated they would need a capital of three hundred and fifty thousand pounds to put into operation their innovative plans, which included issuing titles in both hardback and paperback simultaneously. Carmen Callil, who was then running her own public-relations company, undertook to mastermind the promotion of the new company to the media and gained maximum coverage. Quartet Books became news in the national press. 'The best ideas in years to cut the cost of new books . . . A very different kind of new publishing', was the assessment of the *Sunday Times*. 'Some good publishing brains and bright ideas', wrote *Publishers' Weekly*.

In the event, the board raised two hundred and sixty thousand pounds, which was not as much as they had hoped for but was nevertheless a considerable achievement in the general financial climate of the early 1970s. Significant amounts of interest and goodwill were also generated, and authors such as Angela Carter and Michael Moorcock came forward to offer projects, as did various agents and other publishers. At the Frankfurt Book Fair in the autumn of 1972 they laid out their manifesto: 'Although Quartet plan a wide variety of books – fiction, social history, politics, natural history, the arts and sex – it aims at a sharp identification through the cooperative spirit within the company. It is a socialist company and its theme will be quality without élitism.' It was hoped that, with the help of a small but expert production staff and the backing of experienced editorial freelancers, the first titles would be ready for publication in March 1973. This ambition was slightly over-optimistic as there was a further delay before contracts could be signed and advances paid, pending the incorporation of the company. Distribution arrangements were then put in place and the first titles appeared at the end of May 1973, featuring all three planned formats: hardback originals, semi-hardbacks (christened 'Midways') and traditional paperback reprints. And so the building of the Quartet list could begin.

Quartet Midways represented an entirely new concept: a hardback-sized volume with a heavy paperback binding wrapped in the same jacket as the simultaneous hardback. They were attractive to authors as they allowed an extended print run and gave the public a choice of prices. Hardback editions meanwhile remained essential for libraries, and the media also insisted on receiving only hardback copies for review. There was therefore no getting away from publishing certain titles in dual editions. Soft-cover quality productions are familiar to literary editors, readers and booksellers today, but in 1973 the Midways were ahead of their time in a book trade that was essentially conservative and traditional. The cutting-edge approach was also represented by one title in particular that was seen as being of pivotal importance in Quartet's initial publishing strategy: *The Joy of Sex* by Dr Alex Comfort.

The book was brought to Quartet under conditions of secrecy by James Mitchell and John Beazley, the founders of the progressive book-packaging and publishing company, Mitchell Beazley Ltd. Both men had been with

Thomas Nelson & Sons – as editorial director and production manager respectively – at the time in the 1960s when the venerable Edinburgh firm was seeking to re-establish itself as a London general-books publisher after being bought by the Thomson Group. Among James Mitchell's projects at Nelson there had been an adventurous if short-lived series called 'The Natural History of Society' that came under Alex Comfort's editorship. One of the titles in the series was Dr Comfort's own book, *The Anxiety Makers*, a study of the lengths to which the moral guardians of former times had been prepared to go to abolish masturbation and prevent 'nocturnal emissions', by mechanical means if necessary. Besides his writings on sexual matters, Alex Comfort was also known as a poet, novelist and anarchist, and a distinguished researcher at London's University College into the biology of ageing. After the breakaway from Nelson it was a natural progression for James Mitchell to pursue with him the idea that a new type of sex manual was called for following the watershed defeat of Britain's moral guardians at the *Lady Chatterley's Lover* trial of 1960. It was felt that the public would be ready for a view of sex free from anxieties and guilty hang-ups concerning sexual preferences, with graphic illustrations to show couples in the many varieties of erotic embrace.

For internal reasons, hinted at as relating to objections to the book raised by John Beazley's wife, Mitchell Beazley was looking for a way to avoid publishing the *The Joy of Sex* under its own imprint in the home market. The project fitted well with Quartet's taboo-breaking ethos and the offer was signed up immediately for the first season's publishing, committing a sizeable advance of six thousand pounds. The rights were to run for ten years and were for all UK and Commonwealth editions, hardback and soft cover. Mitchell Beazley were to arrange the printing abroad of all the colour editions and receive a price per copy inclusive of royalty.

The course to publication, however, did not run smoothly. Dr Comfort became nervous about the possibilities of prosecution. There was some reason for concern as aspects of the obscenity laws under liberalized conditions had never been tested, especially with regard to erotic illustration. In 1963, when Neville Armstrong, the proprietor of Neville Spearman Ltd, bought the British rights to a translation of a Swedish sex manual, *An ABZ of Love* by Inge and Sten Hegeler – described as an 'A to Z guide to sex information', he had been advised that some of the drawings it contained would be vulnerable to legal action. He had gone ahead and published, but left blank spaces in the book where the illustrations should have been as a protest against hypocrisy.

In the case of *The Joy of Sex*, it became necessary to seek clearance from the Director of Public Prosecutions before it could be published. This was obtained once it was agreed to drop some erotic Japanese prints from the illustration list, though the negotiations for them had taken many months. Customs and Excise meanwhile would agree to no such dispensation. Mitchell Beazley did succeed in bringing in a hundred and fifty early selling copies through Heathrow, but another two thousand English-language copies were seized at Gatwick and destroyed by order of a magistrate. As a consequence, production of the UK editions had to be done entirely in Britain, thus forgoing the cost advantages of printing abroad and importing the books. Full-colour, full-sized hardback and paperback editions were finally published in Britain in 1974. In late 1975 Quartet followed through with a black-and-white paperback they had originated entirely by themselves, as they were entitled to do under the contract, which stated that only Mitchell Beazley could produce copies in *colour*. They had never thought the colour plates could be converted successfully into black and white, but this edition sold many thousands more copies than the colour versions.

The Joy of Sex, together with its sequel *More Joy of Sex*, also published by Quartet, soon took its place as a legend in publishing history. Alex Comfort enjoyed several years of living in California as an established sexual-lifestyle guru – though towards the end of his life he came to regret the way the notoriety overshadowed all his other achievements. Quartet's sales eventually topped seven hundred thousand copies, but the delays to the original publication had cost them dear, with major effects on budgets and cash-flow.

The 'winter of discontent' took its toll at the end of 1973 as Edward Heath's Conservative administration strove to contain industrial unrest. There were power blackouts and the 'three-day week'. The pound found itself in deep trouble and interest rates for borrowing rose to fifteen per cent, and eventually to seventeen per cent. 'Servicing the debt,' in the recollection of John Boothe, 'became the critical problem for the company.' Despite this shadow, there was no lack of variety or loss of vigour in the way Quartet pursued its goals. In mid 1974 Carmen Callil asked for help with handling production, selling and distribution for a new new feminist imprint, Virago, she was founding with Ursula Owen. Some of the first Virago titles, including Mary Chamberlain's important work of oral history, *Fenwomen* (the very first Virago book), and Nancy Friday's anthology of female sexual fantasies, *My Secret Garden*, were published under a joint Quartet/Virago imprint, though Virago continued to be a financially independent company until it became part of Random House UK in the 1990s.

There was always a pressure on Quartet to publish quickly, and inevitably some of the books they commissioned were delivered in a state far from ready for typesetting. Here the backing of freelance editors, including Peter Ford, who was associated with Quartet from the beginning, grew to be invaluable. Among the books that he 'enabled to come into being' (his definition of the editorial process) were May Hobbs's recollections of a Hoxton childhood, *Born to Struggle*, and the great comedian Max Wall's autobiography, *The Fool on the Hill*, in which Peter was credited as collaborating author. He also worked with the Wearside-born republican, Labour Member of Parliament for West Fife, Willie Hamilton on his dryly entertaining critique of the royal family, *My Queen and I*. Willie Hamilton was well known for his trenchant views on everything associated with the monarchy, usually expressed within the privileged arena of the House of Commons. Despite a rigorous editing to excise any of Willie Hamilton's 'acid drops', as he called them, which might have led to a libel action in the outside world – and a subsequent reading with a toothcomb by the libel lawyer Michael Rubinstein – one small damaging error of fact managed to slip through. The author had referred to Prince Charles's taking 'a crash course in Welsh, taught by a Welsh Nationalist whose party was busy planting bombs at the time'. It turned out that this was quite untrue and the first printing had to be withdrawn for amendment. The book was nevertheless accounted a success and sold two hundred thousand copies, twenty thousand of them in hardback.

The range of titles produced by Quartet in its first four years of publishing was quite remarkable. The paperback-fiction reprint list came to include such works of literary distinction as Shusaku Endo's *Silence*, George Mackay Brown's *Magnus*, B. S. Johnson's *House Mother Normal* and *Christy Malry's Own Double-Entry*, Brian Moore's *The Luck of Ginger Coffey*, Mordechai Richler's *A Choice of Enemies*, Alexander Trocchi's *Cain's Book* and Jack Kerouac's *Satori in Paris*, *Vanity of Duloz* and *Pic*. Among non-fiction reprints were the poet P. J. Kavanagh's *The Perfect Stranger*, Lillian Hellman's biographical volumes, *An Unfinished Woman* and *Pentimento*, Robert Kee's unmatched history of Irish nationalism, *The Green Flag*, in three companion volumes: *The Most Distressful Country*, *Ourselves Alone* and *The Bold Fenian Men*, and Richard Holmes's major biography, *Shelley: The Pursuit*. Holmes also published translations of a selection of Théophile Gautier's supernatural tales, *My Fantoms*, with Quartet.

There was always a strong vein of 'social documentary' in the books that Quartet originated, notable among them being Tom Hart's deeply humane *A Walk with Alan*, an account of a young life ending with a self-hanging in a prison cell after years of troubles and drug addiction. Tom Hart had worked in the children's service all his life and was at the time superintendent of Cumberlow Lodge, a remand centre for under-age female offenders in South London. He was convinced that the young people who came within his care were casualties of society and that society carried a responsibility for what became of them. He went on to publish *The Aura and the Kingfisher*, a novel about an epileptic boy in rural Yorkshire between the wars that was later filmed, and *Safe on a Seesaw: A Book of Children*, a collection of anecdotal reminiscences of the children he had sheltered. Another book of this kind was Noele Arden's autobiographical *Child of a System*, which had a foreword by the psychiatrist Anthony Storr and told of how her troubled childhood in care had led her through children's and remand homes to ECT treatment and incarceration in Rampton High-Security Hospital, certified as mentally deficient. Noele Arden had managed to escape from this cycle of acute emotional deprivation at the age of twenty-five and miraculously gone on to make a normal family life for herself.

In the field of politics there was Des Wilson's *Minority Report: A Diary of Protest 1970–73*, a collection of polemics on behalf of the homeless and minorities, published jointly with Blond & Briggs; and Peter Hain's *Mistaken Identity*, about his experience of wrongful arrest in Britain when, as a South African exile, the future minister of state for Northern Ireland was a notable figure in the anti-apartheid movement. A book that turned out to be a top-selling title was Bob Woodward's *All the President's Men*, published in the same month as Richard Nixon resigned. Topical titles included *In Sickness and in Health* by David Owen (later Lord Owen), written when he was Minister of State for Health within the Callaghan Labour government, and Stuart Holland's *The Socialist Challenge*, a major contribution to the debate on the future direction of Labour politics.

Another bestseller had been *You Always Remember the First Time*, a book of reminiscences of their first sexual experiences by various personalities, including Larry Adler, Brian Aldiss, Michael Moorcock, Emma Tenant and Carmen Callil. The editor of this was B. S. Johnson, who earlier edited *All Bull: The National Servicemen*, a similar collection of memories of National Service, published jointly with Allison & Busby. Johnson was established as the leading experimental modernist writer in English fiction, whose novels explored ways of depicting the layered, fragmented and random nature of memory. They often expressed deep feelings as well as a black sense of comedy. His earlier novels had been published by William Miller and John Boothe at Panther Books in the 1960s. It was a profound blow to Quartet, and a loss to British literature, when Johnson committed suicide while the compilation of *You Always Remember the First Time* was in progress. Michael Bakewell and the late Giles Gordon rallied round to ensure the editing was completed and the book published, and Michael Bakewell contributed a foreword.

Other bestsellers included Ross Russell's biography of Charlie Parker, *Bird Lives*, one of a number of healthy long-term sellers in Quartet's successful jazz list, the foundations for which were laid by Brian Thompson. In the area of fiction Mervyn Jones's novel *Holding On* became a TV drama and sold a hundred thousand copies, and another TV tie-in, Philip Mackie's *Napoleon in Love*, sold fifty thousand. Original fiction of interest featured a novel by the television personality and film commentator Barry Norman called *End Product*, a savage Swiftian satire on a dystopian South Africa where natives are being ranched for meat. Colin Spencer produced a surrealistic satire on relations between the fascist regime of the colonels in Greece and the Nixon administration, *How the Greeks Kidnapped Mrs Nixon* (retitled *Cock-Up* in paperback), and a serious novel on human relations, *Victims of Love*. There was a new novel from Jennifer Dawson, *Strawberry Boy*, and an important collection of stories from Angela Carter, *Fireworks: Nine Profane Pieces*.

All told Quartet had an enlightened list that won it recognition among the Hampstead literati and was not commercially driven as a first priority. Unfortunately the founders had not been sufficiently funded at the outset for their long-term plan, to buy most of the company stock themselves and become truly independent within five years, to be viable. The possibility had receded as other problems of funding developed along the way, and in a sense this was because Quartet's was an old-fashioned approach to publishing. The industry was moving away from an era in which success was the result of an indefinable element of editorial flare and enthusiasm; accountants and sales executives increasingly held sway and demanded a far more rigorous approach. A number of today's famous writers were nurtured by Quartet at the start of their writing careers and owe much of their fame and fortune to the far-reaching vision of Quartet's founding fathers. The strength of the imprint was its radical approach to the pressing issues of the day and its determination to give the underprivileged a forum to air their views and young writers with literary talent a chance to prove themselves. Against this background, however, there was another change in progress that was destined to alter the whole climate of politics in Britain. In 1975 Mrs Thatcher had ousted Edward Heath as leader of the Conservative party and begun her campaign to become prime minister four years later. One inevitable and unfortunate consequence of this would be a marginalization of matters of social conscience.

*

By the time I was involved with the company, the original quartet were down to a trio. Ken Banerji had left the team – to work with Mitchell Beazley. When I acquired eighty-five per cent of the stock and moved into the role of chairman, it brought the corporate strength back up to four. I came with excellent credentials: my birthday, too, was on the first of May.

At that stage I felt confident my entrepreneurial skills could bring an added dimension to a small publishing house such as Quartet and make it commercial enough to survive in a highly competitive marketplace. Rumours were starting to circulate that Quartet was facing financial difficulties. The buzz in town was that the imprint could be in serious jeopardy unless a rescue operation was mounted without delay. The company's initial success in what it had set out to do had won it a large measure of goodwill among the literati, most of whom were left-leaning by temperament. Latterly, however, it had embarked on an expansionist policy and, taking little account of its limited financial resources, had plunged into the mass market through a distribution arrangement with Futura Publications. Up until then, sales and distribution had been handled by Hutchinson, but it was felt that Futura would offer a more aggressive selling approach. Futura was founded and run by Anthony Cheetham, Eton-educated, the son of a well-known diplomat, who was described by many of his contemporaries as being 'too clever by half'. He had set up the company with money from Robert Maxwell, though he and 'the Captain' soon fell out. At the outset of the venture Quartet was getting a large income from its more successful titles, including *All the President's Men*, which was a surprising bestseller that generated large subscription orders in anticipation of the demand for the book continuing at an steady rate. Quartet was therefore temporarily awash with money, which it used to finance its publishing programme. But there were ominous signs on the horizon. The spectre of massive returns of unsold stock soon turned into a reality. Despondency set in among the ranks and the situation became desperate. Quartet had no reserves to fall back on, and things were deteriorating at a frightening pace.

Despite some awareness of this background, I had remained determined not to let the opportunity to acquire Quartet pass me by. I had already had the experience of publishing with the company and I was not going to draw back at this stage. I felt a certain affinity with the founders and had well and truly caught the publishing bug. That Quartet should fail to survive was unthinkable. With its lively independent thinking, it had already played a vital role in the early 1970s when the profession was dominated by the old-established gentlemen publishers and a few notable Jewish immigrants, who between them were able to exert a wide-ranging influence over what the nation was given to read.

When I stepped into the chairman's seat, the financial situation for Quartet was actually far worse than I had anticipated. None the less I convinced myself a way forward could be found and was prepared to stake my whole future on my belief. It was not as if my own finances were solid enough to embark on an adventure of this magnitude. It was a situation that required publishing expertise and ample resources in terms not only of finance but also of managerial know-how. The latter commodity was in short supply. The company's creditors were going to expect me to honour any outstanding debts at the point of takeover. There was a perception that I was a man of great wealth, which was far from the case – a fact that added to the complexity of the equation. Clearing the liabilities was one thing, but active publishing requires a fair amount of venture capital to commission books and buy rights to manuscripts, quite apart from all the production costs. Quartet had exhausted all the capital they had raised when the company was formed. Now they were in urgent need of new capital to sustain their existing list and secure a future product.

It was a dire situation. Certain liabilities, not properly recorded, began to come to light. This was not because they had been deliberately concealed but purely because of the absence of proper managerial competence. The founders' primary interest had centred on literary matters. Being left-wing activists, they had no liking for capitalism; for them money was a necessary evil. On the other hand, they were highly regarded among the publishing fraternity for their zeal and crusading spirit. I managed to muster all my resources and arranged a bank overdraft to cover Quartet's future commitments. The assessment of the funds required was still understated, however. Massive returns of stock from Australia exacerbated the company's plight. These were a consequence of the mass-market collaboration with Futura, and the drain on liquidity became endless. The situation was causing a deep dent in my finances and I was not sure I would be able to weather the storm; it was touch and go.

My priority was to change the sales arrangement and bring the agreement with Futura to an end. Anthony Cheetham in my opinion was a ruthless operator who was never going to do anyone any favours. On the contrary, he gave the impression of being skilled at making sure he always ended up on top in any transaction. I was a tyro in the trade, a man who came from nowhere and an interloper in the eyes of many. I was aware that opinions were divided as to my acceptability within the publishing community. My foray into Cheetham's world was to be my true initiation into the profession. The talks held with Futura were not without their difficulties, but ended successfully in a parting of the ways. Cheetham continued his career with various imprints, following a general pattern of high-profile ventures, not always without a controversial outcome.

The important outcome for Quartet was to be extricated from the Futura situation and from the mass-market publishing business. It could move back to controlling its own destiny without taking incalculable risks. There was one further issue to be resolved, however, and that was the relationship between the company and Carmen Callil's feminist imprint, Virago. Carmen was an Australian of Lebanese extraction and an astute publisher and publicist. There was no denying that the boys at Quartet owed her a great deal for her help in establishing the company, but the nature of the arrangement over Virago was never clarified. It was a symbiotic relationship between the two radical imprints. The early Virago books had been published under the joint imprint and the companies had shared office accommodation at 27 Goodge Street, just off Tottenham Court Road. Early Quartet catalogues contained a section devoted to Virago, and Quartet's editorial and production facilities were available to the sister company. Nevertheless the autonomy of each company was unequivocal and Carmen herself has always stressed the total independence of Virago from Quartet at that time. I continued to be mystified, as I am today, but William Miller urged Carmen to meet me as the new owner of Quartet to make whatever arrangements were appropriate for the altered situation.

Carmen hesitated, and the hesitation continued to the point where, rightly or wrongly, I took her procrastination as a snub. Eventually a meeting did take place in my office at Wellington Court, but the relationship never really recovered from the early *froideur*. Carmen was a formidable woman, as her career in publishing demonstrated. She could be like a steamroller in crushing any obstacle that stood in her path. My perception of the situation between Virago and Quartet was that the advantages were distinctly on one side, and our meeting was formal rather than amicable. It was clear that the publishing relationship had run its course and the only sensible way forward would be to part as civilly and painlessly as possible. The burden I had taken on was too great to stand any additional pressures, and Carmen would never have accepted my direction. The dismantling of the association was inevitable and I worked hard to ensure its smooth conclusion. In the long run, Virago had nothing to fear or lose. It went on from success to success through a combination of astute publishing policy and promotion in the feminist field. If I felt any aggrievement it was only on behalf of the boys, for it seemed to me that there was a singular lack of acknowledgement of the role Quartet had played in getting Virago off the ground in the first place. But perhaps I am being over-sentimental in raising the issue.

Leaving any teething troubles associated with my acquisition of Quartet on one side, the British press was highly supportive. From a public-relations point of view the move was a resounding success. Headlines varied from 'And Now an Arab moves into Publishing' in the *Evening Standard* to 'Namara Secures Control of Quartet Books' in *The Times*. A majority of newspapers reported the event, including the *Financial Times*. A full-page announcement was placed by Quartet to appear simultaneously in the *New Statesman* and the *Spectator*, to assure authors that the intimacy fostered by the company would not be diminished; that the policy of publishing new ideas and new writers on a wide range of subjects would continue. It emphasized that personal links with authors would be maintained to ensure they never became mere names in the catalogue of a conglomerate; that they would continue to have access to all the directors, not excepting Naim Attallah, the new chief executive.

Three

Although embroiled in the serious business of publishing I managed to enjoy a little light relief. Through Namara I acquired two racehorses. One was appropriately named Namara, the other Jona. Namara was a two-year-old filly, the first racehorse to be called after a company, the regulation preventing this having only recently been relaxed. Namara chalked up her first win during the last week in July and then had another the following week at Windsor. The odds were seven to one. Unfortunately, with all the pressures of business, I forgot to place a bet on her. The top racing correspondent, Charles Benson, now tipped her to complete the hat-trick by coming first at Lingfield, which she did. Jona was enjoying a similar success, and it was all put down to beginner's luck. I never claimed to know anything much about horses and hardly ever went to a race meeting. In fact the novelty of owning two horses waned quite quickly. I sold the animals for a healthy profit and congratulated myself on my good fortune in coming out of the chancy experiment so well.

Meanwhile time and effort were being spent unstintingly in getting to know Quartet better. Early suspicions and fears were dispelled as we all became acclimatized to the new situation. Responsibility was now being shared and reporting procedures were firmly in place, while freedom of operation within designated boundaries was in no way restricted. However, I insisted that I must be kept fully informed on the choice of books and the making of any new commitments. Discipline and regular editorial meetings became an important feature. Fortnightly reports on sales figures were instituted and I chaired each meeting to familiarize myself with the workings of my new acquisition and the ins and outs of this unfamiliar trade. I let none of the pressures on my time keep me from a hands-on policy, for I considered my destiny to be firmly linked with that of Quartet and I could ill-afford to fail. My characteristic obsessiveness enabled me to learn quickly. Before long I could see where my own contribution, both editorially and in sales matters, was beginning to yield results. The notion of being just a passenger was out of the question. I had to participate, otherwise I would have lost interest.

As a first step in boosting Quartet's international profile I decided to expand into the American market. Quartet USA was incorporated in New York with Herbert Nagourney, formerly of New York Times Books, at its head. Plans were made to originate the first two titles, one of which was *Tutankhamun: The Last Journey* by William MacQuitty, the film producer and photographer. The book was originally written to accompany the great 'Treasures of Tutankhamun' exhibition in 1972, and published at the time by Sphere and Nelson. Bill MacQuitty described in his memoirs, *A Life to Remember*, how it came to us some years later when the exhibition was about to be set up in America:

> I suggested to Sphere that they might reprint it. By that stage Anthony Cheetham, my former editor at Sphere, had moved on to found Futura Publications, and the new editor turned the idea down. He did, however, graciously sell me the plant for £100. Then I had a tremendous stroke of luck. At a party I met Naim Attallah, who told me that his company, Quartet, were looking for a book to lead them into the American market. I showed him *Tutankhamun*, and he accepted it instantly. To our mutual delight it sold half a million copies.

The other lead book for the American launch was *The Slipper and the Rose* by Bryan Forbes, an illustrated adaptation of the film of the same title, in which Forbes described the making of the musical version of the fairytale in collaboration with Paradine Co-Productions Ltd.

Events were gathering pace back at Quartet's London base. Marilyn Warnick, who had worked with Fred Hift as a publicist for the film of *The Slipper and the Rose*, joined Quartet to become their new PR manager. Subsequently Marilyn introduced me to a book-trade whiz-kid from the late 1960s called David Elliott. David was then running the retail-book chain, Words & Music, and he and I got on like a house on fire. He was not averse to a change of occupation; soon he was in charge of sales at Quartet and taking up the challenge with gusto, as well as betraying early signs of eccentricity. We shared certain characteristics that made for a natural alliance between us. Our working relationship could be serious and flippant at the same time. When the devilment surfaced it caused consternation within the ranks. David began to be viewed as the chairman's eyes and ears; indeed, his position within Quartet gave rise to incessant speculation and a great deal of tittle-tattle that enlivened the atmosphere. He kept me informed of any undercurrents in the rather chaotic life at Goodge Street, accepting the label of sneak with amusement. Many years later he wrote in his own book, *A Trade of Charms*, how the image of publishing he had developed as a bookseller became rather dented. 'To begin with I had thought the fault to be with Quartet, but as the months passed I came to realize that Quartet was no different from most of the other publishing outfits. It was simply more delinquent.'

His book was dedicated to me, which was very flattering, though it might be said that in the matter of delinquency there was more there than met the eye. As seemingly reformed characters, on the face of it at least, we were both in need of reminding ourselves of the early days when mischief played a significant part in our initiation into publishing. These unconventional goings-on gave life an exciting edge and meant I could enjoy hard work while dispensing with any superfluous formalities. Nothing was likely to dampen my enthusiasm once the novelty of publishing had subsided. Boredom was considered the great enemy and the only way to combat it was to have fun. In David Elliott I found a soul-mate with whom I could loosen up because restraint did not count for much in our behaviour.

On another front, I joined forces with Pan-Arab Publications, one of a new brand of companies in London which specialized in Arab magazines and newspapers, to launch a journal called *Marhaba*. Sharif el-Masry was the publisher and the other executives were Anthony Purdy and David Mealing. In Arabic *marhaba* means 'welcome'. The intention was that it should be a London guide for Arab visitors who came to London on a regular basis, year by year, in company with their female relatives. It was towards these relatives that the main thrust of the magazine was directed. One of its first articles warned Arab ladies about the dangers of pickpockets in the metropolis and the heavy penalties the magistrates imposed for shoplifting. In retrospect the magazine was not the good idea it seemed at first. I suspect there was a general feeling of relief all round when within the year it folded. The saving grace of the experiment was that I hired the girl who sold advertising on the magazine to work for me at Wellington Court. Her name was Debbie Jones and she was only eighteen.

Debbie was remarkable for her age. She went about her work like a breath of fresh air – lively, impish, outrageous, sharp and streetwise. Whenever she burst on the scene she brightened things up. Hers was the sort of disarmingly affectionate nature that beguiles even as it wreaks havoc. There were many occasions when inevitably I gave her the sack but routinely re-engaged her soon afterwards. Debbie remained steadfast in her loyalty over the years, and never faltered when the going got tough.

*

In the middle of December 1976 the Asprey family found themselves embroiled in a dispute over the future ownership of Asprey, whose fate was rumoured to be in the balance. Mr Philip Asprey and his son Maurice held forty-seven per cent of the shares, and were accused by Mr Eric Asprey and his son John, who had an equal number of shares, of being in cahoots with an organization called the Tunalt Family Foundation. This mysterious Liechtenstein company was in possession of the balance of six per cent of the shares, acquired from Mr Algernon Asprey when he was pushed out of the firm in 1971. John Asprey suspected a conspiracy to take over the company and leave his side of the family in the doldrums. It all boiled to the surface on the eve of the company's annual general meeting when the board of directors received information that the re-election of Naim Attallah, a director with special responsibility for finance and the Middle East, who had joined the board in 1974, would be opposed. The prime mover in this bid to oust me was understood to be a Mr Alan Grieve, a solicitor with Taylor & Humbert, who represented the foundation. Mr Grieve was believed to have the support of Philip and Maurice Asprey. But when the AGM was held on 18 December, the board of directors, in an unexpected display of solidarity, voted unanimously to support my re-election by a show of hands. Mr Grieve continued to oppose my re-election by virtue of his client's six per cent equity interest and insisted that the matter should go to a poll.

The story of this row prompted a variety of headlines in the British press. The *Daily Mail* took the most sensational line with 'Arab at Centre of Asprey Battle', while the *Daily Telegraph* was more sombre with 'Director's Seat in Peril on Asprey Board'. The *Financial Times* took its usual low-key approach with 'Asprey Control Disagreement Possible'. When the adjourned AGM was eventually reconvened on 14 January the outcome of the poll almost unanimously confirmed my re-election. Mr Grieve swung into a face-saving exercise by explaining that the poll had only been to gain time and now he had given his vote in my favour. There were certain reassurances that he understood had been given by me to the board during a family meeting held earlier in the week. Furthermore, he stated, he was acting on information given to him by Mr Maurice Asprey and his legal advisers, who had said that, in addition to these unspecified 'assurances', a decision had been reached to appoint a merchant bank to act as advisers to the company alongside other moves to strengthen the board. The veracity of these statements was strenuously denied by John Asprey and myself and we asserted categorically that there were no strings attached to my reappointment; and the suggestion of appointing a merchant bank was absolute nonsense. The meeting ended with a truce, but one that did not last long.

The atmosphere at Asprey became tense, though John and I stuck firmly to the principle of business as usual and carried on with our current drive to boost exports; and despite the underlying conflict at home, to improve the figures. Asprey was on an upward spiral and no family feud was going to impede its progress. Board meetings became grim and cheerless affairs where business was conducted in an adversarial mood. There seemed to be a total breakdown of trust between the warring parties. I found myself becoming the main target, accused of being the cause of all the dissension between the family members. The truth was that it was my support for Eric and John that rankled with the other side. It was this support, they reckoned, that was giving Eric and John the tactical edge. If matters remained as they were, then they would certainly be the losers in the battle for the control of Asprey and their ambition to see Maurice become the next chairman of the company would never be fulfilled.

As a matter of record, the next thing to happen was that I was approached through my solicitors, Biddle & Co., with a proposal. If I agreed to withdraw from the family firm, then a large compensation package would come in my direction. It was a third-party approach and the identity of those behind it remained concealed. I flatly refused to have any truck with whoever was behind this treacherous manoeuvre. The battle had turned into a personal one and I was not prepared to back off from the confrontation that would finally determine the fate of Asprey.

Then the unexpected happened. Philip Asprey wrote a letter to his brother Eric, in his capacity as chairman of Asprey, informing him that his side of the family, including his son Maurice, had decided to sell their entire share-holding in the company, though a purchaser had yet to be found. The reason he gave was that the divisions within the family were too deep to be resolved. Eric read the letter to the directors and then tabled it at a board meeting that was held on 7 March 1977.

With this event the battle for Asprey had taken on a new dimension. The power struggle within the family was openly shifting to embrace third parties, with Philip and his family holding the key to any future developments. The decision to sell was a recipe for much wider conflicts in which they were likely to play a crucial part before the sabres were put back in their sheaths for the last time.

*

Such tension as was to be found at Quartet was of a different kind. The frustrations of the past few months, when problems rather than products had been the main preoccupation, gradually fizzled out as progress was made on all fronts. The important thing now was to make up for lost time. It was a race against the odds if we were to transform Quartet into a viable publishing house that would win its place in the market as swiftly as possible. Meanwhile I continued with the Arab list that had catapulted me into publishing in the first place. I commissioned from the Irish novelist Edna O'Brien a coffee-table book on the Gulf State of Abu Dhabi. Her agent, Patrick Seale, talked her into taking up the assignment. Her usual publisher, George Weidenfeld, was furious that she should be doing a book with an Arabian theme, and especially with me. According to informed sources, I was always referred to by George in an undertone at dinner parties as 'that *man* from the PLO'.

Edna left for the Gulf to do her research, with me as her host throughout her stay. On a daily basis she was looked after by my sidekick in the region, Jonathan Mermagen of the Al-Manara Trading Co. Jonathan was very popular locally and able to drive her about and introduce her to anybody who mattered. She was a good travelling companion, though she had her foibles. She could not stand it if the least speck of light invaded her bedroom at night; nor could she tolerate the faintest of sounds. Either of these intrusions would drive her into a state of near paranoia. Before she retired to bed she would mask her eyes and stuff her ears with cotton wool so she could slumber away in the total darkness and silence of the night. Her appearance caused her much concern and she needed constant reassurance about how she looked. Unwittingly she showed signs of vanity but they were charmingly inoffensive, except that at times their repetitive nature made them irritating. After a few drinks her conversation would turn to morbid talk of death and tales of her unhappy childhood and she seemed to have a fascination with the occult. Edna was in love with youth and could not come to terms with the ravages of time. Her ideal would have been to remain eternally beautiful and forever desirable. Some of Edna's personal habits reminded me of that great Italian film actress Anna Magnani, a glamorous Mother Earth totally without inhibition.

The trip itself was filmed by ITV and I appeared briefly in one shot, walking with Edna along the sea front at Abu Dhabi. After she got back to Britain she wrote a prose poem, which the *Observer* newspaper claimed was Edna's way of thanking her host. Whatever her motive, it was a beautiful poem and we incorporated it into the book, which was published in the November of that year under the title *Arabian Days*; we also reproduce it here:

The images cede, recede, because there is so much. Faces of the East, skins like prunes, like peonies; hooded hawks, hooded women. The spires of concrete towering up. Such audacious monstrosities. The mosques' roundness, like basins of white. Inside the praying, stooping, supplicating men – O Allah the Almighty, the All-Merciful. A little file of trees starved for rain. The water merely lodges in the air, the humidity catching the breath and making crinkles of one's hair. In the desert beyond are the blazing torches of flame, the burning bushes, the pillars of fire such as we Christians were forewarned of for the last day. Some women wear capacious dresses, bright blue chiffon with crusts of stars affixed. The workers in the backs of lorries are piled in; their headgear more significant, more noticeable, more telling than their very faces. Coils of baked cloth. A man is what? His genitals? His wives? His mind? His money? A man is what? The city pulsates under the din of cranes, drills and motor cars. The wayside is a shock of sand, white, merciless, unpretty. There is no romance here, how could there be? The air murmurs with money. A bright glaze hovers and simmers across the city. A bird of passage, I wait, I wait.

One literary critic remarked of *Arabian Days*:

such language reveals the author's underlying frustration at being excluded from a society she does not really seem to understand and has not a great deal of sympathy for, although admiration does come through, particularly when dealing with those people still living in the desert. This is interesting enough a book none the less for one highly individual woman's look at a nation far removed from her own experience in the throes of rapid and unprecedented change, illustrated with obvious sensitivity by Dutch photographer Gerard Klijn.

Another illustrated book that I undertook to publish in the same period was *Dhows* by David Howarth, the author of such popular works of naval history as *Sovereign of the Seas* and *Trafalgar*. He was also well known in the Arab world for *The Desert King*, his magnificent biography of King Abdul Aziz, the founder of the kingdom of Saudi Arabia. Dhows were the ancient sailing ships of the Arabian seas and are the oldest type of ship in use today. The largest wooden vessels still being built, they continue to ply the trade routes in the sea lanes they have navigated for four thousand five hundred years. There are at least a dozen different types of dhow, each one of them unique in the modern world. One particular design can be shown to be at least a thousand years old, and even the most recent types date back to the seventeenth century. Among them can be recognized ships of the same shape as those that carried the English armies to Agincourt and Crécy, or that were used by Columbus and Vasco da Gama, or which the Stuart kings sent off to the East in search of spices. In fact the dhows represent a living museum of ship-building history.

David Howarth traced the origin of dhows right back to Sumerian times and even asked, 'Was Noah's ark a dhow?' In the modern world it may not be possible for the dhows to survive much longer, and this was my main motive in commissioning the book, with photographs by Robin Constable. *Dhows* was published in 1977. It was deeply satisfying to be making such an important addition to the record of Arab culture.

Four

With the departure of Virago from the Quartet fold and the emergence of feminism as a serious movement, I felt there was space for a new feminist list that would both reflect one of the most exciting political currents in society and make commercial sense. Early in 1977, William Miller had the vision to suggest that I meet Stephanie Dowrick, who was at the time managing editor of Granada's Triad list of backlist authors. She was a New Zealander, aged twenty-nine, who had been living in Europe for nine years. Before her Triad role, she was managing editor at New English Library, and so had proved her ability to take on huge responsibility. William and his colleague John Boothe had been trying unsuccessfully for a while to persuade her to publish some 'women's interest' titles with Quartet on a consultancy basis. With William's encouragement, I made an approach and at a meeting late one afternoon at my office in Wellington Court found Stephanie matching my enthusiasm for the ideas I was putting forward. As she remembered it many years later, I said, 'We are talking about the wrong thing here' – referring to the possibility of a consultancy with Quartet. 'Have you thought about setting up your own publishing house?'

Having 'arrived curious, but without any real expectations', she said, 'I left with the offer of setting up my own publishing house!' During our meeting, she recollected,

> We talked, summed one another up, laughed and clicked. It wasn't sexual. It was, however, mutual admiration! I have thought about it often and think it is that we are both quick, highly energetic, daring, somewhat impatient (especially you!), passionate and articulate, and, crucially, we were – in London – both outsiders. I am sure I was completely dazzled by this possibility. I know that when I left your office – and I remember walking along the streets outside too elated to get into the tube – I was walking on air. Yet, at the same time, I was almost appalled. (And had I had the slightest idea of how hard it would be to set up and run a publishing house I would have said no. Thank heaven I didn't!)

A week or so later we had another meeting to discuss the framework. I was to take financial responsibility while Stephanie would be in charge of editorial decisions and the day-to-day running of the company. There was to be no outside investment. It was set up with a hundred one-pound shares, with me holding fifty-three per cent and Stephanie the balance of forty-seven per cent. The new company was formed within the Namara Group and given the title of The Women's Press. Its logo was a steam iron, which besides being a play on the word 'press' mocked the repetitive nature of much of women's work and suggested such phrases as 'full steam ahead' or 'don't be oppressed'. To begin with, Stephanie was the only full-time employee and the whole operation was started in her sitting-room in her house in Bow. For a while she continued with her work for Triad and gave The Women's Press her evenings and weekends. Sibyl Grundberg, formerly senior editor at Hart-Davis MacGibbon, joined Stephanie in early 1978, and an aims-and-policy statement was formulated. Stephanie did not see herself as a missionary figure but believed in women working together to take control of their own lives and make their voices heard. The objective of The Women's Press would be to reach a double audience of committed feminists and those non-feminists who wished to read first-class fiction and quality non-fiction across a whole range of subjects, including environment, peace, health, psychoanalysis and social issues. The Press aimed for an initial annual output of about sixteen titles. It eventually grew to be several times that number with an exceptionally active list of perennial sellers. 'Prices,' the early statement added, 'will be as low as financial survival will allow.'

The first titles to appear from The Women's Press were published in February 1978 and had a strong literary flavour. They were Jane Austen's *Love and Freindship* [*sic*], her early burlesque on romantic fiction from her manuscript notebooks, appearing in paperback for the first time; the first edition in Britain of *The Awakening*, the only novel by the American writer Kate Chopin, a work that had been considered scandalous when it was first published in 1899; Sylvia Townsend Warner's first novel, *Lolly Willowes*, originally published in 1926; the first twentieth-century edition of Elizabeth Barrett Browning's 'verse novel' about the life of a woman writer, *Aurora Leigh*, with an introduction by Cora Kaplan; and *Lives of Girls and Women*, an important collection of stories by the contemporary Canadian writer, Alice Munro. That first list was strong, but did not represent the theoretically adventurous books which were to follow. Those more typical books were going to take a little longer to develop and acquire.

Coincidentally, at the Cannes Film Festival I happened to see a film called *The End of August*, adapted from Kate Chopin's *The Awakening*. It was a low-budget film produced in America by an independent company seeking a distributor for it in the UK. The standard of acting was high, the story was hauntingly lyrical and the film had been beautifully produced. Although I had little experience in film distribution, I took a chance and acquired the rights, arranging a limited showing throughout Britain. I continue to believe that the story has a magical feel to it on screen and that *The End of August* has a lasting quality.

Feminism represented a new area of publishing at the time, indeed the word 'pioneering' became a vital part of my vocabulary. I was eager to be in the vanguard of this new cultural revolution, one that was far removed from that in Mao's China in the 1960s. The women's liberation movement, as it was then called, was inspiring women to examine their domestic or business lives and have the courage to assert their rights and make their opinions felt right across society. It was part of the unstoppable wave of social change of which the civil rights movement in the United States was a part. Because of its beginnings as a radical movement, however, the public mind saw feminism as being too strident and extreme and under a largely lesbian influence. As time went by, however, it began not so much to mellow as to broaden its concerns and engage women from the mainstream of the population, who were encouraged to join the ranks. By the late 1970s, feminism was attracting increasing interest from all women concerned with issues as varied as equal pay for equal work, maternity and legal rights, and healthcare, as well as education and other forms of what was called 'consciousness raising'. Women addressing issues from a 'women-focused perspective' was still a provocative concept, but women's publishing was to play a key role in developing and refining the arguments.

There was still a long way to go before feminists would be generally accepted as a force for good, seeking reform and justice in matters of sexual discrimination. The media in Britain was not in the main a supporter of feminism. When the advent of The Women's Press was reported as a 'Diary' news item in the *Evening Standard*, for example, the heading given to the piece was 'Yet More Feminism'. 'I woke up this morning,' the writer expressed his reactions, 'feeling that the sun was shining, the daffodils were blooming and goodwill should be dished out to all mankind. But the moment I picked up a hand-out announcing yet another publishing venture, the sun did rather recede a bit.' With 'yet another' he was referring to the fact that Virago had announced their relaunch the previous week.

The launch of The Women's Press nevertheless got a great deal of press coverage, and Hatchards in Piccadilly devoted a whole window display to the first titles. It was a good start and an office was quite quickly set up in Shoreditch High Street, long before London's East End had gained any sort of fashionable status. Stephanie was soon into what would be a five-year spell as managing director, and the Press was fast moving towards the point where they could begin to publish titles they had themselves commissioned. *In Our Own Hands*, a self-help therapy treatise by Lucy Goodison and Sheila Ernst that was part of a widespread movement to share more broadly the insights of therapy – and was a precursor to the 'self-help' movement that dominates so much of publishing today – was the first originated book to be published by The Women's Press. But many others followed. Among the first novels was Michèlle Roberts's *A Piece of the Night*, which came in under the proposed title 'Swimming towards Blue' and was to be a big success both for the Press and the author.

The look of the books was always a passionate consideration for Stephanie and the attention she gave to their design as well as to the editing was an important factor in their success. Suzanne Perkins was the original designer or art director for most of the covers and publicity materials. Stephanie was adamant that the books should look innovative and smart, despite the financial constraints under which she was working because of the strict limits on The Women's Press overdraft. Stephanie and I, perhaps inevitably given the differences in our experience and ideological allegiances, had our ups and downs in our negotiations, but always ended at a position of mutual respect. At one point Stephanie had to fight to defend her editorial independence when I developed misgivings over whether the list was turning out to be too radical. She won her case, but while she preserved editorial autonomy, it was never possible to add to this the financial autonomy she really must have wished for. She also found herself having to field broadsides from the press, and criticism from some feminists who queried how The Women's Press could be a genuine feminist outfit if it was being bankrolled by a man. (Although, to be fair, she worked very hard to make the Press financially self-sufficient.) Later on the columnist Penny Perrick wrote a piece on me in the *Standard*, headed 'The Man Who Finances Feminism'. It quoted me as comparing the company I ran to a woman, describing it as 'dangerous, unpredictable, attractive'. There were times, too, when I found myself coming under fire from the direction of Shoreditch High Street for publishing material that Stephanie perceived as pandering to male chauvism. My friendship with Stephanie survived everything.

Notwithstanding all the constrictions it had to work under, The Women's Press went from strength to strength. Generating a widespread debate about pornography, they published two books on this subject simultaneously, one by Susan Griffin and the other by Andrea Dworkin. They were also pioneers in the field of art history, publishing ground-breaking books on women artists and on individual artists, such as Gillian Perry's book, *Paula Mondersohn-Becker*. Eventually the Press also had its crime list, with authors like Marcia Muller and

Val McDermid, a science-fiction list under the guidance of Sarah LeFanu, and its teenage Livewire list, which featured titles for young adult women on such topics as teenage pregnancy, vegetarianism and bullying. From the early 1980s there was also The Women's Press Book Club that offered at substantial discounts some of the best of women's writing from across the range of British publishers.

The most spectacular of The Women's Press's commercial successes was Alice Walker's *The Color Purple*, later made into a film by Steven Spielberg. The Women's Press had published Alice Walker's books from the late 1970s, and those of other black woman writers like Toni Cade Bambara, at a time when mainstream British publishing houses were convinced that writing by radical black women could not possibly sell. But over the next two decades there were many other titles that achieved sales figures which would make publishers today feel envious. Among these were Marge Piercy's *Woman on the Edge of Time*, Janet Frame's *An Angel at My Table*, Flannery O'Connor's *A Good Man is Hard to Find*, Elaine Feinstein's *Inheritance* and May Sarton's many books, including her classic, *Journal of Solitude*.

Stephanie left the Press and Britain for a successful writing career in Australia, but several of her books, including the best-selling *Intimacy and Solitude*, were published by the Press in the 1990s. She was followed in the managing director's role first by Ros de Lanerolle and then later by Kathy Gale, each of whom brought their own view of feminism and of publishing to the task. Summing up that early period of truly creative publishing, Stephanie has said what an incredible privilege it was 'to be able to bring together my professional and political passions in the form of The Women's Press'.

> It was, literally, the opportunity of a lifetime and I was hugely grateful. That it was also complex and sometimes extremely challenging didn't take [away] from the amazing opportunities that it gave me to publish books that I believed were genuinely important and even life-changing, and to get to know and work with some truly exceptional writers. The opportunity honed my intellectual life, my professional skills, and I think it significantly contributed to the person I have become. It demanded a great deal of courage, but it also gave me courage.

*

Quartet in the meantime had also been making news, for the company wasted no time in demonstrating to the media and the public that it represented a new force in publishing which was not to be ignored. This was its message on many occasions when it found itself at the centre of some intense controversy. It was also beginning to be noticed in the United States. On 24 June 1977 the *New*

York Times reported that Quartet had, in an unusual arrangement, signed a distribution agreement with Horizon Press. Founded by Ben Raeburn in 1951, Horizon was one of the foremost independents in America. Mr Raeburn, a legendary figure in New York's publishing circles, was most famous for having published the complete works of Frank Lloyd Wright in handsome editions embossed with the late architect-philosopher's signature. He was also well known for his ability to perform each of the dozen and a half tasks needed to see a book into print. Among the writers he published was the powerful but neglected British novelist James Hanley; the literary critic and historian Irving Howe, who wrote *Politics and the Novel: A World More Attractive*; the film critic Parker Tyler; and the art critic Sir Herbert Read. The first batch of Quartet USA titles to be distributed by Horizon would, Herbert Nagourney announced, include *New Irish Writing*, edited by David Marcus, with a preface by V. S. Pritchett; *Arabian Days* by Edna O'Brien; and *In Sickness and In Health* by Dr David Owen, who had by then moved on from the Department of Health to become Britain's Foreign Secretary.

Back at Wellington Court in March 1978 I made another impetuous decision and acquired the distribution rights to a fifty-three-minute documentary about the Holy Shroud of Turin by David Rolfe called *The Silent Witness*. The film's religious content had been thought to put a limitation on its commercial appeal and none of the conventional cinema chains was willing to take the risk of showing it, claiming that it would attract very little attention from the cinema-going public. I was convinced otherwise and acting on the strength of this conviction I formed, in partnership with the film-makers, a joint company called S. J. Film Distributors and set about finding somewhere where the film could be shown. I approached Grand Metropolitan Hotels, who owned what was then the Metropolitan Hotel in Piccadilly, with the proposal that they transform their banqueting hall into a new London cinema expressly to screen *The Silent Witness* for the public at large. They took me up on my idea and we held a special preview for a congregation of interested religious groups of various denominations. The dignitaries attending included four bishops (those of Southwark, Fulham and Gibraltar, Kennington and Stepney), forty vicars and assorted ministers, a number of Salvation Army representatives and the Reverend Chad Varah of the Samaritans.

The film was of the first attempt to use scientific technology to investigate whether the shroud could indeed be the true burial cloth of Jesus Christ, as millions have believed. After it opened on 27 March it was a runaway success with audiences, playing eleven performances a day through to 4 May; then opening again to run through June and July. Against all the odds, it had attracted long queues outside the hotel and the publicity that resulted helped to compound its commercial success. Later it was shown on television in Britain and abroad, and received critical acclaim despite its controversial subject. The experiment confirmed my belief in the use of unconventional means to achieve an objective.

*

At Asprey the truce had been short-lived. The atmosphere had turned so sour that it began to lower morale not only in the boardroom but in every department throughout the firm. The vibes of discord were spilling over into the showrooms and beyond, while John Asprey and I continued in our usual way to do everything we could to safeguard the company's interests while the feud continued to fester. Then it began to take on sinister proportions. Unbeknown to either of us, a Lloyd's underwriter, Michael Poland, who was Maurice Asprey's brother-in-law, had instructed a firm of private detectives to trail us in the hope of unearthing something unsavoury that could be used against us: primarily to oust me from the board and then to secure John's removal in the wake of the coup. The campaign against us came to a head in a court hearing in May 1978, though it had been set in motion in December 1976 by a memorandum addressed to Eric Asprey, John's father, in his capacity as chairman of Asprey. Both John and I, Mr Poland alleged, were engaged in disreputable activities and had been instrumental in publishing a pornographic book, *The Joy of Sex*. Dr Comfort's book, in his opinion, leaned towards perversion and was far from being innocently instructional. Was it in Asprey's interests, he asked, to be associated with neo-pornography? These assertions ignored the fact that the *The Joy of Sex* had been published by Quartet long before I was associated with the company, quite apart from the sheer nonsense of suggesting it was a pornographic book. It was also pushing credibility way beyond its limits to suggest that John could have played an active role in Quartet's publishing programme.

The memorandum was really the culmination of a period of relentless vilification, and by that stage we had both had enough of it. As a result we took great exception to the document, though in retrospect it might have been better if we had ignored it and treated it with the contempt it deserved. We were so angry, however, that reason deserted us and we set in motion libel proceedings against Michael Poland. What we did not foresee was the deluge of unwelcome publicity a scandal of this proportion was likely to bring down upon us. Asprey had always had a high profile through its royal patronage and upper-establishment connections. But by now there was no turning back. We hired Robert Alexander, an eminent QC of the day, and the case came to court before a jury; and inevitably the press went to town and sent the reverberations ringing round the nation. 'A Jewel Duel at Asprey', said one headline. 'Gem Firm Chiefs Sue over Porn Book Libel', shouted another. 'The Memo that Split the Queen's Jewellers', said a third.

Throughout the trial hearing Michael Poland maintained he had given the memorandum to the chairman in strictest confidence and that it was protected by qualified privilege. He denied having sent the memorandum to stir up alarm and animosity within the board of directors, and claimed that as a member of the family by marriage he had a duty to protect its interests in what he saw as the best way possible. Mr Poland's account of his motives was to our ears disingenuous and distorted, yet it seemed to punch a great deal of weight with the jury. They were persuaded that he had acted, however erroneously, to protect his family and there had been no malice in his action. They considered their verdict and they found in his favour. The judge, in his deliberations, proved to be far less concerned with the merits of *The Joy of Sex* than with the technicality of whether the memorandum was protected by qualified privilege.

Yet again the press made a meal of the result and John and I found our pictures emblazoned across the nation's newspapers. We were naturally looking quite shocked and grim, for the way the verdict had gone had taken everyone by surprise, not least the defendants. We were reeling not only at losing the case but also because we were liable for the costs of the action. These came to the then considerable sum of ten thousand pounds. There was nothing we could do except to pick ourselves up, dust ourselves down and resume our normal lives.

*

Uproar erupted on the publishing front with the appearance of two Quartet projects at the end of that September of 1978. The first was an object lesson to any publisher swayed by the twin attractions of controversy and publicity: a book by a journalist, Anthony Pearson, *The Conspiracy of Silence*. It purported to be an investigation into the little-known attack on the US spy ship *Liberty* by Israeli planes and torpedo boats three days into the Six-Day War of 1967. The raid had been carried out off the Egyptian coast in international waters. Despite the ship's clearly visible markings, thirty-four American servicemen were killed and a hundred and seventy-one injured within fifteen minutes. The Israelis always insisted that it was a 'regrettable accident', the *Liberty* having been mistaken for an old Egyptian troopship, and both sides worked to keep the profile of the incident muted. It was reported that the US government eventually paid out four million dollars in compensation to the *Liberty* survivors and the families of the dead. Pearson, a former war correspondent, claimed that during his probings he was offered two hundred and fifty thousand dollars by unknown persons to drop his investigation and had papers burgled from his flat. He was also, he said, shadowed, pressured and cajoled in attempts to get him to withdraw his account of this bizarre political conflict, the details of which were wilder than any invention in spy fiction. His findings were so controversial that no one would publish them in America apart from *Penthouse* magazine, which ran them in two parts in May and June 1976. The book, as published by Quartet, was based on those articles and incorporated additional material in which Pearson described the many threatening things that he said had happened to him subsequently.

This story of the deception and intrigue engaged in by the security forces of both the United States and Israel as they attempted, behind the screen of chaotic events, to change the map of the Middle East in ways to suit their respective purposes was rich material for conspiracy theorists. At the time there had still been no admission from Israel that the Six-Day War was a pre-emptive rather than a defensive action and it suited the Western powers to accept the official Israeli line. Pearson's book was panned by the critics for its implausibilies and flights into fantasy, which undermined the case he was trying to make. Later books have been published about the *Liberty* incident, some of which are just as improbable as Pearson's. The most authoritative is probably *Assault on the Liberty* (1980) by James Ennes, who had been the cryptological officer on board during the attack. It seems that the primary concern of the *Liberty*'s mission in the Mediterranean was to listen for Soviet intercepts, and Israeli radio transmissions were fatally ignored. Sadly it turned out that Anthony Pearson, when he was working on his account, was suffering from the effects of a terminal brain tumour. He died not long after the book was published.

The second event landed far more on target: wickedly biting in concept and hilarious in execution. This was the launching by Quartet of the *Mrs Thatcher's Handbag* kit, ostensibly to celebrate the new leader of the Conservative party, who was already being hailed as a political messiah. 'The Thatcher Bag is full of tricks', said the lapel badge that was to be found among other items inside the facsimile of a handbag fashioned out of stiff card. Mrs Thatcher's worshippers were flocking to her altar in hordes. My oldest friend in Britain, the correspondent George Hutchinson, who knew the British political scene better than anyone, having served the Conservative party and its leadership in various capacities over two decades – he had accompanied Harold Macmillan on his visit to the Kremlin for talks with Nikita Khrushchev – became quite besotted with her. He could not stop singing her praises and seemed striken with awe whenever he was in her presence. In his view, she was the best hope we would ever have of making Britain great again. The sentiment was shared by many who had become disillusioned with the failure of successive Labour and Conservative administrations since the war to bring to heel not only the trade unions but also the fat cats in the City, who were equally guilty of abusing the system. This mood for change and Mrs Thatcher's coming were in precise conjunction. She was a figure to be revered but certainly not lampooned.

The idea for *Mrs Thatcher's Handbag* was dreamed up in a pub by William Miller, David Elliott and Marilyn Warnick, and brought into being by a group whose presiding genius was the satirist John Wells. Apart from the lapel badge there was a postcard with the words 'Greetings from Barnet, Finchley' in the top left-hand corner and a picture of a smiling Mrs Thatcher among her fans giving a two-fingered Churchillian 'V for victory' salute the wrong way round. There was a Mrs Thatcher mask with elastic to enable any admirer to turn themselves into a Mrs Thatcher clone. There was a cardboard paper doll of a naked Mrs Thatcher, which could be coloured in and cut out to be dressed in clothes for different occasions and to be given each day of the week a different hairstyle that was always exactly the same. Among the doll's accoutrements were a brooch, a serviceable wristwatch and a 'defeat knife in back'. A fold-out poster headed 'Mrs Thatcher's Pearls' had a portrait photo of the lady surrounded by a string of her pearls of wisdom, each circle containing one of the famous pronouncements that had marked her political career up to that point. To pick a few of these gems at random:

'Don't forget I'm the grocer's daughter. I lived over the shop. Everyone has to go to the grocer's to buy food, so I met all sorts.'

'The fatuous upper-class image they tried to pin on me is really laughable.'

'We are all unequal. We believe that everyone has the right to be unequal.'

'I can't understand the fuss about student grants. Carol managed to save out of hers. Of course, we paid for her skiing holidays.'

'Rudyard Kipling once said the female of the species is more deadly. You might keep that in mind.'

'My skin's natural. I can't help looking clean. It maddens me sometimes that people don't realize that when you scratch my skin you come up against steel. I'm tougher than Barbara Castle only I don't look it.'

'The charm of Britain has always been the ease with which you can move into the middle class. It has never been simply a matter of income, but of a whole attitude to life, a will to take responsibility for oneself – the middle-class morality that Shaw despised so much.'

There was also a floppy 45 rpm record that had two songs written by George Melly set to music by John Chilton. The first was 'Maggie's Song', sung by Jo Manning-Wilson accompanied by the 'Synco Pinks'. It began with a preamble that parodied *My Fair Lady*:

MAGGIE: Oh, Professor Higgins, I want to be a lady in a flowery hat in Parliament, running Britain instead of selling at the corner shop in Grantham. But they won't take me unless I talk more genteel.

PROFESSOR HIGGINS: I'm sure you're a business girl. How much will you pay me for the lessons?

MAGGIE: Well, our Ted got his French lessons for tenpence an hour from a *real* French gentleman, but I won't give more than fivepence for my *own* language. Take it or leave it.

PROFESSOR HIGGINS: What do you think, Whitelaw?

WILLIE WHITELAW: Higgins, m'old fellow, I'll bet you the expenses of her wardrobe that you can't turn *this* woman into the leader of the Conservative party.

PROFESSOR HIGGINS: I'll go one better. I shall make prime minister of this draggle-tailed creature.

Then Maggie launches into her song:

I'm plucky little Maggie, I've got a little song.
I sing it everywhere I go, it isn't very long.
Though the Lords may think I'm common and the yobs may say I'm posh,
I'm a trueborn Tory lady, and it won't be all by gosh.
I'm Maggie, I'm Maggie, and my teeth are gleaming white.
They shine out like a beacon through the naughty Labour night,
But as Mr Heath can tell you they inflict a nasty bite,
So you'd better cast your vote for Maggie Thatcher.

I'm snappy little Maggie, I'm as neat as apple pie.
My seams are never crooked, I keep my powder dry.
I've a lady name of Peggy, she's employed to take good care
When I speak the table linen doesn't clash with what I wear.
I'm Maggie, I'm Maggie, and I'm clean from top to toe.
My fingernails immaculate, my skin is all aglow.
But when it comes to dirty tricks there's none that I don't know,
So you'd better cast your vote for Maggie Thatcher.

I'm liberated Maggie, wear the trousers, wield the stick.
Stopped Denis giving interviews, he always drops a brick.

They asked him what my hobbies were, he really is a clown,
He told them all I really like was letting my hair down.
I'm Maggie, I'm Maggie, and I won't put up with that.
I won't be misinterpreted and forced to eat my hat.
But I let him pour my double Scotch and then put out the cat,
And of course he'll cast his vote for Maggie Thatcher.

I'm lucky little Maggie, I've almost got it made,
Because you see I'm quite prepared to call a spade a spade.
I'm a friend of Mary Whitehouse, though we only meet at night,
When I lead old Silly Willie to the Festival of Light.
I'm Maggie, I'm Maggie, I know what people think
But don't like to admit to, unless they take a drink.
And so I say it for them and lead them to the brink
To cast their vote for marvellous Maggie Thatcher.

PROFESSOR HIGGINS: All right, you win, Willie, but if I'd had another four
years . . .

On the flip side of the record was the 'Song of the Silent Majority', delivered
by 'More Jelly' ('Good-time George' himself in another guise) accompanied
by the 'Synco Pinks' and 'Sturdy Voices':

List to that hum from every suburb rising,
That murmur on the packed commuters' train.
Hark to the men who meet out exercising
Their labradors in steady Surrey rain.
Over the flick and fizz of gin and tonic
On the eighth green above the driest pond,
We wish to break a silence catatonic
And give a welcome to the wrath to come.
Back the workers not the shirkers,
Send the wogs all back.
Flog the muggers, castrate the buggers,
And abolish income tax.
Gaol those rotters known as squatters,
Force the unions to disband.
Having freed us, Maggie lead us,
Safely to our promised land.

You shall enforce the reign of law and order
On football terrace and in underpass.

Treble the pay of every prison warder
And kick do-gooders firmly up the arse.
No more free milk, school dinners or abortion,
Your orders shall ring out in national lives.
When all's restored to its correct proportion
We'll reap the harvest of free enterprise.
[*Chorus*]
Back the workers, etc.

Oh let the strong deserve the double measure,
Nature itself treats with contempt the weak.
The brigand is entitled to his treasure.
The very birds mob up to kill the freak.
Freedom's a word implying limitations,
Freedom for us to batten on to them.
Britain shall yet again comprise two nations,
So clear your throats of any liberal phlegm.
[*Maggie's voice joins in as cheer leader:*]
'Let's hear it, hot and strong!'
[*Chorus repeats, and fades . . .*]
Back the workers, etc.

Last but not least in the pack there was *Managing: A Guide to Modern Etiquette*, a forty-page booklet penned on Margaret Hilda The*tcher's behalf by John Wells himself on the standards of behaviour needed for the brave new Tory world that was emerging. Its text was brilliantly funny on every page. 'When you enter a Conservative home,' began Chapter Two on 'Home Truths', 'you will sense at once that something is different.'

You know you are among people who *care*.
About *things*.
That is why, as Tories, we favour the neutron bomb.
Because it is *kinder* to *property*.
Of course we care about people as well, about the kind of people we are prepared to have in the house.
And that is where *you* come in. Or not, as the case may be.

As soon as *Mrs Thatcher's Bag* was released, all hell broke loose. The Tory press mislaid its sense of humour. Quartet was condemned for having sunk so low – the *Bag* was the pits, the epitome of bad taste. The Tory faithful were certainly not amused and Mrs Thatcher herself was furious. She demanded to know who was behind this project, only to be told it was a friend of George

Hutchinson's by the name of Naim Attallah. George, who by then had moved close to Mrs Thatcher, found himself being unceremoniously rebuked. My friendship of so many years with George was truly shaken by the incident and there followed a period when he and I were hardly on speaking terms. It took a long time to get back on to our old footing.

In fact the *Bag* did nothing to harm my prestige. In reporting its advent and the controversy it generated, the *Evening News* said how

> the Tory-bashing 'Bag' shows that Palestinian-born Attallah, 47, is no propagandist for any particular viewpoint. Indeed, Quartet's list is one of the most diverse in publishing, with titles ranging from Labour MP Willie Hamilton's *My Queen and I* to Tory MP Ian Gilmour's *Inside Right* and the bestselling *All the President's Men*, not forgetting to mention *In Place of Fear*.

This latter title was by Aneurin Bevan, my first political hero.

Five

Because of the number of high-profile roles I had been assuming, I inevitably found myself in the public eye. Just as inevitably, perhaps, it meant I was turned into a target for *Private Eye*, whose editor at the time was Richard Ingrams. The first shot in a relentless campaign of mockery was fired on 5 January 1979 with the following:

> From Algiers to Afghanistan a distasteful story is being related among Arabs about our dear Queen Mother and her friendship with a London-based Semite called Naim Attallah.
>
> Attallah is a director of Asprey, the royal bauble house, and recently put money into a film called *The Slipper and the Rose*. The Queen Mother was persuaded in the usual way to attend the première – i.e. it was for charity – and later photographed with the grinning Palestinian. Now visitors to his opulent Wellington Court, Knightsbridge, home are shown the picture of him with our sovereign's mother.
>
> Alas, it hangs on the wall next to another picture: that of a young woman displaying naked buttocks. And the nauseating Naim likes to indicate the latter picture to visiting Arabs – 'My friend the Queen Mother.' Needless to say many of the daft desert folk believe it to be true.

I was appalled. The piece was both vulgar and malicious and no one could have claimed it was free of racist overtones. My immediate reaction was that so far as jokes went this one had breached the boundaries of decency and I would have to do something about it. I telephoned our solicitor, Michael Rubinstein, who advised that although I could probably succeed in a libel action against *Private Eye*, it would not be in my long-term interests to do so. Sending them a letter for publication would be more effective, in his view, and was more likely to win me sympathizers than any court proceedings. I held Michael Rubinstein in great respect and took his advice. The following letter duly appeared in the next issue of the journal under the heading 'The Queen Mother':

> Sir – The privilege of being libelled in the *Eye* is not enhanced by the inevitable risk of the undeserving being confused with the deserving. Not infrequently these days an abject apology to those undeservedly maligned

is published (e.g. *Eye* 445) with reference to 'a substantial sum as compensation' and legal costs paid from Lord Gnome's overflowing coffers. I am advised that I would be entitled to join the grateful company of these beneficiaries of Lord Gnome's traditional, if spasmodic, carelessness with facts and words, and of his generosity. On this occasion, however, I shall be satisfied with the publication of this letter, unsullied by snide comments from any of His Lordship's minions, to inform your readers that there is no truth whatever in your malicious report (*Eye* 445) that a photograph of the Queen Mother (with whom, incidentally, I would not presume to claim friendship) shaking hands with me at a film première which she graced with her presence was hung on a wall of my office next to a photograph of 'a young woman displaying naked buttocks'. The former photograph has never hung on any of my walls in juxtaposition with any such photograph as the latter. Your readers will care no more than I do whether you have trusted, yet again, in an unreliable source, or have sub-editorially converted a boring gossip item with a built-in backfire. Even your enemies (amongst whom, in spite of severe provocation, I do not include myself) would surely not wish you to be a rebound victim of the curse of Gnome.

[Signed] Naim Attallah, Chairman, Quartet Books Ltd

The letter was published in *Private Eye* without comment, except that in the same issue a new story appeared that was equally mischievous and inaccurate and this time involved both Quartet and Asprey. It ran as follows:

More news about the business methods of Naim Attallah, owner of Quartet Books, a director of Asprey of Bond Street, friend and partner of David Frost (see Letters). Last year he saw the shapely hackette Val Hennessy on a television programme talking about punk. Naim telephoned her and invited her to lunch, when he asked Val to write a 'quickie' book on punk for his new imprint, The Quartet Diversions. This she did and was paid a considerable sum.

In October he invited Val to Asprey where he introduced her to John Asprey, 40ish grandson of the founder.

Alas! Val was less than impressed and sent up the place – and John Asprey – in her *Evening News* column of October 23rd. Naim was less than pleased. When Val next saw a Quartet employee he hissed at her: 'Naim Attallah wants to smash your face in. I wouldn't want to be in your shoes – he could buy the *Evening News* and you'd be out of a job.'

That was not all – prior to the *Evening News* article, Val had delivered two chapters of her new book to Quartet. When she asked for them back she was told the MS had been mislaid.

The thing that was immediately obvious was that *Private Eye* was delighted to have discovered a prime target for its lampoonery and was not going to let go in a hurry. The Val Hennessy story had been spun from a tangle of half-truths. My introduction to her came about through David Elliott, he and Val being old acquaintancies. During their rebellious youth, they had both belonged to that radical element that marched to ban the bomb or protest at social injustice. Their politics were leftish in a bohemian sort of way. I found Val to be good company and as I began to warm to her I commissioned her to do a book about punk, an anarchic style movement with which she appeared to be closely familiar. The book was unique of its kind and I felt it would demonstrate yet again that Quartet was courageous and innovative and unafraid to take chances. This unpredictability was becoming a source of strength.

Val, in her role of columnist for the *Evening News*, then asked me if she could visit Asprey. She would be fascinated, she said, to have an insider's view of the shop and write about the workings of one of the world's most luxurious establishments. There was no hint of any aggressive intention on her part when she went round the shop. In fact she gave the impression of being enchanted with everything she saw and waxed lyrical about the magnificent range of merchandise on display. Responding to her enthusiasm, I introduced her to some of the key figures behind the scenes, and everyone treated her as if she had been a visiting princess. When the article appeared, the *Evening News* gave it much prominence, but in it, alas, Val lashed out at Asprey and everything it stood for. She mocked the posh establishment accent of John Asprey, who had gone out of his way to be nice to her, and laced her prose with political innuendoes and Trotskyite turns of phrase. For me it was a most unpleasant shock. I was acutely embarrassed as I had to face the Asprey board to explain the meaning of it all, eating humble pie for something I had intended to be both good promotion for the company and a favour to a friend.

The embellishments of the story as recounted in *Private Eye* were totally untrue. I never issued a threat to Val, nor did anyone at Quartet ever mislay her manuscript. It was years before I spoke to Val Hennessy again, and naturally enough David Elliott's relationship with her deteriorated in the wake of the article. He, too, felt it had been an act of treachery and found it hard to forgive her.

*

In February 1979 I expanded the Namara Group's publishing interests by acquiring a recently formed non-fiction paperback list called Robin Clark Ltd. Its founders were Jim Reynolds, who had been managing director of the hardback list at Granada, and R. J. Reilly, a printer. Jim, who was both chairman and managing director, had looked upon it as a sort of 'hobby' venture to see him through his retirement, but it soon ran into trouble. Mr Reilly was short of money for printing costs so I answered the cry for help and bought out the printer. Ever since the parting of the ways between Quartet and Futura there had been a case for acquiring for Namara its own paperback list and Robin Clark seemed the ideal candidate. Jim Reynolds was to retain editorial control and to begin with everything ran harmoniously.

The character of the Robin Clark list was well described by Alex Hamilton in the *Guardian* when he wrote on 29 September 1979 how he 'liked getting little packets of books published by Robin Clark. They come, as it were, unannealed, no PR, no guff. I only know that he has a small list, works somehow with the Namara Group, and has an eclectic eye for books that are *sui generis*, like memoirs of a fairly remote hotel keeper, or a man crazy for rat-catching.' Among the titles in his latest package he was not enamoured of the Duke of Bedford's *Book of Snobs*, which he saw as a piece of 'ermine trailing' well past its sell-by date, but he praised two other reprints as 'little nuggets', one of them being *The Pooh Perplex* (first published in 1963) by Frederick C. Crews. This was a collection of essays on A. A. Milne's children's classics *Winnie the Pooh* and *The House at Pooh Corner*, of which Professor Crews had made an in-depth study, written as parodies of various styles of literary criticism. Equally entertaining and engaging was Lady Mary Clive's *Christmas among the Savages* (1955), an account of her remembered self at an Edwardian country house party as 'a priggish and conceited only child'. Mr Hamilton denied that the appeal of this book had anything to do with nostalgia – 'a term that people increasingly apply to events outside their experience' – but saw it as 'a beautifully distanced piece of writing, simple and apparently artless, which catches every one of the characters at the house party in their immense carelessness, and entertainingly conveys the separate worlds of children and adults, and the equivocations when they connect'.

No one was likely to become enraged by the contents of any of the titles in the Robin Clark list, but it was another matter altogether with many of the books Quartet published in 1979. Alan Brien's treatise on women's breasts, *Domes of Fortune*, described those female attributes in all their variety of shapes and characteristics and met with outrage on every side, not least in the corridors of Quartet itself, where a number of women editors were employed. The press delightedly reported how they were bristling with fury and planning to shame Quartet's proprietor into publishing an equivalent study of a vital piece of the male anatomy. Among the titles being suggested for this counter-blast was *Pricks of Conscience*. Poor Alan Brien, who was married to Jill

Tweedie, found himself coming in for a lot of undeserved flak. The real culprit was me, who had talked him into accepting the commission. It became evident that it had been a mad and tasteless idea, cynically amusing perhaps, yet never meant to be taken too seriously. I had seen it as a caprice, but it misfired badly and did nothing but harm to Quartet's reputation as a serious publisher. It was a case of my taking the company, in my exuberance and enthusiasm, off into territory that would have been better left unexplored.

Quartet's policy of seeking out photographic books of quality had also plunged them into a flurry of controversy back in the autumn of 1977 with the publication of Helmut Newton's first collection of photographs, *White Women*. It carried what was arguably the most erotic book jacket ever, whose sexual charge was heightened by the simplicity of the image and the controlled artistry of Newton's use of the camera. It showed the back view of a woman's lower half as she reclined on a blue satin sofa; the hem of her black lace dress was drawn back and the taut line of a black suspender, fastened to the top of a black stocking, emphasized the natural, subtle curves of her body. Helmut Newton had photographed for American and French *Vogue* for many years and developed a way of bringing fashion to the brink of fetishism. Each of the pictures in the book hinted at the darker, hidden sides of desire in both men and women. There were distinct Freudian overtones, and clear signs of the influence of the German expressionists. It would have been impossible to mistake the images for just fashion photographs and in this sense his work was deeply honest if a little unpalatable at times.

Various of Helmut Newton's contemporaries attempted to emulate the way he subverted fashion but none of them had the same genius for the subject. No one could deny the quality of his work or its artistic validity, yet when *White Women* was published the feminist lobby condemned it out of hand for depicting women as sex objects, abused and enslaved by men, and appealing to a voyeuristic audience. Newton may well have intended these things, but whether that made his pictures pornographic was another question. Stephanie Dowrick, from the viewpoint of The Women's Press, was in no doubt about the category they came into. When, in 1978, she discovered that her Women's Press books were occupying display space next to Helmut Newton on the Quartet stand at the Frankfurt Book Fair, she was so incensed that she declared that never again would the Press be allowed to share the same booth as Quartet.

The book that consolidated Quartet's position in 1979 as a leading publisher of high-quality photography raised no such qualms. This was Norman Parkinson's *Sisters under the Skin*. Parks, as he was generally known, had never, surprisingly, published a collection of his photographs before, despite being another leading talent who had worked for *Vogue* for many years and produced a large number of classic images. While he was more mainstream than Helmut Newton, he was still deeply innovative and *Sisters under the Skin* was designed to show how remarkable had been his empathy with the women he had photographed throughout his career. Some plates were nude studies, others portrait photographs of both the famous and the unknown, and there were informal shots, like his sneaked photos of the camera-shy Garbo in the street at the moment she realizes there is a photographer on her tail. Parks was hardly a self-effacing figure: tall and slender, with a military bearing and flaring handlebar moustache to match, he always wore an embroidered skull-cap when working, even at court.

The idea was to match almost all of the plates in the book with a piece of text placed opposite, written by someone who had an insight into or personal admiration for the subject. To take a few examples, there was Hardy Amies on HM the Queen Mother and James Lees-Milne on Vita Sackville-West; Laurie Lee on Elizabeth Frink and Cecil Beaton on Dame Sybil Thorndike; Lord Longford on Rose Kennedy and Michael Parkinson on Twiggy. The humanitarian journalist James Cameron wrote about a nameless mother and child sleeping on a Bombay pavement. It fell to me to write about Vanessa Redgrave in the role of Isadora Duncan. She was someone I admired, both for her talent as an actress and her political commitment, which was then at the height of its militancy through her association with the Trotskyist faction, the Workers' Revolutionary Party. She arrived at my office dressed in combat fatigues, having lately taken up the cause of the Palestinians in exile and under Israel in the Holy Land. As a result she was coming in for violent criticism along the usual pro-Israeli propagandist line that to question Zionism was a form of anti-Semitism.

Barbara Cartland was the only subject to write on herself. No one else, she declared, could possibly do her justice. Parks visited her to try to persuade her otherwise. 'It would be like masturbation,' he suggested. 'I don't care if I *am* thought to masturbate,' said Dame Barbara, and that was that. Towards the end there was a double-page spread of a nude, nineteen-year-old Tracy Ward settled decorously across an armchair as she examined a copy of *Sisters under the Skin*. Tracy's pedigree was to be found in *Burke's Peerage* and *Debrett's*, and the caption simply reproduced a note she had written: 'Parks, I would like to be in this book!'

Parks himself had undertaken to provide a piece on Diana Vreeland, the powerful, impossible editor of *Vogue* who had decreed so many of the fashions of the 1960s, among them the various ethnic looks. By now she was curator of costume at the Metropolitan Museum of Art in New York. In the event,

Parks developed a total block over writing about the formidable Mrs Vreeland and made an appeal to Peter Ford, who was sub-editing the texts before publication, to get him out of the hole. Peter therefore shaped up the material and no objections were ever forthcoming from Mrs Vreeland. The only person to become infuriated over an item in the book was the Honourable Peter Ward, Tracy's father, who claimed that Norman Parkinson had 'done the dirty' on his daughter by reproducing the nude shot of her in the armchair. On the eve of publication a letter arrived from solicitors acting on behalf of Tracy, presumably at her father's behest, demanding that the picture be withdrawn. I was utterly astonished. The photograph of Tracy was absolutely charming and in perfectly good taste. It could have caused her no harm at all in the modelling career she was setting out to pursue. I flatly declined to remove the picture and nothing more was ever heard from the solicitors.

Another illustrated book of artistic merit, published between the two photographic volumes in 1977, was *Topolski's Buckingham Palace Panoramas*. It was designed to be a contribution to the Queen's Jubilee celebrations in that year. Feliks Topolski had been well known since before the war for his *reportage* style of drawing. He was highly prolific and worked with remarkable coordination of hand and eye and at amazing speed to record impressions in any part of the world his assignments took him to: complex impressionistic lines resolved themselves into recognizable representations of events and individuals. In 1953 he had been an official artist for the Coronation and produced many drawings of the crowds and all the pageantry of the procession and ceremony. His work was especially admired by Prince Philip, who in 1959 suggested a commission for him to paint two spectacular sequences of panels, based on his Coronation drawings, to run along two facing walls of the gallery leading to the state rooms of Buckingham Palace. For the book Prince Philip contributed a foreword and the art critic Bernard Denver provided an appraisal of Topolski's place in art history. Feliks himself worked on the design and layout of the pages with Mike Jarvis, a designer who did much to give Quartet's books their feel and appearance in the early days.

Feliks was also to contribute a commentary on the friezes themselves, but as he was well aware there was a problem with his prose style. This was as idiosyncratic as his drawing, with complex layers of meaning conveyed in sentences with many clauses and sub-clauses and asides in brackets. Unfortunately he fell out with a collaborator, and deadlines loomed. Peter Ford then stepped in as co-author, working with Feliks at his apartment high above the Thames Embankment (once occupied by George Bernard Shaw) and in his studio next to the Royal Festival Hall: a cavernous space in one of the arches under Hungerford Bridge, chaotically hung with work in progress and filled to the roof with racks containing the labour of a lifetime, where Feliks drew and painted and received his many visitors relaxed on a large daybed. As the trains in and out of Charing Cross Station rumbled overhead at regular intervals, they hammered out a solution: a prose 'collage' that interspersed selected passages from Feliks's more exotic writings with a straight commentary. Eventually the book told the story of that magnificent project, arising from a royal commission, and in a series of brilliant reproductions revealed the extraordinary beauty and vitality of Topolski's panels. It was very warmly received and sold well.

Feliks had a keen eye for women, and at about the same time he invited my wife Maria to visit him in his studio under the arches. He was clearly taken with her, especially as they both had Polish origins, and as a mother with a twelve-year-old son she had a certain bloom which he found inspiring. During the visit he tried in his most charming and beguiling way to persuade her to pose for him in the nude. He would like, he proclaimed grandiosely, to celebrate Polish womanhood in the only way he knew how – through his painting brush. Maria was flattered to be asked but declined. The reason, she told him, was that as a mother her modesty would not allow her the privilege of responding to this unique opportunity. If he was disappointed, she assured him, then so was she.

*

A key addition to Quartet's list in 1979 was *The Palestinians* by Jonathan Dimbleby, with photographs by Donald McCullin. It was the sort of book I had long wanted to see published, one that would draw attention to the plight of the Palestinians and chronicle the events surrounding the creation of the state of Israel that had driven so many of them into exile as refugees – and left those who remained on their home soil without control over their destiny. It was high time that their voices were heard; that the reasons behind the upsurge of protest and militant extremism were better understood. One day I phoned up Jonathan and said, 'I like the stuff you've done on television on the Palestinians. Will you write a book about it?' He said he would. Naturally I then became impatient to see the result.

Following on the experience of our working together, in June 1980 Jonathan paid me undeserved compliments as a publisher in an interview profile put together on BBC Radio 4:

His style is unique, one of massive excitement and enthusiasm that propels people along around him. His gift is to enthuse you when you feel uncertain – that 'I've got a lot of other things on and I'm not certain I can get it finished on time'. He doesn't berate you with sticks and say, 'You've got to get it in now, tomorrow, or there'll be trouble.' He says, 'You've got to get it in. If you don't get it in we're all being let down by it,' so that you feel almost a moral obligation to deliver for his sake. Now that's quite unusual, but he is a massively healthy tonic to the industry because of this dynamism that he has and because he is prepared to take risks.

Another early Quartet author, Michael Deakin, in the same broadcast profile, offered the following observations:

Naim is a sort of tornado of enthusiasm. One of the problems is that he's not always aware of the fact that deadlines have a real purpose and sometimes he wants, not yesterday but the day before yesterday, things that other people might want in a month. That's a fault for the good rather than for the bad. Anyone who's trying to do creative things, write books or articles or make films, generally puts off till the last moment what's got to be done. Someone who demands for yesterday somehow composes the mind, because if you don't deliver it you certainly find that not one but twenty-seven pressing telephone calls arrive. Naim's not a financier, Naim's a tornado, and tornadoes have good and bad bits, because the eye of the storm can be a comfortable place to be in a tornado. As a publisher he belongs in the tradition of the great Jewish publishers, who by their own personality put their names on their books. Naim, if he hadn't come late into publishing, would have liked to have a publishing house with his name on it, I think, as the names of George Weidenfeld and André Deutsch are on their imprints.

No doubt Naim has made mistakes through over-enthusiasm, and I'm sure there have been manifestations of one sort or another that he himself, looking back, would not be happy with. Unlike being a banker or stockbroker, publishing is backing your own taste and judgement, and Naim does that. Anyone who knows Naim well will agree he's a man of very high intelligence and is not someone who makes the same mistake repeatedly. I'd say he makes a series of mistakes when coming into a new field, but he doesn't repeat them very often – he learns very quickly on his feet. I think he's in publishing because he thinks it's the business of the wealthy man to give employment to the artisan, that it's the business of people like himself to promote creative work. He sees himself as a patron. He'd dearly like to have been Lorenzo de' Medici – an inspirer of creative work.

The whole idea of *The Palestinians* was to give their side of the story, and the publication was one of the very first non-academic books to have this as a focus. Other contributions to a shift in perspective were underway – Edward Said's *The Question of Palestine*, for instance, was published by Routledge in the same year. But the influential questioning by Jewish historians of the legends attached to the founding of Israel did not begin, on the whole, until ten years later, following the release of much classified material; then such books as *The Birth of Israel: Myths and Realities* by the peace activist Simha Flapan (Croom Helm, 1987) and Benny Morris's *1948 and After: Israel and the Palestinians* (Oxford University Press, 1990) made their appearance. In the meantime there was no shortage of eminent publishers, like George Weiden-feld, to persist in promoting the Israeli side of the picture. Likewise sections of the liberal press in Britain maintained an uncritical loyalty to Israel because of the state's founding fathers' links with European social democracy, failing to recognize how far to the right Israel's politics were being forced by the country's internal lobbyists.

The purpose of Dimbleby's text would be to show how in every dispute there are merits to be considered on both sides, and to challenge public opinion at a time when it was unfashionable to say anything at all in favour of the Palestinians. As a young television journalist who had worked in the Middle East, he was well placed to make the best use of material based on interviews with Palestinians from peasant farmers to doctors, journalists, teachers, political leaders and fighters. The eloquent photographs of Donald McCullin, who had an international reputation for his depictions of harsh reality at the world's flashpoints, were a perfect complement: a visual essay running in parallel with the text.

No one could ignore the book, and as soon as it was published I found myself facing a barrage of questions from journalists. I did not deny that the book was sympathetic to the Palestinians. Why should it not be? I was not a political animal, I insisted, and my main reason for publishing it had been to promote Dimbleby's liberal political views in support of the underdog; which was the understanding on which he had agreed to write it in the first place. A leather-jacketed Dimbleby took the praise of the book in his stride when questioned by the *Evening Standard*. 'The reporter,' he said, 'is an advocate in the court of public opinion. His client is that amorphous chameleon, reality, upon which he occasionally if foolishly confers the truth.' When asked whether that statement was contentious, not to say pompous, he politely replied that he could not see that it was. The book did not exonerate the regimes in neighbouring Arab countries from sharing the blame for the creation of the intractable refugee problem, or neglecting opportunities to help to ameliorate it.

The Zionist press lashed into the book, as was to be expected, and the most dramatic confrontation arose at a press conference held as an 'audience-participation discussion' with Jonathan and Donald at the Institute of Contemporary Arts. 'The audience,' the *Jewish Chronicle* admitted, 'was packed with Zionist supporters who, in the main, behaved in such a manner as to make Mr Dimbleby seem reasonable.' Jonathan and Donald were able to make their point that to do the book had been their choice, both of them having had plenty of opportunity to see the conflict from the Israeli side. 'My experience confirmed my presuppositions,' said Jonathan when asked if writing the book had altered his views in any way. The meeting very soon went into uproar, with members of the audience name-calling each other as well as directing insults at the platform.

The *Jewish Chronicle* itself had contained a review by T. R. Fyvel that Jonathan found insulting. It started by contending that he 'hardly counts as a historian, even in the television sense. All the same, to anyone who has lived through a longer period of modern Jewish history, his account of it reads like a strange fantasy.' He had, said Mr Fyvel, dismissed the unique human disaster of the Holocaust in a few lines. Jonathan defended himself in the letters column, citing his references to the Holocaust and quoting his own statement: 'To acknowledge the Palestinian cause is not to deny the cause of Israel, but to elevate the Palestinians to their proper place in the debate.'

I go on to state my belief that peace in the Middle East, and therefore the peace of the world, depends upon the creation of an environment in which the people of Israel and the Palestinians 'are obliged to recognize that each has an equal and reconcilable claim upon Palestine'.

The crisis in the Middle East has its roots in a double tragedy. To deny the one is as unforgiveable as to neglect the other. I do not expect your readers to agree with my analysis or my conclusions. I do ask them, however, to reject Mr Fyvel's abusive and offensive insinuation that I am an enemy of humanity.

The mainstream reviews in the press were generally in agreement that the true voices of the Palestinians themselves came across in the narrative. As Patrick Seale wrote in the *Observer*:

Jonathan Dimbleby has, with skill and restraint, given a voice to the Palestinians' wretchedness in their exile . . . The wasteland he records of despair relieved only by violence is lit up by Donald McCullin's pictures exploding like mortar bombs.

The Palestinians was reviewed for the *New Statesman* by Christopher

Hitchens, whose sympathies then were leftward-leaning – before he took a lurch to the right after going to live in America. Hitchens was always a powerful advocate from whatever viewpoint he was writing. Jonathan Dimbleby had, he said, found 'Palestinians in their infinite variety of occupations and countries; always passionate, always enterprising, always proud and always extremely keen to talk about themselves'.

As far as he can in what is really a long essay, he has disentangled people from the images [those that others have of them], whether self-imposed or superimposed. Since he has done the book with Donald McCullin, who is the best photographer on this kind of story, there is rarely a description or an anecdote that does not have a vivid illustration to lend it some depth. It would be impossible to turn these pages and retain the conviction that the word 'Palestinian' is just another synonym for terrorist or desperado. Here they are. Judge for yourselves . . . Although he knows them pretty well he hasn't lost the capacity to be surprised at their amazing combination of traditional values with modern revolutionary and international politics.

The book had certainly succeeded in making a contribution towards constructing the platform for debate that was so badly needed if peace in the region was ever to become a reality. It was also important to move on from the attitudes that stereotyped anyone who spoke sympathetically of the Palestinians as either a misguided liberal or a leftist zealot. The rowdy affair at the ICA, with Jewish activists trying to disrupt the meeting, had provided an illustration of how extremism on either side in a dispute can so often lead to conflict.

Then, to my surprise, I received a letter from Moshe Menuhin, the father of Yehudi, congratulating me on the publication of *The Palestinians*. It was high time, he said, that someone stuck up for the Palestinian Arabs and presented their point of view. The letter came from his home in California, where he lived until his death in 1983. To demonstrate his affection for the Palestinians even more, he also sent me a tape recording of an interview he gave to Colin Edwards, who generously agreed to my making use of its contents. The tape began with Moshe's recollections of Palestine and its people after he was sent there from Russia at the age of eleven in 1904 to avoid the pogroms. His grandfather then raised him in the old city of Jerusalem, though later, after being caught in Jaffa by a cholera epidemic, he enrolled at the new Hebrew Gymnasium there and was among its first graduates. The following résumé echoes his words as he spoke them, showing his depth of feeling for the people he was taught to look down on and to treat as if they were usurpers in the Holy Land:

When I was taken to old Jerusalem by my mother I was a little embarrassed because I had ear locks and was wearing a kaftan, like a long nightdress, so the boys of the Jewish colonists, who were already more 'civilized', looked down on this Jewish boy with his ear locks, though no one ever harmed me. The Arabs, I always found, were friendly, decent, kind people, entertaining me, talking to me. We used to hike from Jerusalem to certain places holy to the Arabs, the Jews, the Christians – to certain non-kosher areas where Jews were not supposed to go. Every summer I went to Rehovat to eat grapes on an uncle's estate, eating them till I was sick, though it was supposed to be good for me. At the end of my stay one of the Arabs who worked for my uncle drove me to Ramallah, where in those days not a Jew ever lived. He would let me off the horse and buggy to sit around outside the railway station to wait for the train from Jaffa to take me back to Jerusalem. Nobody ever molested me, I wasn't afraid, I wasn't aware of being a foreigner. (I spoke Arabic fluently by the way.)

Under Turkish Ottoman rule, the officials, the judges, the working people were all Arabs. We – about 35,000 of us when I arrived in Palestine – were just a meek, quiet Jewish bunch. There was no such thing as oppression from the Muslims. I could never apply the word 'oppression'. I cannot recall a single incident. The Arabs gave me more joy than the Jews ever did. They were nearer to life and the Jews had obstructing safeguards against mixing with the world. In those days there was no interest among the Orthodox in Dr Herzl and his Zionist movement. The insane political nationalism that would give rise to the First World War was meanwhile taking its hold in Europe and becoming the religion of the world, and the Zionists swallowed it. I would go to the House of the People in Jerusalem to hear when Zionists – non-religious Jews – gave lectures and used to arouse the people with the slogan, 'Our nation, our country, our homeland,' and of course people fell for the clever speaker.

Already there was the preliminary to warring from the Jews among themselves. You were told don't go to an Arab dentist, don't go to an Arab merchant, or a grocer or fruit trader, even though there weren't enough Jewish traders to go round. People had to buy from Arabs, but there was this constant programme of preaching individually. We had good teachers at the gymnasium in Jaffa, but I would say, to summarize, that underneath the teachings there was one principle premise, repeated again and again, 'Our country, our nation, our homeland.' Yet I cannot recall one student in the entire gymnasium – and they were all nice boys and girls – who'd been born in Arab Palestine. We were all immigrants who'd come from Russia to escape the pogroms, or to get a Jewish education, or a Zionist education in most cases. Day after day we heard the slogan whenever a teacher could stick it in; even in science they somehow managed it. It was to subvert us, to poison us, into becoming Jewish nationalists. I never met a rabbi and there were no religious services of any kind – they were all agnostics or atheists. The gymnasium became a hotbed for wild, insane political nationalism. We were taught to hate the Arabs, to despise them, and to drive them out from 'our' homeland, 'our' country – 'ours' not theirs, quoting the Bible, of course. For five years they were pumping into me the Jewish nationalism, Zionism, happily unsuccessfully – happily for me as a civilized being who belongs to the world and not to any nationalist group.

There were few Jewish colonists: 35,000 Jews where there were 600,000 normal, healthy, hard-working, innocent, unknowledgeable Arabs. There were few farming cooperatives, though I always remember the kibbutzim with affection and admiration. Many a time I slept and worked on the kibbutzim in Galilee during my student days. The kibbutz was the one and only outstanding, eternal contribution that Israel might contribute to the world if it stops going back on itself, as it begins to do already now, and stressing political nationalism. There were 2,000 or 3,000 Jews among the cooperative farms of Galilee. The Arabs could have wiped us out in no time if there had been any organized scheme, but there was no group that planned to do anything among the Arab population. They were individuals. Zionist fanatics and Orthodox fanatics now kept going to Palestine, but most of the Jewish people chose to go to the United States, to Canada, to South Africa, to South America. Even ten or so years after the Balfour Declaration in 1917, Weizmann had to go to Romania to plead with the Jews, 'Look, we extracted the Balfour Declaration out of the British, and now they keep asking us, "Where are your Jews?" If we are to have a *Heretz Israel*, come to Palestine.' There were 9,000 Jews who came in, though 6,000 emigrated. It was only when the Jews had to run away from Germany, or from Russia to work in Palestine, that they came in any numbers – the Jews who were ghetto Jews, who had a hatred for the Gentiles and then had it a hundredfold for the *goy* in Palestine.

As a boy I suffered terribly from bad teeth. They were uneven and some of them protruded to cut my lips. At one point the pain became so unbearable that when I was walking through a narrow alley in the old city and saw a sign indicating an Arab dentist I stopped and went inside. After negotiating some narrow stairs I reached a crowded waiting-room where people sat awaiting their turn to be seen by the dentist. I sat myself down

[63]

in a corner and stayed there till the room had emptied and the dentist had treated his last patient. As he came out of his surgery he saw me sitting there, obviously in great pain. Although he was ready to leave for home, and I had neither appointment nor the money with which to pay him, he invited me to come into the surgery. As he examined my teeth he was horrified by the rotten state in which he found them. If I came to the surgery the same time each day, he suggested, he would attend to me and not expect to be paid for his services. At the end of the treatment I said the day would perhaps come when I could repay my debt to him. He simply replied, 'Ask your people not to stir up trouble, so we can live side by side and share the land of our forefathers.'

Many, many decades later, when I was living in old age in California, I had occasion one day to see a dentist, and he was astounded at the good condition of my teeth. Then I told him the story of that kind and wonderful Palestinian dentist who had looked after my teeth as a boy in Palestine, and treated them with such love and dedication. That is the reason why I find it always traumatic to watch pictures on the television of scenes in the Palestinian refugee camps and the misery surrounding them, wondering whether any descendants of my noble dentist benefactor languish there with no hope of ever seeing their land again.

I was very moved by Moshe's voice on tape expressing views which were clearly against the trend of the time. A friendship between us followed, with a regular exchange of correspondence, though regretfully I never had the opportunity to meet him in person. But, encouraged by his example, Quartet was now more determined than ever to continue to draw attention to the Palestinian tragedy until such time as people of goodwill the world over felt able to stand up and speak out in support of an equitable and just solution to this humanitarian issue.

Six

On the one hand the name of Asprey had once more become synonymous with superb quality and impeccable standards of service that would have been difficult to match elsewhere. On the other, the bizarre twists and turns in the Asprey family feud continued unabated. The incessant squabbling of family members threatened to put at risk the magic resonance the name had recovered with the establishing of a new range of merchandise that retained a classic look yet was very much of its time. This potential impediment to the firm's progress made it an anxious period, but having gone this far, neither John Asprey nor I were prepared to stand aside and see the ruin of all the achievements of the past few years. The obvious solution would be for one side of the family to sell out to the other side. The only question was which one it should be.

These problems were augmented by another that arose in March 1979 when Alfred Dunhill, controlled by Rothmans International, announced it had bought a six-per-cent stake in Asprey from Grovewood Securities, a subsidiary of Eagle Star, for some seven hundred thousand pounds. It was an investment that carried with it the balance of power at Asprey's Bond Street headquarters. The stake had previously been owned by the Tunalt family foundation, who sold it to Grovewood for fifteen pounds a share, so doubling their original purchase price. Grovewood in their turn sold it to Dunhill at a price of twenty-nine pounds a share, which had the effect of valuing Asprey at close on twelve million pounds. Speculation of a takeover bid from Dunhill then became rife in the marketplace, for they had recently paid one point four million pounds for the control of Collingwood, the private jewellers. Unlike the two other recent holders of the six-per-cent stake, who were both investors, Dunhill were traders. Hence the speculation of a takeover was bound to continue, despite the denial by Tony Greener, Dunhill's managing director, that such a move was being contemplated.

Between them, the rumours of a takeover and the family discord were starting to destabilize the company just at the point where its trading was flourishing and showing steady growth. Turnover for the previous five years had risen from five million to sixteen million pounds, with pre-tax profits increasing from one point four million to a record three point two million pounds for 1977–8.

Asprey's many competitors were becoming truly baffled at the speed with which the company was making inroads into the marketplace. Much of this had to do with the working partnership between John and myself, and our rivals could only look on with envy. The choice of merchandise was uniquely rich and the quality of goods unsurpassed. The showrooms bustled with people who came in to buy one thing and left with a variety of items they had never thought of putting on their shopping list. There was a compulsive atmosphere in the place that made purchasing a special delight and inspired the customers to choose the right gift for the right occasion.

In a bid to initiate a family reconciliation I made a persuasive appeal to Eric Asprey, the chairman, that he should let bygones be bygones and receive back into the fold Algernon Asprey, who was facing serious financial problems in the running of his own company, Algernon Asprey & Co. He had founded the company, after a former boardroom disagreement had led to his dismissal from the board, together with his brother Harry in 1971. Eric was far from keen on the idea and forewarned that taking him back would only result in further trouble. Nevertheless he went along with it to avoid yet another scandal involving a family member coming to the notice of the public. In a face-saving move, Asprey Bond Street bought a ninety-per-cent stake in Algernon Asprey & Co., leaving ten per cent in the ownership of Mr Algernon. Together with John Asprey, I then joined the board of Algernon Asprey & Co. and as a first step towards his rehabilitation Algernon was invited to take a seat on the main board of Asprey Bond Street. His company was then closed down in orderly fashion and all creditors paid in full.

What happened next was predictable and Eric Asprey's worst forebodings of a full-scale family drama came to pass. Algernon had ideas of his own, mainly directed towards usurping the power of those who had welcomed him back and given him a reprieve when he needed it most. He was prepared to ally himself with any predator that came in sight, and especially with Alfred Dunhill, who increased their stake to twenty-three per cent and rendered Asprey's position extremely precarious. It was no secret that he was prepared to assume the chairmanship as a quid pro quo for his cooperation.

Nevertheless 1980 began with great promise and a flurry of activity. Trading at Asprey could hardly have been better. A Swiss subsidiary was formed in Geneva to facilitate access to the booming trade in Swiss watches and the special *objets d'art* being manufactured there to satisfy the large demand for such unique and desirable items in the Far East, where Brunei was becoming a major client. Trade in the Middle East was also on the increase, especially in the Gulf States. It was in Oman, however, that John Asprey had forged a special relationship over the years through which the

Sultan had become the firm's most important patron. He used Asprey to order the expensive gifts he needed to present to foreign visitors, including members of Britain's own royal family. As a man with a passion for quality and a love of the arts and music, it seemed entirely fitting that the Sultan should turn to Asprey for his purchases.

John and I hardly ever paused in our search for novel ways to entice our clientele, whose ranks now extended to such non-traditional customers as pop stars and property tycoons. Money changed hands at such a pace that we could only keep abreast of the situation by staying well informed. Intelligence counted for a great deal, together with being in the right place at the right time. It was an integral part of a job in the luxury trade to be visible at all times, otherwise opportunities were lost and competitors stepped in. In general it was a fickle world where loyalties counted for very little.

Being often in Geneva, John and I had the good fortune to meet the legendary Harry Winston, who was undoubtedly the most successful diamond dealer in the world. He maintained a large office in Switzerland to cater for wealthy clients who came to see him in search of important stones, unique for their size and colour. He had set up his own business, the Premier Diamond Company, on Fifth Avenue in New York in 1920 when he was only twenty-eight, and went on to become the most prolific gem salesman of his generation. He revolutionized the way precious stones were set, shifting the emphasis on to the stones themselves and away from the ornate settings popular in the earlier twentieth century. Many of the most famous diamonds in history passed through his hands, including the Hope Diamond, which he donated to the Smithsonian Institution as a gift to the American people. On Oscar nights in Hollywood many of the sparkling diamonds worn by the stars had been loaned to them by Harry Winston. In 1958 his firm created the Nur Il Ain tiara for Queen Farah to wear at her wedding to the Shah of Iran. Among Harry'sroyal clients were members of the House of Saud in Saudi Arabia.

The history of what became known as the Taylor-Burton Diamond turned into one of the most extraordinary episodes of Harry's career. The original stone, of over 240 carats, had been found in 1966 and Harry bought it at once. He and his master cutter then studied it for six months before attempting the cleaving, which was successfully carried out live in front of television cameras. The largest piece eventually yielded a classic pear-shaped gem of 69.42 carats, which was sold to Harriet Annenberg Ames, the sister of Walter Annenberg, an American diplomat. In 1969 it reappeared in the auction room after Mrs Ames tired of having to keep it always hidden in a bank vault. The actor

Richard Burton was well known for his habit of buying diamonds for his wife Elizabeth Taylor, and the Burtons certainly took an interest. The bidding started at two hundred thousand dollars and swiftly rose to a record price of over a million dollars; at which point Burton's representative dropped out and the stone went to the chairman of the Cartier parent company in New York. Richard Burton then became even more determined to acquire it and opened negotiations with the owner's agent, saying, 'I don't care how much it costs – go and buy it.' He got his way, for an undisclosed sum, but only on condition Cartier could first exhibit it in New York and Chicago and it would be named the Taylor-Burton Diamond.

The *New York Times* took a mordant view of this spectacular flaunting of wealth and commented: 'The peasants have been lining up outside Cartier's this week to gawk at a diamond as big as the Ritz that cost well over a million dollars. It is destined to hang around the neck of Mrs Richard Burton. As someone said, "It would have been nice to wear in the tumbrel on the way to the guillotine." ' Miss Taylor wore it for the first time in public in Monaco at Princess Grace's fortieth-birthday party. After her divorce from Richard Burton, she resold it in 1979 for five million dollars, putting part of the proceeds towards building a hospital in Botswana. Harry, who died at the end of 1978, did not, alas, live to see this final act in the drama.

Harry had made it his speciality to purchase from governments and diamond corporations the largest uncut diamonds he could locate and then take the inherent risk of having them cut and polished. Whenever John and I visited him we heard stories of the millions of pounds' worth of diamonds he had sold and of how he achieved this against odds that his competitors (who were few) would have considered unbeatable. He was a rotund, jovial little man with boundless enthusiasm and unquenchable optimism, which had enabled him to do what most people would find impossible. He gave us an insight into the trade, emphasizing above all the importance of perseverance when early signs are discouraging. He taught us a great deal and we looked upon him as our guru in the world of precious stones.

In 1972 Harry Winston had acquired the Star of Sierra Leone, which came from the largest raw diamond ever to be excavated from the Diminco mine in Sierra Leone. Originally it had weighed 968.80 carats and at that point was the third biggest raw diamond ever found. The largest single stone as Harry bought it was 143 carats, emerald cut, brilliant, yet ever so slightly flawed. It was then the largest diamond of his career to date. In what was a tricky operation, he cleaved away the imperfections, thus greatly reducing the size of the stone. Many in the trade called him mad even to consider it. However, the triumphant outcome was a 33-carat D-flawless stone alongside sixteen smaller stones, thirteen of which were flawless. Collectively they far surpassed the value of the original rough stone.

John and I had the privilege not only of seeing the Star of Sierra Leone but also of being responsible for the sale of some of the smaller gems to clients in the Middle East. Harry encouraged us to have faith in our ability to sell important stones by going about it the way he would himself. 'If you have that measure of self-confidence,' he said, 'you'll travel the path of success.' He would insist we take a whole tray of diamonds worth millions on a sales trip. He would not have it otherwise, however much we protested that we could not possibly take the responsibility. 'Listen,' he said, 'it's not your responsibility, it's mine. I'm insured. If anything goes wrong, it's my responsibility.'

To convince us further he would recall the time when he sold over twenty million dollars' worth of gems to a single client, an absolute monarch who was on a visit to Geneva. The monarch's personal secretary phoned Harry in New York telling him to come to Geneva and bring some diamonds with him. Harry called on all the dealers he knew in New York and collected from them on a consignment basis every available quality diamond. He ended by scooping the market in good stones, and when he told his fellow dealers why, they laughed and thought he'd gone crazy. In Geneva he went to see his client with the stones in a black bag and was granted a single audience. The monarch asked him to turn the bag upside down and tip out its contents in the middle of the room. As soon as the glistening treasure lay on the carpet ten or so women appeared from adjoining rooms and fell on it. Within five minutes they had cleared the whole pile. 'Send me the bill,' said the client. The lesson Harry learnt then was that nothing is ever impossible. It gave him great satisfaction to return to New York and tell his colleagues how he had sold the lot.

Faced with tales of such audacity, John and I could no longer refuse to do his bidding. We would take the tray of diamonds worth millions without even signing a receipt and venture forth in the footsteps of the master. To say we ever matched his level of success would be untrue, but we managed to make our mark and he was never disappointed.

Our close association with Harry Winston, the grand master of his trade, continued until his death. The last time we saw him was on a flight to New York in Concorde in the autumn of 1978. He was seated not far from us, and throughout the flight we observed in amazement as he ordered from the stewardess vodka after vodka and never betrayed the faintest sign of inebriation. He was a most extraordinary man. He had a very expressive type of Semitic face and when he spoke about his diamonds his features seemed to become strangely illuminated. His love for and affinity with his stones instilled in us a lasting appreciation of the perfection and beauty that only nature can produce.

*

Among all the many things that happened in 1980 the saddest by far for me was the death of George Hutchinson, who departed far too young at the age of fifty-nine. He was my earliest friend in Britain; I had met him soon after landing in the country in 1949. There were many who mourned him, but for me in particular it was as the last of his kind: a gentlemanly, distinguished journalist with integrity. He had indeed belonged to that rare breed of men whose near-extinction has left the world of journalism a poorer place. The elegance of his writing, coupled with his exquisitely refined manners, made him the darling of that section of society which had an appreciation for such qualities. His readership stretched across the nation at every social level. He was the voice of moderation and invariably he had a message that was tinged with hope and optimism. For the more sophisticated, his political acumen was sharp and incisive, and he was rarely wrong in any assessment he made of an issue of national importance.

There was much I had George to thank for. In 1950, when monetary support from my family in Haifa was blocked by new regulations, the Home Office had been about to repatriate me to Israel, on the grounds that as the holder of a student visa I could no longer sustain myself financially. George's intervention, principally with the Home Office, and his rallying of MPs on my behalf secured my stay in the United Kingdom. Though we each pursued our separate paths, our friendship remained strong over subsequent years. The only blip occurred with Quartet's publication of the *Mrs Thatcher's Handbag* kit. On this one occasion George's sense of humour deserted him, and the resulting *froideur* took some time to thaw. Eventually all was forgiven and Quartet published his biography of Harold Macmillan, *The Last Edwardian at No. 10*. It was the final work he was able to complete. At the book's launch party, a few weeks before his death, the guests included Harold Macmillan with his son Maurice. Harold stood there, leaning on his stick, and demanded, 'Lead me to the author! Lead me to the author!' There was an extraordinary number of writers and politicians among the host of friends and admirers. They thronged about him where he had positioned himself in a corner, awkwardly upright, for the illness had already taken its toll on his handsome frame. Nevertheless his face carried an expression of pleasure and satisfaction. His peers were there to pay him tribute for the last time.

The writer of the obituary in the *Sunday Telegraph* spoke of how kindly,

seen the play and liked it, he was very keen but doubted his ability to rise to such a serious challenge. He promised I would have his answer within a few days. Instead of just waiting for it, however, I telephoned Pamela, asking her to urge him to say yes. Her reaction gave me a heartening boost, for she felt sure that this could be for Billy a good career move. He went into rehearsal almost immediately, though there was one remaining hitch. Because of a previous commitment he could do it for only a few weeks. This being better than nothing, we readily agreed.

The casting of Billy as Beefy turned out to be inspired. He took the part in his stride and if ever he forgot his lines fell back on his variety-act technique of improvisation. There was one seduction scene where he had to rip a girl's knickers clean off, a manoeuvre which dear Simon Callow could only approach with fastidious distaste. Billy, by contrast, tackled the task in a state of heightened heterosexual excitement and performed it with such relish that sometimes he used his teeth as well as his hands. The crowd howled with approval and loved every minute of his antics, not all of which were strictly in the script. They caught the bawdy spirit of the piece, however, and with his manic exuberance Billy never failed to bring comic genius to each perform-ance. The play took on a new lease of life and the queues outside the theatre went round the block, with people hoping either to get tickets or catch a glimpse of their hero. If only Billy had been able to stay on for a few more weeks, then the new capacity audiences would have turned the play into a smash hit in every sense. As it was, it ended up with a good run and earned me the respect of theatre folk for my tenacity and resolve in not being easily dismayed by the capricious nature of theatre.

There were other bonuses. During those few months when I stood every evening in the lobby of the Duke of York's Theatre I encountered a host of people. They would come up to me to talk, and introduce me to whomever they were with. Two meetings in particular were significant. The first was with Sophie Hicks, today a successful architect but then an up-and-coming girl about town who worked at Condé Nast on *Vogue*; the other was Nigella Lawson, a student at Oxford who was up in London to see the play. Sophie in turn introduced me to Arabella Pollen, an ambitious and rather delectable young beauty of eighteen who, with my backing, would become Princess Diana's favourite fashion designer. Nigella, with her persuasive charm and expressive good looks, secured from me a written undertaking to employ her at Quartet after her graduation from Oxford in a year's time.

There was one other interesting footnote to my friendship with J. P. Don-leavy that came years later at the end of the 1990s. He had ended up owning his original publisher, the Olympia Press in Paris, who had brought out his first book, *The Ginger Man*, in 1955, when no other publisher would touch it. The Olympia Press was founded in 1953 by Maurice Girodias, a crusader against censorship and a militant pornographer who had many clashes with the authorities. Among his 'literary' authors were Henry Miller, Vladimir Nabokov, Jean Genet and William S. Burroughs. Donleavy had a long-running legal battle with Girodias, who died in 1990, and his original plan as Olympia's owner was to bring out all his own past and future work under the imprint; but the company was in mothballs and it needed someone enterprising to revive it. The idea was mooted by Sir Paul Getty as a result of a conversation I had with him when he sat next to me at an *Oldie* lunch. We engaged in light banter about our love of beautiful women and this led on to the topic of erotic literature and how it is no longer considered to be taboo. Getty told me about his collection of Olympia Press first editions, bought during his time in Paris. He was nostalgic for that adventurous era and bemoaned the disappearance of the press. With a swift reaction I asked what he would think of its rebirth, especially with eroticism back in vogue. His response was remarkably enthusiastic and to the point. He would be willing to finance such a resurrection, he said, so long as the amount of money needed was not prohibitive. When I pressed him further, he reiterated his commitment and gave me the green light to start on the necessary research.

Encouraged by Paul Getty's show of determination, I telephoned J. P. Donleavy, who welcomed the proposal but qualified his agreement with his usual proviso that, should the Olympia Press be revived, all his books would be published under its banner. The link with Quartet would, he thought, be ideal, with the company's eclectic tradition enhancing the viability of such an association. Then the unexpected happened. Paul began procrastinating, citing 'J. P.'s' reputation for being difficult as a possible stumbling block. I did my best to reassure him that the problem was nothing to worry about, but failed. The real reason for his withdrawal was something else altogether. The moment he realized we were almost home and dry he got cold feet. It had become a question of money and personal status. His advisers would certainly have been opposed to his involvement in the project and would never have agreed happily to furnish the entire capital. More than that, he was very conscious of having rehabilitated his reputation following a rebellious youth. His generosity towards charitable institutions and his efforts to help the nation retain some of its treasures meant the establishment had taken him to its heart. What was it going to think of him now if he embarked on a new career as a pornographic man of letters? By his reckoning, the moment of impulsive enthusiasm shown at the *Oldie* lunch was about to cost him dear. All he could do was contrive a retreat.

I felt badly let down after having devoted a great deal of time to preparing the ground. The revival of the Olympia Press would have generated enormous publicity and interest – enough to attract exciting new authors. Alas, a dream was shattered and a lot of valuable time wasted on a renaissance that was not to be.

*

At Quartet the 1981 party season opened with a celebration of Nicholas Courtney's *The Tiger*. Notable among the guests was Jim Edwards, founder of the Tigertops tiger reserve in Nepal, who came accompanied by Sarah d'Erlanger (daughter of the *Sunday Times*'s editor Frank Giles), who was closely involved with the London side of the operation. Other enthusiasts were our own Davina Woodhouse, soon to marry Earl Alexander of Tunis, Baron Stephen Bentinck, Ingrid Seward (later to join Theo Cowan and marry Ross Benson), Davina Phillips, a jovial Ned Ryan, a close friend of Princess Margaret, and the socialite Homayoun Mazandi.

Another spectacular party was the one held at the RIBA to mark an exhibition of Brian Clarke's paintings and constructions, with which publication of a new Quartet book on Brian coincided. This attracted an odd mixture of people, from the most egregious punks to the *haute bourgeoisie*, reflecting the universal appeal of Clarke's work and the unquestioning zeal of his followers. Piers van Simpson and his wife Lindsey were back in London after a spell of four years with Warburgs in New York. Duggie Fields, Jasper Conran and a coterie of sexy young ladies floated around to enhance the congenial ambiance of the event. Mischa Spierenberg escorted Fiona Thyssen. Her free-spirited daughter Francesca was there; so was Francesca's boyfriend Steve Strange, whose career as a pop star shone but briefly. Francesca was constantly making waves in London's hedonistic sub-culture of rock groups and young painters. Once she arrived at my office in what appeared to be very friendly mode with Jean-Michel Basquiat, the Brooklyn-born son of a Haitian father whose graffiti-based art came to epitomize the youth culture of the 1980s with all its excess and disaffection. If I could have guessed when I met him what a tremendous impact he would have on the art scene before departing from it at the age of twenty-eight as a result of a heroin overdose, I would have invested in some of his paintings. It was a missed opportunity I later regretted. Each one of his paintings that survives today is worth a lot of money.

A more serious affair altogether was the launch of *Palestinian Self-Determination* by Crown Prince Hassan of Jordan, the brother of King Hussein. Prince Hassan was then thirty-four and had been educated at Harrow and Oxford. Writing the book had involved him in two years of research, and he came to

London specially to ensure it received all the attention it deserved. As heir to the throne, he used to act as head of state when his brother, King Hussein, was travelling abroad. When a journalist from the *Evening Standard* asked him to define his exact role, he said, 'I suppose you could describe me as the ombudsman – though I hate the word – of economic development in my country.' The book was important for setting out the legal basis of the claims of the Palestinian Arabs to self-determination and the establishment of their statehood on the West Bank and in the Gaza Strip. For decades they had been denied the independence promised them by the covenant of the League of Nations. In the future, the prince argued, the tensions of the region, which had already erupted into four major wars, were likely to explode into many further conflicts. Only if there was a just solution to give the Palestinians sovereignty could peace follow for the whole region. He discussed how such a solution could be reached according to international law.

Many books on the Palestine issue were published by Quartet over the years. The intention was to create a climate in which people of good will, from all over the world, could work confidently and purposefully for a political solution to the humanitarian tragedy. As a publisher, I never intended to act as an Arab propagandist; my aim all along has been to highlight the sufferings experienced by both sides and condemn violence as the means of achieving the final objective. I still retain the fervent hope that I will be able during my lifetime to visit the Holy Land and find it tranquil and at peace.

Although my office at Namara House was very modern and equipped with all the latest facilities, I continued to look back nostalgically at Wellington Court as the location where everything had begun and the setting in which I had enjoyed true happiness. There the foundation was laid for everything I had achieved so far and was confident I would achieve in the years ahead. Life was fun. Mad ideas came and went. Some were acted upon but others I dismissed because of their implausibility. A typical example of the latter occurred when I was still operating at Wellington Court. I became obsessed with the idea of owning a puma.

It seemed to me that my having a puma as a pet would give Wellington Court a certain cachet and would also provide me with a loyal companion. Yorkshire Television had just completed *The Arab Experience*, and I discussed the question with one of the makers of the programme, my friend Michael Deakin. The idea did not come as a surprise to him for he had always thought I was a bit crazy, and on my behalf he managed to locate a young puma at a private zoo somewhere in the north of England. When the girls at Wellington Court got wind of the proposal, there was general uproar. They were concerned for their personal safety with a puma roaming freely about the office. It only increased their consternation when I told them they would have to take it in turns to exercise it in Hyde Park. At this point they made representations to my wife Maria pointing out that our son Ramsay, then about ten years old, could be in equal danger. Maria took the whole idea with a pinch of salt. She assured the girls it was very doubtful that Westminster Council would allow anyone to walk a puma in the park, since it would constitute a danger to the public. Her advice was simply to ignore this sudden whim which would probably come to nothing.

I had a chauffeur then named Frank who lived with a wife much older than himself who he claimed was very domineering. According to him, she regularly intimidated him. As a peace-loving man he bore it with graceful resignation. Frank drove a long-base Rolls-Royce to ferry me about town and was never far from my elbow. He was like his master's shadow and hardly ever complained. By now I had had the idea of converting the front passenger seat of the Rolls-Royce to accommodate the puma and asked Frank for his suggestions. Perhaps we could purchase a suitable rug for the purpose? The normally sanguine Frank became distraught. How, he demanded, could he be expected to drive the car with a wild animal seated beside him? I appealed to his masculinity, putting the view that no real man would ever allow an animal to put him off his stroke. The puma would warm to him in no time, I reassured him; they would soon become inseparable. Frank was a simple fellow who lacked sophistication and liked his job. He wasn't going to lose it over the small matter of a puma. By the time our conversation ended, he seemed to have simmered down and promised he would think about it seriously over the weekend.

On Monday he arrived for work a different man. He was jubilant and full of confidence, entering the office with a slight swagger. By all means, he said, he would be happy to have the puma riding beside him in the car, but he had one request to make. Would it be possible for him to take the puma home one weekend? I was so taken aback by this complete turnaround that for a moment I was speechless. When I had recovered my equilibrium, I casually asked him the reason behind such a request. He laughed as if it should have been obvious to anyone. If he took the puma home, he explained, then his bossy wife was sure to start pushing the animal around and with any luck would get herself eaten by the beast. This macabre sense of humour was something Frank had kept under wraps until then; or was it that I had underestimated him? At last he had shown how he could rise to the occasion when challenged.

Sadly Maria was right. The City of Westminster would not countenance the idea of having a puma as a resident of the borough, let alone allow it to be promenaded in Hyde Park. Another dream bit the dust.

However, some dreams were more easily realized. One was the seasonal lunch at Wellington Court when a select few young ladies, much favoured by John Asprey and myself, were invited to spend a leisurely afternoon with us. They all happened to be endowed with good looks as well as the gift for being highly entertaining and they made these gatherings into enchanting diversions from the humdrum world of disciplined living. Formalities were banished for the day to give the occasion a more congenial atmosphere. We indulged ourselves with little constraint, feasting on excellent food and a vintage wine such as Léoville Barton 1961, and on one occasion committed the even greater extravagance of opening a bottle of Cheval Blanc 1947. Many years later I gave my dear friend Auberon Waugh a bottle of this extraordinary vintage to celebrate his birthday. The joy on his face as he held the bottle in his hand, caressing it as if it were a beautiful woman, is still etched in my memory. Bron was a true connoisseur, not only of wine but also of the art of fine living.

John Asprey and I spent the early period of our association seeking fulfilment in our work and building for the future. We were very adventurous then and absurdly optimistic. Occasionally we kicked over the traces and escaped briefly from the pressures of work. It had a reinvigorating effect and kept us from stagnating. The strides Asprey took in those days were testimony to our unique collaboration, our singularity of purpose and our ability to make friends and win people over.

Eleven

The rumour around town in early July 1981 was that Davina Woodhouse would soon be leaving my employment. The assumed reason was not because she was about to marry Earl Alexander of Tunis after a two-year romance but that the publication by Quartet of Nigel Dempster's book on Princess Margaret, *A Life Unfulfilled*, was impending and would put her in an embarrassing position. Her own version for leaving was that she hoped to become a conscientious housewife, though if anyone pressed her on the issue she declined to elaborate. Nigel himself gave the rumour much prominence in his *Daily Mail* diary and insisted that any fears Davina might have about the book upsetting the princess would prove to be quite unfounded. I could understand, however, that Davina might wish to distance herself from the book as a matter of protocol. Her original sponsor when she became a full-time lady-in-waiting to Princess Margaret in 1975 was an old chum of her parents, Lady Elizabeth Cavendish, and if Lady Elizabeth took exception to any aspect of the book it would have put Davina in an awkward position. Her loyalties were all with the princess and she did not wish to find herself in a situation where a conflict of interest might arise. In any case, Davina's leaving was natural enough; it would have happened anyway with her marriage to the earl. Her exit was accomplished with warmth and elegance. Our friendship remained over the years and she and her husband were regular attenders at the parties I continued to throw whenever an opportunity arose.

As for Nigel Dempster's book, there was always bound to be a degree of fall-out. Jonathan Cape, as a publisher in the running to take it on at an earlier stage, had dropped out, presumably not wishing to become entangled in a controversial royal affair. The launch for *A Life Unfulfilled* took place at the Arts Club in Dover Street. *Ritz* magazine, which covered the event, hailed it as divine, and according to Ingrid Seward, wall-to-wall hacks were interspersed with blue-blooded young ladies and celebrities could be found everywhere. Personalities who regularly featured in Nigel's column were milling about in force. Peter McKay and Jennifer Sharpe made a big show of friendliness towards the author. In his *Daily Mirror* diary piece, however, McKay claimed the book was heavily slanted in Princess Margaret's favour at the expense of her ex-husband, Lord Snowdon. To place the blame for the breakdown of their marriage on Snowdon for his dalliance with Jackie

Rufus-Isaacs in 1968 was to make too easy an assumption. Dempster asserted that the princess's relationship with Roddy Llewellyn did not begin till much later, in 1973. Would Snowdon retaliate on the point, McKay wondered. Friends believed he might be tempted to set the record straight. In McKay's opinion, that would be unwise, for the Margaret book, though fascinating, was bound to be seen as a whitewash anyway.

Intriguingly the book described how the princess was loved for her beauty and wit yet criticized for her widely publicized emotional liaisons, and always found herself in the shadow of her elder sister. But whatever she did attracted attention and caught the public imagination: whether it was her agony over the enforced loss of her first love, Group Captain Peter Townsend, her bohemian adventures in London's glamorous nightclubs in the 1950s, her fairytale wedding to Anthony Armstrong-Jones in Westminster Abbey and the distressing break-up of the marriage, or her sun-drenched holidays on the romantic West Indies island of Mustique. Nigel, the doyen of gossip columnists, explored the background to her eventful life and the reasons for its turbulence.

Reviews for the book were mixed but that did not stop it being a best-seller. Some people took exception to my having published it, and one particular criticism came from a wholly unexpected source. Victoria Asprey, John's wife, whose mother was married to the owner of the Léoville Barton vineyard, objected fiercely to a passage that named Barton's nephew as having had an amorous episode with the princess. Victoria telephoned me, incensed that I should be publishing a book she described as scurrilous, especially when her husband and I were such close associates, and asked for it to be withdrawn instantly. Her reaction was astonishing and I became angry at this unwarranted interference that she knew perfectly well was out of order. I stood my ground resolutely and our conversation came to a sudden close. Victoria and I did not speak for nearly a year after that. In the end it was John's intervention as peace-maker that restored polite relations.

At the time, most of the British press looked on me in a favourable light. They admired my enthusiasm, not to mention my recklessness. I made news by acting on impulse and occasionally disregarding financial risks if I felt it was in the artistic or public interest to see something published. Headlines in the *Tatler*'s 'Bystander' column encapsulated the prevailing response to me by pointing out that 'with oil millionaire Algy Cluff buying up the *Spectator* and *Quarto* [later to be amalgamated with the *Literary Review*] and wealthy Arab Naim Attallah supporting Quartet Books and the *Literary Review*, who needs the Arts Council?' The article went on to announce that one of Quartet's offshoots, Robin Clark, was to publish three first novels in paperback: Sally

Emerson's *Second Sight*, Julian Barnes's *Metroland* and Dee Phillips's *No, Not I.* *Second Sight* won a *Yorkshire Post* prize for best first work and Julian Barnes landed the Somerset Maugham Award.

I was still very much in a hurry to make our presence felt wherever it mattered most. The cultural future of an advanced nation lies in its emerging talent. For this reason Quartet sought to concentrate on the discovery of new writers rather than the exclusive pursuit of established names. We took chances on relatively unknown authors and worked hard to promote their work. Sometimes we failed through misjudging the prevailing mood or because we were ahead of our time. There were instances where we even lacked the essential resources but did not let that stop us. We improvised and published books that ultimately had to be remaindered despite their excellence, simply because the reading public was not yet ready to accept the subject or the concept. Sadly, this often happens in the publishing world. Books are similar to paintings in that they may be rejected initially only to be recognized as masterpieces after their creators are long dead.

The BBC created another cause for me to espouse in 1978 when it made Dennis Potter's television play *Brimstone and Treacle* and then promptly got cold feet over its theme and put a ban on it, locking the tapes away unshown in the archives. It was a gruelling piece about a brain-damaged paralysed girl being raped by a con man who charms his way into her family's home and turns out to be the devil. Subsequently it had a brief West End run as a stage play, and in October 1981 I joined forces with Dennis to explore making a feature film based on his television script. The director was to be Richard Loncraine and the producer Kenith Trodd. Peter Hannan was signed as director of photography, with Milly Burns as production designer and Robin Douet as production manager. Dennis was put in charge of his own script. Our budget was in the region of five hundred thousand pounds, with my investment, as executive producer, representing half that amount. The shooting schedule was timed to begin on 19 October, based at Shepperton Studios. Among the cast were Denholm Elliott, reprising the part of the girl's father, which he had already acted in the withdrawn television version, and Joan Plowright as the girl's mother. The part of the girl herself went to a gifted newcomer, Suzanna Hamilton.

While our American backers had been attracted by the possibility of David Bowie taking the starring role of the visiting infernal stranger, in the end he was not available. Instead the part went to Sting, the lead singer from the rock band the Police. Sting had some previous experience of working in the movies, having appeared in *Quadrophenia*, a 1979 film about the battles between the

Mods and Rockers in Brighton. He now wanted the chance to do some straight acting, but the Americans insisted on a new Police album as part of the deal. Dennis was prepared to adapt the script to allow Sting a singing role, but this was an idea Loncraine promptly vetoed. He thought it would make it all seem too like a follow-up to *Pennies from Heaven*. In the end it was agreed Sting would sing a nostalgic standard to back the end credits. The number chosen was 'Spread a Little Happiness'. When this was eventually released as a single, to Dennis's chagrin it attracted more public response than the film itself. He was quoted as saying on a Terry Wogan chat show some time afterwards, 'I think I was sent into this world to spread a little misery.'

I first got to know Dennis Potter when Quartet published the novel version of *Pennies from Heaven*. He and I hit it off straight away, though he was a famously complex and cantankerous character. This was largely the result of the terrible chronic illness he suffered from most of his adult life. Known as psoriatic arthropathy, it affected his skin and his joints. He had to endure constant physical pain and was incapacitated in many ways, which gave him a focus for his anger. Despite these handicaps, he was a man of the most remarkable achievements whose delving into the seedy depths of human motivation riveted his audience. He had a feeling for the drama and its need to defy convention which gave his work a rare quality seldom equalled by any of his contemporaries. He had an obsessive nature that in some ways was not dissimilar to my own. Artistically he was driven and inflexible. He loved a quarrel and his relationships with close associates were always tempestuous. This was especially so with Kenith Trodd, who had worked with Potter over many years on his television projects. Theirs was a relationship that oscillated between love and hate and caused consternation within their circle.

Dennis's perception of women was strange as well as intriguing. He was attracted to the dissolute type of woman whose sexual vibes stir man's most basic instincts. He certainly preferred the image of woman as sinful to the idea of her as pure. The seething underbelly of nightlife with all its sexual connotations was a theme he was drawn to explore time and time again. The association between disgust and guilt was very real for him. Somehow he felt at home in an environment where prostitutes lurked or had a dominant presence. But his was a unique talent and his output was prodigious, given the health constraints under which he worked. Of my own involvement I said in an interview with *Screen International* in early 1982 that 'investing in films is a logical progression to my publishing activities', that 'I've always been interested in the media and I've always wanted to take risks. I do not see the point in investing in things that you know are going to work. For me the gamble of doing something you believe in is vitally important.' Dennis told the *Daily Mirror* that in his ambition for the play to be turned into a film he was prepared to work for nothing to see the project through.

The subject matter of *Brimstone and Treacle* was guaranteed to attract controversy. In the mixed reception given the movie by the critics after its London première in September 1982, discussion undoubtedly centred more on its theme than its artistic merit. There was a general consensus that Sting's performance was a triumph, and most commentators agreed he was not its only revelation and *Brimstone and Treacle* was definitely a film to watch out for. It was remarked that it represented 'a most impressive move into film production for the publishing impresario Naim Attallah'. The party following the première was a lavish affair at a mansion in Regent's Park. Billy Connolly and Pamela Stephenson were there, deep in conversation with Captain Sensible (wearing a skirt), while Lyndsey De Paul giggled with her new man, designer Carl Dawson. Sting arrived alone but was soon surrounded by a cluster of beautiful women, including Selina Scott and the singer Marsha Hunt. Everyone at the gathering heaped praise on Sting for his acting ability. 'He was so good, he made me sick,' joked Bob Geldof.

Sting was in his element as he gasped, 'It's all so amazing.' His sudden transition from rock star to film star left him quite bemused. Even the great photographer Helmut Newton, who took the publicity photos for the film and had seen plenty of sights in his time, was dazzled by the event. Only one dissenting voice was raised: that of Virginia Gallico, the mother of Ludmilla Nova, my friend who had been lead dancer in *Arabian Fantasy* at the Royal Albert Hall. Virginia, who was also lady-in-waiting to Princess Grace of Monaco, was outraged and appalled by Dennis's fable. She let me know her views in no uncertain terms but I chose not to engage in any heated exchange with her in case it damaged my relationship with her daughter. Years later, when I bumped into Virginia and Ludmilla by chance in Budapest, the incident was apparently forgotten and all was well.

When Quartet gave Dennis Potter a commission to write a novel treatment for *Brimstone and Treacle*, he passed the task over to his daughter Sarah, whom he was encouraging to do some writing. His utter devotion to Sarah suggested she was the closest to him of all the women in his life.

Twelve

Where the *Literary Review* was concerned, the relationship with Anne Smith began in a flurry of goodwill, mutual respect and affection as she commuted between Edinburgh and London two or three times a month. She was a great character, unconventional in a variety of ways. She exuded the kind of Scottish earnestness that was refreshing, especially in London circles, where superficiality and flattery were a part of everyday intercourse. Anne reminded me of my grandmother in Nazareth, whom I had adored. She had the same physical build, the same gestures, the same matter-of-fact outlook on life. Yet, while my grandmother was illiterate, Anne had literature in her blood. The *Literary Review* under her editorship had turned into a monthly and was doing reasonably well with circulation figures. It enjoyed a staunch and loyal following, who liked it for being different from the other literary magazines and enterprising in its broad coverage of current books. Maybe it was not mainstream, but in a way that was the source of its attraction.

Anne was very ambitious, a trait in her character that began to emerge in the form of frustration at not being given an entrée into the numerous other activities going on within the Namara Group. She felt she was somehow being limited to just editing the *Literary Review* and wanted a new challenge, having accepted a change in her unique mode of operating in return for the funding that was the only way of seeing the magazine continue.

Anne set her sights on The Women's Press, the feminist imprint I had formed with Stephanie Dowrick, feeling that she could make a good job of running it. As her frustrations grew, she became very strung up and suffered the occasional depression. She took to disappearing for up to three days at a time, when no one could discover where to reach her. It began to be a worrying threat to our association. Communication is vitally important to me psychologically and I have never been able to operate efficiently without it. The reason for her disappearances was plausible enough: that she needed to be by herself when she was depressed. We had many discussions on the subject and invariably she was apologetic for her unscheduled absences and each time she made a resolution to be more disciplined in future.

The dilemma here was that The Women's Press was running smoothly enough under its established management. Even if I had wished to make an outside appointment and introduce someone else in a senior position, it would hardly have been possible or appropriate. Stephanie Dowrick, my co-founder and true mother of The Women's Press, had and still has my total loyalty as a friend. I never for a moment doubted her dynamism and talent. To impose Anne Smith or anyone else on the management team at The Women's Press simply did not enter my thoughts. Instead I gave Anne the option of becoming a special editor for Quartet Books, with Nigel Dempster's book on Princess Margaret as her first assignment. She carried out the task admirably, but still there were signs that this sort of responsibility was not enough to satisfy her ambition. She remained unsettled and rather bored, undergoing sharp mood swings. No one could fathom what was the matter and inevitably our relationship began to develop cracks. I still felt a deep affection for her, but a crisis was looming in as much as I could no longer feel as comfortable in our dealings as formerly. She became strangely aloof and the sparkle that endeared her to me in the first place had faded. She had become a problem but the reason was a mystery and I kept asking myself whether it could be something in her private life – an area I never encroached upon; or was it simply that she had tired of me personally, or was jaded with editing the magazine?

Then, on 16 September 1981, she telephoned me and without preamble stated emphatically that she did not wish to edit the magazine any longer and resigned forthwith from her employment with the Namara Group. The only way I could respond to this completely unexpected turn of events was take her at her word and accept her resignation. It never occurred to me that she might intend it as a tactic to pressurize me into granting some future request that she had it in mind to make. If that was the case, how was I to know? I was completely taken aback and my priority was to fill the vacuum created and ensure continuity of production for the *Literary Review*. I turned to Gillian Greenwood, who was in charge of Robin Clark Ltd, and offered her the post of editor to the magazine. She had formerly been deputy editor to *Books and Bookmen* before it folded, so her credentials were excellent. Gillian accepted at once, and the gap she left at Robin Clark was filled by Rebecca Fraser soon afterwards.

As soon as Anne heard that Gillian was in line to succeed her in her old editorial chair, she exploded. And what an explosion! Suddenly a new and totally alien person erupted on to the scene. She was beside herself with fury, levelling one accusation after another against me. All kinds of horrendous reasons were cited for my dispensing with her. The litany of names she called me I could only attribute to her state of mind at the time. Instantly the press was all ears, and in the statements she made to them she portrayed herself as the little person victimized by a greedy entrepreneur who had stolen her brainchild, her magazine, away from her, and was now conducting a war of attrition against her. In one version of her story I became an Arab propagandist who was constantly trying to compromise the editorial independence of the magazine for my own ruthless purposes – hence in part the reason for her 'dismissal'.

Anne had in fact let hardly a moment pass after delivering her telephone bombshell before taking her story to the national press in time to catch their deadlines the same night. On the morning of the 17th, *The Times* had a head-line that read '*Review* editor is to claim her dismissal was unfair'; the *Guardian's* ran 'Editor of *Literary Review* loses job'; 'Row costs magazine founder her job' and 'Magazine editor to be replaced' announced the *Scotsman*; 'Support for sacked editor' stated the *Glasgow Herald* more ominously; and 'Slanging match' said a piece in the *Standard* later that morning. All at once the row, according to her account, centred on a campaign she was running for an increase in annual salary, Anne claiming she had asked for twelve thousand pounds to cover the 'two jobs' she was doing and this had precipitated her dismissal. The one copy-editing assignment she had been offered and carried out was elevated into a post of 'commissioning editor', a job description that implied a senior managerial appointment. According to the *Glasgow Herald* she had been, moreover, a 'director of the publishing firm'. Kenneth Gosling reported in *The Times* that she was 'determined to take the magazine's owner, Mr Naim Attallah, to an industrial tribunal, claiming unfair dismissal. But she made clear last night that her action would be about the simultaneous ending of her job as a commissioning editor with Mr Attallah's publishing concern, Quartet Books, not the ending of the magazine editorship.'

The *Scotsman* had a more detailed account:

Dr Smith admits that she had often expressed discontent over the way Mr Attallah was running the magazine, particularly in his failure to solve distribution problems, but that the main reason for her dismissal was that she had 'hurt his feelings deeply by asking for a rise'.

Another area of disagreement between them was the low rate of payment to contributors. Dr Smith, who got the magazine off the ground by soliciting free articles from famous literary names, claims she was not able to pay the market price as she wanted to.

She now intends to fight the loss of her job as a Quartet editor through an industrial tribunal and hopes that Mr Attallah will recognize that she has a moral right to ownership of the title and give it back to her so that she can look for a new backer.

'I intend to bring the pressure of public opinion to bear on him for his shabby treatment of me,' Dr Smith said at the magazine's editorial office in Edinburgh New Town. 'I hope to shame him into giving me back the title of the magazine when he got it for nothing.'

The *Scotsman* concluded, however, that it was 'almost certain the magazine will now become London-based'. The *Glasgow Herald* also felt that 'its distinctive Scottish character . . . is certain to disappear along with its sacked editor'. It hinted that feelings were likely to run high and a campaign to support Dr Smith 'is now under way among the distinguished literary figures who have contributed reviews to the magazine, including Frederic Raphael, Doris Lessing, Colin Watson, A. S. Byatt and Rebecca West'. First into the lists was Professor Bernard Crick, the biographer of George Orwell, who thundered in a statement to the *Guardian*: 'Mr Attallah has not merely killed the independence of the most lively literary journal that exists in Britain today, but he seems to have taken over a magazine that was entirely created by the capital and unstinting energy of one woman.'

The most outrageous calumny against me appeared the next day in *The Times* 'Diary' column under the heading 'Over and Out':

> Eager for my slice of Sir James Goldsmith's £50,000 award for information about left-wing plots to subvert the media, I can reveal exclusively what lies behind the peremptory dismissal of Anne Smith, founder and editor of the *Literary Review*: it was her refusal to accept Arab propaganda.
>
> When Maim [*sic*] Atallah [*sic*] bought the magazine from Dr Smith he assured her not only that she would remain editor but that she would retain editorial independence. But it was not long before pro-Palestinian articles and reviews signed by Atallah began piling up on her desk for publication.
>
> The split came over Atallah's insistence that the New Year issue should carry an Arab supplement running to 150 pages. Dr Smith says she would not have objected to a small supplement but she dug in her heels at one that would have been three times the size of the magazine in which it appeared.

The misspelling of my name as 'Maim' caused unbridled merriment in the offices of *Private Eye*.

On Saturday, 19 September, I published a letter in the *Guardian* in a doomed attempt to introduce a note of calm reason into the furore, pointing out that their original report had contained several inaccuracies.

> Although not wishing to have a slanging match with Dr Anne Smith, for whom I still retain the highest regard, I would like to be judged on the facts and my record as a supporter of the arts.
>
> The question of money has never been a motivating factor when making decisions of this kind. A cooperation must be based on mutual respect and an ability to work together, unhampered by outside considerations.
>
> The *Literary Review* is not, as suggested, a commercial proposition since

it has never broken even nor is it likely to do so in the future. My interest is purely literary and my initial involvement was only to support Dr Anne Smith, which I have done to a considerable financial extent.

I can assure Professor Bernard Crick that it is not my intention to forsake the *Literary Review* or to affect its independence in any way. I shall continue to support it, and perhaps out of the present crisis a new lease of life will ensure that the review can gain impetus with the passage of time.

It appeared above a letter from P.N. Furbank suggesting that since Anne Smith was such a brilliant editor someone should 'commission her to continue the *Literary Review* under a new title'. On Monday, the 21st, the *Guardian* printed further letters packed with literary rhetoric from Anne Smith supporters. One of them suggested it was time for the Scottish Arts Council to ride into battle with a rescue package for the magazine.

The following Thursday, the 24th, there were two items of significance in the press, the first from Anne to *The Times*, in which she attempted, without loss of face, to soft-pedal on the allegations of Arab bias printed in the diary piece the week before. 'Mr Attallah did not exactly "heap" unwanted pro-Palestinian articles on to my desk,' she admitted, but then went to to make an assertion which would be hard to justify from any scrutiny of *Literary Review* back numbers: 'certainly, the magazine's coverage of Arab books has grown considerably since he took it over, and certainly these books were reviewed, as often as not, at Mr Attallah's "suggestion", by reviewers nominated by him, but with my consent.'

> If I may make a more subtle point, I should add to this that the unspoken possibility was always there that if I were to publish articles or reviews hostile to Mr Attallah's beliefs, that would have spelt the end of the *Literary Review*. He never left me in any doubt that if I incurred his displeasure, e.g. by not returning his phone calls immediately, he would close the magazine down.
>
> Mr Attallah believed that to own a magazine is to have a great say in its content: he would not accept that an editor should have complete control of this.

She went on to perpetuate and enhance the plausible myth she had created about the hundred-and-fifty-page supplement on Arab life and culture:

> I did agree to the publication of a separate supplement of 150 pages on the arts in the Arab world. I was reluctant to do this, because of the amount of work it would involve in such a short time and because my knowledge of the subject is so negligible as to be non-existent. None the less, I was assured by Mr Attallah that I would have complete editorial freedom,

except that I would not be allowed to touch on politics or to include a piece I suggested on public opinion in this country about Arabs.

The other item was a group letter to the *Guardian* signed by eight members of Quartet's office staff, David Elliott, Penny Grant, Olive Coull, Janet Law (later Parker), Renee Knight, Jody Boulting, Gary Grant and Maureen Abdallah, speaking up for the 'people in the back-room' Anne had been claiming to represent in some of her effusions.

> Let us speak for ourselves. If it is of interest to your readers we can willingly, using your columns, discuss our relationship/relationships with Mr Attallah, each other, Dr Smith, and possibly the world at large. It may, however, suffice to say that we feel our relationship with Naim Attallah is both encouraging and rewarding. (We also, by the way, feel flattered that as a collection of publishers we warrant such national attention.)
>
> It is, more seriously, a shame that Anne found it impossible to recognize the same spirit. Perhaps we can all now get back to publishing books and magazines and stop monopolizing your letters column.

From this the conclusion was extrapolated that since only half the staff signed the letter the others perhaps declined and I must be furious. A couple of weeks further on, 'Bookworm' in *Private Eye*'s 'World of Books' column (9 October), picked up on the theme by describing how 'Maim ranted and raged at the letter. He was livid that the entire staff hadn't signed the sycophantic handout.' In the main, however, 'Bookworm' had as much fun with Anne Smith as with me:

> Hardly anyone had heard of Anne Smith before Naim Attullah . . . sacked her from the *Literary Review*, the garrulous magazine she had founded and edited from Edinburgh. Dr Smith, as she likes to be known, conned *Grauniad* hack Martin Walker into presenting her very loaded side of the argument as if it were 'objective' and deluged the Western press with letters declaring how wickedly the Arab Maim, as the *Grauniad* [actually *The Times*] wittily renamed him, had treated her.
>
> It's hard to see how the *Literary Review* could have lost as much money as it reputedly has as Dr Smith didn't believe in paying 'academics' for their reviews: she could offer so little that it was an opportunity for young and third-rate dons to make it in the world of letters. She tried to persuade fiction writers to contribute short stories 'for love'.
>
> Dr Smith insisted to the *Grauniad*'s man that her own first novel, *The Magic Glass*, was published to 'uniformly impressive reviews'. Perhaps Dr Smith didn't show Martin Walker the press cuttings.

The press continued hot on the scent of what promised to continue as a major literary scandal and went on reproducing Anne's accusations, baseless and preposterous as they were, without question. In all of this the fundamental fact was lost to sight: that it was she who tendered her resignation and I who merely accepted it. The columnists loved nothing better than a public quarrel of this magnitude; it made headline news. The movement for the contributors to the magazine and almost the entire literary establishment – journalists and writers – to rally to Anne's support and call for a boycott of the *Literary Review* continued to get up steam. Dark forebodings were expressed that the special quality of the magazine could never now be recreated following Anne's departure. David Gascoyne published a letter in *The Times Literary Supplement* on 2 October in which he said that, although 'he had no practical suggestions to make regarding Dr Smith's dilemma', he was writing,

> principally to express my sense of outrage on learning of the plight of an editor who has by now amply demonstrated her enterprise, discrimination and intellectual independence. It is impossible at present to predict what will be the future of the *Literary Review*, but I only hope that one will find in future issues the work of such fine writers as Anthony Burgess, Doris Lessing, Frederic Raphael, Angus Wilson, Malcolm Bradbury, William Trevor, Michael Schmidt and others of the team of younger, entertainingly astute and professionally equipped critics, all of whose names one has become accustomed to seeing in the *Review*'s contents-lists. Surely there must still be room in Britain, despite the reputedly omnipotent recession, for a literary journal of the range and quality represented by the Edinburgh *Literary Review* under Anne Smith's editorship?

Private Eye, on the other hand, set about debunking the legend of the *Literary Review* being created by the literary partisans who were ready to man the barricades in defence of Anne Smith's reputation. A letter on 20 November, claiming to come from a certain 'Bella Horizonte' of Cricklewood, put the opposing case:

> Sir – I have held back from writing to you on the Dr Anne Smith affair because I assumed that someone with more authority than I would get round to stating the searingly obvious: the *Literary Review* was a cast-iron dud.
>
> All and sundry tried to cash in on the temporary demise of the *TLS* during the Thomson lock-out, and most were pretty ropey. Least incompetent was the *London Review of Books*, then came *Quarto*, and then, a long way behind, came the *Literary Review*.
>
> Because it didn't pay for any contributions (not a normal practice, despite

the claims of one correspondent), it was forced to fill its columns with the outpourings of axe-grinders, opportunists, desperate graduate students, etc. Some people of competence contributed to early issues gratis in the hope that this would earn them favour when the gravy train rolled in: it remained stubbornly in the sidings.

I'm sure Anne Smith, as everyone avers, is a nice person and a good novelist. It may well be that she has been treated shamefully by Naim Attallah. Let not either of these truths mask the equal truth that, for whatever reason, she has backed a loser.

The literary row continued for week after week, becoming so bitter and acrimonious that it lost all touch with reality. In Scotland I had hit the nerve of national pride and was seen as the enemy of all things cultural. Passions became so inflamed that Anne's version of events was the one the public in general accepted.

Eventually I was forced to defend myself. There was a danger that the escalation of feelings would do my reputation and integrity real harm. The time came when I could not let the matter rest without putting forward my own account of the facts. Both sides therefore were using the media to express and rebut accusations and the tradition of fair play can only be served if I offer a glimpse of the copious press coverage at the time. This will allow readers to make up their own minds.

Quartet's publicity manager, Sheila Turnbull, was going through a negative feminist streak that same October. It had clouded her vision on a number of occasions. I was already experiencing some difficulty in my relationship with her, in part because she disapproved of some of the books we published and in part because she deprecated my lifestyle. As publicity manager she was the voice of Quartet, and her attitude was becoming incompatible with her role. She was a nice person, but sometimes misguided on account of her strong views. I had always suspected they were too rigid for her own good and, in a wider sense, that she lacked a sense of humour. I believed her private life had not been easy and she had suffered as a result. She would often misinterpret a gesture or statement as being offensive, especially where it concerned someone of her own sex.

Sheila tended to make any quarrel involving a woman into her own cross to bear. The Anne Smith saga was a typical example. She took it all as a personal affront, despite being aware at first hand of the circumstances leading to the dispute. Anne at that stage was like a hurricane gaining strength, becoming steadily less rational and more unrestrained, her accusations engulfing everyone who had anything to do with me. It was perfectly true that Sheila had flatly refused to lend her name to the letter in the *Guardian*, which left me feeling she was incriminating me without real cause, but nothing followed on from that where I was concerned. In fact she tendered her resignation soon afterwards and gave an interview to *Publishing News*, which they published on 16 October. In this she claimed I had called her a 'rotten apple', but she did agree she had left Quartet of her own volition, having been offered a job with another publisher as foreign-rights manager. She also maintained, however, that while she was in the process of making her mind up about whether to accept the offer, she found out that Juliette Foy, her assistant, had been offered her post as publicity manager and had accepted. According to *Publishing News*, it was this that decided her to quit, having in the meantime also turned down an offer from me of fifty pounds a night to appear nude in J. P. Donleavy's *The Beastly Beatitudes of Balthazar B.*

I could only think at the time that she must have caught the bug from Anne Smith to have come out with such a ludicrous story. *Publishing News* did approach me for my comments and I refuted Sheila's imputations while being able to stress the fact that there were fifteen people at Quartet who had not signed the letter and remained happily working there. Many years later Sheila and I met again and buried the hatchet, though I had never borne her a grudge. A combination of circumstances can sometimes propel the best of us into taking a stance or a course of action we later regret.

During the last quarter of 1981 I was in touch with my legal advisers over instituting proceedings against *The Times* for the description of me as an Arab propagandist. Legal action loomed from the opposite direction when Marina Vaizey, the art historian and critic for the *Sunday Times*, took violent exception to an article on art criticism by Janet Daley that Anne Smith had published in the *Literary Review*. A writ was served by Lady Vaizey and Times Newspapers against Anne Smith, Janet Daley and Namara, as the publishers. Coinciding with the publication of Nigel Dempster's book on Princess Margaret in November, *The Times* 'Diary' reported that the gossip columnist had his sympathies wrung to such an extent by the plight of Anne Smith that he was sending her a cheque for fifteen hundred pounds to compensate for the parsimony of his publishers. Evidently she refused to accept it, but Nigel insisted it should be invested in a new literary magazine she was said to be planning, to be called *The Common Reader*. Meanwhile I had been approached by a friend of Anne Smith's from Scotland, who offered to be a mediator on the grounds that the on-going quarrel was doing no good to any of the parties involved. Her name was Jennifer Bradshaw, now Erdal, and she was a graduate of the University of St Andrews, having studied Russian and philosophy. She was engaged on making a translation of the memoirs of the artist Leonid Pasternak, the father of Boris, which Quartet were to publish.

An offer to intercede in my complaint against *The Times* came from another quarter during a meal at Mark Birley's Harry's Bar, when Nigel Dempster and Tina Brown were in the group. Tina had been close friends at Oxford with Gillian Greenwood, who was now settling in as *Literary Review* editor, and Sally Emerson, a Quartet author. Tina, whose friend I also became and whom I would in due course interview for my book *Women*, was editor of the *Tatler* and married to Harold Evans, the editor of *The Times*. As we talked, Tina asked, 'Do you want me to talk to Harry?' 'Yes, why not?' I said. Consequently, both legal threats were withdrawn by mutual agreement and the situation with *The Times* relaxed on 23 November when it carried the following apology:

On September 18 it was reported in the Diary that Dr Anne Smith, the former editor of the *Literary Review*, had left the magazine because of her refusal to accept Arab propaganda from the proprietor, Mr Naim Attallah. Mr Attallah has asked us to point out – and Dr Smith agrees, as we do – that he is not a propagandist for an Arab or any other political cause and as head of Quartet Books has published a number of works of special Arab interest in the context of world culture. We regret any misunderstanding or embarrassment that may have been caused.

Then, on 23 December, the *Scotsman* carried under the headline 'Ex-editor ends battle over magazine':

Dr Anne Smith, the founder of the *Literary Review* . . . has accepted defeat in her attempt to win the magazine title back . . . [Yesterday] Dr Smith said that Mr Attallah had paid in full all the sums she had claimed and in addition had made her an *ex-gratia* payment.

She said in a statement that she would like 'to make it absolutely plain that I now withdraw unequivocally all the allegations . . . which have been attributed to me in the past few months'. Dr Smith said yesterday that this did not mean that previous statements had been untrue, but that the financial claims which she had made had now been met.

There the matter might finally have been expected to rest, and the *Times* Dairy joined in the general sigh of relief when it wrote on 30 December: 'How pleasant to see that the flickering literary squabble between Dr Anne Smith . . . and Mr Attallah . . . appears to have been resolved amicably.' No 'further legal action', according to Dr Smith, would now 'be taken by either side and they have, accordingly, made up their differences "in all respects" '.

The *Scotsman*, on 15 January 1982, carried a letter from me that, of necessity, clarified a number of issues, including the fact that I had almost immediately after her resignation 'instructed my solicitors to commence negotiations with her and her solicitors so as to settle all outstanding claims amicably'.

> However, as the weeks passed and no specific information was forth-coming, reports began to appear in the press, emanating from Dr Smith, which were highly detrimental to me. Eventually Dr Smith made known the extent of her various claims; a negotiation was effected and settlement made . . . Dr Smith expressed the wish to 'withdraw unequivocally all the allegations which had been attributed to her in the previous few months'. To state now that 'this did not mean that previous statements had been untrue' is to retract upon the earlier statement, and reflects more on Dr Smith's inconsistency than upon the facts of the matter.
>
> I trust that you will publish this letter in order to place on record the above correction as a matter of fact and also to make clear that, to the best of my knowledge, Dr Smith did not begin proceedings for unfair dismissal against me, nor did she ever bring a civil action against me for arrears of salary . . . Nor was there ever any question of her 'winning back the magazine by legal action'.
>
> It only remains for me to wish Dr Smith good fortune in her efforts to found and edit a magazine in the future, and this I do sincerely.

Alas, it seemed that the Christmas and New Year spirit had fully evaporated by 20 January when the *Scotsman* printed a long letter headed 'An ex-editor's regret'. In this Anne set out to challenge my claims on the extent of the *Literary Review*'s losses and said how her 'offer of resignation' had been made in an attempt to force my hand over what she perceived as my refusal to discuss her salary and the 'constant threat' she was under of having the magazine closed down if she displeased me in any way. There was also my 'repeated refusal' to go to an independent arbitrator.

> Finally, the sentence which Mr Attallah quoted from the press release he drew up for me to sign is taken out of context. On his payment of what he owed me, and on his compensating me for the loss of both my jobs, I was prepared to withdraw all allegations I had made with regard to his failure to do this. Of course, *I* can't withdraw 'allegations made by the press' – only the press can do that – but I can and do stand by every word I have said about Mr Attallah's treatment of me, to any member of the press, *unequivocally* . . .
>
> It would seem then that in believing the fervent assurances of Mr Attallah's mediator that the last sentence of that press release could only be

taken to refer to his previous failure to make any sort of financial restitution, in a situation where his moral obligation at least was clear, I behaved as naïvely as I did in the first place, when I sold him the *LR* for £1.

In the circumstances, I bitterly regret having submitted to the sort of unfair pressure I was under to sign that press release.

The next letter in the *Scotsman*, on 26 January, was from Jennifer Bradshaw, protesting that she had undertaken negotiations as a 'close friend' of Anne Smith, having previously written to me a letter in her defence, 'believing her to be the injured party'.

To sign that press release, to accept the payments, and then to re-embark on a smear campaign against Mr Attallah and his management at Quartet, is not acting in good faith, and self-confessed 'naïvety' does not mitigate the bad faith . . .

If there was 'unfair pressure' on anyone during these negotiations, it was on Mr Attallah. I know that to be true since I was applying the pressure and dissuaded him from acting on the advice of his lawyer to go to court.

It would take the 'whole letters page', Anne Smith countered in the *Scotsman* two days later, to refute the question of Mrs Bradshaw's ' "mediation" . . . and my bad faith'. In any case, she said, 'I did not see Mrs Bradshaw as a "close friend"; we had only met three or four times in connection with her translation for Quartet Books and had been acquainted with each other for less than a year.'

She assured me as she had done on so many other points, in particular about going to court, that because I was so emotionally involved I could not interpret it properly, that it could only be read one way, to mean that I withdrew my accusations about Mr Attallah's failure to compensate me . . .

Of course, he can afford, as Mrs Bradshaw so often warned me, to fight me in court till the cows come home, but I have done nothing of which I am ashamed, and if Mr Attallah chooses to waste his time in petty squabbles of the You did/I didn't sort, there seems to be nothing I can do to stop him.

Another upset occurred that January when *Harpers & Queen* published what purported to be a series of extracts from Anne Smith's diary. I had to admit that these did have a certain entertainment value:

CANNES, *April*
Editing Nigel Dempster's life of Princess Margaret. Astonished at how he manages to be so frank and so sympathetic simultaneously. Poor little rich bitch. In Cannes for ten days, having told ND I can only feel free to go if

I know he's working to finish HRH Princess M. in my absence. This is known as the doctrine of substitution in stern Caledonia.

Cannes astonishing: interchangeable young lovelies on the arms of interchangeable pocked and paunchy oldies, in an endless slow promenade on La Croisette to see and be seen. Two facial expressions only: 'I'm being looked at' and 'Am I being looked at?' Am using the Ayatollah's [picking up on the nickname *Private Eye* used for me] flat, rented for film festival: crowning disillusionment of my first and last experience of luxury living – trod on something in the sitting-room, pulled it out of bare foot, to discover it to be a filthy big toenail (somebody else's). Sure, I would have guessed that the toenails of the rich grow just like ours, without the demonstration. But whose? Derek Jarman's? He was the last occupant. No, I spoke to him on the telephone yesterday and he sounded civilized. The Ayatollah's? Doubt it. It's a very old toenail.

Of the later extracts, however, there were three in particular that I felt to be below the belt. They read as follows:

FIFE, *August*

My mother dies. Ayatollah is furious. London Transport turned down two posters for Quartet Books' *Settling Down* and *Sisters under the Skin*, but charged him £2,000 for the space booked. He wanted to brief me to write something nasty about London Transport for the *Literary Review* and my mother, unconscious of this, hands in her dinner pail. I am in darkest Fife, away from telephones. Ayatollah about to set out for holiday in benighted Bulgaria. He yells down the phone to my secretary that he's closing the magazine (only the third threat of this kind in four months – is he tiring?) and buggers off to the Bulgars.

DITTO, *September*

Before the winter of my discontent gets properly under way, I determine to discuss the state of play re the mag, my overworked and underpaid situation, and other little niceties, with the Ayatollah. He keeps me waiting an hour, then hasn't time to discuss anything. I return to work to hear that salary raises are virtually unknown in Namara; that you work and ask until you get tired, read the unemployment figures, and resign yourself to the dignity of labour, poorly rewarded though it may be. As I work, I think. As I think I become outraged. I conclude that the Ayotollah's attitude to me is not unlike that of the Japanese to the POWs on the Burma railway. So I write to him and drop the letter off, together with the article for his approval on London Transport censorship policy, asking for my £12,000 and threatening to resign if it's not forthcoming. The rest is silence, followed by his letter of 15 September, that burbles on about 'irreconcilable difficulties'.

5th October

Bridget Heathcoat-Amory arrives, metamorphosed into the bailiff, to turf me out of my office. I am given two hours to get all that's mine out. All but a desk or two and a typewriter is mine. It is a fraught two hours, but not so fraught as to blind me to the irony that the first issue of the *Literary Review* appeared on 5 October 1979. 'Two years before the masthead' and nothing to show for it but poverty and grief, I muse, feeling temporarily 'Gummidge-ish'.

I could not believe my eyes to find a magazine of the standing of *Harpers & Queen* stooping to publish such scurrilous material, most of it concocted to perpetuate the myth that Anne Smith was a victim of harsh injustice and was continuing to seek some sort of redress. The whole episode had become not only insulting but painful. It was dumbfounding simply to imagine how all my motives behind the monies I had spent to promote new talent and uphold the literary establishment, often to my own deep financial detriment, were being totally traduced by Anne's insinuation that I was a money-grubbing spoiler who did not care a hoot about the poor or the underprivileged. It was a falsehood that I felt must somehow be corrected. Legal proceedings were instituted against the magazine, which later conceded there had been an error of judgement and agreed to make an apology in the High Court on 14 May 1982:

Mr Andrew Pugh, for Mr Attallah, made reference to the feature 'Private Views' which appeared in the January 1982 issue of *Harpers & Queen*. This had contained derogatory reference to Mr Attallah, implying that he and Namara Press Ltd (a company of which he is chairman and managing director) had treated their staff poorly, and underpaid them. Mr Jonathan Hirst, on behalf of the publishers of *Harpers & Queen* and the editor of the article, acknowledged that there was no truth in the allegations and apologized for their publication. Mr Pugh said that Mr Attallah's sole purpose in commencing the proceedings had been to remove the slur on his reputation. The publishers have agreed to indemnify him in respect of his costs.

The Anne Smith saga had not yet run out of steam. It was to continue for some measurable time before a reconciliation took place. (More about that later.) And then, shortly afterwards, the whereabouts of Anne Smith became a total mystery.

Thirteen

In August 1981, I received a phone call from Wilfred Burchett, with whom I had become friends after our first meeting at the Plaza Hotel in New York in the late 1970s. He was in America advising the Nixon administration in its conduct of clandestine talks with the Vietcong with a view to ending the Vietnam conflict. At that time the Americans were sustaining heavy losses and their toll of dead and injured was steadily rising to levels that were politically indefensible. Their problem was to find a way of extricating themselves from the conflict without loss of face. Wilfred was a *bête noir* for the administrations in both America and his native Australia for having covered the Vietnam war from the 'other side', sending out his dispatches from behind the lines in the jungle. His knowledge of and contacts with the Vietcong, however, took on a value that Nixon and his advisers were unable to ignore in the changing political climate of the United States and the rising radical tide of its peace movement.

Wilfred was now retired and living behind the Iron Curtain in Sofia with his Bulgarian wife. His proposal was that I should visit him with my wife Maria and our son Ramsay, if he could manage to secure an invitation for us from the Bulgarian authorities. I was delighted to hear from him in the first place and in the second overwhelmed by this unexpected gesture. My response was immediate and positive: we would love to come. Wilfred was a giant among the journalists of his generation, and a warm-hearted, larger-than-life character. He may have held many controversial political views, but at heart he was a courageous humanitarian, a champion of the poor and the oppressed, and had my unconditional admiration.

Wilfred's initial clash with American interests had come head-on in 1945 when, as a young war correspondent entering Japan with the US invasion forces, he defied the exclusion zone declared by General MacArthur to cover the cities of Hiroshima and Nagasaki after their destruction by atomic bombs. He was the first Western journalist to enter Hiroshima after the attack and sat on a surviving lump of concrete with his Hermes typewriter in the radioactive wilderness, having seen the evidence of obliterated humanity and the plight of those who were dying from their injuries and a mysterious sickness previously unknown to medicine. The technical terms to describe their illness were not yet in place, but Wilfred was in no doubt about the enormity of the implications.

He began his report, published as a world exclusive in Lord Beaverbrook's *Daily Express* in London, with the words: 'I write this as a warning to the world.'

The scenes he went on to describe in graphic detail seemed almost beyond the scope of the human imagination. The official American line on atomic warfare, then and for long afterwards, was that death and destruction were caused by the bomb blast, radiation being a harmless side-effect. From the American point of view, Burchett's talk of 'bomb sickness' needed to be refuted and dismissed as Japanese propaganda. The official press report on Nagasaki, which denied the effects of radiation, was prepared by William Laurence, a science writer on the *New York Times*, who also happened to be in the pay of the US War Department. Laurence and the *New York Times* were awarded a Pulitzer prize for journalism in recognition of their efforts (now seen as dishonourable), but Burchett's forebodings never went away. At a press conference he openly challenged General MacArthur when he made attempts to pour scorn on Burchett's Hiroshima account.

With the polarization of positions and loyalties that inevitably came with the Cold War, Wilfred's sympathies were certainly not in America's favour. His highly controversial dispatches from the Korean war after it began in 1951 were obtained under Chinese press accreditation. He enraged the Americans by revealing that a captured general, William F. Dean, was fit and alive in the north as a prisoner of war when they were trying to use his supposed slaughter to bring pressure to bear on negotiations. The Americans branded Burchett pro-Communist and there were attempts in Australia to have him declared a traitor. Though no formal charges were ever laid against him, the Australian government declined to renew his passport at the start of hostilities in Vietnam, forcing him to remain in exile from his homeland for many years.

At one point his reports from Vietnam from among the Vietcong forces provoked the Nixon administration to such an extent that they put a bounty on his head; but in 1980, one of the most distinguished of American war correspondents, Harrison E. Salisbury, the 1955 Pulitzer prize-winner for international reporting, described him in these terms:

Wilfred Burchett is a man who defies classification. There is hardly a war or revolution in the past forty years at which he as a journalist has not been present. There is hardly a left-wing movement with which he as a radical (or 'progressive', as he likes to call himself) has not sympathized. In his ceaseless travel he has met most of the diplomats and national leaders of his time and most of his fellow correspondents. There is probably no other man living who was on intimate terms with both Ho Chi Minh and Henry Kissinger.

He was reviled by the right in his native Australia, but became a hero for his country's growing peace and anti-nuclear movements. Australian war journalist Pat Burgess wrote: 'No correspondent was better loved by his colleagues or more bitterly detested.' This in itself testified to the power of what he had to say. Burchett himself made clear his standpoint: 'My duties as a citizen of the world go beyond my responsibilities only to my own country. In other words, I reject the "my country – right or wrong".' During a press conference he stated, 'I've certainly not been a traitor to the Allies. I've opposed policies in Vietnam. I oppose Australians being killed on Vietnamese soil. If I were a Vietnamese invading Australian soil, I'd be supporting Australia.'

In Britain another distinguished war correspondent, James Cameron, gave his recollections of him in 1977:

> I have had the good luck to know Wilfred Burchett off and on ever since we toiled together in the Fleet Street vineyard of the Château Beaverbrook. We abandoned this patronage at almost exactly the same time, though for marginally different reasons. To his [Beaverbrook's] dying day, which took a long time to come, the lord believed that our defections had been politically coordinated; he was, as so often, quite wrong. In fact at the time I had never even met Wilfred. Indeed I did not know his name was Wilfred. As an Australian he worked for the *Express* during the war in the Pacific; I was in Asia and Europe. He signed his file simply: Burchett. They had to find an acceptable byline for this gifted but remote correspondent, so someone or other arbitrarily called him 'Peter'. Fleet Street was always pretty cavalier about identities. Nevertheless, for some time after I established a kinship with this wayward old mate, I had a job unscrambling the Peter from the real man. And it is a real man.

Where Burchett's invitation to me and my family was concerned, he was as good as his word. Hardly a week had passed after his phone call before all our travel arrangements were concluded. The official invitation arrived, accompanied by three air tickets on Bulgarian Airlines. We flew to Sofia, where we stayed for one night before taking an onward flight next day to the Black Sea resort of Varna. There we found ourselves occupying a suite in what was then the resort's most luxurious hotel. It had a stunning outlook on to the Black Sea and, as it happened, a grandstand view of the Russian fleet on exercise. We watched their manoeuvres with guarded curiosity and restrained ourselves from taking any pictures in case we found ourselves in breach of some security regulations and landed ourselves in trouble.

Despite the obvious severity of the regime and the signs of Russian influence that were everywhere evident, Wilfred managed to make us feel totally at home with his display of friendly hospitality. The shortage of consumer goods was obvious, and although food was reasonably available, it lacked variety – though not, of course, if you were a government official of some standing. In that case, miraculously, the unobtainable would suddenly appear.

We experienced this phenomenon one lunchtime when we were telephoned by a high-ranking notable from the Ministry of Tourism, who announced that he was waiting for us in the hotel lobby and would like to entertain us to lunch. Normally at that hour we would have been going to take our lunch in the very same restaurant, sampling its minimalistic menu and having any request for something extra acknowledged with a smile and a nod but never fulfilled. Suddenly, as the official snapped his fingers, there was a dramatic transformation of the scene. Trays of food showed up as if from nowhere, their contents equalling anything you would find in the West, with no hint of any shortages in the sizes of the portions being offered. There was also the unusual spectacle of the waiters, who seemed positively panic stricken, running back and forth to satisfy every little whim and gesture of our host. The normally languid service became fast and furious to a point of manic precision. It was an abuse of authority that may have been morally deplorable, but at least it provided us with an excellent meal which was more than welcome in the circumstances.

In Varna leading party and trade-union officials taking their annual vacations by the Black Sea were allocated what were, by their standards, luxurious apartments for their stay. By and large they were the élite, enjoying the perks due to them as a reward for their loyalty to the regime. They were carefully selected individuals and there was no mistaking who they were in our hotel. In the afternoons they took tea and cakes and listened to 'palm court' classical music being performed live by a little ensemble of young musicians. We also spent part of the afternoon having tea and cake since it seemed the thing to do. There was an oddness, however, about the way a generously large pot of tea would arrive but then turn out to contain precisely enough tea to fill three cups. The measurement was so accurate that there was no allowance for any margin of error. The cake portions were cut to a similar exactitude, avoiding any risk of excess and ensuring the size was in compliance with a strict dietary regime. The average American tourist, accustomed to large intakes of food to keep up energy levels when on their travels, would have been disappointed with the culinary rewards of Varna in the Soviet era.

Even so, our stay there was made highly enjoyable by the fact that we spent most evenings with Wilfred and his wife, who entertained us faultlessly. To have the opportunity to get to know the man at close quarters, and hear his own accounts of his exploits together with his insights and conclusions, was a very special privilege. He combined a rare modesty with a zest for living despite the many tragedies he had encountered. The optimism he retained clearly illustrated his belief that in the end the dignity of man would always triumph. His own body had been riddled with bullets and he had had many brushes with death, surviving against the odds. The scars he carried were a testimony to his relentless efforts in the battlefields of South-East Asia to bring the truth to the outside world. He may have been misguided on many issues. His political perspective meant he was slower than others on the left to recognize the real nature of Stalinist control and oppression within the Soviet bloc and the postwar purges and show trials. He wrote in support of the Pol Pot revolution in Kampuchea during its early years, but later altered his opinion after its savagery became all too apparent. His errors of judgement provided his enemies with ammunition to use against him, but while he was fallible in some respects, he was startlingly clear-sighted in others. In Hiroshima he felt that not only was he seeing 'the end of World War II' but also 'the fate of cities all over the world in the first hours of a World War III'. All Wilfred's actions and opinions were informed by humanitarian instincts: the Australian spirit of fair play writ large. This is why I loved the man most dearly. He had never been member of a communist or any other party, he would say if asked, but thought of himself as an international socialist.

The night before our departure from Varna was one we would remember for a long time to come. It was as if all the pent-up forces of history burst in a violent storm around the Black Sea, with a ferocity that seemed to make the hotel rock. The rolling of the thunder, the lightning forking over the sea, the clouds lit up as if by fire – it was awe-inspiring: nature's devastating forces on display in front of our very eyes. It was a dramatic farewell to Varna.

Once back in the capital, Sofia, we were provided with a black Mercedes and a chauffeur to go with it. There was so little traffic we were able to explore the city thoroughly, always in the company of Wilfred and his wife. We dined at the few functioning restaurants and drank dark Bulgarian wine, some of which was really rather nice. The evenings we spent in sorting out the problems of the world.

The qualities in Wilfred that impressed me most were compassion for his fellow human beings and extreme loyalty to his friends. John Pilger, an illustrious war correspondent for the later television age, recalled in one of the pieces in his book *Heroes* (Vintage) how in the spring of 1980, shortly before he was due to leave for an assignment in Kampuchea, he received a phone call from Paris. It was Wilfred on the line.

A familiar, husky voice came quickly to the point. 'Can you postpone,' he said. 'I've heard about a Khmer Rouge list and you're on it. I am worried about you.' That Wilfred was worried about the welfare of another human being was not surprising; the quintessence of the man lay in what he did not say. He neglected to mention not only that he was on the same 'list', but that a few weeks earlier, at the age of seventy and seriously ill, he had survived a bloody ambush laid for him by Khmer Rouge assassins, who wounded a travelling companion. (Wilfred's intelligence was as reliable as ever; I narrowly escaped a similar ambush at the same place he was attacked.) I have known other reporters; I have not known another who, through half a century of risk-taking, demonstrated as much concern for others and such valour on their behalf. He took risks to smuggle Jews out of Germany, to drag American wounded to safety during the Pacific war, and to seek out prisoners of war in Japan, in 1945, to tell them help was coming; the list is long. He sustained a variety of bombardments, from Burma to Korea to Indo-China, yet he retained a compassion coupled with an innocence bordering at times on naïvety which, it would seem, led him into other troubles. Such qualities were shared by none of the vociferous few who were his enemies.

As a publisher I had the privilege of publishing three of Wilfred Burchett's books under the Quartet imprint. They were: *Catapult to Freedom* in 1978; *Memoirs of a Rebel Journalist* in 1980; and *Burchett Reporting the Other Side of the World, 1939–1983*, edited by Ben Kiernan, with a preface by John Pilger in 1986.

Two years after our visit to Bulgaria, Wilfred Burchett died in Sofia in September 1983 from a cancer that he himself was convinced could be attributed to his visit to Hiroshima in 1945. His epitaph should reflect his own words when, in Paris in 1974, he said: 'Truth always turns out to be much richer than you thought.'

Fourteen

With the loss of Sheila Turnbull I had gained Rebecca Fraser, the daughter of Lady Antonia. Rebecca, having worked in the United States as a researcher for the writer Ed Epstein and finished her two-year friendship with Bobby Kennedy Jr, returned to the United Kingdom ready to embark on a fresh challenge. She was among the first of a new breed of young women who would inhabit the offices of Quartet and enhance the literary buzz, extending the company's reach to take in a social circle it had not properly targeted before. The general perception was that we were a left-wing imprint. We needed to shed this restrictive image, considering ourselves to be much more than it implied. Besides being critics of the establishment, we also had to penetrate its protective walls. The reputation we were beginning to forge was of a publisher not labelled in any way but drawing its material from every sector of society. Quartet was on the road to becoming an imprint for its time and we relished the plaudits that would come its way in the following years.

November 1981 had seen the publication of *By Invitation Only*, a softcover book in which Richard Young's lens and Christopher Wilson's pen recorded the famous, the glamorous, the ambitious, the tasteless and the shallow as they socially revered, engineered and mountaineered their way amid the party set of the day. In its pages could be found the chic and cheerful of café society hard at their occupation. The tools of their trade were a champagne glass and a black bow tie; their place of work could be anywhere within the gilded environs of Mayfair. Their only task was to have fun; their only ambition was to come by as many different pasteboard passports to pleasure as possible – each one engraved 'By invitation only'.

Peter Langan, the infamous owner of Langan's Restaurant in Stratton Street, wrote in his foreword to the book, which he had scribbled on the back of David Hockney's menu:

God alone knows why I should introduce you to this book. The people in it veer between the awesome and the awful. Wilson and Young who wrote it and took the pictures are the only two people who can grease their way through a door without opening it. Café society will suffer as a result of its publication. They'll all buy it, and they'll all condemn it. They'll also want to take a quick peek at the index to see whether they're in it. I don't want discarded copies cluttering up my restaurant after they've finished reading it for the 297th time, so I beg you to take it home with you, put it out on your coffee table, and remind yourselves not to be so silly as to want to take part in the high life. They're a lovely lot but sometimes they give you the skids, you know.

The cover of the book featured a dazed looking Lord Montagu clutching a glass with both hands and a cigar between his fingers. The inside cover flap stated that

such is the paradox of café society that many of its components who appear in these pages would, on the whole, prefer to be absent. Many others who have been excluded would prefer to be included in. It must be made clear that some of the more arcane practices described herein apply to the latter grouping and not the former.

The illustration on the back cover showed Peter Langan in a total state of inebriation face down on the floor of his own restaurant. Appropriately enough it was at the restaurant that the book launch was held. On the night, a party for two hundred and fifty people turned into a bash for five hundred of London's most diligent freeloaders, or so reported the *Daily Mail*, which then went on to say:

Naim Attallah's penchant for bacchanalia was put sorely to the test. He played host to the cream of Nescafé society which featured in the tome. But the cast was studded with faces who did not possess the necessary encrusted invitation card. At one point the crush was so great the PR man Peter Stiles felt it necessary to elbow his way out of a corner where he was trapped by columnist John Rendall and his PR wife Liz Brewer. Alex Macmillan the publishing mogul and grandson of Harold Macmillan and Prince Charles's personal valet Stephen Barry made sure they were adjacent to the food, whereas Gary Glitter and Bryan Ferry stuck to the wine on offer.

The book sold extremely well. It was predictably considered scandalous by some, entertainingly outrageous by others, and people outside café society did not give a jot about it either way. I came in for some personal admonishment from certain close friends who thought I should have imposed a more selective policy on who actually got into the book; there were faces whose presence in its pages could cause great embarrassment and even grief to others. They failed to understand how for me, as a publisher, any form of censorship would have gone against the grain.

In stark contrast with the buoyant market Quartet tapped into for *By*

Invitation Only, a book in the same format that we confidently expected to justify a print-run of a hundred thousand copies bombed, with final sales figures of only nine thousand. This was *Settling Down*, the book on Prince Charles by James Whitaker. The mystery of its demise, reported *Tatler*, had caused its publisher 'to work overtime on his worry beads'. It was true enough. To have the title fail so dramatically after Quartet's publicity machine had been relentless in its promotion was for me a serious blow. While some royal observers considered it the best book of its kind that year, the public at large turned its back on it for no apparent reason. It simply would not move out of the warehouse. We kept asking ourselves what went wrong, but were unable to find a satisfactory answer.

Whitaker himself blamed Quartet for the failure, but without producing any evidence to support his contention. The impression he made on me was that he considered himself God's gift to the royal family – an attitude that did not endear him to the public, to whom it came across as pure arrogance. Matters were not helped either when he appeared on *Nationwide* dressed in his wildfowling kit, complete with night-view binoculars. It must have been one of the most unappealing television moments ever. At least Whitaker had the grace to concede that his style was maybe a bit racy for the shires.

One of the things I love about publishing is its unpredictability. You can seldom gauge the mood of the nation when it comes to books. Either you are too late with a trend, or you are ahead of your time; or you happen to choose a subject that turns out to appeal to very few people, of whom you may be one. This very aspect of publishing brings with it exhilarating rewards, so in the end who cares? Long hours of stress may be banished by a single stroke of good fortune, and we all live in anticipation of that happening to us now and then.

From January 1982 the forward impetus continued for Namara in terms of staff expansion and events in a variety of other fields. On the staff side, Virginia Bonham-Carter, the second daughter of the former BBC vice-chairman Mark Bonham-Carter, joined Quartet's publicity department. Shortly before she had been working as a salesgirl at Hatchard's bookshop, so her literary background stood her in good stead in her new appointment. At the same time, Arabella Pollen, daughter of Sotheby's then vice-chairman, Peregrine Pollen, became part of the Namara Group.

Arabella's project was to launch a fashion company under her own name, with my financial backing and the full resources of Namara at her disposal. Though Arabella possessed no formal qualifications in dressmaking or design, I could see she had ability and drive. She combined beauty with energy and her elegance and poise were enhanced by her piercing blue eyes. She was, more-over, being helped in her adventure by one of the rising stars at *Vogue* magazine, Sophie Hicks – today a well-known architect. I was very taken with Arabella, and although fashion was not an area on which I had set my sights, I was carried away by her aura. It was overwhelmingly seductive. She was every man's dream: youthful, zestful and self-assured. There was also that indefinable quality about her that made a man wish to protect her and gave him the impression that she needed him when it was in fact not the case; nevertheless the sensation was gratifying.

She took over my old office at Wellington Court and the process of pro-moting Arabella started in earnest. I was determined to make her a household name. The strategy was to establish Arabella as *the* fashion designer for the young – the new generation of hopefuls who formed the nucleus of a trendy society with their boundless ambition and natural *savoir-faire*. Arabella's beau, Patrick Benson, was referred to by *Tatler* as her chief button-sewer, whereas he was in fact a multi-talented artist whose many sketches provided her with inspiration. Sandra Marr, Viscountess Weir's daughter, was listed in the team as head mannequin, and the indefatigable Sophie Hicks was chief adviser. In due course, a young lady with a lisp, Kathryn Ireland, was appointed special publicity person cum personal assistant.

Katherine was a great operator and a real go-getter. At one point, however, I felt that her influence on Arabella sometimes veered from the positive to the reckless, diverting Arabella towards more recreational pursuits. No doubt I was being over-protective, worried that, because of her youth, she might be led seriously off course. Following through from those early days, Katherine has since moved on to become the hottest property in Hollywood, running her own interior-design company that caters mainly for the stars.

Arabella's rise to prominence happened in no time at all. Among her clients she was soon counting Princess Diana, a fashion icon of her day, and a large majority of the Sloane Rangers who graced the London social scene in that *époque*. Cazzy Neville, a sweet young lady who worked for me briefly at Namara House and later became the Marchioness of Derby, was seconded to Arabella during Fashion Week to help her mount her show. After her marriage I noticed to my chagrin that Cazzy had become rather haughty and lost her former warmth, exhibiting that side of the English upper class that is sometimes hard to relate to.

By now Arabella was the darling of the press and was featured everywhere. A tastefully composed fashion shot of her semi-nude by Bardo Fabiani for *Ritz* magazine showed a beautiful and radiant Arabella topless. Somehow the *News of the World* then managed to pirate the picture and both Arabella and

I were extremely upset by this unwelcome intrusion from a Sunday newspaper. We considered legal proceedings but in the end, to avoid any further adverse publicity, we decided to let the matter drop. With the storm having passed we were back on track with shows in New York and outlets springing up throughout the United States.

Quartet's publishing activities continued in their upbeat way. A biography by Denis MacShane of President François Mitterand came on to the list, the author being a former National Union of Journalists president who was currently a Geneva-based union official. He told the story of how, when Mitterand was working in the French Resistance, he spotted a photograph of a young woman on a co-worker's piano. 'I am going to marry that girl,' he announced, and their marriage took place a few months later, after the couple had met just three times. The woman in question was his wife, Danielle, who became his faithful partner for life.

The book's launch party was described by William Hickey of the *Daily Express* as the left's equivalent of Royal Ascot. Michael Foot and a number of trade-union bosses were there, alongside MPs and various political commentators. There was also a clutch of London-based French journalists who looked on intrigued by the sheer number of people who turned up for the occasion. The book had been published to coincide with the first anniversary of Mitterand's rise to power. Denis MacShane later joined the Blair government as minister with special responsibilities for Europe.

Another Quartet offering unafraid of precipitating a whirlwind of controversy was *Jungle Fever*, the first published collection of photographs by Jean-Paul Goude. On its cover it featured a naked Grace Jones as a caged creature, her sharp glistening teeth eager for the kill. Across the top of the cage was a notice that read: DO NOT FEED THE ANIMAL. The feminist lobby condemned it as the most humiliating and demeaning portrayal of a woman ever published. It could perhaps also have been said to be the most extraordinary portrait ever of a woman by her lover; the artist asserted that it was he who had caged the beast. Some years later Jean-Paul was quoted as saying of their relationship, 'I was Svengali to Grace's talent. As long as I seduced her, and she was in love or infatuated with me, I could do anything I wanted with her creatively, because I was constantly admiring and paying tribute to her. It all ended dramatically when she felt I had started to love the character we had created more than I loved her.' They remained friends, but he regretted the way the relationship had, in his view, ended prematurely, the crunch having come when Grace read the chapter he wrote about her in *Jungle Fever*. She was 'so angry and felt so betrayed that we couldn't go on. Creatively, it was just impossible.'

Jungle Fever was a dazzling trawl through the international underworld of beauty, humour and eroticism. Jean-Paul Goude, the uninhibited graphic genius behind the manipulated images, was once aptly described by *Esquire* magazine as 'The French Correction'. Through his surrealist-influenced techniques, placed at the service of high-profile advertising campaigns, the public probably became more aware of his work than of his name. In many ways, he was always ahead of his time, going beyond kitsch to produce new configurations of images to stretch the imagination afresh. His aim was to make nature conform to his fantasies, as the collection in the book illustrated. Besides Grace Jones, it included Kellie the Evangelist Stripper, Sabu, Gene Kelly, Zouzou, Little Beaver, Judith Jamison, Russ Tamblyn, Toukie, Radiah, the Sex Circus of Eighth Avenue and the nocturnal *flore et faune* of 42nd Street. The only thing these disparate fantasies had in common was Jean-Paul Goude, but even so, as the blurb explained, they formed 'a very special community: they have been made perfect to fit the world as Goude wants it to be – there are stilts for Radiah, a new ass for Toukie, a crew cut for Grace Jones'.

To give an adequate account of Goude's artistic range, his 'work must be considered that of a painter, photographer, sculptor, musician, dancer, couturier, stage director and set designer – all of these and none of them. "To say the truth," Goude says, "I see myself as an artist who uses the best means available to get a point across. What comes first is the necessity to communicate 'my world'. Through the use of different media, I am able to show what to me is important." ' He scornfully dismissed a plastic surgeon who refused to follow his design for a girlfriend's new nose. ' "After all, I am an artist," Goude says. "What does he know?" ' It was the ultimate effect that concerned him: 'the extension of a limb, the padding of a flank, a nip here and a tuck there – and suddenly the fantastic people and places of Jean-Paul Goude have become his for ever and hopefully the reader's too'.

Jungle Fever was another book that sold extremely well, and was destined to become a collector's item. A notice in the *Evening Standard*, under the heading 'Savage Messiah', called it 'an explosive photographic mixture of sex, violence and fun'. As was often the case, Quartet was causing a stir in a variety of quarters. My determination to maintain our reputation for publishing the good, the profane and the thought-provoking was firmer than ever.

We hit the headlines again at the end of June with the merging of the *Literary Review* with *Quarto*, the owner of the latter being Algy Cluff, the oil millionaire. Richard Boston, the editor of *Quarto*, was to step down as a result of the merger, and Gillian Greenwood, Anne Smith's replacement at the *Literary Review*, would take on the job of editing the new combined journal with an estimated circulation of ten thousand. 'It's a genuine merger, not a purely cosmetic alteration,' Gillian explained to the press. 'I think *Quarto* has a high standard of poetry and original writing which we would like to include in the new magazine.' Boston was to remain an associate editor. As the *Evening Standard* reported, 'despite indications that the main direction for the magazine will come from Miss Greenwood and the Attallah empire, Cluff remains adamant that he is not selling *Quarto*. "I was approached by Mr Attallah who suggested a merger. It makes sense for some of these smaller literary magazines to get together. I'm merging it, not getting rid of it," he insists.'

Not long after the merger a super row erupted over a review in the new issue of the *Literary Review* of 'Superwoman' Shirley Conran's new block-busting piece of fiction, *Lace*. The reviewer, the journalist Paul Levy, was so uncomplimentary about the book that many felt his comments were defamatory. Peter Hillmore, writing in his 'Pendennis' column in the *Observer*, had earlier been equally ferocious in his condemnation, writing that:

> It's a book that I cannot recommend too lowly: it's badly written, badly constructed and badly printed. I think I'll call it 'Disgrace' even if she did get over a million dollars' advance. Normally I prefer to curl up with relaxing books like *Principia Mathematica*, but I read 'Disgrace' in the course of duty. Not because Ms Conran used to work for this paper before she went on to worse things – but because of an article in next month's *Literary Review*. The article contains some very interesting speculation about exactly how much collaboration and help 'Superwoman' Conran had on the book. I'd love to tell you more, but the lawyers won't let me.

Against all our expectations the row never went much further. Our lawyer Michael Rubinstein happened to be Shirley Conran's lawyer as well. He telephoned me to express his client's disappointment about Mr Levy's savage review, which perhaps had gone a shade over the top; but he had nevertheless advised her on the basis of fair comment not to institute any proceedings against the magazine, however intemperate the attack she had suffered.

Fifteen

In March 1982 Hugo Williams, the well-known poet, wrote a lengthy profile of me in *Time Out*, after interviewing me at Namara House. The article appeared with a grim-looking but forceful picture of myself, seated with a cane in my hand, beneath which, in bold lettering, was the title, 'The Smile on the Face of the Tiger'. It was eye-catching, to say the least, and given the rather forbidding aspect of the picture, quite dramatic. The article itself started off well enough and had the poetic turn of phrase to be expected from its author. As a prelude it had the following paragraph in italics:

> '*After a long and difficult journey, the tigress arrives in Tiger Heaven. From the build-up of her relationship with Eelie the dog and Harriet the leopardess, through her early attempts at eating a porcupine and her surprise encounter with a bear to her first kill of a Sambar fawn, the reader will be spellbound . . .* ' *So goes the blurb of* Tara, A Tigress, *one of the tiger books published by the Palestinian entrepreneur, Naim Attallah. It sounds like Attallah's own story, with Eelie the dog played by David Frost, Harriet the leopardess played by Mayfair jeweller John Asprey, the porcupine by Times Newspapers and the bear by Lord Grade. The Sambar fawn is clearly Anne Smith, the unfortunate editor of the* Literary Review, *whose sacking last year won Attallah a marzipan pig from Women in Publishing for 'outstanding services to sexism'.*

From that point on the article lost its way, relying on fantasy and recycled gossip rather than properly researched facts. I might have contemplated buying *The Times* newspaper and supplements when they were for sale, as the article speculated, but would never have suggested removing John Gross, the editor of *The Times Literary Supplement*, to replace him with Anne Smith. The notion was preposterous beyond the realms of fantasy: I happened to be a great admirer of John. Far more than by this sort of nonsense, however, I was exercised by a repetition of the old canard that I had swamped the *Literary Review* with pro-Arab propaganda. The article had its interesting side, but this outrageously untrue and easily disproved assertion demeaned it as a whole. There were other inaccuracies relating to the dispute with Anne Smith and the supposed 'sacking' of my close friend Stephanie Dowrick from The Women's Press. These finally robbed the piece of any charm and authenticity it might have possessed and provoked me into contemplating legal proceedings against *Time Out*. It was still a dilemma for me, since I liked Hugo Williams for his wit and nerve, but I could not let these grave accusations go by. Fortunately common sense prevailed and eventually *Time Out* printed an apology detailing the main inaccuracies. Stephanie was also naturally incensed and the editor of *Time Out* reproduced in full the letter she wrote from Australia:

> There was much to object to in your article about Naim Attallah (*TO* 604). However, I will narrow my complaints to what directly concerns myself. Not only was I not dismissed as managing director of The Women's Press by Naim Attallah but I have found him to be, in the five years of our business partnership, an intensely loyal man, capable of putting friendship ahead of all other considerations. When I discussed with him my current sabbatical his support was immediate and has been utterly consistent. Perhaps this kind of loyalty is difficult for your reporter to understand? For the record: Naim Attallah and I continue to own The Women's Press jointly. I continue as a director of the company. Ros de Lanerolle is in a permanent position as managing director of The Women's Press. I will return to The Women's Press in the summer in a chiefly advisory capacity while I continue to write.

Over the years Hugo Williams and I have bumped into each other from time to time. He still remembers the unfortunate *Time Out* incident, but we have both mellowed and our meetings are friendly and warm. What on earth he had in his mind about me in the conclusion he gave his article, however, is still a mystery:

> Attallah once nearly produced an £8 million biopic of King Abdulazzid al Saud [*sic*], Lawrence of Arabia's old adversary. 'It's the most marvellous story,' he told me. 'Can you imagine anyone else in this century founding a nation with the sword?' A tiger smiled at me over his shoulder. '*Why yes, Naim. You.*'

Some time during that summer I received a letter from Auberon Waugh. It was an invitation to a lunch he was hosting at the Gay Hussar restaurant in Soho. The objective was to bring together the leading publishers in England to ask them to debate the merits of their respective imprints and provide fodder for a lengthy article Bron was writing for the *Sunday Telegraph* magazine. I declined the invitation. My feeling over Quartet's position in the publishing hierarchy was that there was not so much an outright rejection as a tacit non-acceptance of our status as an integral part of their world. We were perhaps seen as being on the fringes of the industry, and I did not want to stir the pot before we were ready, convinced as I was that I would only be plunged into a situation not of my choosing. As it turned out, I could have been right.

Details of the lunch were given in the 'Bent's Notes' column in the *Bookseller* of 7 August, which listed the publishers who were there: Tom Maschler of Jonathan Cape, Lord Weidenfeld of Weidenfeld & Nicolson, Christopher Maclehose of Collins, Alan Brooke of Michael Joseph, Matthew Evans of Faber & Faber, André Deutsch of André Deutsch, Christopher Sinclair-Stevenson of Hamish Hamilton and John Murray of John Murray. Among those invited but who failed to turn up, the report concluded, was Naim Attallah of Quartet, who declined to join 'a bunch of Zionists and left-wingers'. When I read this unwarranted distortion of the truth I was naturally furious and demanded that the *Bookseller* retract the statement. 'Bent's Notes' of 21 August duly made a gentlemanly response:

I apologize. I referred to Naim Attallah of Quartet declining an invitation from Auberon Waugh to lunch with Tom Maschler, Lord Weidenfeld, Christopher Maclehose, Alan Brooke, Matthew Evans, André Deutsch, Christopher Sinclair-Stevenson and John Murray. He had not, as I wrote in my column of 7 August, declined to join 'a bunch of Zionists and left-wingers' – that was the paraphrase put on it at the lunch but not what Naim Attallah had said. He had, in fact, replied in these courteous terms: 'My own view concerning publishing is alas not one that other publishers would share and I therefore feel inadequately placed to cope with established figures whose motivations rarely coincide with mine. Their world is one which I feel neither comfort in nor draw any comfort from.' I apologize for any distress or embarrassment I may have caused him.

In the *Sunday Telegraph* article, which appeared later that year, Bron, whom I had not met up to this point, was very complimentary about Quartet, and me personally:

When Naim Attallah of Quartet started publishing six years ago, he gave the impression of being concerned by what he saw as the excessive Zionist influence in British publishing. But his list, which includes among its greater successes Nigel Dempster's *HRH Princess Margaret: A Life Unfulfilled*, does not really support the idea of a holy crusade. There is a surprisingly pleasant and relaxed atmosphere at Quartet under such a dynamic man (Attallah is also the financial director of Asprey's, the jewellers) but the list is unmistakably one of the more interesting around. Currently they are chiefly excited about the recent publication of *Red Square*, a faction novel by Edward Topol and Fridrikh Neznansky, about a supposed plot to topple Brezhnev.

The *Sunday Telegraph* magazine then proceeded to list our turnover as standing at one million four hundred thousand pounds, more than half that of John Murray, founded in 1768.

An indication of how Quartet's profile was increasing in prominence came in the June issue of *Publishing News*, which reported on an idea from the Book Marketing Council for a new wheeze as part of its 'Books are Fun' campaign. Desmond Clarke, as perceptive as ever, observed how the image the man in the street had of the average publisher was of a boring old fart in baggy grey flannels. This he considered not entirely conducive to what the BMC described as a 'book-buying situation'. The first part of Desmond's plan was the creation of an annual Oscars ceremony for publishers. Naturally the proceedings were to be chaired by someone as charismatic as Martyn Goff, Desmond himself or his brother Charles. *Publishing News* lost not a moment in putting forward its own inventions for prize categories alongside nominations for the 1982 ceremony:

> The Edward Victor Award for Services to Agents: Sphere/Pavilion for their £130,000 blockbuster *Hello, Pontiff!*
>
> The Thomas Maschler Award for Self-Promotion: The young lion McCrumb edged out by the old pro himself, Lord Longford.
>
> The Robert Maxwell Award for Services to Printers: Sphere/Pavilion for their lavishly produced *Hello, Pontiff!*
>
> The Au Bak Ling Award for the Encouragement of New Talent: Naim Attallah, who has worked so hard to bring stimulating new blood into Quartet.
>
> The Henry Pordes Award for Services to the Remainder Market: Sphere/Pavilion for their 500,000 copy extravaganza, *Hello, Pontiff!*

I was equally chuffed when, in July, Horace Bent of the *Bookseller*, with whom I had not always seen eye to eye, wrote:

> Having nothing better to do I spent an evening last week poring over old copies of the *Standard*. In one of them I saw Naim Attallah described as 'perhaps the only publisher in the world who compares the company he runs to a woman. Both, he says, are "dangerous, unpredictable, attractive".' Like an Italian sports car I lusted after in my youth.

The reason I was chuffed was because, even in a land of old farts, it is sometimes possible to come across a human specimen with the capacity to step out from the rest. The piece by Horace Bent, despite its tongue-in-cheek tone, was to me most reassuring.

Sixteen

During the protracted Anne Smith saga, which seemed to engulf writers, academics and almost the whole literary establishment, there was one woman in particular who had offered her mediation services out of goodwill. This, as has been told in Chapter Twelve, was Jennifer Bradshaw. Her credentials as mediator were exactly right: she already knew Anne and had been one of her supporters when the dispute over the *Literary Review* first flared up. Although her efforts to find a solution were rejected with some bitterness by Anne, who accused her of gross bias, her intervention led to the forging of a long relationship with Quartet and myself that spanned almost two decades. Initially she was employed as an editor to start a Russian list. Over the years she progressed to become one of my personal assistants, dealing principally with those aspects of my work that involved publishing. Later she became a prolific researcher, working with me on my journalistic output.

Jennifer worked from her home in Scotland and had little to do with Quartet on a daily basis. Occasionally she attended an editorial meeting when invited. She accompanied me to the Frankfurt Book Fair when her presence was complementary to the overall effort of the Quartet team working on our stand. Her first contribution to the Russian list came with the publication in 1982 of *The Memoirs of Leonid Pasternak*, which she had translated, with an introduction by Boris's sister, Josephine Pasternak, who lived in Oxford. Jennifer went on to translate Leonid Borodin's most captivating book, *The Year of Miracle and Grief*, which we published in 1984. As the blurb proclaimed:

> It is a haunting tale of a magical realm where fact and fantasy dissolve into each other. It tells of the blossoming of a young boy's first love in the beautiful setting of Lake Baikal in Siberia. The real world of landscape and nature is skilfully interwoven with an imaginary one of myth, legend and fairy tale, in which the boy is introduced to a mystery which threatens both himself and those he loves.

I read the book many times, and each time I found it even more enchanting. Lyrical and sad, *The Year of Miracle and Grief* remains one of the most beguiling Russian novels I have read.

In the autumn of 1982, Jennifer was asked by Christopher Maclehose of

Collins to be second reader for a Russian manuscript they had under consideration, entitled *Red Square*. She put in an extremely favourable report for Collins, expressing the view that its merits made it far superior to *Gorky Park*, with which she had been asked to make comparisons. On the basis of her recommendations, which coincided with the opinion of Collins's first reader, Maclehose made an offer for the English-language rights. This was rejected by the agent, and so the book came on to the open market. Jennifer then told me about it and I decided Quartet should put in its own bid in view of the topicality of the subject. We made an offer and the agent was happy to accept it.

Red Square had been written by two Russians, the scriptwriter Edward Topol and his co-author, Fridrikh Neznansky, who had worked for more than fifteen years in the office of the public prosecutor in Moscow. As was to be expected, both authors were now living in the West. The novel, completed only that October, anticipated Andropov's succession to the Russian presidency following the death of Brezhnev. By a fortuitous chance Quartet's offer for the rights was accepted only hours before Brezhnev died in reality; but the scheme of the book described a fictional attempt to topple Brezhnev a year earlier. Brezhnev's daughter was revealed to be an intimate friend of Boris the Gypsy, whose arrest opened up an enormous black-market scandal that touched members of the Politburo. According to the novel, the plot was hatched by Yuri Andropov as leader of the KGB to discredit Brezhnev and secure his own succession. It was all very timely and made the book an instant hot property. My dilemma was how we were to translate and publish it in just a few weeks, catching the tide of interest in unfolding events before their topicality faded.

It was a monumental task. The edited translation of the book's hundred and fifty thousand words would have to be delivered to the printers by 1 December to ensure publication early in January 1983. Jennifer recruited a team of three Russian translators besides herself and the mammoth undertaking began in earnest. Jennifer's main role was to iron out any disparities in style and ensure the translation as a whole achieved uniformity. With a deadline for the printers that seemed impossible to achieve, Jennifer and her team made it within eighteen days by working round the clock with very little sleep, sustained by gallons of black coffee to keep the momentum going. Finished copies were ready before Christmas on 23 December. The first print-run of ten thousand copies was immediately distributed to ensure the books would be in the bookshops by the start of January.

In my view it was a performance no other publisher in London could have equalled, but even as we prepared to celebrate a job well done, the inevitable spoiler appeared in *Private Eye* with a scurrilous piece alleging that I had gazumped Collins in the bidding while knowing full well they already had an agreement sewn up to do the book. Jennifer was named as the Russian expert who had acted as a publishing mole, duping Collins into making the manuscript available to her. The story they concocted was deliberately provocative, besides being damaging. Under threat of litigation, *Private Eye* duly published an appropriate retraction. Meanwhile *Red Square* received a great deal of publicity and became a bestseller. Serafina Clarke of Clarke Conway-Gordon, the agent for the book, was highly pleased with the result. In the years ahead she was to put other important Russian manuscripts in our direction to add to the Quartet list.

*

The theatre continued to exercise its hold over me. One evening I went to the Half-Moon pub theatre in Islington to see a play that I heard was enjoying an enthusiastic audience response: Claire Luckham's wrestling-ring marital allegory, *Trafford Tanzi*. I loved it instantly for its originality. It had a rough edge that made it simultaneously dramatic and entertaining. Howard Panter, the impresario, with whom I had earlier collaborated on Donleavy's *The Beastly Beatitudes of Balthazar B*, agreed we should join forces to bring the play to the Mermaid Theatre and ensure it an extended run.

Staging it at that venue meant a radical remodelling of the auditorium, but the Mermaid had been dark for months, leaving us a free hand to revamp it. We subjected it to much ripping out and rebuilding to form four ringsides and increase its seating capacity by a hundred to seven hundred and ten. A bar was also installed at the back of the auditorium to add to the wrestling-hall atmosphere. With licensing regulations overcome, the audience, clutching their glasses of bitter in authentic fashion, would be able to watch Noreen Kershaw as Tanzi hurling her stage family about in the ring. When the show opened in October, they also found themselves caught up in a degree of audience participation as the actors were liable, at unscripted and unscheduled moments, to come hurtling through the ropes, as happens during real-life wrestling matches. It was this sort of realism in the action, coupled with its feminist orientation, that brought the audience to its feet. The *Evening Standard* reported how their man, sitting in the front row, had enjoyed an even more direct experience of participation when one of the actresses, Victoria Hardcastle, appeared from nowhere in fishnet tights and clambered aboard his lap. Miss Hardcastle, whom he considered to be a most comely creature, predisposed him to a new appreciation of feminism. He concluded by describing how I was dressed for the occasion as a 'wrestling promoter'.

Trafford Tanzi was playing to capacity houses in December when two members of the cast took exception to the promotion and sale in the foyer of three Quartet titles, namely Jean-Paul Goude's *Jungle Fever*, featuring on its jacket the naked Grace Jones in a cage, Helmut Newton's *Sleepless Nights*, a recent collection of photographs strong in erotic suggestion, and Janet Reger's *Chastity in Focus*, a celebration of the exquisite lingerie she designed to make women more desirable. The objectors were Victoria Hardcastle and Eve Brand, who spent most of their time in the play in the ring, wrestling men into submission. Victoria rang me up and requested a meeting. In really quite a sweet-natured way, she suggested that the books on sale were unacceptable from her feminist perspective and she would rather I withdrew them from the theatre. It was her gentle persuasion that ultimately won the day, quite apart from the fact that I did not relish the prospect of having to settle the issue in the wrestling ring. When the press came on the line to ask for confirmation of the story, I simply said, 'Since it was the women in *Trafford Tanzi* who objected, how could I be expected to fight?'

The production got a new lease of life in March 1983 when Toyah Wilcox took over the lead. She had to spend several weeks beforehand in training with a bruiser by the name of Howard Lester to cope with being pummelled, arm-locked, sat upon and thrown around in the ring. The following month it was scheduled to open on Broadway, with Debbie Harry, the lead singer from the pop group Blondie, reprising Toyah's role. Debbie was being trained by Brian Maxine, who had been responsible for instructing the London cast in the ungentle art. With a deluge of unanimously favourable critical comment behind it, there was every reason to anticipate an equal triumph for *Tanzi* in America.

The *Sunday Telegraph* had called it 'A rare show', and the *Daily Telegraph* described it as the 'most original, refreshing, surprising, exhilarating and fierce drama to reach London for years'. 'Claire Luckham,' wrote the *Daily Express*, 'has not only written a musical, but a contest that had us going wild in the aisles for feminism', while its competitor, the *Daily Mail*, called it a 'play which brings new meaning to the term action-packed'. The *Guardian* reckoned that 'It's a message you don't forget', and the *New York Times* labelled it a 'feminist play to end all feminist plays'. *Cosmopolitan* magazine thought it the 'most innovative and entertaining show in London', while *Options* went overboard by saying, 'It is, quite simply, unique in the history of the British theatre. Glorious . . . liberating.' The *Tatler* simply said, 'The best night out in London.'

With the critics unanimously on side with their superlatives and the public flocking to see the show, Quartet rushed into print with an illustrated large-format paperback containing the history of the production and an unabridged script. It went on sale in the theatre and to the wider book trade. The success of *Tanzi* made it one of the highlights of my theatrical career. Through it I learnt a great deal about the theatre and what makes a production click with the public. It was also very timely, with feminism becoming such a burning issue.

Then the curtain went up on the Broadway production and I travelled to New York to attend the first night. There was a vast contrast with the London experience and it failed miserably in seducing either the critics or the public: as the saying goes, it closed as soon as it opened. Everyone had agreed at the time that Debbie Harry would make a most refreshing choice in the casting, but in fact she looked uncomfortable in the role. There seemed to be none of the rapport between performers and audience that was the key to its success in London; no sign of the zing and vitality that characterized the Mermaid production. Fortunately we had sold the American rights outright. *Trafford Tanzi*'s failure on Broadway did not involve us in any financial responsibility.

*

The unstuffy and often provocative character of Quartet's list began to attract the attention of young women wanting to work in publishing. Suddenly the imprint had a trendiness about it. One of the many recruits was Sabrina Guinness, who had held various jobs in the past that were quite unrelated to books. Most notably she had been Tatum O'Neal's nanny; during the previous year she had been personal assistant to David Stirling, the founder of the SAS. The task that faced her at Quartet was fronting a new book club called the Academy Bookclub to be associated with the *Literary Review*. The press became quite caustic in reporting the appointment, throwing doubts on Sabrina's ability to run such a venture. She had once stated, they claimed, that 'everyone knows the only book I ever read is *Vogue*'. One reporter, from the *Evening Standard*, phoned her at her David Stirling office to congratulate her on her new job, only to be told, 'She's out, she's gone to Wimbledon for the afternoon.' It gave him just the ammunition he needed to throw in the remark, 'Attallah is a hard taskmaster who demands total commitment from his staff.' The inference was clear: that Sabrina would have to mend her ways to survive the challenges ahead of her.

Simultaneously I employed her brother, Hugo – who had just been laid off by the film producer, Don Boyd – to sell advertising in a special New York edition of the *Literary Review*. This was being produced in conjunction with the Institute of Contemporary Art, which was holding a major New York exhibition that October and November. The appointment of Hugo, which was temporary, had the effect of bolstering Bridget Heathcoat-Amory's efforts in her capacity as commercial manager of the *Literary Review*.

Another addition, but this time to my own office, was a former model, Baroness Andrea von Stumm, considered by many connoisseurs of women to be one of the most beautiful on the international circuit. I first met her through Algy Cluff when she was a close friend of his, and had been impressed not only by her beauty but also by her intellect. She was certainly no dumb blonde. In fact she was extremely well read and was often to be found buried in a book. Once, in my absence, she lit a joss-stick while sitting at my desk reading and unconsciously let it burn its way through the desk's surface. At the time I was very angry, but the incident was soon forgotten. When I took her to the Frankfurt Book Fair she had David Elliott, Quartet's director of sales and my soulmate, completely mesmerized. He was amused to observe that the sensation she caused at the fair could be measured by the number of visitors who flocked to the stand just to get a glimpse of her.

David was then at the height of his madcap phase, smoking and drinking without restraint and doing anything for a laugh. He and I made a good team, indulging our common brand of lunacy in a way that brought us immense satisfaction and a unique sense of camaraderie. David mischievously spread a rumour that Andrea, who was staying in the same hotel as I was, would come to my suite every morning to bathe in vintage champagne. In his fantasy he saw her as a modern Cleopatra and me as her absurdly indulgent Mark Antony. It was all done in good humour and nobody seemed to mind: it was a classic example of Quartet at play.

Nigella Lawson had come down from Oxford earlier in the year and laid claim to the job I had promised her. She joined a strong team of bright young men and women who were providing Quartet with a fresh impetus. To begin with she was assigned the task of reading unsolicited manuscripts, and these she would either reject or pass on for further consideration. It is an interesting first job but it can become tedious after a while. Few unsolicited manuscripts make the grade and become published books, but there is always the possibility of discovering a major new talent. The attitude at Quartet was that we could ill-afford not to be vigilant in case we overlooked a work of great promise. After serving in the apprenticeship for over a year, and having recovered from a bout of glandular fever, Nigella was elevated to the position of editor. It was a promotion she deserved and I felt confident she would do well through being given extra responsibilities and a wider scope. She more than fulfilled the prediction in her remaining years at Quartet.

Another recruit at this period was Caroline Mockett. Her mother, Ann Foxell, who was then head of the press office at *Harpers & Queen*, introduced her to the Namara Group. Eventually Caroline became a notable addition to the Quartet girls. In the following contribution, penned by herself in her own distinctive style, she reveals some aspects of the goings-on at Quartet that sadly had escaped my notice. I can well imagine the wicked glint in her eye as she set out to recall the somewhat nonconformist atmosphere in the Goodge Street offices at the time.

Learning the Ropes
by Caroline Mockett

'Dalleeng. You're pretty. You'll do.' With these words – welcome and verbal contract in five words – I began my tenuous career in publishing.

My introduction to Naim Attallah had been arranged by my mother, exasperated by her daughter's consistent 'failure to launch'. By the age of twenty, I had managed to fail a secretarial course, get chucked off a cooking course and then get sacked from my first five jobs.

I returned home one evening to find mother chatting up a Middle Eastern man. This might not have been anything unusual, except that I noticed that the topic of conversation kept returning to me: my mother's laughter and energetic chat suddenly turning to sighs and sad tales of, 'I don't know what I'm going to do with her.' It took about ten gin and tonics for the charismatic visitor, Anwar Bati, finally to crumble before the twin onslaught of flirtation and sorrow. He agreed to find me a job. 'I know someone,' he said mysteriously, before swaying slightly out of the house.

Wheels turned and I was summoned to Namara House for my brief interview with Naim. Having received the seal of approval, I was whisked away to another address – Wellington Court – where I was shown into a small but pleasant office and told to sit behind a desk. Across the room was an accountant – *the* accountant – a breed I had never before encountered in my years of deb parties and balls. He was nonplussed by me and I was mystified and unimpressed with him. And so it was for the next three months. I had nothing to do (the accountant seemed to have guessed that I was mostly useless) except occasionally answer the phone – and then pass the call over to the accountant, make coffee (the accountant only drank a cup a day) and read the paper. As Beckett might have said in my position (hard to imagine): 'Nothing happens, nobody comes, nobody goes, it's awful!'

My dwindling will to live was given a boost by a change of duties. I was summoned to help with the launch of Bella Pollen's new collection (I thought I had joined a publishing company). I spent a few giddy days helping to hang her fashionable floral skirts and jumpers (it was the 1980s).

For these first three months of working for Naim, I caught only occasional glimpses of him. He seemed to be locked away in his ivory tower at Namara

House, only to appear at parties with a retinue of pretty young women about him, all vying for his attention and favour. Seemingly shut away far from his attention, I began to give up hope of ever escaping the accountant's office and getting involved in the heart of the matter – the great endeavour of publishing. Then, just as I was beginning to work out the best way to get sacked without too many repercussions, I received a summons to Namara House.

'Dalleeng! I need a secretary. Come, sit there.' With that, I took up position at a desk in Naim's office. From the frozen wastes of Wellington Court, I was suddenly bathing in the continual sunshine of Namara House and the launching of the *Literary Review*. My initial panic about actually having to do something and so being discovered to be entirely incapable of doing anything was soon allayed: there was even less to do than there had been at Wellington Court. I sat, looked pretty, chatted to Naim and tidied my desk. A lot. Which seemed to be exactly what my job description required.

After this period of close examination, Naim arranged for me to be given a proper job in Quartet. Not for me the giddy heights of editorial; I was bundled off to sales and marketing. And here my real education began. Naim had found me a slot as post girl and general supplier for David Elliott (who called me either 'the postie' or 'the failed deb') and Penny Grant. Within the friendly chaos of the sales and marketing office, I quickly learnt the essential skills needed for success in publishing. First and foremost was the golden rule: get your work done in the morning because you never know how long lunch is going to last.

I managed to make myself useful by taking David's shaggy dog Tramp for walks and buying toasted bacon and tomato sandwiches for David and myself, a cure for a thumping hangover. And I actually did the post. The post scales I was in command of came in handy when I added to my list of job titles that of 'supplier of soft drugs to the publishing industry'. Marijuana was carefully weighed out and priced alongside letters and stamps, before being delivered – with the mail – around the office.

Occasionally I was sent out on to the front line of publishing to flog books to retailers. This operation involved the donning of an indecently short skirt, plenty of make-up and an innocent smile before targeting Harrods, Smiths and – my favourite – Mole Jazz. I would pile books into the back of my Morris Minor and splutter off to spread the word of Quartet. I soon discovered I was good at the business of flirtation – reps were putty in my hands and I rarely returned with an unsold copy.

Of course it helped that I was selling one of the most controversial lists in British publishing at the time. A mini-skirt and a car-boot load of *The Joy of*

Sex was enough to get even the most jaded rep excited. Back at the office, Quartet ran an impressive after-sales service – I would take calls from keen and interested readers who wanted to discuss details of the positions pictured in *More Joy of Sex*. I happily chatted away, describing various obscene acts to male strangers. Anything to sell a book, I thought, not realizing that I had started probably the first and only free sex-chat line in the world. In the lunch break I sold books to transvestites and other colourful Soho characters. Flexibilty and an open mind was an essential part of the sales technique.

The success of *The Joy of Sex* didn't go down well with The Women's Press, whose presence within Naim's harem of publishing was probably due to a mutual misunderstanding of each other's intentions. Naim must have thought, 'How nice, more women.' The Women's Press probably thought, 'He publishes Dennis Potter – how bad can it be?' The Women's Press had a fearsome reputation; enough to put the fear of woman into David Elliott – his dog Tramp and I would be called upon as escorts when David had to venture into their territory to obtain sales figures. Little was I aware that The Women's Press was making publishing history by releasing classics such as Alice Walker's *The Color Purple*, as well as pioneering texts such as the *Lesbian Mother's Handbook*.

Looking back, I can now appreciate the innovative and risk-taking books Quartet published: Dennis Potter's *Pennies from Heaven*, Jonathan Dimbleby and Don McCullin's *The Palestinians*, Julian Barnes's *Metroland*, as well as publications by Bob Carlos Clarke and Derek Jarman.

My time at Quartet was an education in many ways, a formative experience that taught me the value of originality and of thinking in brave new directions. It all helped in my later career working with artists and other creative types. For all of this, and in particular to Naim, I am thankful.

*   *   *

Meanwhile, in keeping with my policy of diversification, I acquired that September a seventy-five-per-cent share in a wine merchant's, Howell's of Bristol, from the Hood family. The family continued to be involved with the business, Sir Tom Hood remaining as chairman while his son Jim stayed on as a director with a fifteen-per-cent stake in the company. One executive director, Rodney Holt, also remained on the board, and John Lloyd, who had brokered the deal, became managing director with a ten-per-cent holding. Founded in 1785, Howell's of Bristol possessed what were probably the finest cellars in its native city. The firm had a reputation for laying down splendid collections for expatriates through their Bin Club, though in recent years business had dwindled for want of capital. As a first step I therefore injected through Namara Ltd a hundred and fifty thousand pounds for future development. To have John Lloyd at the helm seemed a further advantage. He was a wine expert who had been director of Sotheby's wine department and I felt confident that, with much needed capital in place and fresh blood to revitalize the company, prospects for the future looked rosy enough.

Unfortunately the experiment was soon to come unstuck. This was not through any lack of business opportunities but mainly because the management set-up was not working as planned. Jim Hood and Rodney Holt, having been in charge before the acquisition, found working with John Lloyd quite difficult. Unfortunately the new managing director proved to be rather short on flexibility and given to fits of moodiness; perhaps he lacked the sort of conciliatory disposition needed for creating harmonious relationships.

In the long run, I found the situation unsatisfactory, and have to admit that my sympathies leaned strongly towards Jim and Rodney. Like them I thought John Lloyd's management style was unconducive to establishing a good productive atmosphere in the workplace. It was a situation that I kept in check for a number of years, for I truly enjoyed this involvement in the wine business and learnt a great deal about the trade. As a result of the acquisition I also became a wine collector myself. Financially Namara lost the greater part of its investment in Howell's of Bristol, but it had learnt the golden lesson that, unless management is in unison, riches can be turned to dust; that ultimately any company's most important asset is the quality and drive of its staff. Later I sold the company back to Jim Hood and Rodney Holt, who concentrated their efforts on the Bin Club and made it relatively prosperous. They continued to manage Namara's wine portfolio and we remained on good terms, with no regrets or recriminations to remind us of a period when discord within the firm nearly put an end to our relationship.

*

Private Eye had continued to lampoon me on a regular basis but was now becoming unusually extravagant in its litany of lies and innuendoes. Their vivid imagination was carrying them beyond the realms of plausibility and the offence they gave was unrelieved by humour. Their view of me, which at times verged on the racist, saw nothing in me worthy of praise. For them I evidently embodied everything that was vulgar and nasty in British society and was therefore fair game. Their hostile campaign seemed tantamount to a crusade to demean me wherever and whenever possible, just to satisfy the witless malicious whim of some individual in their midst who had it in for me for an unfathomable reason. Or, I often wondered, was it just another manifestation of the typical British media attitude that seemed to resent anyone who gained a measure of success or possessed a certain amount of chutzpah? It was apparent that success had become a commodity to be sneered at by *Private Eye*, whose sole *raison d'être* at this period was to pander to the credulous masses who read their appalling organ of put-downs.

In the light of all this it was inevitable that Quartet Books would be earmarked for an onslaught in their famous 'The World's Greatest Publishers' series, presumably on account of my proprietorship. The whole thrust of the piece, when it appeared in September 1982, placed me as leading actor, stalking the scene like a heavy in the manner of one of Humphrey Bogart's early roles. All of my achievements were torn to pieces and positive actions I had undertaken, whether in publishing, films or theatre, were denigrated and cast aside as non-events. The highly acclaimed film *The Slipper and the Rose* was described as 'sickly', and, it was stated, my publishing ventures had already lost me over a million pounds. The activities of my other companies were brought into question by sly turns of phrase implying that anyone visiting my headquarters at Namara House had their movements monitored on closed-circuit television to make sure they did not discover the true nature of what went on within its walls. They accused me of publishing pornography, or sub-pornography, and of having reneged on various promises I made to the original founders of Quartet as soon as I was comfortably installed. But probably the most damaging allegation recycled the old accusation that I was an Arab propagandist, publishing books on Arabian themes that 'don't even get into the Quartet catalogues'. Edna O'Brien's *Arabian Days* was an exception to this, since it did get into the catalogues, presumably because of the author's fame. No doubt, they concluded, 'this Arabist publishing is the point of Quartet'.

After that they turned the spotlight on an old chestnut, my supposed relationship with staff within the Namara Group, especially my rumoured inclination to sack anyone I regarded as 'disloyal or incompetent'. The latest casualty, they announced, was Stephanie Dowrick, founder and managing director of The Women's Press, who according to their informed sources was now 'lotus eating and writing a book in her native Australia'. Next in the listing was Dr Anne Smith, 'founder of the *Literary Review* and one time Edinburgh-commuting editorial director of Quartet'. After her came Jim Reynolds, 'old time publisher and managing director of Robin Clark'; and then 'fiery Gloria Ferris, editorial director of Quartet'; and, bringing up the rear, Sheila Turnbull, 'who was dismissed for refusing £50 per night to appear nude in Attallah's production of *The Beastly Beatitudes of Balthazar B*'. The list could go on, they implied: it 'does not include a dozen or so low-paid editors and representatives who were all sacked when unwise enough to ask for a rise'.

The article then took up the tired old theme, so beloved by some sections of the radical press, about my supposed anxiety to be accepted by the publishing establishment, which I was evidently finding 'harder going' than it had been to become 'one of the favourite tycoons of the Tory press'. My latest ruse, it revealed, was to 'hire the nubile daughters of the famous or notorious. One son, too: Hugo Guinness has joined his sister Sabrina and is trying to sell advertising space in the *Literary Review*. Bridget Heathcoat-Amory usually does that.' Then they turned on Rebecca Fraser, 'the Robin Clark editor these days', naming her as 'Magnesia's daughter', hired by me as 'an illustrator (she's done a couple of books with mum) but when she was seen to be too awful at that he gave orders that "in future all the covers will be attributed to Rebecca, because we need the publicity".' Their story about her then ended with the outrageous claim that Alan Bold, the Scots writer and poet, who was commissioned to compile an anthology on writers and drink, received a letter from Rebecca after he delivered his manuscript saying she thought he should not include anything by Norman Douglas, 'because he was a pederast', nor by William Blake, 'because he was mad'. *Private Eye* was reassured, so they said, to 'know that standards of morality are being reasserted at Quartet'.

Private Eye's article stirred the emotions of many, who felt some of its allegations were too vile and underhand to be left unchallenged. Stephanie Dowrick, who was no kitten by any reckoning, fired off a letter from the address of The Women's Press in East London:

Sir – Your fable about Naim Attallah in issue 541 stinks.

It is rotten with lies, though I leave the body of the text to Naim himself to correct.

I should like to point out only, and yet again, that I was not sacked from my position as managing director of The Women's Press. I chose to go to Australia for a whole variety of reasons and was completely supported in this potentially most inconvenient decision by Naim Attallah.

He and I remain joint proprietors of The Women's Press. I continue to be an active director of the company. Naim continues to be a valued and utterly loyal friend.

Far from eating lotuses in Australia, I am, alas, tasting ash in East London.

Stephanie's letter prompted one, in turn, from Jim Reynolds, who saw the chance of giving vent to the spleen he felt over his severance from Robin Clark Ltd, a story already told from my viewpoint in Chapter Seven:

Sir – I don't want to comment on the views of Stephanie Dowrick, for whom I have great affection and respect, except to say that, in the looking-glass world of Namara House, 'loyalty' does not appear to be a virtue that most of Attallah's ex-staff would be likely to attribute to him.

The bitter lesson I learned, all too late in life, as founder and managing editor of Robin Clark Ltd, was not to put my trust in Ayatollahs, and I have little doubt that most of the executives named in your article (nearly all known to me personally) would agree. I only hope that Stephanie will manage to keep both her illusions and her association with The Women's Press, which she founded and so brilliantly ran.

My own letter to *Private Eye* was specific and to the point:

Sir – The honour of my inclusion in your series 'The World's Greatest Publishers' was tarnished by the blemishes in your researches (issue 541).

You had contrived to include inaccuracies, lies and innuendoes at the rate of one per column inch; if that is a record, we should surely be told! But to trot out again the old rubbish that had previously appeared in other organs of 'information' – each forced to retract their stories – suggests that the mighty Gnome is losing his grip. To perform a hatchet job on me *Private Eye* should have come up with something more scandalous and original instead of parodying stale and disredited put-downs.

For the enlightenment of your otherwise misinformed readers kindly correct, first, some major inaccuracies: Namara House is, alas, not worth anywhere near £1m; my reported losses in the publishing field are some-what exaggerated; Bill Miller was third (not first) to leave of the original quartet; Hugo Guinness was employed by us for three weeks only.

And please acknowledge some of your unpardonable fabrications: I have no property in the Channel Isles; I do not own thirty or so companies – or any controlled by nominee shareholders; the Arab titles Quartet have published have all been listed in our catalogues, and none of them do I publish as 'Arabist propaganda'; Stephanie Dowrick was not sacked – indeed she is a valued colleague and friend and very much in evidence; nor were Gloria Ferris and Sheila Turnbull sacked, and the nude extravaganza was not my scene; I have never wished or expressed the wish to be a member of the 'establishment' (I am ecstatic at the suggestion that I have become 'one of the favourite tycoons of the Tory press' – long may they rule, if this is so!); I have never issued any instruction, explicit or implicit, that covers should be wrongly attributed to Rebecca Fraser. Lastly the snide innuendoes: what you imply is, I am reliably assured, out of character – I am open and by no means inaccessible.

So what are you left with? Not enough to make a publishable meal, certainly. To think you missed the opportunity for a bit of fun, however outrageous! But alas *Private Eye*'s current reputation for abysmal unreliability must, it seems, be maintained by foul rather than fair means.

Yours in sorrow, barely tempered by anger.

With this letter I rested my case.

Seventeen

The year 1982 was finishing on a high note. A varied list of books, from politics to photography, from jazz to sex, from music to the City of London, from pop to birds, this time of the animal variety, was successfully published and signalled a turning point in Quartet's fortunes. For this period we were able to report a profit of a hundred and ten thousand pounds on a turnover of one point four million pounds. I was encouraged by the progress achieved and felt bold enough to think in terms of expanding the list even further into more experimental areas or tackling politically charged topics like the Israeli invasion of Lebanon. I was aware of the risks that could be involved, the first being financial and the second being that of alienating the sector of the political establishment that habitually put up the cry of anti-Semitism when any criticism was made of Israel.

We were still in our formative years, and our bullish confidence in Quartet's future can be illustrated by the range of books published in 1982. To take politics first, *The Struggle for Peace in the Middle East* by Mahmoud Riad, Egypt's foreign minister from 1964 to 1972, analysed some of the arguments being put forward for a comprehensive peace in the region, arguing that only a settlement that embraced all the Arab states and Israel could ever be a real solution. The author wrote as one who had taken a leading part in discussions around the world.

Moving to jazz, there was Ian Carr's critical biography of Miles Davis, which chronicled how he burst on to the New York jazz scene in 1945 when he recorded with Charlie Parker for the first time at the age of nineteen. From then on, through the ups and downs of his personal life, Miles repeatedly won his way back into the limelight, a dynamic, controversial figure who became a lasting influence on contemporary music. The development and continuity of his musical career was traced from the formative Charlie Parker years through the small-group ensembles of the early 1950s to the large-scale orchestral collaborations – in which his genius combined with that of the great arranger Gil Evans – and the more rock-based electronic pieces of the 1970s.

The world of pop was represented by *Queen's Greatest Pix*, a compilation edited and designed by Jacques Lowe, for which Lord Snowdon provided a cover photo. In a series of photographs it illustrated Queen's rise to prominence in the 1970s to become one of the great rock groups, known for its high-camp style of presentation. Its tone was established by its lead singer, Freddie Mercury, whose power and range of voice was unique in his generation. Freddie, who also composed many of their numbers, had been born in Zanzibar to Parsee parents, his father being in the British diplomatic service. The group's first remarkable success had been 'Killer Queen', which had become a true classic with its stunning vocal effects and flowing guitar licks fronting a solid rhythm. By 1975 Queen had already produced their unquestioned masterwork 'Bohemian Rhapsody', and their place in the history of popular music was assured. The book was deservedly a great success.

A book that presented sex on an elevated plane was *Oriental Erotic Art* by Philip Rawson, dean of the school of art and design at Goldsmith's College in south London. The author explained the philosophy behind this eastern erotic tradition, showing how sexual love was considered a way of uniting the human with the divine. The volume was lavishly illustrated with reproductions of paintings and sculptures, ranging from the humorous and grotesque to the supremely beautiful.

The subject of philosophy was represented by a biography of Nietzsche by Ronald Hayman. His incisive study explored the life of the man who came to be seen as the most important moral philosopher since Plato. Much of the twentieth century, with its agonizing struggles of belief and conscience, was said to be foreshadowed in his thinking, yet his beliefs changed radically as he developed his ideas. There could be no understanding of his achievements unless they were viewed within the context of his life – a life of isolation blighted by an unremitting deterioration of his mental health and culminating in a descent into madness at the age of forty-four. By analysing Nietzsche's personal and philosophical evolution, the book provided a much-needed reappraisal of this influential pioneer of modern thinking, whose ideas had so often been misrepresented and purloined to justify authoritarian political causes that would have horrified him if he had lived to see them.

A book that confirmed Quartet's standing as an originator of the most luxurious coffee-table books with exciting themes was *The City*, researched by Fiona Pilkington, edited, photographed and designed by Jacques Lowe, and with a text by Sandy McLachlan. Sir Kenneth Cork wrote in his foreword that the book

> penetrates the halls of tradition, power and high finance as never before attempted or permitted. It features the leading personalities from the governor of the Bank of England to the judges in the Old Bailey: the ceremonies of the Lord Mayor's Show to the admittance of a freeman. It goes behind the façade of St Paul's Cathedral and the Barbican Centre

and pictures the markets, the watering places, the rich life of the most powerful financial centre in the world.

Copies were snapped up by all the leading institutions in the City, to be given as gifts to their international customers or used to promote the famous 'Square Mile' in which they operated.

A rich treat for ornithologists was provided by *The Birds of Oman*, commissioned by His Majesty the Sultan of Oman, whose generosity made it possible for Quartet to undertake such a mammoth task. The result was a beautifully produced volume by Michael Gallagher and Martin Woodcock. It was comprehensive and lavishly illustrated, the first systematic guide to all the bird species to be found in Oman. Over three hundred and fifty of them were shown in full colour and the text gave information for each species on their world range and their status in Oman along with data on plumage, form and behaviour. It came complete with maps and indexes: an essential tool for all who study ornithology.

Finally there were the Quartet photography volumes, starting with *Obsession* by Bob Carlos Clarke with a foreword by Patrick Lichfield. Clarke achieved his most striking images by a careful application of montage techniques and tinting, his use of colour being firmly governed by the symbols, fetishes, fears and fantasies of popular icons. The fashion model, urban violence, cars and motor bikes, pornography – his choice of subject developed and extended the dominant themes of the visual language of contemporary culture into hyper-realism, neo-surrealism and a concern with eroticism. His untimely and tragic death in March 2006 robbed the world of a major photographic talent.

Then two more photographic books brought the programme for 1982 to a close, one of them a tribute to a veteran established talent, Angus McBean; the other a celebration of a newly emergent photographer, John Swannell, whose creative sensitivity I admired and recognized as a guarantee of his future success. Angus McBean was the classic old professional whose claim to immortality stemmed from his love of theatre, which had led him to photograph innumerable stage stars in the early 1950s. His portraits of Vivien Leigh were legendary. No wonder they loved working with him. It was said that, like Irving Penn in America, he was incapable of taking an ugly picture. *Angus McBean* had a text by Adrian Woodhouse and a foreword from Lord Snowdon, whose opening statement urged the reader to consider the definition of genius. 'Do look it up,' he wrote. 'I'm sure it applies to Angus.' The launch party was a sumptuous affair, held appropriately on the steeply raked stage of the Old Vic. Guests from many walks of life came to pay tribute to this giant of theatrical portraiture, whose magical evocations of the great performers were unmatched. Among them were the Snowdons, Viscount Moore, Lady Anne Lambton, the Honourable Laura Sandys, Robert Carrier, Bob Geldof, Margaret Rawlings, Marika Rivera and a host of other show-business folk, including a number of McBean's personal friends.

He was a kind and generous man who was anxious to show his appreciation of my publishing the book by offering to take a portrait photograph of me and one of my wife. It was a gesture we gladly welcomed. We turned up at his studio on the appointed day and found it was like stepping back into the early history of photography as he disappeared underneath a black cloth behind his old-fashioned plate camera and, with great precision, exposed five plates each. The following week we received two sets of five signed photographs and found ourselves looking marvellously moody and reflective. Snowdon was right. McBean contrived to make everything he shot reflect his own inner beauty of spirit.

Fine Lines was the title John Swannell chose himself for his book. It accurately conveyed the nature of his photographic gift. John had been David Bailey's assistant for four years, during which time he toured extensively with him. Thereafter he travelled on his own, working for various magazines and advertising agencies. There had been four exhibitions of his work: two in London, one in Hamburg and one in New York. His picture for the book's front cover was provocatively shot and bore comparison with Helmut Newton's for *White Women*, though it did not perhaps have such an overt sexual charge and was more subtle in its connotations. The entire print-run for the book sold out and before long it was a collector's item. As a result John was established in his own style of photography and went on to scale heights which fully justified my expectations.

Eighteen

I had an uncanny premonition that 1983 would be a difficult year. So far my new career as a publisher had been bumpy but without too much discomfort. The controversies of the past twelve months had left my fighting spirit intact. My wife Maria maintained that I always courted trouble because basically I enjoyed adversarial combat. It was my way, she said, of reassuring myself that I was capable of defending what I felt to be right, whether ideological or political. There was an element of truth in that, I had to admit. I function at my best under pressure and relish the art of tactical manoeuvring. I never seek conflict for its own sake, and I would rather win a contest through debate or highly charged negotiation. To pit one's intellect against that of an opponent and win is far more satisfying and morale boosting than entering into some vulgar spat that is undignified for both winner and loser. While I am prone to flare up at the least provocation, I try to leave matters to simmer down before I react.

The start of 1983 was benign enough. The attentions of the press seemed to become focused on Sabrina Guinness, who was causing a great deal of speculation following her appointment to head a book club affiliated with the *Literary Review*. The announcement of the launch party led to various cheap asides in the press questioning her suitability to run such an enterprise. The gossip writers had a field-day delving into her background and claiming she possessed the less serious attributes of a social butterfly. Some reported that she was presently engrossed in books to bring her up to the mark in her new job; others held more cynical views. Sabrina herself showed great reserve, refusing to let her feathers be ruffled by this onslaught of adverse publicity. She proved to have an impressive measure of resilience in coping with the situation and rose above it all with dignity.

Sabrina organized the launch party, which was notable for the rich mixture of people it assembled. The literati were there in force, alongside the gossip mongers who could not resist the chance of picking up more material for their columns. The usual crowd of book-event attenders chattered with delight as they circulated among the beautiful young women there to show their solidarity with Sabrina, whom they considered one of the gang. Roald Dahl, who reputedly never attended a publishing function unless it was to do with one of his own books, had responded to a personal invitation from

Sabrina. He was there with his daughter Tessa, who had had a small part in *The Slipper and the Rose*, the film I had produced with David Frost.

Roald Dahl and I began our conversation with his asking me in which part of Palestine I was raised. He knew the country well, he added, having been stationed there as a fighter pilot with the RAF during the Second World War. Their target at the time had been the Vichy administration in Lebanon. When I told him my home town was Haifa, his face lit up. The mention of it brought back poignant memories, he said. He described how the Arab peasants would wave to signify good luck as the fighter planes flew over Mount Carmel on their outward sortie, and waved to welcome them back when the pilots made a safe return to base. As he was speaking a sudden thought shot into my mind. Quartet was about to publish a book, hard-hitting in its views, on Israel's invasion of Lebanon. Perhaps we could ask Dahl to write a piece about it for the *Literary Review*.

The title was *God Cried* and the author was Tony Clifton, a well-known and respected journalist who worked for *Newsweek*; his collaborator was Catherine LeRoy, a veteran French war photographer who died recently. The book described, in harrowing detail, by way of its words and pictures, the violence and destruction inflicted by the Israeli armed forces on West Beirut through shelling and bombing and the harsh realities of their occupation. Its title derived from a piece of Palestinian black humour circulating in the Middle East at the time, it being said that God had agreed to answer one question each from Ronald Reagan, Leonid Brezhnev and Yasser Arafat. The American president asked his question first, wanting to know when an American would become leader of the whole world. 'In fifty years,' said God. And Reagan cried. When God asked him why he cried, he said, 'Because it won't happen in my lifetime.' Next it was the turn of Brezhnev, who wished to know from God when the whole world would be communist. 'In a hundred years,' said God. And Brezhnev cried for the same reason as Reagan. And when it came to Arafat, he asked God, 'When will my people have a homeland of their own?' And God cried.

Before I could broach my idea for a review from Dahl, I needed to observe the protocol between proprietor and editor and consult with Gillian Greenwood on whether she would agree. Hers was the last word editorially on what went into the magazine and the choice of contributors. I tracked her down in another corner of the launch party and put the question. She gave me the green light at once. Returning to Roald Dahl, I asked him whether he might be interested in writing such a review. His reaction was abrupt to the point of hostility. He received many requests from publishers to review their books, he told me, and never agreed to do one, irrespective of the book's merits. He would certainly make no exception to the rule on this or any other occasion. Dahl could display a rather intimidating side if he was roused and I stood there dumbstruck. The earlier warmth of our conversation evaporated instantly. I mumbled a few meaningless phrases and retreated politely, under the pretext of not wishing to monopolize his company.

After recovering from the shock of this sudden embarrassment – not because of his refusal to write a review but because of the manner in which he had expressed it – I went to seek Tessa Dahl to protest at how I was mortified by her father. She was not in the least surprised to hear my tale, being quite accustomed to his brusque moods. Would she be able to persuade him to change his mind, I wondered, given his interest in Palestine? If we sent her a copy as soon as the book became available, she suggested, she would try her very best to cajole him into a change of heart. I held out very little hope of her succeeding, but sent her *God Cried* even so, just for its promotional value.

Hardly a week had passed before a letter from Dahl arrived enclosing a comprehensive review and informing me that he did not wish to receive any payment for it. I was thrilled until I started to read it, and then my spirits fell in semi-horror. It was couched in language unhoned by diplomacy and without the least regard for the art of gentle censure. Dahl was bold and unrelentingly scathing in his condemnation of Israel for its brutal opportunistic incursion, which had taken its army all the way to Beirut. I knew at once that publication of the piece would send the influential pro-Zionist lobby into a frenzy of rage. It was addressed to the editor of the *Literary Review*, and since the decision on whether to print it would have to be Gillian Greenwood's, I passed it on quickly.

Gillian shared my concerns and we agreed we must first check it out with our lawyer, Michael Rubinstein, whose advice and suggestions would be pertinent since he was himself Jewish. To our utter surprise, Michael liked and approved of Dahl's review. Apart from editing out a few of the more intemperate expressions, he urged us to publish it. The reason he gave was that criticism of Israel should not, when it was deserved, be silenced by those who chose to see only one side of the equation. Michael was a liberal and an ardent champion of the oppressed and dispossessed. His last words to Gillian and myself were: 'Publish and be damned.' We did publish; and we were damned.

The reaction to the review was far more extreme that we had anticipated. Apart from the overreaction of the Jewish lobby, the friends of Israel in the media became virulent in their onslaught on Dahl, myself and the *Literary Review*. The attacks came in from every side, even reaching a pitch where many journalists and politicians of high standing called for a boycott of the magazine and anyone connected with it. Every day something more vicious than the day before appeared somewhere, with accusations of anti-Semitism becoming more strident and preposterous as the campaign to discredit Quartet and the book gained momentum. Dahl did nothing to help matters by growing even more combative and being provoked into making outrageous, inflammatory responses. He was not in the least chastened by all that was being said about him. On the contrary, he expounded on his views and riled the press by being abrasive and dismissing their questions out of hand. There was no way of putting a gag on him and no point in asking him to cool things down. He had the bit between his teeth and nothing would stop him giving our adversaries all the fuel they could have wished for to keep their engines firing.

Time after time I was asked by the press to comment on one or other of his utterances and found myself at a loss for an appropriate response. He was still my contributor and I could not let it seem I was being unsupportive of his right to hold his own views. It was a difficult situation that had gone beyond control. Although we were fighting from the same corner, our temperaments and perceptions of how to get a grip on things were vastly different. In a way, he had dug himself into a hole from which he could not extricate himself without sustaining some damage.

When the whole uproar began I had, in fact, been away for a break in Italy, visiting Lord Lambton, who had invited us for the first time to stay at his villa outside Siena. The holiday was constantly interrupted by the latest reports from London as the drama began to unfold. On the way back to England we travelled via Florence to meet Harold Acton. He had asked us to tea at his famous palazzo overlooking the city, and afterwards took us to walk in the extensive historic gardens, insisting on having his photograph taken with my wife. From that rarefied and civilized experience I plunged into the explosive turmoil back in London, generated, first, by the publication of *God Cried*, and secondly by the furore that was continuing over Dahl's review. Rather than showing signs of blowing over with time, the row seemed to be gaining strength. The entire British press gave the impression of having ganged up to condemn us unjustly – given that in every dispute there are two sides to the issue.

To make matters even worse, Jeffrey Bernard, in his 'Low Life' column in the *Spectator*, went way beyond the bounds of decency by proposing that, as a retaliation for the sentencing of 'a parched man' to six hundred strokes by those 'awful Arabs' (referring to an event in Saudi Arabia), six hundred strokes should be inflicted on an Arab in London. He nominated me for this punishment as the boss of Quartet Books and possibly 'the ugliest man he had ever met'. It was beyond comprehension that the *Spectator* should have published such offensive material, but the *Mail on Sunday* ferreted out a reason to explain 'why the genial Jeffrey is lashing out at Naim in the *Spectator*'. David Skan, the writer of the short piece, speculated that it was 'probably not unconnected with an encounter between Attallah's Quartet book firm and Bernard, who was commissioned to write a book about racing. Deadlines were missed and the book never appeared. Attallah made Bernard repay the advance.'

Then out of the woodwork there came Paul Johnson, known for his Zionist sympathies, with a very trenchant article, again in the *Spectator*, that poured scorn on the *Literary Review*. Dahl's article, said Johnson, was in his view 'the most disgraceful item to have appeared in a respectable British publication for a very long time'. He could not actually recall anything like it. Moreover, he claimed, the *Review* was 'controlled by a wealthy Palestinian who also runs Quartet Books', adding that 'the *Literary Review* has published anti-Israeli material before'. In the face of this I could not remain silent and sent a letter to the editor of the *Spectator* to challenge Johnson to substantiate his charges since he accused Dahl of a 'reckless disregard for facts'.

> Where horrendous loss of life and human misery is at stake, complaints of tendentiousness should be discounted. Johnson has no more need to apologize for the expression of his strong feelings that I have for accepting my editor's decision to publish the expression of Dahl's strong feelings in the *Literary Review*. Nor am I ashamed of my own strong feelings about the current appalling misfortunes of both the Lebanese and the Palestinians; for every comparably suffering Jew I feel no less strongly.
>
> Johnson concludes his diatribe: 'The most effective action the civilized community can take is for reputable writers to refuse to be associated with a journal that publishes such filth.' Contributors to the *Literary Review* are encouraged to write freely within the law. It is not to be assumed that the editor or publisher necessarily agrees with all the opinions of the contributors. Or necessarily disagrees with any of them.

My letter was published by the *Spectator* on 10 September. Meanwhile *Private Eye* had muscled in to comment in their 'World of Books' of 26 August that I had struck again by publishing *God Cried*, and by running a review of the book in the *Literary Review*. They claimed the staff were unhappy with the piece Dahl had produced, but were forced to run it by me, the 'Arab propagandist'. What had appalled them, they said, was the evidence of blatant anti-Semitism in the copy and how *Time Out* had published a slightly sanitized version of the review instead of doing their own. My response to *Private Eye*'s allegations appeared in their 9 September issue.

As Bookworm writes, I own through companies both Quartet Books and the *Literary Review*. Nevertheless, in no sense did I 'force' the *Literary Review* to publish the copy, nor was the staff 'appalled [at] the evidence of blatant anti-Semitism in the copy'.

The suggestion that I am anti-Semitic is as absurd as it is mistaken. If being sympathetic to the Palestinians in their plight justifies condemnation of me as a 'Palestinian propagandist' then I will live with that. But it is a mischievous distortion of the meaning of propagandist – one who disseminates 'information, allegations, etc., to assist or damage the cause of a government, movement, etc.' (Collins). I am prepared to risk such abuse as Bookworm's when I believe that the publication of a book may serve the cause of humanity. I trust the editor of the *Literary Review* to exercise her discretion in the same cause.

Running parallel to all this, a minor scuffle was set off when *The Times* 'Diary', under the heading 'Chutzpah', announced that I had entered *God Cried* for the three-thousand-pound H. H. Wingate Prize, which is awarded to an author who stimulates interest in Jewish affairs, when I knew very well there was scant prospect of the book winning. My reasoning in doing so was that it would at least give the judges the opportunity to look at the book and perhaps recognize the other point of view. The *Jewish Chronicle* came in to say that, for once, it agreed with *The Times*: it was chutzpah indeed, given the nature of the book and the intemperate language used by Dahl in his review of it.

Time Out was also dragged into the firing line for having published its abbreviated version of Dahl's piece. The magazine was flooded with letters of protest and suffered a concerted attack from the media for having dared to publish the article. Philip Kleinman, writing in the *Jewish Chronicle* on 26 August, summed up the situation by threatening that 'if *Time Out* can bash Israel, it may well be that some Jews might want to bash *Time Out*. It has a circulation of 65,000 and is heavily dependent on advertising, most of which could be placed elsewhere (*What's On*, *City Limits*, the *Standard*).' A few days later, in the *Jewish Chronicle* of 2 September, Kleinman picked up on a statement made by Mike Coren (himself Jewish) in the *New Statesman* to the effect that I had, as owner of the *Literary Review*, been put in a difficult position by Dahl's article, since 'not even the crudest Zionist could accuse [me] of anti-Semitism'. Yet in Kleinman's view, my remarks to Coren made it clear that it had been the proprietor not the editor of the *Literary Review* who had got Dahl to write the piece in the first place. According to *Private Eye*, he reported, the *Review*'s staff had been appalled by its anti-Semitism but were forced to use it.

On 9 September the *Jewish Chronicle* carried a letter from me responding to Kleinman's article of the 2nd:

Sir – In Philip Kleinman's article he referred to a report that the *Literary Review* staff were appalled by the anti-Semitism in Roald Dahl's review of *God Cried*, but were forced by me to publish the article. I have already written to *Private Eye* pointing out that there is no grain of truth in this statement.

Because of the controversial nature of the article, we have published a number of hostile letters in the current issue of the *Literary Review* (September 1983). We believe a free discourse on such an important subject can only help to bring about a better understanding of the issue. May I conclude by saying that the killing of innocent people of any race, or creed, is a heinous act, and should be condemned by humanity as a whole.

The previous day, the 8th, *The Times* 'Diary' reported that Peter Hillmore of the *Observer* and their own Frank Johnson were on the point of heeding the call from Paul Johnson to boycott the *Literary Review*. Both had contributed to the current issue but neither of them was sure they wished to do so in future. Hillmore said he considered the article to be 'plain, abusive anti-Semitism which should never have been printed', while Johnson said that 'even by the standards of anti-Israel bias, this piece was above and beyond the call of duty. Gillian Greenwood, when asked for her reaction, said that other contributors to the magazine told her that nobody takes any notice of what Paul Johnson says in the *Spectator*.'

Back on 2 September, the *Evening Standard* reported how I had gone to the extraordinary length of removing from the masthead of the *Literary Review* the name of its poetry editor, Carol Rumens, in the wake of her having written a letter of protest about the Dahl piece in the magazine's letter pages. She wished to dissociate herself from it, she told the *Standard*, as she thought the review inaccurate and inflammatory. It was a bad thing, she added, when the proprietor of a magazine identifies too closely with the views expressed in it. Presumably I had removed her name because I was embarrassed that an employee of the magazine (albeit a freelance) should have criticized any of the magazine's contents. 'But at least,' she said, 'he's printed my letter.'

Again on 2 September, William Hickey of the *Daily Express* informed his readers how an almighty row had blown up in the world of literature, featuring spooky writer Roald Dahl and right-wing columnist Paul Johnson, who was calling for a boycott of the *Literary Review*. When asked to comment on this, 'Mr Attallah dismissed Johnson's call for a boycott by saying: "What do you expect from a man who changes his politics as often as I change my shirts! He has no credibility as far as I am concerned." ' But then the *Express* claimed in the final paragraph that I had bowed to a swarm of protests by agreeing to publish a number of letters putting the opposite point of view. The paper agreed to publish a letter from me in reply under the heading 'Unbowed – a free forum for and against Israel':

> Sir – William Hickey highlights the fact that, following the review by Roald Dahl in the *Literary Review*, published by my company, of the book *God Cried*, about the 1982 Lebanon crisis, columnist Paul Johnson has called for a boycott of the *Review*.
>
> The *Literary Review* provides a forum for the free expression of opinion, and I would not expect reputable writers to refuse to be associated with the journal merely because it has published strongly expressed anti-Israel views by Roald Dahl. William Hickey is, however, wrong to say that I have 'bowed to the swarm of protest' over Dahl's anti-Zionist piece.
>
> Letters putting the opposite point of view to Dahl's have been published in the September issue of the *Literary Review* because that is precisely in accordance with its policy.

As the row continued, Sebastian Faulks wrote in the *Sunday Telegraph* of 18 September about what he called 'a publisher under bombardment over an anti-Jewish book review'. The overall thrust of his article was, in my opinion, objectionable on many fronts. He called the review by Dahl anti-Jewish when it was no such thing. Admittedly Dahl used very strong terms in his condemnation of Israel for invading Lebanon and maltreating the Palestinians, but it was nothing more, nothing less. I also felt angry about what I felt was a misrepresentation by Faulks of the whole issue, not only where it concerned me personally but also for his evaluation of Quartet as a publishing house. The *Sunday Telegraph* agreed to publish a letter from me in reply under the heading 'A publisher's policy':

> While it is unnecessary to take issue with the sillier aspects of Sebastian Faulks's article on myself, I would question his dismissal of our publishing programme as celebrity orientated, erotic and propagandist.
>
> Quartet have some 300 titles in print. Less than 20 of these deal with the Middle East, of which 11 are concerned with the literature, folklore and anthropology of an area whose cultural influence on European civilization has been shamefully neglected. At present we have nine photographic books on our list, and for your journalist to dismiss the talents of Helmut Newton, John Swannell, Deborah Turbeville and Angus McBean simply as 'erotic' is philistine to say the least.

To describe as 'not serious' an imprint that publishes Jessica Mitford, Lillian Hellman, Cesare Pavese, 'Multatuli', Fleur Cowles, Shusaku Endo, Robert Kee, Anaïs Nin (to name a few), and whose autumn list includes Celia Bertin's *Marie Bonaparte*, Ryszard Kapuscinski's *The Emperor* and Sue Davidson Lowe's monograph on her great-uncle, Alfred Steiglitz, rather hints that Faulks and his star-witness, Giles Gordon, might have other reasons for the sneers and innuendoes in the article. Moreover, it would seem a curious strategy for a publisher intent on 'forcing his way into the establishment' to publish Paul Robeson's political writings, Jeremy Seabrook's blistering attack on the inhumanity of unemployment, James Avery Joyce's plea for arms reduction or Ralph Miliband's socialist tract.

Our list speaks for itself and we remain, whatever Faulks and Gordon may say, an independent radical publishing house. And make no mistake, there are all too few of us left.

The *Sunday Telegraph* had printed my letter, but in line with *Private Eye* practice it gave the last word to Sebastian Faulks, who said:

I wrote that Quartet has published a 'wide variety' of books but that its 'hallmarks' (i.e. those books with which it is most clearly and commonly associated) were 'pro-Palestinian books on the Middle East, collections of erotic photographs and volumes by English establishment figures'. I can still see no reason to modify that description either in respect of the 'variety' or of the 'hallmarks'.

My reaction at the time was that Faulks's riposte to my letter was ungracious if not bordering on the bloody-minded. I felt he could have been more conciliatory in the circumstances. More of a reasonable tone was sounded by Alexander Chancellor in the *Spectator* on 10 September when he suggested that the civilized community should suspend its boycott of the *Literary Review* on the grounds that we all publish rotten articles from time to time and that he 'felt a little sympathy for Miss Greenwood's employer, Naim Attallah, who happens to be of Palestinian origin'.

Despite the fact that during the summer he was the object of vulgar abuse in the pages of this paper by Mr Jeffrey Bernard, he wrote a most gentlemanly letter to the *Spectator* in reply to Mr Johnson's attack. The letter was gentlemanly because it failed to point out that Mr Attallah is not the sole proprietor of the *Literary Review*. A chunk of it is owned by the *Spectator*'s revered proprietor, Mr Algy Cluff.

In the end, as the row continued for weeks, it became tiresome, with the same points being laboured over and over again, irrespective of which side they were fired from. I was then challenged to speak to the *Jerusalem Post*, an opportunity I willingly welcomed, for I had nothing to hide or be ashamed of. Their feature article, which covered the whole saga, included a short discourse I had with the newspaper, which prefaced our conversation by saying that neither I, nor the editor of the *Literary Review*, nor Dahl himself had the slightest regrets about the article. It went on to describe how I had been born in Haifa in 1931 but since 1949 had been living in England, where I had become a publisher. My last visit to Israel was six years before when my father died and I had never had any flair for politics.

I did not deny the fact that I was opposed to Zionism and had great sympathy with the Palestinians in their plight for statehood, but was adamant that I never used the magazine to push my own views. The editor decided what to publish, but in cases where an article might cause controversy, then consultation between editor and proprietor was the norm. I also rejected the charge that the article was anti-Semitic, despite its strong language. 'If I thought it was, I would not have published it. I'm the last one to talk about anti-Semitism. The Arabs and the Jews are both Semitic people.' In any case, I told my interlocutor, a healthy debate is far better than resorting to violence. It is an essential part of democracy that people should be free to express their own views. Gillian Greenwood was of the same opinion. She said that a contributor to the magazine should be allowed to express his view and confirmed that she had no regrets about publishing the review in question.

The scale and persistence of the Roald Dahl controversy perhaps deflected some attention from the book itself, which had been the reason for the original upsurge of indignation. When *God Cried* was published in the United States, its fate was rather different. It was virtually ignored at every level by book editors and reviewers as if it did not exist. The well-known Jewish columnist and blues historian, Nat Hentoff, wrote an article around this phenomenon that was published in *Voice* on 14 February 1984. 'Have you forgotten that summer in Beirut so soon?' he asked in his headline, referring to the 1982 massacres of Palestinians at the Sabra and Chatila camps, carried out by the Christian Phalangist militia with the connivance of the Israeli authorities during their invasion. He juxtaposed two quotes on the Lebanon adventure, the first from the Israeli prime minister, Menachem Begin, when he said, 'Never in the past was the great Jewish community in the United States so united around Israel, standing together'; the second came from the respected Israeli diplomat and politician, Abba Eban: 'Beirut for us was like Moscow for Napoleon, a place you'd wished you'd never been.'

'There is a rage in the book, and shock,' wrote Mr Hentoff, 'and much beauty in the faces of the children. I do not know of a more frightening book published last year.' It had been published by a company owned by a Palestinian Arab. 'Aha you say. This must be propaganda.' But then he asked whether, if you took up a strongly pro-Israel book, you looked to see if its publisher was Jewish. 'Yes, I guess some of you do, just as some of you will dismiss this book without looking at it because who can trust a Palestinian? That kind of dumbness cuts across ideological lines, and there's nothing to be done about it. I hope some of the rest of you will judge *God Cried* on its own.'

It was not surprising that Tony Clifton's prose should have been raw, like some of his memories. It had been 'one hell of a bloody, brutal siege of Beirut'. There was the story of an editor on the *New York Times* who cut the adjective 'indiscriminate' from the dispatch of a correspondent reporting the bombing – because he found it hard to believe. 'But . . . the Israeli planes . . . did not give a good goddamn what they hit. The apologists for this most shameful operation in the history of Israel – and many Israelis see it as criminal – can't have it both ways. If there was only precision bombing, why were clearly marked hospitals hit? Repeatedly.'

Hentoff conceded that Arafat and the PLO hierarchy had interspersed themselves among civilians and that it was possible that some of them took shelter in hospitals for the mentally handicapped, 'one of which was bombed five times'; but even so, how could it be worth the cost to 'kill the maimed, the halt, the blind, kids, anything that moved? What would have been worth this terrible price in Israel's first war that was not one of defence?' 'All atrocities should be written about with rage,' said Hentoff, coming to the fundamental point. 'But no one writer has space for all, and I choose Beirut because I am Jewish and feel kinship with those in Israel who do not want Jews, anywhere, to forget what happened in Lebanon in the summer of 1982. Lest it happen again under Jewish auspices, including the support of American Jews.'

Nat Hentoff, writing in America, had finally thrown into relief the meretricious judgements made on *God Cried* by such a large and influential section of the press in Britain.

Nineteen

In the midst of the storm raging around Roald Dahl's review, I carried on with the task of publishing more books. I was not to be deflected from our objective to publish whatever we believed to be of national or political importance by the *God Cried* uproar. I was not for bending, especially in situations where the very tenets of democracy were coming under threat.

Earlier in 1983, it was announced that Georgii Vladimov, one of the most eminent of dissident writers in the Soviet Union, would be allowed to leave Russia as a result of our intervention as his British publisher. Blacklisted by the KGB since 1969 and active in Amnesty International from 1977, Vladimov had been granted permission to leave the Soviet Union with his wife and ailing mother-in-law. Even though he was the author of the highly acclaimed novel, *Faithful Ruslan*, Vladimov had been ordered earlier in the year to write an open letter to Yuri Andropov recanting all his works. To press the point, Andropov sent round one of his old KGB henchmen to threaten reprisals if Vladimov refused. Vladimov complied with the request for a letter, but far from recanting he sought permission to leave, though not without his mother-in-law. At first the Soviet authorities would not allow the old lady to go as well, but they relented in the end. A twelve-thousand-word story by Vladimov, written in a vein of black humour about KGB surveillance, 'Pay No Attention, Maestro', was published in the *Literary Review* on 1 May; and a novel, *Three Minutes' Silence*, was announced for publication in the Quartet catalogue. Jennifer Bradshaw, the editor in charge of the Russian list, told the *Evening Standard* how Vladimov was a household name in his homeland, where, because of his high profile, he could not be persecuted by the authorities with impunity, unlike other less well-known dissident writers. They had tried to tame him and had failed. As his editor, she explained, she had arranged for a Home Office permit to allow him to enter Britain. He was not a writer to be underestimated. 'He is the Solzhenitsyn of the 1980s,' she said.

Rather than report on this example of the serious side of our publishing activities, the press concentrated its attention on a visit by Koo Stark, then much in the news by virtue of her relationship with Prince Andrew. The paparazzi were in relentless pursuit of her wherever she went. No matter how high the level of secrecy surrounding her movements, they always seemed to find her. Sabrina Guinness invited her discreetly to have lunch with me at

Namara House. On the appointed day, no one had an inkling of the invitation or the time of her arrival, yet miraculously the word went round that Koo was there and the building was immediately besieged. We had great trouble smuggling her out. A similar event happened in New York when I escorted her to a party for British agency models, given by the financier Sir Gordon White. The Bentley I kept in New York at the time was literally attacked by a swarm of camera-flashing newshounds, who manhandled us both and pinned us to the ground. It was an ugly and frightening scene I am never likely to forget. Our party consisted of Sabrina Guinness, Bob Geldof, Charlotte Hambro and Norman Parkinson. 'Parks' subsequently became a great friend of Koo's and took her under his wing to advance her photographic ambitions.

In the midst of the *God Cried* turbulence, I threw a party at the Arts Club in Dover Street to launch a Quartet book on the Bee Gees, the vocal trio of the three Gibb brothers who were around in the early days of pop and became one of the world's most successful music groups. It was written and created by David English and produced in gorgeous colour with illustrations and lettering by Alex Brychta. The theme was how funny it is, the way people often resemble animals. 'Think of Barry, Robin and Maurice Gibb . . . Barry as a Lion, Robin the Red Setter and Maurice as an Eager Beaver. Now come with me, says the author, and experience the legend of the Bee Gees.' It was basically a children's book, dedicated to children everywhere and to the fourth Gibb brother. Its style of telling was unique and reflected all the hopes, frustrations – even heartache – as well as the joy and happiness life has in store for us.

Certainly the launch party was a joyous event. The three brothers were there, wrote David Thomas in the *Standard*, 'standing in one corner of the room pretending it was still 1978. Meanwhile the London lit. crit. set, never known for passionate disco fever, milled around asking one another whether they knew what a Bee Gee looked like, pointing at strangers and enquiring, "Do you think that's Barry?" ' Then, Thomas went on to say, 'as if to underline the changes that have come over the pop scene since the days that the Bee Gees ruled the airwaves, there were some newer stars in attendance. Like Marilyn (né Peter Robinson), a good friend of Boy George's who used to model frocks for Vivienne Westwood and who is now, in the best music-biz style, about to sign a six-figure deal with a major company.' Finally Thomas went on to query the purpose of throwing a party when the guests had little to contribute to the selling of books. When he put the question to Juliette Foy, Quartet's press officer, she replied that, 'Primarily we are promoting our publishing house as much as the book.' I thought that was a good response since we could never justify the cost of a party if we were to equate it with the number of books we sell as a result.

My own thoughts are that parties are also useful for meeting people who might have a book in them, and that if, as a publisher, you do not circulate widely, then opportunities will pass you by. The Bee Gee soirée in particular was heavily attended by show-business personalities, including the likes of Billy Connolly, Christopher Reeve, Sting, Bob Geldof and Jeremy Irons. The presence of celebrities will invariably ensure a good deal of press coverage, which in today's world gives a vital boost to any business.

In April the *Literary Review* belatedly celebrated its first year in London, together with the incorporation of its rival journal, *Quarto*, which was owned by Algy Cluff. The political left was well represented at the gathering. Tariq Ali and Chris Mullins fell into deep conversation with Bridget Heathcoat-Amory and her co-workers, Gillian Greenwood and her deputy editor, the delightful Kathy O'Shaughnessy. Among the other guests were Eric Heffer, Anthony Howard, Anthony Holden, Sir Leo Piatzky, Francis Wheen, Peter Hillmore, Piers Paul Read, David Profumo and John Ryle. To introduce the element of glamour, a lively line in literary lolitas (as *Tatler* described them), such as Mary Furness, Camilla Horne and Sally Emerson, turned out in force as a gesture of solidarity.

A month later, Sabrina Guinness's hard work bore fruit and the Academy Bookclub burst on to the scene. It was soon the literary gossip item of the month. Publicized by myself in a high-profile way and structured by Sabrina, it announced its first offer of fourteen titles, which included *Conversations with Graham Greene*, Tom Wolfe's *The Purple Decades*, a *Yellow Book* anthology and novels by Czesław Miłosz and Nobel Prize-winner Heinrich Böll. Sabrina came into her own, enchanting the press corps with the promotion of her first list and slowly winning them over, despite their earlier cynicism.

Also in May, the *Literary Review* launched its special supplement on Ireland and the arts at a party given at the Irish Embassy. Present were Jim Prior, the Northern Ireland secretary; Lord O'Neill, the former Northern Irish prime minister; Sir Hugh Fraser; Lord Moyne; Terence de Vere White and his wife, Victoria Glendinning; and the usual bevy of beautiful young women, gracing the event with their charming presence. Tim Pat Coogan, the editor of the special supplement, greeted the guests with Irish *bonhomie*.

*

Back in February I had been to the Bridge Lane Theatre in Battersea to see the musical *Hollywood Babylon*, based on Kenneth Anger's hard-hitting book about scandals in the Hollywood film community of the 1930s. It looked as if its limited run was going to end there as no central theatre showed any signs of taking it up. I decided to stage it again for three nights at the Camden Palace between 14 and 16 June, feeling that, properly promoted, this might induce a West End management to consider a transfer. The show, in my opinion, was worth another chance.

The play re-enacted fourteen stories from the book, using a mix of music, dance, dialogue, mime and film, assembled by the director Paul Marcus, who was fulfilling a three-year ambition in presenting it for the stage. It was unsentimental and hardcore, whether it was telling of the demise of the Mexican Spitfire, Lupe Velez, bungling a meticulously rehearsed suicide and drowning in vomit and toilet water; or of the kindly Ramon Novarro being murdered by having a dildo rammed down his throat. *Time Out* described it as 'not so much digging the dirt' as 'more of a full-scale excavation'. The critics were confounded by the breakneck pace of the show and the full horror of its story-telling. But they all agreed that Debbie Arnold, playing Lana Turner and Jayne Mansfield, was excellent and a theatrical discovery. Trudie Styler (now Sting's wife) as Velez, Mary Astor and Barbara Le Marr was equally outstanding, and Nick Chagriu as Valentino and Novarro set the seal on the high quality of the acting.

The production was slick and entertaining, so long as you had the stomach for it. In retrospect I could see the reason for its failure. The public on a night out does not necessarily wish to witness scenes of human degradation; and the production's shock tactics were hardly calculated to turn it into anything other than the kind of entertainment that relies on squalor and violence for its appeal. From my own perspective the exercise was another learning experience that would no doubt help my selectivity in future. Debbie Arnold was soon to star opposite Omar Sharif in the stage version of *The Prince and the Showgirl*, in the role made famous by Marilyn Monroe in the movie. This was definitely as a result of her performance in *Hollywood Babylon*. So, on this occasion, something good had come out of my entrepreneurial misjudgement.

*

By the end of September I had made my peace with Carol Rumens, the poetry editor of the *Literary Review*, who had left because of her strong disapproval of Roald Dahl's review of *God Cried*. I was utterly moved when I discovered that a poem she had written about the Arab-Jewish conflict was dedicated to me. It appeared in the *New Statesman* in their issue of 30 September. The poem, which was a cry for peace, was so beautifully worded and full of sympathy for both Jews and Arabs, that it deserves today, as it did then, as large an audience as it can reach. It is as relevant now as it was at the time and I am proud to include it in full.

Carol Rumens
A NEW SONG
(*for Naim Attallah*)

'Thou feedest them with the bread of tears, and givest
them tears to drink in great measure.' (Psalm 80)

Silence of old Europe
Not even the Shofar
Can utter: Maidenek,
Mauthausen, Babi Yar –

Death of the innocent being
Our speciality,
Let us add Lebanon's breaking
Sob to the litany.

So many now to mourn for,
Where can the psalmist start?
Only from where his home is
And his untidy heart.

We pluck our first allegiance
With a curled baby-hand
And peer between its fingers
To see our promised land:

Yours on a hillside clouded
With olives; mine a cot
In a London postal district,
Its trees long spilled as soot.

On a late wartime morning
In Northern Europe, my
First breath seems implicated
In yells of victory.

But it's the quieter voices
That keep on trying to rhyme,
Telling me almost nothing
But filling me with shame.

Germany in the thirties
And half my family tree
Bent to an SS microscope's
Mock genealogy.

Duly pronounced untainted
For his Aryan bride,
My uncle says it's proven,
There are no Jews on his side.

Ancient, unsummoned, shameless,
The burdens of prejudice –
All through my London childhood
Adults with kindly eyes

And sharp throw-away phrases
Like bits of shopfront glass
(Grandfather: 'He's a *schneider*'
– Frowning and treadling fast.)

Later, the flickering movie:
Greyish, diaphanous
Horrors that stared and whispered,
'God has forgotten us.'

Oh, if our unborn children
Must go like us to flame,
Will you consent in silence
Or gasp and burn with them?

It is so late in the century
And still the favourite beast
Whines in the concrete bunker.
And still the trucks roll east

And east and east through whited
Snowfields of the mind
Towards the dark encampment;
Still the Siberian wind

Blows across Prague and Warsaw,
The voices in our head
Baying for a scapegoat:
Historians gone mad,

Thugs on a street corner,
The righteous Gentile who
Pins Lebanon like a yellow star
To the coat of every Jew.

Silences of old Europe,
Be broken; let us seek
The judgement of the silenced
And ask how they would speak.

Then let the street musician
Crouched in the cruel sun
Play for each passing, stateless
Child of Babylon

Conciliatory harmonies
Against the human grain,
A slow psalm of two nations
Mourning a common pain –

Hebrew and Arabic mingling
Their single-rooted vine,
Olives and roses falling
To sweeten Palestine.

Whoever it was said that there is no such thing as bad publicity had it about right if you consider the number of times bad publicity has propelled people of limited talent and quality into celebrity status and brought them fame and fortune. The secret of coping with bad publicity is to withstand the onslaught and never panic. It was for me an ironic twist of fate to find myself presented as a main feature in an issue of *Publishers' Weekly*, the most important organ of the book trade in the United States, solely as a result of my having precipitated a minor earthquake with the publication of *God Cried*. It had been for me personally a most unwelcome and harrowing time as I tried to fend off abuse and gross accusations of anti-Semitism.

My Palestinian sympathies have never prevented me from highlighting the plight of any other repressed minority or race, the Jews being no exception. Nor have they discouraged me from publishing Jewish authors whose work I admire. The emotive argument that any critic of Israeli or Zionist policies is an anti-Semite by definition is harder to maintain today when so much recent history has discredited it by illustration. In the 1980s it was still being bandied about by the defenders of Israel. If people wish to maintain the value of words, then they must use them more selectively. For myself, I think my record speaks for itself. Since the beginning of my stewardship, Quartet has published a significant number of books on Jews or by Jewish writers. The list of titles given below is by no means comprehensive regarding our output in that field. However, it should be sufficient to demonstrate to the reader that Quartet is a publishing company totally free of bias. In the end, as the saying goes, 'Deeds are fruits, words are but leaves.'

Books published by Quartet by Jewish authors or on Jewish topics:

Pearl Abraham, *Giving up America* and *The Romance Reader*. Two novels set in the Hasidic communities of 1990s New York State.

Aharon Appelfeld, *The Age of Wonders, Bedenheim 1939, For Every Sin, The Healer, The Immortal Bartfuss, Katarina, The Retreat, To the Land of the Reeds* and *Unto the Soul*. Eight novels by one of the most revered writer survivors of the Holocaust. Most of Appelfeld's stories are set pre-Second World War and describe Jewish communities unaware of or unresponsive to portents of the tragedy that is about to befall them. He never writes directly about the Holocaust and only occasionally about the aftermath (as in *Bartfuss*).

Giorgio Bassani, *Behind the Door, The Garden of the Finzi-Continis, The Heron* and *The Smell of Hay*. Bassani wrote about the highly assimilated Italian Jews, his masterpiece being *The Garden of the Finzi-Continis*, which tells of the reclusive Finzi-Continis – who open their tennis court to other Jewish young people when the racial laws in Italy exclude them from public courts – and their subsequent wartime fate.

Lesley Chamberlain, *The Secret Artist: A Close Reading of Sigmund Freud*. Gentile author on a Jewish subject.

John Colvin, *Lions of Judah*. Gentile author on a Jewish subject.

Robert Eisenberg, *Boychiks in the Hood*. Highly entertaining travel book cum history of the Hasidic sects of Europe and North America.

Peter and Leni Gillman, *'Collar the Lot!'*. About the British wartime internment of so-called 'enemy aliens', many of whom were Jewish.

Georges-Arthur Goldschmidt, *Worlds of Difference*. Autobiographical novel about a Jewish child separated from his parents and taken to Switzerland.

Louise Lambrichs, *Hannah's Diary*. Novel set in Paris in 1943, in which a Jewish woman feels forced to have an abortion.

Emanuel Litvinoff, *Journey through a Small Planet*. Memoir about the (Jewish) East End of London at the end of the nineteenth century and in the early twentieth.

Arnošt Lustig, *Darkness Has No Shadows*, *Diamonds of the Night*, *Dita Saxova*, *Night and Hope* and *A Prayer for Katarina Horowitzova*. Lustig is another writer survivor, whose work deals much more directly with the Holocaust than Appelfeld's, with books set in the camps (as in *Darkness Has No Shadows*) and others examining the plight of the post-war survivors (as in *Dita Saxova*).

Norman Manea, *October Eight o'Clock*. Stories about the wartime sufferings of Romanian Jews.

Monica Porter, *Deadly Carousel*. Biography by a Gentile author of the Hungarian actress and singer Vali Racz, who sheltered Jews during the war.

Giorgio and Nicola Pressburger, *The Green Elephant*. A Jewish fable.

Milton Shulman, *Voltaire, Goldberg and Others*. A Jewish joke book.

Abram Tertz, *Little Jinx* and *A Voice from the Chorus*. The one a novel by the Soviet dissident, the other his prison notebooks.

Arnold Wesker, *The Birth of Shylock* and *The King's Daughters*. Journals and a short-story collection from the well-known playwright.

Elizabeth Wurtzel, *Bitch*, *The Bitch Rules* and *Prozac Nation*.

Hannele Zurndorfer, *The Ninth of November*. Autobiography telling of the author's experiences as a child refugee from Nazi Germany.

Twenty

In the late 1970s, George Hutchinson had introduced me to his friend Charlie Douglas Home, who subsequently became editor of *The Times*. Charlie was a down-to-earth gentlemanly character, warmly disposed towards his fellow men and bereft of any pretensions. His upper-class background in no way affected his relationships with those who came from other sections of society. Because of these qualities, I found myself drawn to him and felt quite at ease in his company. In the years before I met him he had been battling a drink problem, not uncommon in members of the journalistic profession. Only by resorting to total abstinence did he manage eventually to lick it. Whenever we met for lunch, usually at his office, he would unselfishly offer me a drink, which I then ceremoniously turned down as a gesture of solidarity. Charlie was always easy going and prepared to be a listener, liking nothing better than to engage in light humorous gossip about people we both knew. One thing that fascinated him about me was the way I had become integrated into British society. He thought it quite an achievement, given that I had arrived in the United Kingdom as a student of limited means and had had to make my own way in an environment that must have been harshly alien.

During one of our lunches he had mentioned his cousin, Tony Lambton, now living in Italy following his resignation from his post as a junior defence minister after being secretly photographed smoking cannabis in bed with two prostitutes. It was a public scandal that contributed to the collapse of Edward Heath's Conservative government nine months later. Tony Lambton only came into the conversation because Charlie wanted to find out if, as a publisher, I would be interested in reading the manuscript of a satirical attack his cousin had written in the form of a novel. The subject was George Weidenfeld, loathed by Tony with an intense passion. Weidenfeld was certainly no friend of mine in that epoch; in fact he was my most consistent adversary. His uncompromising Zionist ideology and his blind support for Israel whatever the circumstances placed us in diametric opposition. It therefore intrigued me greatly to have the chance to read the Lambton manuscript, though I was doubtful whether it could ever be made publishable. The word in publishing circles was that it had been going the rounds for a while and had been rejected by various imprints as too antagonistic and probably legally actionable.

Once I had read the manuscript I realized why. Not only could it be interpreted as libellous, but the fact that it was mainly fired by Tony's splenetic loathing of his subject came over more strongly than the storyline. The flaws in the novel rendered it unworthy of its author's talents, which were clearly discernible. My conclusion was that Tony would have better prospects in establishing himself as a fiction writer with a text free from such shortcomings. These views I communicated to Charlie, stressing that my rejection should not be seen as closing the door to other possibilities and that I would be interested in becoming Lambton's publisher, though it would have to be with the right manuscript.

Before very long the right manuscript arrived. It was called *Snow and Other Stories* and heralded a remarkably original début by a storyteller with a calm, laconic eye for the odd and the ordinary alike: as Christmas approaches, a London housewife begins a leisurely diary of her daily life – leisurely, that is, until the snow arrives and its proverbial whiteness turns into a vision of the apocalypse; in 1918 a Russian aristocratic landowner of utopian persuasion is slowly and unwittingly delivered up to the very different utopia of the Bolshevik revolution; an Englishwoman in Italy has premonitions of disaster and prays at the ancient shrine of Minerva, pagan goddess of handicrafts – and of violent conflicts. These were the themes explored in the author's first collection of short stories. Harold Acton wrote of it: 'This illuminating medley . . . brings to mind an eclectic art collection in which oil paintings, pastels, watercolours and etchings are discriminatingly displayed on the walls of a spacious gallery . . . One rubs one's eyes before the revelation of a fresh literary talent.'

The launch party for *Snow and Other Stories* was a grand occasion attended by over three hundred guests who flocked to the Arts Club to celebrate the event. I was anxious to mark the author's return to the London scene in his new role as a writer rather than as the budding politician he had once been. Lambton was spoken of as having had the makings of a future prime minister, had it not been for the scandal that wrecked his chances. He was still considered a most intriguing and charismatic figure. Nearly *tout Londres* was there to greet him, attended by the usual turnout of gossip journalists, anxious to find some mischievous story to fill out their columns. The large number of his friends who were milling about included Angus Ogilvy, Lucien Freud, Lord and Lady Harlech, Woodrow Wyatt, Lady Melchett – as ever in the company of Sir Hugh Fraser – Lady Falkender, Guy Nevill, Auberon Waugh, Taki, Nigel Dempster, Tracy Ward, Katya Gilmour, Valentine Guinness, Liz Brewer, Nicholas Coleridge, Charlie Douglas Home, Lady Liza Campbell, Minnie Scott and Domenica Fraser.

All of Lambton's five daughters were present, as was his son and heir, who arrived with his new bride Christabel (née McEwen). His estranged wife Bindy, with her arm in a sling, was looking rather baffled and out of place, while his long-time mistress, Mrs Claire Ward, was clearly enjoying the party. Lambton himself was in his element, as if to say (to adapt the words of General MacArthur), 'I have returned.' The evening was judged a great success, not only as a public-relations exercise but also for the number of copies of the book sold. Lambton's first published venture as a storyteller was to prove triumphant, and to lead on to even more accomplished and ambitious work.

*

The autumn of 1983 saw Namara House become busier than ever. The bookshop on the ground floor was being staffed by a coterie of socialites known for either their physical attributes or their artistic talent. Models worked there part-time between shoots and university graduates filled in spare hours to earn some extra pocket money. The shop turned into a temporary place of employment for many talented girls who were later to be well-known writers, artists or wives to well-heeled men about town. The person in charge was Charlotte Faber, a twenty-five-year-old artist whose sister Laura was a model. Charlotte oversaw the running of the bookshop with a flair for the bizarre that often caused scandalized consternation among the more sober elements of the clientele. Once she displayed in the window a nude model surrounded by the latest bestsellers to entice passers-by to come inside. She was always brimming with ideas, some of them too avant-garde to contemplate, others worthy of serious consideration.

Charlotte had burst on to the scene through an introduction from my cook, Charlotte Millward. The two Charlottes were close friends and Charlotte Faber often helped out in the kitchen if we had a large lunch gathering. Gradually she became a permanent fixture at Namara House, flitting between kitchen and bookshop and thus making herself indispensable.

By November, Arabella Pollen was becoming the most talked-about fashion designer in town. Still only twenty-one, she was soon being fêted in New York at the trendy Discothèque Xenon, with eight hundred guests in tow. Among them were the cream of New York society, together with Princess Elizabeth of Yugoslavia and her daughter Catherine Oxenburg, who later played Princess Diana in the CBS TV film. Arabella was described as 'the woman who resembles a combination of sophistication and punk and embodies the woman she envisions'. She was quoted by *Women's Wear Daily* as saying, 'I don't go for outlandish things that you wear for three months and then have to throw away. I like to do things with a lasting conservative feel, but things that are different and not just boring.' She went on to explain how 'she is inspired by colour and fabrics, then designs her clothing accordingly. "I thought college or design school would be a waste of time for me. No one can teach you designing – you just have to do it." '

I was in New York for the launch of Arabella's spring and summer collection for the 1984 season and was greatly heartened by the reception she was given. She was undoubtedly a star – quite regardless of her privileged background and her devastating good looks. I felt extremely proud of my protégée and could hardly conceal my excitement that the New York venture was such a roaring success.

In the same month, Quartet published a collection of photographs called *Snap*, assembled by the actress Jenny Agutter, who had taken photos of the two cities between which her time was divided, London and Los Angeles, with the idea of drawing visual parallels. The paparazzi were enthusiastic as they snapped guests at the launch party, focusing attention on Jenny Agutter as she stood next to Nigella Lawson. Jenny's publicity was being handled by Cowan Bellew, which kept the whole operation within the Namara Group and made for a precisely coordinated effort.

Yet another large-format photographic book published by Quartet took a totally different and innovative approach. In *The Self-Portrait Book*, Pat Booth, in the role of photographer, used her own body in place of words to evoke her art, her sexuality and the power of the human form. She visualized every scene is if she were principal actress in a play she herself had written. The accumulation of stark images became a self-portrait, devoid of conventional parameters, which explored the inner depths of her womanhood in provocative poses, revealing her most intimate self without letting the obvious force of eroticism overshadow her art.

Pat, who was born in the East End, began her career as a fashion model, later becoming the owner of two of the most fashionable and well-publicized boutiques in London. She then took up professional photography and published a best-selling novel, *Lady and the Champ*. A second novel, *Rags to Riches*, appeared in 1981, along with a beauty book, *Making Faces*, written jointly with Joan Price. Her most recent novel, *Sparklers*, also came off the press in the summer of 1984. *The Self-Portrait Book* was given a very dramatic black cover showing a topless Pat Booth, camera in hand, as she covers one eye and prepares to pounce on the image she wants to capture. The painter Allen Jones, known as the 'King of Fetish Art', wrote an introduction that gave the book the artistic cachet it deserved.

As soon as the title was announced, there was an upsurge of interest in its subject matter. This sort of self-revelatory approach had never been tried before on such a scale. The question Pat Booth kept being asked was what sort of a publisher would commit himself to this kind of book? Her response was that Quartet was uniquely placed to back projects of this nature and their proprietor was constantly looking for new ground to break in his publishing endeavours. We could hardly have wished for a better testimonial to describe our general aims.

As a diversion from my usual activities, I next staged an exhibition of paintings at the Cadogan Gallery in Pont Street. It featured the work of Michelle Pearson Cooper, an artist well known for her murals (interior and exterior) and her portraits of dogs. In these she created each animal's image in three or four poses rather than producing the conventional single portrait. Michelle was a good friend of mine and I was keen to get her work more widely known to a much larger audience.

Journalistic jokes at my expense continued to be made from time to time. In describing another flat-racing season, Jeffrey Bernard wrote that 'watching a mediocre steeplechaser negotiating twelve fences on a damp and cold winter's afternoon is about as inspiring as watching the Ayatollah Attallah chatting up a beauty at a publisher's cocktail party. You can admire them both for their gall.' Following up on this, 'Pandora's Box' in *Ritz* magazine carried an amusing item:

Naim Attallah
would like: Better looks to appease JEFFREY BERNARD (who wrote in the *Spectator* how ugly Naim is).
would like to give his best friend: 'A smouldering LIZA CAMPBELL' (as described by NIGEL DEMPSTER).
would like to give his worst enemy: A Christmas Carol by Paul Johnson (who also wrote a nasty piece in the *Spectator*).
(The two top cosmetic surgeons in London are Perry Jayes and Freddy Nicolls.)

My friend A. N. Wilson, writing rather entertainingly in *Tatler* on the twentieth-century preoccupation with contemplating one's own navel, commented that 'this autumn, I notice, Channel 4 are launching a series called "Hey, Good Looking". At first I thought this was to be a twenty-part serialization of the life story of London's greatest publisher, Naim Attallah, but it turns out to be a survey of all that is meant by the word "style".'

The *Daily Telegraph*, in its 'Peterborough' column, then reported on 10 December that the 1983 Wingate Prize, presented before the Arts Minister, Lord Gowrie, had gone to Chaim Herzog, the President of Israel, for *The Arab–Israeli Wars*, and to Chaim Raphael for *The Springs of Jewish Life*. The entry of *God Cried* was passed over by the judges as 'a piece of Attallah "chutzpah". However Attallah agreed that the entry could be seen as "antagonistic and bloody cheeky" but argued that the book certainly stimulated interest in Jewish affairs, that critical books were not debarred and that by entering it he forced the judges at least to read it.'

During the same period a reconciliation of sorts was reached when Giles Gordon and I agreed to bury the hatchet, an event reported in the *Bookseller* under the headline 'In celebration of happy endings'. Giles Gordon's remark, quoted in Sebastian Faulks's article in the *Sunday Telegraph*, that he did not consider the proprietor of Quartet, The Women's Press and the *Literary Review* to be a 'serious' publisher, had triggered a chain reaction that would have gone all the way to legal proceedings had it not been for the intervention of our lawyer, Michael Rubinstein. Michael resolved that the affair should be settled in a more civilized manner through the publication of an appropriate letter in the newspaper concerned, and this occurred. With the sting no longer hurting after the passage of several weeks, at Michael Rubinstein's suggestion I invited Giles to lunch as a gesture of goodwill. It was then that he mentioned the problem he was having, as an agent, with placing a manuscript called *Axioms* by Sheila MacLeod, the former wife of the singer and actor Paul Jones.

Axioms was a study of the effects their two teenagers had on the break-up of their parents' marriage. Giles Gordon had delivered a copy of the manuscript to Mr Jones, who was at the time playing at the National Theatre. He at once reacted strongly that the matter had nothing to do with him, that he was no longer married to the author and that the book was a novel in any case. The letter Giles had hoped for, disclaiming any future intention to enter into litigation against its publication, was not therefore forthcoming. The Bodley Head had considered it 'smashing', but nevertheless decided to waive their option, presumably out of fear of legal proceedings. The word at once went about that *Axioms* would be a difficult and risky undertaking and interest in it suddenly waned. Both Daphne Wright, my chief editor at Quartet at the time, and I read the manuscript and decided it should be published. Within four days we had agreed terms and scheduled it for publication on 1 May, my birthday, the following year. The *Bookseller* rounded off its report with this latest piece of news: 'I expect Mr Gordon to be there, raising a celebratory glass, as well as Sebastian Faulks, who might be persuaded to write another article, perhaps on the strange ways in which books and publishers sometimes find one another.'

There was still one last word to come on the Dahl/Attallah controversy over *God Cried*, which had rocked the entire publishing world, when Anthony Blond was asked by the *Literary Review* to give his viewpoint on the whole business. In a lengthy article he condemned both the book and Dahl's review of it. It was, he said, the most badly written book (an opinion with which I disagreed) to be 'published by my good friend Naim Attallah, publisher of this journal'. He then added:

[We] have now descended from international to ballpark politics but *God Cried* has featured so much in the press that there is no need to describe it save to make the point that this is a free country and the author is perfectly entitled to express his indignation and bias (though one would wish he had gone about this task in a more orderly fashion). Equally any editor who spiked Mr Roald Dahl's review on the grounds of intemperance would need to have his or her head examined. The piece from a famous children's writer was, if nothing else, a journalistic scoop. I do not, however, believe Paul Johnson was entitled to write in the *Spectator* that this was 'the most disgraceful item to appear in a respectable British publication for a very long time'.

The year 1983 ended with notable additions of personnel to the Namara Group consisting of yet more recruits to Naim's formidable 'team of bright young things'. They were popping up on every side to promote the group's various activities. Lady Liza Campbell, Lady Cosima Fry, Anna Groundwater and Laura Keen were already making their mark on the social circuit. They all turned up for the launch of *Shooting Stars*, a collection of Sheridan Morley's theatre reviews from *Punch*. It was, as the *Standard* justifiably reported, an occasion for mutual back-slapping. J. P. Donleavy, the playwright, told the paper that Sheridan had written 'the most flattering review I've ever had'; while Morley said of Donleavy's *The Beastly Beatitudes of Balthazar B* that it was 'the best play he ever reviewed'. Arabella Pollen was photographed looking a bit drowsy: the pressure of her work had been mounting. She was wearing pyjamas as part of her latest collection, which enhanced her image by giving it more of a sexual emphasis. She was now being photographed wherever she showed up and was the darling of the Sloane Rangers, who went about mostly attired in the Pollen label.

When *Publishing News* announced the Lejeune Awards for 1983, they chose Nigella Lawson as 'fiction editor of the year'. There would be 'tears in Goodge Street', they feared, but despite the 'competition from Naim's other cut-glass lovelies, it was the vampy daughter of our new chancellor whose stunning hairstyle, frequent mentions in *Tatler* and totally original use of a shoehorn finally landed her the big one'. Sardonically I was voted 'publisher of the year' for the following reasons:

He has the prettiest best bred staff in London. He keeps old roués like Lord

Lambton and Helmut Newton happy by publishing their work. His house magazine commissioned Roald Dahl's zany attack on anything Jewish, and he tried to prevent his top author . . . Nigel Dempster from getting his hands on a £1.50 royalty cheque earned by his book [on] Princess Margaret.

The 'accolades' did not end with my elevation to 'publisher of the year'. The prize for the 'working relationship of the year' went to Sabrina Guinness and myself, in support of which they cited a press release for the Academy Bookclub that gave them another chance to take the mickey:

When he first met her, Attallah was immediately drawn to the effervescent Sabrina Guinness. In her attitude to life . . . she displays a freshness of approach and a new sense of purpose that is at the same time warm-hearted and essentially engaging. The combined talents of the two, he unorthodox and ebullient, she gentle and introspective, augurs well for the future of the Academy Bookclub.

Whoever within the group had been responsible for the press release must have got carried away by a poetic licence which stretched lyricism to its limits. But at least no one could deny the Namara Group and Quartet their place on the map.

Twenty-one

January 1984 began auspiciously with the possibility of acquiring *Apollo*, the prestigious art journal owned by the *Financial Times*. Algy Cluff casually mentioned over lunch that he understood from a recent meeting with the *Financial Times* management that they were keen to dispose of the magazine, feeling it did not sit well within the group. That, at any rate, was their official reason. The reality hinged more on the fact of their having problems with the editor, Denys Sutton, who was a law unto himself and too rigid for their liking. There was also the fact that, with a circulation of only five thousand, it made little economic sense for them. They were therefore opting to shed it rather than continue involving themselves in constant battles with the editor. Since Algy and I already had a working relationship through the merger of *Quarto* with the *Literary Review*, he suggested it would be of mutual benefit if we could add *Apollo* to the equation, thereby making our association even more meaningful.

I did not need much convincing before starting a dialogue with John McLaughlan, the *Financial Times* executive in charge of negotiations. The deal was signed very quickly, to the relief of both parties. I then prepared the ground carefully for a meeting with Denys Sutton, bearing in mind his famous testiness. His reputation for holding uncompromising views on most things was certainly not to be disregarded, but contrary to expectations he and I hit it off well at our first encounter. Naturally I acted with conscious diplomacy and a calculated measure of reserve. It was something Denys appreciated, for he, on his side, had also heard stories about my singularity, considered by some to amount to an autocratic disposition. He was therefore pleasantly surprised to experience the opposite. The first hurdle in the wake of the acquisition was negotiated to the satisfaction of the editor and his new proprietors; and the relationship I forged with Denys over the following months was amicable and fruitful. There were soon signs of *Apollo* making commercial strides in terms of increased circulation and advertising revenues.

In the same month I received a letter from Auberon Waugh, whom I had met casually on a number of occasions without ever really getting to know him. It was a request for me to consider interviewing his eldest daughter, Sophia – described by him as beautiful and fresh out of university – for a possible job at Quartet Books, an outfit he always referred to in the press as 'Naim Attallah's seraglio'. I duly obliged and asked Sophia to come and see me at Namara House. She arrived simply dressed and seemed totally confident and relaxed. She sat opposite me with her legs neatly tucked under her bottom and prattled away with no hint of inhibition or any special concession to formality.

I was won over by the sheer warmth of Sophia's personality and had no hesitation about offering her a job. Her response was spontaneously joyful as she accepted it on the spot and said she was prepared to start as soon as possible. Instead of shaking her hand as she left the office, I bent forward and kissed her. Unbeknown to me, she had already attended another job-seeking interview, with Alexander Chancellor, the editor of the *Spectator* and a close friend of her father. He, too, had offered her a post, and according to his account she had said she would take it. When the news broke that Sophia would be joining Quartet, Alexander complained to her father over his disappointment that she was choosing us over the *Spectator*. Auberon was forthright with his response: 'You should have kissed her as Naim did.'

My private office at the top of Namara House was tastefully furnished with a large modern semi-circular desk and a leather settee that was draped with a tiger skin. The skin was complete with its menacing head, the jaws set open to expose the sharp and deadly teeth. The tiger went by the name of Kaiser and sat imperiously in his place as if he was lord of all he surveyed. Amid the furnishings he was the *pièce de résistance*. Journalists who came to interview me nearly always wanted to include him in any photograph.

The two young ladies who looked after my office at the time were Anna Groundwater and Lady Cosima Fry. They were about the same height and could almost have been taken for twins. They dressed similarly, both wearing black dresses or mini-skirts by the designer Joseph, and they fluffed their hair for effect in a corresponding style. With their attractive looks and good figures, there was no doubting their sex appeal. Both of them were cheekily competitive, and they vied with each other to get the most attention, but they were far from popular with the other girls at Quartet in Goodge Street. Bridget Heathcoat-Amory in particular was highly disapproving of their antics and always referred to them as 'the witches' whenever she left my office after a meeting on her way back to Goodge Street. I must admit I enjoyed their company for its sheer impudence and was amused by the negative reaction this generated in the ranks of the Quartet faction. It would not have been wrong to assume I had a soft spot for them, despite their lack of discipline; though this could be infuriating at times, and in the end reached a point where I gave them the sack – though we remained close. But that is a story for later.

As Quartet's sales director, David Elliott had been urging me for some time to attend the Bahrain Book Fair. He was keen to promote the Arab list and felt it would be a worthwhile trip. He and Cosima Fry flew ahead of me, and I followed two days later. Since I knew Bahrain well and had many friends there, we enjoyed being constantly entertained by both government officials and local merchants. The minister of information, Mr Tareq Almoayed, met Cosima on the day he officially opened the book fair. She must have charmed him during their brief conversation to the extent that he immediately arranged for her to meet the ruler, Sheikh Issa, knowing that they had in common an interest in horses. Sheikh Issa was benevolent and gracious, entertaining her to tea and escorting her to visit his large stable complex. And then, to make our trip even more memorable, it turned out that the singer, Georgie Fame, who was married to Cosima's mother, happened to be in Bahrain for a cabaret season and sent us all an invitation to his opening night. We thoroughly enjoyed the evening, and Cosima was thrilled to catch up with him as she and her stepfather were close.

While all this excitement was going on, back in London Cosima's other half, Anna Groundwater, was ill and had to spend several days in bed. She was feeling very sorry for herself, knowing that Cosima was having such a good time in Bahrain, being fêted and indulged, while she was bedridden, distraught and envious. It became a tricky job for me, trying to avoid accusations of favouritism on one side or the other. If I visited the bazaar in Bahrain, I had to be careful while buying an item for Cosima to find something equivalent to take back to Anna. It was a constant juggling act which pleased neither of them. Ultimately each would have preferred whatever the other was given and both were specially concerned that I had not secretly passed on an additional gift to one without the knowledge of the other.

A few weeks after our return from Bahrain there was a major break-in one weekend at Namara House. My office was ransacked during the night and the items stolen included Kaiser, the tiger skin I had become so closely identified with as my mascot. The police arrived in force on Monday morning, and could not have been more sympathetic and helpful. The only loss from my office that I cared about was Kaiser and the press quickly rallied to mount a hue and cry. The *Standard*, in its edition of 6 February, featured a large picture of me and Kaiser to illustrate a report headed, 'No Smile on Tiger's Face'. Underneath the photograph the caption read: 'Naim and friend. Kaiser is on the right.' The piece was concise:

Kaiser is a tiger with a price on his head. His head and skin were habitually stretched across an armchair in Naim Attallah's Soho office until weekend burglars ransacked the place, stealing thousands of pounds' worth of electronic goods – and Kaiser. The Palestinian-born publishing tycoon was too distraught to speak of the loss this morning, but an aide offered a £1,000 reward for the beast's return.

Nigel Dempster took the same line in the *Daily Mail* next day, mentioning the reward and displaying the same picture of myself and Kaiser with the heading, 'Naim Loses His Head – and Skin'. The piece that followed was similar to the one in the *Standard* the evening before, with the addition of a statement from a Quartet source that 'Kaiser is of great sentimental value and was acquired from West Germany after considerable legal wrangles. The tiger had escaped from a German zoo and afterwards had to be shot.' Nigel then embellished his story with his own satiric comments: 'It is no secret at Quartet that pretty Sloane Rangers, such as Lady Liza Campbell, Virginia Bonham-Carter, Nigella Lawson, Bridget Heathcoat-Amory and Rebecca Fraser, are drawn to Naim's employ by this glamorous creature – even if Naim is under the impression that it is his own charisma!'

The publicity did the trick. An anonymous voice on the phone claimed the reward for Kaiser, saying he had bought the beast in good faith without realizing it was hot property. I asked the caller to ring me again next day to arrange the exact location for the exchange of the reward and the tiger skin. To this the caller agreed, but stressed that any police involvement would result in Kaiser's destruction – and promptly hung up. I then reported the conversation to Asprey's security chief, who was coordinating the operation with the police. They asked me to draw the reward money and entrust it to one of my aides, preferably a girl, to keep the appointment with the robbers. It was vital that she follow their instructions to the letter and be wired up so her whereabouts could be determined at all times. Anna Groundwater volunteered for the mission; so did Cosima. But I felt Anna would be the one best suited to this sort of adventure.

When the caller rang next day to give me his instructions in detail, he made it clear he knew of my connections with Asprey from the press reports and asked who would be bringing the money. He seemed to become more relaxed when he was told it would be one of the girls who worked for me. She was, he said, to carry an Asprey umbrella and walk casually along Bond Street towards Piccadilly. Repeating his dire warnings of the consequences for Kaiser of any police involvement, he said she would be picked up and driven off in a fast-moving car to an unspecified destination where the exchange would take place. Anna then stuffed the money down her tights and set off along Bond Street as instructed, the police having been informed of the plan. Nothing could go wrong, they assured us. They would be out in force in Bond Street undercover. The scheme ran like clockwork as Anna was picked up and rushed as a passenger to King's Cross Station, where it turned out Kaiser had been kept in a left-luggage locker in a black bag. Anna exchanged the money for the bag and, with the mission accomplished, was told to make herself scarce. As if from nowhere, the police then pounced and collared all three of the robbers in one scoop, together with the ransom money that Anna had handed over.

With Kaiser back in Namara House and restored to his former lordly dominance of the scene, Anna was proclaimed a heroine. Nigel Dempster was able to end his account of Kaiser's recovery in his *Daily Mail* diary on a happy note: ' "Naim is eternally grateful to the diary," says Quartet person Juliette Foy.' But the most bizarre aspect of the story was still to unfold when Anna and I were called as witnesses for the prosecution at the trial of the three thieves concerned. As we gave our evidence, the leader of the gang, a big beefy bruiser of a fellow, showed no signs of hostility towards us whatever. On the contrary, he kept smiling at us, and on one occasion even winked, as if to say, 'No hard feelings.' His two partners in crime seemed equally friendly. Strangely enough, both Anna and I ended up feeling sorry for them.

A new recruit was about to join Anna and Cosima in my private office. Catherine Norden was remarkable for many things, but chiefly for her determination to work for the Namara Group, realizing the interaction between Quartet and its sister companies drew no exact demarcation lines, which meant employees could see themselves as belonging to a cohesive unit with openings in various fields. Initially Catherine came to see me through an introduction from Nigella Lawson, but I was put off at our first meeting, not by any lack of intellect but simply by her attire. Her style was reminiscent of Berlin in the 1930s: a very pale complexion with rouged lips and high heels that made her walk seem contrived rather than natural. I reported to Nigella that she had failed the test since I felt she was not someone who would fit in. The message was conveyed to Catherine, who already suspected she had botched the interview through the way she had presented herself. Determined to correct the impression I had formed of her, she tried again. If only, she pleaded, I would allow her to work in my private office for a whole month without pay she was sure she could disperse my misgivings. This show of an enterprising spirit refusing to accept defeat really touched me. I hired her there and then, and waved aside her suggestion of a trial period without pay. So keen was she to prove me wrong that she launched into her work with a zeal that meant she often refused to leave the office till I was ready to go myself. She went even further. Every Friday she enquired whether I intended working over the weekend so she could join me. Her dedication was boundless and it turned into a slightly weird situation. I suddenly developed a compulsion to torment her for being so willing to please. I ribbed her without mercy, not out of spite, for I had come to like her immensely, but just to gain some sort of reaction.

The two witches were intrigued by the development of this bizarre relationship. They began to fish for any bits of gossip that would feed their curiosity. Naturally, this provoked me even more. I started to invent stories to sharpen their appetite for more revelations. Did they know, I suddenly asked, that Catherine wore no knickers? They were flabbergasted. How could I possibly be aware of such a thing? The more they pressed me to tell them, the more I shrugged it off and changed the subject. For days on end I kept them in suspense until, on the eve of a concert by the rock group the Police to which we were all invited, I told them how I knew. Three weeks before, when Catherine was running down the stairs and I was hard on her heels, being late for an appointment, she missed her footing and toppled over, legs in the air, and revealed herself to be knickerless. It was such a shock to my system that instinctively I made the sign of the cross to cleanse my soul and asked the Good Lord for forgiveness. My Catholic upbringing had saved the day. They must never, I urged them, divulge what I had just told them to anyone else. With that, I felt, I had got myself off the hook for having told such lies in the first place and dispelled any notion that there had been some impropriety in my relationship with Catherine. The two girls took it all as the truth, shrieking in unison, 'Oh my God, we'd rather die than have that happen to us. Poor Catherine!' they added sympathetically. 'She must have felt terrible.'

Next evening, after listening to the concert – which caused my poor ears to throb from the music's high level of amplification – we went backstage to have a special celebratory cocktail with the band on what was to be the first night of a tour. Cosima and Anna stood enjoying themselves, both with a drink in hand, but could not stop themselves eyeing Catherine curiously. Suddenly I heard Cosima shout across to Catherine, 'I hear from the boss that you wear no knickers!'

'Oh my God,' responded a dazed Catherine. 'How does he know? I never have worn any!'

If ever I have wished for the earth to open and swallow me, then that was the moment. Many of the guests must have overheard the exchange and would take some convincing that it had only been a made-up story on my part. It went to show how a story without foundation can take on a life of its own. Catherine was a great sport. She never held it against me. Soon afterwards I sent her to New York to help Marilyn Warnick run the Quartet office.

This was a period when I spent a great deal of time in the Big Apple myself, overseeing the Asprey shop in the Trump Tower, located on Fifth Avenue, and attending to our publishing activities in the United States. Asprey was among the first tenants at the Trump Tower – in fact we were approached by Donald Trump long before the building was completed. He wanted the best names to be trading from his prestigious address, to give it an added éclat. His powers of persuasion were prodigious, and any conversation with him was a one-sided affair. Words tumbled from his mouth in machine-gun fashion, leaving him few intervals in which to draw breath.

On one occasion, when John Asprey and I were in New York, he invited us to lunch at the Lutèce, the then most fashionable French restaurant in town. He drove us halfway across the city, stopping at every building of his to demonstrate the might of his empire. On arrival at the restaurant, he was ushered in with great deference and given what was presumably the most sought-after table. As the recital of his achievements continued to take preference over matters of nutrition, it was an upward struggle to get him to look at the menu. Finally the *maître d'hôtel* persuaded him to have freshly made tomato soup, to be followed by grilled Dover sole. To avoid further complications, John and I ordered the same, food being by that stage our topmost priority.

The soup arrived, and although Donald often filled his spoon, it never seemed to reach his mouth. The exercise was repeated over and over without a drop of soup ever touching his lips. When we had finished ours, he signalled to the waiter to take his plate away, virtually untouched. I think he did eat a little of the Dover sole but there was scarcely an interruption in the torrential monologue concerning his vast wealth, his collection of paintings and his power base. The scale of this self-promotion was in my view excessive and seemed to have about it more than a touch of vulgarity. Judging from what we saw, this unrestrained display of verbal energy owed nothing to his food intake, so it must have had its source elsewhere.

Trump began his career by attending business school and getting involved in his family's real-estate business. In property he became a wheeler-dealer on a spectacular scale, creating an empire that took in casinos and sports and transport interests. Later on, in the 1990s, he came close to personal bankruptcy when the recession put pressure on his debts, but the institutions to which he owed hundreds of millions of dollars restructured his loans to avoid losing even more in court actions. Through all his ups and downs, he managed to retain ownership of the Trump Tower, and his gift of the gab stood him in good stead in 2004 when he reinvented himself as host of his own highly popular reality television show. Today America knows him as 'the Donald'. He is certainly a larger-than-life character and in essence represents the American dream; and brash as it may be in his case, he is none the less a true exponent of its aims and aspirations.

At the time when Asprey moved into the Trump Tower, I acquired through Marilyn a magnificent apartment on the thirty-fifth floor of a prestigious building on 58th Street and First Avenue, which became both a home and a private office. The City of New York buzzed with energy and a wealth of talent, and I was entranced by its fast tempo. Every time I came back to London after one of my visits I returned feeling rejuvenated. Our crowd there included the brilliant journalist Christopher Hitchens, whose capacity for alcohol was legendary. He was married to a Greek Cypriot girl and wrote a book about Cyprus that Quartet published. His politics then were generally on the left, but, like Paul Johnson before him, he changed sides to the disappointment of many of his followers, though his journalism remained as brilliant as ever. The claims of the establishment took priority over those of the underprivileged, some of whose causes he had previously championed.

British ex-pats were much in demand in New York society. They were invited everywhere, and most reaped the benefits of their popularity. Many English roses became the toast of New York, with their refined accents and clear elocution. Their sense of humour and lack of inhibition made them irresistible. Their easy-going manner endeared them to their host country, especially to the section of American society that appreciated good breeding enhanced by good looks. Catherine Norden was no stranger to the scene. When she was still at Oxford University she had been snapped up by an American bank and spent a year on Wall Street as a money-market dealer. She settled quickly into her new job, making many friends. Her working relationship with Marilyn Warnick had its ups and downs but eventually each resigned herself to accepting the foibles of the other and a semblance of harmony reigned in the workplace.

Before Catherine's arrival in New York, it was Marilyn who looked after me during my regular visits and spent much of each day helping me with my various tasks. Catherine's arrival changed this to some extent, with Marilyn concentrating on running the Quartet office, except when accompanying me to important meetings. The rest of the time Catherine was constantly at my side, becoming my virtual shadow during working hours and in the evenings as well. Anywhere I went she went, too. She introduced me to many of her girl friends, most of them British but with some notable European exceptions. At one time she stayed with Christina Oxenburg, daughter of Elizabeth of Yugoslavia and sister of the television actress Catherine Oxenburg. At another time she shared a flat with a French sex siren, who eventually departed when her money ran out. Subsequently I became a great friend of Christina's and often escorted her mother Elizabeth to some function or other where she introduced me into her social circle.

Catherine then moved in with Victoria Lockwood, the model later to marry Princess Diana's brother, Earl Spencer, a character I always found slightly affected. The flat they shared was four blocks or so from my apartment, and we spent many exciting evenings discovering the culinary delights of the city. We became part of a social scene where Brits were very much in evidence. Among the many who were there, Lucy Clive, a most desirable young lady with vibrant sex appeal, stood out as a woman to be reckoned with. For a time I saw a lot of her during visits, when we dined at some small restaurant and engaged in animated conversation. New York was to be an important part of my life for the next decade as I commuted from London by Concorde on a six-weekly basis. Indeed, I look back on that as more or less the most exciting period of my entire working career.

In January 1984, David Elliott had flown to Montreal from London to host a sales conference for our North American reps. It was the first time he had undertaken such a trip, brought about by Quartet's expansion in the region. David was there to brief the sales force on those forthcoming publications that were likely to be of interest in their territory. Marilyn Warnick and I flew up from New York to join him – her involvement was vitally important since the whole American operation came under her jurisdiction. My purpose in being there was to become more familiar with what was going on and then to wrap up the conference with a short address to give the occasion an air of *gravitas*.

Beyond its successful outcome, nothing unusual happened except for the weather. It was bitterly cold, with temperatures the lowest I had ever encountered. I had a single worse experience a decade or so later when I visited China in mid February and hired a car to drive me out from Beijing to see the Great Wall of China. I took the precaution of putting on many layers of warm clothing complemented by a fur coat and hat, and a pair of thick gloves, but my ears and eyes were difficult to shield from the cuttingly icy wind that swept in from Mongolia and seemed to penetrate into every fibre of my body. The resulting pain was excruciating as my face was pelted with particles of ice which stung any bit of flesh they managed to land on. I never felt so helpless and desperate as I did when negotiating the Great Wall, hardly daring to open my eyes for fear of some crippling injury to my eyesight.

The Montreal winter, bad as it was, was not in the same league as its Chinese counterpart, though it was still my first taste of extreme weather conditions. Marilyn, David and I wore heavy overcoats as we set out on our last day to brave the elements by taking a walk in the city centre, looking for places of interest, especially the leading bookshops. Our ears and hands were already painfully numb when we chanced on a cinema showing 3D projections for adults only. Marilyn held back, perhaps embarrassed at first, but then decided anything would be better than freezing to death! We bought three tickets at the box office and were given special coloured glasses for viewing the film.

It had to be admitted that the spectacle was technically sensational, though the content was nothing more than a pornographic display of sexual acrobatics. The images hit you from every side until you felt you were yourself a participant in the ongoing orgy. For the first ten minutes the senses were stunned, but the novelty began to wear thin when the action became so confused it was impossible to distinguish who was copulating with whom. When we left the cinema the crisp cold outside air had become less of a problem. The hour spent watching people engaging in libidinous activites had given our blood circulations a boost to fend off the cold. We spent the evening quietly before flying back to New York the next day.

We hardly had time to unpack before heading off to a private viewing of Edwina Sandys's paintings. The cream of New York society had gathered to pay her tribute and buy some of the pictures on display. We bumped into a lot of friends who turned up for the occasion. The city was full of Brits we knew. Anthony Haden-Guest, the journalist who lived in New York for some time and was always referred to in *Private Eye* as 'the Beast', was a regular feature at parties. He tended to be inebriated sooner rather than later, and sometimes towards the end of an evening he became hard to handle, particularly where attractive young women were concerned. He was one of those whose charm was his saving grace. Peter Hillmore was another journalist who visited the city at regular intervals. Meanwhile the likes of Emma Gilbey, Charlotte Dugdale, Bettina von Hase and a score of other desirable young women adorned the party circuit and never failed to give proceedings a certain cachet. Notable among them was Isabella Blow, an icon of the avant-garde arbiters of taste who marvelled at her talent for innovation in style and fashion. Whatever was most outrageous from art's viewpoint she made her own and did it with such flair that she was often the main topic of conversation at the soirées attended by the new breed of young men and women who had found early fame and riches.

Quartet's New York office was beginning to publish more titles specifically for the US market and Marilyn was more and more on the watch for likely books emanating from local contributors. Her most recent discovery was the photographer Robert Mapplethorpe, who was attracting attention not only for his outstanding talent but also because of some of the subjects he chose to photograph. He was already revered and loathed in equal measure. Everyone agreed, however, that with his unique but disturbing style he ranked among the best photographers of his generation. He pushed degeneracy to extremes and stretched the boundaries of homoerotic imagery to a level of debauchery that was wilfully shocking and unashamedly revolting.

Marilyn took me to meet Mapplethorpe in his studio cum apartment in the Bowery. With Quartet having become internationally known for publishing plush photographic books, we both had it in mind that he could be a natural addition to the list. We found him oddly dressed in leather gear, with such fetishistic sex-aids as dildos, chains and whips strewn around his living area. The walls were covered with amazing photographs of young men and women in bizarre but powerful poses. The atmosphere was disturbing and I felt slightly uncomfortable until he led us into an adjoining room to show us some of his exquisite photographs of flowers. By these I was totally enchanted, affected by their beauty and the magic they seemed to generate. There was no doubting that they were masterworks and their creator a genius. I began to warm to him and to feel a growing optimism about the chances of landing him as a Quartet author. He said that he had photographed Rebecca Fraser – who he knew worked at Quartet – when she was in New York, and offered me a signed print. Thus the meeting ended on a positive note as we agreed to think about the most suitable terms for a future collaboration.

After this first encounter I was feeling quite excited about having his name on the list of famous photographers we published. It would add to our prestige, especially in the United States. On my next trip to New York, a couple of months later, I went to see him in the Bowery again. His place was still as cluttered as before with sexual contraptions of every imaginable kind, some of them with sado-masochistic connotations. Again I felt distinctly uncomfortable and had to struggle to maintain an appearance of relaxed unconcern. Robert was as outrageously dressed as usual, all in black leather, and although he lacked a whip he seemed as threatening as if he had one. We exchanged pleasantries and then went straight to the heart of the matter. He would not mind being published by Quartet, he said, but he would have to insist on a large advance against royalties and total editorial control over what appeared in the book. The size of the advance he specified would have been difficult for Quartet to raise, but not impossible; his second demand was another matter. Total control would have been unacceptable under any conditions. My instincts told me that his choice of photographs was likely to be so reprehensible as to make any collaboration between us impossible.

When he had to leave the room to take an urgent telephone call, I wandered into another room that he used to exhibit some of his latest work. There I was brought to a standstill by a series of photographs of fist-fucking so shocking that I experienced a surge of physical nausea. The graphic images were so horribly inhuman and alienating that surely they could only appeal to psychopathic personalities. I darted back to where I had been sitting when he went to answer the phone and tried to regain my composure. When he came back I said I would consider the terms he suggested and made my exit without further ado.

I never saw Robert Mapplethorpe again, nor did Quartet ever publish any book of his. He died of the ravages of AIDS a few years later and was hailed as the most accomplished photographer of his time. His fist-fucking photographs were exhibited in New York amid a barrage of controversy. Today there are collectors worldwide of his photographs, which sell at auction for great sums of money.

Twenty-two

On 28 February 1984 we celebrated the publication of Derek Jarman's auto-biography *Dancing Ledge* by throwing an outrageous party at the Diorama in Regent's Park. All a guest needed to do to gain entry was buy a copy of the paperback edition of the book for a cut price of five pounds. A large proportion of London's gay community converged on the venue in a state of high anticipation and were admitted so long as they were clutching a copy. The numbers who gained access rose dramatically till they reached a figure later estimated at twelve hundred. The crush became so intense that there were fears for public safety and damage to the very fabric of the building. It was far from being an exclusively gay affair. The crowd was made up of a hetero-geneous mix of literati, aristocrats, Sloane Rangers, showbiz personalities and punks. Collectively they represented the most colourful of London's hedonistic high-camp society, as well as its most illustrious. All the beautiful people stood side by side with the ugly, the profane and the bizarre, and were letting their hair down without the least regard for propriety or convention.

The all-night event turned into an orgy of excess resembling a saturnalia. Into the midst of this phantasmagoric confusion and merriment there erupted a surprise cabaret organized by Derek Jarman, the star of which was Elisabeth Welch, the sultry-voiced singer who, at seventy-six years old, was a veteran of numerous musicals and for many a living icon. Escorting Miss Welch was a troupe of fire-eaters who set off total panic among the crowd. The observer who best summed it all up was Auberon Waugh in a piece in *Private Eye*, written in his uncannily insightful style and accompanied by a cartoon by Willie Rushton (the original of which still hangs in my office today):

Latest entertainment idea to hit the London scene is a group of hideous naked women and one man called the New Naturalists. I saw them at a party given by Naim Attallah the Lebanese [*sic*] philanthropist, but now they are everywhere. They come on stage completely naked except for combat boots, their bodies painted in green and blue. Also painted blue is what could be described as the man's generative organ, but might more accurately be called his willie.

They start peeing all over the stage and everybody shrieks with laughter. Those who stayed on at the Quartet party – for a sensitive autobiography called *Dancing Ledge* by 1960s raver Derek Jarman – had the enjoyable experience of seeing it all cleared up by Miss Bridget Heathcoat-Amory, one of the most enduringly beautiful of Naim's string of delicious debs.

I wonder if the Church of England should consider a Thanksgiving Celebration Service of Relief along these lines.

The party was widely covered by the press, with pictures of the Marquess of Worcester with Lady Cosima Fry, Aileen Plunkett with her grand-daughter Marcia Leveson-Gower, and Viscount Althorp, now Lord Spencer, brandishing cash in hand to acquire his passport to entry.

Dancing Ledge was Derek Jarman's first major work of autobiography. He was already established as Britain's most controversial independent film-maker and the book gave a kaleidoscopic account of his life and art up till then, from sexual awakening in post-war rural England to the libidinous excesses of the 1960s and subsequently. He told his story with openness and flair, describing the workings of the imagination that lay behind the making of the films *Sebastiane*, *Jubilee* and *The Tempest* and the frustrations he was suffering over his as yet unrealized project, *Caravaggio*. This was to be made in 1986 with Nigel Terry, Sean Bean and Tilda Swinton, the same year in which he discovered he was HIV positive. *Dancing Ledge* was republished by Quartet in 1991 in response to public demand. Working in the shadow of his diagnosis, Derek Jarman managed to fulfil himself as a unique creative spirit, with an extraordinarily productive output in various fields, in the few years he had left. He was a prophet of punk who linked homoerotic imagery and thought with increasingly profound themes of time and death. More films were produced and he painted and wrote poetry. He died from the effects of AIDS on 19 February 1994 at his Prospect Cottage on the shingle banks at Dungeness in Kent, where he created an extraordinary garden in his closing years. It mixed indigenous maritime plants with stones from the beach and sculptural *objets trouvés* washed in by the sea, and it makes a strangely haunting and touching memorial.

In the spring of 1984 Arabella Pollen's success was at its peak. Her exposure by the media was almost unparalleled for someone still so young because she had managed to capture the fashion scene not only in the United Kingdom but also in the United States and Japan. At some point most of the fashion magazines carried a profile of her, and she was extensively photographed, with gossip columnists following her every step. Among those who became her special supporters was Anna Harvey of *Vogue*, who also acted as a special adviser to Princess Diana. An introduction to the princess led to her finding royal favour. Arabella was not hard to promote, with her striking presence, her magical smile and the gamine look that made her irresistible. The fact that her father was a former president of Sotheby Parke-Bernet in New York and a major shareholder of Sotheby London added to her credentials. While she was was inclined to play down her high-flying background, she wore her casual establishment assurance like a trademark. It was nevertheless her English-rose image that was her greatest asset.

The *Sunday Express* dubbed her 'wonderchild'. The woman journalist who came to interview her had been told by a publicist that, 'She is one of the most ambitious people I have ever met,' and had read an account of her in an article that described her clothes as 'being designed for the scheming woman – the woman who is tougher and sexier'. As a result she had expected to meet 'some horrendous dynamo of infant energy'. Instead she found herself being bowled over by this 'quiet pretty Sloane Ranger blonde dressed in an assortment of pastel woolies and looking exactly like the Princess of Wales'; which, said another journalist, might explain why the new-look princess 'had a scattering of Pollen to her wardrobe. Indeed much of society is now buzzing from Knightsbridge to New York, intent on Pollenation.'

Arabella's design studio was above Zandra Rhodes's in West Kensington. Her brother, Marcus, was now working with her, in charge of production. They were very close and she was keen to have his involvement, with a view eventually to turning the company into a family concern. The idea had certain merits from their viewpoint. From mine it meant that, in practice, some of my original investment was unlikely to be recovered. Fashion is a costly affair and it needs the resources of a large conglomerate if it is to survive the vicissitudes of time and the pressures of competition. The Namara Group was not awash with capital and its main thrust was publishing. Arabella's future expansion was therefore in any case going to depend largely on her ability, now that she was established, to secure an alternative backer and appropriate resources and infrastructure.

In the meantime Gail Rolfe reported in the *Daily Mail*:

Chic, aggressively young like the image of the airline itself – that's the look to be worn by Virgin Atlantic's ground staff and air crews, as these exclusive *Femail* sketches show. And there's no doubt that with uniforms like these, the latest additions to the Gatwick scene will stand out from all their rivals when they make their inaugural flight to New York on June 22. Not surprisingly the designer chosen by Virgin's multi-millionaire boss Richard Branson is that new fashion phenomenon 22-year-old Arabella Pollen, already a firm favourite of the Princess of Wales and the jet-set.

At the start of May I marked my fifty-third birthday by inviting Sheila MacLeod to a lunch to coincide with the publication of her book *Axioms*. In *Guardian Women* Suzanne Lowry wrote:

> Both occasions were elegantly and simultaneously celebrated at a small lunch in the basement of the Quartet Bookshop in Soho. The food was exquisitely prepared and presented by a blonde girl in pearls and with hippos on her apron. Attallah was charming and expansive in a princely sort of way.

Not everyone saw me in such a benign light. *Publishing News* had taken to satirizing me with tedious regularity, though admittedly with less frequency than *Private Eye*. Later that month they included a diary piece commenting on a report in the *Sun* that alleged Nigella Lawson was paid a meagre wage. As the piece, headed 'Life at the Sharp End', was typical of the sort of flak that came my way at the time, I reproduce it here. Presumably my critics could not bear the fact that I was having fun and perhaps doing things they would have loved to do themselves. To me the most important side of it all was that I was giving opportunities to a young and rising generation of people destined to become successful in their chosen fields.

MONDAY

A note under plain cover informs me that, if I so much as mention Naim the Terrible, or the financial status of his pathetically underfed employee Nigella Lawson, I would never work in publishing again.

Awaiting my first call of the day, I ponder the situation. It's true that, in this great go-getting society of ours, wealth-creation not whining about the salaries of junior staff is what it's all about and, heaven knows, I don't want to be thought of as some sort of troublemaker – publishing's answer to the man the *Sun* so brilliantly calls Gruppenführer Scargill. And yet . . .

No, there's no alternative. I must forget the very magical thing that Nigella and I once had between us and apologize to Naim for my rash behaviour. Now that he appears every month in the *Tatler*, nothing can stop him from taking over what's left of British publishing by 1990. Nigella can look after herself from here on.

I do the manly thing and ring Naim personally. He suggests lunch on Thursday which, it so happens, I can manage.

THURSDAY

What a delightful man Naim the Terrible is. Witty, cultured, urbane and astonishingly fluent in English, all things considered.

I met him as agreed at the White Tower and we were soon swapping

Carol Smith stories like the oldest of friends. Being a man of the world, he refrains from mentioning the delicate question of Nigella and her starvation wage until the brandy and then, perhaps rashly, I find myself giving a solemn undertaking that I would never again mention the salary of £5,500 that the *Sun* so inaccurately reported as being paid by the great man. Frankly, if the daughter of the Chancellor of the Exchequer can't look after herself in the money department, then she doesn't deserve to work for one of the greatest publishers of our time.

To lighten the conversation, I sing Naim my rather *risqué* rhyme 'She Was Only a Chancellor's Daughter But She Sure Gave Stock Relief', but the dear man doesn't seem to get the joke.

I confess that I wasn't expecting to pay the bill but I still believe that this was one of Naim's pranks. An invoice from Associates should sort things out.

The publication of *Axioms* went off without incident, the focus of controversy having shifted to another forthcoming Quartet publication, *The Dirty Weekend Book*. One of the participants in the book, Catherine Ledger, decided to jump ship at the last moment after suddenly finding she had principles. Her fellow contributors, Alexandra Shulman, Charlotte Du Cann, Gillian Greenwood, Emma Duncan and Kathy O'Shaughnessy – a dynamic bunch of aspiring, intelligent young women – were naturally disappointed by this change of heart and the sort of publicity it provoked. Miss Ledger, who worked for Virgin Books, gave her reasons, claiming it was too upper class for her liking. The intention, she said, had been to make it self-mocking and funny, but it turned out to be socially divisive, sexist, old fashioned and full of joyless clichés. She asked for her name to be taken off the cover and title-page.

The scheme of the book was to list sixty hotels that would be congenial for an amorous weekend break, mostly in Britain but a few abroad for the more adventurous. Unfortunately the press attention that followed in the wake of Miss Ledger's withdrawal endowed the book with an unwelcome hint of turpitude, calculated to stir up spasms of moral outrage. The newspaper headlines varied from 'The Dirt Flies' to 'Fur Flying', with them all, even such a responsible paper as *The Times*, reporting the same story from different angles. The claim was put forward that certain 'respectable' hotels listed in the book's pages were threatening injunctions to stop its publication unless all references to them were excised. The *Daily Mirror*, despite its sensational headline, 'Lovers Get the Good Sex Guide', was more sympathetic, quoting Mrs Pamela Neil, of the Highbullen Hotel at Chittlehamholt in Devon, who said commonsensically, 'Thirty years ago we would never have accepted an unmarried couple. But nowadays who cares?'

Another headline, this time in the *Standard*, declared 'No sex, please, we are Scottish'. The hypocrisy in the reaction was becoming too ludicrous for words. Mr Ron Lamb, proprietor of the Balcary Bay Hotel at Auchencairn, had his complaint put on record. He objected to his establishment being included, he said, despite the glowing report it was given. He was extremely annoyed that it had been mentioned without his permission and all reference to his hotel should be removed. Furthermore, unless the publishers acknowledged his letter of protest, the matter would be placed in the hands of his solicitors. 'An injunction is a possibility,' he threatened, 'but the least said the soonest mended. I don't want to give the publishers cheap publicity,' he concluded.

As always, I was relishing the fight. 'What kind of a reply did he [Mr Lamb] expect?' I retorted. 'People don't go to hotels for meditation or prayers; as far as I know there are no restrictions on making love in a hotel. If you were to write in your memoirs that on your honeymoon you made love in the Dorchester, is the hotel entitled to sue you?' It was a storm in a teacup. All the hotels that threatened legal action were ignored and melted away without a murmur.

Private Eye remained true to its principle of never missing out on having the last word if it could possibly avoid it. Under 'Books of the Month' at the end of June it included this little squib:

THE DIRTY PUBLISHER'S GUIDE
(Compiled by five young Sloanes who work for Naim Utterlahdisgustin) Utterlahdisgustin comes out tops in this raunchy survey of the world's dirtiest publishers.
(*That's enough books. Ed.*)

The book was not in any sense a sex manual. It was a benign attempt to inject some fun into the concept of a dirty weekend and send up the Anglo-Saxon assumptions behind the phrase. The best way of illustrating the book's intentions is to quote from its introduction:

Strictly speaking, I suppose we would have to say that a dirty weekend is an occasion lasting one or two nights, where two people, not necessarily of opposite sexes, engage in a disproportionately large amount of sexual activity in a location which will tend to be neither of their homes. Of course, that's not what it is at all. It is a window of fantasy, out of the bounds of normal life, where you can do things that are out of bounds in normal life: you can make love with someone you're not supposed to make love with at three in the morning; you can lie in bed and drink Bloody Marys and eat chocolate cake at three in the afternoon; you can lie in a bath pretending you're Cleopatra whose barge has sunk while Antony very softly strokes the soles of your feet. Or you can, if you insist, simply hold hands over a candlelit dinner table while the *maître d'hôtel* tries to catch your eye to point out that since it is *four* in the morning . . .

. . . Only a race as unromantic as ours could call it a dirty weekend. It goes with the bar-room snigger that accompanies the mention of sex; or perhaps it comes from the nursery equation of the sexual with the anal. Either way, the British inability to take sex seriously is pitiable. Imagine asking a Frenchman to go on *un weekend sale* with you. He'd probably take you to feed the pigs on his parents' farm . . .

We've selected the places by word of mouth rather than guidebook, generally from mouths that have been on the same errand as ourselves, and had some idea of what we were looking for. We have been highly critical: if the view is lovely but the food rotten, we say so. The perfect hotel doesn't exist, just as the perfect boiled egg doesn't: if it's right for some people, it's overcooked for others. We liked most things about the ones we've chosen. If a description of a place is less than enthusiastic, it is probably because the man didn't quite live up to the standard of the hotel . . . We also include some Useful Tips for dirty weekends. Not that you need them.

Kathy O'Shaughnessy, the youngest and most disarming collaborator, equipped with lowered eyelids and a devastating blush, according to Stuart Wavell of the *Guardian*, explained how it had been Emma Duncan's spiffing idea in the first place. An approach was then made to Naim Attallah, the owner of Quartet, who embraced the project and came up with the expenses. Each girl was given a thousand pounds to cover her particular weekend. Each wanted to discover for herself the joys and pitfalls of such an adventure. It was all innocent fun since the man could be her boyfriend. The project was conceived in a romantic spirit. Kathy was keen to give the whole exercise its proper perspective. The English, she insisted, only call it a dirty weekend because they are so repressed. The French, on the other hand, would say *un weekend amoureux*. Bravo Kathy! The book was a great success. It was reprinted three times. That was its enduring justification.

Any excuse for a party was the cry at Quartet, and most of its authors became attuned to this type of social exposure and began to expect it. They enjoyed the media attention, which massaged their egos and kept Quartet in the news. It served both sets of interests, one invariably feeding off the other. It tied in, too, with the way I was always keen to promote young talent that was not winning the recognition it deserved. One such talent was Guy Kennaway, who at the age of twenty-six came knocking at Quartet's door because he was getting nowhere with his book called *I Can Feel It Moving*. It had taken Collins nine months to turn him down; Quartet took six months to publish him: a speed of service unheard of in the realm of establishment publishing. The book was a racy satire on the young moneyed socialites about town in the 1980s, its heroine being a gormless American girl who records her observations on sex and the English class system. Her profane monologue is artless, guileful and beguiling: a distant voice the reader hears and overhears.

There was more than a ripple of curiosity about the book among the literati when, instead of the usual picture of the author, they found on the inside flap a photograph of a sultry beauty pouting provocatively over a glass of whisky. 'Guy Kennaway', the blurb claimed to reveal, was the *nom de plume* she had borrowed from a writer *manqué*. It was perfectly obvious, however, that the book was written by Guy and the woman on the jacket was his girlfriend, Melissa Rudd. Tim Willis, writing for *Ritz* magazine, asked Guy whether it worried him being published by Quartet, which employed pretty rich girls. Was he not risking being tarred with the same brush and labelled a snob? Guy's reply was comprehensive:

> I've got worse things to worry about than being labelled a snob. At Quartet they're young and doing things. I've been to other publishers and they're all about forty and pretending to be young wearing denims and when they see 'coke' in a book they think it's the drink. At Quartet's offices in Goodge Street, I must be the oldest person there and Naim must be thirty years older than his oldest employee. They're fun. And so what if they are pretty and rich – some of them are bright too; and even if they are thick, well so are plenty of other publishers. It's better to be thick and rich than thick and poor.

When asked whether the characters in the book were based on real life, Guy's reply was in the negative:

> It is real people who base themselves on the characters in the book. It's marvellous how everyone thinks I am writing about them. They ring up and say 'That's me' or 'You've really caught so and so just right' and I've never heard of them. The great artist in my book has everyone guessing but he's a figment of my imagination. Any man that age would pick up girls if he could get away with it.

Tim Willis then tried to press Guy further, only to receive the reply that the book's young lord was Naim Attallah and the character 'Southie' was Cosima Fry; at which point he decided to abandon his enquiries.

The bookbash for *I Can Feel It Moving* marked the cabaret début of Arabella McNair-Wilson, whose father was a Tory MP and whose fiancé was Nick Ashley, the son of Laura Ashley. She appeared with a group called the Pony Club in the Titanic Ballroom, a favourite night spot for Sloane clubbers, and set about entertaining the throng of young people who were there to enjoy themselves and spread the good word about Guy's book. Arabella made her entrance wearing a slinky black backless dress and was greeted with an enthusiastic round of applause before she had sung a note. Her backing line-up of four dancing girls, consisting of Sasha de Stroumillo, Miranda Culme-Seymour, Kitty Arden and Cat Newton-Graves, dressed in jodhpurs and Princess Anne kerchiefs, supported her in a ribald number about a horsey weekend in the country that had the refrain, 'I can feel it moving and it feels so good'. The night turned out to be a sizzling, hilarious affair, with Simon Callow, Sayo Inaba, Lizzie van Amerongen and the Honourable Sophia Stapleton-Cotton prominent among the guests. Nicholas Coleridge was seen making a brave effort to interview the girl who claimed to be the author, though the well-orchestrated joke was lost amid the noisy banter. Most attention went on the girls in the audience – some of London's prettiest – who had adopted what was described by Christa Worthington, writing from New York, as

> their own élitist uniform – the Grace Kelly elegant garb of Ctolla, the design firm that is the new darling of the more with-it Rangerette. The look is also comprised of Nehru jackets in pale brocades worn over skinny Indian pants, and cotton floral prints in sexy silhouettes reminiscent of the early sixties. Also à la mode – the brocade bathrobe for evening. So attired, they danced to the delight of the evening's host and owner of Quartet Books, Arab entrepreneur Naim Attallah.

The book was well received by the critics, which boded well for Guy Kennaway's future as a novelist. The *Sunday Telegraph* called it a *tour de force* and Godfrey Smith, in the *Sunday Times*, referred to the author as a 'Scottish F. Scott Fitzgerald'. Quentin Crewe said it was 'a damned good book and it made me laugh', while Taki wrote, 'If someone had bet me that one day I would read a book written in the first person by a man writing as a woman that I would be unable to put down, I would have, as they say in America, "gone for broke", and today I'd be broke.'

Within only a matter of weeks we were publishing Guy's second novel. This one was called *The Winner of the Fooker Prize*, the 'F' in the title having been substituted for the 'B' of Booker which was emphatically crossed out in red on the jacket design. It announced itself as the ninth autobiographical novel (the first eight having been turned down) by a young neglected, starving and boundlessly arrogant author. The setting is Malta, where in the bar of a desolate village this stranded and penniless English hack ekes out a living by swallowing each night the most nauseating and inedible substances for the entertainment of an astounded local peasantry. The scene was prophetic of what we often see today on television in such so-called 'reality' shows as *I'm a Celebrity, Get Me Out of Here!*

In between these harrowing acts of consumption, he tells the parallel story of his past as the golden boy of a Carnaby Street advertising company, where for years he devoutly served 'The Glutter', the imaginary and insatiable goddess of all our moneyed consumerist fantasies. The novel weaves its plots into a phatasmagoria of the world as seen from the point of view of the stomach. The literary excesses of our author's gargantuan wit richly merit the distinguished Fooker Prize he awards himself, and which the world has seen fit to award to his creator.

Peter Grosvenor, the distinguished literary editor of the *Daily Express*, under the heading 'Prize-winning title – but will it win?', suggested that the actual winner of the Booker Prize (to be announced that evening) would most certainly not be the winner of the Fooker Prize. 'If that sounds like a tiresome riddle, I will explain. A young novelist, Guy Kennaway (son of the late James Kennaway, who wrote *Tunes of Glory*), has had the impertinence to publish on this very day a wildly eccentric novel called *The Winner of the Fooker Prize*.' The essence of this novel, in Mr Grosvenor's opinion, was more original than anything on that year's Booker short-list. Originality had become one of Quartet's most valued and enduring qualities. The company often sacrificed commerciality in favour of innovative thought so as to provoke the kind of debate likely to enrich the literary scene. The way we were moving forward and unearthing new talent despite the stiff competition from those already established was something that pleased me no end.

*

Quartet continued to be a publisher of the widest contrasts. In the same month as Guy Kennaway's book it also published *The Fate of the Jews* by Roberta Strauss-Feuerlight. It was a title that stirred emotions among the Jewish community in Britain, who were already standing shoulder to shoulder in their condemnation of Quartet whenever the name arose. It had become routine of late that anything published by Quartet that touched on a Jewish theme was likely to land the imprint in a sea of vociferation. *The Fate of the Jews* was by a Jewish author and previously published in the United States by Times Books, a most respectable and conservative publishing house.

Roberta Strauss-Feuerlight was born and brought up in the Jewish community of New York and had written many books on the concept of justice, including the widely praised *Justice Crucified: The Story of Sacco and Vanzetti* and *Joe McCarthy and McCarthyism: The Hate That Haunts America*. *The Fate of the Jews*, which had as its subtitle *A People Torn between Israeli Power and Jewish Ethics*, was a provocative study that took as its subject not those who had persecuted the Jews over the centuries but the Jews themselves. It analysed their successes as a people, to the point where they acquired their own nation state and confronted the difficult moral questions that success raises. The author's view was that, 'Dispersion and exile have so scattered the Jews that the single link that binds them is the legacy of Moses and the prophets – the ethical imperative. Just as we expect Quakers to support peace, we expect Jews to be good.'

David Goldberg started off his review in the *Jewish Chronicle* by saying:

This is a strange, angry, confused book, which covers Jewish history from Abraham to the war in Lebanon in a series of breathtakingly generalized and frequently inaccurate leaps. Its thesis, in so far as there is one, appears to be that 'the heritage of the Jews is not power but ethics' but 'it is a peculiar tragedy of the Jewish people that, having given the world the ethical imperative as well as the concept of an ideal state, they created a state that seems neither ethical nor idealistic'.

Goldberg then went on to dispute the author's perception of the Jews and her analysis of ethics and to question the motive for the publication of such a *tzimmas* by Quartet. He then expounded on what he supposed to be the motive, namely that Quartet 'is of course owned by Naim Attallah', a man who is

wealthy, successful, passionately and understandably committed to the Palestinian cause. It is no more reprehensible of him to commission an anti-Israeli book than it is of Lord Weidenfeld to commission an anti-PLO one. However, he could have come up with a more worthwhile analysis of the dilemmas posed between Israeli statehood and Jewish ethics than this superficial and tendentious effort.

I thought the review was fair enough, except for one vital inaccuracy on Mr Goldberg's part, as my letter to the *Jewish Chronicle* emphasized:

Sir – In your issue of June 15 you published a review of our book *The Fate of the Jews*. The reviewer, David Goldberg, states that the book was commissioned by me. In fact, this was not the case.

The book was first published in the USA by Times Books, a division of the *New York Times*. As Mr Goldberg must surely be aware, the *New York Times* is a great supporter of the State of Israel and has never been particularly sympathetic to the Palestinian cause.

It is therefore ironic that *they* as well as I must have seen some merit in the book to justify its publication.

On the same page the *Jewish Chronicle* quite correctly published a letter from Jillian Becker which is self-explanatory:

Sir – When David Goldberg in his review of the book *The Fate of the Jews* (June 15) writes of Lord Weidenfeld commissioning an anti-PLO book, I take it he is referring to my recent book, *The PLO*. May I please make it clear that Lord Weidenfeld did not 'commission an anti-PLO book'. He commissioned me to write the history of the PLO. As even my one antagonistic critic has conceded, I let the facts speak for themselves. No one can write the history of the PLO without those facts speaking against the organization, unless the writer distorts or omits so much of the truth that what results cannot be described as a history at all.

What is invidious in my opinion about Naim Attallah commissioning an anti-Israel book (if that is what he did) is that he got a Jew to do it. Worse, there was a Jew willing and even eager to do it!

The number of spats I have had throughout my publishing career must make it apparent by now that I court controversy, especially when it relates to international matters of important public concern, or to the repression of a minority, or to some injustice which cries out for wider exposure and rectification. It is the sort of pursuit that, aside from its altruistic aspect, gives one's life a more focused purpose and helps to assuage one's own conscience. It also keeps the mind alert and sharpens the intellect, guarding against cynicism or complacency.

Twenty-three

There were two events in the summer of 1984 to get the antennae of the gossip columnists twitching. The first was the glad tidings that my special assistant Bridget Heathcoat-Amory was about to marry Michael Cockerel, the long-time BBC *Panorama* reporter previously married to Harold Macmillan's eldest granddaughter, Anne Faber. Michael had recently upset the Tory grandees with a *Panorama* report on right-wing infiltration of the party. Selwyn Gummer repudiated the programme as a wicked piece of left-wing trouble-making, but Michael was not to be put off by such a rattling of sabres. He was a rising star and had no fear of causing a political rumpus if the occasion demanded it.

The other, less happy, matter was my dismissal of Anna Groundwater and Cosima Fry, my two personal office assistants at Namara House. I acted on the spur of the moment out of utter frustration. Their repeated failure to arrive on time in the mornings, despite all admonishments, precipitated me into taking this abrupt step. I was out of all patience with their cooked-up excuses for their unpunctuality, having entreated them many times to get their act together and take their responsibilities seriously. They had disregarded my warnings too lightly, being confident that my fondness for them would override all other considerations. On that fateful day, however, my anger reached a pitch where my need for discipline came out on top. Both took their dismissal with ill grace and departed in a huff. Cosima had the more resentful reaction of the two because she felt humiliated. Her boyfriend at the time, Hamish Bullough, found the whole thing utterly hilarious and came to have lunch with me at Namara House. This did not go down well with Cosima, who thought it was tantamount to consorting with the enemy.

The truth is I never meant to sack them, it was more a warning shot across their bows. But the two took it at face value and deprived me of any opportunity to take back my hasty words. I was suddenly quite lost without them. They were the two companions who had kept me amused with their cheek and sauce and brought a glint of youthful devilment back into my life, reminding me of my own younger days. A few weeks later a picture of them in the *Mail on Sunday* showed them looking very glamorous and smiling broadly. The photograph marked the formation of a PR company to be run by them jointly. Among their first clients was Cosima's ex-husband, the inventor Cosmo Fry, and Mark Birley's daughter, the designer India Jane, as well as Thomas Pink the shirtmakers.

I was elated to think my two girls had shown the initiative to branch out on their own in a highly competitive business. Then a phone call came to raise my spirits even further. It was Anna and Cosima on the line, urging me to support their enterprise by coming to the opening of the original Thomas Pink shop in Fulham, for which they were handling the promotion. I was pleased to hear their voices and naturally hankered to see them again and help in any way possible. They fussed about me memorably as I arrived and could hardly contain their delight when I bought four shirts as a gesture of solidarity with the 'two witches', as the Quartet contingent had always called them. They were in their element but the story did not end there. After a few months Cosima decided she would go and live in New York for a while. Anna could not afford to run the PR company on her own and as a result it had to be prematurely disbanded. In looking for a new position she turned to her old boss, who took her back and gave her the challenging task of heading Quartet's PR.

It was not a popular appointment and proved to be highly controversial with the gang in Goodge Street. In fact Anna's forceful temperament and short fuse caused me a long litany of problems at Quartet. She was singular and abrasive with colleagues, and, on a bad day, highly neurotic; yet her personal working relationship with me could not have been better. I never saw at first hand those aspects of her behaviour that raised at Quartet a chorus of protesting voices. But whatever her foibles may have been – and I understood they were many – she served me well and ensured Quartet remained the imprint with the highest exposure in the right places.

August was a busy month. Gillian Greenwood was leaving, having been editor for Robin Clark and then having taken over the editorship of the *Literary Review* from Anne Smith. She had presided over the journal during the most turbulent part of its history, but now was going to join the team for Melvyn Bragg's *South Bank Show*, fulfilling a wish she had always expressed to make a career in television. The opportunity came and she could not pass it by. I was thrilled at the prospect of her finding the niche she was seeking. I had grown very fond of her and admired her courage and tenacity under fire. During the inflated controversy over *God Cried*, she stood resolute and fought her corner, refusing to be intimidated when the onslaught was at its most vituperative.

Bumpy Rides and Gentle Days
by Gillian Greenwood

I first met Naim Attallah in the early 1980s through the late Patrick Cosgrave, a right-wing journalist and former contributor to the magazine *Books and Bookmen* (where I had been assistant editor – my first proper job – until its sudden bankruptcy). Patrick presented me to Naim as a contender to run a small paperback imprint of Quartet Books, Robin Clark. I knew something about books, but little about publishing. None the less Naim decided to give me a go. People have implied that Naim's employment policies were based on the social status of the applicants. That wasn't so in my case, and I like to think it was my ability that he recognized as well as Patrick's recommendation.

A few months further on I got an unexpected summons to Naim's home in Mayfair. This was highly unusual, and my impression was that though he was a flamboyant man, he guarded his domestic life and privacy fiercely. He seemed very anxious, but before embarking on the business of the evening, he played the gracious host and showed me his collection of exquisite Persian rugs. Then came the question. Did I think I could edit the *Literary Review*? He told me that he and the previous editor, who had started up the magazine before selling it to him, had quarrelled and that he now had no editor. I was stunned by his question and his invitation, but with the absolute certainty of youth, I said yes without hesitation.

Twenty-odd years later I have a recurring dream that I am recalled to the *Literary Review*. It is always a pleasant dream and is indicative of the magical time I and all those other young (mainly) women had in Naim's employ. I spent three years editing the *Literary Review* and they were exciting and very happy times, even with the occasional bumpy ride, and I will always be deeply grateful to Naim for the extraordinary opportunity he gave me.

At first our offices were in the Goodge Street rabbit warren, later in a beautiful building in Beak Street. The *Literary Review* office had been Naim's at one point and he had left behind a magnificent chair and desk which I sat on and behind, much to the amusement of my contributors, many of whom liked to visit regularly. In the case of the male contributors this was probably in part because, particularly in the Goodge Street days when we shared premises with Quartet, it must have been like visiting some exotic girls' finishing school. Naim liked young women – that is self-evident – but my recollection is that most of them were clever and efficient. Many of them were also well connected, but their presence wasn't because of some desire on Naim's part to be connected to the British upper classes but a canny understanding of how publicity and the establishment can be worked when cash is short. And cash was short since the whole publishing enterprise was underwritten and, certainly in the case of the magazine, heavily subsidized by Naim. We were very fortunate in having Bridget Heathcoat-Amory as our business manager. She ran a tight, if unprofitable, financial ship, her contacts were spectacular, and her party skills (I have a memory of lethal White Lady cocktails) devastating. Between us (and Kathy O'Shaughnessy, the deputy editor) we managed to persuade all sorts of wonderful establishment novelists, writers and journalists to write for the *Literary Review* for almost nothing.

The bumpiest moment of my relationship with both the magazine and Naim was over a review by Roald Dahl of a book about the plight of the Palestinians, *God Cried*. It was a Quartet publication. Naim had been introduced to Roald Dahl and they had discovered a mutual sympathy for the Palestinian cause. Naim phoned me to suggest that Dahl should review the book. It was unusual for Naim to involve himself with commissioning, but I wasn't going to look a gift horse in the mouth. Roald Dahl was a coup for the magazine. When the piece came in we were aware it was provocative and there was much debate about publication. We consulted our lawyer and mentor, Michael Rubinstein, who assured me that in his opinion the piece was anti-Zionist but not anti-Semitic. I was reassured. We published. All hell broke loose. Dahl, it turned out, had been accused of anti-Semitism by Christopher Hitchens. Editorials were written. Lobbies were mounted. Naim found it challenging and exciting. I found it confusing and stressful, but together we faced it out. With the benefit of hindsight and age I can see two things: one, that for Naim this was an issue of such deep hurt that anything that brought it to attention was justified (and at the time the subject was not the hot subject it is today). He feels passionately about his homeland and will fight for it, but he is not anti-Jewish. Two, I can see the journalistic fracas that followed the publication for what it was, a storm in the proverbial teacup compared to the actual disaster of the Israeli–Palestinian conflict. The spat between the two main protagonists seemed of more interest to most commentators than the principles and arguments at stake.

But this moment of high political drama was not the norm. It was a gentle life of reading and commissioning and trips to the printers, interspersed with magnificent parties, hot tickets in a journalistic pool, presided over by Naim, who stood beaming over the social scene like some Anthony Powell creation. Life in the London of the 1980s would simply have been much duller without him. Above all else, it was fantastic fun, and how rare it is to be able to say that these days about a job. It was a privilege to be a part of it. I left after three years because, although I loved literature and the magazine, I wanted to make films. But I still dream.

*   *   *

Gillian's recollections of how Dahl got involved in reviewing *God Cried* differ from mine in some details. She was not party to the original conversation I had with him during the reception for the launch of the Academy Bookclub, chronicled earlier on. Her love of literature has obviously never left her as John Murray recently published her first novel, *Satisfaction*, a story of family life and friendships in which 'an excess of happiness' becomes a problem.

Finding a replacement for Gillian Greenwood was no easy task. I wanted someone for the review who would maintain the same editorial integrity and carry on its tradition of fair criticism. Eventually I chose Emma Soames, a journalist who was not known for her literary proficiency, but who was acknowledged to be her own woman, both independent and forthright. Her appointment took everyone by surprise. In some quarters the inference was made that I had been more influenced by the idea of employing Winston Churchill's granddaughter than by any credentials she might possess to do the job. The press somewhat cynically referred to her as undoubtedly my highest flyer so far, after citing the illustrious names of the other young ladies I employed – members of my flock, they said.

Emma was then married to James MacManus, who worked for the *Guardian* but soon moved across to join the *Daily Telegraph*. The couple had been living in the Middle East for three years, and she started to look for a suitable vacancy after they got back to London. She was ready for a challenge, and when I offered her the job she welcomed the chance to test her mettle in a completely new direction. *Private Eye*, not unexpectedly, took the mickey out of both of us, calling her 'a busty hackette of yesteryear's *Evening Standard*', adding 'no literateuse she', while describing me as the 'portly Attullah-Disgusting wishing to genuflect to the daughter of Fatty Soames and the granddaughter of W. C. himself'.

For the next three weeks the papers continued to be full of Emma. The *Standard* carried the story twice. The *Daily Mail* and the *Mail on Sunday* did not lag far behind in their coverage. The *Sunday Times*, under the heading 'What's in a Naim?' found a more humorous slant, writing about the party to celebrate the fifth anniversary of the *Literary Review*, which coincided with Emma's appointment as editor and was held at No.10 St James's Square, in other words, Chatham House.

People might wonder why there has not been more of a fuss about this

[227]

stupendous event: a half-holiday for all schools, perhaps, or at least a special issue of stamps from the Post Office featuring the distinguished profile of Atullah [*sic*] alongside the Queen.

Well, it seems that this unlettered isle of ours is strangely unimpressed by the notion of a literary magazine appearing continuously for five years. This is partly a problem of apathy; but also a problem of exclusiveness, since this type of publication mostly sells to people who either write or are written about in its pages.

The commentator went on to remark on my string of female assistants, 'on the whole better known for looks and social connections than any deeply held views on the post-modernist movement in South America'. The Frasers, the Guinnesses and the Sackville-Wests each had a family representative in the firm, and now they were joined by a Soames. The talk was evidently about anything other than books. The critic Jonathan Meades was speculating on the chances of catching AIDS from someone else's wine glass, Paul Levy, the food writer, was describing his confidence in the efficacy of a *cuisine minceur* diet and an overheard conversation was all about the 'impossibility of sex'. At least one publisher declared in a loud voice, amid society's greatest gossips, 'No, this is strictly confidential and absolutely mustn't go beyond these four walls.'

Nicholas Soames, Emma's brother, was there to lend weight, if not *gravitas*, to the occasion, and looked happy. The Greek playboy, Mr Taki Theodoracopulos, was there looking unhappy. Mr Max Hastings was there. Mr Christopher Logue was there. Everyone was there and Naim Atullah was very happy.

Taki gave his own take on the evening in the *Spectator*, in the 'High Life' column, headed 'Confused', describing how he began drinking again on Wednesday, 'and by the evening I was convinced I was an intellectual', a delusion not helped by attending the party for the *Literary Review*, 'now led by the fearless Arabist Emma Mabrouk Soames'.

I've been a friend of Emma's since my Paris days in the late Sixties. Back then she used to work for *Vogue*, and I used to hang around the Place Palais-Bourbon hoping to meet anyone of the fair sex who emerged from the *Vogue* building. Our friendship lapsed for a while when her father took exception to my asking both Emma and her younger sister to marry me. But now that we're both intellectuals, I hope everything is forgiven. After all, unlike a lot of Englishmen on the make, I only asked for the hand of the female side of the Soames family.

The *Jewish Chronicle* was anxious not to miss out on firing off a shot. Under the heading 'Naim Woos and Wins Emma', it commented how appropriate it was for Attallah to engage Soames to edit the *Literary Review*, a publication 'best known for the notorious Roald Dahl review of *God Cried*'. The rumour surrounding the reason for her return to London after spending some months in Jerusalem, they added, was her dislike of Israel.

The party at Chatham House was well attended, not only by the established literary faction but also by faces new to the world of print, such as Melissa Wyndham, Caroline Younger and Charlotte Hambro. Other notables who were there included Robin Day, Auberon Waugh, Charles Moore, Lady Anne Somerset and Nigella Lawson. During the months that followed, Emma settled admirably into her new post. Her main contribution was to widen the range of contributors to the magazine and gain it a higher profile through the invaluable social and political network to which she had access. My hunch that she was the right person for the job at the right time was spot on.

*

That August was a busy time on many fronts. Asprey was doing well, despite the periodic falling out between family members, and John Asprey and I were still on the lookout for opportunities to expand our customer base. It so happened that Avon Products, who owned Tiffany in New York, had made an announcement in June about their willingness to dispose of their subsidiary at the asking price of a hundred and sixty million dollars. Three investor groups had put in bids ranging between a hundred million and a hundred and forty million dollars, so falling short of the price tag. We did not have the resources to enter the arena, but were nevertheless confident that, at the right price, we would have no difficulty in heading a consortium with sufficient funds to qualify us as a serious potential buyer. The name of Asprey was second to none in the luxury world and our progress with building the company into a successful concern during the past few years gave us a certain standing and credibility among our peers – enough to enable us to make the provisional enquiries needed.

The task fell to me to examine the business, with a view to reaching a conclusion as to its viability in commercial terms. Avon Products were highly cooperative. They were keen to shed the subsidiary as quickly as possible and arranged for me to meet the Tiffany management on many occasions. The trouble was that the figures did not add up. They were overstocked and their sales were in decline despite a programme of expansion through the opening of many outlets in recent years. Even so, the Tiffany name still had its magic, despite their focus on the corporate gift market which had become their bread and butter and to some degree had lost them the special cachet they used to have. There was every chance that the glorious past could be revived with a new management intent on restoring the principle of exclusivity. At the time of their artistic supremacy in their splendid *époque* in the 1920s and 1930s, their name and product were cherished by connoisseurs the world over for desirability and craftsmanship. Proof of that statement lies in the prices being fetched today for Tiffany objects from that period. In the event of a successful bid for the company, my strategy would have been to shut down most of the peripheral, insignificant outlets it had recently established and forget about competing in a glorified mass-market. Then we would see Tiffany become again the cathedral of quality on Fifth Avenue to which the rich and successful had once flocked to pay homage.

Perhaps I was carried away by memories of the film of Truman Capote's book, *Breakfast at Tiffany's*, starring Audrey Hepburn. Ever since seeing the movie I had dreamed of being part of that milieu where fairytale combined with vast reservoirs of wealth – the gateway to paradise. It was a dream I almost accomplished. The *New York Times*, in reporting Asprey's interest, quoted me as echoing certain other American retailers, intrigued by Tiffany's potential, when I said I found the asking price 'outrageous'. I had in fact done my homework. Over six weeks I took to spending five days alternately in London and New York, trying to arrive at a sensible deal. I even hired a private jet to take me to visit Walter Hoving, who was on vacation in Newport. Mr Hoving, a legendary figure as a former chairman of Tiffany's and a large investor before the sale to Avon, gave me valuable information. If Avon could get a hundred and fifty million for Tiffany's, then, he said, they ought to grab it. This indicated to me that my own assessment of the value of the business was correct. The story the figures told was that Tiffany's could not be worth more than a hundred million dollars by any stretch of the imagination. However, I was prepared to live with the figure of a hundred and fifty million, provided no more than seventy million was in cash.

Negotiations reached the point when I felt we were almost there. Then, at the eleventh hour, an investment company based in Bahrain upped the stakes and promptly concluded the purchase. Many analysts believed the price they paid was far too high, but when they sold the business many years later, they showed a healthy profit. Had our concern for prudence been too strict for our own good? The wisdom of hindsight returns us only to the realm of dreams of what might have been.

*

For Quartet, August saw the publication of Nicholas Coleridge's *Tunnel Vision*, the product of five years' professional eavesdropping. During this period Nicholas had basked by swimming pools at Tuscan villas, hitchhiked to Yazd, worked as a waiter in San Lorenzo, snooped backstage at both the Royal Shakespeare Company and the Brompton Oratory, run with the paparazzi pack which hounded Lady Diana Spencer, shared dahl with hippies and bull-shots with playboys, and survived to write it all down. *Tunnel Vision* could be described as a hit-and-run report.

A new Helmut Newton collection, *World without Men*, was a fascinating sequel to *White Women* and *Sleepless Nights*, two highly successful photographic books that led the field in the portrayal of sexual ambivalence. *World without Men* developed his themes still further, juxtaposing the naked and the dressed, the rich and the poor, beauty and the beast, in the style that had become his hallmark, placing him among the most famous fashion photographers. The man himself described the secrets of his craft, his preferences and his preoccupations with the erotic side of human physiology.

The Music Master was a biography by Charles Reid of James William Davison, the music critic of *The Times* between 1846 and 1878, with excerpts from his critical writings. These threw a sometimes startling light on the abrasive opinions of the most influential music critic of his era. Davison came across as a true monster in critical terms: Chopin was a flea, he declared; Schubert an impostor; Berlioz a lunatic; Wagner was merely puerile while Tchaikovsky was hideous. The extracts – outrageous, exasperating and uproariously amusing by turn – were taken either from his daily column in *The Times*, which he turned out for over thirty years, or from now forgotten weeklies, such as the *Musical World*, which he edited himself for forty years.

The Time of the Assassins was a study of Arthur Rimbaud by Henry Miller, with an introduction from Anthony Burgess. In Rimbaud, Miller wrote, 'I see myself as in a mirror.' Through this reflection on the French poet, he delivered his apocalyptic judgements on the world, seeing Rimbaud as the prophet of the ultimate collapse of civilization in the twentieth century. This vision of a point of breakdown – the time of the assassins – was shared by Miller who glimpsed the full realization of Rimbaud's horror in the destruction of Hiroshima and Nagasaki. Also in the area of literature, there were three novellas in one volume by Leo Tolstoy, *A Landowner's Morning*, *Family Happiness* and *The Devil*, translated and introduced by Kyril and April Fitzlyon. These, all autobiographical to a large extent, were among Tolstoy's finest shorter pieces, yet were surprisingly little known and rarely translated.

There were two books to make headlines in September, the first of which was *The Nouveaux Pauvres: A Guide to Downward Mobility* by Nicholas Monson and Debra Scott. Its theme was the expanding tribe of the financially deprived aristocracy and gentry of Britain, beset by death duties, costly divorces and inflation. Debra was a journalist and Nicholas, as the heir to a peerage and baronetcy, could himself claim to be pure *nouveau pauvre*. He was the founder editor of a magazine called *The Magazine*, in which the article the book was based on first appeared. 'Being *nouveau pauvre*,' he said, 'is the art of selective poverty. Collapsed sofas and cracked loos are now quite permissible so long as the sofa is antique and the crack in the porcelain is just a hairline.' Education was one of the main preoccupations of social sinkers. He had put down Alexander, his son and heir to his overdraft, for Eton, and then had the anxiety of fearing his cheque for the twenty-pound registration fee might bounce. Among those he interviewed for the book were the premier baron of Ireland, who worked as a silage-pit builder and had a son and heir who was a municipal-drains inspector, and a royal relation with economical party tips to offer to the paupered posh.

For the book's launch party at the Chelsea Town Hall, we adopted the strategy that had proved so successful with Derek Jarman's *Dancing Ledge*: each guest was required to buy a copy at the concessionary price of five pounds as their entry ticket. It was an occasion for the 'not so very hard up', the *Standard* commented. 'The *nouveaux pauvres* may be having us on. After all hundreds of them shelled out a fiver each without a murmur. There was plenty of goodish champagne, some diamonds and not a hired dinner jacket in sight.' In the reporter's view the prize for the most poorly dressed individual was most ill judged. It went to an estate agent, Charles Oliver ('my family gave all their money away to the church'), who so far as he could see did not look at all poor. Close examination revealed a Burberry cashmere jacket, a smart green body-warmer, a striped shirt from Gieves & Hawkes and, on his feet, a pair of Guccis. 'I bought the shoes at least thirteen years ago,' their owner pleaded in mitigation.

The party was full of good-tempered jollity and the bar did a lively trade. There was a buzz of optimistic talk about a new class called the *encore riches*. The highlight of the evening came when the 'Namara Follies' took to the floor to entertain the guests. The line-up was recruited from within the Namara Group: Lucinda Rivett-Carnac (now Lulu Guinness), Virge Gilchrist and Emma Lancaster, an editor at Quartet. Their sizzling cabaret act included a dance routine and, most notably, the song 'Who Wants To Be A Millionaire?' I had been to watch the routine in rehearsal and found it highly amusing, though I teasingly suggested that, to raise the temperature at the finale, they could throw their knickers into the assembly as a gesture of liberating defiance. The expressions on their faces told me the idea fell on stony ground. 'We're not taking our knickers off,' they assured each other, and that was that!

The other book to draw attention that September was *Hashish*, a sumptuous and strikingly beautiful production with stunning photographs by Suomi La Valle and a text by John Julius Norwich. Hashish had long been in use in the Middle East before it was discovered by the European literati of the nineteenth century. It had become part of the alternative culture of the 1980s, being praised and vilified in equal measure, the controversy over the relative benefits and harm done by its pharmacology continuing to the present day. Aside from the arguments, hashish was and is a means of livelihood for many people in Nepal and Lebanon. Suomi La Valle had gained the trust of the peasants who cultivated the plant, *Cannabis sativa*, and taken a series of astonishing photographs. John Julius Norwich, who had lived for three years in Lebanon, wrote about it with deep scholarly knowledge and level-headed lucidity. As he said:

> My own purpose will be to try to put this extraordinary plant in its historical and literary perspective: to assess the effects – political, cultural and even etymological – that it has had over the two and half thousand years or so that have elapsed since its peculiar properties were first discovered; and finally perhaps to remove at least some of the mystique that – among those who have no direct experience of it – has surrounded it for so long.

The *Standard* reported how John Julius Norwich had tried hashish when he was with the British Embassy in Beirut in the early 1960s, smoking the stuff through a hubble-bubble at the home of a Lebanese high-court judge. 'I puffed diligently away,' he recalled, 'but the incident made little lasting impression.' My own experience was similar, though in a different environment. I enjoyed it at a certain stage of my life, but was never dependent. It was a passing phase, like some others one enjoys in the heyday of youth. There are those – mostly politicians – who have problems admitting they ever indulged. Others of us have the courage and honesty to admit it, acknowledging it as a step on the way to becoming more sophisticated and complete human beings.

The party for *Hashish* was attended by a less predictable mixture of guests than usual. Its *risqué* aspect attracted a wider circle than the normal crowd of book-launch attenders. Suomi La Valle's wife, being the owner of an exclusive fashion boutique called Spaghetti in Beauchamp Place, Knightsbridge, invited elements from the fashion industry who were not unfamiliar with 'the weed' and its uses. They joined the motley company of beautiful people who were intent on not being excluded from an event tinged with notoriety because of its subject matter. Leonard Bernstein, new to the London party circuit, was there too. So was the more familiar figure of BBC Television's weatherman, Michael Fish, seen deep in conversation with the model Marie Helvin; which only went to show that modelling and weather forecasting might have more in common than is generally supposed.

Hashish sold quite well, though it never achieved the figures we hoped for. We were definitely dealing with a book ahead of its time and lost out as a result. After the original print run of thirty-five thousand copies was either sold or remaindered, the book was never reprinted, and like various other Quartet titles it has become a collector's item. Whenever copies in good condition surface today, they are sold at a high premium. *Hashish* has become a cult book throughout the world.

Twenty-four

Among the multiple events in October was Arabella Pollen's departure from the Namara Group. She was well established as a fashion designer and wished to work in partnership with her brother Marcus and a girl about town, Kathryn Ireland, who was once engaged to Peter Finch's son, Charles. Since both Marcus and Kathryn were already involved with the company, the proposal would be tantamount to a management buyout. I was not ill-disposed towards the idea. Certainly her family were well enough off to provide the financial safety net to make the transition workable.

My affection for Arabella was never in doubt. She and I had worked very closely for about two years without ever exchanging an angry word. Our relationship was never subject to any discord whatever the business pressures. The negotiations with her financial advisers over the move, however, raised issues that threatened to undermine the amicability of our parting in ways I would never have wished. Neither Arabella nor I were prepared to countenance this. We both used our best endeavours to defuse the situation and prevent a falling-out. I have always had a phobia about financial advisers. In my view more often than not they wreck relationships and advocate breaking deals to justify their fees. My backing for Arabella was more a labour of love than a calculated investment. I was never under any illusion that my original investment in promoting her to become an internationally known designer would bring me any significant return on my money, or even necessarily secure my original investment. On the other hand, I had no wish to be taken for granted or made to feel aggrieved because a third party saw the chance of turning the situation to their own advantage. In the end, with concessions made on both sides, we reached an agreement that gave Arabella the best possible chance to take off under her own steam.

Subsequently, over the years, I have watched Arabella's progress with a sense of personal pride, my affection for her remaining warm and enduring. How could I ever forget those piercing blue eyes and lovely face, etched into my memory from the day I first saw her?

Growing a Business
by Arabella Pollen

When Naim called me out of the blue one day to ask whether I would write something for his memoir, my initial reaction was panic. I have almost zero recall of my twelve-year stint in the fashion business, maybe because it was a long time ago, or maybe it's the onset of premature Alzheimer's. Either way, only the barest threads of memory remain: the up-all-nights and the seven days a week, the brilliance and dedication of my studio workforce. OK, so there was that two-year commute to Paris – Fashion Aid, of course, and the craziness of the Studio 54 shows – but almost all the rest of it, the people, the parties, the excitement, tears, triumphs and disappointments, have merged into one great kaleidoscopic blur stored somewhere deep inside my head. Not Naim, though. Naim Attallah is not a person you forget.

We met in 1980. I was nineteen and a year out of school. I had spent the first six months of that year working odd jobs in advertising and the latter part of it holed up in a crumbling mill in France with a Super 8 movie camera, earnestly attempting to write, shoot and direct a satire on the business. This high-falutin project left me profoundly broke and I was eventually forced to return to London, engage with the real world and look around for a way to make ends meet. Having crashed through my A-levels with a spectacular mix of bad behaviour and complacency, the only asset I had of any real value was a cupboard full of textiles which I'd collected over the years and – for reasons that still escape me – I decided to make clothes out of them. This resulted in a small collection, mostly constructed from stiff and itchy Hebridean tweeds, which somehow caught the attention of an editor at *Vogue* magazine, and before very much time had passed I found myself sitting in the air-conditioned offices of Namara in Poland Street, clutching a portfolio between my knees. 'If he likes you,' the *Vogue* editor had said, 'he'll be back.'

Quite what I was expecting in a publisher who might be interested in starting a fashion business with me, I can't say. Certainly Naim Attallah was not it. First of all, he was extraordinary looking: tall, broad, enormous hands, odd-shaped ears. He was a Palestinian 'Mr Potato Head', but with a charming face and rather beautiful eyes that folded into multiple creases when he smiled. There was his voice: versatile in its range, capable of soaring and dipping through several octaves whenever he became excited. There was his manner: utterly disarming, every gesture expansive. On top of all there, there were his clothes: flamboyant, foreign, yet, conversely, impeccably English. Something bright flashed as he seized my hand. A piece of jewellery, a silk tie? I don't know. There was just so much detail to take in. All I remember is that he gripped my arm, launched forth with great enthusiasm on a variety of seemingly unconnected topics, flipped through my portfolio, and the deal was done.

Later that day, I walked slowly out of the Notting Hill tube station and blinked disbelievingly into the afternoon light. I had a job. More than a job, I was about to have my own business. I assumed he was mad, certifiably insane. But what I came to understand was that Naim didn't believe in business plans or spreadsheets. He believed in people, and once he put his faith in you, it was absolute.

Some of us are dreamers, some are thinkers. Naim is a doer, a nurturer of talent and ideas. Together we put down roots and grew a business. God knows, neither of us knew what we were doing, but we muddled through. It was a lot of fun. We had more than our share of success and I loved how proud that made him.

Random things stick in my mind from those days, like Naim's zeal for cats, not the kittycat variety but animal skins, oil paintings and two enormous white and gold china tigers – maybe kept at Namara, maybe perched on a white rug at his house in Mayfair. I remember the window of our Knightsbridge offices shattering when the Hyde Park bomb exploded. I recently found a gold egg on a chain he gave me from Asprey, which I wore for a while, then temporarily mislaid. I remember the other girls downstairs, bluestocking and studious, working for some mysterious outfit called The Women's Press.

Naim and I would have lunch together. These were three-course affairs, cooked by someone pretty with a cordon-bleu diploma and served with great style. We talked about everything – his myriad of ventures – film, theatre, art. We talked about Palestine, women, publishing, food, love. He was endearing, passionate, funny, enthusiastic, and just a little bit mad. There wasn't a soul who knew him who didn't imitate his delighted shriek of a greeting when you walked into a room. We all took to answering phones 'in the style of Naim'. I think he probably knew. I suspect he kind of liked it. He was happiest being the sun around which lots of interesting people revolved.

From time to time we argued. Then he was infuriating, bombastic, stubborn, arrogant – but so, of course, was I. I was always in a hurry. I wanted Pollen Inc. to be bigger and better. I wanted success and recognition. I wanted greater financing, higher turnover, more staff. He was slower; and a lot wiser. When the time came for us to head off in different directions, I'm pretty sure I was the one who behaved badly, a touch furtively, unsure quite how to approach the matter, while Naim behaved, as usual, like a gentleman. Twenty years later I still count on Naim's loyalty and friendship. When I wrote my first book, a truly dire spoof on the fashion business, it was Naim who, with great generosity of spirit, was the first to review it.

We still have lunch from time to time. The cordon-bleu days might have gone, but the panache remains. Naim's enthusiasm and passion for life have never faltered. I am always more pleased than I can say to see him – and I wear my gold Asprey's egg a lot.

*　　*　　*

In the same month that Arabella took her decision, I commissioned Christina Oxenburg to write a book about New York taxis. From taxis I turned to an attempt to promote jazz, having met Margaux Hemingway, the twenty-eight-year-old granddaughter of Ernest. She had a wonderful husky voice and revealed she was very keen to make a jazz record. I saw this as a golden opportunity and did not hesitate to do my best to make her ambition a reality. The very next weekend I took her to have lunch at Maxim's in Paris to meet Mike Zwerin, a trombonist who had played with Miles Davis in the 1950s. He was a writer on the *Herald Tribune* and the author of many jazz books, one of which Quartet had published – *La Tristesse de Saint Louis: Swing under the Nazis*, the curious story of the protection given by Nazi officers to Jewish jazz musicians in Paris during the Occupation. Mike had the best possible credentials to arrange and produce a disc from a newcomer.

Margaux's voice impressed him as much as it had me. He proceeded to arrange with all the appropriate contacts a few sessions of voice coaching, with everything set for an early recording to follow. Margaux was ecstatic to think she was really about to make her singing début. The combination of her famous name with terrific good looks and vocal talent seemed certain to guarantee for her a whole new future. Unfortunately Margaux was going though a phase where the spirit was ready to go but the body hung back in a lassitude that was impossible to break out of. She had a recurring drink-and-drug problem that was not severe in itself but was enough to drain her energies and sap her motivation. For weeks I kept after her to pull herself together and seize her chance, but although she met my pleas with her habitual charm, she never managed to muster the willpower to shake herself free of her demons. She died a few years later in tragic circumstances, having achieved so little. The gods blessed her with many gifts but failed to grant her the inner strength to put them to good use. It had been a life wasted, with no element of fulfilment.

Also in October *Publishing News* returned like a dog to a well-chewed bone to rib me again about Nigella Lawson's salary:

I am obliged to clarify the Lejeune position on the so-called 'Nigella Lawson scandal'. Naim the Terrible is one of the greatest philanthropists that British publishing has ever known and the fact that he pays his talented and attractive editorial director a generous £5,500 is simply not a subject that I wish to discuss in public. Frankly, my friendship with Naim is too important for both of us to allow it to be jeopardized by mindless gossip.

The tired platitudes about salaries might have sounded amusing when they were first churned out, but constant repetition soon robbed them of any humour. But publishing, like any other branch of the media, has always provided the gossip mongers with a wealth of ammunition. Another missile was fired when Lady Olga Maitland, in her *Sunday Express* diary column, under the heading 'Arab Peerage', reported my interest in acquiring *Burke's Peerage*. Harold Brooks-Baker, a director of Burke's, was quick to confirm the story, saying, 'Naim is very keen. He is a crashing snob but that, of course, is what we make our money on.' It was the first time anyone had ever called me a 'snob' – something I am emphatically not, though I suppose it made good copy. The viability of *Burke's Peerage* as a commercial proposition at the time was a matter of debate. Whatever view you took, the undeniable fact was that it would need substantial refinancing if it were to have any chance of survival. I decided the burden would be too heavy to take on and declined to proceed. That did not prevent *Private Eye* from going into its irresistible parody mode and producing a spoof advertisement for 'Berk's Peerage', now under new management, the definitive guide to Britain's historic nobility, as revised by Naim Attullah-Disgusting. 'NO self-respecting snob can afford this book – whoops! to be without this book, which lists the antecedents of Britain's oldest families.' Then it gave a typical entry, '*showing the ancestry of a highly important personage*', which provided NAIM ATTULLAH with his own heraldic crest: a shield flanked by a unicorn and a greyhound, topped by a crescent, its quarterings juxtaposing the 'Q' for Quartet with sets of moneybags, and underneath it the motto *Dieu et mon argent*.

1. ATTULLAH THE HUN (803–906)
2. SIR NORMAN DE TOULAR (984–1067), Chevalier de Maurice
3. NEAMUS O'TOLER OF THE REEKS (1097–1194), 1st Lord of Galway
4. SIR NIAM MCTULLACH OF THE MCTULLACHS, Lord of Asprey (1280–1569)
5. SIR NIMROD ST JOHN FITZTULLER, Knight of the Order of St John of Jerusalem 1st Crusade – mentioned in despatches twice (1106–1209)
(*That's enough bogus ancestors. Ed.*)

At the foot of the panel were the words: 'Berks – we gottem.'

Another row waiting to flare up concerned Michael Coren, a Jewish author, who came to my rescue in the wake of the great Roald Dahl controversy and stuck his neck out throughout the crisis to defend me publicly. He was a man of great understanding and unbiased views, a good friend to have on one's side. Later, in February 1985, he was to write a letter to the *Sunday Times* objecting to their description of *God Cried* as 'silly':

> With regard to your profile of publisher Naim Attallah (6 January), as the *New Statesman* journalist who opened the floodgates of criticism on the book and its review by Roald Dahl I feel obliged to comment. Your article described the book as 'silly'. An angry, provocative and important volume about massacre and attempted genocide silly? Deserving of discussion yes, silly never.

I mention this background because in November 1984 Quartet published his book, *Theatre Royal: 100 Years of Stratford East*, which gave rise to a war of words between us and the Theatre Royal management at the time. I accused the Theatre Royal of double standards in trying to enforce censorship by disowning the book because it was over-critical. But Philip Hedley, director at Stratford East, claimed I had got hold of the wrong end of the stick and the threat I was making to wage an advertising campaign against the theatre and complain to its funding bodies was uncalled for in the circumstances. He also maintained that the disagreements had been blown out of all proportion.

My argument was that, although the book never claimed to be an official history, the Theatre Royal had encouraged the author and was supposed to be cooperating in a promotional link between publication and its own centenary celebrations. Then, as soon as the book was published, the theatre suddenly took exception to critical references it contained and disowned it. I added that the theatre, famous for its scraps with the establishment since the days when Joan Littlewood brought her progressive Theatre Workshop company to Stratford in the 1950s, was now trying to impose the kind of censorship on a book which they would find abhorrent if it was applied to a theatre production. As my anger rose, the language I used became perhaps slightly intemperate. The management of the theatre, I said, were a disgraceful bunch who were arrogant enough to believe themselves above criticism and were guilty of inconsistency.

Hedley, for his part, claimed that far from being offended by critical references in the book, he found it was almost too nice about his own five-year tenure. He admitted he had cooperated fully with Michael Coren and had insisted from the outset that the book must be a critical, independent assessment of the theatre's contribution. As it turned out, it had then become imperative for him to distance himself from the finished volume on account of certain factual errors and the fact that he himself came in for so much praise. He was highly sensitive to the idea that people might gain a notion he had sought to influence Coren in some way or was endorsing the book as an official history or a whitewash of the current management. My personal feeling was that the theatre management took exception to a number of the illustration captions, which Hedley considered particularly flashy – though the *Standard* described them as rather anodyne. One of them referred to a production as 'the height of mediocrity'; another said of a pair of performers standing outside the theatre, that 'most critics wished they had stayed there'. Eventually the rumpus petered out but left me feeling that I must accept conflict and controversy as part of my staple diet.

Start Again Britain was another book that received a great deal of attention, though of quite a different kind. The author was Sir Charles Villiers, the chairman of British Steel. It was a book for people either to love or to hate or both at once. It consisted of an unflinching examination of Britain's need for bold, imaginative change. The manufacturing disaster, the reluctant industrialists, the 'them and us' syndrome, the new start, the unions, the education failure, the threat and example from Japan, the promise of micro-processors, the need for thousands of new businesses, the anaesthetic effect of North Sea oil – a wasting asset indeed – all these issues were explored with unusual candour from a background of experience. On the back cover Sir Michael Edwardes was quoted as saying: 'Sir Charles Villiers has dedicated *Start Again Britain* to present and future managers in Britain. They would be well advised to "read, mark, learn and inwardly digest" (whether or not they come to agree with it), because, as he says, "the management of anything is everything".'

The launch party for *Start Again Britain* was held in the newly completed office block above Victoria Station called Victoria Plaza. Beneath a glass atrium many leaders of industry gathered to pay their respects to the author, who was surrounded by a great number of friends, there to lend their support. It was Sir Charles's first book, and his proud wife, a much decorated heroine of the Belgian Resistance, greeted the guests with a captivating continental charm. The book was yet another benchmark for Quartet in its push to widen its readership base.

In November Nigella Lawson announced her intention to leave Quartet after two years to take up a job in journalism on one of Rupert Murdoch's newspapers. The response of *Publishing News* was to give her the Lejeune award for ex-publisher of the year, for being grossly overpaid by the saintly Attallah and for being thoroughly overrated by lovesick trade journalists.

During the same month Quartet threw a charity party at Merediana, a restaurant in the Fulham Road, to celebrate the publication of *What Mummy Said* by Jane Mitchell. The proceeds from the book were designed to 'refresh' the coffers of a charity providing holidays for disabled young people with respiratory problems. Mrs Mitchell, who had no children of her own and was married to the producer of the *Irish RM* series on television, told the assembled guests how, when she was bidding farewell rather prematurely to the Mother Superior of her convent school, she was instructed never, before marriage, to let a man touch her below the neck or above the knee; while the advice she got from her mother was never to allow her husband to see her cleaning the bath. Quite what the connection was between these two anecdotes escaped me then and leaves me no wiser today.

About this time Denis Norden, whose sense of humour is second to none, had to undergo a hernia operation and was advised by his doctors to avoid laughing. When pressed by the *Standard* to comment on this injunction, he retorted, 'God help the "Londoner's Diary" if that's all you've got to write about. Can't you find another story about Naim Attallah?' It was certainly true that the constant press attention being given to my various activities was causing irritation in certain humourless quarters of the British establishment. There was a minority who considered me to be mad. My response was simple. To be mad and institutionalized must be a terrible thing, but to be mad and on the loose is the ultimate in living for fun. I was doing things that most men only dream about. So far as the whiners were concerned, they could whinge on; I was content to reap the benefits of a more fulfilled and mirth-loving existence. This was the positive note on which, for me, the year 1984 came to an end. There was a less positive note in the departure of editorial director Daphne Wright, later to be reborn as the successful crime novelist Natasha Cooper. Her recollections of her time at Quartet round off this chapter.

Life at Quartet in the Mid 1980s
by Daphne Wright

There was no drowning involved when my life began to flash before my eyes this morning. Naim's telephone call got me out of bed. Somehow it seems typical that I should have been dressed in nothing but drops of water and an immense yellow towel when I spoke to him for the first time in more than twenty years.

Would I write him a short piece about my memories of Quartet? How could I refuse?

Names, faces, incidents began to swim in my mind: Zelfa Hourani, like the

[242]

Sibyl in her office at the front of the building, knowing everything about everyone and saying discreetly little; Sabrina Guinness dashing in to find the shoes she'd just had mended but left in the office, asking whether I was the same Daphne Wright who'd been brought up only yards from her. I was, which is why my baby brother had shared her parents' nursery governess for his first steps in education. Then there was Rebecca Fraser, whose grandfather, Frank Pakenham, had taught my mother at Oxford and given her a job when he was Chancellor of the Duchy of Lancaster in the 1940s; and Nigella Lawson, whose copy of *The Secrets of the Hungry Monk* I have shamefully never returned after she lent it to me. (I console myself with the thought that maybe she has enough cookery books to manage without it.)

I can see Nigella now, coming into my office one day, auburn hair flying, to say she doesn't feel very well and will I give her permission to have a Dover sole at Bertorelli's on the account for lunch? No, I won't, I tell her, shocked at the very idea of such extravagance. Only moments later, the telephone rings and our boss wants to know why I am being so totally cruel to Nigella, who must have her sole.

There weren't only women, of course. Naim employed lots of men. I don't remember them all, but some are vivid in my mind as I write. Paul Keegan, staggeringly well read and beautiful with his wild Irish hair and bright blue eyes, would have made a far more adventurous editorial director than I. An apparently mythical Pickles, whom I'd never seen, was reputed to bring tribute to Naim in the form of records from the shop he managed in those days. The wonderful Tim Binyon, who became a friend and whose untimely death I still mourn, dropped in to discuss the crime list he ran and how we could raise money to translate the then deeply unfashionable European crime fiction that interested us both. David Elliott was the unlikely point of warmth and stability at the heart of the circus.

Then there was Naim himself, the King-Emperor of all he surveyed, generous, eccentric, flamboyant and mischievous. I remember a moment at the Frankfurt Book Fair when he was planning to send a magnificent selection of flowers (orchids mainly, I think) to one of 'the girls' (could it have been Nigella? – or was it Rebecca?) in order to make the rest of them jealous.

Another memory swims out of the past. Naim is planning to hire the vast Theatre Royal, Drury Lane, to put on a French farce. All the staff will be required to perform. One of my few moments of outright horror leads me to say, 'I won't.' 'Don't worry, darling, we'll give you a part with authority,' says the King-Emperor. 'Tot–ally. We make you the *madame*.' No, you won't, I think to myself, and luckily never have to face the realization of this particular dream.

Then there's the day when I arrive at our grotty offices in Goodge Street to find we've been burgled. (Actually, the offices themselves weren't grotty: it was the common parts and in particular the loos that were grotty.) Nothing has been taken from the offices – not the calculators, typewriters (long before computers then), loose change, shoes, bags or jewellery left by 'the girls', nothing – but every filing cabinet has been opened and clearly rifled. Later that morning, the telephone call from Naim, who works out of offices that are far from grotty with immaculate loos, a good twenty minutes' walk away from us: 'Darling, I have Inspector — [I've forgotten his name, alas] from Special Branch here. Why have you been corresponding with arms dealers?'

I hadn't. My nascent crime-writing brain instantly decided that Special Branch had had something to do with the burglary. Later, reading Peter (no relation) Wright's memories of burgling and bugging around London, I wasn't so sure it had been members of Special Branch; some other strange arm of law-enforcement seemed likelier. Discussing it with a man-in-the-know only a week or so after the incident, I was told he knew the name of the journalist who must have made the allegation that led to the burglary. I could never get him to tell me any more and decided it would be politic to keep my head well below the parapet.

An editorial meeting surfaces next. The text and illustrations of a long-awaited academic book arrive. It is to be an expensive exhaustive tome about a surrealist artist. Naim is not taken with the artist's photographs of his wife tied up with wire and other fetishistic images. Naim has previously been assured by the commissioning editor involved that the book will be erotic. These illustrations do not pass muster. Trying, as always, to be diplomatic and make peace between two warring factions, I murmur something: 'I suppose you could say it's a cerebral eroticism.' Naim, mishearing my half-hearted murmurs, bellows down the long boardroom table: 'Saleable? It's not *saleable*.'

There was no lunch involved that day, but there were often lunches. Sometimes one of 'the girls' would be summoned to share Naim's delicious and carefully calorie-controlled food in the basement dining-room of his office building. But his chosen companion would often be someone who had been rude about him in the press. There were plenty of those. Some would be sued; others invited to lunch and – always – charmed. I could never understand the rationale for who was considered to deserve which treatment.

Now I think about it, I see the flirty atmosphere made many people behave oddly, not just the cook.

The first time I meet freelance editor Jennie, down from Scotland, she shows me how she has just shocked her mother-in-law by taking out of her capacious bag a Braun Styler (a gas-fired device for curling the hair). Apparently she has told her mother-in-law that this is a vibrator, adding as she whips off the plastic cover to reveal the black spikes of the curler, 'and this is for when you want a rough ride'.

There wasn't always flirtation and mischief. When I resign from my job in a babyishly tearful rage after a misunderstanding about the removal of my secretary, Emma Lancaster, Naim gives me an Asprey watch and sends me kindly on my way.

Back in the office, David Elliott asks me what I'm going to do now. I answer that I know what I want to do but am not sure whether it'll work and would rather not say until I know. (Who, moving out of publishing in order to try to write, would confess her ambition until she knew whether she could create publishable fiction?) David asks quite seriously if I'm intending to become a nun.

Did I really seem so prissy as I made my way through the colourful, rickety, emotional circus that was Quartet almost a quarter of a century ago?

Twenty-five

January 1985 kicked off with my profile in the *Observer*, written (anonymously) by Geoffrey Wheatcroft and given the bold title, 'Tiger at the Media Gates'. It contained a few inaccuracies, as such pieces usually do. It claimed that some of the Arab-interest books I had published were 'agit-prop for the Palestinian cause', and expressed the dismissive view of *God Cried* which was counter-attacked by Michael Coren in his subsequent letter. Not only did it call the book silly and tendentious, but also referred to Roald Dahl's review as much sillier and even more tendentious, saying that its publication in the *Literary Review* had been a gross error of judgement. Otherwise the profile was well balanced and dispelled any notion of my being remotely anti-Semitic.

> The Namara group is clearly not some sort of laundering operation for the PLO, as the *mauvaises langues* have suggested. Nor can anyone honestly accuse Attallah himself of anti-Semitism (or, to be more precise, Jew-hating). Not only some of his best friends but some of his employees have been Jewish – for example, Nigella Lawson the Chancellor's daughter. Equally, Attallah has never disguised the very strong and natural sympathies which he feels for his fellow-countrymen and the very different fate from his own which fortune has brought many of them.

It suggested my broader ambitions were now set on 'the "media" in all its facets', and that what I wanted to be was 'not rich but influential'. 'If men of Australian and sub-Carpathian birth can be major British press proprietors, why not a Palestinian? Why not indeed, if he has the money . . . [though] this gifted and ambitious man is as yet in nothing like the mega-magnet category.' Fleet Street, wrote Wheatcroft, was going to have to wait a little longer to see if the tiger pounced.

Meanwhile the distant rumblings of another literary *cause célèbre* in the making were heard in March, when the *Sunday Telegraph* carried a report of the intentions of the Countess of Dudley, the former actress Maureen Swanson, to sue the *Literary Review* for libel. Her claim was that Alastair Forbes had libelled her in a review of the book *Ladies in Waiting* by Lady Anne Somerset under the headline 'Leaves in Vallombrosa'. When the paper approached me for my comments on the claim, I indicated that any action would be vigorously contested. The Dudleys were taking an aggressive stance and evidently spoiling for a fight. The finances of the *Literary Review* were, on their own, incapable of supporting any libel battle, but I felt our whole prestige was at stake and was reluctant to let anything create the impression that we might be an easy target. During the following months, the fight would escalate into a major confrontation in the high court and a running spat, with sniping from both sides, in newspaper columns and magazines, especially the *Spectator*.

Quartet's immediate attention was focused on the promotion of Tony Lambton's new book, *Elizabeth and Alexandra*, for which we were mustering all our energies. We considered this to be a potential bestseller, and planned the campaign with the precision of a blitzkrieg on all fronts. The launch party was to be hosted by the Marchioness of Dufferin and Ava and myself at the Dufferin London home in Holland Park, where guests could spread out and drift in the neoclassical garden. The invitation card was so heavily embossed that, as some journalists remarked, it must have broken half the thumbnails in London. Catering was arranged by my cook, Charlotte Millward, aided and abetted by Charlotte Faber. Both were talented cooks and artists and the sublime ideas they introduced achieved a new high in buffet presentation. The sumptuous cocktail they devised had pieces of real gold leaf floating on the surface of each drink. The Quartet girls were provided with specially designed, slightly transparent, flowing evening dresses in lilac to wear while circulating among the guests, their exquisitely toned, gold-painted bodies shining through from underneath. The concept and stage management of all this were down to the two Charlottes, whose creative imaginations knew no bounds. Among the Quartet girls was a new recruit, Richard Ingrams's daughter Jubby, who was already making her mark, both within the ranks at Goodge Street and in the world beyond. Jubby was a free spirit whose sense of fun was to find a place on the London scene, though sometimes to the dismay of those encumbered with a stuffy outlook. Her impishness had a whimsical appeal for the literary set as well as for the young ravers who clustered around her, always on the lookout for mischief.

At the party itself there were four hundred guests from every walk of life. Aristocrats were there in hordes to celebrate Lambton's first major novel, including his family. Lady Lambton (Bindy), unmissable because of her imposing presence, was seen chatting to Lady Soames. She stood at a distance from his companion of many years, Claire Ward, the mother of the film actress Rachel Ward. The tension between the two women seemed to be allayed by the grandeur of the occasion. Sir Jack Colville and old political colleagues like Lord Jellicoe and Viscountess Lymington mingled with the group round Lady Sylvie Thynne, who was drawn in turn to the *haute art* set, among them Lucien Freud and Kasmin. Princess Michael of Kent and Nicky Haslam were engaged in good-humoured conversation. Others busy circulating included the satirist John Wells, the novelist A. N. Wilson and the columnist Nigel Dempster; Auberon Waugh and Richard Ingrams; John Saumarez-Smith from the Heywood Hill bookshop; Lord Durham, the Earl of Wilton, Emma Soames, Susan Ryan, Countess Fitzwilliam, Arabella Weir, Roc Sandford, Lady Delves-Broughton, Lynn Arial, Ari Ashley, Dennis Walker MP and Mrs Walker, Nigella Lawson, Laura Faber and Amanda Lyster, to pick names from the guest list at random. The Quartet girls looked stunning and entertained the guests with their usual social aplomb. In his account of the party Auberon Waugh waxed lyrical, describing Lambton as 'the great swordsman turned novelist, being fêted by the most glittering people in England and the most beautiful young women'.

Tony Lambton was definitely back in the limelight, but this time in triumph rather than for reasons of political disgrace. The scandal that had wrecked his political career was relegated to the past and no longer mattered. His emergence as a first-class novelist was a clear sign of a new dawn for the man who had once been a rising politician. The difference was a change in direction, and in his new role he would excel. Significantly hidden behind dark glasses, he was delighted to see the large number of celebrities who had answered his invitation call. Among the crowd of people who were keen to shake his hand were David Dimbleby and Diana Rigg. His indiscretions had clearly been forgiven by the establishment, while to the bohemian section largely made up of the young set, many of whom referred to him as Uncle Tony, he remained a hero. Possibly they admired his wicked sense of humour, which could be biting indeed, and a disregard for conformity he tempered with a certain aristocratic fastidiousness.

Elizabeth and Alexandra was well received by the critics. *The Times* wrote that, 'Antony Lambton shows himself to be a considerable novelist, deftly handling a large cast of characters from Queen Victoria to Joseph Stalin.' The *Listener* called the book 'a good solid read'. The *Daily Telegraph* concluded that, 'Antony Lambton's research has clearly been prodigious, and his description of the stifling atmosphere of the Russian court is memorably convincing.' In line with that opinion, the *Observer* considered 'it accumulates respect . . . by sheer archival industry'. And the *Literary Review* called it 'a massive achievement'. The book attained the bestseller status we had anticipated for it. Quartet's promotional campaign proved highly effective.

The prevailing party mood that year was summed up by Auberon Waugh in his 'Diary' column in *Private Eye*:

Naim has many talents – he can sing all the arias from Verdi's *Ernani* while accompanying himself on the french horn, he is a yachtsman, no mean shot, and very good at balancing lumps of sugar on his nose. But above all, he is the greatest party giver of our time.

Among the 500 guests who flock to the Arts Club in Dover Street are about 100 of the most beautiful young women in England, most of them called Emma or Sophia. They are not only beautiful to look at but shapely, well-mannered, cheerful, intelligent, and juicy. Some of them even wear black stockings.

I find myself gasping that so many delicious creatures should have emerged from the last decade of comprehensive education, fluoride in the water and watching filth like Roy Hattersley on television. Then it occurs to me that these lovely ladies are all that is left in England. Consider the less lovely ladies who go to parties given by Lord Weidenfeld, the plain women who seem to be creeping into *Spectator* parties, the frankly hideous old slags to be seen at *New Statesman* dos. Then reflect on all the embittered females who never get asked to any parties at all. The country is a dung-heap. This is just the glorious foliage on top of it.

Earlier in the year we published paperback editions under the Robin Clark imprint of all the five novels Bron had written at the start of his career. Bron recorded the event:

THURSDAY

My paperback publisher who mysteriously calls himself Robin Clark (his real name is Rebecca Fraser) has decided to reissue five novels I wrote in my youth. They have names like *Buttercups and Daisies*, *Hypodermic Syringe* and *Cowslips Over the Moon*. In order to publicize them I summon a hack from the *Gruniad* and ply him with champagne in my penthouse suite at Gnome House.

Unfortunately, he becomes over-excited by this treatment. In a confused account of his experience, he omits to mention the name of the publisher (Robin Clark) or the books (*Buttercups and Daisies* etc.). I have decided to ask Naim Atullah, the Christian philanthropist who owns Robin Clark, Rebecca Fraser, Harrods stores etc. if he will give a party to celebrate the books.

*

Back in the previous October at the 1984 Frankfurt Book Fair, Jennifer Bradshaw had suggested the introduction of a new literary Quartet series.

The objective was going to be to publish twentieth-century European authors in translation, with forewords from distinguished British or foreign academics to explain the merits of each book. The concept for the series was Jennifer Bradshaw's, but work on the books was in the hands of Janet Law (now Parker), Daphne Wright, Paul Keegan and Nigella Lawson, with guidance from Kyril Fitzlyon, a freelance translator. The first six titles were launched in April 1985, comprising the following:

Aharon Appelfeld, *The Retreat*, translated from the Hebrew by Jeffrey M. Green, with an introduction by Irma Kurtz: a story about a group of Jews from Central Europe who go to a hilltop retreat to learn how to talk, look and act like Gentiles on the brink of the Nazi holocaust.

Grazia Deledda (winner of the Nobel Prize for Literature in 1926), *After the Divorce*, translated from the Italian by Susan Ashe, with an introduction by Sheila MacLeod: a young wife in a primitive Sardinian community is left alone to look after her baby son and ageing mother when her husband is sent to prison for murder, her only hope being a new law allowing convicts' wives to divorce and remarry.

Carlo Emilio Gadda, *That Awful Mess on Via Merulana*, translated by William Feaver, with an introduction by Italo Calvino: two crimes are committed in the same apartment house, a robbery and a stabbing – events behind which lie the creeping corruption of Mussolini's early fascist state.

Gustav Janouch, *Conversations with Kafka*, translated from the German by Goronwy Rees, with an introduction by Hugh Haughton: a record of conversations revealing insights into the mind of the great writer, written down when their author was an admiring adolescent.

Henry de Montherlant, *The Bachelors*, translated and introduced by Terence Kilmartin: two bachelors, uncle and nephew, impoverished aristocrats who have turned their backs on the modern world and live in squalor, desperately try to find a strategy to preserve their home against encroaching financial realities.

Stanisław Ignacy Witkiewicz, *Insatiability*, translated from the Polish by Louis Iribarne, with an introduction by Czesław Miłosz: a striking piece of experimental and futuristic prose fiction that sets the fate of a social group against the background of a Communist Chinese invasion which brings about the fall of Western civilization.

City Limits welcomed the new series at once. It had, they said, the 'best translators, expert introductions . . . elegant design', and the books were good value, with cover prices ranging between £3.95 and £7.95. The 'Encounter' series was away to a good start – or so we thought until Melvin J. Lasky, the current editor of *Encounter*, the prestigious review of politics, culture and literature that had been running since 1953, took umbrage at our use of the word 'Encounter' to describe our new venture. The argument flared into a legal battle when Lasky went to the high court, claiming the series title chosen by Quartet would cause confusion and winning a limited injunction to restrain Quartet from publishing any further volumes under that name, though the books already issued would be allowed to remain in circulation.

It was a setback no one had foreseen. The injunction stunned me, especially since Lasky implied we had only settled on the word 'Encounter' to gain respectability and increase sales by riding on the back of his journal's reputation. To me the claim seemed complete nonsense. *Encounter* had only a limited and select circulation and our sales were unlikely to be boosted by an imagined connection. We were simply using the word in its literary sense. The publicity arising from the case, on the other hand, did help with the launch of the series, though the downside was the temporary freezing order, which took the wind out of our sails. Our solicitors launched an immediate appeal and the case was heard before Sir John Donaldson, the Master of the Rolls. To our further bemusement, Sir John promptly ruled that the title 'Encounter' for our series might indeed be confused too easily with the monthly academic journal, *Encounter*. An 's' should therefore be added, he said, making our series title 'Encounters', if Quartet wished to retain the name.

This legal compromise left us with ten thousand copies of books in the warehouse, all of which were required to have a sticky label affixed to correct the title before they could be marketed. It might be claimed as the most expensive 's' in publishing history, quite apart from the legal costs we had to bear as a result of losing the appeal. I continued to feel it had been a bloody-minded decision, though we may have been trespassing more seriously than we realized since, as history later revealed, the finances for *Encounter* depended on CIA contributions in return for which the journal maintained an anti-Soviet philosophic stance. It was hard for most people to see that the whole dispute was about anything more than a minor semantic point, not worthy of a legal confrontation between 'two literary godfathers' as one press report expressed it.

*

Having been launched with Sabrina Guinness at its helm, the Academy

Bookclub was then run by the beautiful Liza Campbell for a short period. Lady Liza Campbell had been the last child of her family to be born in Cawdor Castle, which had been the Campbell family seat for six hundred years. Later she wrote about her Scottish childhood in *Title Deeds: Growing Up in Macbeth's Castle*, published by Doubleday. The experience had been like a fairytale, but one with dark undertones, for she saw her father descend into destructive excess and madness under enormous financial pressures and ultimately lose the family heritage.

In May 1985 the Academy Bookclub was totally revitalized by the appointment of Sophia Sackville-West, who had formerly worked in Quartet's publicity department. She was so keen to take the book club under her wing that, as a relation of Vita Sackville-West and the daughter of Lord Savile, she enthusiastically told the *Observer*, 'I'm prepared to prostitute my family name to push it.' She set about writing to all her friends and the people she had known at Oxford, urging them to subscribe, arguing that even the grandest of families appreciate a discount on books. *Private Eye* had pre-empted the appointment in late April by devising an advert of their own:

CASTING NOW: *Literary Follies*, a musical extravaganza from the producers of *Gold Diggers of 1982, 1983, 1984, 1985*, etc. Only lovely girls from lovely homes required. Hyphenated surnames an advantage. Literacy not. Call N. Atullah on 01 636 1968.

Private Eye was relentless in its pursuit of me, and they redoubled their efforts as soon as they discovered that September that I was about to launch a range of toiletries. A piece in the 'Grovel' column was a prelude to what would follow:

Who is the mysterious 'N' to whom the Rev. A. N. Wilson dedicates his masterly new novel?

I am told that it is Arab-born publisher Naim Attullah-Disgusting for whom the fogey scribbler entertains a warm admiration.

But there are limits apparently. Naim was hoping that the Rev. Wilson would help to write publicity material for his new perfumes 'Before' and 'After Sex'. But when Rev. A. N. Wilson saw the revolting phallic-shaped bottle in which the perfume is to be marketed, he adamantly refused to cooperate.

Speculation was set off at the same time by the news that I had suddenly bought on a whim what the *Standard* called the 'Villa Disraeli', the horribly uncomfortable house in the Dordogne that had been owned by *Private Eye*. Could it possibly be that I was thinking of retiring? 'Pendennis' in the *Observer* weaved an altogether more elaborate story around the purchase, the gist of this being that André Deutsch had been making imploring telephone calls to *Private Eye*, reminding them of his total loyalty and the fact that he was the publisher of the *Eye*'s profitable books, solely for the reason that he wanted to buy the same property. According to the report, he had wanted it badly, while I, at the same time, had been been making the same sort of imploring telephone calls, reminding the *Eye* that I employed the daughter of Richard Ingrams, the magazine's editor. The piece ended with recording my successful purchase, putting it down to a triumph of 'filial . . . over corporate loyalty'.

If André Deutsch was truly disappointed not to have secured the property then he need not have been. The fabric was in terrible condition and the few facilities it possessed were so low grade that the place was hardly habitable. If you described it as spartan, then that would have given it a luxury status that it did not have. The house lay in the middle of a forest choked with wild, uncontrolled undergrowth in which serpents lurked and other beasts roamed freely once darkness fell. After dusk an eerie silence descended over the place and the wilderness took on a threatening aspect. It was a crazy impulse that led me to buy the property without seeing it first. The asking price of twenty-nine and a half thousand pounds was very modest, and would not, I calculated, be much of a gamble, especially since there were several acres of land to go with the house.

Maria set off with our son Ramsay and Jubby Ingrams on a reconnaissance mission, but their voyage of discovery soon turned sour. Maria was adamant that she could not stay in the ruin and found a room in the hotel in the next village. Ramsay and Jubby managed to camp out in the house and went to Maria's hotel to take baths. The trip was cut short and they all returned to London to regale me with tales of the horrors they had found. I refused to be downcast. It was yet another challenge, and one that I rose to in transforming the dereliction and wilderness into a most desirable property over the years that followed.

The summer of 1985 was noteworthy for the recruitment of more staff, both in my office at Namara House and for Quartet in Goodge Street. Enter: Amanda Lyster, whose sister Lucy later married the comedian Harry Enfield; Laura Keen, whose mother, Lady Mary Keen, was a well-known garden journalist; Princess Katarina of Yugoslavia, daughter of Prince Tomislav; Candida Crewe, the daughter of my great friend Quentin Crewe; Emma Williams, an ambitious young woman, to be my secretary, though it was predicted that since she had a degree and a wicked way with a lacrosse stick I would not be able to hold on to her for long. Emma later became a doctor and married Lord Gilmour's youngest son. She went with her three small children and husband to work in Jerusalem as a doctor in 2000, a month before the eruption of the Palestinian intifada. Her book, *It's Easier to Reach Heaven than the End of the Street: A Jerusalem Memoir*, was published by Bloomsbury, and told of her experiences of working and living with Palestinians and Israelis on the volatile border between East and West Jerusalem. She gave birth to her fourth child in Bethlehem when the city was under siege.

Exit: Baroness Andrea von Stumm, who at twenty-seven returned to the fatherland to work for a television company in Munich, leaving behind William Hickey's description of her in the *Daily Express* as 'a cerebral steel heiress who broke many aristocratic hearts'.

Recollections of an Epoch
by Andrea von Stumm

For Naim, with 'celestial' affection!

All cultures have eleven names to divide the visible light frequencies into colours. This seems to be true, regardless of levels of literacy, industrialization or tradition. By sharing in these standard categories – black, white, grey, red, blue, brown, yellow and so on – our own culture confirms this surprising rule. The only exceptions occur within ethnicities that gather under one name the combinations of two colours: blue and green, red and pink or orange and yellow. These therefore use only ten visual names, or so the *Proceedings of the National Academy of Sciences* for 22 July 2003 inform us. Various controversial talents, as diverse as Baudelaire (*Correspondences*), Rimbaud (sonnets or vocals), Wagner, Scriabin, Kandinsky and Nabokov, are endowed with the gift to project – rather then perceive – emotions, or even mathematics, in terms of specific colours. The technical term for such phenomena is synaesthesia.

Well, dear Naim, that is all as may be, but I have to say I suffer from partial colour blindness so far as my memory of my Namara House days is concerned. Peaks of luminosity, and the lack of them, punctuate my spectrum of bygone times. Whole stretches of the past merge into a rather blurred light and dark, a chiaroscuro that one might call affective insignificance. So please forgive me for depicting in this sketch of a privileged epoch only certain subjective flashes in the mind, reminders of an age before they and we became digital.

Beyond remembering your shrill ties, your ostentatiously ill-assorted socks and your flamboyant, colourful self, it is the brightness in the gloomiest days that I shall always recall most vividly. Thanks to you, every day brought some new insight. Learning was fun. As to the flashes of light, they were galore to one who was your personal assistant. The fascination with the unusual often upsets one's sense of balance. By that I mean not only a tendency to talk about oneself while declaiming generalities (my French education), but also because I venture to suggest that, in different ways, we shared a peculiar addiction to disorder.

Cringe not! What I mean is that, unlike other successful people, you are not a one-track-minded person. You are much too curious to follow tramlines of taste and do not believe the fastest route will follow a straight line. Organized chaos, given your lucid mind and Levantine charm, produced the most creative sparks. (Too sad that I arrived after your forays into music producing and film-making.)

I always marvelled at how, in the course of just one day, you could generate so much energy around you. You *are* a generator, which is at its most efficient in situations of power failure, besides being a magnet in eliciting allegiance and enthusiasm. Your life, in so far as I can gather from all you have told and written, proves it.

Are you as genuine as you seem, and as naïve as you want to appear? Who knows? What I do know for sure is that you are not entrapped by envy and never bear rancour, neither looking back in anger nor ahead with suspicion. Trenchant but not harsh, you are a well-meaning, deeply good person, but always careful not to let anyone tread on your toes. In disappointment, you always struggled hard, surmounting setbacks with panache. Your family – the pillar of pragmatic wisdom and unconditional support throughout your life – deserves much of the credit for your manifold achievements. As I said when we spoke the other day, your wife is a hero in my vision of your personal saga! My devoted affection for you is also rooted in my esteem and admiration for Maria – and for Ramsay.

But to return to recollections of that epoch. Could I type in those days. Yes, with two fingers. Did my LSE degree qualify me for the job? No, not really. Did I have an Oxbridge accent? By Jove, noooh! Was I the first to arrive and the last to leave? No comment. Yet the alchemy worked. Having been given the benefit of the doubt, I was given the job, and it was all due to an introduction by a mutual friend; the friend and gentleman in question being Algy Cluff. What an unlikely combination you two made: he, flying his eternal silver-grey tie; you, your phosphorescent ones, as big as flags. He, wearing his late uncle's work watch; yours all gold and glitter. He, elevating discretion to the point of mannerism; you, provoking attention in purest dandy tradition (or am I inverting roles?). Be that as it may, Algy was the epitome of understatement and discretion; and you, of exuberance and extremes. As for me, I was considered a member of the 'eurotrash set', with multilingual non-chalance as its lucky scar.

If opposites attract, then your association in publishing (through the *Literary Review* and *Apollo*, I forget what else) crystallized an alliance of interests and spirit. You and Algy shared, beyond appearances, a relentless drive for knowledge, the same humanistic, generous selflessness, a need for recognition and, above all, an attuned sense of humour and honour. A broad tolerance helped with electing your affinities. You also shared a trust and affection for me. I owe to both of you what have been among the happiest times of my life.

What we all had in common was curiosity – for life, for people, for the 'exploration and drilling' for ideas. (Did that make us idealists? Don't ask me.) Curiosity may kill cats, but it cements deep and lasting bonds between people. Curiosity is a drug, and its cure is a weakness requiring strength, an upwards march and ascending a cliff (not Cluff – frog humour for the bored reader, sorry!). Curiosity is dangerous. It often involves risk-taking, a facet of your personality stressed in your earlier *mémoires* which will keep you eternally young. He who loses that also loses the ability to marvel and to fight, to give and receive – the humility to let experience temper impulse. I could go on and on (my French education again).

Bref. I listened a lot and relished doing so in admiration and awe. Today I thank you for the FUN – for fun it was! Then, however, I was idiotically unaware of the transitory nature of happy times . . . Now, what do I remember in particular, other than one book that excited us no end, *The Palestinians* by Jonathan Dimbleby, which helped open my eyes to their plight, and a memorable, hilarious trip to the Frankfurt Book Fair?

- Can't remember exact dates.
- Remember vividly not the whiffs but the positive tornadoes of eau de toilette that preceded your arrival in the office, where I sat rubbing my eyes.
- Therefore not being surprised when you decided to create your own perfumes, even though, in those days, i.e. still a flower of innocence, your 'naiming' them 'Avant l'Amour' and 'Après l'Amour' did not altogether convince me. (More French lack of subtlety.)
- Being constantly amazed by how you paddled through the Babylonian stack of papers on your desk with an efficiency assisted by the fact that I had not touched any of it.
- What *did* I do, in fact, apart from answering the phone and providing an often puzzled witness to your conversations, decisions and dealings? Fog.
- Being most impressed by your barking into a battery of telephones to the general drift of 'What's new?', 'How much?', 'When?', 'Why?', 'Immediately!'

- How, having rallied and mobilized your troops, you went on to what really amused you: to let people come and go, talking of whatever subject or project they had in mind, all the while being your open-minded maverick self.
- In between came conversations with Asprey. Fog again.
- You occasionally asking me to fetch a coffee, and me doing so, despite my French distaste – for it was repulsive – but happy to smoke a guilty cigarette.
- Lunches in the basement, all sorts of fascinating people accepting invitations: occasions known for their entertainment value (you) and their gourmet quality (achieved by pretty lady cooks). Being asked to assist on occasions, though these were all too few and far between for my liking.
- Afternoons. More phone calls, more meetings, more unabated vitality (yours), for by then, quite often, (my) desk-dreaming had begun.

I also remember vividly how it was to wake up every morning looking forward to the day, how bicycling across town to get to Poland Street was pure joy. Loads of working people never had such luck.

The flashiness that helped you forge your public image (never a mask – I just discovered in a French dictionary that the English translation of *ludique*, which I would have thought to be 'playfulness', is 'Cartesian devil' [*Hachette*, 1946]) was offset by the discretion you have always shown as a private man, coupled with a paradoxical disregard for mundane values. An acquired expertise in selective *refoulement* of reality's and personal shortcomings is perhaps not a moral strength but can be a mental one: casting a beam to light the way for those who, 'day and night, never nearer to their goal, feel the trouble of a wanderer in their soul'. In that sense, too, we are a little similar. I often miss you, and wish I could come to London more frequently. *Insh'allah*.

With a mischievous twinkle in my heart and mucho love from Spain, where I now live,

Your loner friend and fan club all in one, Andrea.

*   *   *

Stephen Pickles was a talented young man of some distinction who had worked for a number of years at a classical record shop in Great Marlborough Street, round the corner from Namara House. I used to buy my classical CDs in the shop and in due course a kind of friendship grew up between us that resulted in his joining Quartet to oversee the editorial department. The first personal contribution that he made to Quartet was his book *Queens*, a brilliant study of some of those who inhabit the London gay scene. Glamorous and sordid by turns, it described, among many characters, 'The Northern Queen', 'The

Opera Queen', 'The Screaming Queen', 'The YMCA Queen' and 'The Rent Boy'. The elements of drama, documentary, diary and monologue were brought together to create what was the first mainstream book to chart the labyrinths of gay metropolitan life. It combined sympathy with acid comment and was both an anatomy of a subculture and a virtuosic celebration. *Queens* received critical acclaim while also achieving commercial success.

Pickles was a formidable character, gifted with prodigious talent and singularity of mind. His mood swings could sometimes seem bewildering and contradictory and he was uncompromising in his judgements. In that respect he ressembled Auberon Waugh: if he got a bee in his bonnet about someone, his dislike would manifest itself in no uncertain terms. My own relationship with Pickles was consistently cordial and warm, and I do not recall any discord between us during the time he remained with Quartet. Anthony Blond, in his autobiography *Jew Made in England* (Timewell Press and Elliott & Thompson, 2004), described him as someone who had influenced my musical tastes, coaxing me from Tchaikovsky to Bartók. He then went on to paint a little word picture of Pickles:

> Delicate in stature and address, with big swimming eyes, he passed so much of his life propping up the bar in the Coach and Horses in Romilly Street that I warned him he might get clamped.
>
> Pickles was tricky and touchy, a militant homosexual with an air of having been scarred in some terrible romantic battle. He loved Naim and glowed . . . when complimented by him. Naim, on the other hand, when accused by a not totally sober Pickles of homophobia, one evening at the Frankfurt Book Fair, just smiled.

The office Pickles occupied at Goodge Street became like a Chinese opium den of the nineteenth century, but filled with books and personal treasures rather than narcotic fumes. It always remained locked, for it was his very private domain where no chance intruder might trespass.

The contribution that Pickles made to the eclecticism of Quartet's list in giving it a more emphatic literary orientation was tremendous. During his years as editorial director he lifted the imprint's literary output to place it on a level with the likes of the Penguin Modern Classics. The Encounters series grew to the point where it contained over a hundred titles, representing on the British publishing scene an unprecedented selection of European novels of outstanding merit. It was a brave attempt to bring European twentieth-century literature to a wider audience at a time when the political link with Europe was becoming an actuality. Commercial success eluded us, it is true, but perhaps that was because we were ahead of the field. The critical acclaim was resounding and established Quartet's image as an imprint that left no avenue unexplored in its search for innovative ideas.

There will be a later chapter to present a full assessment of the impact and significance of the Encounters list. Meanwhile here is a brief round-up of critical opinion. The *Daily Telegraph* wrote how, 'Since 1985, Quartet publishers have been doing their bit to promote a free market in European writing with the "Encounters" imprint, which offers translations of work by distinguished, and sometimes neglected, modern European authors.' 'The best of world writing in translation, Quartet Encounters has an editorial policy of real vision and imagination. Long may it flourish,' wrote Gabriel Josipovici. John Banville in the *Observer* said, 'Quartet are to be warmly commended for their courage and enterprise in making available to English-speaking readers so many modern European authors'; and Michael Tanner wrote, 'Quartet Encounters strikes me as one of the most enterprising and worthwhile ventures in contemporary publishing.' 'Not only extraordinary variety,' said John Bayley, 'but remarkable quality too. A comparativists' paradise.' The *Spectator* was even more fulsome in its praise: 'The series as a whole is a landmark in responsible, original and stimulating publishing.'

Pickles also acted as mentor to the host of gifted young men and women who flocked to Quartet to exercise their talents in an environment free of conventional humbug. There was no doubt he could be brutally frank on occasions when his tolerance wore thin, but his influence was far-reaching and enduring.

Twenty-six

In 1985 an event took place that was stranger than fiction. It began as a whimsical exercise in curiosity. Word had reached my ears of a beautiful Syrian girl called Rana Kabbani, said to be full of cultural graces and exceptional talents. She was married, twice, to the Palestinian poet, Mahmoud Darwish, and when the marriage failed the second time she left Paris, where she was living, and returned to Damascus, the city of her birth. There, I was told, she was contemplating her future. The details were sketchy, but the more I heard about her the more intrigued I became. I grew intent on finding out as much as I could before making any overtures. In time the pieces of the jigsaw came together to reveal more: she was a Cambridge graduate who had broken many hearts during her sojourn at the university; an Eastern beauty who was endowed with outstanding intellectual gifts; a woman whose abilities could take her in any direction she chose.

I became determined to bring her into the Quartet fold. My obsessive nature gave me no rest until I had managed to track her down. As we spoke on the telephone I found myself babbling about a job at Quartet to someone who was a complete stranger. She must have thought me a dangerous lunatic, ringing from London for a reason beyond her comprehension.

That conversation was the first of many. In the end I persuaded her to pack her bags and head for the airport and a new life. The strangest thing about the whole business was that neither of us had laid eyes on the other, yet both were willing to be hostages to fate. For me it was an inspired gamble, though I cannot guess what went through Rana's mind. That is why she has penned her side of the story especially for this book and given me permission to reproduce it along with a letter she wrote a week after joining Quartet. My own recollection is as vivid and vibrant today as it was when she came into my office for the first time, bringing with her a bright light that somehow illuminated the premises.

Naim's Harem
by Rana Kabbani

I came to London in 1985 in answer to a job offer from Naim Attallah.

I had lived in many of the world's great cities – Damascus, New York,

Djakarta, Washington, Beirut, Paris, Tunis, Cambridge – and was native to the very oldest of them, Damascus. But London would prove to be the most significant for me. It was the place I came to consider my home, where I would throw myself into work and political causes; where I would marry and have children; where I would make my most important, sustaining and wonderful friendships. And all because of Naim, that improbable *deus ex machina*.

I had lived in England before, spending three years at Jesus College, Cambridge. From there I came away with a PhD, my first published book and something of a broken heart. My plan was to return to my country of origin and look for a university teaching post, which was what I did in 1985. Syria in the meantime had become a very sinister place. Two years earlier an armed uprising by the Muslim Brotherhood had been put down by the regime in the most violent and ruthless manner, resulting in a massacre in the city of Hama, where thousands of civilians were slaughtered. The regime then extended its crackdown to crush all dissent and, besides, every shade of Islamist, targeted leftists, communists, Nasserites, students, poets, teachers and actors – activists and intellectuals of every kind. These found themselves in horrifying dungeons from which there was often no way out alive. In this way they were silenced from speaking out against the macabre methods of the state. Thus did many of my generation perish and join the unaccounted for, the 'disappeared', who to this day in Syria number some 14,000 missing.

To survive in the country, get a job, remain free, remain alive, one had to show total allegiance to Big Brother. The army was on the street; the vicious security services ruled everywhere, helping themselves to whatever and whom- ever they wanted. You crossed them at your peril. I had applied to the English faculty at Damascus University to teach the nineteenth-century literature that had always been my passion. I was well qualified for the job, but it was soon made clear to me that I would only get it if I became a Baath party member. But I was not a joiner and one-party rule sickened me.

My family had been deeply implicated in the making of Syria's history. On both sides its members had respectively served the Ottoman Empire, fought the Ottoman Empire, fought French colonial rule and been imprisoned; had penned the Syrian constitution, had thrown themselves into establishing democratic elections after independence; had been elected to ministries and premierships; had been outstanding citizens and patriots; had used their personal fortunes and patrician positions to serve their country in every con- ceivable field. It may therefore have been in my genes to look askance at the angry country boys who had come to power on the back of tanks, replacing a budding, democratic Syria with fascism and thuggery. Urbane, middle-class professionals had already left the country, realizing that Baathist Syria saw them as class enemies and would never treat them with justice. Yet still I lingered a little longer. I did not want to be cut off from my language and family, or to become dispossessed – the invariable fate of exiles.

Then a man I had never heard of, let alone met, began to ring me persistently from London, insisting he had a job for me. Since he sounded like a demented cartoon character, calling me 'Dahling' in an extraordinary accent and an over-excited manner, I became intrigued. I promised I'd consider his offer, but this wasn't good enough. Naim Attallah wouldn't leave it there, but rang me every day, four times a day, demanding to know when I would arrive. He cajoled, scolded, joked, pleaded, ordered. Finally I cracked and thought it best to get on a plane to London. It is only now, as I write this twenty years later, that I realize Naim Attallah probably saved my life.

Quartet Books, where I arrived to work, was in a broken-down area off the Tottenham Court Road, miles away from the gentrified bit of Kensington where I was staying. The buildings were Dickensian in their ramshackle mess; everyone working there looked like a character from a novel – lush, mad, exotic and highly strung, with a hilarious sense of humour. Naim operated, like the Wizard of Oz, from somewhere else and was still no more than a voice to me as I climbed the stairs to find my office. I was in luck. The spirit of the place, a man possessed of the most beautiful eyes I had ever seen, Stephen Pickles, took a shine to me. With my very high heels and very long hair, my scarlet nail polish and lipstick, I was everything his rigorous, homosexual rules wanted a woman to be – overtly feminine and utterly unapproachable.

Pickles at once voted me the perfect arm candy to take to swish London parties. We settled into a comfortable routine: books and gossip by day; more books and gossip on our evening prowls. It would have been hard to find two more contented cats. In Pickles I had discovered a sensitive, ferociously well-read, elegant and sardonic navigator and translator. London was a mysterious place where everyone spoke in code. Thanks to Pickles I was given the key to break the code, and very soon break it I did.

On my first morning, right on cue, having checked me out first, Pickles walked me through a few streets and across Oxford Street to meet Naim. We went into the most amazing office, full of colours I had never seen used before on walls and floors in such extravagant profusion. Entering Naim's inner sanctum was a mind-altering experience: all shocking pinks and animal skins and precious, eroticized objects. Naim himself was larger than life: very tall, elegant in a startling and unforgettably vivid way, with an amazing lining to his jacket and a brilliant tie. His features were all wrong if you took their components separately, but joined together they made a unique and loveable face that was forever working itself up into spasms of high excitement, like a child's. Pickles slipped easily into being the gruff, nonchalant, understating foil to his boss's florid dramas, and I could see within a few seconds that everything was going to be fine. I had landed in a sort of recherché zoo, and being a wild animal myself – part panther, part peacock – I began to feel immensely happy.

'Is your office comfortable, my dahling?' Naim enquired as he hugged me again and again, as though recognizing a soul-mate.

'No,' I said as petulantly as I could manage. 'My office is awful, because there's no bed in it, and I need a bed so I can have a siesta in the afternoon, as I always do at home.'

Naim froze in horror – not, as it turned out, in a reaction to my utterly preposterous demand but because he felt he had been found wanting.

'We must get you a bed at once!' he announced, turning pale. 'Pickles, who should we call? Harrods?'

Next morning I had a bed, which soon became the social focus of the building, just as in a student bedsit. Pickles would sometimes sit on it as he ploughed through a typescript he was working on. Then rumour began to circulate that this was no mere bed, but a harem divan covered in silks that Naim had had made for the new Sultana Valideh, who could wrap him round her little finger and made her terrifying demands in Arabic. Quartet was a rumour mill and the pecking order among Naim's harem of women employees was as ferocious as it must have been at Topkapi. The bed story duly reached the ears of the two Great Beauties who shared an office down-stairs: Nigella Lawson and Rebecca Fraser, who had shared power quite amicably prior to my arrival. Rebecca, who possessed a fierce intelligence, extraordinary beauty and the skills of a virtuoso fencing master, decided she must see for herself what was going on. She came up to introduce herself, saying we must have lunch in a few days. On her way out of the office she smiled and said in her most imperious tone, pointing at the bed, 'Oh! How sweet!' Thus I was put in my place for ever as her second in command.

In this respect, too, Naim had come to my rescue, saving me from existential loneliness in the England that gradually became my home through a precious introduction to the formidable Rebecca Fraser. She was to become my dearest friend, and her family was to adopt me as yet another wild and wayward 'gel'. Her clan – generous, rowdy, erudite, affectionate, supportive and inhumanly clever – was all you could wish for. Rebecca's mother, Lady Antonia Fraser, and Rebecca's sister Flora also became my adored friends. Her daughter, Atalanta Fitzgerald, born years after our Quartet era, is my goddaughter, of whom I am more than usually proud.

Naim had an uncanny ability to talent-spot. Many of those he employed, or whose careers he supported or encouraged, became high-flyers in their fields. A list of their names would come close to constituting a British cultural who's who. Despite an *embarrasse de richesse*, my favourite of Naim's 'discoveries' is the use made in Jonathan Dimbleby's book *The Palestinians* of photographs by Don McCullin, showing haunting images of people in refugee camps. Don was then known only as a photo-journalist within press circles, but he has since come to rank, quite rightly, as one of the world's most moving, profound and serious artists. Naim could see this quality from the start. But then Naim was always in advance of everyone else, blazing ahead in a flurry of ideas and enthusiasms. It always makes me secretly pleased that a maverick Palestinian, and a self-made one at that, should have had such a profound effect on English society, giving such a tremendous leg-up to so many of its gifted sons and daughters from such a range of social backgrounds.

Whenever he entertained he was wildly extravagant and generous. His parties – whether they were seated affairs for a few in his office, with delicious food served by stunning employees, or cocktail gatherings for hundreds of the famous, where champagne flowed and canapés never stopped circulating – were forerunners in the 1980s of what would become 'lifestyle' events in the 1990s. No one in England, certainly no publisher, had thought before to entertain as he did. He was the king of parties. Everyone who was anyone wanted to be included. Other people's book launches were shrivelled, mean, puritanical affairs by comparison, with undrinkable plonk.

The person I came to worship most at Quartet was Olive, Naim's amazing accountant. She was a great woman, 'worth a guinea a minute', as Jeremy Beale, my fellow editor, liked to describe her. Olive was matter-of-fact and funny at the same time. She came out with the best throwaway one-liners I have ever heard, delivered in her inimitable Aberdonian accent. She was scary and made you want to behave; and behave I always did, when she was around at least. I was dumbfounded when, on the eve of my marriage, she called me up to her office and gave me the most beautiful porcelain candlesticks and bonbonnière, ornately worked with delicate grey and gold roses. These, she told me, had been given as a present at her own marriage, half a century before. To this day they remain my most treasured possessions.

Working at Quartet was a dream. I was doing what I liked – reading and editing books. I was partying with friends and discovering a great city, all on Naim's time and pay. No boss could have been more magnanimous or asked for so little in return. He allowed me to be myself – lazy, free, crazy and ungovernable. He understood me instinctively and never tried to change me.

If only the men I became involved with could have had his wisdom! I loved him then, as a true and great friend, and all the years that have since passed have never dimmed the memory of that first phone call.

*   *   *

The letter Rana wrote me soon after arriving in London was as follows:

> Dear Naim – A strange Sunday afternoon this as I read *The Shah of Shahs*. This Polish man [the distinguished journalist Ryszard Kapuscinski who died recently] knows more about our displaced history than all the specialists; for in the end, it is his own wound which he is describing, his own country's wrench between fragrant church and the sorrowing democrat's dream. Certain lines stay in my mind like Mozart's phrases: ousted politicians entering history, blinded children singing their pointless tragedies – all of our untidiness is here, all our panic and passion.
>
> I go for a walk in the park on this first Sunday of my new existence. I'm settling in with the frenzy of a bird after rain. A woman on a nearby bench is exiled in a particular sorrow. She must be Iranian, her eyebrows and hair come straight out of Hafiz. She sits on this green bench in remote Holland Park – how very far from Tabriz! A park full of exiles stunned by the sudden sun.
>
> I'm happy, and bursting with language. I think our commerce will be rich beyond calculation. Leave me some scope to wander and some freedom to dash off to Beijing when the mood hits me and I will always meander back to the genteelly shabby premises of drab Goodge Street. Whatever I make of myself in the heady and luxuriant years to come will be of your making too. I am so excited by possibilities, by the wandering restless fanatical mind's voyages. And I am utterly contented in the choice I've made to come under your wing.
>
> Yours, Rana

During her time at Quartet, Rana married my good friend, the writer Patrick Seale. I was a witness at their wedding in the registry office. My admiration and love for her have never wavered throughout the years: it is a friendship for perpetuity.

Today she lives with her husband and family in Paris, working as an essayist and historian. As the author of *Letter to Christendom*, a reasoned attempt to convey the essence and truth of Muslim culture to Westerners, she has become an important voice for Islamic womanhood. Prejudice, she says, has always been a part of the West's attitude towards Islam. 'Arab-hating remains the last permissible form of racism,' she told Suzie Mackenzie in an interview for the *Guardian* in 1991. The West has always had a vested interest in lumping together the world's eight hundred million Muslims as barbarians, who would be lost, it thinks, without the West's 'civilizing' influence. Fifteen years later, with the war in Iraq continuing as a 'peace' operation, her views sound prophetic.

> For politicians in the West [she said], the most dangerous thing is to portray Iraqis as normal human beings. Far better to see them as people who don't matter, don't suffer. If they are Arabs, somehow they must deserve it. People want to believe their prejudices are there for a good reason . . .
>
> There is [for a migrant in exile] a great pressure to confirm to Western audiences what they have been led to believe. And you are rewarded for that. Britain has had 300 years of colonial power, secular power, affluent power. I come from a world which is poorer, less powerful, that has had much suffering, and I owe it emotionally to that world to look at it more profoundly, honestly. But I do not want to denounce it completely. If I do that, who am I? I am lost to both worlds. My history determines me.

She saw herself and her husband as, from their different angles, bridges between the two worlds. Her social role in the West was important: 'to challenge your assumptions. The immigrants who make up [the new minorities in] Britain can revive your [Western] culture in all kinds of ways through the cultures they come from.'

*

In September 1985 I was putting the finishing touches to the planned launch of two perfumes I had created. One was called 'Avant l'Amour', the other 'Après l'Amour'. As a preview to the launch, which was scheduled for the end of October, samples were being tested at various events to gauge the public reaction. One such occasion was a party to celebrate the publication by André Deutsch of *A Turbulent Decade: The Diaries of Auberon Waugh, 1976–1985*. Bron himself wrote up the event for his *Private Eye* 'Diary':

TUESDAY
To Gnome House for the publishing event of the century. Not since Shakespeare's First Folio appeared in 1622 has there been anything like it. All the elegance, beauty and talent in London parade themselves on the floodlit lawns. In silk-walled drawing-rooms there are fountains of champagne with lovely topless Quartettes splashing in them (by gracious permission of His Highness Sir Naim Attallah), disguised as mermaids, to the sublime music of the London Symphony Orchestra playing snatches from Gilbert and

Sullivan; . . . [in] those familiar rooms, the scene of so many momentous events, where now the indescribably delicious perfumes of Avant l'Amour and Après l'Amour compete tantalizingly with each other.

A lot of press coverage followed. The *Sunday Times* announced my foray into the world of beauty by calling me the whimsical entrepreneur whose Parfums Namara was bringing out two scents, the 'sweet relaxing Après l'Amour and the more stirring Avant l'Amour'. My secretary, Amanda Lyster, told them 'this is the latest venture by a man who likes to try all walks of life'. The *Sunday Express* went for a more sensational approach, citing my liking for pretty girls, the unashamed names I had chosen for the scents and then quoting the blurb:

Enter my fragrant world and discover the age-old secret of perfume's seductive spell . . . For the women whose nights of passion dissolve into clear mornings of tenderness and tranquillity, I bring Avant and Après l'Amour . . . They are created out of love, created for women who enjoy love and dare to show it . . .

In retrospect, I should have used less flowery language but I let my enthusiasm run away with me. I would have achieved far less in life without this tendency, however, even if it did occasionally expose me to comments that verged on ridicule. The launch party was an exotic affair. Charlotte Faber's creativity as usual knew no bounds. She dressed eight of the Namara girls, including several from Quartet, in rubber dresses with laces up the back and velvet at the hem and collar. Four of the dresses were in white rubber, and four in black. It needed a lot of talcum powder to squeeze the girls into the garments, and much giggling was involved as they struggled and helped each other. But once they were in they looked weirdly evocative – 'rather like Sloanes in bondage', as one journalist went so far as to put it. Then a problem no one had foreseen occurred to them. If one of them needed to go to the loo, she was going to have to take the dress off first, and there was no way she could cope with the manoeuvre on her own. 'You will just have to go in twos,' I told them.

The guest list was fragrant with aristocratic, political and social names. Auberon Waugh was accompanied by his daughter Sophia. Others included Tony Lambton, Annabel Heseltine, Vanessa Llewellyn with her estranged husband Dai, Laura Ashley's son Nick, the model Camilla Scott and Christina Oxenburg. Two huge promotional bottles containing three thousand pounds' worth of the perfumes were on display, prompting Henry Porter of the *Sunday Times* to be fearful that, 'if one should fracture, it could represent a considerable hazard to either the emotions or the ecology of Central London'. The *Observer* described me as scurrying around, 'like a gleeful genie out of one of his own cut-glass bottles, giving away samples in frilly velvet pouches'. Anna Groundwater, Quartet's PR person, went on to a fashionable restaurant after the party, still wearing her rubber dress. She claimed that all the diners rose to give her a standing ovation.

Even 'the ebullient Attallah', the *Observer* said the next week, 'has been amazed by the response; people *want* his scent'.

> Harrods has taken it exclusively for the first two weeks of its new perfume hall; it's selling well, and from next week it will be available in other major stores, at £75 for a ½-oz bottle and £30 for a 2-oz bottle of *eau de parfum*. For which prices you could buy a goodly number of books.

Namara was now definitely in the perfume business. An office was established in Paris, run by a very attractive lady, Annie Faure, to oversee the marketing and distribution on a worldwide basis. In London, all the famous stores, along with Harrods, were maintaining a stock; Harvey Nichols, Fortnum & Mason and Selfridges were among the first to take it. Elizabeth Arkus, arguably the doyenne of the French beauty industry, wrote a piece for the magazine *Les Nouvelles Esthétiques*, printed opposite a full-page picture that juxtaposed the stretched-back silhouette of a beautiful naked young woman with one of the bottles, its sensuous shape adapted from an art-nouveau design. 'Perfume is always being reborn,' said Elizabeth Arkus. 'Who,' she asked, 'will be the woman to choose "Avant l'Amour" and who the one to choose "Après l'Amour"?'

> What, you don't yet know these amazing perfumes produced by Namara, i.e. Naim Attallah? The first comes in a black glass bottle, the second in a container of the same sculpted shape, but transparent as (a very relative!) innocence regained. Both bottles have the same shape, with a broad base and a carved phallic stopper. This is the first time we have been presented so boldly with a passionate perfume in such a frankly erotic flask.

Avant she characterized as, 'dark, mysterious and deep as night'. Its fine floral fragrance carried an element of chypre and a 'trace of tuberose hinting at sin'; its lingering scent of musk was 'archly tinged with iris and peach'. Après was also floral, 'with a hint of powder . . . made sensual with vanilla, elegant with myrrh'. 'Avant is full of warmth, Après is bright, joyful, scintillating.'

> They certainly do not leave us indifferent. And since the perfume was created to gratify the senses, we hope [Naim Attallah] will continue to

astonish, amuse us or trouble us. Will he produce the perfume of the twenty-first century?

All the posters advertising the perfumes were shot to a high graphic standard and the Namara girls took turns to act as models in promoting them. Jubby Ingrams was without doubt the model *par excellence*. She displayed a natural affinity with the product and was always willing to try out some novel idea. Her delightfully mischievous responses were inspired, and watching her turn a photo session into a hilarious event was pure joy. From then on *Private Eye* began to refer to me as the 'seedy parfumier' in addition to its usual sobriquet of 'Attullah-Disgusting'.

Peter McKay, in the *Mail on Sunday*, wondered what anxieties about his twenty-year-old daughter went through the head of the proprietor of *Private Eye*, Richard Ingrams, as he sat pounding away at the organ of his parish church, knowing she had been 'the model on a suggestive colour poster designed to advance the sales of a new scent' concocted by her employer, who was quoted as having boasted, 'I have created the perfumes of love.' 'When I called this man a seedy parfumier,' Richard Ingrams was said to have countered, 'he called in Jubby and asked her what "seedy" meant.'

Two years after the perfume party Jubby remembered her white rubber dress without any fondness. 'First of all,' she told an interviewer for the *Telegraph Sunday Magazine*, 'it's freezing cold on bare skin and it takes half an hour to get on. And once it is on, it's impossible to go to the loo, and I look like a top-heavy milk bottle. I can't wear any knickers under it. I can't walk fast in it. My boobs bulge out at the front and fat bulges through laces at the back. I sweat in it and when I finally manage to peel it off, I stink of rubber.'

*   *   *

Quartet published three coffee-table books in the autumn of 1985, each in its different way thoroughly eccentric and bizarre. The first was *Eighties in the Shade*, a collection of photographs by Arabella McNair-Wilson with a text by Adrian Woodhouse. The blurb launched into a gush to explain who the subjects of the photos were:

> They're talented, they're tantalizing, they're the toast of their generation. Who are they? They're the Eighties Girls, who combine brains and beauty more stunningly than those from any previous decade. Here, for the first time, the Eighties Girls have been captured and collected.

These representatives of their generation, who were 'making the most of Britain in the Eighties – and whom Britain should be making the most of', included cooks and countesses, circus artistes and stockbrokers, who had all agreed to be placed before the camera of a gifted young photographer and to undergo the interrogation of an incisive young columnist. There were eighty of them in all, and to give a flavour of the book they included Emma Hope, shoemaker, Joely Richardson, actress, Sophie Hicks, fashion editor (later an architect), Anne Somerset, historian, Penny McDonald, journalist, Jessica Berens, pop writer, Charlotte Faber, inventor, Teresa Manners, gossip-column fodder, Candida Crewe, writer, and Natasha Richardson, another actress. The 'champagne-showjumper, the girl who is knocking Paris into a wine glass, the girl who put chocolate on the map' were there, the blurb continued, along with seventy-seven others

> who show that British girls are the brightest and best-looking in the world. People have suspected that for years. *Eighties in the Shade*, with its words and pictures, provides the proof.

The *Observer* noted how the girl on the cover was Charlotte Faber, 'an erstwhile member of the Naim team' who had designed the rubber dresses the Namara girls wore at the perfume launch. At twenty pounds the book was 'little more than a photographic catalogue of yet more stunners and ravers (and some achievers) of the upper crust'. Inevitably some ex-Quartettes featured in it, including Candida Crewe and Emma Williams. 'Why do they work for him?' the *Observer* wondered. ' "He makes it so exciting," said an Amanda.'

> Naim reckons it's the lack of hierarchy; his personal explanation for his classy entourage . . . he says merely that he grew up surrounded by women and always prefers their company. 'Is that so strange?' In England, perhaps, yes.

An envious commentator was then quoted as saying, 'I never quite under-stand what Naim's up to. Is he social climbing? Is he a propagandist for Palestine? Where does the money come from? He must be up to something. Those without a suspicious nature might say that he is up to having a ball.' I may have been a puzzle to some, but the last point hit the nail on the head. *Eighties in the Shade* prompted Wendy Ledrum of *Nouvelle* to say, 'If you really want to be where-it-is-at, follow a Quartet party. Always enormous fun. It's like being in a 3-D *Tatler* page. Everyone young and talented is there for the spotting.'

Another of the three books was *Forbidden Dreams* by Rebecca Blake, originally published by Quartet Inc. in the United States the previous year, consisting of seventy-eight highly individual and sometimes profoundly disquieting images. Rebecca Blake had been a fashion photographer, working for all the leading fashion magazines since 1972. These images derived from her work, but took it into another dimension with 'photographs that sear – and chill – with a dry-ice intensity', as the blurb described their effect. The conventions of portraiture gave way to themes that came through from the unconscious, sometimes cinematic and touching on the violent and the ambiguous. There were layers of meaning in a world that belonged to the night after the 'normal' life of daylight hours had packed up and gone home.

The party for this one had been held in New York and become a glamorous assembly of the city's artistic set and a roaring success. Rebecca Blake had arranged it and we made our own contribution to the guest list, with Marilyn Warnick and Catherine Norden, both stalwarts of our New York office, helping with the organization. I attended with Ros Forestier-Walker, formerly PR for Quartet London. The beautiful people loved every minute and were reluctant to leave when the party closed. Quartet was becoming very well known in the Big Apple, and gaining a lot of recognition for the diversity of its product and its flare for 'bold publishing'. To be British was also an advantage at the time. The ex-pat enclave consisted of the most sought-after girls from London. They walked tall and were much in demand, as Compton Miller reported in the *Daily Express*:

> You only have to watch local TV soap operas to understand why American men might climb the Trump Tower for them. My top ten for class, style and wit must include: the new 'in' model Victoria Lockwood, banking heiress Sabrina Guinness, publishing assistant Evgenia Citkovitz, painter Laura Faber, Princess Elizabeth of Yugoslavia's daughter Christina Oxenburg, assistant Françoise Gillard, Naim Attallah's Girl Friday Catherine Norden, West Indies heiress Sarah St George, cover girl Isabel Townsend and film costume designer Eliza Dugdale.

Ros Forestier-Walker, who accompanied me to New York, had a most varied career at Namara House. First she worked with Bertram Rope in Namara Public Relations, then moved to Quartet to become a publicist.

Namara House, 1983–5
by Ros Forestier-Walker

The first thing I was told by the others on joining Namara House in September 1983 was: 'Don't get too close to Naim, like Icarus you will fly too near to the sun'; and: 'Above all, don't let him invite you to the Frankfurt Book Fair.'

Like many completely useless English Lit. graduates, my main ambitions were either (1) to be a famous novelist or (2) a high-powered fiction editor. My entrée into publishing was via Namara PR, whose clients disappointingly were Wimpey Construction and Crown House Engineering. My first task was to write a feature for *Heating and Ventilating Contractors' Association News* (better known in the trade as *HEVAC*). I found myself in a world of *Concrete Quarterly* and *Contract Journal* rather than the *TLS*, the *Spectator* and the *Literary Review*.

Being called up to Naim's exotic penthouse office, furnished with huge leather sofas, was a welcome escape. Naim collected real tiger skins and shiny green plants that gave a tropical theme to the many photographs that he took of his girls. When, only a week after I had started, he asked me to the Frankfurt Book Fair, I was secretly thrilled, but the uproar downstairs at Namara PR was such that I was persuaded to refuse the offer on the grounds that 'my grandmother was coming to stay'.

Twenty-two years later, the 'grandmother' excuse (dead, coming to stay, having a bad turn) never washes with me – as it certainly didn't with Naim. I was sent to Coventry for several weeks, banished to the world of building sites and topping-out ceremonies. We made up eventually and I was promoted to press officer at Quartet Books and moved to Goodge Street.

It was believed that Naim's policy was to 'divide and rule'. The competition between the staff at Quartet was ferocious. Everyone wanted their chance to succeed and opportunities in publishing were fiercely fought over. It is ultimately to Naim's credit that he gave us all the chance – and that so many have developed successful careers from this start. There was an unwritten understanding that Naim's attentions were deemed to be unwanted, whereas in reality everyone wanted to be the 'chosen one'. Naim had a magnetism and energy that were irresistible, but in a typical English manner we all felt compelled to feign reluctance.

One such favour was to be invited to lunch in Naim's private dining-room in the basement of Namara House. Allegedly he had a wine cellar that ran the breadth of Poland Street, though I never saw it. Only imagine the thrill of meeting Ian Hislop, Christopher Hitchens and other journalists and authors!

Shortly after I started my new role at Quartet, Naim asked me to join him in New York to launch a new book, Rebecca Blake's *Forbidden Dreams*. I jumped at the chance. My great friend Catherine Norden had been promoted from working as Naim's PA to helping run the New York office and I looked forward to spending ten days with her in a city I had always wanted to visit. Going anywhere with Naim was an adventure!

We launched *Forbidden Dreams* at the Area night club – a vast underground warren of decadence with living statues of St Sebastien displayed at every corner and in each alcove. I still have polaroids of me and Catherine sporting the new leather jackets Naim asked us to wear at the party.

Back in London, the books I remember most clearly are *Hashish* by Suomi La Valle, *Queens* by Pickles and *Sexual Exercises for Women* by Anon. I remember running after Wayne Sleep as he left the *Hashish* launch party and pressing a copy of the book into his hands. On the publication of *Sexual Exercises*, I promoted the book quite freely to the women's pages of every publication I could think of, without knowing that my predecessor had promised an exclusive to *Good Housekeeping* magazine. When the *Daily Express* printed a full-page feature on *Sexual Exercises*, the editor of *Good Housekeeping* was incandescent.

I don't think I made a very good publicist. My denouement came when Naim was featured as the main profile in the *Observer*. Early that Monday morning I thought: 'I must call Naim immediately – what a fantastic piece,' and then promptly forgot until 3.00 p.m. It was too late. I was fired.

We made it up eventually, but my career moved away from publishing, journalism and PR, and I can safely concur with the view that, as I have never published a word, my initial literary ambitions are unlikely ever to be fulfilled. However, Naim did open my eyes to the endless range of opportunities and surprises that life has to offer and I will always be grateful to him for giving me my first job.

*   *   *

The third book to be mentioned in this round-up was *Tattoo* by Stefan Richter, who had travelled extensively to gather his material. Initially his enterprise aroused suspicion from the artists and their models, but Richter had been able to forge friendships with many of them and gain their confidence. They came from a wide cross-section of society, and were 'normal' in every respect except for their admiration for an ancient art form from the Far East that the West had chosen to relegate to a symbol of decadence. Richter's aim was to restore the tattoo to its rightful status as a visual embellishment of high quality and by so doing reassert the credibility of those who wore them and rescue them from the stigma of freak-show connotations. Many fascinating details emerged about the art and the painstaking perfectionism which always surrounded its creation. *Tattoo* attested to the imaginative brilliance of a select group of artist designers who made the human body their canvas. Yet, as well as beauty and intricacy, some of the designs could also reflect deeply disturbing under-currents, especially when they touched on the bizarre, the occult and the primitive. Then the beauty could be perverted into something so weird that it shocked the senses. There were those who chose to have their entire bodies tattooed from top to toe so that no area of natural flesh remained and even their genitals became hardly distinguishable. For some of them this was a devastatingly flagrant gesture of sheer exhibitionism but the motives of others were perhaps more disturbing.

The book was costly to produce and a great gamble. Some might have found it offensive, representing a desecration of the human body. Others, while appreciating its art, might have found it most unsettling or simply too peculiar. The potential audience for it was an unknown quality and those to whom it could be expected to appeal directly were not likely to be among the ordinary reading public. It was hard to see, either, where it would fit in with traditional press expectations. As it happened, the book's cultish status was to save the day. While it did not become a bestseller, neither was it a failure. The experiment was worth the effort and helped to reinforce the view that Quartet's vision was infinitely enterprising. There were, however, to be consequences I could never have foreseen and which I did not link at first with *Tattoo*.

Every year, when attending the Frankfurt Book Fair, I stayed at the celebrated Nassauer Hof Hotel at Wiesbaden, where I was exceptionally well treated and had a magnificent suite allocated to me. On one of these trips, several years after the publication of *Tattoo*, I ran into problems at Heathrow, before I had even left England, when I found my flight reservations had been cancelled for no apparent reason. I then had a most difficult time securing an alternative flight, but managed it in the end. On arrival at the Nassauer Hof I found an embarrassed staff at reception who were perplexed to see me. Only two days before, they said, my secretary had phoned to cancel my reservation. I assured them that this was not the case. Alas, the hotel was now full to capacity. The reception manager spent a long time on the telephone to try to find me acceptable accommodation, and in the end he secured a suite for me at a nearby hotel that was on a par with my usual accommodation. I checked in at the new hotel with a great sense of relief and a growing suspicion as to who the perpetrator might be.

Despite the good sales we had achieved for *Tattoo*, a dispute had arisen with Stefan Richter over the royalty applicable to five hundred copies which he had himself sold at a fifty-per-cent discount. Quartet maintained that, according to the terms of the contract, the royalties should be calculated on the price received, whereas Richter insisted they should be levied on the full cover price. I held my ground and refused to budge. Richter then became abusive over the telephone, but I would have none of it. He took to haranguing David Elliott on a regular basis, threatening to use less conventional methods, including force if necessary, to get what he saw as his due. I would not be intimidated and told David to take no notice of these ravings. In his last conversation with David, Richter hinted that strong-arm tactics would now be put in motion and I would live to regret my obstinacy.

Richter was a manic personality who, because of his particular interest, frequented a milieu in which psychedelia was the prevailing style and exponents subverted the art of the tattoo by representing visions of the Gothic or the visually provocative, including explicit sexual postures. The sinister shadow of this world fell on the book fair and the question became to what lengths would the disgruntled author be prepared to go? We were soon to find out when David Elliott and I arrived at our stand in the International Hall to be greeted by a pungent smell so nauseating that we had to flee before it overcame us. We alerted security, who quickly confirmed that a powerful chemical compound had been left exposed at the back of the stand, and some of it had been sprayed on the carpet to make sure of its overwhelming effect. The odour was so vile that we could not venture into the vicinity for several hours while the work of removing the residue and thoroughly washing the carpet went ahead. Simultaneously it emerged that pornographic leaflets, showing myself at the centre of an orgy with various naked females – one of them giving me a blow-job while the others ravaged different parts of my body – had been left on every British publisher's stand alongside an obscene poem.

Whenever the Frankfurt Book Fair was on, Richter used to come to it almost every day with his heavily made-up English wife, both of them dressed outlandishly. Her customary gear was a tight black-leather outfit, sometimes with body-hugging trousers to create a highly erotic effect, and a pair of exceptionally elevated high-heeled shoes. She looked like the living subject of an Allen Jones painting. His outfit was in a similar vein, though without the high-heeled shoes, and as an equivalent to her make-up, he usually wore some weird punkish ornaments to signal his bohemian proclivities. We felt sure a visitation from him must be imminent and reported the matter to the police. They showed very little interest in the affair, even though we emphasized he was capable of extreme recklessness and perhaps bold enough to inflict some physical harm. Reluctantly they agreed to question him if he should show up and went away with our full description. Sure enough, as we had anticipated, he was unable to resist the temptation of coming to the fair to survey the havoc his actions had caused. As always he arrived with his wife in tow. She was instantly recognized from her bizarre get-up and apprehended on the spot. Richter was not far away and was similarly stopped. With a disarming smile, he denied all knowledge of anything that had happened and accused us of waging a war of attrition against him for having demanded his proper rights. The police took the matter no further and he was set loose to roam the fair in a defiant mood.

I never stayed the full course at Frankfurt but always returned to London after four nights to get on with other tasks. News of my mishaps had preceded me and Andrew Moncur of the *Guardian* was already at work preparing a diary piece declaring how the Frankfurt Book Fair had 'turned out to be a real stinker – perfectly foul – for Naim Attallah' and trying to account for 'the sheer, ripsnorting campaign of sabotage'. The only thing to be auctioned at Frankfurt, according to one publisher, had been copies of the defamatory leaflet, while the tale of the 'foul stench' had grown in the telling to where it included 'buckets of ordure being dumped around'. 'Who could possibly do these things?' asked Mr Moncur. 'If Quartet has suspicions, it isn't saying.' All he could think of was a dispute with The Women's Press in 1991 that had led to staff changes and angered some of their published authors, though it was inconceivable 'that the faintest trace of suspicion should fall there'.

Meanwhile David had been left holding the fort at Frankfurt prior to its close. As soon as I was out of the way, Richter approached him for a chat in a less bellicose frame of mind. He was still reeling, he said, from our refusal to pay him the full amount of royalties according to his interpretation of the agreement and would be instituting legal proceedings against us in London. None the less Richter managed to sweet-talk David, who was now leaning more towards finding a way to resolve the dispute amicably. The line David took was that *Tattoo*, having been the moderate success it was, could never justify a legal battle that would be to no one's benefit. Leaving principles aside, a sensible approach might save both parties from a mutually damaging confrontation. He told me that, underneath it all, Richter had a soft spot for us both and would love to close the matter on a happy note.

I decided to heed David's advice and paid Richter the additional royalties he was claiming. The following year at Frankfurt he visited the Quartet stand regularly and inscribed a copy of his latest book to me (not published by us) with some warm words that helped to make up for the bad things he had been saying about me twelve months earlier. Richter was a complex character who craved recognition and, according to his own and his wife's account, was prone to fits of depression that involved self-harm. Sometimes, as a result, he became hospitalized, often after frenzied scenes reminiscent of Jean-Jacques Beinex's film *Betty Blue*, where one of the lead protagonists, played by Béatrice Dalle, suffers similar traumas. These episodes were cries for help from a man who sought to give dramatic expression to many of the artistic creations he captured on film. We both recognized the bizarre bond that existed between us, notwithstanding its inexplicability.

Back at Goodge Street, Sophia Waugh, Bron's daughter, was bidding fare-well to Quartet. She had worked there since 1983 and felt that a career change would be beneficial. I leave her to tell her own story.

Looking for Graham Greene
by Sophia Watson (née Waugh)

For a hick from Somerset via Durham, Naim's office was the smartest thing I had ever seen. A top floor in Poland Street, an impossibly glamorous PA/secretary and, at the far end of the room, a big table behind which was Naim. My father, having recently written a piece about publishing, had organized a row of interviews for me. I wasn't at all sure I wanted to be a publisher; was totally sure I wanted to be the next Ellen Terry and take the West End stage by storm, and was equally sure I didn't approve of nepotism. Still . . .

Naim disarmed me at once. Exuberant, warm, enthusiastic (the latter one of his favourite words), I was enthralled by the end of the interview. He hired me on the spot, and made me believe that I would find, among the endless manuscripts sent to Quartet, 'the new Graham Greene'. I had stopped believing in Father Christmas years before, but somehow he returned. I read every manuscript diligently, searching for Graham Greene but never (alas) finding him.

The Quartet days were happy days. I soon discovered that to be one of 'Naim's girls' had a certain cachet. He was famous – and somewhat mocked – for his stable of well-bred girls with surnames. Nigella Lawson, Helena Bonham-Carter, Rebecca Fraser, Sophia Sackville-West were all there at the same time as I was. And yes, we were girls with surnames, but we worked hard as well as played hard.

Naim was famous for his parties – I remember refusing to wear black rubber to one on the grounds I was Catholic – very spurious, but Naim (also Catholic) took the joke and let me off. The parties were theoretically for book publication, but no other publisher gave parties to match them. There was a whole lot more than cheap wine and stale canapés on offer. There were lunches in Naim's basement, too – how pleased we were to be called to these delicious, elegant meals with the great and good of the writing world.

My father worked in London and we would meet for lunch – a dozen oysters and vodka-martini cocktails before I wove my way back to my duties at the desk. On dull days, my friend Emma Lancaster and I competed to see who could type rejection letters fastest (with their toes), but on the whole we did work hard.

I only stayed a year with Naim. I was asked to go and work for Edmund

Fisher's new publishing company. It was a promotion to full editor, and better pay, but perhaps it was a mistake as the company folded after only a year.

It mustn't be forgotten that 'the girls' were not the only people to make up Quartet Books. Perhaps the biggest driving force after Naim was David Elliott, the sales director. He, too, was a wonderful character. He had sat on Paul Robeson's knee and had 'My Curly-Headed Baby' sung to him. I think David's father was a left-wing political activist (he or I might have invented that), but in any event he was a glorious contrast to the girls with surnames out of Oxbridge (and Durham). He, like Naim, was full of energy, and he teased us all unmercifully and made us laugh. He introduced us to a wonderful driving instructor called Edwin O'Cansey, a first-generation (and indeed fairly recent) immigrant from Jamaica. Edwin took over both David and the girls, teaching us all to drive and acting as a sort of taxi service between us. Sophia Sackville-West, Nigella Lawson (I think), possibly Rebecca Fraser and I were all among those he taught (and amazingly got through the test – in my case, after four recorded failures). I remember one lesson which involved taking David home through the rush hour – I'm sure it was against all the rules.

I kept in touch with Naim after I left. One day he rang and sounded me out about the possibility of my father taking over the editorship of the *Literary Review*. I was not sure Papa would want to do it, but to my amazement he was more than interested in the idea. How odd it was that Papa had brokered my job with Naim, and then the tables were turned. I think Naim was too shy to ask Papa directly. And yet from that there came a real partnership, a mutual admiration and trust and even, on my father's side certainly, and certainly on Naim's, even a love that lasted until Papa's death. Papa loved the *Literary Review* and the Academy Club, which Naim, with his characteristic energy, generosity and enthusiasm, backed. He would never hear the faintest criticism of Naim from anyone. They both shared loyalty, I think. Naim has often said to me that I was responsible for Papa taking the job – not true at all, but it warms me to think that, however erroneously, they both gave me some of the credit for such a successful partnership.

Twenty-seven

At the end of October Emma Soames announced she would be resigning as editor of the *Literary Review*: her good friend, Anna Wintour, was to become editor of *Vogue* in London and had offered her the position of features editor. It was an opportunity Emma could not pass up. She had always hoped to return to the prestigious fashion journal. Her departure, however, would be contingent on a suitable replacement being found at the *Literary Review*. This generosity on her part was a gesture I appreciated immensely. The arduous task of finding the right person to take over the helm proved challenging. I wanted an established name whose presence would help to boost the circulation figures from their present level since the state of the magazine's finances was causing me some concern. I was determined to keep the *Literary Review* alive irrespective of the cost or sacrifice. However, any established figure was likely to ask for terms that would stifle any hopes of seeing it break even in the foreseeable future. The problem was how to solve this conundrum. It was a tall order that needed reflection and rigorous financial consideration.

Various names came to mind, but I reduced these to a short-list of about five people I thought might seriously consider the position, not so much for its salary level but more because of the literary nature of the magazine and the forum it would provide them with. First I spoke to Anne Somerset, who was flattered to be asked and enthusiastic about the challenge, but had to decline because of other commitments. Then I approached Antonia Douro. She was equally chuffed to be considered, but while she would have loved the chance to fill the vacancy, she felt she wouldn't be able to devote enough time to the magazine. Blake Morrison was another candidate, for it seemed he had the makings of a first-rate editor for a literary magazine. After a candid discussion of the various possibilities, however, he too decided that the commitment would far outweigh the many undoubted benefits it could offer.

A. N. Wilson was by now my most promising target. He had just been dismissed from the *Spectator* and he and I always got on extremely well. While there is no denying he could be mischievous at times, his status as biographer and novelist would give the *Literary Review* a decided cachet. He had a way with words, and like Auberon Waugh, he courted controversy. He certainly had the qualities we needed to boost the high public profile the magazine had nurtured over the years. We had lunch at Namara House and I worked hard to convince him that the vacancy was tailor-made for him The magazine would undoubtedly provide him with a platform from which he could provoke lively literary debate with no holds barred. The idea seemed to appeal to him and I felt confident he was going to say yes. First, however, he needed time to consider whether such a commitment would in any way impinge on his writing career.

The meeting left me feeling thrilled. Prematurely I was sure the problem of the editorship had been solved in the best possible way. Sadly, twenty-four hours later A. N. Wilson phoned to say that, having given deep thought to the matter and agonized over the offer, he would have to pass it over regretfully. It was not the right time for him to be taking such a responsibility and tying himself down in a position that would need his constant attention. Naturally I was very disappointed, especially as I was aware that Emma was anxious to move on and get to grips with her new job at *Vogue*. I suspected she was under pressure to name a date for taking up her new appointment. Naturally, I was keen to release her as soon as possible and did not wish to presume on the immaculate sense of responsibility she had displayed throughout the period of our association. Francis Wheen was mentioned as another highly eligible candidate, but before the possibility had been properly explored progress was made in another direction.

Sophia, Auberon Waugh's daughter, who was working at Quartet as an editor, to my utter delight replied positively when I asked her if I should try approaching her father. She knew he was thinking about leaving *Private Eye* after many years, feeling the urge to take a new direction. The *Literary Review*, she thought, could be just the stimulus he was looking for. But, she warned, I was not to have high hopes in case he turned me down. Sophia offered to speak to her father, who was already at Combe Florey in Somerset for the Christmas break, and in response Bron phoned me to say he would give the matter some thought over the festive season, suggesting we meet for lunch in the New Year. Though he was noncommittal at that stage, I somehow began to feel a cautious optimism. When we did meet early in January, I found he was beaming with excitement and ready to spill the glad tidings: he would be willing to fill the post of editor to the *Literary Review*. That only left the matter of fixing his salary, and apologetically I mentioned a figure that was much too modest for such an appointment by anyone's standards. Brushing the figure aside, he said he would not accept it. It was far too high and I ought to reduce it by a third. If I was agreeable, he would be able to start as soon as he had given the usual terms of notice to *Private Eye*. Once he had taken the editorial chair at the *Literary Review*, he said, he would no longer be able to continue with his contributions to *Private Eye*. In this way we settled on Bron's salary, which was to remain the same until his untimely death fifteen years later. Whenever the question arose of a wage increase he always refused it. There were others, he said, who worked for the *Literary Review* out of devotion and were more deserving by far. The amount of the suggested increase should be distributed among them. A new epoch began for me the day Auberon Waugh came into my life.

Securing Bron as editor for the *Literary Review* was a remarkable coup. He honed his wit in the first piece he wrote for the magazine before he had actually taken over the editorship:

> By the time you read this, you will probably be in the middle of your two-week Christmas 'break'. The Institute of Directors has now urged factories and firms to stop work for a fortnight after Christmas. It all seems lamentably boring. In the old days, when the majority of Christians believed that God had taken human flesh in Bethlehem, the feasting was all over by Boxing Day. Now, when the majority of bishops and theologians do not believe that Jesus was God, and doubt whether he ever went near Bethlehem, we are all obliged to celebrate for a fortnight. At least the problem of presents was solved for me this year by the proprietor of this paper, Mr Naim Attallah. I have given most of my close friends boxed sets of the stunningly alluring *Avant l'Amour* scent, with its accompanying *Après l'Amour*. Clearly, this stuff works! I have had a most suggestive thank-you letter from the ever-lovely Suzanne Lowry, suggesting that we spend a two-week break together on a Hebridean island, watching the crones weaving tweed underwear on the looms. I will let you know how we passed this *vacance* in the next issue.

Bron was always supportive of his family and friends, so it was typical of him to plug Parfums Namara as a first gesture of solidarity.

The next step was to bid Emma Soames farewell and to welcome Bron into the Namara fold. A party was scheduled for February, when Bron was officially due to assume the editorship. Meanwhile the press had been surprised and intrigued by the appointment. The headlines varied. 'Bron Sacks *Private Eye*' was how the *Sunday Times* expressed it, while Peter Hillmore in *Punch* referred to what was going on as a 'Waugh Game'. He added that all sorts of fierce disputes with Richard Ingrams were being put down as the reason for Bron's departure. Bron himself stated, however, that there was no animosity between him and Richard, who apparently told him that 'it is stupid of you to go and work for Naim', who 'is a madman'.

In fact the press announcement took Richard Ingrams as much by surprise as anyone. He could not bear the fact of Bron's leaving *Private Eye*, and, in the view of many observers, his vacating of the editorial chair at *Private Eye* in favour of Ian Hislop only a month or so later came about as a direct result. I can well understand Richard's feelings on this score. Bron's uniqueness made him irreplaceable. I too felt the gap in my life after Bron died many happy years later.

Private Eye revealed a hint of pique when it printed a column asking what was he really like, this man who was dismaying and horrifying his friends and colleagues by 'storming out of the most important job he has ever held'? Might his resignation be because he had devised 'some long-term game plan to carry him to even dizzier heights in his career'? More probably, it implied, the reason was nothing more than 'the reckless, impulsive action of a middle-aged man in the throes of a mid-life crisis'. As soon as the dust had settled, it predicted, Mr Auberon Waugh would 'never be heard of again'. Meanwhile Bernard Levin in *The Times*, assuming Bron had departed from *Private Eye* before he had actually left, took the chance to fire off another shot in their long-running personal feud, attacking Bron for the 'terrible' column he had contributed to *The Times* fifteen years earlier. In Bron's opinion, the dig was provoked by his review published in the *Daily Mail* of Bernard's latest book, in which he said, 'In twenty years of reviewing I can think of few books which were more penny-chasing and bogus.'

Nothing daunted, Bron then proceeded to round off one of his last pieces in *Private Eye* with yet another salvo:

> Bernard spent his mid-life crisis on the Bagwash's *ashram* in Poona with a Greek pudding for company. I will spend mine on the *Literary Review* surrounded by beautiful and intelligent young women from the Attallah Seraglio. After that I shall retire and drink my way through the huge cellar of wine which has been quietly maturing in Somerset. But what does one do with a tiny fifty-seven-year-old bachelor journalist who has seen better days? Someone must have the answer.

While all this excitement was still in the offing, *Tatler* had published its Christmas issue, featuring under the heading 'Special Treat' what various friends, acquaintances and famous people had said in answer to the question what sort of Christmas treat would make them feel beautiful. With some measure of flippancy, I came up with the saucy reply that it would be having my toes sucked by a beautiful woman. Unlike Bron, who was amused by my frivolous reply, many people reacted with outrage and it took me a number of years to live down the remark. Byron Rogers was one of the first to seize on it as a piece of good copy in his television-review column in the *Sunday*

Times at the end of January. Channel 4 had asked me to fill the 'Comment' slot after the end of the *Seven o'Clock News* and I took the chance to attack the moral standards of politicians then in government. Mr Rogers wrote:

> [On] Tuesday night a figure crying 'Woe, woe,' like Solomon Eagle during the London Plague, burst on to Channel 4. Mr Naim Attallah, probably the most mysterious figure of his time – publisher, parfumier, employer of Auberon Waugh, and now prophet – was delivering the Comment . . . [the same] Mr Attallah who a month ago was telling *Tatler* readers of his dream of having his toes sucked by a beautiful woman . . . A dark-eyed figure, his tie lit by red, blue and green flashes, he stared grimly out of the television set. 'And now a look at the weather,' said the announcer.

*

There had been mutterings in the press about a forthcoming Quartet photographic book called *Naked London*. It was not planned to come out till later in 1987, but speculation was already rife over which celebrities were likely to appear nude in its pages. The photographer was Katya Grenfell, described by *Private Eye* as a 'lissom young photographer with the right connections'. Peter Hillmore in *Punch* that November was being more speculative than most when he said the MP Brian Sedgemore was to be one of the subjects to be seen in the book. He asked readers to note he did not say 'heard' but 'seen', in the 'first book that ought to carry a Government Health Warning'. As a publisher, he said, Naim Attallah was proud to subscribe to some loony ideas, 'but this could be one of the looniest – a book of celebrated figures in the nude'. He had once seen a politician naked – Edward Heath in the sauna at Grosvenor House – and vouched for the fact it was 'not a particularly pleasant sight'.

Jubby Ingrams, the *Standard* reported, had nervously informed her father Richard that she and her brother Fred would be appearing nude in the book. 'I did it for fun,' she said. 'I have never posed naked before, but I enjoyed it very much. It is all very tasteful. You do not see any naughty bits, but I suppose you do see my boobs. My dad didn't say much about it. He just grunted and said, "Do what you like." ' The *Standard* then went on to gild the lily somewhat by claiming I had been persuaded to strip for a family pose with my wife and son. Had I been blessed with the perfect torso, I would not have hesitated. As things were, there was no question of my exposing myself in this fashion. Katya meanwhile was getting on with her project of photographing the up-and-coming young men and women on the quirkier side of London society, together with some downright eccentrics, all in a state of undress. She was looking for those who were willing to pose in the nude, or nearly so, in attitudes that reflected their personality. Many volunteered, but then got cold feet when put to the test.

Meanwhile, I was worried that Jubby's inclusion in the book could lead me into crossing swords with her father, who as editor of *Private Eye* was already causing me problems with his attacks in the magazine. There was a danger that any further stirring of the pot might finally make life intolerable. But nothing could persuade her to change her mind. Eventually, when I saw how resolved she was, I withdrew any objections and resigned myself to facing whatever consequences of my folly emerged. Samantha Baring, of the banking dynasty, was another attractive young women, barely nineteen years old, who not only expressed a desire to be in the book but insisted she must feature on the cover.

Samantha was a somewhat crazy character, full of energy and verve but perhaps a little highly strung. She had arrived at Namara House to deputize temporarily for my secretary while she was on holiday and somehow managed to stay on afterwards. Chaos and disruption spread in her wake through Namara House and unsettled all the other female staff. Samantha became highly protective, trying to distance me from the other girls and assuming the role of my assistant without ever having been asked. Her remarkable nerve endeared her to me to the extent that I actually bought her a Vespa to facilitate her getting to work. I must have been as loony as Peter Hillmore implied in *Punch*. I even asked Katya to include Samantha in the book on the grounds that she was a real character with immaculate breeding and really quite pretty and youthful. Katya was happy to oblige and arrange a photo shoot at dawn (to avoid a crowd of onlookers gathering) on the Chelsea Embankment, close to the Albert Bridge. The result was unsuccessful for some odd reason and the whole idea of using Samantha fell by the wayside. The bravado that was her trademark must have deserted her on the day and the photographs bore witness to it.

The ripples of publicity continued, *Publishing News* taking up where the *Standard* had left off with the additional titbit that Jubby Ingrams's colleague, Anna Groundwater, had also been invited to appear, but 'decided against it for professional reasons. "I felt I couldn't publicize the book properly if I was too close to it," she declared.' In March the *Evening News* reported the development of a change of author for the 'much touted tome', the 'international name-dropper and professional Greek, Taki Theodoracopulos', having been signed up to take over.

The choice of Taki as wordsmith is a piquant one. For two of the book's subjects are children of *Private Eye* chairman Richard Ingrams, whom Taki despises. He has threatened in print, after being insulted in *Private Eye*, to visit Ingrams's Berkshire manor armed with a baseball bat. Perhaps he will find a subtler method of revenge when he has to describe Fred and Jubby Ingrams.

Following this, *Private Eye* in 'Grovel' fired off its own salvo of shots the same month:

> I am told that an unseemly disagreement has arisen between the seedy Palestinian parfumier and publisher Naim Ayatollah and the world's most famous cottager Adrian Woodhouse . . . Woodhouse apparently accepted gelt from Naim to write the text for a book of soft-porn photographs featuring London's glitterati in their naked glory . . . But as . . . no words have sprung forth from Woodhouse's pen, [the] camel herder has resorted to employing the glue-sniffing dope smuggler Taki Theodoracopulos to write the text instead.

In April 'Grovel' was expounding on the story, announcing the further difficulties he heard the 'seedy Palestinian publisher' was having with 'his absurd book'. Meanwhile 'the book is proving to be a disaster'.

> Unfortunately several so-called celebrities have decided to withdraw their pictures at the last minute, including Margaux Hemingway, Samantha Baring and even Oliver Gilmour – Katya Grenfell's husband. In desperation, therefore, Katya has had to persuade cadaverous wino Jeff Bernard to lend her his body. Thankfully, his vitals were 'draped' with a racing-form book.

Naked London was finally published in September 1987.

*   *   *

Back at the start of 1986 things got off on a happy note after Sophia Sackville-West had recruited her sister Victoria to help part-time with the running of the Academy Bookclub. They made a formidable pair: Sophia, a bright bubbly blonde with a gentle air of enthusiasm, and Victoria, as dark as her sister is fair, with the same keen interest in the book project. *Debrett's Magazine* photographed them together in brilliant colour, surrounded by all the stock in the relative calm of their shop at 51 Beak Street in Soho. They looked glamorous, confident and inspiring.

In January Bron announced in *Private Eye* how he planned to revolutionize the *Literary Review*:

> Next month I will go and take the lovely Emma Soames's place . . . It might

be argued that the *Literary Review* carries no advertisements for messages, or, indeed, any classified advertisements at all, but all this may change under my Editorship if the ladies of the staff agree. There may even be free space for those wishing to advertise London's newest diversion, the Literary Massage, where beautiful young graduates offer to recite *Lepanto* or *The Little Revenge* as they go about their soothing ministrations.

The party to wish Emma farewell and welcome Bron was held at the Travellers' Club on 25 February, with the guests 'Bronning' Bron all over the place, according to the *Standard*'s 'Londoner's Diary'. They included Donald Trelford from the *Observer*, Anna Ford, Rachel Billington and Count Nikolai Tolstoy, flamboyant in Georgian national dress, as well as 'a liberal smattering of the famous writer clans – Pakenham, Guinness – [adding] lustre to the event'. By comparison, Chaucer's *Parlement of Foules* wasn't a patch on it, with every 'writerly egret and starling in town' seemingly there – 'if not looking for a mate, at least talking to his mates'. 'The last time I edited a magazine was at school,' Bron was declaiming, 'and that never came out. The worst thing about this new job is sending back all the poems, but I shall enjoy commissioning people – mostly students, because I think that's all we can afford.' Nigel Dempster in the *Daily Mail* asserted that Bron, at forty-six, was a better critic and journalist than his late father, Evelyn, then picked up a comment that Bron threw off about those not present at the gathering – 'the egregious Karl Miller, a former literary luminary, and the appalling Charles Osborne, who caused such pain when at the Arts Council as Literature Director'.

Anne Smith, as founder editor of the *Literary Review*, had turned down an invitation to come to the party, but felt no constraint about coming forward with comments on the new development in an article in *Women's Review* that March. She felt she ought to 'respond with something stronger than mild, passing interest', though in fact 'found the strange turn in Mr Waugh's brilliant career more interesting then anything happening to the magazine'. Meanwhile she was 'still trying to figure out what made Mr Attallah imagine that I would be glad to accept the expenses-paid invitation to his party to celebrate five years of the magazine's existence'. She continued to rake over her version of the events surrounding her departure and picked up a remark made by Bron in *Private Eye* that one serious libel award could ruin the *Literary Review*. 'For the owner of the *Literary Review* to worry about ruination from a libel suit,' she said, 'is about as real as Marie Antoinette playing at shepherdesses.' Perhaps she had been naïve, she said, but the worst part of her experience had been 'the realization that there are no "ethics" in business, that most businessmen succeed on lies and bluff. That was gradual, and sickening. At the end of it, I was not just confirmed in my socialism, I found myself leaning to communism.' Against the 'blatant roguery of commerce' she set those, among her erstwhile contributors, 'who insist on the relationship between art and life, art and truth – people who could not be bought'.

I was not prepared to let this case of emotionalism distorting the facts pass me by and *Women's Review* printed my response in its next issue. I described how Anne Smith had immediately cast herself in the role of victim after I accepted her offered resignation and how we subsequently arrived at a settlement. Now for Anne to 're-embark on a campaign of denigration which continues even today suggests an absence of good faith, and self-confessed naïvety does not mitigate the bad faith'. I questioned how a businessman who acquired a loss-making literary magazine and sustained it to the tune of half a million pounds could be described as unethical or motivated by the prospect of financial gain. While she professed her regard for 'people who insist on the relationship between art and life, art and truth' and disdained 'hypocrisy', there had been one outstanding instance during our association where such lofty principles could have been put to the test.

This concerned an issue in which Janet Daley wrote a vigorous piece on art criticism and what she called 'the shallow and turgid reflections' of the art critics. One celebrated art critic claimed that the article lacked objectivity and a libel suit was threatened. Both Janet Daley and Anne Smith assured me that the article was fair comment. I decided to back my editor and her contributor unequivocally: they had asked for my support and, despite the inherent risk, I would give it unstintingly. But the fight was overtaken by events. In September 1981 Anne Smith resigned, and the principles of which she had spoken so passionately were suddenly forsaken in order to impugn me. Readers may thus draw their own conclusions about the flexibility of Anne Smith's regard for truth and her attitude towards hypocrisy.

The unkindest cut of all had been her sneering reference to the party invitation when there was no mystery attached to it at all: it was quite simply a straightforward gesture of goodwill and conciliation. To have stated, as she did, that 'I wouldn't care if I were never to hear of the *Literary Review* again' was disingenuous in the extreme. 'Were it not, she would hardly have taken the trouble to write the article in question.'

The *Literary Review* has evolved since the days of Anne Smith . . . and it has won a place among the best and most distinguished literary magazines.

Under its new editor, Auberon Waugh, it will no doubt broaden its base, and consolidate and expand its field of influence. The tragedy is that had circumstances been different, the *Literary Review* could have been Anne Smith's monument.

On a lighter and unconnected note, *Tatler*, a week or two later, published a cheeky pastiche advertisement, purporting to be from Quartet, announcing *The Collected Party Invitations*, translated from the Arabic by Antony Lambton (LORD Lambton): 'A beautifully bound and lavish reprint of the original invitations to Naim Attallah's book-launch parties. Of particular interest to collectors with limited shelf-space, who will now be able to throw away the originals.' ' "What do you mean I have to pay for any extra drink?" – N. Monson. "Marvellous, perfect. And the other's a Scotch" – Lady Elizabeth Anson.'

Bron was able to start indulging his own brand of serious playfulness when he finally assumed the editor's chair for the *Literary Review* in April and produced his first editorial: 'Lord Gnaim Writes: Not a Manifesto'. As the magazine's first male editor, he had no objection to correspondents continuing to address the editorial chair as 'Dear Madam'. Emma Soames was leaving the magazine in good shape and he had no intention of being 'a new broom in the stables of the London literary establishment'. Having said that, he tilted his cap against state patronage of the arts that had led to 'affectation, mediocrity and pretentiousness [swarming] like dung flies round a cow pat wherever the state milch-cow lifts its tail'.

> So far as I have any revolutionary intention in becoming a literary editor, it is to produce a magazine which will be enjoyed by intelligent, educated people who read books, rather than flatter the socially and intellectually insecure by claiming some deeper meaning for whatever is obscure, muddled, incomprehensible or frankly meaningless. The cult of the 'difficult' in literature may be assailed from time to time, but without too much reference to its supporting structure of academic idlers, journalistic pseuds and Arts Council scroungers.

Poetry was likely to be a problem because of the torrents of it that were being submitted, Bron's own impression being 'that the Free Verse movement has run its course. Many more people wish to write it than wish to read it.' However, he admitted, 'Our poetry editor, on whom the task of reading this drivel falls, Carol Rumens, takes a more sanguine view' and would continue to 'produce her selections of modern poetry to delight its dwindling band of enthusiasts'. Meanwhile she was hopelessly overstocked with material awaiting publication and asked that no more unsolicited material should be submitted till further notice. To counter the situation and keep poetry in the picture, he therefore announced a monthly poetry competition with a £50 first prize, a £20 second prize and several £10 prizes for runners up. The subject of the first competition would be a simple English sonnet of fourteen lines in iambic pentameters on the theme of Spring.

Since the *Literary Review*, like all unsubsidized magazines, could only pay its contributors peanuts, this meant that they wrote for enjoyment and the need arose to find as many readers as possible to share that enjoyment. The magazine could not survive or improve unless it increased its circulation. Friends and relations, local libraries, schools, dentists' waiting-rooms should all be encouraged to subscribe. 'Our only purpose is to spread happiness, light, commonsense and joy in the language we share.' With that statement the scene was set for the *Literary Review* to consolidate its reputation for independence of mind and an idiosyncratic attitude that set it apart from the fashionable orthodoxies. Emma Soames remembers her time at the *Review* with affection.

Métier in Beak Street
by Emma Soames

Until Naim Attallah rang me up with the proposal that I take on the editorship of the *Literary Review* after the departure of Gilly Greenwood, I had never edited anything in my life. Nor could I boast a degree in English literature or indeed any other academic tag. I had worked in journalism since I first pulled a salary at the tender age of twenty, but this was entirely confined to the diary and feature pages of the *Evening Standard* and two stints on that famous hotbed of literary content, *Vogue*.

Despite this, it seemed to me like a crazy but fine idea. I had just returned from nearly three years living in the Middle East. My then husband, James MacManus, was Middle East correspondent of the *Guardian* and we had spent three fascinating years living and working in Cairo and Jerusalem. Well, in my case working was possibly too strong a word for what I did. Looking after my baby and filing the occasional piece as a freelance was as close as I came to the coalface of earning during those years. On our return to London, we were homeless with one job between us, and it fast became clear that two jobs were needed to fund a fancy Clapham lifestyle. So Naim's timing was good from my point of view. And without further thought – never my strong suit – I clambered aboard.

I don't know whether, at this later stage in my life, I would have the chutzpah to accept such a challenge, but in retrospect Attallah's bold and risky casting provided me with a huge opportunity and nearly two years of exhilarating fun and useful experience finding my feet as a commissioning editor.

Both of us had to contend with a backwash of press comment which centred on my lack of qualification for the editorship, combined with Naim's tendency to hire posh girls. Both of us rose above it. Naim had heard it all before, and my rather weak line of justification was that I had slept with Martin Amis, which, given the media's obsession, must represent some sort of left-field qualification.

I fast developed a taste for this editing lark. I loved commissioning reviews – sometimes from rather left-field reviewers – that would get some chemistry bubbling up in the encounter of book and reviewer. Kathy O'Shaughnessy and I had a ball thinking up unlikely castings in a pleasant little office in Beak Street. She provided some much-needed literary high-minded ballast to my sometimes mischievous and often philistine tendencies. The greatest sin I think I committed in Kathy's eyes was in my approach to poetry. I have never 'got' the medium – it made me distinctly nervous – and I suggested to the deputy editor that we should file the countless submissions by length and only print them when a correctly sized hole appeared on the proofs: poetry by the inch.

I did not, however, take that line over the book reviewing which formed the backbone of the magazine's content. Here, I adopted the same approach to casting reviewers as I had to writing pieces for newspapers. The first responsibility of any printed piece is to grab the reader's interest. Their hearts and minds may or may not follow, but engaging their interest in the first place is the prime responsibility of both editor and writer. This strategy appeared to work as we quite quickly doubled the sales of the *Literary Review* from five figures starting with a one to five figures beginning with a two. Not that I could claim to have found the elixir of profit, for the magazine never became commercially viable. It was then, as it ever was, dependent on the generosity of Naim Attallah, who underwrote the entire operation.

None the less I found my *métier* in Beak Street, and editing magazines is what I have done with enormous satisfaction ever since. At the *Literary Review* I learnt first and last that a good editor should be able to produce a magazine on any subject.

Indeed, a bit of distance is very healthy. Early on in my days in Beak Street I formed the impression that the literary world was a closed and cliquey fraternity and many reviewers regarded it as their God-given right both to review certain titles and, in some cases, to treat somewhat unqualified editors with open disdain. It was like an eightsome reel with a small cast and a few titles swirling in some strange parallel universe inhabited by dons and clever young men in tweed suits. Coming from a different – and dare I say it wider – world, I saw no reason why the *Literary Review* should necessarily be a part of this. It needed its own identity.

I know that my approach did not endear me to many reviewers, but my hide had to be thick enough to withstand a certain amount of bullying. My already rocky friendship with Ali Forbes foundered as he demanded titles to review and I found excuses not to give them to him. And when I succumbed to his terrifying blandishments, and reluctantly thrust Lord Mountbatten's biography through the bars of his cage, he promptly reviewed it for another paper.

The most extraordinary (and flattering) fact about my editorship of the *Literary Review* was that I was replaced by Auberon Waugh. If life were some parlour game, and I was offered odds that I would hold a job where I would be succeeded by that giant of Doughty Street, that pillar of *Private Eye*, I would never have believed it possible. I was rubbing my eyes in disbelief as I crossed Regent Street to rejoin *Vogue* – doubtless to the relief of the literary world.

Twenty-eight

Charlotte Chandler was a mysteriously influential American lady whom I met in London through the public-relations office of the Savoy Hotel. She was born in California, an only child, and used to write short stories. That was the total extent of her printed biography, and it was as much as she considered anyone needed to know about her. No one knew her age. She once said she stopped counting when she reached nineteen. Her background was no less obscure: it was shrouded in mystery. In Hollywood she had somehow got to know most of the stars and celebrities, from Charlie Chaplin to Douglas Fairbanks, and had interviewed many of them. Fairbanks used to address her as 'Cha Cha' when he wrote to her, to distinguish her from Chaplin, whom he called 'Ch Ch'. With her engaging manner and bouffant style of piled-up curls, she listened to them all and gathered anecdotes wherever she went. Mae West told her, 'You know, honey, I see something men must like about you – you're a brilliant listener.' All the time Charlotte was interviewing Miss West, she was aware of a sound like small birds rustling their wings. It turned out to be caused by Miss West fluttering her false eyelashes.

Having gained access to the notoriously difficult-to-interview Groucho Marx for *Playboy*, she then wrote a book about him called *Hello, I Must Be Going*. Now, in May 1986, Quartet were publishing her latest book, *The Ultimate Seduction*. All those she had known were in its pages, including the famous film directors Billy Wilder and Federico Fellini. With Fellini she had a particular friendship and a drawing he did of her was on the jacket. Picasso also drew her but signed it 'Pica', saying it was only half a Picasso since she had declined to disrobe completely. Marc Chagall told her how fame was a ghetto when she called on him with a picture painted by Groucho that friends told him was 'very Chagall'. Chagall then reciprocated with a book that he signed 'Very Chagall'. Over teacakes from Fortnum & Mason, Henry Moore told her how his mother used to watch him sculpt, shaking her head and saying, 'And you could have been a teacher.' Tennessee Williams, with whom she stayed many times, remarked, 'Nobody who knew my day-to-day life would envy me at all.'

The title of the book came from a quote by Picasso: 'It is your work in life that is the ultimate seduction.' Charlotte explained the reason for her book of conversational interviews, which was like no other in existence:

The ultimate seduction is not about sex, but about passion. It is the thrill that cannot be surpassed. For the people in this book, that passion is their work. Sex is the ultimate distraction, work the ultimate satisfaction. They all followed strong drives towards goals not always known, and found – themselves. All were able to work at what they wanted to do and do it successfully. All were willing to risk everything when the chances of success seemed small. All gave everything to their work and received everything from it. All began by defining their work, and then were defined by it.

Besides celebrities from the world of show business, she included in her collection the president of Hermès in Paris. Charlotte never took no for an answer and was full of surprises. She had arrived at teatime in Madrid to visit Isabelita and Juan Perón in exile, to find the late Eva Perón being attended in her coffin by her consultant embalmer, Dr Ara, who was carefully combing her hair. Perón had particularly wanted her to come on that day and pay her respects to Evita.

I don't know if I thought Eva Perón would look like a body or a man-nequin or a wax doll or something else. She looked like all of those or none of those. She was wearing a white dress which had acquired a shroud-like appearance. But her face was even whiter. Perón said to me, 'She was fair, like you.'

Dr Ara was offered some tea as well, but declined. He was too absorbed in his work of preserving the hair, tufts of which kept falling on to the polished parquet flooring. 'There was only one crack in her,' said Isabelita. 'But it was a shame about the hairpins. They rusted in her hair.'

Charlotte befriended academics and rogues and knew the true value of working the circuit. In New York she was a regular attender at the grandest social functions and always seemed on intimate terms with those who wielded power in publishing and the artistic world. Famous restaurants in New York accorded her special treatment and she was often seen being ceremoniously ushered to her favourite table. No one could fathom the secret of her influence or how she achieved it all on an income that was modest by the standards of those with whom she kept company. She lived at the right address and had neighbours, such as Pavarotti, with whom she was on the friendliest of terms. The way she operated and how well informed she always was could only be marvelled at. Over the years she and I have become good friends, meeting regularly in New York and London.

The Ultimate Seduction is full of revelations and it packs a punch without being threatening. Her interviewees became her close friends and each relationship is unique in its own way. She keeps her manner very low key and her voice at the same low register. She is a slow eater and a sympathetic listener. To engage in conversation with Charlotte is to find time irrelevant, her languid attitude being perhaps her greatest strength. She is seductive without being aware of it and quick to make anyone feel at ease without any visible effort on her part.

The book launch for *The Ultimate Seduction* was held in the Beaufort Room at the Savoy Hotel, where Martin, the fifth-floor waiter who usually served Charlotte and other illustrious visitors, was this time on the guest list with his wife Teresa. Show-business luminaries who were there included Robert Morley, Adolph Green, Emlyn Williams and the widows of Sean O'Casey and Jack Hawkins. The Beaufort Room was decorated with pink balloons and large colour blow-ups of Charlotte with some of the people from her book, such as Henry Fonda, Bette Davis, Tennessee Williams and Fellini. The Fortnum & Mason pastry chef created the cake in the shape of a large book that looked as if you could actually turn the pages and recreated the jacket with Fellini's drawing. At the end of it all, half the cake remained uneaten and was donated to an orphanage.

Other outstanding Quartet Books that year included a reissue in paperback of *The Monocled Mutineer*, originally published in 1981 to coincide with a major BBC 1 drama series that received critical acclaim. Written by William Allison and John Fairley, it told the story of a bizarre event on the Western Front in 1917, on the eve of the battle of Passchendaele, when British troops in France erupted into mutiny. It remained one of the British army's most carefully guarded secrets. At the centre of the revolt was Private Percy Toplis. A court martial sentenced him to death by firing squad, but he escaped to England and took to the life of a colourful outlaw, masquerading under a multitude of disguises. He organized a unique black market in army stores, even re-enlisting in the army under his own name, apparently with impunity. Finally the authorities made ready to pounce, and for six desperate weeks he was pursued the length and breadth of Britain in a manhunt that ended bloodily in a police ambush in 1920.

The critics were unanimous in their praise for the book when it first came out. 'An amazing disclosure after sixty years,' wrote *The Times*, 'of how 100,000 men were immobilized in a murderous protest against brutality.' 'A sensational story the British army tried to suppress . . . a sensational book,' said the *Evening Standard*. The *Guardian* affirmed that there was no doubt the authors had 'opened out a rotten piece in the woodwork'. In the opinion of the *Daily Mirror*, the book had, 'Revealed at last a shameful, secret story which, for so long, the establishment has tried to hide.'

At the same time, a new novel from Antony Lambton, *The Abbey in the Wood*, confirmed him as a fine writer with a remarkable imaginative reach. After his historical novel *Elizabeth and Alexandra*, about the fall of the Romanovs, he turned to a Gothic-romance theme, full of power and enchantment, set in Germany early in the nineteenth century. It told the story of how a hangman's beautiful daughter grows up in an old house built amid the ruins of a medieval abbey, surrounded by forest and doomed to live out her days among her family clan of executioners – till a young poet spies her and falls in love. The tale was suggested by a fragment of memory written down by the dying German poet, Heinrich Heine, 'usually considered to have been a figment of his fevered mind'. 'My additions are entirely figments of my fevered mind,' wrote Lambton in his epigraph to the book.

A very different sort of book, which Quartet published in 1986, was Peter Clark's *Marmaduke Pickthall: British Muslim*. Pickthall, the son of an East Anglian clergymen, whose translation of the Qur'an is still held in high regard by Islamic scholars, converted to Islam in 1917. As well as being a writer and novelist on Near Eastern themes, he led a highly adventurous life and espoused unfashionable causes that won him criticism in his homeland. Peter Clark regarded him as a figure who was overdue for reappraisal, and also wrote an introduction for his finest novel, *Said the Fisherman*, which Quartet reprinted at the same time. It told a colourful story of events following a massacre of Christians by Muslims and Druze in Damascus in 1860, Said being a Muslim fisherman who takes cynical advantage of the chaos but ends facing his fate in riots in Alexandria. Pickthall's appreciation of the power of the Muslim faith was almost unprecedented in Western writers. E. M. Forster thought him 'the only contemporary novelist who understands the nearer East', and D. H. Lawrence said that 'in imagination he goes native. And that thoroughly.'

Quartet Inc. had not been dragging its heels in New York. That October it published Christina Oxenburg's *Taxi*. The book received a great deal of coverage in the States, partly on account of the author's identity as one of the daughters of Princess Elizabeth of Yugoslavia – the other daughter being the Hollywood star, Catherine Oxenburg – and partly because its subject matter had an appeal for New Yorkers. In Christina Oxenburg's view, they regarded riding a cab in the city as a bit of an adventure and occasionally a risk. The hundred or so taxi stories she had gathered from either side of the partition, to represent both drivers and passengers, made that an understatement. To say all cab drivers are crazy would seem to be near to the truth from her examples. There was the intellectual who drove so he could subsidize his search for the 'negative' *scienza nuovo* of Giambattista Vico; and the immigrant who took the wheel because 'it requires no prior experience, no knowledge of English and no familiarity with the geography of New York'. There was 'Nico', whose attitude was, 'People are nice to me, I'm nice to them. But a lot of people, they try to take advantage of nice guys, so sometimes I have to break their ribs with a baseball bat. It's not like I enjoy to do it. But a lot of strange people in New York.' The writer Alastair Forbes once got into a cab and noticed the driver's name was Giuseppe Verdi. Before he could say a word, the driver rounded on him with: 'Don't give me any more of that crap about my name! Every goddam passenger tells me the same thing every goddam day. And you know what, I HATE music!'

Helen Gurley Brown, the head of *Cosmopolitan* magazine, remembered how, when she first arrived in New York, a lot of people told her to 'beware of cab drivers because they were difficult to get along with and if you didn't like what you were faced with you should just get out and take another one'.

I always thought they were paranoid but as the years have gone by, I have realized they they are more right than wrong. It does seem that about 30 per cent are really seriously troubled.

Humorous experiences? I think mine are more apt to be tragic, which is likely to be the case with anybody who has lived in New York for many years. I have joined the paranoid ones and all I have are complaints!

Another driver was described by the author as 'the living embodiment of urban paranoia', but to judge by some celebrities' responses to her request for stories, the tag could apply equally to many of the passengers. A designer, John Weitz, declared, 'I get into cabs with fear and trepidation: two great friends of mine, Irving Fear and Bobby Trepidation. I only hope I will get out with reasonably the same skin.' There were those who refused the request for an anecdote, and who had the exact words of their refusals reproduced in facsimile, such as Christina Onassis, whose social secretary wrote that, 'Regrettably Mrs Onassis does not have a story to recount to you.' The author could only assume this was because she had never ridden in a cab. Others who were more forthcoming included Douglas Fairbanks Jr, Diana Vreeland, Quentin Crisp and Andy Warhol. There was also Catherine Oxenburg, whose driver, in a bid to make a date, promised he could get her a spot on *Dynasty* if she would give him her phone number.

Taxi was fully illustrated with line drawings, which made it as redolent of New York as the yellow cab it was describing. The back of the cab could serve as an arena for metaphysical discussion, for copulation, for homicide, for drug abuse, for literary quotation. Apart from the celebrities, there was the incontinent lion cub whose owner then panicked, stopped the cab, handed the driver a ten-dollar bill and decamped, leaving the result on the back seat. The cab was promptly rehired by an old lady. It had only gone half a block before it screeched to a halt and the old lady staggered out and began belabouring the vehicle with her umbrella. There was also Franco Rossellini's puppy Gramophone, callously flung into a shop window by a demented driver during a row with its owner. As Christina said, the only thing that usually got flung was the tip you offered – back in your face. 'Taxi driving is not a passive sport,' she drily observed. Diana Vreeland told her:

> Compared to any other city, in the Western world anyway, there does seem to be something that makes New York taxi drivers unique. Perhaps it is just the pressure of driving in such conditions. I don't know what it is. I'm beginning to think that they really are a breed on their own! There was a time, years before you were born, when there was such a scare about the Mafia that it was unheard of to take taxis after dark. Mobsters used to use them for their own purposes, like the St Valentine's Day massacre.

Sharp observation and a diligent disregard for contributors' requests to remain anonymous gave Christina's book an extra edge when it came to press coverage. She knew everyone who mattered in New York and beyond. Her own publicity machine went into full gear. On publication it was almost impossible to open a newspaper or magazine in America without seeing a mention of *Taxi* and a picture of the author.

The first New Yorker to import an English taxi for use as a personal limousine was a banking heiress, Mrs Evelyn Lehman, who, when asked why she had chosen the boxy, high-roofed black cab in preference to a Rolls-Royce, explained, 'Why would I want to own a car that is going to live longer than I will.' When *Taxi* was published in London, however, the publicity was far more low key. London had its own taxi culture and a high degree of interest in the yellow cab of New York could not have been expected. Even so, the gossip columnists were alert for nuggets likely to amuse their readership that they could lift from the book's pages. Quentin Crisp pointed up what he considered to be an essential distinction between taxi drivers in London and New York:

> In England, NEVER tell the driver how to reach your destination; you won't be halfway through your instructions before he will say, 'D'you want to drive the damned thing yourself?' American drivers, on the other hand, expect guidance – but give it in a cooing voice.

*

Following the phenomenal success of Avant l'Amour and Après l'Amour, a new fragrance from Parfums Namara was about to hit the market. Harvey Nichols and Harrods both listed the two scents among those heading up the popularity charts, and a new line of toiletries for men had also been successfully launched to complement the feminine products. The great event now was the razzmatazz preceding and following the launch of Naïdor, which completed the trilogy of scents. The dangerous power of scent had been acknowledged by Parliament in a bill it introduced in 1770:

> That all women . . . whether virgins, maids, or widows, that shall . . . impose upon, seduce, and betray into marriage, any of His Majesty's subjects by scents, paints, cosmetic washes, artificial teeth . . . high-heeled shoes, bolstered hips, shall incur the penalty of the law now in force against witchcraft . . . and that marriage, upon conviction, shall stand null and void.

Susan Irvine commented in an article that, had such an edict ever become law, 'a man today might have been able to divorce you on the strength of your L'Air du Temps', but even

> more overt connotations of a perfume's powers are on the market. Naim Attallah's strong-smelling stuff, Avant l'Amour and Après l'Amour, gets the message across in its packaging. The first has a gargantuan phallic stopper towering lustfully over the bottle; the second – to be applied after the first round – has a detumescent, post-coital lid.

My initial venture into the heady world of fragrances, the *Daily Telegraph* reported, had 'sent a few shock waves through the cosmetics industry when I presented the first two . . . in suggestively sculptured bottles'. Now, with the latest offering of Naïdor, the shock was about to be perpetuated by using the same design of bottle, but this time covered in gold leaf. Hence its name: 'Naï' for its creator and 'd'or' for its glitzy bottle. Naïdor was being marketed as a provocative perfume for the extravagant woman. It had a flowery amber fragrance and its price tag never pretended to do anything but reflect its exclusivity – £45 for the *eau de parfum*, £105 for the ½ oz, £2,200 for the giant 25-oz version. 'It's going to be a peach-scented winter for those who can afford it,' commented the *Daily Express*.

The launch took place at a celebrity-spattered party at the ultra trendy Bill Stickers restaurant in Soho. The Namara Girls, described by *You* magazine of the *Mail on Sunday* as having 'brains, beauty and a touch of class', were there in a throng. They turned out in force, dressed in gold lamé sack-like gowns designed by my cook, Charlotte Millward. Suzy Menkes, the doyenne of fashion, writing in *The Times*, caught the mood of the party with her lively report:

> Alice Jay, 18, greeted guests including her father Peter and his new wife Emma, and Auberon Waugh was in his element when he posed with the line-up of golden girls for the paparazzi. Margaux Hemingway was there wrapped up to her ears in fur and the diminutive Lyndsey De Paul tossed her blonde mane over the canapés . . . In case this sparkling crowd still missed the point, Soraya Khashoggi, clad in white lace like a benevolent fairy godmother, distributed silver lamé pouches (presumably also run up by the cook) containing gold phials of the fragrance.

The reason for Alice Jay welcoming the guests can be explained by 'Grovel' of *Private Eye*, who had got wind of the fact that 'seedy Arab publisher Naim Attullah-Disgusting has enticed a new beauty into his web'.

> She is gorgeous, pouting Alice Jaybotham, daughter of former ambassador Sir Peter, who has signed on as the Ayatollah's secretary.
> Alice has now been selected from all the Quartet Girls to accompany Attullah-Disgusting to the Frankfurt Book Fair.
> She will need to keep her wits about her.

Apollo magazine had been running smoothly since Algy Cluff and I acquired it from the *Financial Times*. It had turned out to be no financial burden and Denys Sutton had proved less difficult as its editor than we had been led to believe. His tenure, however, was coming to an end with his wish to retire. He had been connected with *Apollo* for a number of years and was inextricably associated with its character and style. Although he was very singular in his views and not easily persuaded to change any of his ways, his contribution to the arts scene was undoubtedly tremendous. His like today would be hard to find. Over lunch I said to Godfrey Smith of the *Sunday Times* that what I really needed for *Apollo* was another Auberon Waugh. Godfrey wrote in his column the following week, 'I wish him well but fear he faces a labour of Sisyphus. There have been many Waughs and rumours of Waughs; but there is only one Bron.'

Among the candidates proposed by my partner in *Apollo*, Algy Cluff, was Norman St John Stevas, with whom he was well acquainted. He suggested I ought to meet Norman since I was the one in overall charge of the magazine. The meeting took place promptly as I was anxious to find a quick replacement for Denys, who, having made up his mind to retire, had become eager to go as soon as possible. Norman gave me the impression that he would be well-equipped for the job, but I also found him irritatingly grand and a bit of a prima donna. I could see there might be a clash of personalities in the long term, but was willing to take the chance and risk the appointment. As a former arts minister, he had a stature that could have counterbalanced any reservations I had over his pomposity. The good of the magazine was my main concern. I never doubted he would have made an excellent editor. But a new factor came to the surface. He regarded the task of editing the magazine as a part-time assignment whereas I viewed it as a full-time job. The more we discussed the matter, the more convinced I became that he was not going to be able to commit to the magazine the time it deserved. I also began to conclude that he was the type of person so used to getting his own way that a meeting of minds would be hard to achieve. The chemistry was not right, and as a result the appointment of St John Stevas to the editorship of *Apollo* was never made.

A month later, when I was on a visit to New York, Algy telephoned me to suggest I meet a lady friend of his called Anna Somers Cocks, who also happened to be in the city at the time. He thought it would be worth discussing the possibility of her taking the editorial chair at *Apollo*. She was thirty-six, I was told, and her provenance was the Victoria and Albert Museum, where she had organized the Renaissance Jewels Exhibition of 1980. She had trained as an art historian at the Courtauld Institute, but had no previous journalistic experience. Yet she certainly possessed an unusual combination of qualities: marvellous looks, a disciplined intelligence and the assured manner of one with a privileged, cosmopolitan background. Together these made her one of the most impressive people in the art world, or so wrote the journalist Sheila Hale when the appointment of Anna as editor of *Apollo* was announced.

It did not take me long to be intellectually captivated by her, which was not to discount for a moment her physical attributes – the combination was devastating. When I met her in the New York apartment, I had not a moment's hesitation in offering her the job, which she accepted. Her policy, she declared, was to make *Apollo* more topical, more readable, more like the *Giornale dell Arte*, which covered all arts-related news, views and politics. From that day on Anna was to become my muse in all matters connected with the arts.

In 1986, Princess Katarina of Yugoslavia moved on after having spent the best part of 1985–6 at Namara House, working in my private office. She was recruited to help me launch Parfums Namara and participate later in the promotion and marketing of the products. She was a tall, handsome young lady with stunning long hair and the figure of a model, shy but extremely personable. She had the Eastern European captivating look and a sparkle to match. Here she remembers a couple of the roles she was called upon to play.

The Namara Follies
by Princess Katarina of Yugoslavia

I came to work for Naim during the heyday of his entrepreneurial activities that were in many ways the talk of the town. Assembled around him was a coterie of the most desirable young ladies, all of them noted for their high profiles, intelligence and social graces. The atmosphere throughout the group was mesmeric. The papers seemed to pounce constantly to catch the titbits and cover every nuance of all that happened. They unabashedly reported in full what amounted to high-octane gossip, as any girl who worked in the group became newsworthy and was likely to find herself turning up in the diary columns of leading newspapers. I was no exception, especially when I found myself as one of the six Namara girls dressed in rubber dresses for the launch party of Avant l'Amour and Après l'Amour. Black rubber stood for Avant, white rubber for Après. I was chosen to represent Après. Heaven knows why.

We first had to be photographed in the basement at Namara House, which was transformed into a studio for the occasion. We had chiffon arranged round our bare shoulders and were professionally made up, with our hair done in readiness – my hair being quite long and curly, like a subject in a Pre-Raphaelite painting. As I faced the camera, I had to gaze up at the ceiling as if at someone I was in love with. This was in order to make my neck profile seem quite elongated with the shape to echo the erotic curves of the scent bottle designs. When the prints arrived back for Naim to check, we were perturbed at how transparent the chiffon looked in the photographs. At the launch party it intrigued the press to find me there attired in a rubber costume as well as appearing on a six-foot poster.

This was one of many incidents that kept us *au fait* with the latest follies that were always a feature of the place. All in all, working for Naim was a madly unpredictable but enlivening experience. His energy and lack of inhibition were object lessons in how to work and play, and all those who had the chance to share in his merry-go-round of remarkable adventures have been touched by them ever after.

Twenty-nine

In the summer of 1986 I lost Rebecca Fraser as well as Kathy O'Shaughnessy. Rebecca had been with Quartet for many years in a variety of roles, culminating in her running of Robin Clark. Kathy was deputy editor of the *Literary Review* under the stewardship of Gillian Greenwood, Emma Soames and, later, Auberon Waugh. She was, so to speak, the cornerstone of the magazine, having seen it evolve over a long period into the literary force it had become. I was saddened to see them leave, but chuffed to have recognized and nurtured their early talent before they went on to greater things. Here, in their own words, they recall their time spent in the bosom of the Namara Group with their usual incisiveness and warmth.

For Naim: A Tribute
by Rebecca Fraser

Almost a quarter of a century ago, in the autumn of 1982, I arrived at the publishers called Quartet Books, to work in the art department. I was very interested in book production and illustration as I had just illustrated two books myself, and had also done so as a child for Sidgwick & Jackson.

Having a mother who was a writer brought additional interest to working in publishing. I liked the whole pernickety process of bookmaking which I had seen going on in our house from my earliest youth – the book-jacket proofs, the colour plates, the prelims, the acknowledgements, the footnotes, the index. Just how complex the whole process was had recently been brought home in New York where I had been a researcher for the investigative journalist Edward Jay Epstein on two complex books, one about diamonds and the other about Armand Hammer.

But Quartet was a publisher with a difference or 'a tweeest!' as my new employer liked to say, drawing the word out as he always did into a sort of shriek of highly contagious excitement. Like everything to do with Quartet, starting with my immediate hiring over a delicious lunch, the whole experience would be faintly surreal, but wonderful. Mr Naim Attallah, the boss, was absolute emperor and lived in a magnificent and flamboyant fashion. Every day his uniformed chauffeur was to be seen whizzing about London in a large Rolls-Royce, mainly taking Naim to power breakfasts, or occasionally rushing proofs to a libel lawyer far away in the Temple if Naim or an editor had got the wind up about a book. I found that by and large Naim aimed to be in the newspapers a great deal, whether on his own account or with his publishing, which was daring and challenged the status quo – as all good publishers do. Naim had the mind of a Bletchley Park computer, strangely allied to the exuberant temperament and creative passion of a conductor or a great opera star. Having been a banker, he insisted that he personally rechecked all the costings which are the integral part of the publishing process. He never stood still.

As in *Alice in Wonderland*, what I thought was a publishing house was always becoming something else as well: a chocolate shop, parfumerie, jewellers and so on. For like a true empire it expanded all the time with the sort of relentless energy of my new employer. And oh the extravaganzas that flowed from Naim's fertile and enthusiastic mind – the plays, like *The Beastly Beatitudes of Balthazar B* and *Trafford Tanzi* starring Toyah Wilcox, then at the height of her fame, the magazines, many of which have become literary institutions – the *Literary Review*, the *Oldie*, the *Wire* – and the Academy Bookclub. The whole operation was backed by the legendary PR company Namara, also housed in the empire's engine room, Namara House in Poland Street. At the top of this narrow house sat the imposing, enormously tall figure of the charming Naim behind his vast custom-made desk, while in and out rushed captains of industry, famous figures like Fleur Cowles, editors, reporters and photographers. They were all desperate to be published by Naim and wined and dined and promoted by him. For Naim loved people and they usually returned his affection. Naim was kind-hearted, generous and trusting in the extreme.

I soon realized that my real passion was editing, and after a period learning the black arts of publicity, I moved to edit Robin Clark books. This was a very nice little paperback imprint that had begun as a humorous classics list but which I was keen to make a showcase for exquisite first novels and literary non-fiction. We discovered some terrific writers even off what was known as the 'slush pile' – novels sent in without an agent, something unimaginable today with uberagents presiding as chick lit goes for six-figure sums. The great thing about Naim was that he was prepared to take the risk on first novels which other, bigger houses would not. We began to specialize in literary trade paperbacks like the Bloomsbury Frances Partridge's *Memories*, Allan Massie, Peter Vansittart and Auberon Waugh's five novels. We published Peter Handke, Julian Barnes's first novel and Heathcote Williams's classic *The Speakers*. Christine Sutherland's marvellous *Princess of Siberia*, which continues to sell twenty years later, was a huge hit, as were *Marie Walewska* and *Monica: Heroine of the Danish Resistance*.

No. 27 Goodge Street, a tiny little walk-up opposite a stationer's just off Tottenham Court Road, was the nerve centre of the editorial department. It contained within it many fierce spirits battling for dominion. They were also battling with Naim's taste, as most of them were women and most of them had an inbuilt resistance to Naim's default position *vis-à-vis* publishing. Despite his passionate interest in current affairs, what made Naim really happy was a photography or art book – 'Very erotic, beloved!' he would call out happily – and the saucier the better. There was usually a great deal of annoyance and rolling of eyes about the photography books at 27 Goodge Street, to which Naim paid very little attention. He continued to commission them imperturbably and they rolled inexorably off the presses. At the same time Naim was also truly contributing to feminist power by bankrolling the ground-breaking feminist publishers The Women's Press, which published seminal works by Elaine Showalter and Kate Millett, while Quartet itself published the 1980s classic, Anne Dickson's *A Woman in Your Own Right*.

Some of the Namara empire's contradictions were embodied in the figure of the sales director, David Elliott. David, who now has his own publishing company, was rather like Naim in character. He was extremely kind and very mischievous. Although he was also the sales manager of The Women's Press, he took huge pleasure in annoying every member of their staff. He rushed about in his combat jacket and his desert boots, thinking of remarks to enrage 'the Sisters', as he called them, his black eyes snapping with pleasure, his bushy hair bristling with aggro for the sake of it. His close ally was the Scots accountant, Olive, who had very black eyebrows and white hair. Every week, as she distributed the pay slips made out in her tiny precise writing, Olive sniffed in a way that suggested that Naim was quite mad to pay anyone except herself. She was guarded by her huge Dobermann pinscher which she had bought as a tiny sweet puppy. But David also enjoyed baiting the blue-stocking editors at Quartet. Just when everyone had had enough and would rush round to kill him, he and his terrible dog Tramp, the worse-tempered mongrel I have ever known, would make you scream with laughter.

Despite his naughtiness, David was extremely well-read, had been in books for years and had all kinds of brilliant ideas. He forced me to seek an audience with Dame Nora Smallwood to get her permission to do a V. S. Pritchett omnibus. That was quite terrifying – she was then the doyen of English publishers – as was meeting the great man V. S. Pritchett himself in Gloucester Terrace. The *Pritchett Omnibus* was a smash hit for Robin Clark, which under Jeremy Beale began to expand. Since then the imprint has published a great many jewels of English writing that should always remain in print: Thackeray's *The Book of Snobs*, Herbert Read's *The Green Child* and

W. W. Jacobs's terrifying 'The Monkey's Paw', with a selection of his humorous stories. Of course, we could never compete with the bigger trade paperbacks starting up at the time, but we published many literary books which in today's climate might remain unpublished.

At night as the dusk fell and the office workers started leaving Goodge Street, it was a perfect life for a twenty-four-year-old. One could either work late in the cosy little offices looking out on Fitzrovia and roam through the amazing Quartet backlist, or increasingly one could go to Naim's parties! By the time I left in 1986, having begun to write a biography of Charlotte Brontë, Naim was one of the most fêted men in London. He had begun a successful literary career of his own with several wonderful books published. His warmth, charm and sheer niceness persuaded many icons of our age to 'fess up all to him.

I met some of my greatest friends at Quartet, where the atmosphere was serious, hardworking and enormous fun. We all wanted to get on and Naim had a wonderful ability to give responsibility to the young. The thought of children and marriage left me cold. The word was what mattered. I then went on to work for a Maxwell paper and *Tatler* magazine as features editor, but the seminal period in my life was working for Naim. Gentle, kind and thoughtful, he was a great creative force and true Maecenas. There should be more like him.

Life at the *Literary Review*
by Kathy O'Shaughnessy

I hadn't spoken to Naim for years, when out of the blue came a phone call, asking me to write a piece about the *Literary Review*. Within minutes I was experiencing his personality in full, just like in the old days. He was telling me not only I could write anything I liked, but – 'If I was a monster, you can say I was a monster!' (voice rising to an excited, already indignant little scream).

'Only a very benign monster,' I replied, but I was laughing away, as Naim's enthusiasm and unEnglish lack of restraint took me back twenty years. He was far and away the most enthusiastic employer I ever had, with a generosity, theatricality and warmth that was extremely endearing, and a long way from corporate publishing as it is today.

I was twenty-three when I went to work for the *Literary Review*. I had abandoned my post-graduate degree at Oxford on Byron ('See you at the end of the term,' my supervisor had said on day one, somewhat dispiritingly) and begun writing book reviews for *Time Out* and the *Spectator*. Shortly after that I heard about an impossibly perfect vacancy – deputy editor at the *Literary*

Review. I applied and was interviewed by Gillian Greenwood, the editor, who seemed at once interesting, funny, lively – the sort of person you'd like as a friend, let alone to work for. Happily she took me on, and the next day I went to meet the already legendary Naim. 'Welcome to the family!' he said, as he vigorously shook my hand. My eyes were wandering, however, to the far end of the office, where a stupendously good-looking blonde had materialized as out of nowhere; and *this* was to be a recurring feature of working for Naim: beauties popping up in doorways and offices and desks like hallucinations, each more splendid than the last.

The *Literary Review* offices were above a hairdresser's and a strong-smelling restaurant: you had to climb three flights of rickety stairs to get to the two rooms in question – one for editorial (Gillian and myself), one for business (Bridget Heathcoat-Amory). And that, beguilingly, was it – so small-scale, so DIY, so very hands on! On one trestle table lay the books ready to be reviewed. Gillian sat at the large leather-topped boss's desk; I sat at a suitably smaller desk facing the traffic of Goodge Street, and so began my career in literary journalism. (So, too, my intense career as a passive smoker, as all of the magazine's editors smoked with a will, a few feet away from me; yet I have to admit to a nostalgic fondness for that smoky office of the past, with its piled-up books and tottering, over-spilling ashtrays, redolent of a more relaxed and less health-'n'-self-obsessed era.)

It was a dream of a job for a twenty-three-year-old. Each morning began with a pile of post: cardboard-encased books, which, like a cluster of presents, looked all the more promising for being wrapped; and the copy – typewritten, of course. It was a thrill to open the envelope and discover the copy. The type-written pages had a presence and shadowy sort of character that today's computer print-out could never aspire to – maybe the n's didn't print properly, the page might be clotted with inky crossing-outs; the very letters bore the imprint of effort expended. Then, if the copy was unexpectedly funny, or clever or just felicitous, you had the feeling of treasure-in-the- making. If it was flaccid or lacklustre – well, cutting and editing could accomplish a lot. This was my editing apprenticeship, and I loved it.

Gillian was my first and main boss at the *Literary Review*. Like most fine editors, she was herself a gifted writer, and I learnt all about editing and commissioning and putting a magazine together from her. It was a tiny operation, just the two of us, and it felt lucky to be part of this two-man or rather two-woman team – the job so enjoyable it was like being a child in a sweetshop. I soon began writing for the magazine myself, as well as helping with the commissioning. But then we had to do everything: sometimes even driving round London and dropping off batches of the newly printed issue at the not-so-many booksellers that took it at the time; and always spending one exhausting but satisfying day a month putting the magazine to bed at 'the printers'. The printers were in fact a husband and wife team, Ken and May, operating out of a small house in Chatham, Kent. There we spent many hours in the dank and indeed dark basement correcting the final proofs as the magazine went to film. It was a bonding experience and we became close friends.

Part of the job was of course meeting the writers. Broke! solitary! talented, not so talented – satirical – worthy – brilliant – the whole gamut passed through the doors of the *Literary Review*; and if they didn't pass through our office they very likely appeared at Naim's parties or at his dining table in Poland Street, where you might meet Ryszard Kapuscinski on one day, J. P. Donleavy on another, Hilary Mantel on another, and so on. In the early days our contributors included, to take a random sample from the time: Francis Wheen, David Profumo, A. N. Wilson, Colin MacCabe, A. L. Rowse, John Lahr, Carlo Gebler, Max Egremont, Geoff Dyer, Sheila MacLeod, John Orr, Christopher Hawtree, Martin Walker, Antony Beevor, Richard Williams, Christopher Hitchens, Grey Gowrie, Lucretia Stewart, Neil Berry, Kyril Fitzlyon and others. For their pains, they were paid the princely sums of £10 or £20! But the world of books was different then: there was less money around, marketing was less to the forefront, and those mergers between the publishing houses were still an evil mirage on the horizon.

The magazine's offices were in Goodge Street, busy and lively with its sandwich bars, Italian delis, shoe shops, bikers dashing in and out with their important packages, and Charlotte Street with its restaurants round the corner (the Spaghetti House being our top budget outing). It was a short walk from there to Naim's office, where we would either have lunch (his cook Charlotte was a maestro of the kitchen as well as a beauty, *ça va sans dire*); or debate the perennial problems of circulation, advertising and distribution; or receive Naim's advice, and above all, almost intravenously it was so intense, his enthusiasm. Clapping his hands, exclaiming, he would tell us his idea for a mischievous article that would stir up controversy, and so help the magazine's ailing circulation; and indeed circulation was part of the aim, but so, it must be said, was Naim's badly concealed and infectious joy in taking on the British establishment.

At a certain point the *Literary Review* moved its offices to 51 Beak Street, future site of the Academy Club. But wherever we were, the spirit of Naim was always hovering around. He would ring up on the telephone, and somehow his voice lingered in the office, with its rolled r's, and his favourite phrases – 'at the end of the day' – or, my particular favourite, the exclamation,

'Bobby's your uncle!' In short, the experience of working on the *Literary Review* could not be disentangled from the experience of working for Naim, because you were always conscious of the increasingly wide-ranging activities of your unpredictable impresario boss, who had this protean fund of energy and will, to the point of metamorphosis. One moment he was publishing books, the next he was launching perfumes with the titles Avant l'Amour and Après l'Amour, unmistakable variations on a certain theme, and doubtless there would be a party held in some splendid arena such as the Reform Club or the Travellers' Club. As Naim held one party after another, London seemed to open its doors to reveal an endless number of potential party venues.

The *Literary Review* filled a niche determined in part by its competitors. The *London Review of Books* clearly occupied the intellectual high ground; *The Times Literary Supplement* had its firm allegiance to matters academic; and so the *Literary Review* was there to be perhaps more comfortably on the ground, not highbrow, but not lowbrow either; distinctly lively; drawing on journalists as well as writers. The writers ranged from the famous to the little known, and that was one of the pleasures of working on the magazine – coming into contact with many relatively unsung writers who wanted to bring their particular sensibility and encounter with literature to paper in some form. It always seemed to me that this 'middle ground' gave the *Literary Review* freedom to run, for example, exhaustive interviews with writers that went at a serious ruminative pace, giving place to all kinds of unshowy detail that was nevertheless of literary interest.

Gradually the *Literary Review* became a home for maverick columnists such as A. N. Wilson or Cosmo Landesman, where humorous or odder and more free-wheeling sentiments could be expressed in pieces that were short but piquant; later on, when Auberon Waugh became editor, this bent, the sense of the magazine's character as idiosyncratic, was to become more developed, as Auberon Waugh stamped his own exceedingly British and in some ways divinely eccentric personality on it.

There were three editors at the *Literary Review* during the period I worked there: Gillian, Emma Soames and Auberon Waugh. I shall always be grateful to Gillian or Gilly for taking me on. Gilly had diplomacy, patience, sensitivity and an unerring feeling for whether or not a piece worked. We ran early pieces by David Sexton (two particularly good ones I still remember, one on Tolstoy's diaries, another on father and son in fiction, focusing on the Waughs), Paul Taylor and Andrew Graham-Dixon, and many others. The magazine was going from strength to strength when she left, to go to the *South Bank Show*, and a new editor was appointed, Emma Soames.

Emma was confident and instinctively clever in her judgements, and gifted with wit in abundance (certain jokes still make me laugh – '*TAXI!*' to be shrieked when you want to get out of a situation). The magazine began to take off in new directions: we changed its typeface and logo, got in a very funny cartoon from Nick Newman and Ian Hislop, thought up the anonymous column 'Scrivener' (usually about the nefarious goings-on behind the scenes in newspapers); I persuaded Richard Curtis to do a television column, which was hilarious, and which he later passed on to Stephen Fry, who, perhaps less funny than Richard, was nevertheless an elegant, fluent and reliable contributor. In a relatively short time Emma had made her decisive mark as editor, and we had become great friends (we really did have a lot of laughs), but change was afoot again. Anna Wintour had come back from New York to edit *Vogue* and was claiming Emma as her features editor. Once more the editorship was vacant and this time Naim appointed Auberon Waugh.

I had met Bron, as he was universally known, at a *Spectator* lunch, but nevertheless his columns at the time, which could be so provocative, filled me with apprehension. The *Literary Review* was an extremely small ship. As deputy you sat about five feet away from the editor, and all day you shared an office, just the two of you in the one room; if one of you was on the telephone, for example, the other heard everything you said. In short, it was essential to get on.

However, when Bron did appear, wearing that memorable hat, I liked him immediately. It was in fact impossible not to. He was courteous, kind, considerate, but none of these words (though true) get what was fun about him, which was his drollery, his immensely discerning eye, his effortless dry intelligence – which he wore, almost as a point of honour, lightly. Nor was he ever affected. I couldn't imagine him ever adopting a sentiment that wasn't truly his. He had an original interesting mind, and was without fail interesting to talk to.

I think Bron was grateful for my help because of course it was new to him, running a literary magazine. But it was clear to me that he viewed me sometimes as a sentimental leftie. We always tried to run a short story and we were inundated by short stories, most of which were, to put it bluntly, screamingly terrible. But I remember one on the slush pile depicting a mining community devastated by pit closure. It seemed to me a moving story, that felt authentic, even though the treatment of the subject was in no way surprising; and I showed it to Bron. He read it and was horrified by my suggestion that we run it, seeing it as predictable in the nth degree. I suspect we both had a bit of a case.

As a team, we had our comic moments. I remember that if I arrived and Bron had got there first, perhaps even just fractionally earlier than me, and was sitting ensconced at his desk, I would feel extremely guilty, as if his silent diligence were a reproach. Later, as we became more relaxed colleagues, it turned out that he experienced the identically persecuted sensation if I had preceded *his* arrival.

With such a small staff there was always a great deal to do. There were proofs to correct and re-correct, proofs to be sent out to authors, authors' corrections to transfer, 'shouts' on the cover to be decided, illustrations from publishers to be chased up, short stories to read, and so on; and it was characteristic of Bron that shortly after arriving he advertised for a 'slave' to work gratis in the *LR* office, on the grounds that this menial apprenticeship would be the gateway to future triumphs. I was sceptical if amused, but sure enough, the next month found Grub Smith, whose very name seemed to beggar belief, like some fantastic projection of a Dickensian imagination, sitting at an exceedingly small and low table, almost child-level, below the intercom phone near the door, our slave for the immediate future. Bron was proved right.

Auberon Waugh did to a degree re-mint the magazine in his own image, with his opening column 'From the Pulpit', and that was very good for the magazine's profile. At the same time the magazine became more hospitable to a strand of literary activity that was in some ways proudly anti-intellectual (I always remember him saying that Proust would have written a good book had he kept it to one volume), yet in other ways deeply committed to the concept of the literary, even if it came to that notion by ranging it against a partly exaggerated foe, the too-intellectual or the narrowly academic. Perhaps this battle too found its secret expression in Bron's commitment to placing, at all costs, the word 'sex' on the cover (no dry magazine this). Thus it became a running and well-known joke: even if this month's literary offerings refused to yield anything involving sex, there might be a piece by David Sexton, that would then get cover billing, as in – 'David SEXton on Kingsley Amis', and so on. And then obviously there followed all sorts of things like the 'Bad Sex' competition, all of which earned the *Literary Review* more publicity. But by this time I had followed Emma to Condé Nast, to edit the arts and books section of *Vogue*.

During all this time Naim was the kindest and most supportive of bosses. Although he sometimes got a mixed press, being often depicted as a very sexist employer, the truth is that Naim defied simple labelling. In the world of British publishing he always seemed to me to be something of an innocent who, like all essentially good-hearted people, expected the same in return – windfalls of goodwill. One has to remember certain things about Naim: that it was he who also owned and funded The Women's Press, and published an imprint like Quartet Encounters, run by Stephen Pickles – a less commercial, more riskily high-minded list would be hard to find.

When I came to leave the *Literary Review*, I helped Bron find a successor (pointing him in the directon of Kate Kellaway, for which he was always grateful). But before then various candidates came along, including the sadly late Linda Brandon. Linda – who was to die tragically young – was extremely intelligent, with an exceptional CV. She had also become a lesbian, and wore short hair and dungarees. Accordingly we had an interview: Naim, Bron, Linda and myself. Bron, who was usually utterly unlike the persona of his more extreme kind of column, behaved briefly like the said invented persona – as soon as Linda had gone, he dismissed her completely. Naim on the other hand was perplexed by the single-mindedness of Bron's response. All he could see was this incredibly impressive CV, and her pleasantness as a person. Naim and I argued for her, but Bron was resolute.

That was typical of Naim, who had a disinterested open-minded respect for achievement, and at the risk of stating the obvious, an appreciation of women above and beyond their appearance.

Well, to be fair he liked that, too. But then, to recycle that great last line in cinema, nobody's perfect.

*   *   *

In 1986 I met the young delectable model Jeny Howorth and was immediately entranced by her uncomplicated view of life. She was breathtakingly pretty and had begun modelling at the age of seventeen when she discovered that her bodily assets had developed into a marketable product. Her motto was, 'Keep eating the garlic. Twenty-three years of sunshine, that's how it's been, that's how it's going to be.' She became a regular at the Quartet parties and was one of the two hundred and eighty-nine women I interviewed for *Women*. The book had its genesis that summer when I was beginning to feel that my life could never be complete unless I embarked on a literary adventure I could really call my own. Words had fascinated me ever since childhood and I had tried to express myself through their medium, whether in a social, political or philosophical context. The language in which I was strongest at the time was Arabic and in that language I was able to put pen to paper and achieve a certain fluency. I abhorred anything I produced that I felt to be mediocre or falling below par. Now, with my total change of circumstances, living in a literary world where I had achieved my dream and become a publisher, the time seemed right to direct my surplus energies into a book project that would further my ambition to be remembered as a man of letters. I had never had the opportunity of going to university but I prided myself on being self-taught and having a natural curiosity and sharp, incisive powers of observation. In my teens I read voraciously, and went through a period of flirting with the classics, especially those from Europe, which gave me a sound grounding. Having reached the age of forty-five, I felt the time had come to try my own hand at writing.

An opportunity to prove myself came out of the blue during one of our editorial meetings. Pickles, Quartet's editorial director, challenged me teasingly, saying I ought to write a book about women, seeing that I was so besotted with them and obviously had a special insight into the subject. To begin with, I took the challenge as a piece of cynical ribbing, but the idea began to take root as the days went on. For me to write about women would have been too formidable an undertaking, but to talk to women about their lives and aspirations could make a most worthwhile project, particularly in the late 1980s, when the ideas behind the 'women's movement' were becoming more widely accepted and women were beginning to make their way in professions considered till then to be male preserves.

The more I thought about the idea, the more enthusiastic I became. However, as I saw it, there were two major stumbling blocks. The first was that, to give the book a total originality, I would need to talk to as many women as possible: those who had achieved their success despite prejudice or adversity; others who had been fortunate enough to sail through life convinced their gender was an advantage rather than a disadvantage. Would enough women agree to talk to me? The second stumbling block was more complex. I had no journalistic experience to qualify me in this field. In the circumstances, would I be able to persuade women to talk to me? I was anxious that the book should not in any way be a sociological survey. My 'credentials' came down to the fact that I had always been known to admire women – that I often employed them in preference to men and was conscious of their ability to juggle the demands of career and motherhood. I also enjoyed their company and felt at ease in their presence.

As soon as Quartet made it known it was planning to publish a book on women with me as its author and circulated an information pack, the British press erupted into a babble of speculation. *The Times* wrote:

As if in answer to Anna Ford's indigestible tome on *Men*, publisher Naim Attallah has commissioned himself to write a book on the other sex. One of the people he applied to interview was La Ford. She turned him down.

Private Eye was quick off the starting blocks to catch the bandwagon:

Naim Attullah-Disgusting – head of seedy Quartet Books – has thought of a new scheme to engage in discussion with the opposite sex. He has circulated a number of gorgeous pouters with a letter in which he claims to be writing an 'in-depth book on the evolution of women' and requests an interview. The idea of Attullah-Disgusting writing anything, let alone an 'in-depth book', is too ridiculous to contemplate.

The 'Quick' column in the *Sunday Times* commented how 'Mr Attallah . . . presumably one of the new brand of author-publishers, is well known for his appearances in little columns such as this.'

At last, we are told . . . he is combining his love of words and women, and writing a book about them. Women from all over the world (they wouldn't tell us who), stars of stage and screen, feminists (as opposed to the aforementioned categories) and aristocrats. It will be a book, say the cover notes in a shamelessly juxtaposed reference to Simone de Beauvoir's *Second Sex*, which presents 'a remarkable case for the radical reappraisal of women as the First Sex'. Fascinating. The only problem being that Attallah hasn't written a word. Text by July, we're assured. If he's going to manage addressing, as he says, that long-standing injustice, women's position in relation to men, drawing on mythological, religious, philosophical and literary evidence, as well as interviewing all these people about their upbringing, sexuality, aspirations, fears and hopes, he'd better get a move on.

Veronica Howell, under 'Observatory' in the *Observer*, then said that, rather than hearing what the forthcoming book was going to be like,

we want to know . . . just who in his house of Quartet Books wrote the blurb currently causing so many giggles. We quote: he 'has long been fascinated by words and enchanted with women. Now with singular intent, he has combined both passions and written a book of seminal importance, working to a formidable regimen . . . stars of stage and screen . . . speak candidly.'

Jennifer Bradshaw (Erdal), who had gradually been acting more in the role of a personal assistant, particularly in the literary field, had been put in charge of the *Women* project and the logistical tasks it involved. Letters were then sent off to scores of women in the public eye – writers, academics, actresses, scientists, doctors, lawyers, politicians – inviting them to talk to me (as *Private Eye* accurately reported) and explaining the book's format and objectives. Initial reactions were not encouraging. 'La Ford' did turn me down as *The Times* reported, and she was not alone. I needed to start somewhere, but it had to be on a positive note. Lady Camilla Dempster, the wife of Nigel, the *Daily Mail* diarist, was the first to agree to appear in the book. Her support proved invaluable. This did not, on the other hand, deter her husband from writing the following in his column:

> Anyone who attended the launch of publisher Naim Attallah's 'aphrodisiac' perfume last year – his Quartet girls were squeezed into rubber bondage-style suits – will be surprised to hear he is writing a book on the liberation of women. 'It's a very serious work – I've talked to many women, some famous, some not famous. It shows how women have become more independent and less under man's influence,' he explained, giving one of his young female aides a liberated cuddle.

Camilla brought me luck. From then on, the initial difficulties were slowly overcome. More and more women came into the fold and were willing to air their views with a candid and sometimes devastating openness. Even more remarkable was the flurry of women who then volunteered to be in the book without being asked. Word went around on the grapevine, with various names bandied about, and somehow it became fashionable to be part of the list. In the end it reached the number of two hundred and eighty-nine women, and the figure could easily have gone higher. I put the brakes on simply because there was a danger the tome might become so heavy as to undermine its commercial viability.

Most of the press coverage continued to be so negative that it was clear they were determined to give the book the thumbs down before it even appeared. I was seen as an entrepeneur and familiar character about town by the literary establishment, not as an arbiter of human thought or a collater of women's views and aspirations. They could not but think the book was just a publicity stunt to satisfy my vanity and add another string to my bow. Val Hennessy was her usual acerbic self as she joined the trend of press opinion, revealing in *She* magazine how she had already been interviewed and describing to her readers the kind of questions I had put to her. I was taken aback by the way she reported our encounter, deliberately placing the emphasis on certain questions taken out of context. It was an obvious put-down as she ended her piece by saying I had left her 'with a strong impression that his in-depth book to be published by Quartet will be a mere floundering in the shallow end . . . '

'Grovel' of *Private Eye* redoubled the sarcastic tone when he referred to

> the gorgeous pouting hackette Val Hennessy [as] one of the hapless victims of the swarthy Lebanese parfumier who asked her such questions as 'Is orgasm a female obsession?'; 'Why do some women enjoy being beaten up by men?'; 'Do you wish there were brothels for women?'

Disgusting's dirty tapes, transcribed by tearful secretaries, will be sold to the public as a serious feminist tract by a leading Catholic moralist impelled by a sense of 'spiritual purpose'. Says the blurb: 'The book addresses a long-standing social injustice: women's position in relation to men.'

As it happens, this is a subject on which Ayatollah is something of an expert. So much so that I am now conducting interviews in the hope of a glossy book called *Naim*.

Finally I earned a place under 'Sayings of the Week' in the *Observer* of 22 March: 'A man who is nothing values himself ten times what he is; with a woman it is the other way round.'

Completing the task was to take me a whole year, during which I made regular journeys to New York to interview women there; sometimes as many as five in the course of one day. It was hard work, but it had its rewards. The experience was unparalleled, absorbing and so intensive that at times it left me drained. Yet it also had an addictive effect and I became preoccupied to the point of being unaware of the surrounding realities. The interviews could be deeply emotional as one woman after another confided a tragic experience or expressed her innermost feelings about love or sexuality with a candour I had not been prepared for.

I was left with countless stories to tell about the interviews I conducted in New York. There was the young and dashing socialite who seriously suggested that if I really wanted to remain in touch, then I should adopt her. There was the princess who arrived at the apartment block in her white chauffeur-driven Cadillac to be interviewed after the hour of midnight. There was the famous Hollywood actress who collected me in her car and drove me to the town where she was rehearsing for a play, so the interview could take place during the two-hour journey. There was the stunning international model – an early participant in the project – who became a close friend and introduced me to everyone she knew in New York and Los Angeles.

I felt I was fortunate to have had this unique experience, and when I was called upon by my French publisher to add interviews with an additional thirty Frenchwomen I was delighted to oblige, since I was suffering with-drawal symptoms back in the real world.

A small diversion from my many activities came about when the *Sunday Times* magazine included me in a set of party-goers asked to take a camera along to any party of their choice and come up with some unusual snaps. Each of us was provided with a fully automatic 35AF2 Kodak camera loaded with Kodacolour Gold film. We had three months in which to deliver the pictures.

According to the magazine, most of those approached said 'Great!' to the proposal, others declined. Derek Jameson said he would love to do it, but he never went to parties. Tony James of Sigue Sigue Sputnik also said he would love to, but never came up with any pictures. Those of us who took the commission seriously produced our results from the social frontline in due course. Peter Stringfellow offered his perspective on an evening of entertainment; Elaine Page photographed a group of her own guests; Ian Botham, who was occupied with Amnesty International, found time to work the pavilion at Lords. My own choice was to cover the party for the tenth anniversary of punk at the Limelight Club in Shaftesbury Avenue.

The idea of being behind the camera in the manner of the paparazzi, observing punk in all its shapes and forms, was something I was looking forward to. I felt I had a special interest in the subject as the publisher of Val Hennessy's definitive book on the phenomenon and also of Stefan Richter's *Tattoo*. The correlation between punk and tattoo was inescapable. Each used colour and the human form to send out some sort of signal or make a statement. Each could in a way be said to disfigure the natural grace of the body by imposing outside elements to give it more impact visually and conform with an artificial tribalism. More often than not it was cocking a snook at the aesthetic of beauty, turning beauty into a freak display of weird images designed to shock and draw attention. The result was an improvised sort of wilful ugliness with no definitive characteristics of its own.

The party at the Limelight Club was not the kind I would usually have gone to for pleasure, but I had an assignment I had to carry out. To bolster my morale in an alien setting I took along two of my girls: my cook, Charlotte Millward, who was an extrovert beauty and as cool as a cat, and Amanda Tress, who was then in charge of the Quartet Bookshop; she was equally cool and had a wickedly contagious sense of humour. They dressed in the black-rubber outfits they had worn for the launch of Avant l'Amour and Après l'Amour. The suggestion was made that I, too, ought to be dressed in black rubber. I vetoed the idea and opted instead for a red silk shirt and black trousers.

Charlotte and Amanda made the most of the evening amid a near-demented crowd of young people who whirled, capered and jived to tempos hard to pick out of the ear-shattering noise. The notion of taking pictures seemed an impossible challenge. The floor was jammed and everything was happening in pitch darkness. Only the fear of failure *vis-à-vis* the *Sunday Times* induced me to keep trying. Eventually I discerned the figure of a young woman – at least I thought it was a young woman. It was extremely hard to tell the difference. The styles of youth made the sexes almost interchangeable, but the creature I targeted seemed very colourful and sexy, irrespective of gender. I managed to snap a picture, and then another face beamed out of the darkness. I clicked the camera again and and kept on clicking at random, trying to capture the mood of the party. Some of the visual effects were fascinating, but others you just couldn't cope with. In the end I couldn't stand any more of it.

As it turned out, my efforts were not in vain. The *Sunday Times* were very pleased with what I had achieved and published the fruits of my endeavours, giving them some prominence in the feature article. Among the contributors I was apparently the only one who failed to include a self-portrait in the selection. As a result, they had to find one for themselves and I was referred to for the first time as 'the self-effacing Naim Attallah'.

*

Early in 1987 I was involved in a theatrical venture that turned sour. *The Old Man of Lochnagar*, Prince Charles's much praised children's yarn, was transformed into an expensive flop when adapted for the stage. It was based on the Goon-like humour that the prince is known to favour and told the story of a Highland character with a lavatory contraption that played 'Scotland the Brave'. As one of the show's main backers I sustained a sizeable loss. Its three-week run in the West End at the Albery Theatre left a deficit of forty thousand pounds with not a single house achieving a sell-out. All in all, the exercise was a big disappointment. Prince Charles had been expected to turn up to see the show with Princes William and Harry but he never came. It deserved a better fate at the box office than the one it received. Prince Charles's staying away did nothing to help the situation. When the deflated cast members questioned his absence, after they had done so much to capture the spirit of his book, they were told bluntly by a palace aide, 'He chose not to go.' Had he been too busy, they wondered. The response was a crisply repeated: 'He just chose not to go.' The whole attitude of the palace was a public-relations disaster. It certainly came over as one of Prince Charles's less gracious moments: a *faux pas* verging on the arrogant.

A project that was more of a sure-fire entertainment in ways it never intended was a book published by Quartet a month later. The hilarity arose partly because of its subject and partly because of the identity of its author, who happened to be married to David Stevens, the press baron of Express Newspapers who had been created a life peer as Lord Stevens of Ludgate. Melissa Sadoff, as she called herself, possessed an inherited family title from central Europe and was, formally speaking, Melissa, Countess Andrassy. The book she had written was *Woman as Chameleon: or How To Be the Ideal Woman*. It was the very antithesis of feminist doctrine, aiming to teach women ways to keep their marriage exciting by pampering their man and acceding to his every wish and whim. Melissa was flamboyant in her views and Lord Stevens gave the impression of taking his wife's attentions in his stride. She described the treatment she gave him in rather embarrassing detail, which opened up an opportunity for the critics to have a field-day in leg-pulling.

'Grovel' of *Private Eye* immediately dubbed Melissa 'Countess Undressy' and claimed to have suggested the book after hearing her speak about her husband's 'Ugandan preferences'. He was able to quote her verbatim for his own purposes.

> 'There is *nothing*,' she says, 'that can be called perverse between husband and wife so long as it relates to the husband's need and the wife's willingness to do it.'
>
> I have advised her to put it all on paper with a view to publication in book form. I tell her that my friend the seedy Lebanese parfumier Mr Attullah-Disgusting could well be interested, as he is currently obsessed by all aspects of the Ugandan situation.

Two weeks later 'Grovel' followed through with the latest development:

> As I suggested, the Countess Undressy . . . is to write a book of Ugandan hints, which will shortly be published by the swarthy Lebanese sex-fiend Naim Attullah-Disgusting.
>
> The 'Countess' will not mince words when she describes how she sees the duties of a wife.
>
> 'Always kiss your husband's body, starting from his toes,' she writes. 'After kissing his toes and sucking them, proceed to kiss every inch of his legs . . .
>
> 'She should then perform the oral act. Many women feel an aversion towards this form of sex . . . Women who feel this way need to be asked what they would prefer – to have their husband go to a prostitute for such a service?'
>
> (*What's the oral act?* © *Norman Fowler* '87)
> (That's enough filth. Ed.)

The launch for *Woman as Chameleon* was held on 10 February, with 'Londoner's Diary' of the *Evening Standard* citing the toe-kissing routine before asking 'a pale, nervous and uncomfortable' David Stevens, 'Well, does she always?' He had to confess that he hadn't yet read the book, and didn't intend to do so till he'd sifted through the reviews. 'Otherwise I might be embarrassed.'

The nearest the party came to being *risqué* was when Jubby Ingrams's shoe was removed from her foot by an admirer with a view to kissing her from the toes upwards. Ms Sadoff rushed over to intervene. 'No,' she cried with a Transylvanian lilt. 'It must be the other way round.'

Henry Porter in the *Sunday Times* 'Notebook' judged David Stevens to be 'rather more reticent about his home life' than was his wife.

I would estimate that this book . . . is going to cause considerable embarrassment to Mr Stevens . . . None the less, he has taken steps to purchase the serial rights if only to keep it out of the hands of the *Daily Mail* group, which naturally was keen to enhance his discomfort by publishing extracts like this: 'Become your husband's own prostitute . . . if your husband is in his study, workroom or garage in the wintertime put on a sexy slip, wrap yourself in a coat, slip on suspenders, black stockings and surprise him wherever he may be.'

Unfortunately the fun and games of the press diverted attention from the rest of the book, which threw many a light on relationships, friendships, motherhood and divorce, with sound philosophical reflections. Melissa was of Hungarian origin, a talented concert pianist and an accomplished hostess. She was perhaps a shade over the top in her enthusiasm, but being an eternal optimist her heart was in the right place. In retrospect, I believe she deserved more praise for the book than she ever received.

Throughout the merciless lampooning from *Private Eye* and the barrage of snide sarcasm aimed by the rest of the press against the book, which inevitably earned the displeasure of the feminist lobby, she remained in control and outwardly unaffected by it all. Her husband, despite the newspapers' determination to embarrass him, was extremely supportive. He did not seem to be in any way phased by the teasing of friends over the rumpus caused by some of the book's intimate passages. Sadly, only two years later, Melissa died when she got up in the middle of the night to eat a peach and choked on the stone. I was in Los Angeles at the time and was woken to hear the dreadful news. It left me feeling very emotional. I had grown to like Melissa immensely. Her colourful personality and boundless zest for life were her enduring strengths and ensured she could not be easily forgotten.

*

In January 1987 I met Mrs Shelley Vaughan Williams, a very attractive and personable woman who was closely connected with the Jersey Scriptorium in the Channel Islands. Her keen interest in calligraphy stemmed from a belief in the value of clear communication, whether this took the form of a beautifully hand-lettered poem or the kind of text fonts being developed for computer programs. She stressed the fact that calligraphers trained in the visual side of lettering had a crucial role to play in determining the optical spacing used on computers and in satellite communications. From 1979 onwards, an exquisitely inscribed and decorated birthday card had been presented each year to the Queen Mother from the Jersey Scriptorium. Now, for the first time, the chance was there for the public to share in the enjoyment of the superb workmanship that went into producing one of the cards. Having secured the permission of the Queen Mother, I agreed to take the project on board. I would provide the financial backing and Quartet would print the card, designed by Charles Stooks, and arrange its distribution in the marketplace.

It bemused me slightly to find myself suddenly involved in the business of royal birthday cards without any warning. The culprit was Mrs Shelley Vaughan Williams herself, who, with her energy and evangelical zeal for the calligraphic arts, was responsible for my seduction. This was not too difficult. I was always prone to do the bidding of a determined woman, especially one who had the charm and persuasive power of Mrs Vaughan Williams. The fact that she was a member of the Worshipful Company of Painter-Stainers and a freeman of the City of London will give some idea of her status. There was another reason for my support. As was the case with Asprey, I wanted to help with ensuring that individual skills and handicrafts were maintained and survived in a world where mechanization threatened them with extinction. If artists, calligraphers and bookbinders were no longer encouraged and rewarded, then their particular skills would die out and we would all suffer for it, finding ourselves in a vastly impoverished world.

Mrs Vaughan Williams printed a letter of appreciation in the *Jersey Evening Post* of 4 February:

> Not only is it Mr Attallah's generosity of action that is appreciated, it is also his regard for the innate value of the Scriptorium's work. It is his wish to encourage us to continue helping not only the young but people of all ages and from all walks of life in pursuing avenues of excellence in the world of communication that will open up their personal and working lives.

The Queen Mother's card was a one-off venture, the rewards for which were not financial so much as useful public-relations-wise. The Jersey Scriptorium benefited from the extra publicity, Quartet came to have its profile known in new quarters and I forged a close friendship with Mrs Shelley Vaughan Williams. She figured in due course as an interviewee in *Women*.

No one could have ever accused Quartet of turning its back on an unusual celebrity offering which had a particular merit and was likely to engage public attention. One such instance was Susan George's book of poems, *Songs to Bedroom Walls*. Susan George was best known as an actress and for having been a one-time friend of Prince Charles. The book consisted of sixteen poems, with sixteen paintings by Andrew Hewkin. It was printed on cream vellum in a calligraphic script and hand-bound in cloth. A cassette of Susan George reading her poems, and singing three of them that had been set to music, was also included. The whole production was stamped with a seal bearing the initials of the poet and the illustrator and it came gift-wrapped in ribbons and tissue paper. Peter Ustinov wrote the preface. The edition was limited to five hundred copies at seventy-five pounds each, available only by direct order from Quartet.

The launch was held at the Savoy Hotel, with a reading by Susan George against a strummed guitar accompaniment. Her husband, the actor Simon MacCorkindale, described the book as 'an emotional outpouring' and said stoically that he knew what poems were written about which people and under what circumstances. They had been composed by Susan over a period of ten years, telling of poignant moments with loves past and present. 'It was always a private thing, until such time as I was ready to share it,' she said. She explained in an interview with *You* magazine how, 'One morning I woke up and I wrote. I don't know where the talent came from, I only know God gave it to me.' The book was full of emotion of the sort expressed in the following poem:

The Performer

Sometimes your bitterness wears deep within my soul,
But you wouldn't know as you cannot feel the pain inside.
Often I can't distinguish laughter from the tears,
Often I'm afraid, for there's nowhere to hide.
It's a game that we play and yours is to win.
First you open your heart, then you don't let me in.
I can't believe you're here to hurt me.
I know you came to love me.

'There's much that David Frost can be held accountable for,' said 'Londoner's Diary' in the *Standard*, '[but] it is only now that I learn Frostie is responsible for one of the more bizarre cultural firsts of the year, the collected poetry of the no-longer-youthful starlet Susan George.'

It was he who contacted Quartet publisher Naim Attallah on the Fragrant One's behalf . . . 'He was full of enthusiasm,' Attallah tells me, 'and as I'm an enthusiastic person I said, "Why not?" '

Whether his enthusiasm will be repaid is another matter. So far 100 copies of the limited edition have been sold, but whether there are enough fans of Miss George still around and interested in finding out whether her poetry is as great as her contribution to the dramatic arts, I do not know.

The book was in fact well received by the many admirers of the author. Despite its restricted appeal for the public at large, it captured the section of the market at which it had been aimed. As an exercise in publishing versatility, it established a new Quartet departure and gained an exposure for the imprint in a field that was entirely outside its normal range.

Another celebrity book, again concerning an actress, was *Charlotte Rampling with Compliments*. It was a collation of snapshots, fashion shots and movie stills of the star over a period of twenty years. The *Standard* commented this time:

> The divine Charlotte Rampling has been turning strong men to porridge ever since her début in 1965 as a water-skiing nymph in Richard Lester's *The Knack*. Now one of her most devoted fans, Mr Naim Attallah, the Arabian connoisseur of the fair sex, is bringing out a book . . .

Another admirer, Dirk Bogarde, who starred with her in *The Night Porter*, contributed an introductory portrait of the actress: 'She was as free, simple and skittish as a foal, hair tumbling in a golden fall about her . . . the grace of a panther . . . the almost incredible perfection of her bone structure.' The Japanese film director Nagisa Oshima, who had recently directed her in *Max My Love*, in which she co-starred with an ape, contributed four pages of painstakingly drawn Japanese ideograms in celebration of his leading lady. Both contributions gushed shamelessly and showed the amount of love and admiration people in show business felt for her.

I was particularly glad to be publishing this book. In 1973, when Charlotte Rampling starred in *The Night Porter* with Dirk Bogarde, she began to inhabit the dreams of a whole generation of men. I, for one, had never recovered from the sight of her straddling Dirk Bogarde, and the image remained in my mind like an old sepia photograph. In the film she played a young girl who blossomed into a sophisticated woman, and her performance was so haunting as to move one critic to compare her with Garbo. Two years later, in the 1975 remake of *Farewell My Lovely*, her seductiveness was supreme yet perfectly contained.

When I met her in the 1980s, I found the real Rampling even more compelling than the screen version. She struck me as both exotic and English – a near contradiction in terms – and she underplayed her sex-symbol status with a rare intelligence, despite the allure of her emerald-green eyes, her velvety voice and the perfection of her bone structure.

Underneath the poise, however, Charlotte Rampling seemed haunted by demons. As the daughter of an army colonel, she had had an unsettled – and sometimes unhappy – childhood. She had felt rejected by her mother in favour of her older sister, who later died tragically at the age of only twenty-three. Charlotte reacted by exceeding the traditional boundaries of women's lives. During the 1960s, when everyone else was on CND marches or off to India doing ashrams, she went to live with gypsies in Afghanistan (a dangerous and violent experience) and later to a Tibetan monastery in Scotland. By the time she was twenty-two, she was in Hollywood and had earned herself the title of 'Europe's kinky sex-film queen' by living in a *ménage à trois* with Brian Southcombe and a male model. Later she told me that she had loved both men but, to spare her parents' feelings, thought it best to marry one of them.

In 1976, she met Jean-Michel Jarre at the Cannes Film Festival after what she described as a *coup de foudre*, and the following year they married; unfortunately they are now divorced. Jarre was a highly successful composer and musician with an international following. Looked at from the outside, they seemed like a dream couple, combining art, beauty, glamour and intelligence in enviable proportions. It could have been an ideal partnership, but it was never likely that Charlotte Rampling would subscribe to the Jane Austen view of marriage as a woman's principal act of self-definition. Rampling was always far too unconventional ever to be defined by marriage. 'Jean-Michel and I are very *marginale*, as we say in French,' she told me. 'We do things which are off the beaten track.'

Just as she had always chosen cinematic roles that explored the darker side of human nature, so she was given to delving deep into her own soul. More than once she had suffered depression and come close to nervous breakdown.

Evidently it was improbable that marriage would ever bring her stability in the conventional sense; rather, it was always likely to be a continuation of the restlessness from which she could never find a refuge. *Plus ça change, plus c'est la même chose*. She was truly a woman to break boundaries.

Charlotte Rampling with Compliments was virtually a biography, but it told its story visually. It illustrated the early modelling career of the beautiful girl in the London of the swinging sixties as well as documenting the international film career that followed for her soon after. Fashion photographers, including the world-famous Helmut Newton, David Bailey and Cecil Beaton, captured her compelling, enigmatic moods, which were often mysteriously melancholic and invariably conveyed an erotic aura of unique intensity. The volume was also beautifully produced and it did well commercially. It created a good rapport with Charlotte, which led to her becoming yet another candidate for my projected book of interviews with women.

In March Quartet published *Last of a Kind: The Sinking of Lew Grade* by Quentin Falk and Dominic Prince. Lew Grade was then Britain's biggest show-business mogul, in the mould of Darryl F. Zanuck and Sam Goldwyn in the United States: he was a species on the verge of extinction. For a quarter of a century his position of dominance in the entertainment industry had seemed unassailable, first as a theatrical agent and then as a television executive. He was also a pre-eminent salesman who had a tremendous rapport with the press and revelled in the most uncritical coverage ever enjoyed by a top British businessman. He held them in the palm of his hand with his one-liners and they, in turn, fed the public with tales of his workaholism, his unswerving patriotism, his sales figures and his long cigars. Then, when he was almost seventy, he decided to take on Hollywood. Within two years the Grade fiefdom had collapsed under relentless public gaze. Amid a flurry of plunging profits, pay-off rows and inept movies, his business empire was swept away after one of the most insidious takeover battles in the history of the City.

Last of a Kind chronicled the demise of a man who extravagantly built and launched a '*Titanic*' venture, only to have it sink to the bottom, taking with it the colourful tycoon who was its creator. Lew Grade was none too pleased about the book being published. Another title from Quartet earlier in the 1980s, *The Television Barons* by the *Daily Mail* theatre critic Jack Tinker, still rankled. In that case Jack had taken a clear-eyed critical look at the men for whom the independent television franchises had been 'a licence to print money'. He examined the history of the various companies and the role of the Independent Broadcasting Authority (the IBA) and went on to raise long overdue questions about the ethics of the situation in broadcasting at the time, when the franchises were being fiercely contested. Lew had been irritated by the contents of Tinker's book and hinted that legal proceedings were an option he was considering. Yet nothing further was heard from him until *Last of a Kind* arrived on the bookstalls, being partly a biography and partly a chronicle of his company's collapse. He demanded that all copies of the book be withdrawn within twenty-four hours, otherwise he would seek an injunction banning its sale, the focus of his objection being not his business history but one paragraph concerning his adopted son, Paul. Again no more was heard, beyond the lawyers of the ennobled Lew Grade saying they 'were considering the position'.

I never had an axe to grind with Lew Grade or any of the other television barons, beyond the fact that having secured franchises that bestowed on them great wealth and immense power they seemed to have become a law unto themselves. For too long they had been 'the untouchables' and resented anyone who dared to criticize the system. It was high time their wings were clipped.

Thirty

In March 1987 the Countess of Dudley's libel complaint against the *Literary Review*, which went back to the time before Auberon Waugh became editor, finally had a hearing and we needed to defend our position in court. The passage that caused the commotion had occurred in just a few sentences of a seventeen-hundred-word review by Alastair Forbes of Anne Somerset's book *Ladies in Waiting* in the July 1984 issue of the magazine. Two years before that the countess had acted as an 'unofficial' unpaid lady-in-waiting to Princess Michael of Kent on a 'flag waving' tour of the United States. In the wake of the trip her husband, Lord Dudley, had taken to reciting a scurrilous poem about the princess, which he called 'Our Val', in the privacy of London clubs and smoking rooms. It was 'biting, bitchy and along the lines of "Eskimo Nell" ', as the *Daily Mail* described it without contradiction. The poem had then unintentionally taken on a life of its own by being retailed on the social circuit, on one occasion, it was said, making Princess Margaret fall off her chair with laughter after she heard it. When word of all this got back to Princess Michael, she naturally became upset. Alastair Forbes referred to the episode in his review, saying how the Earl of Dudley had spent much of 1983 giving 'Tennysonian after-dinner readings of his most un-Tennysonian tirade against poor Princess Michael of Kent'.

> Her only offence had lain in her proven unwisdom in inviting Dudley's humbly born but avid countess to accompany her to the United States as a lady-in-waiting, who would be expected to pay her own way.
>
> Dudley's scurrilously bad poetasting, coarse and clumsy attempts to clothe criminal libel in Clive Jamesian mode, had the effect in due course of winning considerable sympathy [for the princess], not least from the Queen.
>
> The unprecedented outcome was that Dudley received a *lettre de cachet* from the palace solicitors that has since effectively zipped his wife's lips.

Dudley had done the least he could do and written a letter of apology to Princess Michael, which was delivered in person to the royal solicitor by Lord Goodman. Subsequently it came into the public domain when part of its text was printed in the *Mail on Sunday* in 1985:

I write on behalf of my wife and myself to place on record our most sincere regret for the grave distress and embarrassment which we have caused you, Prince Michael, and your family and we unreservedly express our deep apologies. We acknowledge that the statements are untruthful and should never have been made. We undertake that we will never repeat or publish this offensive material again or anything similar relating to you or your family.

Later Lord Dudley, when questioned by the press, put out a statement that he was confident no copy of the poem had got out at the time. 'All copies of it were destroyed.'

Lady Dudley's lawyer told the press: 'Our action concerns allegations in the review about the countess's attitude.' The burden of their case was that Alastair Forbes's article, by stating that the countess's lips had needed to be 'zipped' by the Queen's solicitors, implied she had fed libellous stories against Princess Michael to her husband and verbally stabbed the princess in the back, other parts of the review portraying her as 'vulgar, greedy, grasping and pushy'. It had been, claimed her counsel in court, 'a scurrilous and damaging attack' on Lady Dudley's character. 'It is quite a serious attack on her loyalty, her integrity, and her character as a whole.'

There were undoubtedly social sensitivities involved in the Dudley family background. Lady Dudley herself was irked by the tendency of the press to refer to her as a former 'Rank starlet'. The publicity arising from the libel hearing compelled her to circulate a CV to the editors of Fleet Street to correct any misapprehensions: ' . . . my claim is that I should be regarded as having been a serious actress and dancer who only appeared in leading roles in films, on the stage and on television'. As Maureen Swanson, a talented twelve-year-old schoolgirl from Glasgow – the daughter of a hairdresser's assistant – she had arrived in London to study with the Sadler's Wells Theatre Company and moved on to graduate as dancer from the Royal School of Ballet. From there she was talent-spotted for stage and screen, gaining a part in the first London production of *Carousel* at the Theatre Royal, Drury Lane in 1950. The following year John Huston cast her for a role in his film *Moulin Rouge* and she began to widen her social circle, becoming a friend of Dr Stephen Ward before he was engulfed and destroyed through his links with the Christine Keeler–John Profumo scandal.

Later films in which she had supporting roles included Jack Lee's *A Town Like Alice* in 1956, with Peter Finch and Virginia McKenna, based on Nevil Shute's novel; and in the same year there was a film version of A. J. Cronin's novel *The Spanish Gardener*, with Dirk Bogarde, in which she played a 'sultry peasant girl (strangely endowed with vowels of purist Pinewood)', in the words of the commentator, Hugh Montgomery-Massingberd, in the *Daily Telegraph* on 1 April 1987. In the 1950s film fans were not so troubled by such incongruous inauthenticities as they were likely to be half a century later. Then, in 1957, she had a role in Jack Lee's *Robbery under Arms*, with Peter Finch and Ronald Lewis, but the promising acting career ended in 1961 when she married the 4th Earl of Dudley after a six-year courtship and joined the long tradition of show girls who have merged into the aristocracy. Their marriage had been delayed until the earl's divorce from his first wife became absolute.

The actress had therefore 'metamorphosed into the peeress', but the 'finest performance of her career', in the words of Mr Montgomery-Massingberd, basing his judgement on the way she handled her evidence during the libel hearing before a jury, had now been as the Countess of Dudley.

The vision of the Countess of Dudley crying in court over Mr Alastair Forbes's uncomfortable revelations, published a mere three years ago in the *Literary Review*, could well provoke polemics on the gross absurdity of the libel laws or the sickening hypocrisy of the upper classes, but it also affords a striking example of the apotheosis of the 'actressocracy'.

Both Bron and I had confidence in the total logic of the magazine's defence, which was that Alastair Forbes's words, as given in the *Literary Review*, were not capable of bearing the meaning complained of. The hearing lasted four and a half hours and the jury, consisting of seven men and five women, retired for a further two hours to consider all they had seen and heard. The *Daily Mail* next day, on 31 March, printed a headline that told the whole story: 'Earl's wife in tears after she wins "zipped lip" libel case'. The spirit of the 'actressocracy' had won the jury round, and a 'tearful Countess was comforted by her husband after the hearing at which she was awarded £5,000 damages and costs estimated at £20,000'. 'I feel absolutely vindicated,' said Lady Dudley. 'It was just the result I wanted.'

Writer Auberon Waugh, recently appointed editor of the *Literary Review*, said after the case: 'We are very sad indeed because it all depended on whether the jury understood English or not. Obviously it didn't.'

Asked if there would be any problems in paying the award and legal costs, he replied: 'I imagine there will be, but I am keeping quiet about that.'

Bron also won himself a place in 'Quote of the Day' in the *London Daily News* the following morning: 'Our defence was that what we said was true, but that we didn't say it.' The result initially got him down and 'Londoner's

Diary' in the *Evening Standard* drew a depressed response from him, finding him 'trying to talk himself out of a job'.

> Though the proprietor, the parfumier and publisher Naim Attallah, sings in his sweet Palestinian voice that he'll find the money somewhere – and he shouldn't find it difficult – Waugh says it might be the time for the mag to go to the great library in the sky.
>
> 'It should have gone under years ago,' he sighs. 'I have put the sub-scription up to £15 but haven't got any in yet. The future is parlous.'

The only thought that cheered him up a little was that if the magazine folded the countess was going to have to start all over again with a fresh action 'against Attallah or the printers if she wanted her money'. Meanwhile Lady Dudley was complaining that I had not stayed to shake her hand in a sporting way, but had 'slunk' off after the verdict, and fuming against Bron for his 'élitist attitude' in patronizing the jury with his assertion that they did not understand English. It was a theme Bron was not going to let drop in a hurry. He returned to it with fresh vigour in his column in the *Sunday Telegraph* of 5 April, saying how he observed that 'three of the jurors had some difficulty in reading the jury oath and one could not do it at all. It was read to him by the Clerk.'

> The case revolved around the meaning to be put upon some words in a fairly abstruse piece of literary criticism. The countess claimed that they suggested she was a 'greedy and vulgar woman', who despite an undertaking to do so, refused to pay her expenses on a trip with Princess Michael, but instead furnished her husband, the Earl of Dudley, with material for a scurrilous poem which he wrote about the princess and circulated until requested to stop by the palace.
>
> The *Literary Review* . . . pointed out that the words meant nothing of the sort. Since that was the point at issue, the judge, Mr Justice Drake, declined to take sides. The jury decided after [two] hours that the words were indeed capable of some such meaning . . .
>
> I do not know what governs Parliament in its choice of qualifications for jury service, but even a Labour government should be able to understand that a case involving interpretation of the written word is unlikely to be helped by a juror who cannot actually read. This was undoubtedly the case with one juror, but several others had the utmost difficulty. Perhaps, in the great explosion of illiteracy which has been observed since the education reforms of the last decade, court officials might divide their cases into those which require an ability to read and those which don't.

Mercifully enough, said Bron, the hearing had lasted less than a day.

In summing up, Mr Justice Drake seemed to invite the jury to share his disappointment that the *Literary Review* had not mounted a more comprehensive defence. But he must have been aware that tiny magazines like the *Literary Review* cannot begin to afford the cost of such an enterprise. At the time of the alleged libel – long before I became editor – its circulation was apparently only 2,000 copies. The sum at stake in this one-day hearing – about £20,000 as it turned out – may be nothing to the Dudleys, who are extremely rich, but to the *Literary Review* it represents the entire annual revenue from 2,000 subscriptions . . .

There is hope that something good will come out of this sorry little episode. I had supposed that immediately after the result, Lady Dudley would announce she was giving the £5,000 to charity. Unfortunately the announcement seems to have been delayed, but when it comes it will prove even more conclusively than the jury's decision that she is neither 'greedy' nor 'grasping' nor any of the horrid things of which she thought she had been accused.

Lord Dudley mounted a counter-attack in a letter printed on 19 April, summarizing Bron's case and adding that readers of the *Sunday Telegraph* would be surprised to know that Alastair Forbes had 'admitted over two years ago in a letter dated January 24, 1985 to Naim Attallah, owner of the *Literary Review*, of which I have a copy, sent to her by the *Review*'s solicitors, that the passages in his article objectionable to my wife did in fact carry the meaning she attached to them; . . . and apologized to my wife . . . ' Auberon Waugh, he accused, had unhesitatingly used his access to the press to portray the defeat in court in a less unfavourable light while hinting at a 'possible mistrial'. His advice to Lady Dudley on how to use her damages had only added insult to injury and his comments had already involved the Dudleys in extra legal expenses. They were therefore instituting a 'fighting fund or Waugh chest, fortified by the jury's award'.

Then, as a challenge to a further account of the hearing Bron had given in the *Spectator*, Lord Dudley wrote a letter to that journal too, quoting at greater length from Alastair Forbes's apology:

'Having too credulously but in perfect good faith accepted as authoritative a circumstantial account of the matter from a cousin of the sovereign whom I mistakingly assumed to be in a position to know, I hinted in my review that the two ladies had subsequently fallen out . . . over the matter of expenses incurred . . . I have since been informed that this was not the correct *casus* . . . I unreservedly accept . . . that "filthy lucre" played no part . . . I apologize to Lady Dudley for my inadvertently inaccurate interpretation.'

Bron and I must therefore have known, Lord Dudley asserted, that the words complained about did carry the meaning Lady Dudley had imputed to them, which meant we were now paying dearly for an error of judgement. Auberon Waugh had been a 'liar' when he wrote that Lady Dudley 'wept in the dock [*sic*] while describing how she had six children' and that she 'did not give the impression of quick appreciation of the English language'. Bron had made the assertion that an effective defence could have been mounted for costs of a hundred thousand pounds, and Lord Dudley challenged him to substantiate this 'untrue and defamatory innuendo'.

> If he is unable to respond to my challenge, and to justify those passages in his article in which I accuse him of deceit, lies and unfair innuendo, he will condemn himself in the eyes of readers of your periodical, and the wider readership that has access to it, as a bad loser and a bad sport, all whose past comments on the case are attributable to these defective qualities.

There must be more honest and honourable ways of defending the *Literary Review*'s reputation, thought the earl, than more mud slinging at Lady Dudley or attempts to 'take the edge off her well-deserved triumph'. 'Auberon Waugh,' added an editor's note, 'when asked to comment, groaned.'

At this point I stepped into the firing line and wrote my own letter from Namara House to the *Spectator* on 25 April:

> Sir: I was amazed by Lord Dudley's partial quotation . . . from a letter Alastair Forbes wrote to the *Literary Review* on 24 January 1985.
>
> If Lord Dudley wishes people to know why the *Literary Review* never published the letter, then I suggest he quotes it in full; or, better still, he could challenge the *Literary Review* to publish it.

In the *Sunday Telegraph* of 26 April I printed a letter clarifying the position over this further:

> What [Lord Dudley] does not divulge is that the same letter also contained inflammatory material about the Dudleys which the *Literary Review* quite rightly chose not to publish. The magazine was not prepared to find itself embroiled in a family squabble not of its making.
>
> Much fuss has been made of the original review of which Lady Dudley complains; the reality of the situation is that all could have been settled amicably had the Dudleys, at the outset, chosen diplomacy rather than heavy-handedness.

Simultaneously, Alastair Forbes was joining in the letter-writing fray, denying Lord Dudley's claim that there had ever been an admission from him that the passage complained about did indeed carry the meaning Lady Dudley saw in it. He had, he said, admitted to no such thing. In his view, Lord Dudley was attempting to bamboozle and mislead the *Sunday Telegraph*'s readers by disingenuously quoting out of context. He greatly hoped that Lord Dudley would take up my challenge to print in full the text as he originally wrote it. The part that was true, he told the *Spectator*, was that

> after refusing to provide the grovelling apology and withdrawal demanded by Lady Dudley's solicitors, I sent to the latter a copy of the 'Apology and clarification' I had thought it appropriate to offer to the *Literary Review* . . . In this document I corrected and apologized for a minor error, attributing one cause of the admitted 1982 dispute between Princess Michael and Lady Dudley . . . to a tiff over tipping in a British Embassy.
>
> My clarification reminded readers of the *Literary Review* that Lady Dudley was only one of 'the sixty or so persons, titled and untitled, to have received appropriate contextual mention' in my notice of *Ladies in Waiting*. 'Likewise her husband,' I went on, 'who, it has nowhere been disputed, was the author and publisher of a scurrilous libel and slander grossly defamatory of HRH Princess Michael of Kent whom Lady Dudley at one time accompanied as companion and unofficial lady-in-waiting on a most successful fund-raising trip to the US undertaken by the princess, both roles being performed to the latter's satisfaction . . . I have since been informed that this [i.e. the tiff over tips] was not the correct *casus* of the Dudleys' bitterly belligerent ballad . . . I unreservedly accept Lady Dudley's assertion that "filthy lucre" played no part in the genesis of her husband's filthy poem' . . .
>
> I went on to suggest that nevertheless the princess had been ill-advised to choose as companion 'anyone capable of suddenly becoming so avid of encouraging the public pillorying and ridicule of a member of the royal family, whose much-loved parents-in-law, I cannot help recalling, began their honeymoon as guests of Lord Dudley's father at Himley Hall'.

It was a pity, he concluded, that the jury had heard nothing of all this background, or of the letter of apology written by Lord Dudley to Princess Michael.

At the end of April there was an 'At Home' party for the *Literary Review* at the Groucho Club, ostensibly to mark a change of staff and to boast about the enrolment of the five-thousandth subscriber, though really as 'a riotous excuse for authors to meet authors and for hacks to play in the conversational surf', as 'Londoner's Diary' in the *Evening Standard* reported it.

Guests included novelist Piers Paul Read (a bit of *gravitas* there), for foreign glamour Count Adam Zamoyski, for beauty the bevy of Waugh girls and for respectability Jeffrey Bernard.

Literary Review's publisher, Naim Attallah . . . waved aside suggestions that the costs of the recent Lady Dudley libel case may sink the mag. 'It's an occupational hazard,' he said with painful grandeur.

Lord Dudley returned to the lists with a final letter to the *Spectator* on 2 May, apparently unaware of how it reflected on the way the *hubris* of his uncouth calumny against Princess Michael must continue to haunt him long after he had lodged his apology.

Alastair Forbes speculates in his letter, and in his review, about the contents of my poem, of which he knows nothing from me, nor, I suspect, from any other source. Unlike his defamatory article, no jury has been asked to decide if it was libellous. It reflected my anger more than four years ago at what I believed to be unfair treatment of my wife, as explained in the covering letter to Prince Michael accompanying my apology, subject to a legal agreement that the contents should remain confidential to those persons having heard or read the poem.

I firmly deny that the poem could justifiably have been compared to 'Eskimo Nell' in style, meter, or content, as anyone with knowledge of it would confirm. Otherwise I continue, despite the leak of my apology, to honour my side of the agreement.

I can also state as a positive fact for which I have conclusive evidence that there was no 'unprecedented outcome' to the existence of the poem, as stated by Alastair Forbes in his book review . . . and that it is untrue that my wife's lips were effectively zipped up by any such letter, or that any letter exists likely to have influenced the jury to reach a different verdict.

Finally, on 16 May, Bron put on a demonstration of how formidable he could be when roused, as he gathered up and summarized all the implications in an article for the *Spectator* headed: 'Time for Dudley to act like an earl and belt up'. While away in Spain for a week, he had debated whether maintaining a dignified silence was really appropriate in the face of a letter that accused him of 'deceit, lies and unfair innuendo'.

To say of an established member of the journalistic profession that he is a deliberate deceiver, etc., is a fairly dangerous thing, especially if it is based on a single matter whose truth is easily established. In my experience of the libel law, which may be more extensive than Lord Dudley's, I would put it at £20,000 in out-of-court settlement, and any sum you care to mention after litigation. Perhaps someone told him that respectable journalists do not sue for libel unless they are accused of treason or taking bribes. That has always been my rule . . .

But dignified silence does not always work, either, as I found to my irritation when returning from abroad, by which time another long, tendentious and, I am sorry to say, rather misleading letter from Lord Dudley had appeared . . . My earlier silence was inspired, more than anything else, by an earnest desire not to bore *Spectator* readers with a continuation of other people's troubles. However, they have already been bored to tears, and I now feel I have an obligation to explain to them, in as unboring a way as possible, what it is all about. So here goes.

In October 1982 Lady Dudley . . . was asked to accompany Princess Michael of Kent on an American tour. In the course of that tour, they spent a weekend at the Washington Embassy where certain events either occurred or did not occur – I do not know whether they did or not – which caused Lord Dudley to write to Mr John Barratt, Prince Michael's secretary, in August 1983 that criticism of his wife's conduct had been made by Princess Michael as early as the previous November (1982), 'when she told Mrs Jonathan Aitken that the British Ambassador in Washington (Sir Oliver Wright) had told her, Princess Michael personally, that my wife's conduct in Washington had been so odious and outrageous that the Ambassador would never invite her to the Embassy again'.

That is Lord Dudley's account. Mr Barratt gives a slightly different one. Whatever the rights and wrongs of it, Lord Dudley under 'emotions of deep resentment', as he described them in a letter to Prince Michael, and feeling that his wife had been unfairly treated, composed and circulated a poem about Princess Michael, which was variously described as scurrilous and obscene. I have not read it. What is possibly the only surviving copy of the poem is now in the safekeeping of Sir Rex Williams, senior partner of Messrs Clifford Turner, the royal solicitors.

It was Alastair Forbes's reference to this incident in his article in the *Literary Review*, said Bron, which attracted the letter from Lady Dudley's solicitor and led to the libel action.

The second string to Lady Dudley's plaint, and the one on which I judged that a defence of fair comment would have been available to the defendants, if they could have afforded the gamble, was where Forbes claimed that activity by the royal solicitors had 'effectively zipped his [Lord Dudley's] and his wife's lips'. Lord Dudley challenged me to produce the letters which would support this opinion under threat of being thought a deceiver by *Spectator* readers.

'I can also state as a positive fact for which I have conclusive evidence,' he wrote to the *Spectator* on 2 May, '. . . that it is untrue that my wife's lips were effectively zipped by any such letter, or that any letter exists likely to have influenced the jury to reach a different verdict.' He also states as a 'positive fact' for which he has 'conclusive evidence' that no letter was ever received from 'the "Royal" solicitors or any other solicitors'.

Very well. I suppose I had better produce the letters. On the second point, I have in front of me the photocopy of a letter from Sir Rex Williams, Princess Michael's solicitor, to Lord Goodman, Dudley's representative, dated 20 December 1983. He acknowledges receipt of Lord Dudley's letter to Princess Michael and confirms that his client will not pursue her complaint or seek any further remedy in return for indemnification of her costs and the surrender of copies of the poem by Lord Goodman's client.

On the first point, on whether or not Lady Dudley's lips were effectively zipped, it is true that we have not seen any letter from solicitors making a complaint, but we have seen Lord Dudley's own letter to Princess Michael, delivered to her solicitor and written 'on behalf of my wife and myself', in which he places on record their most sincere regret and unreservedly expresses their deep apologies for the poem. Lord Dudley's letter continues: 'We acknowledge the statements are untruthful and should never have been made. We undertake that we will never repeat or publish this offensive material again or anything similar relating to you or your family.'

I do not think it unreasonable to argue that Lady Dudley's lips were effectively zipped up by this letter, which was plainly written at the royal solicitors' insistence. Perhaps Lord Dudley puts some other interpretation on his own words.

Perhaps he was advised by his lawyers that these letters were somehow 'privileged' and unable to be produced. If so, he was badly advised, but in any case it would have been an act of extreme folly to rely on such advice in denying their existence, of which he was perfectly well aware. Perhaps again he sees himself as some knight in shining armour, vicariously defending his pretty, sensitive, unvulgar, ungreedy wife against the calumnies of Princess Michael, and joining in Lady Dudley's 'well-deserved triumph' against the *Literary Review*. Has he no friends who can tell him he is pushing his luck?

The whole dismal affair had been blown up out of all proportion. The Dudleys were unwise to persist in suing a literary magazine that was struggling to survive, especially since the spat was not of its own making. The dispute could easily have been settled in a civilized fashion without resorting to an acrimonious display in court and in the press which verged on the ludicrous. Their insistence, as it appeared, on airing their complaint through the law courts did neither party any credit. On the contrary, washing one's dirty linen in public invariably ends in tears, as was the case with Lady Dudley when she seemingly became overcome with emotion during her cross-examination on the witness stand. Whatever her motives may have been – and one can only speculate about those – they won her no friends. The Goliath-like approach the Dudleys adopted towards a small magazine committed to literary excellence was perceived by many to be excessive and uncalled-for. The magazine lost the case, but nevertheless emerged with much greater sympathy. In the process, it had thrown into question a form of judicial procedure that was much in need of reform.

Thirty-one

In 1987 the coveted Betty Trask Award for a work of fiction traditional or romantic in nature was unexpectedly won by a Quartet book called *Hard Luck*. The author was James Maw. His novel told the story of a pair of scallywag twins, Richard and Tom, who had been born in the late 1950s on a new housing estate named Prospect. They grew up in a world of pubs and allotments where television was still a novelty and the Welfare a frequent necessity. The council house that was their home was known as Timbuctoo. Here they lived with their devoted mother Ellen and their father Frank – till he deserted them. After Ellen had obtained her divorce, the twins took up matchmaking on her behalf, leaving notes for the milkman and holding the rent collector, Mr Bannister, in reserve. When Ellen had to go into hospital, the twins' hilarious adventures continued in the same vein in the Crab Apple Road Home, to which they were sent by the authorities, and it was while they were there that they learnt the fateful results of their eleven-plus exams. Tom had won a place at St Saviour's Technical High School, but Richard, having failed, was condemned to go to Broadfield Secondary. Their touching and comical attempts to reverse this inequality brought their childhood history to a close.

James Maw had written his book with a keen sense of period and social detail. His comic gift, coupled with extraordinarily insight into the lives of two mischievous boys, created a novel that with its colour and uniqueness bore comparison with Dickens's *Oliver Twist* and Mark Twain's *Huckleberry Finn*. It had come about, the author told the London *Standard*, after rather more misfortune than he deserved, but now *Hard Luck* had turned into good luck. 'It's ironic,' he said, 'that all the hard luck that caused me to write the book is finally making money for me. I'd had a tough spell in London, having lost my job as a television presenter and had forgotten to pay my taxes – which I now have – on an earlier book; and then lost all my money in a theatrical venture. Inspiration came after I retreated to a housing estate in Northolt, but even then publication was not easy. I had to swop for it. I talked my editor at Quartet into forgetting a book I was commissioned to write on apes and taking *Hard Luck* instead.'

Another book in keeping with Quartet's tradition of providing a forum for left-leaning thought and ideology that we published at this time was Fenner

Brockway's final exercise in autobiography, *98 Not Out*. Brockway dated his conversion to socialism to the time he went to interview Keir Hardie in 1907 as a young liberal journalist and after an hour emerged convinced. Thereafter he came to occupy a controversial position in the Labour movement and remained on its pacifist wing during the First World War, when he actively opposed conscription and was for a time imprisoned in the Tower of London as a traitor. Between the wars he worked on the campaign for the independence of India and won his first parliamentary seat as the member for East Leyton in 1929, losing it in 1931 after opposing the National Government. He was then responsible for disaffiliating the Independent Labour party (the ILP) from the national Labour party in 1932. When he saw the rise of the fascist dictators in Europe, he put his pacifism on hold for the duration and actively helped to organize resistance to Hitler in Germany and Franco in Spain. In 1936 he went to Spain to help with rescuing ILP volunteers with the International Brigades, including George Orwell, from persecution by the communists, who were following the dictates of the Stalinists and operating purges behind the republican lines. He then helped with getting Orwell's *Homage to Catalonia* published.

After the war he took up the causes of world peace and the Campaign for Nuclear Disarmament (CND), and in 1950 became the MP for Eton and Slough. In 1964 he accepted a life peerage and pursued the principles that had governed his political career.

In writing *98 Not Out* he was able to draw on a vast experience in British and international politics and showed he had not dropped behind in addressing contemporary issues. He argued against the hereditary base for the House of Lords and proposed a properly democratic second chamber. In that respect he was ahead of his time. He launched an attack on the economic imperialism of the 1980s and the poverty and starvation in the world that were the needless result. Above all, he made an unanswerable case for world disarmament. His arguments shone with the integrity of the philosophy and values that had motivated him down the years, most especially with his version of the brotherhood of man, in which he saw the whole world as a family. *98 Not Out* was both an important political memoir and a persuasive polemic for socialist ideals. During the book's promotion, and subsequent to its publication, I got to know the ninety-eight-year-old Labour veteran well enough to be certain he remained committed to his pursuit of a better world, convinced it was possible to create one where poverty and oppression would be things of the past. I took an immense liking to him on a personal level. He stood apart from the usual run of politicians in being far too honest ever to be one of their number. All his life he had to fight alone against great odds to make his voice heard. Like Aneurin Bevan, he left his mark on society. He died a year later, just six months short of attaining his century.

*

There was an important development at Quartet in August when the publisher Anthony Blond and I joined forces to form a partnership that according to the London *Standard*, under the headline 'Terrible Twins!', had 'all the incendiary potential of a latter-day gunpowder plot'. Blond's own company, Muller, Blond & White, had gone down earlier in the year, having reached the point where, as he said in his autobiography *Jew Made in England*, 'We couldn't even pay the grappa bill from the friendly neighbourhood Italian restaurant.' Although he had managed to clear all his debts, he no longer wanted the hassle of refinancing and starting up again from the beginning. He was considered to have brilliant flare as a publisher but less acumen as a businessman. Now he was seeking a home within an established publishing house, from where he could operate and supply ideas for projects, in return for which his name would appear in any books which might materialize. It was his wife Laura who suggested he give me a ring and I invited him to Namara House.

> I climbed the four flights of stairs to Naim's offices. There I encountered a macho lair, strewn with tiger skins and occupied by young ladies who supplied his occasional needs, like a glass of water or a pullover when the air-conditioning became too intense. I explained I only needed 'walking money' – an expression employed by the late Dominic Elwes.
> 'How much?' asked Naim.
> 'Ten thousand.'
> 'Too much, that would upset the others.'
> 'OK, then five thousand.'
> 'No,' said Naim, 'six thousand.'
> And so it was.

My relationship with Anthony Blond had always been warm, a warmth strengthened by recognition of the support he gave me in my early days as a publisher when I was being sneered at and referred to as a 'cowboy' in the trade. He defended me when others stood aside and took no part in the furore that followed the publication of *God Cried* and Roald Dahl's subsequent notice of it in the *Literary Review*. While he personally condemned the book, he refrained from using any intemperate language and was deeply unhappy about the torrents of vitriol that flowed from many of the commentators. Throughout the crisis he remained staunch in my defence, rejecting the accusations of anti-Semitism being levelled against me in certain quarters and arguing that free speech should never be sacrificed to suit any particular ideology or viewpoint. He never questioned my entitlement to publish material sympathetic to the Palestinian cause and considered my rights in this to be equal with George Weidenfeld's when he published similar material in favour of the Israelis. Each of us was conducting a crusade of our own and affirming the democratic right of free expression in our society.

I did not always agree with Blond, but our disparities and our different ethnic backgrounds proved a strength rather than a weakness and we forged a good working relationship. I am a Palestinian Arab, while he is an English Jew from a distinguished assimilated background. Even our sexuality was of quite a different kind in its orientation, he being drawn to both sexes whereas I was passionately heterosexual. He became a practising Jew at the time when my Catholic faith was wavering. He drank and smoked heavily while I hardly ever touched alcohol and had given up the latter many moons before. In an interview with *Publishing News*, Blond said he and I in fact had a lot in common, he even went so far as to describe us as kindred spirits. We both liked pretty, well-heeled girls with double-barrelled names from aristocratic families (his wife Laura was a daughter of Colonel Roger Hesketh, whose father-in-law was an earl). Of his Quartet tie-up he said,

It's a wonderful arrangement. I'm not much of a dab hand at admin or finance, but I am good at acquiring. So I'll just get on publishing around a dozen books a year. Naim and I both believe in eccentric rather than category publishing. It will be anything from the official biography of J. R. Jaywardine, president of Sri Lanka, to a book version of Muran Buch-stansangur. I also have in mind books from two new English novelists. It's such a relief to feel all these jewels are no longer unwanted.

I trust Naim fully to take care of all the financial arrangements. He is very pro-Arab of course, and I'm a Jew, but Naim isn't anti-Jewish, he's anti-Zionist. I used to be a Zionist, but now I'm one of the Jews for Peace. I'm for a multi-racial Israel.

In addition he argued that these factors could be seen as bringing an extra piquancy to our working relationship. 'But it's an irrelevance,' he added firmly. 'The kind of irrelevance I enjoy . . . ' *Private Eye* put its usual more jaundiced spin on events:

Veteran publisher Anthony Blond is certainly down on his luck. Not so long ago he had to wind up his publishing company Blond & Briggs [*sic*] and last year he even resorted to the catering trade, accompanying his wife, the former Laura Hesketh, as she distributed cold sandwiches to office workers in the City. Now, however, he has had to accept the most ignominious fate in the world of publishing – a job with the crazed pro-Arab publisher Naim Attallah. A press release announces that Blond has been offered his own private imprint and list within the Quartet empire. He will liaise with Attallah's main editor, the leery Stephen Pickles, author of *Queens* . . .

Of Blond's proposed list, *Private Eye* commented that the official biography of the president of Sri Lanka – 'more hagiography than biography' – should 'sit easily alongside the tedious memoirs of obscure Middle Eastern politicians that Attallah is fond of publishing'.

Anthony described his new workplace thus:

Quartet Books occupied two adjacent rickety houses in Goodge Street, between which, it was always being mooted, a door would one day be breached. To the young ladies who clattered and chattered up and down the two flights of stairs, I was presented by Pickles as 'seasoned timber' and by David Elliott, the sales director, known as 'dump-bin Dave', as 'a living legend'. The young ladies, however, were understandably more interested in stealing each other's boyfriends on unmonitored telephones than talking to me. The circus mistress of the *salle de manège* was Jubby, daughter of Richard Ingrams, who cracked a condescending whip and out-lasted them all. She was to look after me. Jubby was the Saint-Simon at the court of King Naim, registering his movements, moods and reactions.

On one occasion Anthony tried to set up a television interview with Simon Raven at the Reform Club in their library, which he felt to be 'the most splendid room in London'. He received a curt no to the idea of any television cameras entering the portals of the Reform, the reason to emerge being that Jubby once

hired the Reform for a photo shoot and subsequently the secretary was horrified to be sent a copy of *Playboy*, to which surely neither he nor the club subscribed. I am sure the magazine featured a naked girl standing on one of Sir Charles Barry's horsehair sofas, next to the bust of the young Queen Victoria, in the marbled atrium.

'I was never allowed to attend editorial meetings,' Anthony recorded, 'though my modest suggestions were nearly always agreed to.' The partnership produced a handful of titles, including biographies of Hugh Montefiore, the former bishop of Birmingham, who had been bar mitzvahed at Blond's own synagogue, as he reminded him, and Justin de Blank. It was odd, he reflected, 'that these titles, from a Jewish editor, should emerge from a publisher who is Arab'. He almost had one coup in introducing to Quartet Jennifer Patterson, of future 'Fat Lady' best-selling-cookery-books fame, but unfortunately his letter of recommendation, advising that we might get her 'cheap', was sent to Jennifer by mistake and she went to John Murray instead. Jennifer, a fellow Catholic, was to become one of my dearest friends. Without fail on the morning of every first of May she would ring me to sing 'Happy Birthday' over the phone.

In the end Anthony Blond decided to go and live in France, though I continued to pay his honorarium for a while. We also published his book *Blond's Roman Emperors* but, 'Eventually he [Naim] wrote me a most elegant letter of farewell.' Blond was widely known for discovering many novelists, his most outstanding protégé being Simon Raven, whom I interviewed some ten years later. Raven was perhaps the most outrageous writer of his generation, frowned on by the whole establishment, defying convention and writing explicitly about his own bi-sexuality. Blond has an enduring reputation as a publisher and retains an admiring and faithful following. As a preface to *Jew Made in England* he printed his own obituary, full of honest self-appraisal. Muller, Blond & White had gone bankrupt after publishing 'a lavish volume on the Sistine Chapel, on every copy of which the company contrived to lose money'. Of his coming to Quartet he wrote:

> Although an energetic spotter of talent, Blond lacked the discipline and temperance to make a good businessman, and was, according to his friends, trusting and gullible. He was now bereft, having regarded an imprint as a form of self-expression.
>
> Blond attempted to secure work through his extensive network in what he liked to call the 'publishing game'. No one wanted to know: and Blond was quoted as saying, 'None of my best friends are Jews.' Nevertheless, he was taken up, out of charity, by the Palestinian Arab Naim Attallah, as a consultant to his firm, Quartet.

The continuing speculation on who was and who was not included in Katya Grenfell's book *Naked London* came to an end with its publication in September. It became caught up in the general uproar surrounding my book *Women*, which will be given a chapter to itself later on. Both books fell foul of the intellectual snobbery endemic in literary circles. In actual fact, notwithstanding its provocative title, the notoriety *Naked London* attracted was created by the media. Its sensational content was more mythical than real; but when it came to the crunch the participants, with very few exceptions, lost their nerve and confined their state of *déshabillé* to something symbolic which did not reveal all that much. The advertising that is common in the glossies of the twenty-first century makes more explicit use of erotic nakedness than anything in Katya Grenfell's relatively tame collection. Even the outrageous Taki, posing in a display of physical prowess, guarded his modesty, unlike my friend, the actor Simon Callow, who revealed all in a somewhat defiant mood. Julian Sands, another actor, was more adventurous, showing his well-proportioned torso while holding a child. Jeffrey Bernard, the turf correspondent, journalist and frequenter of the Coach and Horses in Soho, sat imperiously on a chair while shielding his genitals with a book. Anthony Blond was cautious for a change, sitting at his desk with a bare chest. Dai Llewellyn lay on the floor, covering his midriff and his lower region – the hub of his activities at the time – with various bottles of booze. Neil Norman, critic, stood outside the Groucho Club fully dressed on top but dangling his penis to air it in the gentle breezes of Soho. Matthew Freud, PR executive, was protected by his telephone unit amid his many newspapers. Marco Pierre White relaxed with a piglet, displaying a macho bare chest and naked legs. David Jenkins, TV producer and now eminent feature writer, showed a naked cool, lying on his stomach on the floor as he watched a television with his feet crossed in the air behind him.

On the whole the women tended to be less inhibited. Patsy Kensit, who graced the cover, was visibly naked but draped in a film of celluloid, which made the image more titillating than revealing. Caroline Kellett made herself less exposed by wearing rows of beads and adopting a sitting posture. Nicki Freud, unmistakably pregnant, with her daughter Martha lying on the bed beside her, made an inspiring shot, beautifully composed and full of human passion. Kyle Morison, chef, lay totally naked on a bed of fruit and vegetables, looking extremely feminine and rather delectable. Sally-Ann Lasson, interior designer, stood behind a column in lush surroundings and showed a glimpse of one breast, while her long black hair, cascading in total uniformity, conveyed a distinctly slinky look that was irresistible. Jeopardy Control and Harriet Hall, two mud wrestlers, engaged in their bizarre sport and seemed jolly pleased to be photographed. Equally pleased was Naomi Coke, university student, who posed topless to display huge breasts fit to overwhelm any hot-blooded male.

Over eighty people appeared in *Naked London* and showed good humour, taking a pride in being able to overcome some of those inhibitions natural to us all. The critics found it hard to attack the book for fear of tarnishing their avant-garde and go-ahead image by showing old-fashioned or boringly traditionalist tendencies. Instead the media kept its focus on the gossipy aspects rather than the artistic dimensions. Of them all, as I said before, the only photos to cause me personal worries were those of Jubby Ingrams and her brother Fred.

Jubby first came into my employment through Bron, when he suggested to me that I might give Richard Ingrams's daughter a job at Quartet. She was not particularly qualified academically to be an editor, he said, but she was very bright and energetic and I was bound to like her. My immediate reaction was a deep sense of relief. Surely the never-ending attacks on me in *Private Eye* would stop once Richard's daughter was working for me. Bron predicted correctly that I would take to Jubby, but my assumption regarding *Private Eye* turned out to be completely misplaced. The thing that actually happened was that Jubby went home each evening to tell her dad whatever had been going on that day at Quartet. The next morning, after she arrived for work, she would come to me and say disarmingly, 'You're going to kill me. I promise I didn't mean to tell him; it was an accident. I can't control what he does.' Jubby was irrepressible; there was no way she could keep anything bottled up. Employing Jubby was not in any way the sort of insurance I had hoped for, and the sniping from *Private Eye* continued as relentlessly as ever.

My reaction when Jubby first told me she was going to pose naked for the photographs with her brother was to say, 'Oh, no, Jubby. Your dad will slaughter me. I get into enough trouble with *Private Eye* without you posing in the nude.' I felt certain it was not going to go down well. Quite apart from any other considerations, there was always a deep-seated puritanism at the root of Richard's satirical style. Nothing I could say made any difference and Jubby went ahead with the photo session. When it was done she telephoned me, quite delighted, and said, 'Nami, Nami,' using the nickname she had coined for me, 'it was really great. I'm coming round to show you the Polaroids.' Along she came with three prints of herself, and I knew at once that, left to herself, she would show them to all and sundry, so I confiscated them despite her protests and put them away in my wallet. Three days later I had an appointment in New York to see a bank manager. During the course of our conversation I happened to take out my wallet and Jubby's prints fell out face up on to the table. The humiliation of that moment is with me to this day. I imagine something went through his mind along the lines of, who is this seedy customer, carrying photos of naked young women about with him – some sort of sex maniac?

Before long Jubby was on the phone again, this time with the news that Richard had summoned her to *Private Eye*. He was finding the whole thing very funny, she told me, and had already phoned the *Evening Standard* to tell them Brian Sedgemore MP, one of Quartet's authors, was to feature in the book naked – which explained how that story had got around. I had to admit that the photos of Jubby and her brother Fred, when they appeared in *Naked London*, were sensationally good. In one pose Fred was standing while Jubby sat in front of him, blocking her brother's lower part while displaying her glorious bosom, which would have been the envy of many a woman. In another pose, Fred was made to seem as if he was taking a punch at one of Jubby's breasts as part of a joyful prank. In fairness to Richard, he never made a fuss and was able to see the funny side. This was not to say he was pleased for his son and daughter to have appeared in the book. The way-out nature of many of Quartet's parties, like the one where Jubby and the other girls were dressed in rubber, caused Richard some distaste and disquiet on her behalf, but he found himself torn between that and a father's loyalty to his daughter. He was amazingly supportive and always found a reason not be angry with her. Later on he confided in me that any displeasure the book caused him seemed to evaporate when it failed to attain bestseller status. It was impossible not to love Jubby dearly for her free spirit. That was her great attraction, but she got us all into such trouble. She even got Bron and me banned for life from the Reform Club after using the gents and being found out.

The last word on *Naked London* went to the *Literary Review* of March 1988, in which Bron printed a lampooning letter of legal advice to Henry Root of the *Bookseller*, who was given to printing disparaging remarks about my publishing activities. It concerned an imagined review of the book and purported to come from Susan Grabbit of the firm of Sue Grabbit and Run in Grays Inn. The following are extracts from what was a sustained burst of wit:

3. You suggest that the book's publisher, Mr Naim Attallah, is a personal friend of yours. Such an assertion certainly defames Mr Attallah. The fact that you have, as you put it, 'twice lunched with him without ejaculation, the plovers' eggs and the choice of wine on each occasion being served by pretty girls with double-barrelled names and unearned incomes' would be no defence. He might have thought you were someone else, you could have been there as a bet or an editorial joke, or to make the other guests appear less common . . .

5. I do not understand your reference to Mr Dai Llewellyn, the Welsh nightclub greeter, as Princess Margaret's walker-in-law. I further notice that you refer to all the naked men in this book either as 'flower-arrangers' or 'a friend of Princess Margaret'. I am familiar with the expression 'a friend of Dorothy'. Has this been replaced by 'a friend of Princess Margaret'? I am aware, of course, that both Mr Kenny Everett and Mr Elton John are welcome at Kensington Palace . . .

7. You say that Mr Taki, the little Greek, recently visited a Turkish bath.

He took off all his clothes and waited in a queue for the attention of a Nubian masseur. When the steam cleared he found he was in a fish and chip shop. 'I'll have sixpennyworth of that,' said the man standing next to him, 'but go easy on the vinegar.' Is this true? I do not think Mr Taki would sue, but he looks formidable still in the upper arm and has a reputation for settling legal disputes with a display of Eastern fighting techniques up alleys. I would advise caution.

8. Your description of the art dealer in high-heels as a 'a floppy-bottomed fairy' is dangerous. 'Floppy-bottomed' can no longer be predicated of a person since the actress Charlotte Cornwall called Miss Nina Myskow 'a floppy-bottomed journalist', the latter receiving substantial damages on appeal. I suggest you substitute 'theatrical' for 'floppy-bottomed' and 'angel' for 'fairy' . . .

9. You say that Miss Emma Freud, the talkative TV person, is a pretty lass but that she recently confused her KY Jelly with a tube of industrial putty with the result that all her windows fell out. I don't understand this. Further, the claim that you recently ejected her father, Lord Freud, from your flat because he gave your cats asthma is possibly defamatory.

10. I am unhappy with your description of the two girls on page 5 as 'being joined at the G-spot in a sapphic embrace'. 'The G-spot,' you say, 'was discovered in 1980 by Dr Theodore Whipple as a result of experiments carried out at the San Diego Institute of Advanced Sexological Research. The G-spot lies directly behind the pubic bone on the anterior wall of the uterus. Imagine a small clock inside the uteral tube with 12 o'clock pointing towards the navel. Most women will find their G-spots at approximately 12.25 a.m. Alternatively imagine a street map of London with St Pancras on the navel. Go up Pont Street and turn left into Hans Place – the G-spot is just behind Harrods where the old Jacaranda Club used to be.' I would be unhappy with the inclusion of this passage without a sight of Dr Whipple's paper.

11. What evidence do you have for saying that Mr George Michael wears a frozen chicken down his trousers?

The publication of *Women* in the autumn of 1987 was drawing ever closer, but earlier in 1987 we had published, on the twentieth anniversary of the occupation by Israel of the West Bank, a book called *Prisoners of God* by the journalist and television commentator David Smith. He subtitled it *The Modern-Day Conflict of Arab and Jew*. It traced the profound changes that had taken place since the Six-Day War for a generation of Palestinians that, in twenty years, had grown up knowing only Israeli rule and an occupation which had become *de facto* ownership through expropriation, enforced purchase or settlement. Despite sharing a common interest in seeing the economic development of the West Bank, the Palestinians and their Israeli landlords remained locked in a seemingly insoluble conflict. Both claimed that the land had been granted to them by God, and in seeking to justify their claims by force, had become the prisoners of God, trapped together in a land where each sought to fulfil the divine promise. With humanity and understanding, David Smith explored the feelings and aspirations of the two peoples, besides chronicling the fruitless search for peace and the failures of the Western World to seize the opportunities that had been there to bring the two sides together. The author's sympathies were with both the occupied and the occupier, for each had suffered oppression and the misery of circumstances not altogether of their making. As a foreign correspondent for Reuters and ITN, David Smith had reported from Europe, Africa and the Middle East. In 1983 his dispatches from Lebanon won him the Royal Television Society's International Award. Between 1984 and 1986 he was ITN's Middle East correspondent, based in Israel. His insights into the conflict were therefore refreshingly unbiased.

Alastair Forbes, writing for the *Spectator*, said that

> On a different level of mankind's cruelty and folly, *Prisoners of God*, by the young journalist David Smith, struck me as a remarkably fair assessment of the bloody Arab–Israeli predicament, for which the English-speaking world can scarcely escape blame. This book certainly seems to have received less than its just deserts, perhaps because of its Palestinian publisher, whose own interminable tape-wormcasts engendered in the press almost as much further type-tripe as they contained.

This broadside was directed at *Women*, which was attracting a rising storm of media interest, but Alastair Forbes had hit the nail on the head in some respects. The press obsession with *Women* became so intense that little attention was paid for some time to the more serious titles that continued to emanate from Quartet. *Women* was to become a *cause célèbre* that dwarfed anything not linked with scandal. Luckily the novelty wore thin in time, and *Women* was consigned to history, as with everything else. Today's news, as the saying goes, is tomorrow's chip wrapping.

However, mindful of Ezra Pound's dictum that 'literature is news that stays news', there was a crop of haunting novels that we published in 1987, including a personal favourite of mine, *The Dream of Heroes* by Adolfo Bioy Casares. It had originally been published in Portuguese in Buenos Aires in 1954, when the author's friend and collaborator Jorge Luis Borges proclaimed it his masterpiece. Bioy had collaborated with Borges in the past, and in *The Dream of Heroes* he produced a book that was a strange but compelling blend of magic and realism, a contribution to that stratum in Latin American literature which deserved to be more widely known. It was grounded in a solid sense of time and space – the suburbs of Beunos Aires in the 1920s – but from there moved effortlessly into a realm of magic and metaphysics. With a brilliant ear for dialogue, the author considered, among many other themes, the nature of courage and the 'macho' image, which was a central preoccupation in Buenos Aires at the time. Born in 1914, Bioy developed into one of Latin America's most outstanding writers, almost all of whose works were characterized by the same mingling of fantasy and reality, skilfully constructed plots and a fine ironic wit. Many besides Borges considered *The Dream of Heroes* to be Bioy's finest achievement, and this was its first translation into English.

A book of a very different kind, representing a distinct coup for Quartet, was Grey Gowrie's *Derek Hill: An Appreciation*. Grey was then chairman of Sotheby's in London, and had been Minister for the Arts from 1983 to 1985. Derek Hill was acknowledged as one of Britain's leading portraitists, but Grey considered this reputation to overshadow his standing as a landscape artist unjustly. Much of Hill's most impressive landscape painting had been done on the remote and wild island of Tory, off the north-west coast of Donegal, where he helped to found a school of primitive artists. He himself had lived at the Glebe at Churchill near Letterkenny, a house he gifted to the Irish nation together with the extraordinary collection it contained of work by other twentieth-century artists. Grey had grown up near by at his family home at Dunlewy and a special intimate understanding existed between them. This was evident in the interview that formed the main text of the book, in which Hill talked uninhibitedly about his life, work and influences, providing a commentary for the reproductions of landscapes and portraits in both colour and black and white. It made a handsome, intriguing volume.

When he was in his late teens in 1934, Derek Hill had gone to study stage design in Munich and come under the influence of the Bauhaus before going on to the Soviet Union to meet some of the leading exponents of the amazing avant-garde Russian theatre of the time, just before the Stalinist crack-down on everything creative and the appalling purges and persecutions that followed. He finally left stage design behind shortly after the war and concentrated on pursuing a life as a painter. One of the points of the book was to look beyond his reputation for being a conservative artist who opted to paint in the manner of Constable, Corot and Courbet in order to stress his twentieth-century significance. As he himself said, there was, at the basis of his best landscapes, 'a completely abstract geometrical drawing'. The book was something more than just a selection of Hill's best work with an appreciative introduction. So much of his personality showed through in the text that it developed a real sense of the connection between the man and his paintings. The result was a tribute to an artist seen by Grey Gowrie as one of Britain's foremost painters, whose importance was too often misunderstood, being more appreciated in Ireland, where he spent so much of his life, than in his home country.

The reception to mark the book's publication was hosted by Grey Gowrie at Sotheby's in Bond Street. Prince Charles was among the guests, since he counted Derek among his closest friends. It was a well-known fact that Derek had helped and encouraged the young Prince Charles to pursue his painting hobby during visits to Balmoral. Derek felt entirely at ease among the royals and the aristocracy. He was a frequent visitor to the Queen Mother at Clarence House and his close friendship with her lasted till the end of his life.

As a result of publishing the book I came to know Derek well. He was a complex character, who could overflow with charm one moment and be overbearingly rude, offhand and pompous the next. The female staff who had to deal with him at Quartet loathed him for his abrupt dismissive manner over the telephone. He was intolerant and lacked patience, and was in the habit of complaining incessantly about one thing or another, mainly about the inadequate amount of publicity the book was getting, in his opinion, or the inefficiency of its distribution in the marketplace. Yet whenever he contacted me he would adopt an entirely different tone, the message being similar but more tactfully put. There was no denying he was a snob whose proximity to the royals and the high and mighty of the land had warped his vision of the real world. Somehow he became too grand to relate to ordinary mortals, most of whom he considered mere minions – a category that could be extended to taxi drivers or even the wives of friends, to their intense anger. Yet he also possessed an undoubted gift for friendship and prided himself on having the common touch with those gardeners, housekeepers or Tory islanders who were his special favourites. It was all part of his contradictory nature.

Despite these misgivings my relationship with Derek developed to the point of friendship. He came to stay with us in France at the invitation of my wife Maria, in spite of the doubts I expressed about the wisdom of having him with us at close quarters. My worst fears were more than justified. Derek was insufferable as a house guest. His demands for service and attention were constant; at breakfast I found myself ceaselessly getting up and down to appease one or another whim in the selection of food items. As soon as he had finished one course, he would wait for the next with irritated impatience. His treatment of the household staff was positively feudal and I soon felt highly embarrassed by his behaviour. One morning I became so provoked that I was was forced to remind him of his status as a guest in my house. I, too, could be a prima donna, I said, and could outdo him in the role any day. He then mended his ways to the extent of becoming more courteous, though there was no material change in his requirements. Derek loved his food, and while in France was determined to make the most of whatever the local cuisine had to offer. Because of his ill-health and overweight, I was assigned to go to the market every day with a list he had made specifying what he fancied for lunch. In the evenings we dined at one of the famous restaurants in the region, where Derek indulged himself on *foie gras* despite his weight problem. In his better moments, he could be a marvellous raconteur, very much in the manner of writer and *bon viveur* Quentin Crewe, telling such stories as how Unity Mitford came to him when he was living in Munich to ask him to help her find a way to meet Hitler. Derek telephoned her when he knew the Führer had stopped at a favourite coffee shop on his way back from Berchtesgaden. Unity rushed straight round in a taxi and so got her first glimpse of her hero in the flesh, surrounded by his henchmen – the first fateful step along the road to the point at which, when Britain declared war on Germany, she shot herself, inflicted brain damage and was repatriated to wartime England as an invalid.

Greatly as I liked Derek – and he was someone who could inspire a genuine fondness – about four days of living with him was as much as I could stand. I fled back to London, fearing my level of tolerance would otherwise reach snapping point. I had no wish to hurt him. He was brave in the way he endured a great deal of pain and coped with his physical decline, pursuing a lifestyle that took him back and forth between the cottage he had retained at Churchill in Ireland and his Hampstead house on Holly Hill with a dogged determination. In France I left him in Maria's care and they formed a real bond. Derek painted her as a sign of affection, and his fondness for her never wavered through to the last days of his life, when she often visited him in hospital. After he was dead I missed the old curmudgeon. He had insisted on doing a portrait of me as well, to mark his appreciation of my having published the book. When the time came to tackle the job I had a high fever, the cause for which was diagnosed as pleurisy. I was almost in a delirious state, but Derek had travelled from Ireland specially to paint me so I felt I could not let him down. For three mornings, against doctor's orders, I rose from my sickbed to go into my office till noon and sit for Derek. The result was a portrait which he called 'Pleurisy'. It bore witness to my sickness and captured it on canvas for all time.

The Frankfurt Book Fair of 1987 was an eventful one for us, with the appearance of *Women* looming large against a background of the already described incidents concerning Mr Richter and his book *Tattoo*. As the whole book trade knows, the fair takes place early in October each year, when publishers from across the world converge on the city to exhibit their books and acquire and sell manuscripts. It is a kind of jamboree where publishers shed their inhibitions once a year and behave as if it were one enormous office Christmas party, similar in format but on a far larger scale. The liberals, those with high ideals, mingle with their more sedate and conservative counterparts; the pious and the profane go arm in arm; pornography to suit all tastes displays for the initiated its explicit art, which has flourished since the advent of civilization. The book fair in itself is a great arena of learning. No taboos exist except in the minds of a negligible minority and nothing is forbidden so long as it sells. Presentation and the ability to deal with any subject under the sun are what matter most, along with the conceptual arguments and ambiguous phrases that are a publisher's stock-in-trade and induce a belief in a magic art that only publishers are privy to.

In the airless and sometimes stifling atmosphere of the vast main hall, the sense of competition rises to a crescendo as the big fish of publishing attempt to outdo each other, showing off their financial muscle to gain the ascendancy in the bidding wars. In the midst of all this the small publisher hardly has a toehold. He is a minnow among the leviathans and can only watch in awe and wish he could rank alongside them. Yet no publisher worth his salt can afford to stay away. Ideas are formulated, concepts take shape and random encounters often lead to worthwhile acquisitions.

My first visit to Frankfurt had been in 1976 when I was completely new to publishing. I was a tyro in a world where most things were strange to me. I had to keep my wits about me and take in as much as I could. At the same time, I had to pretend I had more insight into the arcane business of publishing than I actually possessed. Any display of ignorance or naïvety would have worked to my disadvantage, making fair game of me as an inexperienced newcomer. Hardened publishers are a breed apart. They are very protective of their own areas of expertise and are seldom generous in paying tribute to competitors. They do not embrace change easily, nor do they welcome strangers into their midst with open arms. Their view of their own profession is somewhat élitist, and they close ranks to shun those whom they consider to be parvenus – not for the reason that they lack ability, but simply because they do not possess the right credentials. Well, I thought, I was now one of them whether they liked it or not, and I was certainly not for turning.

That book fair of 1976 was memorable for me for many reasons. It gave me the chance to get to know William Miller and John Boothe better. They were there with Brian Thompson and our newly recruited sales director, David Elliott, who was still working out his notice with Words & Music. David was due to join us that December, but meanwhile he was spending a great deal of time with us and he bonded with the group from the start. Another major reason for the memorable nature of that Frankfurt was that I suddenly became aware of the distance I had to travel before becoming a publisher of note. Enthusiasm and determination I had in abundance, but there was no short cut I could take to avoid the blood, sweat, toil and tears.

Subsequently the book fair became an annual ritual I kept up religiously, despite the increase in my other commitments. For more than two decades, the first two weeks in October were reserved for what I called intellectual pursuits and the chance to fraternize with booksellers from all over the world. The change of scenery, and one's immersion in every aspect of the written word, confirmed one's belief in the fellowship of the pen. The multitude of people, merchants of their own languages, of different races and creeds, packing the large complex of exhibition halls, proved at the very least that words are still the currency of communication and a potent force for both good and evil.

The lighter and brighter side of the Frankfurt Book Fair was the opportunity it gave me to get to know the Quartet staff in a more personal way, in a different environment and at a more leisurely pace than was usually possible. Formalities were dispensed with and a camaraderie of equals developed naturally. Whereas in London I was far too occupied to develop that sort of relationship, at Frankfurt it simply happened. My mode of operation in London focused on my immediate circle of young ladies, with whom I communicated frequently, dispensing with formalities in favour of a more relaxed atmosphere. They handled the most sensitive information and had the advantage of free access to me at all times. Their close proximity became an integral part of the merry-go-round that made Quartet not only a formidable force in publishing terms, but also a place of learning where fun was intrinsic to its culture.

Quartet became a finishing school, not of manners and graces, but of self-discovery and how best to bring out a latent talent with the right encouragement. There was no inculcation. It was a gradual evolution that brought with it an unshakeable self-assurance. We operated to the envy and consternation of others. Some found us impossible to understand; a few wondered how we ticked and what drove us forward; the rest were simply baffled. However, incessant speculation kept us in the public eye to such a degree that promotional advertising began to become superfluous. We were getting it all for free.

Private Eye naturally extended its coverage to Frankfurt. A typical 'Grovel' piece ran as follows:

I hear that gorgeous pouting Selina Blow has been selected from his harem to accompany Naim Attullah-Disgusting to this year's Frankfurt Book Fair [1987]. The vivacious Ms Blow tells me that she is required to get into training for the fair by playing ping-pong with the Ayatollah in the basement of his luxury Poland Street HQ. The pair has been entered for the Ugandan mixed doubles event, I understand.

It was customary for me to take a young lady to Frankfurt to act as my assistant during the four days I spent there. This had nothing to do with the contingent from Quartet who manned our stand. My visit, though part of Quartet's presence, was independently planned so as to leave me the maximum flexibility. My assistant stayed with me at the Nassauer Hof, Wiesbaden, while the people from Quartet were booked in at different locations in the same town. Each party retained its autonomy, but we all dined together in the evenings to debrief and review the day's happenings.

Over the two decades of my attendances at Frankfurt I had the good fortune to enjoy the company of scores of young women who travelled with me. Some worked at Quartet, others came from within the Namara Group or as a result of some propitious social encounter. In every case it was gratifying to think that I had perhaps contributed in some small measure to the future development of young women who went on to become symbols of success for their generation.

Meanwhile there was a new exit from the *Literary Review*. Kate Kellaway reminisces:

The Nine-Month Party
by Kate Kellaway

Working at the *Literary Review* as deputy literary editor was as near as any salaried job could come to being paid to attend a party. It was a party which lasted, for me, for nine glorious months, ending in April 1987. When I left, I remember reflecting that parties, after all, cannot be expected to last for ever. At the *Literary Review*'s light, airy offices on the first floor of Beak Street, Soho, there was an endless supply of books and of nice people willing to review them for a tiny wage. Bron Waugh (contrary to everything I had supposed before I worked with him) was the most charming colleague. I was devoted to him. Bron feared boredom. Jokes were not optional adornments. They were necessary. He was seriously frivolous. It was essential to find life amusing. And we did. 'You are looking a little off colour,' I remember him saying to me one morning, at eleven o'clock, correctly diagnosing a broken heart and opening a particularly fine bottle of pink champagne.

It was not a problem that I was a *Guardian* reader or a Labour voter. Nor was it disconcerting to him that I had recently returned from teaching English in a township school in Harare, Zimbabwe. Bron loved difference, dissent and edge, and was heartened by the possibility of an argument (I must have disappointed him by not arguing enough). We agreed about more than I would ever have thought possible. We were in accord about everything from literary style to broad beans, although, as always, he was ready to be more dramatically emphatic than I was. ('There is no one in the world who doesn't love broad beans.') Bron was as loyal as the day was long. But the day wasn't long at all. Sometimes it had more or less finished by midday, helped on its way by lunch. (Fish was a favourite as Bron used to insist it was 'good for the brain'.)

Reviewers dropped in throughout the day, often unannounced, to help themselves to a novel or just to gossip. Bron would pick up the phone and charm the grandest people into reviewing the most unlikely books. He was never afraid to ask. He was ruthless with his editor's red pen, especially after lunch. I picture him sitting in a swanky leather director's chair (I loved those chairs of ours) and pronouncing: 'There is nothing in the world that cannot be improved by cutting.'

He was right. Sometimes, I wanted to do more than cut. I wanted to kill. But when I was offended by some bigoted review Bron had commissoned, or when he had asked some pretty girl he'd met on a train whether she'd like to review a novel (as happened more than once) and the result turned out to be unprintably banal, I learnt not to say too much. Bron would brighten if I sounded indignant. The most effective thing was to *yawn*. Whatever happened, we must not bore our readers or ourselves.

If the *Literary Review* was a party, then there were were two hosts: Bron and Naim Attallah, the magazine's owner. Naim was a tall, handsome, improbable presence. He wore beautiful suits and cut such a dash that he looked more as though he were about to sponsor, or even take part in, a Merchant Ivory film than to bother himself with a literary magazine. Not that 'bother' was a word that suited Naim in any way. He was mavellously calm. I was grateful and amazed at his charming way of welcoming me from the start, with a twinkle in his eye, before he knew anything much about me – there was gallantry in this. He had tremendous warmth – something I can never resist. He was not a flirt, though. There was no banter, thank goodness. But there was a sympathetic intelligence and, I think, a great wish to please. I remember being presented by Naim with a small, stylish black and gold Asprey watch. I adored it. But I worried faintly that it might be some sort of bribe, then felt ashamed of the thought. It was nice to be spoilt – and an unfamiliar feeling – although, like my time at the *Literary Review*, the watch didn't last for long. Its time ran out. But Naim was nothing if not generous.

Naim has a reputation for being a ladies' man and this was something Bron relished and liked to discuss. I remember the endless jokes in the *Literary Review*'s offices about the beauty of the girls with whom Naim worked at Quartet. I remember vividly feeling daunted by their languid glamour – some of them definitely, I remember thinking at the time, looked too beautiful to work.

But then glamour was Naim's thing. He had a flair for decorous, delicious literary lunches too. Looking back on those lunches now, I think invitations should have been extended to struggling writers only, to those starving in garrets. They would have speedily recovered, although it might have taken the edge off their literary hunger. These lunches were as unexpected as Naim was. I remember Germaine Greer coming to one of them – charmed, I like to think, against her better judgement by Bron or Naim; or most likely by both of them. Naim contributed hugely to the sense that our purpose in life was to enjoy ourselves.

People used to assume that Naim must have an editorial stranglehold on the magazine and be breathing down Bron's neck, instructing him to have reviewers rave about all books published by Quartet. This was not the case at all. I don't remember any editorial interference whatsoever from Naim – although I guess that if he had been consulted, Naim might have been on Bron's side in encouraging reviews written by the pretty girls encountered on trains – the Railway Children. But then, if I'd protested or appealed to him, it would have been difficult for Naim to take sides. My impression was that he was a man who would wish to shy away from conflict. He was a benign influence, in every way.

Bron used always to talk as if he wanted to please Naim – he would make it sound like a joke. But he meant it. Bron started many of his sentences with the words: 'The sad truth is . . . ' The ends of most sentences that started in this way were funny. The 'sad truth' was that Bron was unapologetically nepotistic. It was a matter of loyalty. And loyalty was something Naim and Bron had in common. Naim would not have dreamt of asking Bron to look favourably on his own books. But had he been the sort of person to insist on a good review, Bron would have been absolutely and robustly corruptible. The truth – sad or the reverse – is that Naim must have known he did not need to ask.

Bron liked to shock, even in small ways. He once told me that if you had not read a book, you should always praise it when reviewing it. I couldn't believe that he was owning up to not reading some of the books he reviewed. I later came to regard the words, 'She writes like an angel', when they issued from Bron's pen, with particular suspicion. The extraordinary thing was that the party atmosphere at the *Literary Review* did not prevent a magazine from appearing every month. I like to think that instead it made the magazine what it was: entertaining, generous, unpredictable. Much of what Bron did, he did only to annoy because he knew it pleases. Meanwhile Naim allowed the party to go on, and for that everyone involved will continue to thank him.

Thirty-two

Women was launched at the Victoria and Albert Museum in the Raphael Room. It was the first time the museum trustees had allowed the room to be used for such an occasion. The party was planned meticulously, with nothing left to chance. Again the two Charlottes, Millward and Faber, were put in charge of organization and showed their usual flair for originality and extravagance. The hostesses, endearingly referred to by the press as the 'nymphettes', came from Quartet and my private office. They were dressed in gorgeous blue velvet evening gowns with gold leaves in their hair, the outfits especially designed for the occasion by the two Charlottes. They looked breathtakingly beautiful. As the guests arrived, they were greeted by the bright radiance of these splendid creatures, who stood on either side of the entrance to the Raphael Room, handing out long-stemmed blue flowers from a basket they each carried. The flowers matched perfectly the book's cover, which was reproduced by photographing a lapis lazuli block from Asprey. A bevy of waiters with silver trays served blue champagne, in keeping with the general theme of the party, and three lady violinists from the London Symphony Orchestra provided the background music.

The catering was exquisite, the brainchild of Charlotte Millward, who never failed to astonish with her culinary gifts. *Tout Londres* came to the V & A to celebrate the appearance of the book at what turned out to be the party of the year. In the midst of all the revelry a murmur of wonder went through the crowd as one of the statues in the room suddenly moved. The two Charlottes had arranged for a young model, Danielle Minns, to be dusted with plaster to look like the other classical figures in the hall. She was partially nude and fooled the whole assembly into thinking she was a genuine artwork, till all at once she decided to cause a ripple or two and lifted an arm. A guest standing near by, who had been indulging her enthusiasm for the champagne, nearly passed out with shock and needed to be calmed down. She was sure she must have seen a marble statue come to life.

The bash was considered to have been a great success. The guests had lingered on well after it was time to leave. They found it difficult to wrench themselves away from those magnificent surroundings in the V & A, particularly with such a feast of mouthwatering food, blue champagne and heavenly music.

The intention behind the book was quite simple: to convey the views of women from many walks of life in answer to the questions I put to them on the important topics of early influences, the advantages and disadvantages of being a woman, feminism, sexuality, motherhood, creativity, relationships and the differences existing between men and women. In the interviewing process I refrained from expressing any views of my own, except to solicit a response or clarify a point. My only sin, if that is the right word, was to entice my interviewees to speak to me candidly on sensitive issues, often of a personal nature – the sort of thing they would not normally have discussed with a stranger, or have exposed to public scrutiny. I only succeeded because my intentions were genuinely honourable and my approach allowed them to feel comfortable within themselves. To begin with, I was very nervous and unsure of my ground. I was careful not to offend or to press my subjects to a degree where they began to show signs of irritation. My lack of experience as an interviewer was a clear advantage at the time. The women treated me more gently because I was not one of the hard-nosed professional journalists with whom they would have had to be more on their guard.

Whereas the normal press approach was to see an interview as an adversarial process, I wished only to arrive at a social discourse that had no competitive edge. There was no question of my pitting my intellect against theirs; the issue never arose. By the time I finished the book, having interviewed an amazing total of two hundred and eighty-nine women – at which point I was compelled to draw the line – an inner serenity had replaced my earlier state of nervousness. Over the months the task had ceased to be laborious and become something that was a pleasurable, self-enhancing and mind-enriching experience. I was therefore shaken to the core to find myself the target of a vicious campaign directed against the book itself. One would have been hard put to it to find a pejorative word in the English language that was not used in the attack.

With the first serial rights having been purchased by *The Times*, there was initial resentment in the trade at the embargo this involved. In his column 'Shelf Life' in the *New Statesman*, Malcolm Imrie had written:

Quartet publishes Attallah's magnum opus on *Women* later this month. Review copies come complete with stern warnings that they have been sent on the strict understanding that, due to contractual obligations, no review of, or material from, the book will appear before 18 October. What this means is that Quartet has sold first serial rights to Murdoch's *Times*. The legality of the warning is about as doubtful as the wisdom of feminists like Angela Carter, Jeanette Winterson and Jill Tweedie (among 289 'successful' women interviewed) in participating in such a superficial and overblown project. But with a promotion budget of £50,000 Attallah can afford to put a few literary editors' backs up. I wonder if the *Literary Review* (owned by Attallah) will trash it.

Yet the bizarre paradox was that notwithstanding the hostile reaction the book generated, newspapers and magazines began falling over themselves to acquire second serial rights (as in the case of the *Sunday Mirror*). *The Times* in fact ran extracts for only five days, yet spent a great deal of money promoting their acquisition on national television. A large number of periodicals also took chunks, all of which helped to boost the book's sales in no uncertain terms. Quartet had a considerable hit on its hands and no amount of slagging off from the media was going to reverse the momentum. As I went around the country promoting the book on regional radio and television and in newspapers, I had a feeling of being almost immune to slings and arrows. It was as if the commercial success of the book was creating a protective shield, and without a conscious effort, I became unaware of anything beyond the task in hand.

Only now, two decades after those events, when rummaging through the press cuttings, do I begin to realize the intensity of feeling the book generated. There seems to be no rationale to account for the concerted onslaught. It is impossible to avoid the implication that, by working so hard to discredit the book, the critics were waging an assault on the women who had agreed to talk to me. I was simply penning their views, my role being that of a master of ceremonies and messenger. Maybe it was a clear case of shooting the interviewer rather than having the courage to get to grips with the crux of the matter. My interviewees included:

Diana Athill, Joan Bakewell, Heather Brigstocke, Tina Brown, Joan Juliet Buck, Carmen Callil, Susan Crosland, Margaret Drabble, Sally Emerson, Christina Foyle, Lynne Franks, Pam Gems, Felicity Green, Baroness Grimond, Miriam Gross, Anna Huffington, Lucy Hughes-Hallett, Angela Huth, Tama Janowitz, Margaret Jay, Doris Lessing, Bel Mooney, Rabbi Julia Neuberger, Christine Ockrent, Diana Parker, Baroness Plowden, Marjorie Proops, Esther Rantzen, Anita Roddick, Joan Ruddock MP, Dame Cicely Saunders, Claire Short MP, Lady Anne Somerset, Christine Sutherland, Lisa St Aubin de Terán, Claire Tomalin, Polly Toynbee, Jill Tweedie, Diana Vreeland, Marina Warner, Katherine Whitehorn, Jeanette Winterson and Anna Wintour.

No one in their right mind would describe the views and thoughts emanating from such a group of women as a load of twaddle. Yet that was the overriding criticism as it came in from every direction.

Anita Brookner, writing for the *Observer*, took a more considered approach:

Although great candour is displayed one has the feeling, on reading this book, that the whole story has not been told, or that it has been told in capsule form. All women love to confide in men, and some see it as the ultimate intimacy. . . Although weighty enough in both scope and format the book is not satisfying, and for an unexpected reason: it lacks evidence of human weakness. All these women could answer Freud's question, 'What do women want?' But in their eagerness to reply they have shown that, contrary to expectation, more is somehow the equivalent of less.

Barbara Amiel, reviewing the book for *The Times*, was surprisingly shallow, citing as her example Jerry Hall, who is not known for her intellectual depth, and basing her whole judgement on a single pronouncement made by the model that, in pregnancy, a woman's body gets 'deformed for the benefit of both sexes'. Ms Amiel concluded:

The level of discourse in the book reflects this. [The author] would probably have been better off looking for accomplished women among scientists and others who for their achievement had to undergo a more rigorous level of mental training than that of a television presenter.

Kingsley Amis got into his stride in the *Sunday Telegraph*, his opening paragraph setting the tone for all that followed:

This book weighs something like a kilogram and a half, which fact the literary editor of this newspaper omitted to mention when he persuaded me by telephone to agree to review it. Treating it so that it will lie open on a desk or lap is impossible to one of normal muscular power. This might matter less if closing it on purpose were not such a constantly attractive option.

Commenting on my selection of women who participated, Amis said:

But wherever he got them from he certainly came up with a bumper crop of raging egotists, pompous buffoons and unstoppable talkers, because that is what most of those who would take part in such an enterprise are inevitably going to be, with all humour and power of detachment virtually ruled out. To hear them go on, you would think that no female before them had even been a child, got a job, met a man, had an affair, got married, had a baby or noticed that women are different from men and often have a different sort of life in certain respects . . . Luckily for the rest of us, a few human beings have managed to slip past his selection procedures, though not enough to save the book or make it worth while.

Sally Vincent complained in *New Society* that

The 289 women quoted here at such exhausting length do not include one agricultural worker, nor yet any other ordinary working woman. He has travelled far and wide in pursuit of the blatant plurality of his avowed theme, yet his chosen 289 are, to a woman, rich-born, rich-mated or richly endowed and known in these benighted times of winners and losers as Successful Women.

Such women have a tendency to be what mainstream media recognize as articulate. They dance, publicly at any rate, to the tune of the culture that allows them centre stage. You might think they would have little need of a forum for self-expression offered on the terms of another's limitations, Attallah's or any other whip-handed man. And yet they do. Vanity calls to itself and is never denied. Perhaps inclusion in this uninformative, uninspiring and humourless tome was a lesser risk than exclusion

In the *Sunday Express* Graham Lord set out to be deliberately scathing, heading his review 'A to Z of Women by Attallah the Hype' and making it the pretext for an unwarranted attack on me. The pontification in his first paragraphs was meant to hurt me as a publisher:

A writer whose book is rejected time and again may decide to pay thousands of pounds to some printer to publish it.

This pathetic last resort, 'vanity publishing', usually results in the author losing most of the money.

But the ultimate in vanity publishing is surely when an established publisher blithely issues his own book as his company's lead title of the year.

This week, to a fanfare of publicity, London publisher Naim Attallah launches his own grossly long collection of interviews with women . . . in the most blatant literary ego trip since Jeffrey Archer created *Kane and Abel* and rested on the seventh day.

It would be pointless to continue quoting from this review, and the only thing to say for Mr Lord's benefit, and the benefit of others who made similar assumptions, would be that, contrary to his assertion about 'vanity publishing', in my case the book *Women* made more money for Quartet than any other book they published, with the exception of *The Joy of Sex*. I am sorry to say that Mr Lord's philosophical exposition let him down badly on this occasion.

Craig Brown told readers of the *Mail on Sunday* that:

> At 1,150 pages the book called *Women* is much, much longer than any of the classic works of literature on women.
>
> It is three times as long as *Madame Bovary*, ten times as long as *Hedda Gabler*, and about as long as all Jane Austen's novels put together.
>
> Which publisher has so much confidence that this man who has never written a book before has so much more to say on the subject than the great artists of the past. The answer is, of course, Naim Attallah himself. As the owner of Quartet Books he was in the perfect position to have his book accepted for publication by them.

It was the same theme and inference of vanity publishing as Graham Lord's, but put more subtly. He then went on to compare the dialogue in the book with the sort of conversation 'one has in the early hours of the morning at a London media dinner party, with people droning on and on about Mrs Thatcher and whether men are better than women and how important sex is', before adding:

> There is no consensus whatsoever on any subject at all. Women constitute half the population of the world, and any sane person knows that they are as different and disparate as the men who constitute the other half. To treat them as Naim Attallah does, as if they were some obscure Brazilian jungle-tribe to be peered at, is the height of sexism, the intellectualization of the ogler's regressive fantasies.

After having a go at Koo Stark, Barbara Cartland and Molly Parkin, he moved to the close of his piece by saying, 'It is a sorry reflection on this sprawling, worthless, self-indulgent book that the silly, slightly grotesque women for whom Attallah has a penchant linger in the mind longer than the many thoughtful and decent women he interviewed,' and came to his *coup de grâce*: 'You will learn a lot more about women from reading one page of *Anna Karenina* than from slogging through all the 1,150 pages of *Women*.'

This last assertion totally astonished me. Maybe I never did go to university and gain the great privilege of a higher cultural insight into the classics, but *Anna Karenina* is a work of fiction and its heroine the product of Tolstoy's imagination. His creation was not necessarily a role model for every woman in the modern world, whatever its insights into human nature. What on earth was the purpose behind this comparison? I was not remotely setting myself up to compete with Tolstoy; such a thought would never have occurred to me. The disparity between the two works represented an unbridgeable gulf. So Craig Brown had read his Tolstoy. So what?

Deborah Moggach in the *Sunday Times* was more gentle and humorous. She proclaimed she had no doubt that 'the author is profoundly womanstruck and, like a passion for the theatre, if infected at an early age one is hooked for life. In a curiously earnest introduction he cites his female relatives, in whose cloistered Palestinian quarters he grew to manhood, as the growing conditions for what has flowered into his lifelong obsession with the female sex.' Coming to the theme of the book, she then had something positive to say:

> His subjects cover a wide spectrum – politicians, actresses, writers, models, tycoons, princesses – and they are mostly rather good value. The platitude quota is low, except when they talk about the feelings of giving birth, for which there are no words except 'wonderful' and 'marvellous'. But on the whole the tone of the book is bracing, honest, highly intelligent and often funny . . . In fact it's impossible to come to any conclusion except that this would make a good Christmas present for a man, and when he's finished it, would make a handy bedside table. If, however, he refuses to read it, saying he knows all he needs to know about women, then it would make a most effective missile to throw at him.

At first glance Libby Purves in *Punch* gave the impression that her review was going to be more temperate perhaps than some of those by her sisters, who seemed mainly intent on giving vent to a deep resentment – dare it be said – that they had not been invited to express their own views in the big tome they were now out to condemn. Libby's headline quote – 'Never having myself been asked to eat quails with Naim Attallah and spill out my philosophy on motherhood, creativity or sexuality, I tread cautiously' – was phrased in a way to give false comfort. It promised caution, but in reality it was a shot of anaesthetic which numbed the senses briefly before its effects wore off. It was misleading in that the promise was never lived up to. The piece was long and rambling and darted off at various tangents. At one point she discovered from a stained copy of the *Sunday Times*, retrieved from the hutch of a friend's son's rabbit, that 'this Naim Attallah is indeed the same chap who keeps recruiting privately-educated young gels with connections, and getting them to wear rubber dresses and things to promote perfume, feminist literature and Mr Auberon Waugh'. Whatever, she asked, could have lured 'an adored headmistress and a clutch of Hampstead lady writers into an open-ended dinner interview on the "evolution of women" with the pasty-faced Palestinian tycoon?' It could have been the 'classic trapster's formula of curiosity and vanity'. Then, in a typical *Punch* vein of humour, she let drop such pearls of wisdom as, 'All of us from puberty are disastrously prone to confession, theorizing and wild extrapolation from the state of our own ovaries.' Finally she recalled how I referred to *Women* as not just a book but also a much needed forum for women to express their views. Or that was what she thought I had said in the *Sunday Times* interview. 'Can't quite read it. The rabbit appears to have shat on that bit.' Charming!

Only a week later, again in *Punch*, Roy Hattersley made it his mission to lay into *The Times* for having serialized the book and boasted that 'some women were even ready to discuss the delicate subject [of the evolution of women] in interviews carried out over breakfast as much as during lunch or dinner'.

> Do not be deceived by the abysmal grammar. The idea that there is some-thing deeply significant about agreeing to discuss sex over eggs and bacon rather than steak and chips is intrinsically ridiculous. It is, of course, an idea intended to appeal to an essentially trivial meretricious readership.

Again I felt amazed to find how my book seemed to have induced a load of claptrap from even such a seasoned politician of the calibre of Mr Hattersley. Who cared where the interviews took place, or at what time of day? Was it that, by having a go at *The Times*, he was striking two birds with one stone? It was certainly an ingenious way of starting his review by demonstrating to the public how the Old Thunderer was lowering its standards by acquiring the serial rights, before going on to question the sort of power I possessed to make Pamela Armstrong ('television presenter') tell me, 'I would love to see what could happen if someone set up a brothel full of glorious, wonderful men,' or encouraged Lady Falkender to opine that, 'Eventually, if you are in women's company alone, they'll reduce the conversation back to the level of home and family.' Lady Falkender, said Mr Hattersley, 'worked for the wrong prime minister'.

> Mr Attallah's virus is clearly contagious. Penny Perrick (who ought not to have cast herself as *The Times* femininity correspondent) wrote about his researches immediately after their serialization ended. She gushed about the writing, and the author's 'exquisite line in delicious but non-fattening lunches'. For her, Maureen Lipman (actress), Susan Crosland (journalist widow of cabinet minister Tony Crosland), Joan Bakewell (television presenter), Margaret Drabble (author) and Marghanita Laski (critic), I have only one question. What do you think George Eliot (novelist) would have answered to Naim Attallah's impertinent questions?

Ann Leslie, airing her views in the *Daily Mail* under the heading 'The Lady Killer!', declared that 'only a man could make women so utterly boring'. 'Hey everyone,' she began on a light note, 'I've just finished cobbling together this really great book called *Women*! . . . I'll now stagger round with the hefty result to some nice publisher, like, say, Naim Attallah of Quartet Books, and try to con him into printing it.' All I could say to this was that if it only occurred to a fair number of people to stagger round to Quartet with similar books, then the imprint would have been made prosperous beyond Ann Leslie's imagining. As the saying goes, the proof of the pudding is in the eating. Her assertion that I had made women 'so utterly boring' was in no way reflected in the staggering success of the book commercially and the publicity it generated. Her sour grapes at the end of the piece were too transparent to be taken seriously: '*Women*'s 1,184 pages will make great bedding for the gerbil.'

Alice Thomas Ellis was on the whole complimentary in the London *Evening Standard*:

> I once knew a girl who was training to be a doctor. As she went through an intensive obstetrics course she gloomily remarked one day that she'd be quite happy if she never saw another woman in her life. I neither understood nor sympathized at the time.
>
> Now, having read Naim Attallah's book, I feel rather like my medical student friend and begin to discern the point and purpose of men – they *do* make a nice change.
>
> It's not that this book is boring – it is just that there are 1,155 pages of it and most of the ladies are thinking about men most of the time. One feels they ought to shut up and go off for a drink with the boys . . .
>
> I feel I have been unfair to Naim Attallah. He certainly did a lot of listening. Just because I am familiar with the views expressed doesn't mean they won't bear restating. Being female, I have always been a good listener. Too many men say, 'I've made up my mind, now kindly don't confuse me with facts.' They might from this book learn something to their advantage.
>
> Not understanding men as I understand women, I was greatly interested in Naim Attallah's account of his early life.
>
> He writes well. Perhaps he will give us an extended version – though not, I hope, 1,155 pages. At the moment I feel like the *Private Eye* footnote: *That's enough wimmin* (Ed.).

Isabel Colegate in the *Spectator* explained how the book was conceived and brought to fruition, while hastening to state that 'it isn't a serious work or even an interesting one, partly because the team [who worked on it] haven't, after all, organized it properly . . . the need to refer all the time to the brief biographies at the back of the book becomes irksome.' The only part of the book she liked, 'which seems to be Mr Attallah's unaided work', was the 'four-page autobiographical prelude. This is charming; it seems a pity the team did not encourage him to continue on the same lines.' She concluded her piece,

> Taken *en masse* and all jumbled up the mixture of opinions becomes indigestible; for everyone saying one thing there is someone else saying the opposite; confusion sets in. The overall effect is a bit like one of those evenings when the women leave the dinner table before the men and the men seem to stay in the dining-room for hours and hours and however much one likes the women one is sitting with it is *such* a relief when the men come in because then one can go home.

The *Bookseller* could not resist the opportunity to lambaste the band of discontented critics under the heading 'Hype is the Naim of the Game'. It set off by saying:

> It never ceases to amaze me how, every time it happens, newspapers, even normally quite sane ones, fall for an extreme hype when it comes to books. Somehow they seem to lose all sense of proportion, presumably because those in charge of the papers concerned are semi-illiterate and think that if something is between hard covers it must be important. And they are never persuaded otherwise. Seldom can it have happened over less worthy a book than Naim Attallah's *Women* (Quartet) which for no rational reason was given large space all over the place.
>
> I had expected hysteria from the populars, and they duly obliged, but it was really quite astonishing to see people of the weight of Anita Brookner (*Observer*) and Kingsley Amis (*Sunday Telegraph*) writing about the book. It must have been the money that persuaded them.

The author of the piece, Quentin Oates, was allocated an unusual amount of space by the editor of the *Bookseller* to round up and summarize all the least favourable reviews. Small publishers cannot afford lavish amounts of advertising and so become an easy target. To judge by what happens in the media, it seems it is a part of our English culture to build up a person in order to have the satisfaction of bringing him or her down at a later stage. Is it the disease of envy, which seems to be endemic in our society? I have often wondered about the reason for this unhealthy tendency, which is more prevalent in the United Kingdom than anywhere else in Europe. In France authors are revered, especially first timers, so as to give them a chance to develop. Critics there are more likely to appreciate the effort whatever the resulting product, being alert to the danger of stifling a talent still in its period of gestation. For the *Bookseller* to have gone on the offensive in this way demonstrated, with unprecedented clarity, the ill-will that lurked within the doors of the highly respected organ of the book trade. Surely it is the smaller independent publisher which should be encouraged rather than made the subject of snide remarks from every jackass with a self-serving claim to superiority of intellect and knowledge.

Piers Paul Read commented in the *Literary Review* that,

> It is common enough to review a book by a friend, but rare when that friend is not just the publisher of the book but of the magazine in which the review appears. Such is the chutzpah of Naim Attallah – the ebullient and energetic Palestinian who began his life in England as a steeplejack and has since scaled the spires of literary London. *Women* might have been a fiasco: so many of us make fools of ourselves when we sound off about the opposite sex. If it turns out to be something of a triumph this is because Attallah cleverly limits his own contribution to a charming 'Prelude' which in five pages tells us of the influence of women upon his childhood in Haifa and Nazareth . . . [The] meat of the book [is] a thousand pages in which over two hundred women speak their mind. Attallah's talent here was to persuade this number to talk to him and allow what they said to appear under their own names . . .
>
> Towards the end I began to wonder whether perhaps the book said more about the author than I had at first supposed? Was it possible that Attallah had chosen to talk to the women who fascinate him, but not to those he admires? Do these interviews perhaps represent the whimsical, vicarious infidelities of a man whose heart remains faithful to those good Christian women who raised him in Nazareth and to his delightful wife Maria to whom he dedicates the book in which she wisely and modestly does not appear?

Valery McConnell maintained in the *Financial Times* that I chose only to interview women I found interesting, which meant they were career achievers, beauties or privileged in terms of wealth. 'The title *Women* is a pretentious misnomer. These are not typical women.' There was a lack of coherence in the book, she added, 'and to pretend that the snippets it contained add up to a major statement on women in the 1980s is the kind of misjudgement a major publisher should blush to have made'.

Linda Colley, in a long review in the *London Review of Books*, called the book 'rather silly and sporadically illuminating [but] explicitly devoted to female achievers'. She said that 'Attallah interviewed his 289 women, of whom 150 are British, 76 are American, 37 from Continental Europe, and the rest straggle in from Australia, New Zealand, South Africa and the Third World . . . [by] jetting between London, New York and Paris and enticing his subjects to a series of lavish lunches', achieving all this 'with formidable energy and no less formidable expense'. Linda Colley's review was more in-depth and analytical than most. She never resorted to the sort of vindictive claptrap that characterized so many others and hindered any serious debate on the subject. Where she disagreed with an aspect, she gave valid reasons and refrained from point scoring. The book, she concluded, 'is none the less fun; it is cheap at this price [£15]; and if you can carry it, it will last you through many a long plane trip'.

Another Quartet author, Tony Lambton, tackled *Women* for the *Sunday Telegraph*. 'It has taken a man to write the most revealing book about women,' he said.

A book of more than a thousand pages in which women talk about their thoughts on love, life and aspirations does not sound all that promising. The trouble with this sort of compendium is that the interviewer's ego usually keeps intruding into the conversations. In this instance, however, not the faintest ghost of the author, Naim Attallah, is to be found.

The women speak almost literally for themselves for their remarks were taped – a clever idea for women will often say what they will not write down. His victims were asked to come to an excellent recorded luncheon, given what they wished to drink and then interviewed by a man who gave them to think by his inquisitive, questioning, expressive face that they were brilliant and fascinating conversationalists.

In England such delightful treatment is a rarity, as the majority of Englishmen do not like women's company. They have developed over the years such defences as sitting at port after dinner while the women withdraw, often angry but pretending to be amused by each other's company. Such a habit was and is unknown on the civilized Continent . . . However intelligent the women in Mr Attallah's book, it seems to me that his élitist aristocrats sometimes forget that their privileges and opportunities are not shared by ordinary women.

Mr Bill Grundy of Stockport, Cheshire, was provoked to pen a letter to the editor of the *Daily Telegraph* complaining about certain aspects of this review, specifically the assertion that 'the majority of Englishmen' did not like women's company and had developed the tradition of 'port after dinner' as a defence. 'The majority of Englishmen?' Grundy questioned. 'Port after dinner?'

May I tell Lord Lambton that, at least in the north-west, a lot of us actually like women's company, and not many of us sit knocking back misogynistic port after dinner, the women having withdrawn. Withdrawn to where?

Now I come to think of it, in the north-west it's the women who prefer the port, usually with a drop of lemon.

Private Eye had launched straight on to the offensive under the heading 'Naim Droppings'. After saying of books by publishers that 'all they're up to is fondling their sensibilities', and citing 'the late Michael Joseph's prose poems about eroticism with his cats' as an example, the 'Bookworm' piece continued:

> In this appalling genre Naim Attallah has gone straight to the top. For his hobby is a little more interesting: women. And he likes them not just one at a time, not in twos or threes, but in great gabbling throngs. Poshly gabbling for preference. Namara House, where he concocts his phallic perfumes and saucy picture books, is thickly carpeted with gorgeous pouting Naimbirds of noble birth, if little brain. They are popularly known as Naim's harem. But really what they find themselves in is that other rich man's fancy: a private zoo.
>
> Now, with Oriental generosity, Mr Attallah has flung open the doors and allowed us all a peek. Indeed he has been out on safari and brought back no less than 289 prime specimens of ripe womanhood from around the world. The old, the young, the rich, the mad . . .
>
> The noise from this collection is, frankly, appalling, not to mention the smell. None of these women agree; all want to be heard.
>
> Most of this snuffling and screeching is pretty dull. Yet Naim listened to it all . . .

And that's enough of that too. The rest is typical *Private Eye* garbage and they were never going to be content with the one onslaught.

Germaine Greer had her main chance ahead of the field when the *Observer* commissioned *her* to interview *me* before the other reviewers got started on pouring scorn on the whole undertaking and lighting the fuse to try to blast me and the book into oblivion. She kicked off with a definition of vanity publishing and how it had become the preserve of writers unable to find a publisher. Then she described the book, although she only had a proof copy, and its lapis lazuli cover. She mentioned the number of women interviewed and how the book was being puffed in glossy magazines with a studio portrait of its author, whose 'effrontery is balanced only by his charm, which many (men) find oleaginous'.

> The day I went to interview him, I had a badly blistered mouth, four broken teeth and one leg hugely swollen and leaking from an insect bite. The dog-like gaze of the brown eyes gave no hint that I looked anything but adorable.

The interview was hard-hitting, laden with sarcasm and not a little bitchiness, peppered with words like 'bullshit' and such observations as, 'Attallah's elephantine innocence surrounded him like a scented fog.' Germaine was provocative at every turn as she tried to make me lose my composure and put up some platitudes that she could then shoot out of the air like clay pigeons. In fact I enjoyed the encounter; I had the sense that she was somehow struggling within herself to cast aside her brashness in favour of a more sympathetic approach. The chemistry between us turned out to be less conducive to hostility than expected and neither of us minded the cut and thrust of the exchange. At the close of the interview she said: 'It's nice to think that rich women are working out a new dance in which the woman isn't always travelling backwards, but that hasn't altered the fact that most women are not even on the floor. To the women living in misery in this country, your book is a mockery.'

'But the book itself isn't against these women,' I challenged her.

No. It is innocent of their very existence. In Australia we used to have a system where you bored a hole through a book and hung it on a string in the lavatory. You'd read a page, rip it off and wipe your behind on it. 1,200 double sheets for £15. Looked at that way, *Women*'s not such bad value.

According to Greer, my reaction to this remark was to laugh disarmingly, 'widening the brown eyes'. 'OK, OK. But do you think the book's a fiasco? Really?'

'Yep. But you'll probably get away with it.'

The idea of Germaine Greer using my book to wipe her behind gave me a measure of comfort. It is not every day that a book embodying the thoughts and aspirations of 289 women is used to cleanse the lower regions of the body of a feminist icon. I felt I was in good company.

A month after the contentious but curiously affectionate article appeared in the *Observer* magazine, I happened to find myself sitting next to Germaine at a luncheon hosted by the editor of 'Londoner's Diary' in the *Standard*. Whether this placement was accidental or a deliberate tactic to liven up matters I do not know. I decided to take it all in my stride and refused to betray any embarrassment. Germaine, in fact, seemed more on edge than I was, but she adopted the policy of attack as the best form of defence and opened the conversation by saying she had listened to BBC radio's *Any Questions* programme, chaired by Jonathan Dimbleby, when I was on the panel. To her utter surprise she had heard me say that, if I were to be a woman, I would choose to be Mrs Thatcher. Quite aside from her obvious disapproval of my choice, she said that if only I could be less flippant and give the matter more serious consideration, I would surely realize, in my misguided confusion, that being Mrs Thatcher must mean having to sleep with Denis. Perish the thought! I was reduced to speechlessness and had to admit Germaine had got the better of me on this occasion.

'Now we have Naim Attallah's cheerful gossipy compendium *Women*,' wrote Lorna Sage in *The Times Literary Supplement* (in a review bracketed with Andrea Dworkin's feminist polemic *Intercourse*), 'which goes to show, if nothing else, that women are almost pathologically patient.'

> Attallah's strategy was to ask the questions then excise them. As a result the women (289 of them in over 1,000 pages) are reduced to presenting themselves as eagerly interested in the after-dinner topics that intrigue him. It's a method as old as social documentary: Henry Mayhew in *London Labour and the London Poor*, interviewing the underclass of Victorian England, did the same, and teased the bourgeoisie with the spectre of street urchins aggressively denying all the pieties. No, they said, seemingly without being asked, I never go to church. No, I don't know who my father is. The results, with this technique, depend, however, on the quality and motive of the questions.
>
> Here, the women – the privileged class of their sex whatever that means (and we're not going to find out) – almost all say yes. Or possibly the naysayers have been eliminated from the miles of tape, having nothing positive to contribute. They are for the most part public women, public figures even, but what the questions are after is their privacy – on the assumption that that is where they exist *as women*. The questions not asked are those about the wide world. God hardly comes into it (reasonably perhaps) but nor does the work of these women who 'have all, in some way, made their mark in the world'. Here, they might as well sign themselves with a cross.

Lorna Sage's conclusion was that *Women* was a non-book though that was not anything that was going to interfere with its success.

> What it does is take the interests of the tabloid press and the chat-show up-market. What it reveals is the poverty of 'dialogue', never mind 'intercourse'. No wonder Andrea Dworkin talks to herself.

Private Eye continued to make the most of its field-day with *Women*, a topic that provided them with such rich pickings that they flogged it to death and carried on flogging it even after its burial. 'Grovel' had two items at the end of October:

> My fragrant friend Sarah Giles tells a curious tale.

Sarah, daughter of Frank and Lady Kitty, was visited in New York some time ago by Naim Attullah-Disgusting, the ubiquitous Palestinian parfumier. She assumed it was a social call.

Imagine her surprise when as he ran to leave, the Ayatollah whipped a small tape recorder out of his pocket and switched it off, grinning roguishly.

Now, to her consternation, she finds herself quoted at length on the subject of Englishmen's sexual fantasies in Attallah's book *Women*.

I can reassure her. Since nobody will read the Ayatollah's ridiculous tome, her bedroom secrets are quite safe.

The second was particularly ripe with racist overtones:

Meanwhile Stalinist yuppie Julie Burchill tells me that she was one of the many women to turn down the Ayatollah's invitation to be interviewed for his book.

She wrote back to him in no uncertain terms: 'No, I will not be in your book. One, because I don't like Arabs in general. Two , because I don't like Palestinians in particular. And three, because I particularly don't like you. Now sling your hook.'

In recognition of this act of bravery, Grovel is compiling a roll of honour to commemorate those women who declined to be interviewed by Attallah. My list so far includes Anita Brookner, Fay Weldon, Lady Teresa Waugh, Germaine Greer, Nigella Lawson and Sue Townsend. The usual 5p for any additional names.

There was also a cod book notice:

THE NAIM OF THE ROWS OF SILLY WOMEN WHO WERE STUPID ENOUGH TO TALK
TO THIS CLAPPED-OUT OLD ARAB
by Ayatallah Disgusting
Cortit Books, £899.99
How was it that a seedy Arab perfumier could lure millions of the world's women into his Soho basements to pour out their innermost secrets? Was it that they thought he was Lord Lucan? Perhaps we shall never know.

In November 'Grovel' followed through:

Further to my item in the last issue, I discover the names of two wise ladies who resolutely refused to be interviewed by Naim Attullah-Disgusting for his ludicrous book *Women*. Grovel's roll of honour has therefore expanded to include historical biographer Lady Antonia Fraser and literary agent Pat Kavanagh.

In December a genuine letter from Charles Glass was printed, headed 'Palestine Liberation Affront':

> Would Grovel in your recent issue have quoted Julie Burchill so approvingly on her dislike for Arabs in general and Palestinians in particular if she had referred to some other race? If her remarks had been made to publisher Lord Weidenfeld instead of Naim Attallah, would Grovel have pointed out her wisdom and courage; or instead condemned her justly for infantile racism? One wonders whether Miss or Mrs Burchill really told Attallah as Grovel said she did (and as Chris Hutchins said she did in *Today*, 28 October), 'I don't like Arabs in general, I do not like Palestinians in particular and I particularly do not like Palestinians like yourself.'
>
> Her letter to Mr Attallah . . . , in which she responds to his request for an interview, says only: 'Dear Mr Attallah, I am very sorry but I am much too busy to give interviews. Yours sincerely, Julie Burchill.'
>
> Were the racist remarks attributed to Miss Burchill something she said later to others? Or did they spring from the fertile imagination of Grovel and Chris Hutchins. If so, why?

Like a naughty schoolboy sticking his tongue out to show he doesn't give a damn about being reproved, *Private Eye* finally cooked up a letter from 'Wedge Antilles of Birmingham Polytechnic':

> It is always nice to read complaints about ghastly, petrifying Julie Brainill/Bitchkill/Bastard. Her racist tendencies should come as no surprise though. After all it was her remark about 'Argies' that was the beginning of the end at *Time Out* and a reference to Arabs as 'camelfuckers' has also been attributed to her.
>
> In December 1986 she told *Q* magazine of her (largely unreciprocated except by her hubby Cosmo Landesman) idolization of and deep identification with a New York-based 'Jewish literary/intellectual establishment'. By the age of 12, she claims she knew that 'I was really one of these people'.
>
> Deducing a difficulty with Arabs in general and 'Palestinians in particular' isn't too difficult then.
>
> May the force be with you.

As the ripples spread outwards, 'Gibson at Large' in the Edinburgh *Evening News* said:

> Mr Attallah . . . struck me as being a genuine seeker of candour and wisdom. He fully expects the book to be a bestseller despite the controversy. 'Men who don't particularly care for women have attacked it and women who are not in it have savaged it, saying those in it are unimportant.'

I suggest you give *Women*, price £15, to the man or woman in your life for Christmas, as a two-way investment. If he or she ever walks out on you and happens to drop the book, it will break their foot. It weights about a kilo.

Mary Maher in the *Irish Times* considered that my diligence had 'produced a curious and provoking documentary' and the overall impact had 'very little to do with the fact that the women testifying included such divergent luminaries as Koo Stark, Princess Elizabeth of Yugoslavia, Jerry Hall, Margaux Hemingway, Ariana Stassinopolous, Doris Lessing, Charlotte Rampling, Juliet Mitchell, Katherine Whitehorn, Marina Warner, Jill Tweedie, Gloria Steinem'.

The celebrated names lend the cachet necessary to promotion by publishers, of course. There is a certain voyeuristic relish in reading what Mandy Rice-Davies thinks about lust (it leaves you in a desert afterwards), or what comparison Molly Parkin draws between marriage and one-night stands (four-course meal to a bag of crisps, each has its satisfactions). But it isn't the notoriety of the contributors that gives the book real interest, it's the candid and reflective nature of their contributions to four central issues: feminism, sexuality, motherhood, creativity.

And while there isn't consensus, there most certainly is shared ground. There is the eternal and somewhat exasperated puzzle as to whether the male sexual drive really is fundamentally different, or whether that's a convenient bit of male codology. There is the dilemma of women's relatively poor showing in the annals of art, literature, music: lack of opportunity, or genetic limitation, nurture or nature? . . .

But if all this is vastly entertaining, and some of it is very worth while, the chapter on feminism I found pretty depressing. This is partly due to the number of celebrities who coyly embrace what one describes as the 'imbalance' between men and women: considering how richly over-privileged most of these particular women are, this is gagging to read.

I thought Mary Maher's review of the book extremely intelligent. It had the right balance. She took the subject seriously and treated it in the manner it deserved.

The *Ham and High* of Hampstead commented:

The splutterings of women who think they, and their sex, have been misrepresented in Naim Attallah's tome, *Women*, . . . is nothing compared to the pique felt by women who were not asked to be in it. As lecturer and local politician Enid Wistrach (one of the chosen 289) says: 'Such an ego trip; who can resist talking about their feelings to someone who is so prepared to listen?'

Not many apparently, as only 10 per cent of those approached turned Attallah down.

Suzanne Lowry, in the *International Herald Tribune*, described the text of *Women* as 'a patchwork quilt of chat, opinions and recollections; not tales from a Vienna couch, but from a Soho lunch table'.

Naim Attallah is a figure who flirts simultaneously with notoriety and establishment respectability. He is famous in London for his staff of upper-class aides with names like Bonham-Carter and Fraser and Sackville-West and Guinness ('Naim's Harem') but also owns The Women's Press, a leading feminist imprint, and the *Literary Review*, edited by Auberon Waugh. He makes perfumes with blatantly erotic names ('Avant l'Amour' and 'Après l'Amour') and is finance director of Asprey's, the grand Bond Street jewelers and silversmiths. He owns a jazz magazine, *Wire*, and a fine arts journal, *Apollo*. He backs dress designers and television shows. He is colorful and urbane, presiding over his little empire from the rather cramped headquarters of his Namara Group in Soho.

All in all, he contrives to be a walking, talking, lunching affront to the British idea of a businessman and gentleman. He is charming, but seems happily to lack any violent undertow in his manner, of the sort so common among 'charming' Anglo-Saxon men . . .

Even Germaine Greer, who was furious with him, admitted that he would probably 'get away with it [*Women*]'. The reason may be that it is not at all anguished, as so many books about women have been. It is entertaining and not, in the end, abusive. Here is not woman as problem, but woman as lunch companion. And it gives some flavor, for better, for worse or for sillier, of what conversation or 'communication' with educated, privileged women of the late 20th century is like. And even a few clues to what they want.

Patrice Chaplin, in the *Jewish Chronicle*, picked on my remark in the introduction that

'Arranging the interviews drew exhaustively on my reserves of patience. Sometimes I found the whole exercise most exasperating and despite my initial drive my spirit was in constant danger of weakening.'

It sounded as though he was trying to locate a rare, doomed strain of wildlife rather than a group of mostly desk-bound women. I think his emotional investment could have been used to much better purpose. Perhaps writing more fully about his own life and relation to women, which he does very well, although briefly, in the foreword.

Women works best as something to open at random but you need big hands. There are some hilarious quotes. Margaux Hemingway on sex: 'Sometimes the need for sex goes through cycles. I know I need to have it when the moon is less full. I think it's all gravitational pull.'

It makes you realize life is surely a subjective business.

The most supportive coverage I received was perhaps from David Litchfield, the editor and proprietor of *Ritz* magazine. He must have seen the savage onslaught on *Women* as being uncalled for and as having a very suspect motivation. He interviewed me at length, giving me ample opportunity to put across my point of view and my side of the argument, while at the same time gauging my reaction to the vitriol that the publication of the book had uncorked. He summed up his own thoughts in his introduction to the piece with a brilliant few words whose clarity of meaning was never in doubt:

A man for all seasons – a man whose past is as undefinable as his present – a man who rescued Asprey quietly and publishes noisily – a man who champions the Palestinians without frightening the Jews – a man who loves women so much that he interviewed three hundred and nine of them and recorded their six hundred thousand words in a book he entitled *Women*, which could be the world's largest literary indulgence or the definitive statement on the coming trends in women's thought. Whatever. Its creation was more fun than foreign-exchange dealing.

Its critics have spent most of their time forgetting who wrote the book while Craig Brown said that one could learn more of women by reading *Anna Karenina*, forgetting, or probably never knowing, that Tolstoy hated women. *Women* is a work of love, not hate.

Another staunch defender was David Elliott, who published a letter in the *Bookseller* drawing attention to several fundamental issues of book-trade ethics raised by the Quentin Oates 'Critics Crowner' piece and pointing out how this had 'sought to destroy all credibility for Naim Attallah's *Women*'.

It was clear he was prepared to use his influence in any way he could to damage the book trade's opinion of Mr Attallah and his book. I cannot recall any article in the *Bookseller* (and I have been reading the magazine for over twenty years) ever calling a book 'worthless'.

Women was sold to *The Times* for a serialization over five days, second serial rights were sold to the *Sunday Mirror* for two weekly extracts and magazine rights were sold to *Women's World*; Australian, Swedish, Dutch, German, Spanish, French and South African serialization rights are sold . . . Interviews have already appeared in six major provincial newspapers and two Sunday colour supplements. The author is presently engaged on a tour of Scotland and other parts of England and Wales appearing on regional TV programmes, local radio stations and being interviewed by provincial newspapers.

Any book which generates this torrent of attention and activity usually wins glittering prizes from the trade journals – not so with Mr Oates. With a sniff he dismisses it all as 'hype'. What does he want? Every time any book generates controversy and attention it is good for all the trade. He has ignored the good reviews altogether . . .

These reviews were as pleasing and praising as Craig Brown's (quoted at great length by Mr Oates) was nasty and damning. Oates's précis of Anita Brookner's review left out her obvious fascination with aspects of the book and when Deborah Moggach's review for the *Sunday Times* actually praises *Women*, Oates declares he couldn't be bothered with reading it. Precisely, Mr Oates! When Deborah Moggach writes: '. . . the tone of this book is bracing, honest, highly intelligent and often funny', it does not suit your brief.

Finally the marketplace decides if a book is to sell or not. And this is my real annoyance with Mr Oates and the *Bookseller*. He chooses to deride, in a vindictive manner, a book launched with incredible coverage and attention whilst that launch is still in progress – *Women* was published only two days before Oates's article appeared. Since his name is pseudonymous, I can only imagine his motives, but if the *Bookseller* is to take sides on controversial books, can it do so in a more balanced fashion?

To coincide with the publication of *Women*, the *Sunday Telegraph Magazine* had commissioned Candida Crewe, an ex-employee of Quartet and daughter of my good friend Quentin Crewe and Angela Huth, to write an article about my love of working with women and what they, in turn, thought of me. When the article appeared, I did not mind its tone but I did take exception to statements attributed to Bridget Heathcoat-Amory. Some were inaccurate; others were over the top and had a catty resonance:

'Because he was brought up in a matriarchal society, Naim is more comfortable with women. He gets platonic crushes: a girl will be flavour of the month and the relationship is then very intense. He rings her up eight times a day to tell her *all* the news about everything. I was favourite for too long – there was nobody immediately to replace me. But it's better not to be in the limelight. I used to stand up for myself in front of him. Now I think of Naim as a friend, but I remember once shouting at him, "You think you're God." He was furious, but respected me more in the end.

He gets completely loony about some girls, taking them on a whim or connection. I remember going to see him and his PA, the then favourite, was in a mini-skirt and with bare feet. She sat cross-legged on his desk putting lipstick on, gazing into a compact. And he let her get away with it! I think he thought it rather cool.

'He never advertises for people, never needs to. He pays the girls very badly, but they're grateful for a job. And every now and then he picks a winner, like Rebecca Fraser. About one in three of these grand girls turns out to be really good.'

I begged to disagree on various counts, especially on the last statement. Ninety-five per cent of the girls who worked for the Namara Group, which included Quartet, went on to forge illustrious careers to the extent that some became household names. In some way or another they made their mark in society. The other gossipy platitudes are not worthy of comment.

In sharp contrast, the actress Patsy Kensit, who starred in *Absolute Beginners*, was quoted as saying:

'When I first met Naim I was madly in love with an Italian playboy. Naim had asked me to lunch in his basement dining-room in order to interview me for *Women*. I instantly found him so approachable and felt I could talk to him about boys, anything. So I confided in him about the playboy, said I even contemplated marrying him. Naim advised me against it, thank God. "Don't be so ridiculous," he told me heatedly. "You can't marry yet." I'm grateful to him for that.

'I stayed talking to him for hours that day. The next morning he sent me flowers, a card, some scent and two books he wanted me to read. One was a love story. And as for the interview, he wanted to hear my answers, not just for the sake of the book, but because he was really interested. He made me feel as if I was the only woman he'd ever met in his life.'

Again Bridget postulated:

'Naim's not a great publisher, but he is a great force in publishing. I'm longing for the day when he's Sir Naim. Though he'd deny it was one of his ambitions, it would give him such pleasure.'

The difference between being a great publisher and a great force in publishing escaped me. However, I have no wish to be too harsh in my condemnation of Bridget's remarks in the article which, looking back, I see were affectionate at best and theatrically inspired at worst. They nevertheless touched a raw nerve at the time.

Siobhan Crozier at least stood alone in her frenzy of condemnation of *Women* when she stated it was 'more pornographic than the *Sunday Sport*'. In writing her essay, she seemed to lose her marbles entirely.

Attallah gored [*sic* – 'gorged'] himself on these women in long 'questing' interviews with those he'd enveigled into his master plan, the ones who still haven't learnt to say no. He directs them to their fake marble pedestals as if he's running a literary Miss World and then flays them of their private thoughts.

We are left pondering how many of Attallah's subjects wish they'd had more sense for many of them emerge from the exercise more naked than their sisters in the *Sunday Sport*.

The person who derives the real satisfaction from *Women* has to be Naim Attallah himself, for many of his subjects must be cringing at what they've revealed to him.

He's had the pleasure which he anticipated in meeting all these women whom he already admired. There's no craft in it – it's titillation in a fancy package for readers of the *Sunday Times* who can't allow themselves a peek into the *Sunday Sport*. Attallah emerges from it not as a writer but like a schoolboy after a binge in the sweetshop. In his case, it's his ego and not his belly that's inflated.

Following the publication of *Women* in October 1987, I was approached by Carrere, the French media group and publishers, with a view to producing a French edition. Their only stipulation was that I should interview an additonal thirty Frenchwomen almost immediately. They were in a great hurry to bring out the French-language version in March 1988, a mere six months after the appearance of the English edition. It looked an almost impossible task. They hired a team of translators to work round the clock on the English text while I frantically set about conducting the necessary interviews. The choice of women and arrangements to interview them were all done in conjunction with my own office in Paris. It was just left to me to brush up on my French and plunge into another voyage of discovery with renewed vigour and optimism. Strangely I had remained unaffected by the adverse critical reception I had received in the UK and felt undaunted by the idea that the whole thing might involve a repetition of the experience in France. My new list included writers, bankers, artists and stars of stage and screen, such as Arletty and Emmanuelle Béart, who had recently starred in *Manon des Sources*, the continuation of Claude Berri's hit film based on Marcel Pagnol's novel *Jean de Florette*, with Daniel Auteuil. Also there, among the politicians, was Edith Cresson, who was to become the first woman prime minister of France not many years later.

Despite the shortage of time, the French edition was published as planned and Carrere arranged for a launch party to be held on 22 March at the famous Parisian night-spot, Le Privilège. It was a most glamorous occasion, extensively covered by the French media and attended by hordes of celebrities. I was seated at dinner between Hélène Rochas, the *parfumière*, and Joan Juliet Buck, the American writer and then editor of French *Vogue*. The room teemed with beautiful women. Over the next few days I appeared on French television, discussing the book with some of the stars who featured in its pages. The French critics were unanimous in their plaudits, in sharp contrast with their counterparts in the UK. It was impossible to open a French newspaper without seeing some reference to the book. I felt euphoric at this unexpected show of appreciation and enthusiasm. And to crown it all, the book sold extremely well in France and our efforts were richly rewarded.

Looking through my archives, the retrospective impression is that more was written about the French edition than the already phenomenal amount about the English edition in Britain. The difference in coverage lay in the fact that while the Gallic approach was constructive the trend in the book's home country was certainly destructive. Even after the furore surrounding the original publication of *Women* in hardback had died down, the appearance of a paperback edition in Britain a year later precipitated the same spitting of venom as before. It was as if those who had missed their chance at first publication now climbed aboard to make their voices heard from the bandwagon. But this was a new wave of women, some not so well known as their predecessors of a year earlier. They entered the fray as if to proclaim solidarity with their dissenting sisters.

In the meantime, a Japanese edition was in preparation. The divergence of opinion between the public at large, who welcomed the book, and the band of its detractors, who did not, posed many questions. Who matters most? Is it the reading public or the self-proclaimed arbiters whose judgement has proved on many occasions to be out of touch with the prevailing mood? Is our cultural life totally dependent on a select few whose opinions seldom reflect the thinking or aspirations of the ordinary man or woman? These questions have continued to trouble me. We seem to be burdened with an élitist literary establishment intent on keeping the myth of its infallibility going at all costs. In saying this I could hardly be accused of 'sour grapes'; I laughed all the way to the bank.

It was pleasing, when the dust died down, to read in the London *Evening Standard* that a sharp-eyed commentator had spotted three books prominently on display in a photograph of Michael Caine taken in the library of his Beverly Hills home and printed in *Hello!* magazine. Alongside Paul Johnson's *Intellectuals* and Orville Shell's *Discos and Democracy* was my book *Women*.

Thirty-three

In early March 1988 Eric Asprey died as a result of a fall. He was eighty-five. Two years before his death I persuaded him to step down as chairman in favour of John, his son, and to assume the title of president, a non-executive position. He loved being chairman in charge of proceedings at board meetings and found it hard to relinquish his responsibilities and with them his pacifying role in a family bruised by years of internal conflict. His benign and fatherly presence helped us all to keep our feet on the ground and not be carried away by the success the company had achieved under his stewardship. His most endearing feature was the way he won the loyalty of his staff and inspired in them a common interest in the continuing prosperity of the business. He dismissed wealth and money as being volatile and transitory, and passionately believed that the Asprey business should always remain the focus of our attention.

For their obituary of him, the *Daily Telegraph* asked me to write a tribute:

> I first met Eric Asprey in the early 1970s when he had just taken over the chairmanship of Asprey from his brother Philip, who had occupied the chair for more than thirty years.
>
> He was naturally new to the demands of such a position and one could detect a certain apprehension at the weight of the responsibilities suddenly thrust upon him; for Asprey was then undergoing difficult times both internally as a family business and as an established concern that needed to evolve if it were to meet the challenges of a changing market at home and abroad.
>
> I was very struck by Eric's warmth, by his ability to make you feel at ease and his direct, uncomplicated view of the world. He had no interest in intricacies of high finance, neither did he appreciate the entrepreneurial activities of some of his contemporaries. He believed in a solid base, that base being the shop; and that no amount of money in the world could be a substitute for a sound continuing business whose standards would pass from one generation to the next.
>
> He shunned publicity, frowned on extravagant living and led a simple life free from pretension.
>
> He was very popular among his staff. He spoke to everyone and they respected him, not because he carried the mantle of authority, but rather

because 'Mr Eric' was a most genial man. I will always remember him as the guiding force who brought Asprey into a new century, and whose compassion and wit made life all the merrier for those of us who worked with him.

For some considerable time afterwards, Eric's death left a feeling in the shop which was hard to define, as if a robust and healthy tree had suddenly shed its leaves out of season. His jovial face was no longer to be seen as he strolled in the shop, greeting the staff and surveying the scene, as he had done every day of his long working life. He was the soul of the institution without being conscious of it, and he left his mark quietly with a dignity that was always regarded as his finest attribute. In 1992 the dedication of my third book of interviews, *Of a Certain Age*, was to Eric's memory.

Eight years later, when Asprey was facing a turbulent period for a variety of reasons – some of them beyond its control – Eric's influence on events would have been not only beneficial, but would have also rallied the family together. John had his incontestable talents, but he was never strong enough to face adversity and stand up to members of his own family who put pressure on him at every turn. The constant battering was something he was unable to withstand; he began to lose his equilibrium and rational judgement. Then panic set in, to the consternation of those who saw matters in a totally different light. I was the main advocate for calm and optimism, but my voice was drowned by the sheer force of the opposition.

If only Eric were still alive, Asprey would remain today a family concern. That it is one no longer is a tragic example of how disunity, compounded by fear, can lead to the loss of a thriving business.

*

At Quartet we seem to have been unfazed by the uproar that followed the publication of *Women*. In fact we were feeling stronger for the experience. Manoli Olympitis, whom Nigel Dempster described as the poker-playing merchant-bank director, had written a thriller, *By Victories Undone*, with a barrister friend, Raymond Lewis, as co-author. Quartet published it and the launch was held at Aspinall's in Mayfair. The venue was appropriate as the book told the story of Jamie Stuart, the heir to a baronetcy and a vast fortune, whose great passion was poker. The death of his father meant he could leave Oxford and immerse himself in gambling clubs and high-class brothels. But hanging over his new-found freedom was the memory of his grandfather, Clarence, whose ability to mind-read drove him to insanity. Jamie has inherited this ability of his grandfather's, and it enables him to humiliate a

Greek shipping millionaire, Spiros Virakis, at the poker table, thus making him into an implacable enemy.

Guests at the launch included many of Manoli's friends, as Nigel Dempster reported in the *Daily Mail*:

> Princess Ira von Fürstenberg, the niece of Italy's richest man Fiat chief Gianni Agnelli; financier Sir Gordon White's mini-skirted daughter Sita, 27; a suavely suited Viscount Althorp; and his publisher Naim Attallah. Manoli was missing one crucial catalyst in the creative process. Screen siren Valerie Perrine, with whom the hard-grafting Greek had a doomed engagement, was absent from the celebrations, although they remain friends.

Manoli was at the time chief executive officer of Aitken Hume and was responsible for boosting its net worth to thirty-nine million pounds. The late Ross Benson, reporting the launch of *By Victories Undone* in the *Daily Express*, wrote a rather humorous piece:

> This morning I shall just call him Manoli O. In the past this King's School Canterbury-educated businessman has been worried that my reference to him in the company of a whole series of shapely bimbos might endanger his business cred . . .
>
> Since O has begged for anonymity in the past lest he should be by conquests undone, I won't name him now that he courts publicity.
>
> Suffice it to say that his guests . . . hardly blinked as ever-attentive O swung into his old routine and whispered sweet nothings in the ear of Princess Ira von Furstenberg.

Both Manoli and his co-author Raymond Lewis played poker with some of the best-known figures in gaming circles, including Norman Mailer, who prophesied that their forthcoming book would prove to be 'the thinking man's bestseller'. Was Mailer right? Perhaps it was the lack of 'thinking men' in the world that prevented it from attaining that status.

Another book was *Cutting Timber* by Thomas Bernhard, translated by Ewald Osers. The previous year Quartet had published Bernhard's novel *Wittgenstein's Nephew*, also translated by Osers. Bernhard had been born in Holland but raised in Austria. He was the author of much poetry together with several novels and plays and three volumes of autobiography. His awards included many European prizes, including the Bremen Prize, the Austrian National Prize and Le Prix Seguier. *Cutting Timber* was a novel in which he vented his anger on the Viennese cultural community.

The narrator, having spent the last thirty years in London, meets the

Auersbergers, a couple he knew in his youth. They tell him of the suicide of a mutual friend, Joanna, and invite him to an 'artistic evening'. This has been arranged in honour of a well-known Burgtheatre actor, the sort of person the narrator feels he heartily despises. As he sits in a wing chair in the Auersbergers' entrance hall, his thoughts dwell misanthropically on the sudden death of Joanna, on the bohemian life and on his own early times in Vienna. He had been good friends with the Auersbergers in those days, but now they strike him as superficial and uncultured; their 'artistic evening' fills him with contempt. The surprise of the evening is the famous actor from the Burgtheatre himself, a man whom he has been fully prepared to scorn, but who turns out to be a clever critic of the theatre world, of Viennese society and indeed of civilization itself.

A book of some topicality was *Rudolf Hess: The Deputy* by Wulf Schwarzwäller. It came out in translation just a few months after Hess's death and the immense public interest aroused by his passing after his years of imprisonment in Spandau. Hess was born in Alexandria, the son of a respected merchant, though he was educated in Germany. He enlisted at the start of the First World War, and in the chaos that followed the Armistice, joined the group fighting the communist insurrection in Munich. There, in 1920, he met Adolf Hitler and quickly became his most devoted supporter. After the failed *Putsch* of 1923 they were imprisoned together, the experience cementing their mutual loyalty still further. Hess's influence began to wane, however, with the Nazi rise to power in the 1930s. He was no match for the gang of power-hungry men who gathered about the Führer. After the Second World War had begun, he made his absurd lone flight to Scotland in 1941, apparently to try to broker a peace with Britain through a duke known for his right-wing sympathies.

Historians have long argued over the significance of this eccentric adventure, which Schwarzwäller's book documented in great detail, showing what a truly amazing feat it was at that stage of the war. The conventional view has been that Hess became unbalanced and was acting on an independent initiative, but the author argued that the plot had the tacit support of Hitler, who shared the delusion that powerful fascist sympathizers in the British establishment might help to bring pressure for peace with Germany. The subsequent announcement by the Nazis that Hess suffered from mental illness was designed to distance the Führer from a plan that had badly misfired.

Another controversial book of social significance, published that June, was Russell Lewis's *Anti-Racism: A Mania Exposed*, which carried an introduction by Enoch Powell. This set out to ask the question of whether the anti-racist movement in Britain had become a latter-day witch-hunt. Abhorrence at the crimes of Nazism had been right and proper, Lewis agreed, but he felt it had also set the climate for the establishment and growth of a 'race-relations industry' in the country. His thesis was that legislation designed to foil racial prejudice had invariably had the opposite effect. Tolerance would never be born of legislation or activism, he maintained, but could only flow naturally from the depoliticization of education and the phasing out of those institutions that had a vested interest in racial strife.

Salman Rushdie, as one of the 'ethnics' Lewis referred to, took the book apart in his *Observer* review:

> In this allegedly 'fascinating and well-researched' volume, Mr Lewis offers a series of diagnoses and prescriptions which are, alas, variously risible, inept and predictable. His contention is that anti-racism is a form of witch-hunting, that anti-racist agencies largely create the problems they were set up to alleviate, and that, anyway, it's all part of the higher craziness of loony-leftism . . . What black Britons must recognize, he concludes, is one thing: precisely because it is colour-blind the free market is their friend . . .
>
> Not long ago a book as poor as this would have had trouble finding a respectable publisher; it's a sign of the times that it has now found lodgings at Uncle Naim's Cabin . . . and . . . here is aged Enoch still prophesying civil war: Enoch, to whom the country remains in debt for his great speech about the river of blood.

Salman Rushdie was perfectly entitled to express strong views about theories advanced by an author with whom he clearly disagreed. It was a step too far in his criticism to denigrate the book by claiming that no respectable publisher would have touched it in the past. 'Uncle Naim's Cabin', as he called Quartet, had been responsible for publishing more left-wing books than one could begin to count. We had consistently been champions of the underdog, the dispossessed, the oppressed minorities, the unemployed, and had highlighted a wide diversity of views to create an environment in which debate could replace violence and conflict. We had often disregarded commercial considerations in our pursuit of this aim and had defied convention to our own disadvantage. The book Salman was reviewing carried a valid warning which in some respects seems to have come true. Debate is now muffled by political correctness, which, while well-meaning in concept, has worked against free speech and robbed us of certain civil liberties, for which we are all culturally the poorer. The greatness of Britain stems from its commitment to freedom of expression, and this is now under severe threat of being gagged by accusations of 'racism'. The new obsession with racism in this context will eventually have the opposite effect to that intended. We are all equal under the legislation, and we should ensure that preserving these freedoms is our main objective and dispense with 'political correctness' as it is being interpreted today.

Emmett Murphy's *Great Bordellos of the World* was a magnificently illustrated history of the bordello as an institution that has flourished in many societies over three thousand years of civilization. He describes the range of women recruited, from the supremely intelligent *hetaerae* of Classical Greece to the poverty-stricken denizens of Hogarth's Gin Lane, from the devout temple prostitutes of Babylon to the massage-parlour girls of Times Square. It often made startling reading as it threw light on the relations between social norms and marginalized sexuality.

The connection between narcotics and the rock and pop scene was the subject of Harry Shapiro's *Waiting for the Man: The Story of Drugs and Popular Music*. He showed how drugs had been an issue for the popular-music industry from the undoubted link between jazz and marijuana in the 1920s through to the anti-drug campaigns of the 1980s. He detailed the downfall of many victims of substance abuse, from Charlie Parker to Sid Vicious, and gave accounts of such high-profile drugs busts as those involving the Rolling Stones and Boy George. It was a well-researched and gripping narrative.

The spotlight moved to the Turf with *No Regard for Money* by Charles Benson, the correspondent who had for many years been 'the Scout' on the *Daily Express*. Benson combined his career as racing pundit with friendships with such high-profile figures as Lord Lucan, Dominic Elwes, Lady Charlotte Curzon and John Aspinall. His autobiography contained many entertaining observations and original anecdotes on life in the circles in which Benson moved, which took in as well as the Aga Khan and Graham Hill, glitzy jet-set personalities like Mick Jagger and Jerry Hall. 'No regard for money,' wrote *W* magazine, 'means holidaying in Gstaad, Barbados and Dubai possibly within the same week, and probably – in the case of Charles Benson – as someone's guest.'

No Regard for Money also means a major London launch: shoulders being rubbed – and becoming rather sore on the crowded premises of the Aspinall Curzon – with celebs like Robert Sangster, Albert Finney, dishevelled Annabel Croft and a conspicuously unaccompanied Bill Wiggins. Charles beamed unflinchingly throughout, and heat waves from his smile almost reached glacial Earl Howe's daughters. No amount of extrovert exertions, however, brought a hint of a grin on grim Naim Attallah's face.

[385]

Back on 22 January 1988 two items had appeared in the press announcing the resignation of David Elliott from Quartet. The *Bookseller* reported that David, 'who had worked for Quartet for ten years, intends to take an extended sabbatical' and that 'no date has been set for his departure, which he and Naim Attallah describe as "entirely amicable" '. *Private Eye* put an entirely different twist on the story:

> Crisis has struck at Quartet, the publishing arm of Naim Attullah-Disgusting's business empire.
>
> Hot on the heels of the acquisition of the tired and emotional Anthony ('Fine old piece of seasoned timber') Blond comes the resignation of David Elliott, the publishing director. Known in the book trade as 'Dump-bin Dave', Elliott was the only person at Quartet with any grasp of publishing. His departure, which follows a major row with Attullah-Disgusting, is likely to throw the firm into turmoil.

Over the years I had known David our relationship was such that, no matter what occasional disagreements we had, the bond between us remained steadfast. We had a deep understanding that was not easy to define. David's mode of work and mine sometimes clashed, but the infrequent eruptions that followed were soon forgotten. Each had a soft spot for the other and the possibility of a rift was out of the question. Our close comradeship created unrest within the group, especially at Pipeline Books and to some degree at the The Women's Press. At Quartet our playfulness was considered juvenile, with David being referred to as 'the spy'. We regarded all this with a degree of insouciance that was beyond the comprehension of others.

An argument with David arose as a result of his sanctioning one of the Quartet reps, Maurice Vidowsky, to accept the return of some copies of *Women* from Liberty's book department. Rightly or wrongly I felt I should have been consulted before such a decision was taken. A flare-up was understandable. The barrage of negative publicity surrounding the publication of *Women* had brought nerves to snapping point and it needed the least provocation to set tempers rising. It was then, in a sudden moment of pique, that David decided it was time for him to depart the fold – at least in terms of his physical presence. He left Quartet six months later to act as adviser to two small publishing outfits while remaining on the Namara payroll for a few further years. While his role with us had outwardly changed, in essence it remained the same. Whatever function he fulfilled from then on, it was as if the watchful eye of Namara never left him. Today, after an even longer passage of time, the camaraderie and friendship we shared retain their original freshness and we are as close as ever.

The Chairman Publishes
by David Elliott

Fourteen years ago I wrote a book about the book trade, including my years at Quartet. It was an attempt to tell of my experience during what seemed to me was the greatest change to our cultural ethos since the first industrial revolution: the wanton destruction of sustainable work by technology, and the worship of the market.

I do think it lucky I was able to enter the book trade when editorial staff still told their salesmen what was expected of them. I was lucky when Claude Gill Books was bought by a US conglomerate and I saw the last great flowering of the US trade, after the seminal influence of the European *émigrés* who had fled Nazi Europe transformed American attitudes. I was lucky to run a chain of aggressive metropolitan bookshops able to challenge Net Book Agreement certainty and antiquated retail practices. And, most of all, I was lucky to work at Quartet and The Women's Press.

It was a very special atmosphere. Fourteen years later, I still rejoice that I shared such good times with so diverse an assortment of people, all trying to publish books: radicals and wide boys; captains of industry's daughters; toffs, wastrels and débutantes; feminists and celebrities; earnest and not so earnest writers; intellectuals, wankers and raving loonies. Each day was different, but everything that happened hinged on the attitudes and opinions of the man I called 'The Chairman'.

Anthony Blond, in his memoir *A Jew Made in England*, likened 27 Goodge Street to the court of Louis XIV. He had a point. Naim once published a brilliant account of life at the Ethiopian court of Haile Selassie – *The Emperor* by Ryszard Kapuscinski – yet always denied its description of the intrigue and chaos as having any similarity to the dramas and tensions of Goodge Street or the feminist retreat in Shoreditch. Not that the dramas ever interfered with the parties.

I remember being driven terrifyingly fast into a dark German forest by a beautiful princess to drink champagne by a floodlit swimming pool; eating Sunday brunch at Elaine's; being asked to leave the Plaza for wearing inappropriate clothes; watching a man in a gorilla suit doing something rude with a banana in an Amsterdam night club; seeing the sunset over Manama having eaten so many huge lobsters I was ill; my first Broadway show; Covent Garden in the early hours, after a party where champagne and caviare had been consumed by over five hundred guests; telling the Chairman I thought he was nuts not to let Ruby Wax interview Leni Riefenstahl; driving to the Frankfurt Book Fair, and back, in a London taxi cab; escorting Lady Stevens of Ludgate to tea at the Ritz or lunch at the Four Seasons (and she was a Hungarian aristocrat, to boot!). And there are, to paraphrase Bennett Cerf's fine publishing memoir, just some memories at random.

Cerf wrote an obituary for Horace Liveright. Now long forgotten, Liveright was a gambler and autocratic publisher whose New York list was one of the most vibrant around in the 1920s. He did change things, founded The Modern Library, but destroyed himself in the process. After a somewhat ambivalent account of Liveright's career, Cerf concludes he 'had an amazing faculty for winning the unquestioning loyalty of a great number of fine men and women. They love him still. They probably always will . . . [He had] a rare love of life and a reckless generosity they could not resist.' Like Horace Liveright, the Chairman led a disparate team into many adventures. I remain convinced the real achievement of that unique time was the diversity of talent which was published. Quartet and The Women's Press produced some extraordinary books.

Years later, when a memoir portrayed Naim to be an illiterate bully, incapable of empathy or compromise, written by a woman who had been part of Quartet and whose life, she claimed, had been wasted and abused by a monster, all of us old Quartet staff signed a letter to the *New Statesman*, which had hailed the book as wonderful. What pleased me the most about this action, apart from the chance to rebuff the book's vicious sentiment, was the spontaneous manner in which we all sought to contact each other, reunite and nail our colours, yet again, to his remarkable mast.

*   *   *

Looking back back on 1988, I felt I had been like an actor-manager in that I had spent so much time travelling the country to promote the paperback edition of *Women*. This experience reinforced my conviction that every city, town and village needs well-stocked bookshops. It was disagreeable to see the big bookselling chains jockeying for prime high-street sites in towns that were already adequately served by existing bookshops.

Following on the previous year's success with the Quartet Encounters list, I decided the time had come to stand the list firmly on its own imprint and issue a separate catalogue with point-of-sale material while orchestrating a major sales campaign in June. Other highlights from the Quartet list at this time were Julia Voznesenskaya's *Letters of Love*, an anthology of messages smuggled out of prisons, asylums and institutions by women prisoners in the Soviet Union; *On the Outside Looking In* which told the harrowing but ultimately uplifting life story of Michael, the adopted son of Ronald Reagan; and *Women & Fashion: A New Look* by Caroline Evans and Minna Thornton, who had written a fascinating exploration of an intriguing subject that was an instant classic text for anyone with an interest in questions of style.

The award of the Nobel Prize for Literature that year to the great Egyptian writer Naguib Mahfouz created a buzz for Quartet as we had one of his novels in our backlist and suddenly there was a demand for copies. 'Penguin,' said 'Grovel' in *Private Eye*, 'who had sniffily turned down the paperback rights some time ago were begging to be given a second chance. Attullah-Disgusting, whose feeling for the language is beyond question, gleefully told his staff that Penguin could "stick their bums up their fingers".'

My greatest personal excitement, however, lay in presiding over the publication in English of the Mexican masterpiece *Pulinuro of Mexico* by Fernando del Paso. When it was originally published in 1977, it had won the Romulo Gallego Prize, which was awarded only once every five years for the best Spanish-language novel. The French translation won the Meilleur Livre Étranger in 1985. I was determined that when this epic Joycean tale was published in Britain, in a translation by Elisabeth Plaister, it would meet with a similar success. In the Latin American canon it had been compared with the best work of Gabriel García Marquez, Carlos Fuentes and Mario Vargas Llosa. It was set in Mexico City, where a medical student, Palinuro, has loved his first cousin Estefania with a consuming passion since childhood. Together they gratify their rampant desire in a room in Plaza Santo Domingo. Palinuro comes from an eccentric, polygenetic family. His Uncle Estaban fled from Hungary during the First World War and travelled across the world to Mexico; his Uncle Austin is an ex-mariner from Britain; his grandfather, Francisco, was a freemason and companion of Pancho Villa. Added to this are his grandmothers and a host of aunts and other cousins. The great labyrinth of the city in which they live their lives becomes like an additional living character in the novel, evoking a cultural cornucopia and drawing in themes from mythology, science, politics, pornography and the collective unconscious.

In its French edition *L'Express* had called it 'an immense book in scope, length and beauty [with] pages of romantic lyricism, heady erudition, unbridled eroticism'. 'Read it:' exhorted *Madame Figaro*, 'it is a breath of fresh air; it has a universal voice rarely heard . . . it runs the gamut from laughter to tears, from the crude to the tender, with an incredible virtuosity.' The English-language version soon gathered many similar tributes. The *Los Angeles Times Book Review* summed it up by calling it 'an inspired roller-coaster of a book about life and love in Mexico City'.

Dreamlike and fantastic, filled with sensuous, poetic language, a positively orgiastic love of life, bubbling humor and a special brand of literary alchemy, this pulsating novel still carries the same explosive punch of its first appearance in Spanish nearly twenty years ago . . . What's impressive about *Palinuro of Mexico* is that it transforms a potentially daunting literary experiment into something that's enormous fun to read . . . Few other novels have so much color, so many metaphors, so much of the feel, smell, sight and sound of human experience, so much life.

'This tour de force is the novel of modern Mexico and its sprawling capital . . . warm and very funny . . . Elisabeth Plaister's translation is brilliant,' said the *Sunday Telegraph*; and in the opinion of *The Times Literary Supplement*: 'At its deepest level, the narrative of *Palinuro of Mexico* embodies a totalizing ambition, reminiscent of Joyce, to investigate the conditions of culture and knowledge, to explore the relationship between myth and history, and to demonstrate the potential of literary language to revolutionize our ways of seeing the world.' For a publisher the book represented a rare privilege which dwarfed all other considerations.

A publishing anniversary worth celebrating had been the tenth birthday of The Women's Press in April. Ros de Lanerolle had been working since 1981 on the foundations for the feminist imprint laid down by Stephanie Dowrick. The naysayers who thought a publisher with such a title as 'The Women's Press' could never succeed had been proved misguided in their opinion. The imprint now had an annual turnover of one and a half million pounds and was publishing sixty titles a year, figures bringing it from the margins into the mainstream of the book trade. To the general titles and books on sexual politics they had added a practical-handbook series in 1983 and a crime list in 1984; and had a world first with their feminist science-fiction series, started in 1985. Livewire, a series for teenage readers, had been running just a year and had proved an immediate hit.

A title of particular significance in the anniversary catalogue was *The Life and Death of Emily Wilding Davison* by Liz Stanley and Ann Morley, which incorporated the first reprint in seventy-five years of *The Life of Emily Davison* by Gertrude Colmore. Emily Davison had become a martyr and an icon to the women's movement when, in 1913, she ran on to the racetrack during the annual Derby steeplechase and made a grab for the reins of George V's horse, suffering fatal injuries as a result. Her funeral had been an occasion of one of the most impressive displays of feminist solidarity ever seen in Britain. Gertrude Colmore's personal and moving tribute was written within a few months of the event, and to this Liz Stanley and Ann Morley added a reassessment of Emily Davison as a courageous woman of ideas rather than a fanatic from the lunatic fringe as the popular press had depicted her.

Sarah LeFanu published her exploratory study of science fiction written by women, *In the Chinks of the World Machine: Feminism and Science Fiction*, while working as an editor for The Women's Press. She took the view that this genre offered women writers a particular freedom to explore its radical and progressive potential to arrive at a fusion of feminist politics with the imagination. In contrast with this was a book that reached back in time. Fadhma Amrouche's *My Life Story: The Autobiography of a Berber Woman* was established as a classic in its French version, and its first publication in English was in this translation by Dorothy Blair. Fadhma Amrouche was eighty when she finished writing her memoirs in 1962. She had been born illegitimate in the mountainous North African region of Kabylia, but went to live in Tunis when she married at sixteen. Later she arrived in Paris, bringing with her the wild, plaintive songs of her place of origin. Her singing of the songs made her famous, as did her poetry, and her life came to embody the tension between colonist and colonized, Christian and Muslim, Berber and Arab that became North Africa's post-colonial legacy.

More poetry was represented in *Right of Way: Prose and Poetry from the Asian Women's Writers Workshop*, the subjects coming from a diverse array of sources – India, Pakistan, South Africa and Britain; and Suniti Namjoshi's *The Blue Donkey Fables*, which mixed her significant cautionary tales with poems of elegance and wit. The opening of the title fable gave a taster of her style:

Once upon a time a blue donkey lived by a red bridge. 'Inartistic,' said the councillors who governed the town. 'A donkey who lives by our bright red bridge must be of the purest and silkiest white or we require that the said donkey be required to move on.' The matter soon turned into a political issue . . .

Fiction was represented by Norma Klein's *Older Men*, which told the story of a daughter having to confront a powerful doctor father who has committed her mother to a mental hospital following a 'breakdown'; and Millie Murray's first novel *Kiesha*, about how a thirteen-year-old learns to cope with her parents' separation after all she has done to try to bring them back together again has failed. There was also a set of vivid stories about women's inner lives in various situations, translated from the Japanese by Geraldine Harcourt and called *The Shooting Gallery and Other Stories*.

Of the handbooks, an important title was *In Our Experience: Workshops at the Women's Therapy Centre*, edited by Sue Krzowski and Pat Land. The workshops had, over ten years, covered a wide variety of experiences – including relationships as daughters with fathers and mothers; roles as mothers, as workers, as leaders; and problems with sexuality and with bodily identity – amounting to a wealth of unparalleled know-how; the book made this available to women everywhere while providing an encouraging account of what happens when women work together.

In an interview with Angela Neustatter in the *Guardian*, headed a 'A Cause for Celebration', Ros de Lanerolle rose spiritedly to counter any suggestion that the work published by feminist publishing houses was somehow inferior in quality to that acceptable to the major imprints.

> Who decides what is quality or merit? I'll tell you. It is a mafia of white, Oxbridge-educated males with a particular style of thinking and taste. Look at who heads publishing houses, who is in charge and influential in the literary press, who does the reviewing and you'll find I am right. There are exceptions but they are not setting the standards.

> The most original, exciting work is coming from women . . . And I defy anyone to say that the quality of our writing is not good. It may not be conventional but I can point to stunning prose from women from all over the world I am proud to have published . . .

> I believe we now have one of the most international lists in publishing. Now it is important to hear what women with different experiences and from different backgrounds have to say . . .

> In the beginning we were very careful about defining women's issues but now we feel all issues are women's and we publish books on a range of subjects you could find in any list, but by women. An example is Rosalie Bertelli's *No Immediate Danger* about low-level radiation, and soon we will publish a book about homelessness . . .

> I believe feminism is about taking on all issues of repression.

Thirty-four

On Sunday, 8 January 1989, I was invited by Mapam, the left-wing Zionist movement in London, to put my views on feminism to a paying audience at Hashomer House in North London. The organizer for the evening's event was Ms Lucy Seifert, an executive member of Mapam. It all came about as a result of *Women*, the controversial reception the book received having cut across party politics. A largely Jewish gathering of people who were perfectly aware of my Palestinian roots and my crusade on behalf of the Palestinians was there to quiz me on quite another topic. The hall was full to capacity and the evening went without incident. I felt at ease as I took questions from the floor and had not the least sense of any hostility from the audience. In fact the opposite was true. The difficult audience I anticipated because of our political disparities turned out to be most sympathetic. I even sold copies of *Women* to a delighted crowd and was fêted for having cared enough to write a book about women. I left the hall feeling gratified, pondering on the thought that if only politicians could behave more like ordinary human beings the world would be a far happier place.

In the February issue of the *Literary Review* Auberon Waugh announced to the British public our intention to form 'The Academy Club' and invited applications for membership. It was to be housed in the basement of No. 51 Beak Street, a building the Namara Group owned, the basement itself having been a recreation room with tables for snooker and table tennis. Earlier on I had used it to indulge my weakness for table tennis especially, but such leisure activities became neglected as pressure of work mounted with the expansion of my field of interests. The Academy Bookclub still occupied the ground floor, and was still being run by Sophia Sackville-West with her sister helping her on a part-time basis. The *Literary Review* took up the first floor and the rest of the available space, with the exception of the top floor, was utilized by the accounts department of the Namara Group. Right at the top was a small flat I occasionally occupied when overcome with exhaustion or in need of relaxation.

The idea for the club was first proposed by Bron and Victoria Glendinning during a casual meeting at my office. I was taken aback, to put it mildly, not so much on the grounds that I was reluctant to give up the basement as because it seemed obvious there was just not enough space. In the end their keenness disarmed me. They made it clear that no practical consideration was going to deter them from pursuing their objective. I went along with the idea, and without enquiring as to what it would cost or its commercial viability, I simply said, 'Do it!' Work soon began on transforming the basement into a Soho club, and Bron's brother Septimus, an inspired carpenter, was commissioned to refit the place with solid wooden benches and tables as well as chairs to give it a simple but robust look.

In his 'Pulpit' announcement in the *Literary Review*, Bron described the projected club as being 'primarily designed for writers who are too poor, too mean, or too proud to join the Groucho'. Applicants were to submit a copy of what they considered to be their best book. This would join the club library once its author was deemed worthy of election by the club committee, consisting of Bron, his deputy editor Laura Cumming, Victoria Glendinning, Sophia Sackville-West, Robert Posner and myself – whom Bron referred to as 'the philanthropist'. The applications began to flood in on this basis, but included many from *Literary Review* subscribers who, while they would have liked to join, did not qualify. This set Bron brooding on the matter and he amended his original concept.

> I decided that a club made up exclusively of writers was not a very good idea because (1) they are often quite unpleasant people, (2) they do not always want to meet each other and (3) it would do them good to meet the nice, intelligent readers of the *Literary Review*. The problem is to devise a system which will deter all the bores, pigs and PR men who make the Groucho so disagreeable. What I have decided is a variant of the old 'cinema club' practice, whereby to see a dirty film you had to buy a ticket and return next day. Membership will be open to all who have been subscribers to the *LR* for two years – that is to say, who have renewed a one-year subscription before applying. They must also offer a published author as their reference, and submit a few lines of self-description in their letters of application. The Club, which should be open at the end of April or beginning of May, will be limited to 600 members, 30 present at any one moment. It will offer a club room, bar, good wine and light meals.

I was still convinced that the basement was never going to be spacious enough in the long term. It began to look inevitable that the ground floor would have to be sacrificed and with it the Academy Bookclub, a move which was bound to upset Sophia Sackville-West deeply. She had nurtured her project with an enthusiasm and a dedication I had never seen equalled. The book club, alas, did not attract enough customers to pay its way, though in ordinary circumstances I would have maintained it if only because it meant so much to her. When the axe fell a year later her disappointment was heartbreaking, as was apparent from a piece she penned for the *Literary Review*, headed 'And So Farewell – In Memoriam: A Great Little Bookclub':

> Once upon a time there was a literary bookclub who lived in the middle of Soho. This bookclub often went hungry because his father, try as he might, had too many children to feed them all equally. But the little bookclub, who was called the Academy Bookclub, had many friends and managed to grow quite well on the nourishing berries which came his way. But one day the father came to him and said, 'Great news. I have a son of unparalleled beauty and strength. And because you have always been a brave little sort I have named him The Academy Club and you will live together in peace and harmony.' But the Academy Bookclub was much afraid. His old friends soon forgot him as they rushed to worship at the paragon brother's shrine, and as the latter grew bigger and bigger the Academy Bookclub began to waste away. Until one day his father came to him and said, 'Academy Bookclub, although it breaks my heart to say this, now that you are so thin and your brother is so fat, you must give up your space in the house to him.' So the Academy Bookclub set off to seek his fortune. But without a roof to protect him from the driving rain, he soon sickened and died. THE END.
>
> I hope that all Academy Bookclub members received a letter informing them of the Academy Bookclub's demise back in June. It tried hard but never quite made it through.
>
> No flowers, please. Donations and offers of employment to: Sophia Sackville-West, c/o Knole, Sevenoaks, Kent.

The pattern at Namara House, as at Quartet, was that people came and went. They served their apprenticeship, then moved on to make a name for themselves elsewhere. The two locations were always bursting with energy and there was seldom a murmur of discontent. All were granted the space in which to discover themselves and develop whatever talents they possessed. They enjoyed a transitional period of freedom before making passage into the more exacting world outside. When opportunities beckoned, they flew the nest, but always remembered the formative months or years they spent learning the ropes. Where else in the world of publishing in London could they have found a workplace brimming with interesting books and eccentric ideas? The one thing they all had in common was a desire to find out what life was really all about before settling down to the rigours of a demanding career.

A recent arrival was Sonamara Sainsbury, a lanky lass with lovely features, who had recently finished four years at Edinburgh University. The *Evening Standard* announced her arrival in 'Londoner's Diary':

The exotic publisher Naim Attallah has a new addition to his collection of beautiful and brainy women who shelter in his Soho offices. She is Sonamara Sainsbury, twenty-three-year-old daughter of oriental-carpet dealer Barry Sainsbury and a member of the grocer dynasty. Her name is taken from her late grandfather Paul Sainsbury's yacht . . .

Attallah's Quartet Books and Namara empire are seen by many as a perfect finishing school.

A reunion of 'Old Naim' girls was expected to take place on St Valentine's Day, a date coinciding with the launch of a new Parfums Namara bath gel.

The girls ['Londoner's Diary' continued] are lavished with attention and occasional gifts but the salaries are modest.

'I'm his personal assistant, organize publicity and do some editing,' Sonamara tells me. She admits it took a little time to get used to her boss, but they get on famously now.

Sonamara, with whom I enjoyed a close working relationship, travelled round the country with me when I was promoting the paperback edition of *Women*. I even took her to the Frankfurt Book Fair. Throughout her time at Namara House she remained a favourite with a magically inspiring presence and the aura of a queen bee. In herself she was low key, diffident and had no pretensions. Her name, Sonamara, had a special resonance and its chiming with Namara seemed a happy accident; had fate brought her into the company? Who knows?

Her abrupt departure from Namara House was shrouded in mystery. It happened without warning, with ill health the reason she gave. She would not expound on this. I felt more than a little concerned; so much so that I walked with her from Namara House in Poland Street to the Italian Catholic church in Soho Square, and there lit a candle for her rapid recovery. The next day I gave her a rosary I had always treasured for sentimental reasons: my mother had purchased it years before at the Church of the Holy Sepulchre in Jerusalem. Then a week after Sonamara left she failed to turn up at a farewell lunch in her honour, meticulously prepared by my great cook, Charlotte Millward, to include some of her favourite dishes. It was so out of character as to defy reasonable explanation. She never phoned me or wrote me a note to say what had happened. It seems none of her colleagues at Namara House heard anything more from her. It was a disappearing act without precedence.

Many years later I bumped into her at a charity reception, where we came face to face. She greeted me and my wife Maria with an embarrassed embrace then turned and simply walked away. The Sonamara of yesteryear was no more; a new person had taken her place. Alas, I was never to lay eyes on her again. Only the memories and the many photographs I took of her remain.

The launch of the new Parfums Namara cosmetic products had meanwhile taken place as planned in February. They included bath and shower gels to go with both Avant l'Amour and Après l'Amour, as well as a 'Miss Asprey' scent, elegantly packaged in the Asprey colours. I commissioned my friend Nicholas Haslam to come up with ideas to give the occasion an air of extravagance laced with decadence. It was a tall order, but Nicholas rose to the occasion with his usual flair. 'Londoner's Diary' in the *Evening Standard* described the launch so succinctly that it would be hard to find a better account. By giving the piece the heading 'Smell of Excess', it evoked the ambiance splendidly. Both title and piece were spot on. Among the untutored at the fragrant launch, it said, there was a slight confusion between Naim Attallah's 'retired nymphets, his present "harem" and the waitresses at the Pal Joey nightclub'.

One obvious distinction was that former employees wore dresses of a respectable length, reigning beauties wore dresses that barely scraped their thighs and the waitresses wore black tails and nothing else.

In the midst of the sea of blondes and Auberon Waugh stood a triumphant Naim by a luridly lit bowl of ice containing his new bath gel and, by some curious kink, caviare. This was all that remained of Nicholas Haslam's 'design concept', which had been dismantled by fire officers during the afternoon.

Pamella Bordes, a photographer and a former 'Miss India', was destined to hit the headlines as an alleged high-society prostitute who was also mistress to many well-known individuals in the worlds of both politics and journalism. She was often escorted socially by Andrew Neil, then editor of the *Sunday Times*, and it was reported that Colin Moynihan, a junior Conservative minister, had taken her to a Conservative winter ball. It also emerged that she held a House of Commons pass arranged for her by the MPs David Shaw and Henry Bellingham. When, in March 1989, the *Evening Standard* printed allegations linking her with a Libyan security officer named as Ahmed Gadaff al-Daim, the scandal threatened to raise the spectre of the Profumo affair or, perhaps more aptly, the career of Mata Hari. Bertram Rope, the head of Namara's public relations, reminded me at this time of how Miss Bordes had applied for a job at Namara House the previous November. It was something I had completely forgotten about. She had ascended the stairs to Bertie's third-floor office, directly underneath mine, wearing a red suit with a very short skirt, and sat down in front of him, sending his heart into a flutter. It seemed she had been mentioned to Namara by a property developer who said there was this 'Indian princess' who was interested in public relations.

Bertie lost no time in wheeling her up to my office, fully expecting me to be as bowled over as he was. Despite her good looks and sexy attire, she failed to impress me. Everything about her seemed artificial, especially her unsubtle technique with men. She lacked the innocence that some women put out, which in my view is the more potent aphrodisiac by far. Our conversation felt contrived and superficial. I told her she should take up typing lessons if she really wanted to go into PR. Once she had got that qualification we would consider giving her a job. That was all I could remember about our meeting, apart from her perfume, which was overwhelming.

The incident was soon forgotten, until Auberon Waugh announced to me a few months later that he had met a delightful girl called Pamella Bordes, who had enchanted him to the point where he had bent the rules of the Academy Club, which he himself had formulated, and accepted her as a member. He thought she would bring a welcome *frisson* of notoriety to the club. It was a vintage gesture from Bron, who was contrariwise by nature and relished the tittle-tattle his action would provoke. I was told Pamella then turned up at the club on several occasions, though mysteriously our paths never crossed again. I did, however, mention her to my friend and barber, Tony of Knightsbridge, a Greek Cypriot who, unlike many in his profession, exudes a macho image. He also has among his clientele a good few of the business élite from the City and other high flyers so that his premises often become a positive hotbed of establishment gossip. I visited him early every morning so he could exercise his artistry on my thinning hair, about which I felt self-conscious, so as to ensure the remaining strands were firmly anchored to my scalp. (That was until it all became too much of a bore: one heavy shower or a gust of wind and the whole process had to begin again from scratch.) Of Pamella Bordes Tony remarked that she and another girl had at one time rented a flat he owned in Battersea. On the first occasion when he went round to collect the rent, she greeted him with, 'Oh my God, you remind me so much of Omar Sharif! We had a wonderful time with him when he was here. Now really, tell me, do you want the rent in cash or in kind?' 'So which was it – in cash or in kind?' I asked Tony. 'No comment,' he replied, but his wicked smile said it all – though since all Tony's stories are apocryphal, I suppose I shall never know the truth.

*   *   *

May 1989 marked the tenth anniversary of the *Literary Review*, an event that was celebrated in the library of the Reform Club in Pall Mall. The magazine was redesigned for the occasion and issued in a special edition which traced the entire period of its existence, from its beginnings under the editorship of its founder, Anne Smith. The party went on far longer than expected as people arrived in a continuous stream with no sign of a break in the flow. Each one of the four hundred and fifty guests invited showed up and all piled into a space not normally expected to accommodate more than three hundred. Most of those who attended were journalists, writers, literary editors, publishers and other media folk who favoured casual wear and therefore had to borrow ties from the club management before being allowed in. There were no circumstances in which the strict clubland taboo against entering the portals tieless could be waived, and the club's supply of spare ties was not unlimited. The minor hitch this caused seemed to do nothing to spoil the fun and guests formed themselves into a tie chain at the door, so that those going out could pass theirs to those coming in. The close proximity of the guests, one to another, only made the atmosphere more intimate and encouraged the outflow and consumption of wine, so that supplies had to be boosted from time to time. The mix of people was quite remarkable. The cartoonist Willie Rushton stood next to the Duchess of Argyle, while the Marquess of Worcester chatted with literary agent Ed Victor and newscaster Anna Ford. Richard Ingrams headed the *Private Eye* contingent and Bron worked the crowd with his usual *bonhomie*.

As the appointed hour of nine o'clock for departure came round, there were no signs of the tempo of the party winding down and guests refused to leave. In fact the momentum gave every indication of gathering itself afresh. Only one happening introduced a sour note before festivities closed, for this was the occasion when Jubby Ingrams was discovered by a club official in the gentleman's lavatories. With the assistance of Louis Vause, a Quartet employee and a free spirit like herself, she was relieving herself in one of the basins. Jubby was certainly high on spirits in every sense, having had her share of the drinks available. She apologized at once to the Reform, saying she had been bursting for a pee and the ladies was too far off for her to make it in time. Nevertheless she was unceremoniously marched out of the club.

I expected the matter would end there. To hush things up and preserve the dignity of both parties seemed the natural course, especially given the Reform's long-standing liberal tradition, which would surely wish to avoid any unwelcome repercussions. I was wrong. A reception due to be held at the Reform by The Women's Press for Alice Walker's *The Temple of My Familiar* had the plug pulled on it at the last minute. A letter from the catering manager informed me of the cancellation of the party and of any other such parties in the future. He omitted to give any reason for the ban, which applied to both Auberon Waugh and myself and our respective organizations. Nor did he specify any limit on how long the ban was to run. Bron was outraged at the stupidity of this preposterous prohibition. He issued advice to any ladies attending future receptions at the Reform that they should take chamber pots with them as a precautionary measure. It took many years before common sense prevailed and the ban was suddenly lifted.

Louis Vause, who had aided and abetted Jubby in her emergency, was one of many who passed through the doors of Quartet without the press taking any notice. Quartet was never just a refuge for girls from the upper classes, it was also a seedbed for talents of all kinds in their period of germination. The mixture of people from every stratum of society worked extremely well and reinforced my view that by drawing its staff from such varying backgrounds Quartet was enabled to venture into all sorts of areas and subjects without carrying the stigma of élitism. Louis had a chequered upbringing after being born on St Valentine's Day in Edinburgh in 1958. His family had gone to live on a barge lined with books on the Lancaster Canal when he was six. His father had been a talented amateur musician, but developed multiple sclerosis, and Louis remained with him on the barge from the age of fourteen after his mother moved out with his brother and sister. In 1988 Quartet Books was his day job while he played piano or keyboard with bands at night. He was one of Quartet's true originals who, one felt sure, was destined to make his mark somewhere sooner or later. Subsequently he coped as a single parent with monetary difficulties, working for uncertain returns as an actor and musician on the fringe. The two albums he has recently produced under his own name are intriguingly titled: *Pianophernalia* (2001) and *Mecanicatastrophe* (2006), whose fame has reached Slovakia. The first is 'all about capturing the magic of the exact moment of recording and expressing emotion on what is a combination of plastic, wood and strings'; the second is based on material well received at the Brighton Festival. He seems at last on the way to finding the idiosyncratic, discerning niche for his art that he deserves.

Back in 1988 I was part of a team seeking the franchise to run the new Greater London FM radio station. Commercial radio was rapidly growing in popularity as an advertising medium, with revenues rising at twenty-five per cent a year, a fact which attracted a wide range of contenders with influential backing in the music world. There were thirty-two applications, among them one from Cleo Lane, who was pushing for London Jazz Radio together with Bishop Trevor Huddleston, Michael Caine and Earl Alexander of Tunis. Lord Hanson of the Hanson Trust wanted a station devoted to 'easy listening' from big band to country music. A rock station claimed that round-the-clock classical rock would please more listeners than 'extra jazz, golden oldies or easy listening'. Our team, Classical City Radio, was led by Joan Bakewell and included myself, Terry Maher, Carmen Callil and Cameron Mackintosh. We almost got there with our proposals, but were pipped at the post by Andrew Lloyd Webber, who had André Previn, Kiri Te Kanawa and Lady Christie of Glyndebourne on his board. Thus was Classic FM born.

*

One of Quartet's books that summer was Kieran Tunney's *Interrupted Biography*, that incorporated the text of his play *Aurora*, which for various reasons had never been published or staged. I first met him the year before. He was proposing to write a portrait of Margot Fontaine as a follow-up to the success he had had on both sides of the Atlantic in the early 1970s with his bestselling life of Tallulah Bankhead, *Tallulah, Darling of the Gods*. Before our encounter I knew nothing of the rather engaging man who walked into my office one morning, having had to climb four flights of stairs and being as a result visibly out of breath. He conveyed a sense of vulnerability which was gently tempered by an old-fashioned, rather distinguished manner seldom found in more recent generations. The old romantic values were there; the glamour and glitter of the Noël Coward era, and the appreciation of beauty and excellence shone through his tired frame. I tried to imagine what it must have been like in those glorious 1930s: favoured with good looks, endowed with wit and humour, the world at one's feet. Kieran was certainly in the midst of it all then: youthful, debonair and talented, with a great zest for living. A portrait of Margot Fontaine was not the sort of book normally associated with Quartet, but I felt a compulsion to commission it because I was enchanted with the idea. I could only attribute this to the romanticism we both shared.

The months went by and progress on the book was slow. Kieran had to undergo a series of operations that left him extremely weak. He had the energy neither to research the book nor put pen to paper. With great sadness the project was abandoned. Despite his shortage of funds, he returned the advance at great sacrifice to his own needs. I was deeply touched by this gesture and the dignity he showed. In today's world, everyday pressures tend to lead to an undervaluing of tradition and personal honour. Six months later, Kieran was restored to health and ready to resume writing. This time it was his autobiography. Two chapters had been written and submitted to Robert Lantz, his agent in New York, who was highly encouraging in his response to them. When Kieran then approached me with his new project, I, too, was supportive and urged him to complete it as soon as possible. But again his health deteriorated and he found himself unable to sustain the original impetus.

Rather than throw in the towel again, Kieran then had an idea. Why not publish *Aurora* along with the two chapters, since they in part related to the play? I felt some deep misgivings since Quartet had never published a play text before and could not visualize any obvious link between it and the two chapters. Then I read the play and my attitude changed. It was a beautifully crafted surrealistic concept, unlike anything I had read before. The central character, Aurora, was on the face of it almost uncastable, but I felt exhilarated by the play's mystery and originality and the strength of its dialogue. I was seduced not only into publishing the project but also into dreaming of being able to realize the play on stage, with its potential for vivid imagery, whatever the formidable difficulties might be.

When the book came out the reviews were mixed. Shaun Usher in the *Daily Mail* was ecstatic:

> Salute a supremely romantic venture and quixotic gamble . . . publisher Naim Attallah has turned just two chapters of a fascinating figure's life story, plus a piece of theatrical treasure trove, into a unique book. The treasure is Kieran Tunney's gorgeous comedy of manners, updating *Sleeping Beauty* to high society in the roaring twenties. Written some forty years ago, its wit, originality and charm won praise from Shaw, Coward and Somerset Maugham, all of whom read it in manuscript.

Hugo Vickers, on the other hand, under the headline 'What's in a Name Dropper?' in the *Spectator*, was very dismissive. His opening line, 'Only Naim Attallah could have published this book', was clearly meant to indicate that no one else would have done so, not because it was controversial but because of its contents. His tone at the end became increasingly damning:

> I wonder if Naim Attallah will stage it. *Aurora* has slept for twenty years, the play has slept for forty. If he gives the critics enough Brandy Alexanders before the curtain rises, they'll find some smart lines to laugh at. In conclusion the part I admire in all this is Mr Tunney's determination to press on against all odds.

Diana Mosley in the *Daily Telegraph* was equally unconvinced. She called the autobiography 'a name-dropping exercise of extreme triviality'.

> It is only partly redeemed by the writer's worship of the most beautiful woman of her time, Greta Garbo. With none of the vulgarities of Cecil Beaton when he 'told all' about his affair with the lovely actress, Kieran Tunney recalls worship from afar . . .
>
> When the play was written more than forty years ago, the bomb loomed more menacingly than it does now. London is still here, getting uglier

year by year. The scene in the cave no longer convinces. All the actresses suggested for the part of the heroine died long since. Naim Attallah, however, is so taken that, not content with publishing the play, he also intends to put it on the stage.

Diana's concluding sentence was perfectly accurate. I did try to stage it, but no one would collaborate on the grounds that it was dated and could have no appeal for a modern audience. No director worth his salt was willing to undertake such a project. To go it alone would have been impossible. Maybe everyone else was right in their assessment of the commercial viability of the play; maybe I was wrong. Because it never happened the verdict must remain open and I am happy to be left with a vision of what might have been.

The weather must have been very cold at the end of November 1989. The girls at Goodge Street began complaining to the *Evening Standard* that they were freezing because of Quartet's lack of central heating. The paper was quick to make a story out of it, though it got the location wrong, saying that 'Antarctica' was at Poland Street rather than Goodge Street. The trio who led the protest against their spartan work conditions were Anna Pasternak, Jubby Ingrams and Nina Train. They went so far as to claim they had resorted to thermal underwear in their efforts to keep warm. The *Standard* went on to embroider the piece:

> But Attallah, who once spent six months as a steeplejack in the south of England, is deaf to their heart-rending entreaties. 'My girls will stay slim and beautiful operating in the cold,' he told me wisely. 'And carting books up and down stairs will certainly add to their fitness.'

That was one of the most endearing aspects of the place, the way it was viewed by many as a nest of left-wing idealists and blue-blooded socialites who loved the *frisson* of perversity. Quartet was many different things to many different people. It was a paradox that challenged conventional analysis and the unpredictability of its publishing programme won it a high share of public attention.

The Quartet jazz list was a case in point. In 1989 Chris Parker departed after having spent six years in charge of it. He had taken the list over in 1983 after being a Quartet proof-reader for one year. The first book he commissioned was a jazz autobiography, Mike Zwerin's *Close Enough for Jazz*, to add to such titles as Ross Russell's biography of Charlie Parker *Bird Lives*, and John Chilton's acclaimed *Billie's Blues: A Survey of Billie Holiday's Career, 1933–1959*. Chris was aware of jazz's being notoriously divided by ideological factions, whose loyalties lay towards either the traditional or modern schools. Put three jazz *aficionados* in a room together, it was said, and they'll produce four conflicting definitions of the music. Commercially speaking, there was also the saying that the best way to make a million pounds out of a jazz venture was to start off with two million.

His appraisal of the existing list was that it mainly comprised biographies of legendary jazz figures from the undisputed canon: Miles Davis, Dizzy Gillespie, Duke Ellington and Charles Mingus to take other examples. The 1980s, however, was a period that saw the exploration of types of jazz that were not based solely on US models but drew on European musical traditions as much as they did on spirituals, blues and ragtime. This became an important thread in the way the list developed. Titles reflecting the trend were Leo Feigin's *Russian Jazz: New Identity*, Jim Godbolt's *A History of Jazz in Britain, 1919–50* and Chris Stapleton and Chris May's study of African music, *African All-stars: The Pop Music of a Continent*. Graham Lock's *Forces in Motion: Anthony Braxton and the Meta-reality of Creative Music* combined a tour diary with a biographical account of a musician who had been influenced as much by European free style and classical music as by the blues. Another title by Mike Zwerin, *La Tristesse de Saint Louis: Swing under the Nazis*, took an ironic, entertaining, sideways look at the fortunes and significance of jazz in Europe under the totalitarian dominance of Hitler's Germany.

Another growing awareness was that the stereotypical image of a jazz musician – African-American male with a raffish lifestyle – was totally inadequate to account for the music's evolution. Bruce Turner's *Hot Air, Cool Music*, for instance, was the autobiography of a UK musician who happened to be a white teetotaller vegetarian with a penchant for confectionary. The contribution made by women to jazz was covered by Linda Dahl's *Stormy Weather: The Music and Lives of a Century of Jazz Women*, a book that sold out within three months of being published in paperback, presumably because it 'crossed over' from having an exclusive appeal for a jazz audience to the area of those interested in the reclamation of women's history. Leonard Feather's *The Jazz Years: Earwitness to an Era* was a study written by a UK-born critic and writer, whose *Encyclopedia of Jazz* we republished in a revised edition. Robert Gordon's *Jazz West Coast: The Los Angeles Scene of the 1950s* exploded a prevailing myth that California-based jazz in that era had been only a palid, anaemic, over-arranged version of the harder jazz from the East Coast.

From Chris Parker's point of view, *Wire* magazine (dealt with later) made a useful complement to the book list, being able to react immediately to changes or innovations in jazz. The founder of the magazine, Anthony Wood, however, had personified the factionalism rife in the 1980s. As a strong believer in 'free music', he threw up his hands in horror at the idea of being linked in a launch party with Bruce Turner, who had been a mainstream clarinetist and saxophonist playing with the likes of Acker Bilk and Humphrey Lyttelton. Along with this tendency to insular defensiveness there were also those who claimed that jazz was a 'black art form' that had been highjacked and commercialized by whites, ignoring the fact that the truth was far more complex and nuanced than their thesis implied. The Quartet jazz list was regularly castigated for featuring too many white musicians and writers. Any attempts to hitch the jazz wagon to the notoriously fickle and ephemeral star of fashion were also, Chris felt, misplaced and inappropriate. They simply left musicians and projects stranded as the modish surge of popularity moved elsewhere.

During his time working on the list, Chris managed to steer it around these hazards with a great degree of success. He found a positive reward awaiting him when he visited America and discovered just how important the Quartet jazz list (mainly sold on to be published there by the Da Capo Press) was proving to be for US listeners. They were fed up with the way their music was not taken seriously by the mainstream media in their country. The manager of City Lights in San Francisco told him – before he even knew there was any personal connection – that the list and *Wire* together contained the best current writing on the music. When his identity became known, Chris found himself being spotlit and applauded in the jazz clubs. In a typical working week at Quartet he would be contacted by 'a Finn, a Hungarian, a Pole, several Americans and the odd Australian'.

> As encouraging . . . is the sight of Quartet jazz books in libraries all over the country . . . and the experience of authors telling me how much they have earned from Public Lending Right. People out there are reading and listening!

Given that the market was 'almost unidentifiable, totally unpredictable and select – not to say small', he wrote in an article for a German publication, how had it been possible 'to apply meaningful criteria in a selection process'? Some of the most successful books had come about through unsolicited approaches.

> It would be easy to pretend that a lot of hard-nosed commercially minded market-oriented strategic planning went into the ensuing selection/ rejection decision, but in all honesty it must be admitted that, given that one customarily views oneself as a model of fair-mindedness and perspicacity, a

much simpler criterion is generally applied: would I want to read *this* book on *that* topic?

*

With the amalgamation with Theo Cowan back in 1983, I concluded that a coordinated working relationship between Theo's show-business outfit and Namara Public Relations, run by Bertram Rope, would be beneficial to both sides. Each would retain its autonomy, but there were instances when their joint effort was likely to add a certain *gravitas* to the proceedings and ensure augmented efficiency and a more practical measure of continuity. Theo was unused to operating in concert, yet showed no signs of disquiet. All the same he instinctively guarded his independence and contacts with unusual zeal. He must have been fearful of working himself out of a job by sharing some of his vital connections in the world of show business.

As matters stood, these assets rendered him indispensable, but he felt he still needed to play his cards close to his chest. He was much too astute to risk vulnerability. On the contrary, he weaved around himself a cocoon of security and calm. When he had no choice, however, he toed the line, but otherwise stopped short of implementing anything he disagreed with. The evasion was masterly and his *savoir-faire* and natural charm negated any possible backfire. Janie Ironside-Wood, who joined the Namara Group in 1985, was well placed to perceive the intricacies of the situation. She has penned her recollections of the period and the various characters involved. Her piece is atmospheric as well as incisive. It brings to life the many aspects of a complex interaction in which she was a participant and a keen observer.

Namara Round-Up
by Janie Ironside-Wood

Returning to work in 1985 after a five-year career/maternity break, I don't think I had any idea of the extraordinary and eclectic hive of industry that lurked above the small Quartet Bookshop in Poland Street. This was the heart of Naim's empire, which encompassed a glorious array of businesses (some profitable, some not so profitable), as well as the base from where he managed his legendary fortune.

There was considerable speculation, both within Namara and more widely, about the size of this legendary fortune, and also about how it had been accrued. Rumours ranged from the prosaic to the outlandish. Since the smaller businesses lay mostly in the arts and literary sector, however, very few people were actually qualified to answer questions of this nature, and most were in any case so passionately involved in their particular venture that they soon lost interest in the conversation anyway – unless, of course, they thought they could engineer a sizeable cash injection for their endeavour, which was sometimes forthcoming, sometimes not. For the businesses he loved, Naim was a generous benefactor.

Naim's portfolio of businesses at that time consisted mainly of magazines (the *Literary Review*, *Wire*, *Apollo*), publishing (Quartet and The Women's Press) and Public Relations (property and showbiz). Heaving your way up the challenging six flights of stairs (this was strictly a walk-up), you first passed the showbiz floors, run by Theo Cowan and Laurie Bellew. On up you reached the property team, run by ex-Wellingtonian and elegantly side-burned Bertie Rope. And finally, beetroot red in the face and gasping, you came to Naim's airy penthouse office. This was loft-style living with light streaming in on a jungle of plants, leather sofas and an expansive tiger skin. Naim sat at the far end behind an imposing desk with a bank of telephones that he answered with alacrity, no matter who he was meeting with at the time.

I had heard of Naim, usually from *Private Eye* and usually something vaguely scurrilous. He also loomed large in newspaper diaries, famed for his premières, launches and parties – and also for the bevy of beautiful girls who worked with him and lent a fragrant glamour to the events. The world of diaries – and the influential characters from politics, business, arts and publishing who flitted across those pages – was the world that he loved. He was entirely clear about the sector of British society that fascinated him and the place that he wanted to occupy within it. Although Naim loved all things glamorous, his hard-wired career in banking, finance and the Asprey group provided a sharp focus that offset any mistaken impressions of frivolity. His beady eyes could harden up in an instant if he smelt a good business opportunity – or suspected anyone of trying to pull a fast one on him. By contrast, a sentimental streak could mean ongoing life support for businesses that would have died a natural death much earlier without his intervention.

Naim's workforce divided roughly into two: the above-mentioned beautiful girls of influential parentage (many of whom went on to brilliant careers) and a rather more grizzled bunch of old pro's. Sadly, I'd say I was in the latter category.

I joined Bertie Rope's property consultancy – actually Bertie announced that I'd joined it while I will still taking stock of the building and the bewildering nature of the set-up in general. But it was a good decision. Bertie's clients were large construction companies (such as Wimpey Construction), architects, estate agents and designers – and also Scope (then called the Spastics Society) for whom we were tasked with fundraising. We did see through some extraordinary ventures: the move of the newspapers from Fleet Street to Docklands (Wimpey built many of the huge printing plants), the complete redesign of old department stores into glittering architectural office spaces and their reoccupation, and the restoration of some of Liverpool's Georgian heritage. However, in time, I was made a director of Naim's PR businesses – and my brief was widened to include the magazines and also to work with Laurie and Theo on the showbiz side.

Theo and Laurie were without doubt the absolute doyens of British showbiz PR. Theo had worked with some of the greatest of the Hollywood greats: Bette Davis, David Niven, Michael Caine, Peter Sellers; and Laurie's clients had included Robert Mitchum and James Stewart. In the mid 1980s, the roster still included Channel 4 Television and Michael Caine, as well as other British luminaries such as Jeremy Irons, Roy Marsden and Jenny Agutter. Theo, who had also presided over publicity for the Rank Organization in its heyday, was large, amiable and shambolic. On the face of it, an expansive and genial character, he was actually a very private man. Among his finest traits was his dry, offbeat sense of humour – and a repertoire of brilliant one-liners. I asked him one day if he'd caught up with a memo I'd sent him and he replied he was a bit behind – 'in fact, I think there's going to be trouble with Hitler – but I'll let you know'.

Laurie Bellew, his long-term professional partner, was the quieter of the two, but none the less an effective operator. He'd grown up in Liverpool and started out as a teenager writing gags for Ken Dodd. In the mid 1980s he continued to look after Dodd, as well as Tommy Steele and James Stewart, among others. Where Theo painted the big picture, Laurie provided the kind of detailed planning and media 'wiliness' that I've tried to draw on ever since.

Like many long-term partnerships, commercial or marital, there was considerable tension between the two. Locked into their business with each other, they occupied separate floors and did not, as I remember, communicate directly with any regularity. As my widened brief developed, I would tread a discreet and subtle line in trying to bridge between the two.

Other enjoyable tasks for the showbiz arm at this time included the launch in the UK of the American buy-in *Thirty Something* and also the return of *Batman*, which I think provided something of a challenge in terms of generating publicity. Then, somehow or another, we took on the Monkees' reunion tour (1988). Little had been seen or heard of them in the UK since the television series in the 1960s and the media interest was huge. It was probably my first experience of dealing with a 'campaign' of this size and also in managing media interest strategically to a specific objective – in this case, bums on seats. With the Monkees themselves (minus Mike Nesmith), plus two wives and a girlfriend, plus a tour manager, most of whom were in a complicated state of total disagreement with each other, this also called for considerable people-management skills. The tour was nevertheless a sell-out and provided me with a solution to a dilemma.

There was an urgent need to come up with a substantial cash-raising venture for Scope – with a rather hair-raising figure attached. Fundraising was definitely not a speciality of mine and I was frantic as to how to achieve this aim. The answer of course was right in front of me: I asked the Monkees to do an extra date at the Royal Albert Hall and to donate as much as possible of the proceeds to the charity. It was a testament to their good natures that they agreed, and we were able to hand over a sizeable cheque.

Around the corner in Beak Street, Auberon Waugh edited the *Literary Review*. The offices, no less Dickensian than the lower floors of Poland Street, were warm, paper-strewn, somewhat chaotic and always welcoming. Bron's reputation, tinged perhaps with that of his father, was a mixture of wit, bile, intellect and charm – and, as such, he was a slightly awe-inspiring character to meet. In person, he was gentle, warm – and utterly uncompromising when it came to his magazine, which he loved as fiercely and protectively as one would a child. The atmosphere of the *Literary Review* in those days was redolent of the fusty, literary, old-world Fleet Street milieu – inhabited by the Willie Rushtons and John Wellses, as well, of course, as the authors of the day.

Across town, in a separate universe in Cleveland Street, were the offices of *Wire* magazine. *Wire* (a wide-ranging jazz magazine for the seriously knowledgeable – and for people who took their jazz very seriously) was a beautiful piece of work. It was edited by Richard Cook, a jazz critic of note, and was not only cutting edge in its content, but also exquisite in its design. With Naim's help, and as part of a bid to bring *Wire* to greater prominence, we mounted the first British Jazz Awards. Having scoured London for suitable venues, we settled for Katherine Hamnet's ultra-cool store on the Brompton Road and set the event in the midst of it. A combination of bluff and bravado (and Naim's contact book) resulted in a line-up of presenters including Jools Holland, Sting, Salman Rushdie, Linford Christie, Marie Helvin, Robbie Coltrane and Moira Stuart.

The challenge for Naim at this time was to try and draw the various strands of his business together and to make sure they were as cash efficient as possible. This presented considerable difficulties. The property PR arm was relatively healthy but it was more difficult to get to grips with the showbiz side. While the Channel 4 contract paid a decent retainer, it was much harder to fathom what, if anything, the various celebrity clients were paying. It was also, in brutal terms, desirable to ensure that the business would continue to be viable if anything were to happen to Theo, who was now into his seventies. As any seasoned celebrity PR will avow, the currency on which the relationship rests is the personal bond between client and consultant. Theo was well aware of this – and played a crafty game, appearing on the one hand to be completely open to Naim's intended integration of his business and on the other ensuring that no one – but no one – got near any of his clients. When I left Namara to join TV-am, this elegant Mexican stand-off was still playing out.

Further difficulties arose when Naim appointed Richard Cook publisher of the *Literary Review* and asked his team to redesign it to give it a touch of modernity. Bron was appalled – and loathed every proposal put forward. One day I wandered into his office, holding a copy of *Wire*. Bron's eyes fastened on it and he said, 'I loathe that magazine. I loathe everything about it.' The result, in the end, was a gentle facelift for the *Literary Review*, with its three columns reduced to two and a slightly rounder typeface. The two teams, however, as different from one another as it's possible to imagine, were never going to gel.

Looking back on my time at Namara twenty years ago, I regard it with fondness and considerable admiration. Naim presided over a small empire of significant talent, fame and enterprise. Many of the people who worked with him were already pre-eminent in their particular spheres of operation; many were fledgling talents who went on to notable success in later years. Naim was certainly thought of as autocratic in some quarters, but in my personal dealings with him I found him to be shrewd and straightforward. He showed great personal loyalty to his staff and expected the same from them. He was dedicated to supporting the businesses he loved and would give them the necessary freedom and headroom to operate effectively.

The Namara years were certainly a formative time – both for me, and I suspect for everyone else working there – in one way or another.

Thirty-five

In October 1989 Quartet had announced my forthcoming book *Singular Encounters*, to be published in the autumn of 1990. This time the subject was men. It was to consist of an exhaustive study of twenty-five of them. The interviews, designed to unlock the subjects' innermost secrets, would cover their private and professional lives, their ambitions and aspirations, and would delve into areas that carried the warning: 'proceed at your own risk'. The first assumption made by the press was that it was out to make Anna Ford's recent book on the same subject seem like a toe in the water compared with the murky revelations I would try to uncover. 'It's not going to be yet another book of interviews,' I told the *Evening Standard* firmly. 'I'm doing it for the challenge. My reputation as a writer will rise or fall on the book.'

From the start I saw *Singular Encounters* as a highly ambitious project, one that was bound to determine my future as an interviewer. The men I was seeking to engage were leaders in their respective fields and were unlikely to make any concessions to the fact that I was a novice in this journalistic medium. The women's book was comparatively simple. My natural affinity with women had been an immeasurable help. I could not as yet advance the claim to have a similar affinity with men. Whether or not the right empathy was there would only emerge with time. Moreover, where the women's book had been, broadly speaking, a compendium of their views on subjects affecting women in general, the men's book must aim to present an individual in-depth study of each participant. As such it needed more background research and a more focused concentration during the interviews.

The difficulties were exacerbated by the slating *Women* had received at the hands of a large majority of critics and commentators. The general tone had been to hold up to ridicule the two hundred and eighty-nine women who had accepted the invitation to appear in its pages. I was anxious that this might now become a discouraging factor, deterring some men from agreeing to a serious encounter with me. Fortunately my fears turned out to be without foundation and most of the men I approached were happy to oblige. A. N. Wilson had his reservations at first, though he soon relented, and they had been on entirely different grounds, as he explained in a 'Diary' piece in the *Spectator*.

My friend Naim Attallah . . . is compiling a volume of interviews with the thirty most important men in the world. I believe it [will include] revealing conversations with Yehudi Menuhin, Lord Goodman, Monsignor Gilbey, J. K. Galbraith and Richard Ingrams. I was flattered to be asked to be of their number. The company is so grand that it really feels better than being given the OM . . . I said no at first, because I was frightened that Naim would only want to ask me about sex, but in the event he twisted my arm by saying that if I did not consent there would be no *young* men in his book. In the event, he did not ask me about sex at all, having covered the subject exhaustively with the others. I was glad to help him out by being the voice of youth.

In fact I got him on to the subject of sex by way of Christianity's disapproval of sex, which brought him out firmly against St Augustine, St Paul and the puritans. But what about the puritan argument that sex was addictive, I asked, and that from addiction comes perversion? 'Obviously, if you're a healthy grown-up person, your sexual impulses go on, but that's not the same as saying something is addictive. To say that is like saying food is addictive.' 'But if you suddenly had three or four women, and you start having sex with them, wouldn't you want to have more and more?' I pressed him. 'What an adventurous life you must have led, Naim,' Andrew replied. 'I'm not qualified to answer that question.' Despite his reluctance to rise to the bait, the riposte was very much vintage Wilson in its sharpness and humour.

Another reluctant target was Mark Birley of Harry's Bar and Annabel's. He procrastinated but in the end agreed as well. Until then he had always refused to submit to any press coverage and his inclusion in the book was a bit of a coup. However, it was a chance I almost missed. On the appointed day I was struck down with flu. If I had cancelled he would no doubt have jumped at the excuse not to reconvene the session at another time. To ensure this could not happen, I rose from my sickbed suffering from a fevered, aching body, swallowed two codeine tablets and phoned Mark's secretary to confirm I would be arriving for our appointment. To my astonishment, as if by a conjunction of fate, she told me Mark had the flu as well but would be willing to do the interview at home if I was happy to make the effort. We ended up sipping champagne together in a state of near delirium and conducting a serious conversation in a codeine-induced haze. The unusual encounter marked the beginning of a friendship that remained strong over the years.

Lord Goodman raised a stumbling block of a different order. I saw him over a lavish breakfast at his London flat, initially to be assessed for my suitability to be an interviewer of this giant among men. I outlined the concept of the book for him and mentioned several people who had agreed to participate, including Lord Alexander QC and Lord Rees-Mogg. Evidently I passed muster because a month later I conducted the interview itself. Then, a few days later, a letter arrived from Lord Goodman withdrawing his permission for publication on the grounds that Richard Ingrams would be appearing in the same volume: 'It was inexcusable to have lured me with a number of respectable names and to have withheld the fact that Mr Ingrams is to be included in the book.'

I replied with a soothing letter, reminding him of his avowed opposition to censorship and questioning the wisdom of bowing out in vexation. The strategy worked, though his reply was designed to put me in my place: 'In view of your pathetic plea, I am prepared, albeit reluctantly, to allow the interview to appear.'

I heaved a sigh of relief. Lord Goodman, a staunch defender of the cause of the arts, commanded great respect as a legal adviser to both political wings and the establishment itself. He knew nearly everyone in British public life and had been called upon to advise virtually every great national institution. Indeed, he came close to being a national institution himself. It seemed strange that he should have felt so strongly about the one-time editor of *Private Eye*, though the magazine had once allegedly libelled him. He talked only in general terms about libel in our interview. 'I've always deterred people from becoming involved,' he said. It seemed that in the case of *Private Eye* he was unable to follow his own advice. The whole little episode was completely at odds with the image he cultivated of being a sage, invulnerable in his judgement.

Harold Acton made a sharp contrast: though he had the reputation befitting a grand aesthete, I found him easy-going and charm itself. Our interview took place in Florence over dinner at his home, La Pietra, a Renaissance villa that was like a domestic museum full of countless *objets d'art* and priceless paintings collected by his family over the years. I had visited him there many times, mostly for tea or dinner, when he would engage in affectionate gossip about his great friend Tony Lambton, or regale me with the latest scandals making the rounds in the small circle of Florentine society, taking especial delight in any sexual peccadilloes. He considered me an amusing dinner companion – a welcome change from certain other guests, who tended to be academic and whom he labelled stuffy and boring. He often cancelled a dinner date with them in preference for spending an evening of banter with me.

As a student at Oxford, Harold had been well known for flouting convention and mixing in male undergraduate circles where bisexuality was in vogue. His close friends included Auberon Waugh's father, Evelyn, who reputedly used him as a model for some of the more outrageous characters in his novels. I used to tease Harold about girls and enquire if he had ever slept with one. He would put on a show of being greatly shocked at this sudden intrusion into his private life before rolling his eyes and smiling an enigmatic smile. Then he would tap me coyly on the hand as if chastising me for being such a 'naughty boy'. This only encouraged me to urge him on, and on one occasion he told me about an intimate encounter with a young Chinese girl during the time when he lived in China, teaching English at Peking National University in the 1930s. He described the silky skin of her naked body with obvious relish, but that was as far as he ever went. The mystery of whether he actually slept with any girl remained unsolved.

During one of our conversations, he expressed his regret at the way Oxford University had turned down his offer to bequeath them La Pietra with its collection of priceless art works, forty thousand rare books and fifty-seven acres of grounds in his will. They felt they could not have afforded the cost of repairs and restoration. Instead, after he died in 1994, La Pietra went to New York University as a study and conference centre. Although he had an American mother, he would have preferred the legacy to have gone to a British institution. In the years after his death, the estate became the subject of a long-running counter-claim from the descendants of Harold's illegit-imate half-sister, with a judge giving authority for the exhumation of his father's body from the family grave in Florence. Happily, it seems there has been no need to disturb Harold's remains, though his father's were reported as confirming the DNA link.

Harold entertained well, but he had one curious phobia about electricity consumption. When I needed to visit the cloakroom he would escort me to switch on the light and linger in the vicinity to make sure it was switched off again after I emerged. It was part of his economy drive to maintain his lifestyle without compromising it with waste. Or that was how he explained it.

John Kenneth Galbraith, the world-renowned economist, was a difficult proposition: he was imperious and patronizing. From the outset he tried to dwarf me by orchestrating every aspect of our conversation, refusing to give me a straight answer when he felt a question might compromise him. Instead he would skirt around it and avoid tackling its essence; or refrain from being specific when challenged. Whenever I tried to insist on a proper response to a question, he brushed it aside with a curt dismissal: 'Move on to the next question.' The tone in his voice made it clear he meant what he said and I knew that, if I stood my ground, I would soon be shown the door. Since he was a name to be reckoned with, I swallowed my pride and moved on under his overbearing direction. Eating humble pie was better than having no portion of pie at all. He was a man totally secure in his self-confidence and impressively grand in his immense knowledge. The experience of meeting him was worth it for the painful lesson it gave me in self-control.

The ennobled Gordon White was another example of someone who made me feel uneasy. This was not because of any display of high intellect, but it had everything to do with the fact that he was a right-wing bigot, bereft of any compassion for the underprivileged and under no compulsion to conceal it. He was without doubt a brilliant market operator, who had found his niche in the United States and been a perfect counterbalance for his partner, Lord Hanson, who was altogether more mellow and less strident.

Lord White was also working hard to re-enact his youth at the time I met him. He had a young girlfriend, with whom he was desperately trying to keep up physically by exerting himself in the gym. His motivation was so transparent as to make it open to ridicule. The adage, 'There is no fool like an old fool,' was particularly apposite in his case. I somehow found myself unable to relate to him at any level. A tone of self-congratulation ran through the interview and even impinged on what he would like to have been if not a businessman – a major figure in the sporting world or an actor. 'I was once offered a screen test,' he said, 'but didn't have the courage to do it. I was afraid of failure. You see, I looked right. I was a very good-looking guy when I was younger.' He was an ardent admirer of Mrs Thatcher, to whom he owed his elevation to the Lords.

With the broadcaster, Michael Aspel, who was introduced to me by Theo Cowan, I had a different kind of problem – one that threatened to blow up into a major row. The interview itself went extremely well. I was particularly struck by Michael's total candour and his willingness to touch on matters that had at certain points blighted his life. His was a story full of pathos and sorrow, and it was indeed moving. The chemistry between us must have worked most effectively and I felt delighted to have extracted from him some gems that would help to make the final version a most absorbing and sympathetic lesson in soul baring. Away from the limelight of his profession, Michael revealed his true self and showed his skills and vulnerabilities in a human light.

A few days later I received a phone call from his agent requesting a sight of the edited interview. It seemed Michael was beginning to feel concerned about certain aspects that he would like to reassess and perhaps omit. Instinctively I felt the agent was angling to doctor the interview and thus fillet out its quality of spontaneity, reducing it to the usual homogenized, polished sort of interview so common in show business – the kind that avoids delving too deeply into inner feelings or dwelling on the frailties of the subject's life. My reaction was not the one the agent had expected. I fought hard to maintain the integrity of the interview as I saw it, while also feeling some embarrassment at the prospect of having to air our views in public with the indignities likely to follow.

Theo Cowan was keen to prevent any falling out and took on himself the role of peace broker. He worked tirelessly to arrive at a solution to avoid a rumpus that was going to benefit no one. Peace was eventually restored, but at a price. Compromise is not always the best way forward. In the event, we ended up with something more like an *entente cordiale*, having had to sacrifice some deeply held principles for the preservation of something called 'image'. That, alas, is more or less the way of the world.

Dominick Dunne became a household name in the United States when, after producing a number of Hollywood films, he turned to being an author and a contributing editor at *Vanity Fair*. A recovered alcoholic, he had tragedy in his background, his daughter having been murdered by her boyfriend in 1983. The impression I had gained on meeting him was that he would have been more at ease doing the interview than being interviewed. He had an irritable impatience and I found it hard going to keep him focused. He did not appear to be interested in any of my questions, but would rather have been formulating his own and then giving what he considered to be appropriate answers. I persevered to the very end without seeming to be rattled. He was not a person I would have chosen to be marooned with on a desert island. I felt that his demons had never left him and he sadly remained a tortured soul. Possibly our encounter was ill-timed, or perhaps I myself was in a state of mental turmoil that I mistakenly projected on to him. All I could remember sub-sequently was my sense of relief when the interview was over. As I walked away, revived by a light breeze, the sun was shining and New York looked at its best.

Monsignor Alfred Gilbey, the ultra-orthodox Catholic Society priest who resided, till his death a few months after I interviewed him, at the Travellers' Club in Pall Mall, was for decades a chaplain at Cambridge. He lived in grand style and entertained his guests for dinner at the club with healthy measures of good wine, obviously not believing that abstinence from culinary pleasures was needed to ensure an easy passage to heaven. For the interview, I met him for dinner and then retired with him to a quiet corner to conduct it. He certainly had a rare eloquence and gave the impression of a single-minded individual who was not afraid to court controversy, especially when it came to his views on women. Tackled directly on the subject, he swiftly emerged as a woman-hater *extraordinaire*, nostalgic for the days when universities and other institutions were strictly male preserves. His view, he considered, was 'wholly compatible with the God-given design of women as complementary to men', which was to say they were not the equal of men. I could only feel he was taking an unnecessary risk. What if God turned out to be a woman? What then for Monsignor Gilbey?

The distinguished writer Edmund White remains the most explicit individual I have ever interviewed. Endowed with formidable powers of communication and an elegant prose style, he had the ability to shock while retaining an icy composure. His life was marred as a boy by a violent father and he was later to experience the trauma of losing his male lover to AIDS. Yet his eloquence never deserted him, even when discussing the most explosive of subjects, such as a homosexual son's incestuous feelings for his father.

Many of the homosexuals he had known, he said, 'had strong erotic fantasies about their fathers, and have even slept with their fathers or brothers. It's not unusual . . . I definitely had strong erotic feelings towards my father.' An extraordinary story then emerged from his family situation.

I think the idea was that whoever was sleeping in my father's bed was in a privileged position in the family and would gain power. In other words, my father was a tyrant, and at first my mother was in his bed and a privileged person; then my stepmother became a privileged person; then my father had an affair with my sister, and my sister was elevated in the family because of it. I didn't know about it at the time, but I sensed it because I once walked in on them when my father was brushing my sister's hair. She had very long blonde hair, and looked quite a bit like his mother, who was very pretty . . .

Anyway, my father was brushing my sister's hair, standing behind her and crying as he did so. It was the only time I saw my father cry. I sensed there was something going on, but I wasn't certain to what extent. It was only later, when my sister had a complete breakdown and was in a mental hospital, that I knew for sure. She had tried to kill herself and it all came out, but that was many years later. I guessed she had always had strong guilt feelings about this relationship with my father, maybe partly because she liked it.

I think she had loved him very much. It was extremely dramatic when my father died, because we had a farm in the north of Ohio where he wanted to be buried, and that was terribly inconvenient for everybody because it took hours to get there. We finally arrived in the small town with its little farmers' church, and there he was in an open coffin, which I hated. But my sister went up to the coffin and talked to my father a long time, rather angrily and crying. Then she took off her wedding ring and put it on his finger. She was forty something at the time.

It was one of the most surprising moments of revelation in the whole book.

I particularly wanted to interview John Updike. He was the American writer of his generation with the most distinguished and prolific output, who had dissected the suburban sexual mores of small-town America. The snag was that he then rarely gave interviews. As André Deutsch was his publisher in Britain, I asked him if he thought he could persuade Updike to meet me. André said he would do what he could but could promise nothing. Eventually he came back and said Updike would be willing to see me in Boston, but had stipulated that the interview must be restricted to forty-five minutes. I naturally gibbed at this impossibly meagre concession, but André said well, it was either that or nothing. I flew to Boston specially and Updike came to my hotel room as arranged. Once he got going, our conversation went on for almost two hours. In his own memoirs he had described himself as malicious, greedy for a quota of life's pleasures, an obnoxious show-off, rapacious and sneaky. This did not really match the public perception of him, I suggested.

I think that anybody who knows me would agree with all those adjectives. I was an only child who never had to compete with a sibling, and my parents were both, in their way, very loving and indulgent. Just the fact that I had the presumption to become an artist is rather ridiculous, isn't it, with no qualifications except that I felt treasured as a child. When my mother died, among the things in the attic was a scrapbook containing many of my drawings done when I was three or four. Not every child gets that kind of attention. The good side of it is that I have a certain confidence, and by and large I've acted confidently in my life and had good results. The bad side is that I like to be the centre of attention.

As for being malicious, I think I am more than unusually malicious. That joy, that *Schadenfreude* we take in other people's misfortunes, is highly developed in me, though I try to repress it. I detect within myself a certain sadism, a certain pleasure in the misfortunes of others. I don't know whether I'm average in this or whether it's exceptional, but I'm interested to a degree in the question of sadism. People who are sadistic are very sensitive to pain, and it's a way of exorcizing the demon of pain.

I'm so aware of my enviousness that I try not to review books by contemporary Americans. I'm not sure that I would really give an honest opinion, and that's sneaky. People who are cowardly and don't especially enjoy confrontation or battle tend to be sneaky. In this unflattering self-characterization though, I was no doubt just doing my Christian duty of confessing sins. Human nature is mightily mixed, but surely all these malicious and cruel aspects are there along with everything else.

I then raised the question of a reviewer of his novel *Couples* calling him 'the pornographer of marriage'. Did he resent this tag, I asked.

Not too much. I wasn't trying to be pornographic. I was trying to describe sexual behaviour among people, and the effect was probably the opposite of pornographic. Pornography creates a world without consequences, where women don't get pregnant, nobody gets venereal disease and no one gets tired. In *Couples* I was trying, to the limits of my own knowledge, to describe sexual situations and show them with consequences. Without resenting that phrase, I don't think it describes very well what I was trying to do . . .

I think *Couples* was certainly of its time, just in the fact that it spans very specific years and refers to a lot of historical events. In a funny way, the book is about the Kennedy assassination. It's also about the introduction of the contraceptive pill, the fact that the danger of getting pregnant was almost entirely removed and that a certain amount of promiscuity resulted directly from this technology. It also turns out that it was the pre-AIDS, pre-herpes paradise, so it was a moment that's gone, a moment of liberation which broke not upon a bunch of San Francisco hippies, but upon middle-aged couples, yet was a revolution of a kind. It is very much of its historic moment.

There was general agreement that Yehudi Menuhin was not only a great musician but also a great human being. I had already been in contact with his father, Moshe, over *The Palestinians*, and was interested to hear the son's views on some of the issues involved. My lead-in to the subject was a question about Wilhelm Furtwängler, who had remained in Germany and continued his career as a conductor almost till the end of the Nazi era. As a result he had been much criticized. Yehudi Menuhin's assessment was both eminently sane and full of insight.

A very great conductor and an absolutely clean man, no question of that. He stood up for Hindemith, he protected a great many Jews, helped many out of Germany, and himself had to escape towards the end of the war. He happened to conduct the orchestra when some of the German leaders were there, but we can't expect everyone to behave in the same way. Sometimes it takes more courage to remain in your country than to leave it. Those who stayed suffered a pretty bad fate, and those who came out, after all, escaped. Yet there was this feeling of superiority among those who escaped, thinking that they showed great determination in leaving it behind. I would say, Jew or Gentile, you can't blame those who stayed, you can't blame those who escaped. It's just the way things went. But Furtwängler himself was a man of integrity.

The anti-Semitism I have seen in my lifetime has had a psychological impact on me only to the extent that I know it is important to maintain the dignity of the Jew and to avoid a kind of behaviour that might prompt a response. The caricature of the Jew is the businessman with the big cigar, who does exist sometimes. They can be charming and interesting people. What bothers me sometimes is that they are a little like desert flowers. When they have only a drop of water they blossom. They make the most of the opportunity, as they did in Germany before the Nazi days, when they occupied extremely powerful positions. That must have created a certain amount of resentment. Of course, it gives no excuse for anti-Semitism, but you can understand it. The Jew does not stand out in Italy or Greece, nor would he in China, since the Chinese are far cleverer at business than the Jews. There are so many different types of Jew, but traditionally people have fastened on the Jew who is obviously different from them. But there are so many that are in no way different. It's like the problem of the black in the United States. There are almost a majority of blacks that are nearly white, and no one bothers about them.

It is true that the Jews are far too sensitive, though they have perhaps been sensitized by history. They are too ready to imagine an insult; they are not prepared to give enough leeway, even to allow for a certain mis-behaviour; and it is part of the psychology. One can understand that too, and one must understand it. They have to compensate for certain established assumptions. If it's not one thing it's another. If it's not religion, it's jealousy or it's race. Yet it's none of these things actually. It's simply that people are nasty and want to condemn anything if they can find a little difference; can say that hair is frizzed instead of straight or there's a detectable accent. Then they pounce on it.

Unfortunately the Jews have come to Israel with the narrow aim of making themselves an independent nation, to a large extent disregarding the environment and the rest of the world. They didn't come to establish a nation with the Palestinians and a wonderful federation (though now they realize that perhaps they should have done). They came instead with the pure desire to establish a Jewish state to the exclusion of everything else. They did it very successfully, but they did it ruthlessly, and probably the sense of fear is equal on both sides. I feel that the only solution lies in a federation, totally equal, as in Switzerland. If both have an equal title to the land, what else can you do? Meanwhile there is something cruel about all of us. We are capable of the most horrid things, especially if we have suffered them ourselves.

Yehudi left an indelible impression on me: a shining example of goodness and humility. He would never have thanked you to feel humbled in his presence, but that was the effect.

In December 1992, three years after my interview with Yehudi, Richard Ingrams, a friend of the Menuhins, asked me to interview Lady Menuhin for the *Oldie* magazine. The interview never appeared for two reasons: first, because of its length there were difficulties over successfully abridging it to fit three pages of the magazine without losing the natural flow; secondly, Lady Menuhin had concerns, as she expressed them to Richard, that some aspects of the interview might cause her embarrassment or even trigger off the kind of controversy that would be extremely harmful to her husband. Richard, not always known for his understanding in such matters, surprisingly refrained from running the interview in any form. I believe Richard took the right decision at the time, but now that the Menuhins are dead it will be enlightening to read some of Lady Menuhin's thoughts on life with Yehudi and the dangers he had faced because of his support for Furtwängler.

As she told it in her own autobiography, Diana Menuhin came from a rigorous background, having had an Edwardian Christian Scientist mother, and a chequered career as a ballet dancer in which you could never afford to be ill, along with a love life that had gained no permanence at its centre. The disciplines she had been through made her, she felt, 'very serviceable for life with darling Yehudi, who prefers to live on cloud nine, which he seems to have rented for most of his life'. She had met him after being in the Middle East during the war and enduring a deeply unhappy end to a love affair.

'When I met Yehudi, my metaphysical attitude to life made me realize that he was my destiny. He fell in love with me, and I was in love with him, but as he was married with two small children I never told him. It took two and a half really terrible years for him to get his divorce, because he was so angelic he couldn't hurt anybody, even if he knew he was not to blame for his first mistake. I may have been his second mistake, but he hasn't found out yet.'

In her book she described her life with Yehudi as 'service in its highest sense'.

I'm an incurable, incorrigible worker. I think that's what Yehudi liked so much, and he recognized with great relief that we had a tremendous amount in common, that we'd both had aspirations since we were born, that I had enormous experience because I hadn't been protected by wonderful parents who had given up everything for me. He remains to this day the most incredibly modest man, and I think that's what the audience feels. Yehudi's a medium – the music comes through him; he feels responsible to the composer, dead or alive. He was very sad and very lonely when I met him, because his marriage had really broken up, and Yehudi wouldn't admit it; and if he had admitted it, he would have blamed himself. Yehudi never blames anyone else, ever, for anything. He told me that when he first saw me at my mother's house he went away to sit on a pouffe at the end of the drawing-room, and thought, 'I'm going to have her.' I said, 'Don't be ridiculous, it was your daughter's fifth birthday,' for I didn't know then that the marriage was no good, but Yehudi has a way of knowing what he wants, and he gets it.

Before they could marry in 1947, there were two and half 'dark years' while Yehudi was separating from his first wife, but Diana never doubted she was herself doing the right thing.

I never raised a finger to help him get rid of his first wife. I never told him I was in love with him, because I didn't want him to feel any obligation towards me. Of course he knew, but I never said it, and when he told his wife about me and mentioned the word marriage, she just said no, although she had God knows how many lovers herself. And Yehudi, who is utterly good and sweet, but can also lack a certain will, blamed himself for everything . . .

But I was in love with him, the way I'd hoped to be in love ever since I can remember. I hadn't met his wife, though I had heard rumours of her behaviour and of course I'd seen the results in him. He was completely broken by it and had even decided he would give up playing the violin. I remember saying to him – we spoke mostly in French in those days – 'Yehudi, j'ai peur.' Finally his wife told him that he had to stay with her and the children. It trailed on and on with her promising divorce and then breaking her promise over and over again. Then, thank God, she realized that from a practical point of view it would be better for her to marry whichever lover she had at that time, and so after two years she let Yehudi go.

Attacks on Yehudi in the Jewish press for marrying outside the faith had bothered her not at all.

In any case, the whole of that was not because he'd married a Gentile, but because he had insisted on going to Germany. He has incredible courage, Yehudi, immense courage. He went to Germany and played night and day for every cause, Jewish and German. When we were there we heard that

Furtwängler had had to run away in the middle of the night because the Gestapo had come for him. He had done nothing except get on with his job and stay in the country. I knew Furtwängler because my mother had a musical salon to which every musician in the world came, and Furtwängler had lunch with mummy when he was over to conduct the opera; but Yehudi had never even met him. Furtwängler was decent and had helped Jewish members of the orchestra to get to America. He also wrote very dangerous letters from Denmark to my sister – he adored blondes and was mad about her. He wrote: 'When I think I am writing from this country, occupied by my people, it makes me ill.' One night his friends came to him and said, 'Run, because the Gestapo is coming for you,' and he escaped at night with his second wife, the lovely Lizavet. Yehudi was told that the Americans wouldn't give Furtwängler his purification trial, so Yehudi sent off a two-page telegram to America – Yehudi's telegrams are full of notwithstandings and neverthelesses – saying it was a disgrace to the Americans that they hadn't at least given him the chance to clear his name. Furtwängler got his purification trial, he passed a hundred per cent clean, but of course you can imagine what the cabal in New York did about it: the ones who were jealous of Yehudi were heard to say, 'At last we've got Menuhin.' So the press reports were not really because he had married a Gentile but because he had defended a German . . .

Before Hitler one didn't analyse Jewishness or non-Jewishness. For example, I realized only afterwards that many of the musicians who came to my mother's house were Jews, but to me they were Russian, or Hungarian, or German, or Austrian. Until the time of the Hitler incitement, one wasn't Jewish-conscious – I had a very broad spectrum, but it was different for Yehudi. His father had sensibly taken him away from Europe when Hitler came to power, but his American experience was very limited because his parents simply didn't go out anywhere. . .

When I first married Yehudi, he was more or less estranged from his family because they very foolishly condemned his first wife, the last thing to do to a man who refuses to condemn anybody. So when I first went to California I told Yehudi that no Jew was ever separated or estranged from his family, above all from his mother, and I persuaded him that he should go and visit them. Abba loved America because he felt he could trust people; everywhere else in the world he thought everyone was cheating him. Mamina was a completely emancipated Jewess, totally and absolutely Russian, though she spoke six languages beautifully. When Yehudi made his incredible début at the age of nine or ten, all the Jewish community in New York naturally wanted to claim him as their star. She held them off, which led to a feeling among the Jewish community that she didn't want to have anything to do with them.

Abba was an inspector of Hebrew schools, but they didn't often go to synagogues, and Yehudi was brought up with no sense of what is kosher; there was nothing kosher at home at all. So there was no question of their being ritual Jews. Mamina would never touch Yiddish, and in fact spoke good German, which laid the foundation for Yehudi's assertion that his entire culture came from Germany and Austria. After that the Jews saw their opportunity to murder him. Yehudi's father was only anti-Israel because he had divided loyalties. He was very proud to be American, yet he was of course a Jew, the grandson of a rabbi. When he and Mamina first went to look for rooms in New Jersey when their baby was about to be born, they found a very nice landlady who must have found them an attractive pair – Abba was extremely handsome, blue eyes, blond hair, and Mamina was quite incredibly beautiful, with golden hair she could sit on and Tartar-blue eyes. As they left, the landlady said, 'Well, I'm very glad to have you two young things, because I simply hate Jews, and I won't have them here.' Whereupon Mamina turned and said, 'Well, you won't be having us because we are both Jews.' And as they walked away, she tapped her tummy where Yehudi was prenatally stored, and said, 'This child is going to be called Yehudi, the Jew.' And yet that was the last Jewish gesture she made.

For Abba, the greatest thing on earth was his American passport; it made him feel that he was somebody, because Mamina certainly didn't make him feel that. Zionism threatened to break apart the feeling of being American; it was going to demand a dual loyalty, so he joined the Philadelphia lot, a group of very distinguished Jews. It was called the American Council of Judaism, and it was made up of all those first- and second-generation Americans who felt that it was terrible to be asked to be less than a hundred per cent loyal to their American naturalization; and this was the basis of his anti-Zionism. Secondly, the Menuhins were Jews who had never suffered. Abba didn't know how important it was for the Jews to have a homeland. I talked to them and explained what it must have been like to have been a Jew in Europe . . . The Menuhins didn't know how necessary it was for the Jews to try to escape the pogroms; they had never been through a pogrom.

Yehudi was not really pro-Israel. He hated militant Zionism, yet he realized the necessity for a land for the Jews, while at the same time refusing to talk about it. Yehudi was not one of your pro-Isrealis at all, and that is why they tried to kill us when we first went to Israel. With a certain amount of counselling from me, he realized that something had to be done about the Jews, what was left of them, but he never wanted to be a militant Zionist. He played at concerts to raise money for the Jewish fund, of course – that was the least he could do. But because we had already been to Germany, there followed a period [in America] of Jews being told to boycott his concerts. His concerts were always sold out, but only Gentiles were sitting in Carnegie Hall. The Jews were told by all the Jewish newspapers to send their tickets back too late to have them resold, and that Menuhin was anti-Israel. It wasn't true. He was only anti the militancy which was being shouted from the rooftops.

He went everywhere where the Jews had really suffered, where they had been taken out and burned. He even gave a concert in Berlin for the displaced-persons camp. Unless you've seen what had befallen those wretched Jews who had survived what was done to them by the Germans, you wouldn't believe it. And they came crowding round the car in a wave of hate such as you've never seen. The military police accompanied us into the hall where people were literally hanging on to the players, and the howl of rage was really quite terrifying. But Yehudi has a radiance that makes people suddenly understand what he is trying to be. He got up on the platform, with a huge policeman each side. There was an *agent provocateur* with a club foot, and he was trying to incite the crowd even more. Yehudi said, 'Let me speak. Let me speak.' And he spoke to them in excellent German, telling them that Jews did not go begging to others because they had been maltreated – 'We are a great race and nothing can extinguish us.' Then they clapped, they applauded, they said, 'Yehudi, Yehudi, you are wonderful . . . ' He changed the whole mood of the crowd, and when the *agent provocateur* got up, he was booed. When we left people were crowding round the car, saying, 'Yehudi, please come and play to us again, please.'

It was the most moving thing you can imagine. Yehudi hates talking about this and he may be angry if this comes out, but it was a wonderful moment in his life.

Thirty-six

Also in October 1989, in the middle of the month, an unusual new project was announced, though this one involved my wife Maria. A shop was to be opened in Shepherd Market, Mayfair, and called 'Aphrodisia'. The idea had its roots essentially in the premise that products that are life-enhancing promote a healthy well-being which in turn improves one's love life. Artificial aids and stimulants had no place in this scheme of things. Nature's way was to be the answer. Maria would run the shop and assemble the stock. Aphrodisia's diverse merchandise would all be guaranteed to combat the stress of modern living. Handcrafted gifts and natural products would be evident everywhere. Rare honeys, both bitter and sweet, gathered from a variety of locations from the Mediterranean to the Pacific, would be placed alongside the finest ginseng and pure mineral sea salts. Chocolates to excite the palate, based on an exclusive Aphrodisia recipe, would be available, as would cold-pressed olive oils, rich in aromas and full-bodied, with jars of wild berries to make the mouth water.

Maria's artistic flair was ideally suited to the enterprise. Acting as the sole interior decorator for the Namara Group she had received unequivocal praise for her ingenuity and good taste. The new undertaking was to give her the opportunity to display her many talents in a field primarily aimed at boosting the romantic side of life. The shop would be an Aladdin's cave with love as its theme and *raison d'être*. The London *Evening Standard* seemed taken with the whole idea:

> I'm delighted to hear that the publisher Naim Attallah is to set up his wife in an aphrodisiac shop in Shepherd Market, the notorious stretch of Mayfair so enjoyed by businessmen and authors. The excellent Maria Attallah is sometimes forgotten in all the excitement of the publisher's famous gaggle of nymphets at Quartet Books, so it is heartening to find that Naim is redressing the balance. Among the shop's products will be a 24-carat-gold powder to sprinkle on your bread-and-butter pudding.

Three months later the shop opened. Among the first of its illustrious customers was Auberon Waugh. After his visit, writing in the *Spectator*, he bemoaned the loss of innocence, until

> I chanced on a shop in Shepherd Market called Aphrodisia. It is kept by

Maria Attallah, wife of the Palestinian philanthropist, whose purpose, she tells me, is to sell things which make men and women feel natural and good. Some are toilet preparations, but there are books, too: *The New Sensual Massage: Learn to Give Pleasure with Your Hands*; *Love Spells*; *Shakespeare's Sonnets*; *The Japanese Bath*; books on roses; love poems; foods of love; books of pretty Edwardian nudes; beeswax candles; green-apple candles . . . 'all my objects point towards sensual passion', says Attallah. Single ostrich feathers; silk damask copes with gold fringes for those with religious fantasies; pretty painted-wood putti; Japanese tea; honey from Hawaii; hearts made of crystal, yellow and rose quartz; amethyst matrices, silver hearts, eggs of agate; little trinkets of affection; gold love chains; ginseng roots pickled in vodka and brandy . . .

At 25 Shepherd Market, Maria Attallah has collected everything that is innocent and pure, everything worth saving from the Sixties. There is a philosophy and a truth in sensuality which need to be separated from the destructive guilt which once supported the drug culture. Apart from anything else, I felt that all my Christmas-present problems are solved as long as Aphrodisia lasts.

No one could have described the shop better.

The opening of the Academy Club was on 12 December 1989, an event temporarily marred by an oversight. Both Bron and I had forgotten to have the drinks licence rubber stamped by Marylebone Road Magistrates' Court. Bron was therefore to be seen scampering to the court to get the formalities completed. In the absence of both Bron and the licence, the barman, Jock Scott, and the club secretary, Robert Posner, were not allowed to charge for drinks. 'Any member can now get blottoed,' sighed Posner, whose other role was managing the *Literary Review*. But cheers were soon heard from across the road as Bron came into view triumphant and waving the approved licence. This signalled the start of what was to become the most talked-about dive in Soho. In the weird chronicles of clubland tales, few could match the bizarre goings-on at the Academy. It established itself as a place where fame and notoriety intertwined, where cultural conversations were heard alongside juicy gossip, where social status counted for nothing; where, while boorish behaviour was frowned upon, decadence with style was accepted as quite the norm. The atmosphere of the club was merely the reflection of its rules as Bron had formulated them. Here is a sample of the eccentricities:

1. Dress shall be informal, but shoes must be worn.
2. Members are invited to make civilized conversation with other members, unless seeking solace behind a newspaper.

3. The Academy is a private club and nothing that is seen or heard in the club may be reported outside, on pain of instant expulsion without refund of membership fee.
4. Smoking is encouraged, but cigars and pipes are not allowed.
5. Poets are banned from the club.
6. Any member who has the misfortune of being sent to prison may take up the unused part of their membership upon release.

After a few weeks of the club's existence, Joseph Connolly of *The Times* 'Diary' phoned Robert Posner to see how it was doing, 'only to be told that it was policy not to talk to the press because it did not want any publicity – which is one of the funniest things I have heard in ages'. Later *The Economist*, in a summary of the merits or otherwise of London's clubs under the heading 'Change and Decay in Clubland', put the Academy in the 'Fun' category (there was only one other).

> The Academy Club was founded by a cantankerous writer, Auberon Waugh, in a fit of fury at the stuffiness of the old clubs. The Reform had complained about a party he had held there: many turned up without ties and a woman was said to have relieved herself in the gentleman's lavatory. The Academy has only one rule – shoes must be worn – but members may be expelled for being boring.

Bron was the main attraction, the club's life, its very soul. I was reminded of my student days years before, when I joined a club in Paris at St Germain le Pré, where Jean-Paul Sartre used to hold court, dispensing his existentialist philosophy surrounded by his flock of adoring young men and women. Juliette Greco was often there, and at night would sing some of her melancholic ballads to an audience of left-wing intellectuals. Yet Sartre was in some ways a messenger of doom, whereas Bron was a purveyor of joy and wit. The similarity was only in the setting. Bron's following was usually made up of pretty young women with a high level of intelligence and a cheeky disregard for convention. They hovered around him with pure delight written on their faces. They sat at his table in the club, listening to every utterance, smoking, drinking and enjoying the whole ambiance. They would also berate him – which he liked – whenever he went overboard with an attack on feminism or a particular contrariness that made them shriek. But it was all done with great humour and no trace of malice. The club was Bron's haven and he took to it as if it were his natural habitat.

All sorts of characters worked in the club. Jock Scott, the one-time barman, was a pub poet with whom the actress Anna Chancellor fell in love one night when seeing him perform in a London dungeon. The romance yielded a daughter named Poppy. In my view, Jock, like many performance poets, had never written anything good after the age of eighteen, but he went on repeating his old act till he was forty-five. His tenure at the club was short-lived. Anna, on the other hand, was a club regular. She used to stretch out her beautiful body on the leather Chesterfield, commenting on any man who came down the stairs. Club members used to finding her there were surprised to see her on the screen as 'Duckface' in *Four Weddings and a Funeral*.

Lucy Cohn, a stunningly beautiful half-French actress, the sister of the former *Telegraph* columnist Will Cohn, worked behind the bar for several years when 'resting' between acting spots. She was to star later as Princess Margaret in a Channel 4 documentary drama about the life of the princess. In one scene she appeared naked, but she never took her clothes off during working hours at the club. Lucinda Galloway, another actress, was employed as a waitress for a couple of years. She was very beautiful and intelligent but away with the fairies much of the time. For his memories of her and others I am indebted to Robert Posner, who recollects his time at the club:

Memories of the Academy
by Robert Posner

Lucinda was in the Star Café in Soho, passionately kissing her boyfriend goodbye at the door, wearing the smallest red leather mini-skirt invented and an almost see-through top. A movie producer came up to her and asked if she would like a part in his latest film, which happened to be *Robin Hood – Prince of Thieves*, starring Kevin Costner, Morgan Freeman and the brilliant Alan Rickman as the evil Sheriff of Nottingham. Lucinda can be seen in the film, naked apart from a small bearskin rug, when Alan Rickman comes up to her and says, 'You – be in my bedroom at ten o'clock. And bring a friend.' I don't think she got any other parts.

Remember the wretched Arnold Arnold, who was eased out from the club? The row started because he had reduced Lucinda to tears, shouting at her when she borrowed his dreadful book from the Academy shelves and forgot to return it in time for him to show off about to one of his guests. When Arnold Arnold sent in his application for membership when the club first opened in 1989, he included a photograph of himself. Bron took one look at him and said no. I begged Bron to accept him because he looked like a big friendly bearded bear in great thick spectacles. Bron then said, 'All right, Posner – you can have him as a member – BUT ON YOUR OWN HEAD BE IT.' Rather prescient of him, as it turned out.

Lucinda's boyfriend, James Richmond, was a lovely guy but suffered from severe manic depression and had to be permanently medicated with lithium to keep him on an even keel. Unwisely he stopped taking it on the advice of some friend and went completely nuts in the club one afternoon. Bron, unaware of his illness or his missing medication, wrote him a letter terminating his membership. A week later, we received a humble apology explaining his behaviour and begging to be allowed back. It was on the headed paper of a psychiatric clinic, so we invited him back.

Diana Rigg came to the club on the opening day as the guest of a film producer Colin Campbell. She looked at the menu, but each time she chose something to eat, we had run out of that particular dish because we were so amateurish and disorganized during the first week. Eventually, she glumly settled for her fourth choice, a pork pie. She started to chew her way through it and stuck up her hand to ask if we had any mustard. Embarrassingly, we had to admit we had none. Ten minutes later, she stuck up her hand again and said, 'Do you have any toilets here? Or have you run out?'

Several months before the club was even fitted out, Bron wrote a letter which I sent to about 900 prospective members gathered from Naim's, his and the *Literary Review*'s address books. In his letter, he asked that anyone who wished to join should send a cheque for £75 together with a copy of their best book, in order to start filling the empty and, as yet unbuilt, bookshelves. Three hundred people responded with books and cheques, eight months before the club opened, such was Bron and Naim's reputation. By mistake, half the books that arrived in the post were immediately put on the reviewing shelves of the *Literary Review* and duly disappeared off to the second-hand bookshop in Charing Cross Road. We used to empty the shelves every month to clear the way for the next 500 books from publishers seeking reviews of their latest output. We received a telephone call from the puzzled bookshop several days later. They couldn't understand why several dozen books contained £75 cheques made out to something called 'The Academy Club'. Unfortunately, many books, possibly containing similar cheques, had already been bought by their customers. The fate of those cheques was never resolved.

David Irving, who lived in Mayfair, applied for membership. The membership committee – Naim, Bron, Laura Cumming, Sophia Sackville-West and me – considered his application, but apart from me, the only Jewish member, were absolutely against electing him. I lost the argument. Naim and the others were right, as it turned out. I thought that although he was a neo-Nazi sympathizer, he was the leading expert on modern German history and would make an interesting member. Whoops!

Regarding Rule 6, I received a letter from Dr Roger Cooper from his prison cell in Teheran in April 1990. He had been arrested by the Ayatollahs' regime for spying (he probably was a sort of spy, being a member of Chatham House). He had been sentenced to sixteen years in the infamous Evin Prison and for some strange reason he was denied any publications apart from the *Spectator*, in which Bron had announced the birth of the Academy and printed the rules as well. Roger Cooper's imprisonment was the subject of a lot of activity by human-rights activists at the time. He was not allowed to write or receive any letters from the UK, but for some mysterious and bizarre reason had been allowed to write a single letter to me at the club address in Beak Street. In this letter he wrote, *inter alia*:

2 April 1990

Dear Captain Posner – I have just read Auberon Waugh's article about the Academy in the *Spectator* and would like to apply for membership. It sounds an ideal club for people like myself . . .

You will note from my address that I would not at present be able to utilize my membership and indeed have been sentenced to sixteen years' imprisonment, expiring on 4 July 2003, but I am an incurable optimist and membership of the Academy would be most useful to me if I am set free at an earlier date. It would also be comforting to imagine myself there from time to time, even if this is not possible at present . . .

Unfortunately, they let him out a couple of years later and he often came to the club, where in the opinion of certain other regulars he nearly bored them all to death. Perhaps that was the reason the Iranians let him out.

There was a well-known *Daily Telegraph* correspondent who used to drink himself senseless in the club several nights a week and could sometimes be found sitting on the pavement outside the club doors at 1 a.m., weeping and declaring his love for Victoria Glendinning's beautiful son, Matthew, who used to manage the bar most evenings. I was very concerned and asked Bron if there was anything we should do to modify his drinking. Bron's reply was that there was nothing we could do and that, in any event, it was our job to serve him drinks. I know this journalist very well. He has not had a drink since 1994 and thinks this is the funniest story he has ever heard about himself.

Michael Bywater, a brilliant columnist and diarist, was the last member to leave the club on the last night, having concealed himself from the staff by hiding under the stairs. He wrote for the *Independent on Sunday* a wonderful article on the club after it closed down in Beak Street, 'The End of Life as I Know It'. 'A hole has opened up in my life,' he announced. 'Do you want to hear about it?'

So you shall. It's a deep yawning hole. A deep yawning *black* hole. What you'd call a pit of melancholy, a chasm of accidie, a gulf of gloom. Do you begin to get the picture? Good.

I have had holes like this before. They can be caused by debt, women, deadlines or foreclosure . . . But this hole is different. This hole has been brought on neither by financial defalcation nor by sexual incontinence. This hole has been dug by others. And how have they dug it?

They have closed my club . . .

There are other sorts of clubs, it's true . . . But the Academy Club was different. The people there were civilized. Nobody ever gained or sought advantage by being a member of it, because all that being a member of the Academy said about you was that you were a member of the Academy. It was just sort of . . . *there*. The rules were few and enlightened. Members were obliged to wear shoes. Cigarette smoking was encouraged. Members who had the misfortune to be sent to prison could claim the unexpired portion of their subscription on their release. Members were expected to talk to each other, unless hiding behind a newspaper (or engaged in intense rapid conversation, in which case they were *not to be homed in on*). The best rule was: no poets.

The application of the rules was capricious. One man was barred for several months for the offence of coming to the club too often. 'He's down here every evening, drinking brandy-and-ginger and beaming at people,' said the barman, petitioning for a ban.

It was, in short, a haven for amiable, civilized misfits who wouldn't have liked it anywhere else, and now that haven has been closed off I feel at sea. Where can I go? Where can I go where I don't have to contend with ball-ripping music, surly barmen, barking yuppies, stinking microwaved food and the sense that I am enriching some filthy coterie of brewery executives? Where can I go, on the offchance, and be reasonably sure of bumping into someone affable? Where there's nobody on the make, nobody trying to impress, nobody who even *owns* a cellular telephone, nobody dressed in black. Where people say 'Hello' and *mean* it? Where nobody laughs at my hat? Where nobody will hit us if we burst into song?

There is talk of reviving the club at some unspecified time, in some unspecified place. But you can't go back. No; it's over. The best thing to do is climb into my pit and pull the rotting boards over my head. Don't bother to call; from now on, I'm staying in.

*   *   *

On Thursday evening, 7 December 1989, in the crowded Green Room at the

Queen Elizabeth Hall, the actress Fiona Fullerton was invited to present the prizes in the jazz awards, which I organized in conjunction with the *Wire* magazine, owned by the Namara Group. Fiona, described by many as the most beautiful woman in the world, said she would prefer to be referred to as the 'former Bond girl'. The two compères for the event, David Roper and Gary Rice, introduced her as the person who once played the blue fairy and went on to become a Max Factor model. After a long-suffering glance at the audience, which included her parents, she summoned all her considerable acting skills to grin and rise above it, but was visibly rattled. Afterwards there was no containing her anger. 'I am a serious actress and don't have to be treated like this,' she told me, close to tears. She strongly objected to the way the compères had worded their introduction. Theo Cowan came to my rescue and together we did all we could to placate her.

Meanwhile, at the other end of the room, Earl Alexander of Tunis was hammering out some ragtime on the piano. He informed the guests that he was probably the best worst jazz pianist in the world. His admirers disagreed. Later, when Fiona presented the best newcomer award to Orphy Robinson of the Jazz Warriors, she was in a more jovial mood. 'I must say I have never heard of them,' she giggled. The evening ended harmoniously with an audible sigh of relief from the organizers.

The year came to an end with my purchase of Algy Cluff's half-interest in *Apollo* magazine. This was to give me, as sole owner, the opportunity to make every conceivable effort to bring it to a wider audience and promote it in every way I could. One feature, however, that was not going to change was the magazine's most glamorous and charismatic editor, Anna Somers Cocks, whose editorial never failed to cause some trepidation among the buffs of the art world. She had established a reputation for forthright thinking and seemed to have become more *formidable* as the months went by.

In an interview she gave to the *New York Times* a few weeks later, in January 1990, she said that the art world 'is a microcosm of the world. It has economics, commercialism, politics, religion, gossip, scandal, all aspects.' During her three years as editor, she had transformed the once starchy publication, declared the newspaper, into a thoughtful but lively look at all art's facets. Since she took over, the circulation had risen to nine thousand copies, a respectable figure for a glossy art magazine of that calibre. The choice of Anna as editor had been a most shrewd and enlightened appointment.

New recruits to the Namara Group were also a feature of the start of 1990. Anna Pasternak, a great niece of Boris Pasternak, joined Quartet's publicity department, while Lady Cressida Ward, a daughter of the Earl of Dudley, became one of my personal assistants when Claudia Ward, whose father is the actor Simon Ward, left to write a children's book. Claudia is gifted with a natural wit and a wicked sense of humour. She could describe events or encounters with a wry turn of phrase that I found hilarious. I used to encourage her to put pen to paper if only for my benefit and entertainment. Reading her poetic prose was a sheer joy and I missed her when she left. Meanwhile the employment of Cressida did not escape the attention of the *Evening Standard*, especially in view of her mother's legal tangle with the *Literary Review* that had won her five thousand pounds in libel damages. But, the Earl of Dudley told the paper, 'It's all history, and it would be sensible to forget the whole business because, let's face it, we must really give a lot of credit to Cressida for getting the job in the first place, in spite of the handicap against her.' The *Standard*'s comment was typical: 'Being an earl's daughter, and pretty, is no great handicap when the prospective employer is Mr Attallah.'

My press coverage, as was often the case, went from the ridiculous to the sublime when the 'Peterborough' column in the *Daily Telegraph* reported a book launch for *Namibia – Birth of a Nation*, an album of 'rather polemical photographs' by Jenny Matthews, which had a text by Glenys Kinnock, whose husband was then leader of the Labour Opposition in Parliament:

> The launch was held in the private dining-room of the book's publisher, Palestinian-born millionaire Naim Attallah – not quite the unfamiliar territory for Mrs Kinnock that one might imagine. 'We've known him for years. He's a friend of oppressed peoples all over the world,' she insisted, somewhat to Attallah's surprise. 'Am I?' he said. 'That's nice.'

It was heartening to read a quotation from Glenys that reflected my commitment towards speaking up through Quartet for the less privileged and the dispossessed wherever they happened to be. Being able to do that is for me one of the more positive aspects of being a publisher.

Thirty-seven

Among the first assignments to fall to Anna Pasternak at Quartet in May 1990 was to publicize Catherine Olsen's first novel, *Songbird*. The author, a well-known journalist, had been born in Brisbane and was married to the former president of the Seychelles, Sir James Mancham, whom she had met when she interviewed him. A large contingent of Fleet Street correspondents came to the launch party at the Arts Club in Dover Street to congratulate her on her first novel being published. She was a popular figure among journalists, combining glamorous good looks with a disarming manner and feminine charm. All the stops had been pulled out, commented *Boardroom Magazine*, 'for what Quartet obviously expects to become a monumental bestseller, and the fashionable and journalistic estates were out in force to celebrate the event'.

Every London press column was represented, from Neil Mackwood of the *Sunday Correspondent* through to Nigel Dempster, Ross Benson, John Rendall and Lady Olga Maitland, and the press cameramen were kept clicking away at the famous faces they saw in the assembled crowd. Among those to be spotted were Baroness Falkender, Princess Katarina of Yugoslavia, Princess Charlotte of Luxembourg, Lady Cressida Ward, Margaret Duchess of Argyle, Lord Kinsdale, Sir Nigel and Lady Seely, the Honourable Nicholas and Mrs Monson, Mandy Rice-Davies with her husband Ken Foreman, Daniel Topolski, the Shah of Iran's *chef de protocol* Pari Taghizedeh with her husband Reza and at least one Saudi prince.

The theme of *Songbird* was a love triangle in which a husband paid visits to his girlfriend next door through a revolving bookcase – an extra-marital love story mixed with touches of black comedy. It had been inspired, Catherine said, by 'the bizarre falling apart of a friend's marriage [when] she and her husband took some LSD on holiday and he started telling her about all the mistresses he'd had for years. And I thought what a great idea for a novel.' In the opinion of one reviewer the story 'was a cross between soap opera and black comedy, between the rich, the titled and the inventive'. The *Sunday Express* placed the book in the category of designer psychopathology: 'It fulfils all the criteria. But there is more to this book than high heels and *haute couture*. What starts as a designer novel full of sun and sex develops a psychopathic edge.' Penny Perrick in the *Sunday Times* provided the voice of dissent:

If you really want to find out what's in store for women who love too much you would be better off reading *Madame Bovary* and *Anna Karenina*, books where the characters are something more than tanned limbs and couture wardrobes. We read novels like *Songbird* not for insight into the human condition but for information as to what is currently smart. To give Olsen her due, there is plenty of this.

The tremendous coverage *Songbird* received was partly the result of the sustained efforts of Anna Pasternak. Aided in part by Lucy Blackburn, she had done a tremendous job. Another satisfying project, launched in the same month, was *Elena: A Life in Soho*, written by Elena Salvoni in collaboration with Sandy Fawkes. Elena's memoirs told of how, after being born in Clerkenwell to Italian parents, she had arrived in Soho to be a waitress at the Café Bleu in wartime London; she then moved on to Bianchi's for many years before becoming the presiding *génie* at L'Escargot. Over many years she knew and was known by many legendary figures in the arts and show business, from Ella Fitzgerald and Vincent Price to Albert Finney, Stephen Spender and Barry Humphries. She had memories of Dylan Thomas and Brendan Behan drinking together; of Maria Callas refusing to be parted from her mink coat before being seated; of Donald Maclean dining 'in all innocence' two days before he defected to Russia. Her account was both personal and a slice of Soho's history.

Elena's launch party was held, appropriately, at L'Escargot and attracted a glittering array of illustrious names: Timothy West and Prunella Scales were there, alongside Anna Ford, Keith Waterhouse, Michael Frayn, Dan Topolski, Michael Palin, Auberon Waugh, Ned Sherrin, Nigel Hawthorne, A. N. Wilson, Anthony Howard, Elizabeth Squires and Ladies Cressida, Amelia and Victoria Ward. 'Londoner's Diary' in the *Standard* recorded that the celebrations, 'hosted by the effulgent Naim Attallah', had gone on into the early hours, 'when survivors grouped round a piano for a rousing chorus of "I'm In The Mood For Love" '. They had caught Melvyn Bragg in nostalgic mode, declaiming emotionally that, 'Elena is our mum. After she left Bianchi's we arrived here the next day. There are no other mums like Elena in Soho, although there are plenty of madams.'

A more problematic book published that year had its origin in a meeting that took place early in 1988 with a young author called Elisabeth Barillé, after I had been introduced to her by the French cosmetic journalist Elizabeth Arkus. Elisabeth Barillé's novel *Corps de jeune fille* was just then the latest literary sensation in Paris. She was Parisian born in 1960 and had gained degrees in English and Russian before becoming a freelance journalist contributing to *Paris-Match*, *Depêche Mode*, *Femme* and *Geo*.

She was currently literary editor of *L'Eventail*. I was entranced by her at our meeting. She had that kind of sexuality which disturbs the senses. I bought a copy of the book and started reading it on the plane back to London. It was a book I could not put down. Its appeal was more attuned to the avant-garde French reading public, but her use of language and the depth of insight into the human condition were impressive. I was determined that Quartet would publish an English version, even though certain expressions she used were going to be hard to translate into English without losing their nuances.

It told the story of twenty-three-year-old Elisa, audacious and sensual, who is accosted by a middle-aged writer in the Jardin du Luxembourg. She is intrigued and troubled by him after he seduces her and says he wants her to be the heroine of his next book. As he interrogates her on her childhood and aspects of her sexual awakening, the tone of the narrative darkens and they begin to play a game in which it is no longer clear who is preying on whom.

The French press had given the book some very positive reviews: 'A revelation . . . unpretentious and direct . . . truly liberated,' said *Marie-Claire*; 'Gay, tender, biting, playful . . . written with enthusiasm and zest,' said *France-Soir*; 'Vigorous, direct and lucid, sparing nothing and nobody,' said *Le Figaro Littéraire*. The English literary establishment was more ambivalent in its reception of the translated version under the title *Body of a Girl*. It came as no surprise, however, for I had always been aware that its appeal here would be limited. It belonged to a *genre* that had that intrinsically cerebral quality more consonant with European culture. Clarence de Roch in *Tatler* chose to focus on the book's erotic side. His opening paragraph set the mood of his piece: 'There's a brilliantly funny scene in Elisabeth Barillé's first novel, in which Elisa, the heroine, brings her suitor's amorous *élan* to an abrupt halt by staring at his exposed penis and describing it witheringly (literally so as it turns out) as looking "just like Cyrano's nose!" ' Cara Chanteau in the *Listener* was rather more dismissive:

> Jane Austen once wrote that in *Emma* she was planning a heroine 'which no one but myself would like': Barillé might, with a lot more justification, have said the same for *Body of a Girl*. It is a problem from which her novel never really recovers . . . [But] Barillé has a good and very fluent style; one could wish to see it employed on more searching subject matter. Perhaps the successor to *Body of a Girl* might be a little more sparing with the body and reveal rather more about the girl.

Janet Barron, for the *Literary Review*, found a degree of merit in the book, though she confessed that the use of some words made her blush:

I wouldn't recommend reading some of this in public; try convincing the chap who's peering over your shoulder that 'fanny' is a symbol of women's liberation. Barillé takes the obsessions of male erotic writing and attributes them to her narrator Elisa. The result is often witty. Barillé has a sardonic sense of humour and Parisian bohemianism is given a sarcastic twist.

Rebecca O'Rourke's reaction in the *Guardian* was especially damning:

Elisa's sexual history contains much that is surprising and some that is shocking. It's a joyless account, rehearsing without exploring the idea that women's autonomous sexuality is the province of whores and sluts. The special secret Elisa keeps to herself is compulsive masturbation, fuel to shameful self-hatred. Britain often looks to France, impressed by the latter's sexual freedoms and sophistication. Colette, Violette Leduc and Simone de Beauvoir made enormous contributions to women's writing by pioneering sensual, erotic and sexual themes. On the evidence of *Body of a Girl*, this pre-eminence is now receding.

In late 1990, Quartet published Elisabeth Barillé's second novel, *Marie Ensnared*. This time the author's obsession with prostitution manifested itself even more clearly. The story had the same resonance as *Body of a Girl*, but in this one the heroine began to lead a double life. To summarize the plot, Marie and her husband Luc, a charming and talented architect, apparently make the perfect bourgeois couple. While he provides her with a life of comfort and security, she is his perfect companion and hostess to the cosy, if complacent, dinner parties that are the cornerstone of his success. Then Luc accepts a commission to build a vast palace in the Moroccan desert for a rich megalomaniac Aloui, whose escort is Nalège, a malicious manipulative call-girl. Marie becomes fascinated by Nalège's lifestyle, seeing it as an emancipation from the trap of comfort that is her life with Luc. She becomes her understudy, but when Nalège sends her the obese, alcoholic Aloui, the arrangement ends in a disastrous surfacing of guilt and self-loathing, with Marie now the victim of male cruelty and her own emotional confusion.

When I read *Marie Ensnared* I strongly suspected that the book had an autobiographical basis and that Barillé's fictional account was a clever way of expressing her own dark secrets. Barillé's own explanation for her theme was that, 'Eroticism interests me more than sex. It's the staging of our sexual impulses.' But in the view of Jane O'Grady in the *Observer*, 'chic, pretty Marie' was both 'directing and starring in the film of her life, and Barillé's slim novelette resembles a soft-porn movie minus eroticism'. Neither *Body of a Girl* nor *Marie Ensnared* made the impact I personally had anticipated.

Somehow they failed to catch the mood of the literary public in Britain. *La différance* was once again manifesting itself.

Another book Quartet published that year was *A Woman's Story* by Annie Ernaux, translated from the French by Tanya Leslie. This was in a different genre, being an autobiographical novel by a daughter whose mother had died in an old people's home, a victim of Alzheimer's disease. For the author it was a literary venture designed to find out the truth about her mother, who with her husband had managed a grocer's shop in Normandy. She had been strong-willed and industrious, a voracious reader who encouraged her daughter not to speak in dialect so she would get on in the world and fulfil her mother's own thwarted ambitions. With the mother's decline, the daughter found she was having to deal within herself with ambivalent feelings of love and hate, tenderness and irritation. It was a moving, universal tale told with a stringent economy.

Quartet entered *A Woman's Story* for the *Independent* Foreign Fiction Award, just in case the unexpected happened, but apart from that it received almost no coverage in the UK. It was another case of modern French literature failing to travel well across the English Channel. One solitary mention of the book by Zoë Heller in the *Independent on Sunday* was typically brief: 'It is a cross between literature, sociology and history but with its confused oscillation between rage and "objectivity" it can only enact the crude anguish of a wake.' Literary editors were not prepared to devote space to these translated titles. In Britain the appetite for foreign literature has declined since the days of Camus, Sartre, de Beauvoir and even Françoise Sagan.

There were two biographical volumes published that year, both relating to aspects of modern German history. One of these was Robert C. Bachmann's *Karajan: Notes on a Career*, translated by Shaun Whiteside, and the other was Giles MacDonogh's *A Good German: Adam von Trott zu Solz*. In his study of von Karajan, Bachmann set out to penetrate the tangle of myth, flattery and half-truths with which the controversial career of this great German conductor was hedged about. He took a long, hard look at von Karajan's rise to power during the Third Reich, his role within Hitler's Germany, his bitter rivalry with Wilhelm Furtwängler and his fanatical devotion to his work, which often led him to deny the truth. Bachmann argued that it was his very fear of the truth that drove him to realize the 'cult of beauty' in his flawless interpretations.

MacDonogh's *A Good German* was an account of the life of a patriot and hero who was consistent in his opposition to the Nazis and was hanged in 1944 for his part in the bomb plot that failed to kill Hitler. It was also a powerful indictment of the British Foreign Office attitudes of suspicion that undermined his position and failed to take advantage of the opportunity he represented for ending the war at an earlier stage. MacDonogh had the cooperation of Adam von Trott's friends and family in writing the book, as well as access to newly released cabinet papers and an FBI file relating to von Trott's attempts to avert war during a visit to America. David Profumo in the *Sunday Times* said he had 'produced a work that is both witty and informative, and he wears his erudition with commendable lightness'. The wider aspects of European culture continued to figure prominently in Quartet's catalogue.

*

At midnight on Monday, 16 July 1990, fourteen hours after a dramatic smash-and-grab robbery at Asprey's showrooms in Bond Street that resulted in the loss of a diamond necklace worth seven hundred and fifty thousand pounds, I telephoned John Asprey at home to tell him we should be ready in about half an hour to sign with Sears for the takeover of the Mappin & Webb Group, which included Garrard, the Crown Jewellers. It was a telephone call John was anxiously awaiting. In the meantime, George Magan and Odile Griffith of Hambro Magan, merchant bankers to Asprey, were putting the final touches to a complex agreement with Geoffrey Maitland-Smith, chairman of Sears, and his advisers to seal this important transaction for a consideration of seventy-five million pounds in shares. No cash was involved. A long day and night ended only at 3 a.m., when the agreement was finally signed, and champagne glasses were raised to mark this momentous event before the exhausted parties retired to bed feeling ecstatic at having turned a dream into reality.

It had all begun long before, in the late 1950s, when Sir Charles Clore, the father of Sears Holdings, acquired the Mappin & Webb Group. The whole of his dream, however, was never fully realized. He had wanted Asprey as well. Looking on it longingly, he was wont to declare it would be 'the jewel in my crown'. His successors never totally ruled out the idea, but they were hampered by problems within the Mappin & Webb Group that made it impossible for them to contemplate an expansion of their jewellery interests until they had managed to stabilize what they possessed already. Nevertheless they continued to be attracted by the prospect of some sort of link-up with Asprey, if not outright acquisition. The wish was fuelled by the success Asprey were having in overtaking their competitors and growing faster than any observer had forecast. The chance of a link-up arose at last for Sears in 1979 when they bought from Maurice Asprey and his father their twenty-per-cent holding, so raising Sears's stake in Asprey to twenty-five point four per cent. The purchase earned Geoffrey Maitland-Smith a non-executive seat on the board of Asprey. In 1981 Asprey joined the Unlisted Securities Market, and thereafter, by virtue of the seat they had secured on the board, Sears became privy to the inner workings of Asprey and could see the potential of an enlarged group at first hand. The idea of an even closer link began to make sense, but Sears were biding their time.

The chief architect of that vision was Geoffrey Maitland-Smith, who saw clearly the advantages of a marriage between the two companies. It took him ten years to arrive at his objective. In the spring of 1990 he had requested a meeting with John Asprey and myself in isolation from the board. It was at this time that he suggested a merger between the two companies in which the Asprey family would not only still retain a controlling interest but would also be in charge of the overall management of the enlarged group. John's immediate reaction was to dismiss the idea. He was not in the least enthusiastic, and so far as I could see he did not give the proposal a moment's thought before rejecting it out of hand. His reaction took me aback. I moved swiftly to try and play down John's negative response by assuring Geoffrey that the matter would be given the most serious consideration; and made it clear at the same time that it had my unequivocal support.

John was often impulsive, reacting before he had thought things through. On this occasion the enormity of the challenge had taken him by surprise and unsettled him. It had made him admit to himself that he would not be confident enough to cope with such an enlarged group. He feared that we would immediately lose our way. I spelt out my own view, explaining that, while our profit growth was showing a steady rise year-by-year of twenty per cent, we could only maintain this by expanding our customer base. Otherwise we would inevitably become more vulnerable to dips in both profit and turn-over. Our aim should be not only to consolidate our present growth but also ensure that it was not going to come to a sudden standstill. This, I was adamant, could only be done by targeting a much larger share of the market. To do this we desperately needed to seek as many outlets as possible, and the Mappin & Webb Group would provide us with more than we needed. Eventually John was won over and he became as enthused by the prospect as I was. After such a long voyage to reach the goal, we could ill-afford to let it slip away in 1990.

At that point we felt truly masters of our destiny. Under the terms of the deal with Sears, the Asprey family retained fifty point seven per cent of the Ordinary shares and was given management control of three separate chains. Added to Asprey's showrooms in London and New York, as well as its cluster of related subsidiaries such as an art gallery and a bookbinders, were twelve Mappin & Webb outlets and three Garrard shops that were a part of Mappin.

Sears received eighteen point five million new participating preferred shares and increased its interest in Asprey's earnings to thirty-eight point five per cent. In 1989, Asprey had reached a record profit of twenty-one point nine million pounds on a turnover of seventy-five point three million pounds. With Mappin and Garrard as additional trading entities, the market now had the expectation that Asprey's group profits would hit twenty-seven million pounds.

Rufus Olin, writing in the *Sunday Times*, commented:

> A key figure in Asprey's new commercial edge is Naim Attallah, the Palestinian-born proprietor of Quartet Publishing, and author of *Women*, a book of 289 interviews with the rich and accomplished. He first met John Asprey as a customer, joined the board in 1974, and now controls the group's financial affairs as joint managing director. Attallah said that Asprey is not unduly worried by the slowdown in consumer spending. 'Money doesn't disappear. It changes hands and we target the people who have it.'

In an interview for the *Daily Mail*, I said:

> It will give us tremendous opportunities to expand by covering the middle ground which Asprey could not do because it is established at the top end of the market. But there will be no fall in standards. Asprey's secret has been the quality of its service and the fact that we look after any item you buy for as long as you own it.

According to the *Independent*, the merger was also going to give Asprey useful contacts in the Japanese markets, where both Mappin and Garrard already had outlets in the leading department stores, Seibu and Mitsukoshi. 'The businesses will continue to be run separately and Asprey intends to inject a new management into Garrard, currently run as one with Mappin & Webb.'

As soon as the euphoria had subsided I had to come to terms with the gigantic task that faced me. I was put in charge of the new acquisition in addition to my existing responsibilities at Asprey. The first priority was to streamline the two operations so that they became complementary while their autonomy remained unaffected. It was the biggest challenge I had so far encountered and was destined to change my life dramatically. I was going to have to organize my time more efficiently, and a pattern emerged where I spent most mornings at my office in Namara House but moved on in the afternoons to occupy my new offices four floors above the Garrard showrooms in Regent Street. My assistant at the time, Lucy Wastnage, an attractive young lady of mixed English and Italian parentage, loyally accompanied me from one office to the other until the day came when commuting between offices was proving irksome and unworkable. Sadly I had to leave Namara House after so many happy years and install myself permanently in my new suite of offices, taking Lucy with me.

On 11 September the *Financial Times* announced the restructuring I had so far achieved in the separation of Garrard from Mappin & Webb:

> Mr Naim Attallah, joint managing director of Asprey, has assumed the role of managing director of Mappin & Webb; Mr Paul Clayman remains as deputy managing director; Mr David Beckett, previously group financial director, now becomes financial and administrative director of Mappin & Webb; Mr Edward Green resigns from the board of Mappin & Webb, but remains managing director of Garrard & Co.

The *Daily Telegraph* in 'City Diary', under the heading 'Belt-tightening at Mappin & Webb', managed to present the item in a more popular tone to appeal to a non-specialist readership:

> That urban social butterfly Naim Attallah, famed for his flock of dewy-eyed personal assistants and for his publishing flair at Quartet Books, is having to dirty his hands with some 'tightening' at Mappin & Webb. Attallah has become managing director there following the acquisition of Mappin by Asprey (where he is group finance director and joint managing director).
>
> 'In certain areas we feel we're overmanned,' mused Attallah yesterday. 'Although in other areas we're undermanned.' The net result, though, will be fewer faces at Mappin, particularly in the financial and marketing departments. Attallah also refused to condemn Peter Palumbo's long-running plan to tear down Mappin's building in Poultry, by far its best publicity asset. 'I like traditions but we musn't stand in the way of progress: I'm flexible,' he purred.

While I was conducting the serious business of reorganizing the Mappin & Webb Group, an event occurred which gave me some much needed cheer: the recovery of my diary. It had been lost, along with my keys and bank statements, when my chauffeur inadvertently left my briefcase on the pavement outside Namara House after he opened the door for me to climb into the car. By the time we returned three minutes later, the case had vanished. The diary, bound in crocodile skin, had been made specially for me by Asprey. I would have given up all hope of recovering it, but the thieves lost no time in making contact, phoning half an hour later to ask what the reward would be. They scoffed at my offer of a hundred pounds, demanded five hundred instead, and promptly hung up. A further call followed after they had presumably inspected the contents of the briefcase more thoroughly. This time the figure had escalated to a staggering four thousand pounds, the reason being, the villains explained, 'You got money, man, and we haven't.' As petty thieves they were sure they had stumbled on a gold mine, but after I refused to consider their revised offer, there were no more calls. I accepted the loss as the weeks passed, but then received a call from a total stranger who lived on a barge on the Thames. He had seen my crocodile diary floating in the river and recovered it. Although he could barely make out the address, he did manage to decipher the phone number.

The diary was in a terrible state when my chauffeur collected it. The water had ruined everything inside, leaving nothing legible. It had a mouldy smell and so far as I could judge the beautiful crocodile cover was spoilt beyond repair. It was bloated and the edges had begun to disintegrate from the water pollution. Even so, I decided to show it to Asprey's leather workshop, where it had been made in the first place, to see if anything could be done. The workshop head, a highly renowned craftsman, took it in his hands, gently stroking it as if it was the corpse of a beloved dead bird, and said, 'Leave it with me. I can't promise miracles, but I will try to salvage whatever's possible.' Four weeks later, the crocodile diary was delivered to my office. It was slightly reduced in size, but looked magnificent. The skin had a glow that was better than new and its renovation represented craftsmanship at its very best: a tribute to the unparalleled expertise Asprey's leather workshop provided. The diary is still in my possession. It has never been used again but is preserved as a small monument to a conservation miracle. I often touch it gently, pondering on its history and its resurrection.

At the same time as I recovered my diary, however, I lost my chauffeur. Chris Parsons had been in my employment about eighteen months when the call of fame proved to be too much of a temptation to keep him behind the dashboard of even a Bentley. He had won a Tom Jones lookalike contest. He could sing like his hero besides looking like him and having his hair styled in the same way. When he told me about his ambition to take up a singing career, I advised caution, pointing out all the pitfalls of such a move and the downside of the competitive world he would be taking on. Nevertheless, I said, if he was determined enough he should have a go. If he made it I would be the first to ask for his autograph.

By some strange chance, the story came to the notice of Chris Hutchins, a journalist on the *Today* newspaper, who telephoned me to gauge my reaction. My chauffeur was a very nice chap, I told him, but he was starstruck. I knew that if he was offered the chance of spending a night with one of Tom's ladies or Tom himself, he'd choose Tom. Parsons confirmed the point when Hutchins put it to him, saying, 'The boss is right. If I could choose between a night with a group of beautiful girls and a few beers with Tom I would choose the latter. I drive my wife mad!'

For me it only confirmed what a truly bizarre world we live in. How could a red-blooded young man pass over the chance of spending a night with a bevy of beautiful young women for Tom Jones? I thought Chris Parsons must be barmy, and if I had been a psychiatrist, I would have recommended shutting him away on the grounds that the balance of his mind was disturbed.

It took me a short while to familiarize myself with every aspect of the Mappin Group; and having done that, I decided my first priority must be to cut down on overheads and cancel all current consultancies with outside firms. My belief has always been that resorting to third parties for help to sell or market one's product was to admit one had limitations. I wanted the group to be self-sufficient in every way, capable of servicing all its requirements in-house instead of relying on some whiz-kid whose theoretical expertise was unlikely to achieve results. The process of selling is simple if the basic rules are under-stood. Belief in the product is, in the first instance, the key to success, the next step being to persuade the client into sharing that belief. The rest becomes a natural progression towards the desired result. The art of selling lies in targeting the right customer with the right product; otherwise the exercise becomes a waste of energy and, invariably, the loss of an opportunity.

The human resources side to marketing was an area I studied carefully. Energy, flexibility and an aptitutude for creative thinking were more important to me than the much respected experience factor. A long-held job without these qualities is no yardstick by which to assess the worth of an individual or his or her potential usefulness to the company. It is the hunger in people that interests me the most, but it takes different forms and falls into different categories. Physical hunger is easily satisfied by the intake of an appropriate amount of food, while hunger for achievement, as with lust, is never satiated. It recognizes no boundaries and is therefore limitless in its appetite. It is a driving force that enlists our intellect in the pursuit of our ambitions, yet maintains us in a permanent state of want, of desire, of seeking fulfilment, of recklessness and sometimes of total ruthlessness. I have always viewed this form of hunger with a mixture of admiration and apprehension. It can be a force for good, or equally a force for evil, but without it our lives will lose momentum and come to a monotonous standstill. Since action is my maxim, I invariably take the risk where a person's hunger strikes me as being both strong and controlled. And I have never been afraid to test youth by giving it greater responsibility than is usual. With such a policy in mind, I began the task of overhauling the whole structure of Mappin, with no department excluded, the aim being to give it new impetus and inject new blood.

The good image formerly enjoyed by Mappin & Webb had been steadily eroded through the use of its outlets to market merchandise that had failed to sell at Garrard. Mappin became the dumping ground for slow-moving stock, or stock that had failed to appeal to its intended customers. The strategy behind this was to postpone the writing down of stock that would have affected the Mappin Group's profitability. It was one of the anomalies I discovered and refused to sanction in future. The autonomy concept must be adhered to and no interchange of merchandise was to take place without my written consent. The mere fact that both companies were part of the same group made the practice more unacceptable. There were no circumstances in which stock cycling or the bolstering of sales through inter-company transactions would be tolerated. These were merely ways of delaying the inevitable instead of taking the bull by the horns and getting rid of surplus stock by any means available. It was a matter of accepting a loss sooner rather than later. Realism in retailing is crucial and must always take into account the public mood when assessing market requirements. As soon as stock becomes redundant, it must be replaced by new merchandise reflecting current trends.

My ambitions for Mappin & Webb were twofold. On the one hand, I wanted to see it return to being a vibrant retailing outfit, with a special appeal to traditionalists who remembered its glory days when the name was synonymous with high-quality silver objects. On the other, I wanted to see it attracting the new generation of fashion-conscious consumers which had become a potent force that no forward-looking retailer could afford to ignore. These were my main reasons for a clean sweep at the executive level, starting with the marketing department, headed by Tom Goldstaub, whose wife was Jane Procter, *Tatler*'s editor in the wake of Emma Soames's sudden departure from the magazine. I felt Tom was high maintenance in his approach and the department itself was overstaffed. The whole marketing department was therefore reduced to two people. One of these was Jenny Aeron-Thomas, aged twenty-six, who was placed in charge of advertising. The other was Tania Foster-Brown, aged twenty-three, who took over publicity.

Both girls had a certain spark and their elevation proved to be an inspired piece of decision-making. Their brief was to work with Paul Clayman, the newly appointed deputy managing director of Mappin & Webb, while also reporting to me directly. Their office was in the suite of offices on the fourth floor above the Garrard showrooms where I had my new base. The close proximity of our offices enabled the fostering of a working relationship that was to revolutionize the public's perception of Mappin and place it at the forefront of shops with fashionable *élan*, thereby distinguishing it from other retailers who lacked the drive and innovation we were introducing to the marketplace. These were exciting days, when creativity and pioneering methods worked in tandem and where our vision of the future shaped our experiments of today, with emerging individual talent being given the freedom to explore its full potential.

It took a year before we were able to break through decades of stagnation. A new range of carefully chosen merchandise was giving the shops a revitalized look. The window displays were dramatic and eye-catching. Our advertising campaign reflected the new sophisticated image, with adverts that were truly works of art targeting a new generation of shoppers who were often dazzled by our mode of presentation and the glamour of our design. The shops had pizzazz. They were no longer drab and uninspiring but were pulsating with vitality. It was infectious. The staff felt it; so did the customers. The first stage in the grand strategy had been completed.

Thirty-eight

Preparations had meanwhile been going ahead at Quartet for the launch in the autumn of 1990 of my second book, *Singular Encounters*. Its pre-publication coverage had more or less matched that accorded to *Women*. Snippets from the book had appeared in the gossip columns of many news-papers and the stage was set, or so I thought, for another mauling at the hands of the sanctimonious few – and of those who had missed the opportunity to join in the onslaught on *Women*. This time, however, I felt seasoned and hardened by the first experience and was totally prepared. Nothing short of an earthquake was going to shatter my equanimity this time. Whereas the first book had been more of an experimental under-taking, an initiation into the art of interviewing, this one showed how far I had advanced along the learning curve. The experience had proved to be indispensable, given my determination to succeed in what had now become my chosen field.

As it turned out, my worst fears came to nothing. The reviews were com-plimentary in general, leaving to one side the inevitable bursts of cynicism. There were some who came up with a blend of spleen and qualified praise, as in the case of Lynn Barber, whose known trademark is vitriol. Reviewing the book for the *Independent on Sunday*, she began dismissively so no one could accuse her of failing to live up to her reputation:

> This is an easy way to throw a book together: interview twenty-nine elderly men at great length, get some poor sucker to transcribe the text and presto – a 628-page tome. The typist must be admired, if not the author. In his foreword, Mr Attallah mentions that his previous doorstop, *Women*, entailed doing 318 interviews in a year. That's almost one a day, so this effort presumably took slightly over a month. Choosing his subjects must have taken all of half an hour with the Rotalex.
>
> Having vented my spleen, I must now say that Naim Attallah is a good interviewer . . . [He] has the art of relaxing his subjects, so much so indeed that they often patronize him, perhaps because he is a foreigner with a funny hairdo. So much the better.

Fiona MacCarthy in the *Observer*, under the heading 'Pontificator's Paradise', called it 'fundamentally a book of fogeys' and 'an exercise in private hero worship and secret masochism'. Her verdict in the end was more self-revelatory than she intended:

> Attallah meant this book to entertain and inform. It is certainly enthralling as a study of male reticence, the reticence both of the subject and the author. But I also found it hauntingly depressing in its picture of male ageing, the ambitions running out . . . The general air of gentlemanly wryness emphasizes that men's lives have peculiar limitations; more so than many women's. Is it ecstasy they miss?

Sean French in the *New Statesman* drew attention to the 'change of title, from the all-embracing, monolithic *Women* to the assembly of particulars. Each man is awarded a discrete interview', which, he claimed, 'inferred that men have coherent, individual viewpoints, while women are part of a mysterious unity'. This was an assumption I totally rejected. In fact the book *Women* undermined the myth that their majority talk in unison about issues affecting their own lives or the lives of others. I had found them to be more intellectually independent than most men and the wealth of their different views constituted their strength and superiority in a diversity of fields. I wrote a letter to the *New Statesman* to correct this misrepresentation, saying how he had distorted and trivialized the project's integrity in order to 'present himself as a champion of feminism, or so it seems'.

> The hypocrisy behind the piece is breathtaking. What exactly are Sean French's credentials in this area? What contribution beyond lip-service has he made to the cause of women?
> My own support for women has been practical, not just theoretical. In the group of companies I control, I employ more women than men, and for the past thirteen years I have sustained The Women's Press not out of commercial motives but in the belief that women's voices should be heard.

Mr French continued his review by going on about my deep interest in sex:

> Even in this collection, it is still women who obtrusively preoccupy the interviewer. Attallah's concern for the public lives of his subjects is frequently perfunctory and dull. What he's really interested in is sex, and especially the question of how to get more of it. To the wheelchair-bound womanizer, Quentin Crewe: 'You have a legendary reputation for seducing women in general and beautiful young women in particular. What is your secret?'

The bit he wrote on Sir Gordon White, however, I thought was illuminating:

Sir Gordon White, carnivorous capitalist and partner of Lord Hanson, rejects feminism for this reason: 'My mother brought me up to believe that if I was in an aeroplane which was about to crash and there was one parachute I should give the parachute to the girl and should go down with the plane – exactly what happened with the *Titanic*. The men went down with the ship. The band played, and officers stood by with guns and pistols in case men tried to get into the lifeboats ahead of the women and children.'

What a pity the grand old code had to be enforced with firearms brandished by functionaries, who then got into the boats themselves, leaving hundreds of women and children with cheap tickets to go down with the ship. Since White's own business practice is the commercial equivalent of seizing boats and then making the women and children walk the plank, it's difficult to take his credo too seriously.

French ended his review in the same vein as he began:

The subjects are overwhelmingly right wing. The left's sole representative seems to be A. N. Wilson, who emerges as the most likeable of the inter-viewees. It is fascinating to see the contortions these misogynistic men undergo when they discuss Mrs Thatcher. They admire but dislike her, and her success does nothing to change their view that women don't belong in politics.

The twenty-nine men are a motley collection, composed largely of *Spectator*-ish contributors to the *Literary Review*, with a few of the sort of people Attallah probably bumps into at parties. After more than 600 pages of being harangued by them, I felt that Andrea Dworkin may have a point after all.

In making this intended *coup de grâce* with a sympathetic reference to Andrea Dworkin, he was possibly unaware that I had published two of her books: her radical *Pornography: Men Possessing Women* and *Right-Wing Women*.

Emma Soames, having referred previously to *Women* as 'a dog's dinner', was full of praise for the new volume in her review for the *Evening Standard*:

In this collection of interviews with thirty [*sic*] men of some degree of fame and *gravitas*, Naim Attallah proves himself to be a deft and sensitive questioner who appears both to have done his homework and – more originally – to have listened to the answers provided by the objects of his curiosity. Students of public life in Britain could do a lot worse than invest in this volume about men who, if not actually in public life themselves,

[450]

have spent most of their lives basking in the light cast by the Establishment or, in some cases, gnawing like moths at the edge of its fabric.

She also ended her piece on a positive note:

> The subjects discussed range broadly, depending on the speciality of the interviewee; but childhood, the opposite sex, politics and religion are common to most. The closing questions to some of the older men elicit much wisdom and thoughtfulness.

Andrew Billen in the *Listener* attempted to make his piece humorous at the expense of the author and his subjects. In this he was only partially successful in my view. He seemed to have tried too hard to achieve his objective and ran out of ideas in midstream. The humour then lost its originality and became wearying towards the end. He adopted a question-and-answer mode like that in the book:

> *The best thing about Attallah's previous collection of interviews,* Women, *was his subjects' views on sex. Is there much about sex in this volume?*
>
> Most of the conversations get round to it in the end, although Richard Ingrams, Auberon Waugh and A. N. Wilson refused to play. If you were being priggish you might object to him provoking Quentin Crewe into accounting for his conquests by the thought that women want to know what it is like to go to bed with someone who is disabled. You wonder if Attallah doesn't half agree with Gordon White, another Casanova apparently, when he says: 'All men are led by their cock.' He shamelessly leaves in some knowing references to his own libido. Fred Warner observes: 'Some people need it two or three times a day – you, if I may say so, have quite a reputation round the town.'
>
> *You talked earlier about extracting 'a line' from an interview. What lines would you take from Attallah?*
>
> In most cases here it would be no trouble at all. You have got to admit that most of his subjects, with the odd exception, like A. N. Wilson and Yehudi Menuhin, have opened up to him to an unusual degree. He has done his homework and that usually inspires a kind of flattered intimacy. All the following was new to me: Michael Aspel did have an affair with a Miss World contestant; Raymond Carr claims he and Philip Toynbee competed with each other to see how many women they could sleep with; Lord Lambton liked Oswald Mosley 'very much'; poor old Monsignor Gilbey never converted anyone in his life; Edmund White has fallen out with Susan Sondheim (surely some mistake?) because she thinks he put her in one of his novels; Gordon White, even more unpleasant than you

expected, believes blacks in South Africa should have the vote only if they are over fifty. These are not world exclusives, but they'd make any interviewer, or diary editor, pretty happy.

In some cases though, take Galbraith or Acton, there's nothing much surprising at all, is there?

You've got me there.

So what's the point of them being in the book?

I have answered five questions, and that is enough. Don't give yourself airs. Do you think I can listen all day to such stuff? Be off, or I'll kick you downstairs.

In *The Times Literary Supplement*, Aisling Foster was critical that the author had not done enough probing. As an example, she cited my interview with Edmund White,

[who] talked almost exclusively about homosexuality, gay writing and AIDS; his own brush with insanity and his sister's incestuous relationship with the father are mentioned but ignored. One wishes Attallah would intervene, probe, go back, but always he defers to his subject's determination to stick to the set text. Confronted by his apparently liberal stance, one can almost hear Monsignor Gilbey's quiet chuckle as he turns an intransigent cheek: 'The idea of the church changing is as foreign to me as equality or democracy.'

The way she ended the review was both curious and enlightening:

A large number of interviewees are more lyrical. At first, claims by the likes of Auberon Waugh of a preference for women's company seem suspect, a sort of modern flag of liberation. It is only as one reads on and on through all this talk, man-to-man, that one recognizes a real need for masks to slip. Despite some prurient prompting, sex is usually shrugged off as irrelevant or a thing of the past, with only Sir Gordon White (chairman of Hanson Industries) mentioning a current young girlfriend 'who is very much interested in the body'. Finally one is left wondering how much one can believe of what these men say they think. More than 600 pages of hard talking only confirms a suspicion long held by women: that men, when alone, do not really talk to one another at all.

Francis Wheen in the *Spectator* was teasingly funny without pomposity or cynicism. His piece was lighthearted and evoked the book's general thrust:

Long before the phrase 'positive discrimination' had been coined, the owner of Quartet Books, Naim Attallah, devised the admirable employment strategy which he follows to this day: he would hire a dozen women for every man. The only slight qualification was that the women must be called Sackville-West, Bonham-Carter or Heathcoat-Amory. No, I'm being unfair. Several women with no more than a single barrel to their surnames have been recruited in recent years. And who are they? Oh, Anna Pasternak, Sonamara Sainsbury, Jubby Ingrams . . .

What is it with Naim and these young things? There are two schools of thought. One holds that his females-only rule is proof that Naim, unlike most men, 'actually likes women'. The other is hinted at by Arthur Schlesinger in this book. In reply to a question about President Kennedy's womanizing, the historian of Camelot says to Attallah: 'I was not aware of anything undue going on. If you went to the Kennedys' for dinner, there were always pretty girls, but I'm all in favour of that. So I understand are you.'

Poor old Naim. He tells us that when he conducted the twenty-nine interviews whose transcripts make up this book, 'I set out to be as invisible as possible.' Try as he may, however, his subjects (all of whom are men) will insist on turning the questions back on him . . . Attallah's book – the vastly superior sequel to his 1986 production, *Women* – reveals what hilarious rot most men talk on the subject of the opposite sex. 'Women don't like each other's company, don't form clubs,' Monsignor Gilbey pronounces confidently. 'They don't like that to be said, of course, but the fact is plain to see.' Plain, that is, to an unmarried priest living in the Travellers' Club who has apparently never heard of the Women's Institute. 'The major part of your leisure hours must be spent with men,' Nigel Dempster warns, as if disclosing an Eleventh Commandment. Why? Because 'you can't play squash with a woman, or golf with a woman, or tennis with a woman . . . women are not very good at it'.

The fact Anna Ford had written her own book about men made her a natural choice for the *Daily Telegraph* as a reviewer for my book. It was a challenging task for her to undertake, and she did it with grace and intelligence. Notwithstanding her strong views on the inequality between men and women in our society, she produced a well-balanced piece. I always had a soft spot for Anna, despite our falling-out for a brief period over a misunderstanding concerning my book *Women*. It was an estrangement we both regretted, but we soon made up for lost time after we became friends again. The final paragraph of her review was somehow philosophical:

I would have liked Naim to have taken a leaf from Studs Terkel, who says he was impelled by the lyrics of a Mahalia Jackson gospel song he had heard years before – 'Dig a little deeper.' What is best about so many men is what is buried deep, but as some have learnt, it may be too painful a process to dig it out.

Victoria Mather in the *Literary Review* liked the book. In her conclusion to a comprehensive review she commented:

> The fascination of *Singular Encounters*, and it is compulsive entertainment, is its gossipy, conversational nature. The men let Naim Attallah in by the front door. What he has done is nipped through and unlocked the back door for us.

The *Daily Mail*, which usually took a hostile line where I was concerned, had a friendly piece from Polly Sansom, who later married David Gilmour of the leading rock band Pink Floyd. I was famed for my fascination with women, she said, eulogizing them at every opportunity, though 'the real Naim Attallah is not as his sugar-daddyesque image might suggest'. The overall effect of the new book was 'rather like being at a gentleman's club as the port is passed around. Witty, indiscreet but sometimes incoherent. The fact that the men in this volume talk so openly is surely a testament to his charm which until now was only really known to women.'

But the response to the book I remember best was the skit, in lieu of a review, penned by the late Humphrey Carpenter for the *Sunday Times*. It was beyond doubt a send-up, but its wit and hilarity were its saving grace. He constructed it so as to beguile the reader with its originality. I loved it for what it was: a little gem encapsulating the English sense of humour at its best. I wrote to Humphrey, whom I had never met, to tell him how brilliant I thought his piece was and invited him to lunch. It thrilled him that I had taken no offence at his ribbing. I have continued to admire the piece to this day, but to enjoy it means it must be reproduced in its entirety. I hope the reader will appreciate it as much as I have done. It is a joyful piece of writing, skilfully crafted and irresistibly amusing.

Hallowed Be Thy Naim

1. And the Lord created Naim Attallah and sent him from Palestine to London to be chairman of Quartet Books. And the Lord God said to his servant Naim, Increase and multiply.
2. And Naim Attallah published *The Joy of Sex* and *More Joy of Sex*, and showed his balance sheet to the Lord, and said, Lord, I have increased and multiplied, and done thy bidding. And the Lord God said, That was not quite what I had in mind.

3. And the Lord God said unto Naim Attallah, If thou art going to be a prominent London publisher, then thou wilt have to get thyself a lot of women, so that people will talk about thee. And Naim said unto the Lord, Lord, I will do thy bidding.

4. And Naim Attallah went into the highways and byways of Sloane Square, and hired a lot of young women with double-barrelled names to work for him, and said Lord, I have done Thy bidding. And the Lord God said, That was not quite what I had in mind.

5. And the Lord God said unto Naim Attallah, If people are are going to talk about thee, and if thou art going to make the gossip columns, thou wilt have to become intimate with a lot of successful members of the opposite sex. And Naim Attallah said unto the Lord, Lord, I understand, and will do Thy bidding.

6. And Naim Attallah went into the highways and byways and found 318 remarkable women whose common denominator was achievement. And Naim Attallah published the interviews in a book called *Women*, and said unto the Lord, Lord, I have done Thy bidding. And the Lord God sighed and said, That was not quite what I had in mind.

7. And Naim Attallah said unto the Lord, Lord, I am bored and dejected now that the excitement of publishing my book *Women* is over, so I will go and publish a book on men. And the Lord God said, Naim, my servant, why on earth do you suppose anyone wants to read a book about men?

8. And Naim, the servant of the Lord, said Lord, I will call it *Singular Encounters*, because then some people will suppose it to be a sequel to *More Joy of Sex*, but actually, Lord, it will be a book of interviews with twenty-nine remarkable men whose common denominator is achievement.

9. And the Lord said, Naim, didst thou say twenty-nine? Why hast thou not interviewed 318 like last time? And Naim said, Lord, I am not as young as I was, and anyway, I do not like men as much as women, because I was not at an English public school.

10. And anyway, went on Naim, it was very difficult to persuade even twenty-nine men to take part. Most of those I approached, Lord (as I say in my introduction), were over-cautious. But then Richard Ingrams said yes, and encouraged some others, and soon Auberon Waugh agreed too.

11. And the Lord God said, Who is this Richard Ingrams and this Auberon Waugh? And Naim said, Lord, Ingrams is a man whose daughter works for one of my companies, and Waugh is the editor of the *Literary*

Review, of which I am the proprietor. And the Lord God hid a smile and said, I see, I see.

12. And the Lord God said unto Naim his servant, Naim, who are the other twenty-seven that thou hast persuaded to take part? And Naim said, Lord, there is Willie Rushton, Nigel Dempster and A. N. Wilson. And the Lord God said, Who are these people? And Naim said, They have all written for *Private Eye*, as have Ingrams and Waugh. And the Lord God said, Naim, thou dost not appear to have a very big circle of friends.

13. And Naim said, Lord, there is also Sir Harold Acton and Monsignor Alfred Gilbey. And the Lord God said, Who are they? And Naim said, Acton was a friend of Waugh's father and Gilbey is well known unto Wilson. And the Lord God said, That leaves twenty-two to go. Thou hast not covered much ground yet.

14. And Naim, the servant of the Lord, said, Lord there is also Michael Aspel, J. K. Galbraith, Yehudi Menuhin and Lord Rees-Mogg. And the Lord God said, And what made you choose these men? And Naim the servant of the Lord said, Lord, they all great and famous men. And the Lord God said, I see. I was beginning to think they were just chaps you just happen to have met at dinner-parties.

15. And the Lord God said, Naim, what questions hast thou asked? And Naim said, I have asked two of my interviewees whether it is true they have long-running feuds with Gore Vidal. And I have asked Willie Rushton whether he has opened a lot of fêtes. And I have asked the Warden of St Anthony's College, Oxford, what is the secret of his charm. And I have asked . . .

16. And the Lord God interrupted Naim and said, Naim, how on earth did you think of such daft questions? And Naim not listening went on, And I have asked André Deutsch about his disagreement with Tom Rosenthal and I have asked Lord Lambton why young journalists find Margaret Thatcher sexually attractive. And the Lord God said, I do not believe this.

17. And Naim, the servant of the Lord, smiled and said, Maybe, Lord, but I have featured in magazines and have made the front page of the Style section of the *Sunday Times*, and I have never had such coverage before in my life. So maybe, Lord, I know what I am doing after all.

18. And the Lord God nodded, and said, Naim, my servant, maybe you do.

My admiration for the piece notwithstanding, I succumbed to the temptation of writing a letter to the *Sunday Times*, which they published. It was meant to reciprocate the humour:

Your celestial mole has misinformed Humphrey Carpenter. The Lord's original bidding was done by William Miller, a founding father of Quartet Books. He continues the work of the Lord in Japan while I, a humble disciple, carry on in the highways and byways of Sloane Square and Soho. The Lord God knows there is no mystery about the 'daft questions'. His servant has become a journalist.

There was a final amusing shot in the *Sunday Times* from Mr Simon Kamlinsky in Manchester:

And the Lord God said unto Naim Attallah his servant, Why have you not included Humphrey Carpenter in your book *Singular Encounters*.

He is distinguished in the field of jazz and letters, has written biographies of Auden, Pound and Tolkien, besides children's tales and a study of Jesus, a subject very dear to my heart, though regrettably issued in the Past Masters series.

Furthermore, he seems to have written on, if not been acquainted with, Sir Harold Acton and Evelyn Waugh, who both feature in your book, the latter albeit at second-hand.

And Naim said unto the Lord, Not only is this Carpenter not related to my twenty-nine chosen men, but his daughters are not yet of an age to be endowed with the attributes necessary to serve under me. Moreover, he has worked for the BBC and is thus very likely to be a bit of a Bolshie, a word which I am told is common coin in English public schools. Finally, he is published by others whom I would not sully my lips or offend your ears by mentioning.

And the Lord God said unto Naim, My servant, you have acted wisely. Long may you prosper in my tents. Go thou now out and hearken unto others so that you may spread my Word and feather your nest at the same time.

In Scotland the *Scotsman*, through its 'Tibbie Sheil's Diary' column, could see little that was publicizable about *Singular Encounters*, with the interviewees being mostly past the first flush of youth and originating from a handful of public schools, and Scots being 'noticeably absent'. Yet perhaps the most balanced appraisal of all came from Betty Kirkpatrick in the *Glasgow Herald*, under the heading 'Encounters of the most quotable kind'. She made the point that even the best-written autobiographies have their boring patches, but 'a book just published' – *Singular Encounters* – managed to avoid 'this pitfall'. It adopted the 'interview approach which makes for more lively reading than the average biography'.

But what I like most about the book is the diversity and breadth of its coverage – 'by design a rare miscellany', writes the author – and the fact that you can dip into it at will. Many books I devour at a gulp but I like to keep at least one book by me for occasional savouring, and *Singular Encounters* fits the latter category perfectly.

With such a book you feel no compulsion to start at the beginning. You can put a toe in the water at any point. I chose to start with Updike and found his interview/biography, like so many of the others, a treasure-chest of quotable quotes. After-dinner speakers take note . . . there's someone for everyone here – musicians, publishers, economists, businessmen and the odd one of whom I've said, 'Who's he?' But that's part of the charm of the book.

Publication was marked in Scotland by a reception at the Royal Society of Edinburgh. 'Why then,' asked Julie Morrice tartly, as 'Gatecrasher' in *Scotland on Sunday*, 'should the great Mr Attallah suffer the indignity of a flight up to Edinburgh, cocktails, dinner, and a night in the Caledonian?'

Mr Attallah's pilgrimage to Edinburgh was not, as scurrilous gossip suggested, in order to buy up the Canongate imprint, but simply because Anne Smith, *grande dame* of the Scottish literary scene, 'decided to give this party for us'.

It behoved me to seek out this Lady Bountiful, and eventually I found her, stubbing out a cigarette in the dregs of a glass of Leith claret. But as I approached, a distant tinkling ushered in a memory of some past unpleasantness. Could these be the self-same Anne Smith and Naim Attallah who fell out over the *Literary Review* . . . ?

Understandably shaken, I accepted a spiral-bound tuna on brown bread, and dropped into a nearby seat. Something cold and inflexible caused me to jump slightly, and out from under my thigh slipped an invitation card, edged in gold, and large and stiff enough to double as a tea-tray. Sure enough 'Anne Smith and Naim Attallah request the pleasure of your company . . . ', a public reconciliation. How charming, and indeed, what a Singular Encounter.

For the London launch a few days earlier, more than four hundred guests crowded into the ballroom of the Hyde Park Hotel for a cocktail party. Among them were the Marquess of Worcester, Patrick Ryecart with his wife, Viscount Linley, Sir Robin Day, Gordon Honeycombe, Cheri Lunghi, Imran Khan, Robert Kilroy-Silk and several of those who featured in the book, including Colonel Henry Townsend, Nigel Dempster, Sir Raymond Carr, Richard Ingrams and Auberon Waugh.

As Kate Saunders recorded in her 'Style and Travel' piece in the *Sunday Times*, 'the fragrant young things in Chanel jackets' had been arriving in a fit of sniggers 'at the way the top-hatted porters' at the hotel 'kept asking if one was headed for the "Ayatollah Party"'.

> Honestly, as if one would miss *Twin Peaks* for a party thrown by some dull old Ayatollah.
>
> The host's proper name was Naim Attallah. 'Attallah the Fun' to his friends. . . .
>
> Thirteen of Attallah's victims are classically public school and Oxbridge, and most of the rest behave is if they were. Not the types to drop amazing revelations, you may think – but the guests who had read *Singular Encounters* were giggling over Sir Harold Acton's confessions about his Chinese mistress, and the ancient Monsignor Gilbey's antediluvian comments about women. Had the old boy, who has lived for years in a gents' club, ever seen one? And how on earth did Naim persuade him to talk so frankly? The Monsignor did not leave his monkish retreat for the party.

Nigel Dempster declared to Kate that I had conned him into doing the interview. 'He's very cunning, you know. I fell for that Palestinian charm.'

> Attallah's charm is so dazzling that it has conquered the tweedy old heart of the British Establishment – a near impossible feat for a foreign johnny who wasn't at anyone's house at public school. Tuesday's turn-out was proof of his influence among the upper crust. The 400 or so guests, tipping back champagne beneath a chandelier while a string quartet sawed away at Mozart, were mainly a colourful mix of literary style-leaders . . . and lovely young females who knew somebody who knew somebody . . .
>
> Attallah stood at the entrance to the ballroom, greeting each guest with a little personalized effusion. Male guests had their hands pumped energetically, and basked in the soothing torrent of his accented English. The female guests were caressed, squeezed and generally bombed with love. He was thrilled to see absolutely everybody, and the feeling was mutual.

One unidentified posh gent was overheard saying, 'He doesn't need to write books, you know. It's just his hobby.'

> To the upper classes, there is something intrinsically admirable about chaps who write books just for a hoot, and never think of anything as vulgar as cash . . . He has won influential friends in this quarter by giving jobs to their bright and willing daughters, often freshly down from Oxford

and dying to get into publishing. Known as 'Naim's Harem', Attallah's penthouse office is always decorated with fresh-faced maidens whose names have the snob appeal of fine old crusted port. Many a clever gel began her career in Attallah's empire . . .

Attallah himself sighs and rolls his eyes whenever he hears the word 'harem'. 'People have called Quartet a finishing school for posh girls. And now, whenever a girl comes to work for me, people try to frighten the life out of her. As if she had to be warned against me! . . . When you get an upper-class girl to work for you,' he said, 'she doesn't mind what you ask her to do – she doesn't have a big chip on her shoulder, so she won't say it is not her place to lick stamps or make coffee. I personally don't agree with the British class system. I firmly believe that it is wrong to evaluate people by their accent, or which school they went to. But unfortunately, that is the way this country works. If you come from a comfortable background, you are likely to be more confident and secure . . .

'There is no secret to the interviews in my books, except that I care about people. And I get very involved – if you tell me about your feelings in depth, I might start to cry. It would no longer be just an interview.'

By 10 p.m. the party was beginning to thin out after three hours, though the champagne had not yet all gone. I could stand down from waiting by the door, feeling more relaxed and mingling with those guests who remained.

Attallah surveyed his guests benignly. 'I hate meanness, you know. I hate to be cruel. I never get any enjoyment from it. All relationships have their ups and downs, but I only remember the good things. People are very important to me. At the end of a hectic day, you should put your head on your pillow and go to sleep easily, knowing you have done no harm to anyone.'

His chauffeur was waiting. Naim went home to his pillow in Mayfair, feeling as satisfied as Longfellow's village blacksmith. Something attempted, something done and several hundred important pals filled with champagne had earned him a night's repose.

'Naim Attallah's massively expensive book launch is paying dividends,' announced *Private Eye*, '(even if at £20,000 this works out to be a grand per copy sold).'

It generated not only a slavish piece by Anneka-Rice lookalike Kate Saunders in the *Sunday Times*, but an appearance for Naim-Dropper on Radio 4's *Start the Week*.

Naim plugged his book which, as the programme's host Melvyn Bragg explained, consisted of interviews with twenty-nine important men. This innocent observation provoked another guest, Sir Robin Day, to declare that none of the men in the book is important, particularly Michael Aspel. Surely Sir Robin is not suggesting that Aspel should have been excluded because he is a mere television personality?

The *Bookseller*, the organ of the book trade, had rarely been kind to me or appreciative of Quartet's efforts during the years of my proprietorship. Their dismissive attitude to our contribution to publishing in general and their constant sneers at me personally had both become tediously tiresome. The magazine never lost an opportunity to be disparaging and I felt the editorial staff had it in for us, though I was never able to fathom the reason. I would not have minded their sniping if it had been witty or illuminating. It was invariably acidic and mocking, and discarded accuracy in favour of sensationalism. With *Singular Encounters* they decided on a change of tack. Instead of a frontal attack, they opted for the more subtle device of inventing an award. In February 1991, Jonathan Sale, whoever he may have been, suggested under the heading of 'Fairly Glittering Prizes' that there was a gap to be filled in the list of literary awards. This was to be called 'The Naim Attallah Vanity Publishing Award'. Its citation went as follows: 'Open only to publishers who have persuaded themselves, against their better judgement, to print their own scribblings. Winners have all unsold copies from the massive print run taken off their hands at half-price, and pulped.'

The joke had by then worn so thin as no longer to be remotely funny, yet it was the sort of rubbish the *Bookseller* kept on publishing, and it included an assertion that had no basis in fact, as I clearly indicated in my letter to the editor:

I am sure I am not alone in finding Jonathan Sale's Naim Attallah Vanity Publishing Award (22nd February) a rather laboured joke. My book *Women* grossed around £60,000 in serialization sales alone, and sold almost 20,000 copies in hardcover. The *Sunday Telegraph* and *Observer* took extracts from *Singular Encounters*, which is selling well and continues to arouse great interest.

Neither book will be remaindered; indeed, *Women* remains one of Quartet's all time bestsellers, the profits from which enable us to publish new translations of classics like *The Brothers Karamazov* and other less famous but highly distinguished works of literature. If such are the benefits of 'vanity' publishing to one of the few enterprising and independent publishing houses left, then by all means let us have vanity in abundance.

Publishing News, the other organ of the book trade, featured me on a regular basis, but in sharp contrast with the *Bookseller* was more imaginative. Its editorials were also genuinely funny. They had the indirect effect of encouraging me to laugh at myself and to appreciate humour even when it was at my own expense. None of their pieces ever made me feel threatened or left me suspecting a malicious intent. Nor did I believe that they showed signs of a bias against me personally or Quartet as a publishing enterprise. It was a case of lampooning a character whom they considered a fair target on account of his high public profile and the many strings he had to his bow. I accepted their jesting with amused resignation.

By an accident of delayed effect, one of the last judgements passed on *Singular Encounters* came in June 1991 from David George of the *Jerusalem Post*, in a notice which toiled through a litany of negative comments with a plodding determination, starting with a description of *Women* as 'a jumble of misinterpretations of what those women really had to say'. Mr George then took up the publicity claim that the new book was remarkable: 'He is correct; it's remarkably dull.'

> Without any real focus or direction to these interviews, twenty-nine well-known and not-so-well-known men ramble on interminably about anything that comes to mind. William F. Buckley Jr reflects on the joys of political conservatism; John Kenneth Galbraith bemoans the fact that John F. Kennedy failed to take his advice about Vietnam; John Updike mumbles a few words about whether he finds writing easy; and Lord Arnold Goodman reflects on why lawyers never seem popular as a group . . . All in all, this is a collection of biographical interviews well worth ignoring.

The publication of *Singular Encounters* in the United States took place in May, with a launch party held at Mortimer's, one of the trendiest restaurants in New York at the time. Even more significant was the agreement of Nan Kempner, the famous American socialite, to co-host the party with Whitney Tower Jr, another figure on the New York social scene, who also happened to be a good friend of mine. (Sadly, Nan Kempner died earlier in 2006, as I was working on this book.) 'Suzy', the chronicler of New York's celebrities and their doings, heralded the evening as a forthcoming event in her column in the *New York Post*:

> You've heard about power breakfasts. How about power book parties to celebrate books about powerful men? The big boys written about in a new tome titled *Singular Encounters* are symbols of success, talent, wealth, glamour and other aphrodisiacs, and *Singular Encounters* and its author Naim Attallah will be celebrated at a party at Mortimer's tomorrow

evening . . . Expected at Mortimer's for the fun are such terminal bookworms as Fernanda and Jamie Niven, Mica and Ahmet Ertegun, Nina Griscom Baker, Shelley Wagner Mortimer, Alexandra and Arthur Schlesinger, Blaine and Robert Trump, Marianne Strong, John H. Davis and, of course, Pat Buckley. Why should she miss a party when, after all, her husband is one of the book's subjects. Why, indeed?

Singular Encounters was the book that consolidated my working relationship with Jennie Bradshaw (now Erdal). It began with *Women* and after that spanned fifteen years of close literary collaboration and a whole series of titles. The first two books were very much a team effort, spearheaded by Jennie. They could never have been produced on schedule, as they were, without the back-up of many others at Quartet or Peter Ford's self-effacing but substantial contribution to the often complex work of editing. Rosemary Graham (now Gray) described the process from the viewpoint of the Goodge Street office: 'After Jennie had edited the material from the transcripts and the shape of the text was in its final form, it was sent to Peter Ford for an over-all copy-edit; in due course I received the finished typescript and tried to spot any remaining errors. I would then phone Jennie to discuss anything I had found and raise any queries of my own. Once all problems had been resolved, the end result went off to be typeset. Then followed the painstaking task of reading the proofs!'

Considering the historical background to the remarkably productive partnership I had with Jennie, I found it heartbreaking, long after it had ceased, to see her pull it all apart in public. The book she wrote bears witness to her indifference to any version of the truth but her own. It is a one-sided account and her motive in writing it is still unclear to me. Our relationship had always been a model of professionalism, and one that existed, as I thought, between close friends. The nagging question remains: why turn on our unique collaboration and destroy the memory of it – a memory I would have treasured for the rest of my life?

I remain at a loss to unravel the mystery, even after the passage of time. The word 'regret' has never had a place in my vocabulary, yet it is the only word to use on this single sad occasion. However, for the sake of maintaining a sensible impartiality, I intend in the pages that follow to remain faithful to the past as I viewed it then with unsuspecting eyes.

Thirty-nine

When Ros de Lanerolle celebrated the tenth anniversary of The Women's Press in 1988, the mood was very bullish with a turnover of one and a half million pounds achieved and a production rate of sixty titles a year. The reputation of the Press had also placed it firmly alongside the major publishing houses. In an interview she gave to Angela Neustatter in the *Guardian* in April 1988, she had pointed out how both Virago and The Women's Press had done more than produce books of worth. They had also created a market for feminist writing, launched many leading women writers and succeeded in making feminist writing fashionable. She also made an emphatic statement on her own future policy:

> We may have got the books where we want them but we certainly don't have a society which can get its head around the notion that women are half the population, so we have to go on demonstrating that they are both mainstream and have something interesting and important to contribute.

Ros hailed from South Africa and had her own good credentials as a writer and editor of radical publications. She was also a founder member of Women in Publishing. When she took over the helm of The Women's Press in 1981, she had the approval of both myself as backer and Stephanie Dowrick as outgoing editor. Her achievements at the Press were by no means inconsiderable, but by the early 1990s the early promise she had shown and her sharp eye for talent were failing to have the same impact. She was passionate in her idealism as a radical publisher, intent on upholding minority rights and highlighting the oppression of women worldwide, especially with reference to the African continent. The failure, in the end, was in not seeing the wider picture from a commercial perspective. She seemed to become locked into publishing material from South Africa, India, Iran, Algeria, Central America, Canada and China that at the time made little impression on the lucrative European market on which our livelihood depended.

Maybe she was working ahead of cultural trends, but in the meantime our very survival was at stake. With the years there had been a gradual erosion of the commercial appeal of the The Women's Press list, till it reached the point where it was firmly in the doldrums, with a diminished profile and a lack of press coverage. Ros was blinkered to these signs of impending disaster and could not see any need for a change of direction. She remained convinced that the emergence of markets in Africa, the Far East and Central America would in no time restore profitability. Unfortunately the reality was rather different. Meanwhile Stephanie Dowrick, who remained chairwoman of the Press and had been its guiding light throughout, became disillusioned with the path the imprint she had founded was taking. For its income the Press had been reliant on the backlist built up by Stephanie, but this was now beginning to show signs of its age and was clearly in need of a fresh creative drive.

I tried very hard to persuade Ros that it would be possible for her to seek out more commercial manuscripts without in any way compromising the declared aims or the integrity of the Press. It was simply a matter of reinstating its original concept by not forgetting its European roots. The balance of the list, I stressed, should take into account the market trends and be geared accordingly. But her vision of the markets was clouded by the strong idealism that, strangely enough, was both her strength and her weakness. She was unable to disassociate one from the other. My working relationship with Ros had been exceptionally good over the years, and she had enjoyed total editorial freedom, even if, on occasion, I had disapproved of some of the books she published. My support began to wane as it became clear that her editorial policy was having a negative effect on the Press finances and giving everyone involved a cause for concern. Both Stephanie and I felt we could no longer sustain our backing in the light of Ros's reluctance to change and adapt.

Another worrying aspect involved office politics. Stella Kane, who later became Quartet's production manager, has written a snapshot of how life was at The Women's Press when she joined it in the mid 1980s.

The Sisterhood
by Stella Kane

In May 1986 I left Penguin Books to join The Women's Press as their production manager, working for Ros de Lanerolle, the managing director, and with a team that included Mary Hemming, sales director, Suzanne Perkins, art director, Katy Nicholson and Jacqui Roach in publicity and, in editorial, Lorraine Gamman, Jen Green, Sarah LeFanu and Rachel Pyper. The Women's Press Book Club was run by Alison Hennigan.

Ahead of the times, we were one of the first wave of creatives to move into the Clerkenwell area, turning a dilapidated loft space into a modern open-plan minimalist office. Despite the revolutionary feminist fervour in the air, all was not a bed of roses in the Sisterhood. Not a day would go by without arguments about political correctness, accusations of racism, endless debates over whether we should allow the male postman to come into our work space or leave the post outside the front door, and the monthly premenstrual tantrums that often ended in someone locking themselves in the 'wimmin's' loo and sobbing for hours on end.

I had been there only a matter of weeks when I was invited to join Martin Maloney, the production assistant to Gary Grant at Quartet Books, on a day trip to the printers. On the train journey, I made the big mistake of telling Martin how much I was being paid. Within days I was summoned to meet Naim for the first time, in his Poland Street offices, to explain myself, as Martin had run straight to Naim, demanding a pay rise or else threatening to leave. I had the good sense to wear a pair of high heels, short skirt and leopard-print blouse, and to plead with Naim not to sack me. Luckily he took pity on me and let me stay, but reduced my salary as a punishment. Naim never knew, but Ros de Lanerolle secretly paid me the missing salary through petty cash every month.

Martin kept his word and resigned, deciding to spend some time on his great passion for painting, and the rest is history. Martin Maloney is one of the Brit Art stars, collected by Saatchi, his career launched in the infamous 'Sensation' exhibition alongside Tracy Emin and Damien Hirst.

*   *   *

By 1988 the bickering was constant between Ros de Lanerolle and Mary Hemming, who had been recruited by Stephanie as sales director in the early days of the Press. Their styles of management were in sharp contrast. Whereas Ros was laid back, Mary was a stickler for discipline. As a result, tensions between them began to tear The Women's Press apart. It was made even worse when, during Ros's leave of absence to spend Christmas in South Africa, I elevated Mary to the post of deputy managing director. This precipitated a serious crisis with open rebellion. Mary herself was not the easiest of people to work with and lacked popularity among the staff. While she cared deeply about the imprint, she was highly strung and confrontational. Her radical views were uncompromising and she was not known for her tact. She and I had many arguments over the years. On various occasions she had challenged me with a touch of aggression in her manner and taken the challenge to the brink of a showdown before withdrawing at the last moment to avoid losing face. Mary was a survivor, but unfortunately set in her ways. Any prospect of her working in unison with Ros seemed, in my view, to have become an impossibility.

Given the reservations Stephanie and I already held over the current policies of the Press, I decided sadly that the only way forward would be for Ros to be replaced. What happened next was not entirely unexpected. A majority of key staff also resigned as a mark of solidarity with Ros. As in the case of Anne Smith and the *Literary Review*, a public row erupted, with Ros sticking to her guns. The policy she followed, she maintained, had been the right one and she felt victimized by the whole affair. Her anger was real but not intemperate. She was basically a woman of high integrity with a consummate passion for the repressed among her gender. It was the reality of the situation she had failed to grasp. A weakened Press was never going to have the means to fund her aspirations. She refused to see that her lofty ideals could never be implemented unless The Women's Press maintained a financially solid base.

Inevitably a variety of comment and an exchange of correspondence appeared in the newspapers, with me being initially disadvantaged in the general perception as a man meddling in women's business. 'The Women's Press was set up as one of Britain's first feminist publishing houses, so what's it doing now with a man in charge?' asked David Pallister in the *Guardian* on 27 March.

[Attallah's] intervention, after more than a decade of hands-off management and the rejection of a management buy-out offer [of £500,000], has caused consternation in feminist publishing circles. It coincides with what *Publishing News* headline as 'The Blackest Week', with 250 jobs axed in the recession.

But behind The Women's Press débâcle there lie tales of coups and betrayal, vengeance and manipulation. In the past week, two senior commissioning editors, Sarah LeFanu and Hannah Kanter, the publicity director Judith Palmer, the contracts manager Morven Houston, and one of two desk editors, Judith Murray, have all followed de Lanerolle. The arts director, Suzanne Perkins, has stayed on but resigned from the board. The senior person left, out of a full- and part-time staff, is Mary Hemming, the deputy managing director in charge of sales. Hemming, it is said, has Attallah's ear . . .

The troubles at the Press began about eighteen months ago . . . Last autumn matters came to a head when Hemming was appointed deputy managing director against the wishes of some of the senior staff . . . De Lanerolle was put in a difficult position: either sue for unfair dismissal and take her chances with the vagaries of the law or accept redundancy terms. She decided to pick up the cheque.

Two days later, on 29 March, a letter appeared in the *Guardian* signed by twenty-three Women's Press authors, including Michèle Roberts, Anna Carteret, Merle Collins, Joan Riley and Gillian Slovo, supporting Ros and dissociating themselves from the new management 'as best we can'. 'Some of us, as it happens, are "Third World" women. In the light of Mr Attallah's remarks it is only too evident that anything we might have to say would be entirely irrelevant to his purposes.'

Immediately following it in the column was a letter from David Elliott, as a director, clarifying what de Lanerolle was representing as 'small losses'.

'Small' losses over the past three years have totalled £250,000, and projected for this current year is a loss in excess of £100,000. Until last week few sensible suggestions about how to stop these 'small' losses had come from the Press's senior management.

Stephanie Dowrick put her own point of view forward on 4 April:

Under Ros de Lanerolle's direction, the company has lost a great deal of money. It is unlikely, therefore, that Naim Attallah would think it wise to sell her the company he and I founded together in 1977.

Since 1977 Naim Attallah has consistently supported feminist politics as financial backer of The Women's Press. The deal between us during my years as managing director was crystal clear: run the company efficiently and there will be no editorial interference . . .

Following normal business procedures, Attallah would have 'interfered' as soon as the Press went seriously into the red. That he held off for so long speaks volumes for his unwillingness to do what he is now accused of – taking over a women's concern.

Readers and authors can be reassured that he has now acted. The Women's Press has an exceptional backlist, and continues to have talented staff who are loyal to feminist ideals and sensible business practices, and a backer who, over fourteen years, has proved himself unusually willing to 'back off' when the viability of the Press is assured.

In turn I wrote from my home in France, where I was on holiday, on 6 April. I was particularly anxious to clarify what I had actually said about Third World authors, my remarks having been taken out of context. 'All I said was that the list should fairly represent women from all over the world, including the Third World, and that since we are a part of Europe, European women writers should also be covered.' Ros herself swung into the fray on 10 April, disputing the scale of losses claimed by David Elliott and Stephanie, though adding:

> These figures are of course far from satisfactory, but ours was not the only publishing company with a problem, and reviews of the situation took place regularly between me, Naim Attallah and the sales director.
>
> There did emerge serious differences between us on how the Press should develop. My own understanding has been that the kind of adventurous publishing for which The Women's Press has always stood inevitably risks uncertain profit margins. That is what the best of British publishing has always been about. And until a year ago it seemed that Naim Attallah supported me in this attitude . . .
>
> Unfortunately the 'talented staff who are loyal to feminist ideals and sensible business practices' to which Ms Dowrick pays proper tribute have almost to a woman left.

According to *Wiplash*, the newsletter of Women in Publishing, there was consternation at the group's May meeting that The Women's Press now had 'a male managing director', who would personally be appointing new staff. 'This is clearly an inappropriate role for a man at a feminist press.'

> Market forces are now set to prevail upon the Press in a way which is incongruous with the risk-taking nature of a radical publisher. The profit motive is suddenly taking centre stage with an injection of capital which had previously been begged for in vain. It seems that Naim, having taken up management, is determined to turn the Press into a purely commercial venture. Unfortunately this may be at the cost of a fine feminist list.
>
> It is Ros's view that the editorial policy of The Women's Press has been thrown out with the editors. As yet no definitive statement has been issued, but indications are that there is likely to be a move away from Third World writers to European writers, despite major interest in the former.
>
> 'Bonk busters', or even books of a Thatcherite ilk, may be seen to issue from the Press.

Management Week in May gave the opinion in its headline that, despite my reputation, I had not 'mastered the art of managing women', though the article which followed gave me the chance to voice my position clearly:

> 'A company which is divided is no longer viable. I didn't step in earlier because I really hoped they could sort it out for themselves. It's a very sad situation but the imprint will survive and go from strength to strength because I am determined that it should do so.'

Attallah has been accused of forcing the situation due to his interference but he said: 'The Women's Press has been losing money for the last three years. An imprint weakened by financial losses has neither the strength nor the scope to champion the cause of women. I could not sit back and allow the Press to lose its impetus after its dramatic evolution over almost fifteen years.'

The Women's Press is now advertising for new staff but it will be run in a completely different manner. Said Attallah: 'I will interview all the applicants. I don't want people to be under any illusion about it – they have got to talk to me. All my life I have supported women and I don't see why now, to placate the feminists, I shouldn't appear to be involved.' . . . Attallah will oversee the day-to-day management of The Women's Press for the next few months until he feels it is back on its feet. 'But then I see it becoming an autonomous unit. It's very important that they have total authority because it must be by women and for women. All I want is for The Women's Press to be more international and appeal to a larger section of the women's community.'

In a measured article in *Spare Rib*, Rulchsana Ahmad commented that 'it was obvious that the dispute was a murky cocktail of personal hostilities and political differences, barbed with manipulation and intrigue, which might have earned the title of boardroom coup if the cast had been all-male'. She went on to consider the background crisis in feminist publishing in general, where the smaller publishing houses were increasingly at a disadvantage. 'They all claim that they are not in the business just to make money. They are forced to respect the laws of the marketplace simply because all money that is around is "male" money, whether it is Naim Attallah's or the City's or an individual bank's money.'

Perhaps the slump in sales indicates not so much a fatigue with feminism, as some publishers suspect, but a boredom with the predictability of the books being pushed at them. How good are the communication channels between publishers and readers? Can publishers lead more and generate demand, as they once claimed that they did, or can they only slavishly follow the trends they used to set? Perhaps a new dynamism is needed to overcome the crisis.

The controversy generated by the departure of Ros de Lanerolle from The Women's Press continued to rumble in the background long after the appointment of Kathy Gale to be joint managing director with Mary Hemming. The reverberations from former events haunted the Press as the sisters had difficulty in divorcing the past from the present. The situation was not helped by yet another falling-out, this time between Mary Hemming and Carole Spedding, another close member of the partnership. Again I found myself embroiled in a highly charged affair where love had turned to hatred and the Press was suffering. The warring sides became totally irrational, airing their disagreements with an intensity of feeling that ran right out of control. There was no solution possible but the sacrifice of one person to placate the other. Both parties were equally resistant to my attempts to bring them together. The hurt between them seemed beyond repair and I was faced with the worst sort of dilemma. I decided to remove Carole from the premises where the Press operated and relocate her to Namara House in Poland Street, from where she would take full control of The Women's Press Book Club while remaining series editor for the Livewire Books for Teenagers.

On 21 June the *Bookseller* announced our new personnel line-up along with changes to the board,

> now chaired by co-founder Stephanie Dowrick. Ms Gale joins, as do Nina Kidron, a founder and former managing director of Pluto Press, and Jennifer Bradshaw, an independent editor based in Scotland. Co-founder and proprietor Naim Attallah, sales director Mary Hemming and David Elliott, freelance literary consultant to Granada Television, remain board members.
>
> Ms Dowrick described Ms Gale's appointment, which follows managing director Ros de Lanerolle's much-publicized resignation last March, as 'marking a new and extremely positive phase in the life of the Press'. The Press 'will continue to publish with the integrity which has been its hallmark', but she believed that Ms Gale would bring with her 'a necessary commercial expertise'.

These arrangements had by no means been easy to implement, but I was determined to see them through, and for a short period at least they became workable. I considered that we now had a revitalized team consisting of the 'three musketeers', Kathy, Mary and Carole. The problems we had needed to iron out to reach this point were illustrated in *Private Eye*'s revelations, which while inaccurate in detail, nevertheless reflected the goings-on in its own distinctive style! As 'Grovel's' report had it on 10 April:

> Poor old Naim Attallah has blundered into a minefield by sacking Ros de Lanerolle from the top job at The Women's Press, the feminist imprint which Naim Dropper (rather incongruously) owns.
>
> For months the Ayatollah had been aware of a power struggle between de Lanerolle and her deputy, Mary Hemming. So out of touch was he,

however, that he thought it was Hemming who enjoyed the support of her colleagues; thus his decision to force out her boss.

Last Friday, at a meeting of all the remaining staff, Naim discovered the awful truth: Hemming is universally unpopular. As the assembled wimmin harangued him the wretched man shook his head sadly: 'I lurrve women,' he drooled. 'Why cannot I have some gratitude and lurve back?' He also promised that the hated Hemming would 'sit in her office and be sweet' in future.

Still Attullah-Disgusting stands by his choice. As he told his board recently, 'some of the happiest moments of my life have been those times when Mary was sitting on my lap'.

On 26 April 'Grovel' announced, 'More news, I am afraid, of Naim Attullah-Disgusting and problems with . . . Women's Press':

As I noted in the last *Eye*, Naim has sided with the hated Mary Hemming, the scheming deputy chief of the Press, in the mistaken impression that she enjoys the support of her staff. However, from his recent comment to a board meeting . . . some readers might have inferred that he is enjoying some sort of sexual hanky-panky with her.

Far from it: for as I perhaps should have mentioned, Ms Hemming is a committed Sapphist.

To improve her beleaguered position at the office, on Hemming's recommendation, Naim has now appointed one Carole Spedding as bookclub manager at The Women's Press. Carole Spedding is Mary Hemming's lover.

Pip Pip!

We only enjoyed a brief period of calm before the next explosion occurred. It was a great pity to be faced with more turmoil just as the omens for the Press were looking better. On 7 June, 'Bookworm' in *Private Eye* reported further trouble at The Women's Press, 'Attullah-Disgusting' having been 'sent a most interesting parcel of documents relating to his two protégées at the Press, Mary Hemming and her lover Carole Spedding'.

The ambitious Hemming engineered the recent dismissal of her boss, Ros de Lanerolle, by revealing that de Lanerolle had been consulted unofficially by another feminist publisher. If it could be shown that Hemming herself had actually been a director of a rival company while simultaneously being employed by The Women's Press, there might be a spot of embarrassment for Attullah-Disgusting.

This is precisely what the documents do show. In February 1989 both

Spedding and Hemming – who was then sales director of The Women's Press and a member of its board – quietly became directors of a rival firm called Silver Moon Ltd trading under the name of Beryl's Book Publishing Company. It had been set up by two women called Jane Cholomley and Sue Butterworth, who worked at Silver Moon bookshop in Charing Cross Road. The purpose of Beryl's Company was to publish lesbian fiction. No one at The Women's Press knew of Hemming's involvement with their would-be competitor.

In October 1989 there was a quite amicable parting of the ways between, on the one side, Cholomley and Butterworth and, on the other, Hemming and Spedding. 'It is right that we should resign from the company, as it was yours in the first place,' Spedding wrote to Butterworth on behalf of herself and Mary Hemming. 'What is not so clear is what we might decide to do next . . . i.e. whether we go on with a publishing project ourselves.' She urged Butterworth to 'keep this matter completely confidential' – not least, presumably, because of what Attullah-Disgusting might do if he discovered his sales director's duplicity.

In spite of offering to resign as directors [of Beryl's Company], Spedding and Hemming then refused to sign the necessary forms unless they were paid a handsome 'consultancy fee'. Meanwhile, they also declined to pay their share of the legal bills the company had incurred. As far as anyone knows, Hemming and Spedding are still both directors of the firm.

The documents proving his employees' moonlighting were sent to Attullah-Disgusting on 26 April by registered post. He has yet to reply.

The Women's Press was never to be the same company without Stephanie Dowrick at the helm. Her presence, dedication and charisma were unique. The Press would continue into the years ahead, with periodic traumas along the way and between them phases of recovery, but it never had the same thrust or meaning for me personally without Stephanie. In her case, our occasional differences were also a source of strength. I knew from the day I met her that, whatever vicissitudes time had in store, our love and friendship would be enduring.

Forty

On 30 December 1990, Graham Lord wrote in the *Sunday Express* that one of his most amusing Christmas cards had come from 'the awesomely energetic Naim Attallah, the author, boss of Quartet Books, publisher of the *Literary Review* and managing director of Mappin & Webb. It shows a manic leaping Santa, and Mr Attallah claims that this is his latest new job. I don't think he is joking, either.'

In January 1991 *Publishing News* reported that Christina Foyle, a favourite of mine, had just finished reading *Singular Encounters* and found it quite diverting. Christina and I had got on remarkably well when I interviewed her for *Women*. She told me how she had adored her father and how much she had learned from him.

> My father was really rather a gambler. He was always up to something. Once, coming back from America, he kept playing cards with some rather sharp people. First of all, he won quite a lot, about a thousand pounds a day – this was in the 1930s – and then he lost it all and a lot more besides. He told these men – they were real sharpers – that he couldn't pay, but they accepted a cheque. Then I had to get off the boat very quickly at Southampton to stop the cheque. He used to give me all those sorts of things to do. And then there was a lot of money owing him from the Soviet Union, with all kinds of bad debts, and he sent me over there to collect them. I went to Russia, by myself, when I was twenty-one. I went all over Russia, but most of the people who owed us money had either been executed or gone to Siberia. I didn't have much luck.

Christina was very entertaining and a good raconteur:

> When I first came to Foyle's, it was a wonderful time. There were very many great writers about: Bernard Shaw and Wells and Kipling, Conan Doyle. They all used to come into the shop, and they were charming to me. That's why I started my luncheons, because customers used to say you're so lucky, you meet all these great people, I wish I had your opportunities. So I said to my father, we ought to give a luncheon and let our customers come and meet these writers. So my father said, well, you've nothing much to do, why don't you arrange it? That's how our luncheons came about. But I

found that, although I was so young, they never patronized me or talked down to me at all. I used to go round and call on these people, asking them to come and speak, and they always said yes. And we've had them from that day to this. The first lunch we gave was for Lord Darling, the famous Lord Chief Justice, and Lord Alfred Douglas came, who had been involved in the Wilde affair years before; and then our most recent lunch was for Jeffrey Archer, who wasn't born when we started them. So it's been marvellous, and I can hardly think of a time when I've had any unpleasant experiences.

She was a woman to whom I could relate. She often invited me to a Foyle's luncheon, usually held at Grosvenor House Hotel, and invariably seated me next to her. She was worldly and gossipy and it was enchanting to be in her company. On one occasion she told me how Colonel Gadaffi of Libya would send Foyle's a cheque for two hundred and fifty thousand dollars and ask her to chose the books for him. She loved her profession and she loved people. The two strands were completely interlinked in her life.

On the Quartet front, the newspaper coverage of the imprint continued to be incessant, maybe because of the illustrious young women who worked there or the number of media friends who appreciated us. No matter what the reason, it kept us in the frame of public awareness. Eliza Pakenham, the granddaughter of Lord Longford, was a case in point, having joined Quartet in 1990. The *Evening Standard*'s 'Londoner's Diary' reported in February 1991 that she was about to see the first fruits of her work as a commissioning editor published: Philip Purser's *Poeted: The Final Quest of Edward James* and *A Pinch of Salt*, an Afghan cookery book.

Naim tells me that Eliza has inherited literary flair from her father, the author Tom Pakenham. 'I give her a lot of important things to do,' he says. These include sifting through unsolicited manuscripts. 'I have to do a fair number of rejections,' Eliza tells me. 'I'm quite used to it by now.'

Edward James was a 'forgotten' figure of British culture, a multi-millionaire eccentric who had been a patron of the Surrealists and of Savador Dali in particular. He harboured ambitions to be recognized for his own creativity, especially his poetry, and devoted much time in his later years to a never-finished project to turn a jungle enclave in Mexico into a surrealist garden with wild beasts and concrete fantasy architecture. At the end of March 2007, James became the subject of an exhibition, *Surreal Things*, at the Victoria and Albert Museum, to reassess his influence. Quartet had published Philip Purser's book in its original form as *Where Is He Now?* in 1978; *Poeted* was a revised, expanded edition that completed the story up to James's death in 1984.

Another title from Philip Purser already published was his playful satire *Friedrich Harris: Shooting the Hero*, which told the story of a purported wartime German plot to subvert Laurence Olivier's shooting of his film of *Henry V* in neutral Ireland. It seemed a natural topic for sale of film rights, but though there were nibbles of interest, nothing ever firmed up. The idea foundered on who on earth could have played Olivier.

Catherine Bennett, writing in the *Guardian* at the end of January, had been her usual cynical self in surveying the 'sometimes calm, occasionally fractious world of Britain's literary magazines', asking, as a new editor took over at *The Times Literary Supplement*, 'whether they got the editors they deserve'. She took a quote from Bron about his preference for rhyming verse as her starting point:

> 'I just think the modern movement [in poetry] really ran out of all vitality about thirty years ago,' Waugh maintains at the Academy Club, a smoky cellar beneath the *Literary Review*'s confined premises, all of it owned by Naim Attallah, the Levantine parfumier and woman expert who bought the magazine for £1 in 1979, for motives nobody has yet fathomed. Sense, yes – and scansion, up to a point – but why rhyme?

Claudia Ward was often pictured in the press after she became my assistant, and I could understand why. She combined great beauty with a charm that transformed a mischievous streak into an attractive facet of her personality. She would be forgiven anything for the smile that lit up her face and set her eyes twinkling. During my time at Namara House, before I moved to Regent Street, I was passionately fond of photography. I used most of the girls who worked for the Namara Group as models, especially those with whom I got on best. It was a hobby on which I expended a great deal of time and I achieved some stunning shots. Claudia being one of the most photogenic of my subjects, I took scores of pictures of her; despite the habitual nonchalance she displayed when facing the camera, she could not avoid looking incredibly good. Had she opted for a modelling career, she would surely have reached great heights, but alas, she was not interested. Her sights were set on other ambitions, having also, as the daughter of the actor Simon Ward, turned her back on the stage. 'I have written some children's books, though none have been published yet,' she told 'Londoner's Diary' in the *Standard* of 26 March.

> She is currently assistant to urbane publisher Naim Attallah, to whom she turned when she decided acting was not for her. She candidly admits: 'I didn't like performing. When it came to improvisation I trembled and scuttled out of the room.'

April that year was full of activities. There was a party for David Tack's book of photography, *Impressions of Spain*. It took place at the National Theatre, co-hosted by Lady Soames, the chairman of the Theatre Trust. The event was commented on by both the *Evening Standard* and the *Sunday Times*, though they differed in their assessments. The *Standard* told how the evening had drawn a huge throng to the theatre, but the *Sunday Times* seemed to think the opposite, asking whether my party skills were on the wane. While London publishers had 'locked away their warm white wine and stale peanuts for the duration of the recession', said the *Standard*, 'Attallah himself has not become infected by the general gloom'.

'There are more things in life than money,' Attallah told me. 'Other publishers may be mean, but I like to have a good party.' All the more commendable, given that he is a teetotaller.

Despite having detected a lack of 'razzmatazz', the *Sunday Times* noticed Tuck leading the Spanish ambassador and his wife around the exhibition.

The paparazzi had turned out in force, and they practically swamped Bubbles Rothermere and Lady Soames, who appeared to be the only snap-worthy party-goers. Desperation set in and they spent the evening photographing each other . . .

Throughout the evening Naim was flanked faithfully by his new Chanel-clad personal assistant, Lucy Wastnage, whose duty was to act as a portable ashtray. 'All this harem business is very tiring. Even my parents get relentlessly teased about my job,' she fumed, as another of her employer's guests extinguished a cigarette. Naim, however, rose above it all. Despite the hullabaloo over his temporary donning of the managing director's hat of The Women's Press, he claimed: 'Men need to be strong and powerful to support women.'

The *Sunday Express*, who were putting together a guide for turning forty, asked me for my opinion on love and sex. Here is what I told them apropos the forty-year-old looking for love:

A forty-year-old man should never attempt to compete physically with a man of twenty-five. What he lacks in stamina is quite adequately compensated for by his worldly knowledge and his refinement of the art of love.

What a forty-year-old woman should not do is play the little girl. It detracts from her womanhood.

After forty a man should have two assets: charm and power, the ability to entertain and capture a woman through worldly goods.

A forty-year-old woman with sophistication can entice the otherwise unenticable. Her womanhood is at its peak and her wiles are tempered with a softness and sensuality harder to find in a younger woman.

To illustrate the guide was a gorgeous picture of Selina Scott, who must have turned forty at the time. She was a most cherished friend and I found her devastatingly attractive. The flirtatious glint in her eye made her irresistible. I first met her when I was planning *Women*, and greatly enjoyed her company, but we fell out when she withdrew from an interview for the book. A chill wind blew for some years till we met again at a BAFTA dinner, where we kissed and made up. We used to have tête-à-tête lunches in my private dining-room above Garrard. How I miss those occasions now. I have not seen her for many years, ever since she moved to Scotland, but I often think of her fondly.

Selina had a colourful career in television, starting out as a newsreader on ITV's prestigious *News at Ten* and then being the first woman to front the BBC's *Breakfast Time* in 1983. She went on to present the first fashion-magazine programme, *The Clothes Show*, again for the BBC. She produced documentaries, among them a profile of Prince Charles which was enhanced by the personal *frisson* between them. She went on to work in America on news and chat shows for CBS and NBC, and was the first journalist to expose the cruel trade in ivory in Kenya. But then, on a more sombre note, came her most notorious claim to fame with her contretemps with Donald Trump when she interviewed him on television in the mid 1990s. Her portrait of the fast-talking tycoon was violently at odds with his own self-image. His male ego dented, he fired a barrage of invective in her direction from across the Atlantic. Paradoxically, the nature of the insults shed more light on Trump's character than the most penetrating interview could have done. The manner of his attack was particularly instructive. In a letter to Selina, he first of all established his own position of pre-eminence: 'Up until last spring, I had not heard of you.' (Subtext: *The fact that I had never heard of you is clear evidence of your inferior status.*) With Selina's ratings on Sky 1's talk show having plummeted, Trump was once again firing off poison darts. They appear to have hit their target, since Selina was claiming that his persecutory behaviour towards her was tantamount to mental stalking. She was the least deserving of this kind of treatment and remains one of the most delectable women I have ever known.

At Mappin & Webb I was still in pursuit of a more upmarket image. I embarked on a range of platinum jewellery I had designed with the full backing of the Platinum Council. Always keen to try out my creative ideas, I had been dying to do something like this. A trade magazine carried a story about my making a special presentation of the prize of a platinum heart with a little diamond at the centre to Sergeant Gary Boughton of the South Yorkshire police. It was his reward for answering questions on the theme of romance and love in a St Valentine's Day Competition in the *Daily Telegraph*. Donated jointly by Mappin & Webb and the Diamond Information Centre, it went to prove 'that policemen do have a heart, in more ways than one'. The platinum heart was basically an expensive upgrade of a solid silver heart of the same design I had previously produced to market at Mappin & Webb. It was a great success and I often used it as the perfect gift for promotional purposes.

A number of celebrities carried the silver heart in their pockets to bring them good luck, including Auberon Waugh and Richard Ingrams. During the course of a conversation with the *Sunday Times* when he was attending a Lynn Barber book bash at the Groucho Club, Richard said he would not care to be interviewed by Lynn, but added, gesturing in the direction of 'a beaming Naim Attallah', 'I've already told Naim all my secrets for his book and he's now given me a silver heart from Mappin & Webb to keep in my pocket.'

Where Asprey was concerned, I was by now feeling very confident about the prospects of the group with the incorporation of Mappin & Webb and Garrard. I continued with my strategy of revitalizing and streamlining every part of the conglomerate. A write-up in the April issue of *Tatler* shed some light on what we were trying to do, and in part explained my own perspective in building up the group and dealing with the recession. I was breathing optimism, they said: 'The prospects are fantastic. My prediction is that the jewellery trade will prosper despite the recession – there's so much enthusiasm and creativity around.' A recently launched unique line in blue gold – perfected in Switzerland for Mappin & Webb – supported this prediction. 'People want to be able to buy something no one else has got. They're becoming more fussy and demanding, and the upshot is that competition has become much fiercer.'

Although the three businesses are inextricably linked, Attallah is determined that they will maintain complete autonomy. Garrard's strength lies in the fact that it is the Crown Jeweller. It is renowned above all for its antique silver and customized jewellery – designed for the more traditional taste. Asprey, on the other hand, has been described as the world's most luxurious gift shop – an Aladdin's cave of irresistible, decadent goodies – while Mappin & Webb stands alone in that it was the first European jeweller to break into the Japanese market, creating decorative baubles for emperors at the turn of the century. Now Attallah plans to revamp its image infusing it with a 'zest for youth'. 'We want to make the shop more up-to-date and more accessible to the young – those who will be the tycoons of the future.' Dismissing the problems of a recession Attallah adds: 'Money does not simply disappear. It merely changes hands, and there is always going to be someone rich enough to afford anything.'

This was a period of my life when I was bubbling with energy and reluctant to miss an opportunity to express my feelings on any subject I felt competent to tackle. It therefore came as a fresh challenge when I was asked by the *Telegraph Magazine* to write an article on scent. It was benign by today's standards, but when it was published it raised a few eyebrows in the sheltered drawing-rooms of Asprey's traditional customers. My wearing my writer's hat did not always go down well at Asprey. There was always an underlying conflict, but it failed to curtail my other activities. I insisted on a kind of individual autonomy that was rare in those days, otherwise I could not have operated properly. The article is as relevant today as it was at the time it was written, so I reproduce it in full.

Scent Signals
Naim Attallah

From an early age, I have had a highly developed sense of smell. This may be attributable to the simple fact of having a large nose, but whatever the reason, it has served me like an extremely sensitive barometer over the years.

As the only boy in a large family, I was weaned on female fragrances. In school holidays I spent a great deal of time with my grandmother in Nazareth, where her garden was full of scented flowers and trees of every description. It was an aromatic enclave unspoiled by exhaust fumes.

I often think of women as flowers whose fragrance varies according to age and the environment in which they grow. There are women whose native odour can be very sensual. While their own redolent freshness would seem to need no additions, a discreet dash of scent can enhance their desirability, and at the same time heighten their sense of well-being.

Those women whose bodies do not emit a natural fragrance tend to use scent as an essential part of their make-up. This can be catastrophic if it is done too liberally. How often have I come home with a headache after a night at the opera sitting in the midst of pungent perfumes, or felt the lingering ill-effects of taking a lift recently vacated by a heavily scented woman.

Beauty is proverbially in the eye of the beholder, but an unpleasant smell is usually unequivocal. Although we are invariably guided and influenced by the visible, there is no doubt that an attendant bad smell seriously compromises beauty, whereas ugliness can often be transformed by a lovely fragrance.

Animals are attracted by smell in courtship; so too with people. When I left home to come to England, I was beginning to take a serious interest in girls. My heart would pound at the briefest encounter with a pretty girl, and if her perfume was seductive my heartbeat would reach a crescendo. If the smell was not pleasing, the boredom of normality would descend suddenly and decisively, replacing all desire.

In today's world, where the air in our cities is thick with various pollutants, and people rush around trying to earn their living, there is very little opportunity to feel fresh and relaxed. This is particularly true in summer, when the atmosphere is oppressive. In these circumstances some women use scent as a means of freshening up. This is what I regard as a serious abuse of the whole *soins de beauté*. The result is always displeasing; the staleness remains and resists any cover-up. There can be few things less appealing than a rank smell overlaid with scent. Conversely, there are few things more alluring than the smell of newly shampooed hair and the aroma of a woman's body after a warm scented bath.

When I interviewed some 300 women for my book *Women*, the first whiff on meeting told me a great deal about my subject. An excessively perfumed woman I found neither sexy nor, usually, intellectually sophisticated. The more discreet the scent, the more interesting and charismatic the woman – or so it seemed to me.

All my entrepreneurial adventures have a common goal: love in some form or other. I have recently launched an aphrodisiac chocolate which I believe is to the palate what scent is to the olfactory senses. Four years ago I launched two scents: Avant l'Amour and Après l'Amour. The first is designed to relax the woman and at the same time to stimulate her gently. The unique blend is made up of rose, jasmine, tuberose, iris, peach, sandalwood, vetiver, clove, civet and musk. Après l'Amour is a blend of ylang-ylang, rose of Bulgaria, jasmine, iris, Florence, violet, vetiver, vanilla and myrrh. With this scent I wanted serenity to prevail.

It is very important that women should use scent judiciously, the correct amount is crucial. A little dab behind the ears prepares the ground for a tender assault on the senses, whereas the merest suggestion on the inside of the thighs is irresistibly erotic.

In love-making the importance of conducive smells cannot be exaggerated. I believe the earth-moving sensation sought by so many is reached not simply by the union of two bodies, but ultimately by the fusion of two sensual aromas.

*   *   *

Life in my new Asprey offices above Garrard was now taking on a more permanent pattern. On my floor I had nine young ladies who looked after me, shielded me from unwelcome intrusions and were particularly adept in their efficiency, diligence and total commitment. Besides being a source of fun, they made my task easier. It was not long before I turned Mappin & Webb into a self-sufficient outfit: catalogues, advertising artwork and photo shoots were done on the premises under my direct supervision. No outside agencies were used for any of our promotional material and all artistic assignments were carried out in-house. This helped save the corporation a great deal of money and ensured the creation of the right concept for the right product.

I had a photographic studio especially built on my floor. Its resident photographer was Seresa Hearne, otherwise known as Sissy. I met Sissy through her friend Wiz Marshall, who stayed with me one summer at the family's house in the Dordogne, where I used to go intermittently whenever the pressures in London became too stifling. Sissy visited me at the house on one occasion when Wiz was unable to come. We seemed to hit it off and it marked the beginning of a fruitful association. She was then working at Christie's photographic section in South Kensington. Her recruitment to take charge of the newly built photographic studio at Mappin was an inspired choice, in line with the strategy I had kept in mind since the takeover of the group. The experiment reaffirmed our belief that reliance on our own efforts was the key to future success. Deadlines were no longer dependent on third parties, over whom we exerted little control. It was up to us to keep to schedules and maintain quality of product with our priorities strictly defined. Above all, it gave us a much-needed flexibility to operate without the hampering rigidity that so often plagues contractual arrangements.

Many attractive and talented young ladies inhabited my floor. Being prepared to work hard was always a prerequisite for being part of the team, and a sense of humour was essential. The atmosphere was charged with every kind of excitement. New ideas – often outrageously original – were bandied about. Intoxicating new projects were thought up daily. The buzz was so contagious that each one of the girls had her own theories, perceptions and striking images to contribute. After so many years I still cannot tell whether the energetic environment was the catalyst or vice versa. Each one of them was a character worth describing, either for her singularity or her eccentric disposition. But since I consider food to be one of life's most pleasurable diversions, I will begin with my cook, Hattie Beaumont.

Hattie was endowed with exceptional culinary talents and used them with remarkable originality. She improvised almost on a daily basis, creating the most delicious dishes that seemed effortless but always had the required effect. She ranked alongside Charlotte Millward, my cook at Namara House, who likewise never failed to dazzle everyone with her exquisite cuisine. Charlotte herself was not without her eccentricities, but in Hattie it was her skittishness that was her most lovable trademark. Both were cheekily attractive to suit their personalities, Charlotte being more controlled while Hattie was a bit of a loose cannon. When Hattie was on her best behaviour, she had no equal, and conversely, if she was being naughty, her equal would also have been hard to find. She was adorable and exasperating in equal measure. Her exploits were hilarious and sometimes played havoc with her life and ours. But once you loved her, nothing mattered. She became irresistibly addictive and there was no getting her out from under your skin. Her secret was eternal youth, for she looks no different today from the way she looked then: radiant with optimism and *joie de vivre*.

Work and Antics
by Hattie Beaumont

I worked for Naim for several years, moving with him from Namara House to Regent Street, where he then presided as chief executive of the Asprey group. When I look back on those years, I do so with much nostalgia, for they were indeed some of the happiest of my life. We were an eclectic gaggle of girls working for him with a fierce loyalty that we maintain to this day. Most of us agree that he was endlessly forgiving, even when he felt compelled to sack us for chronic misbehaviour, which in my case was not a rare occurrence. But he always relented in the end.

He was more of an indulgent father figure who managed us all charmingly well. Even with so many hormones flying around, we never fell out. In fact we looked forward to every morning breezing into work with a skip in our steps and a smile on our faces that reflected our pleasure in working for such an enigmatic and caring man. Along with the normal workload, we had time for many amusing antics, which we played on our wonderfully patient boss. He would turn the tables on us occasionally, like the time when I was meeting a potential boyfriend at the local pub and he and some of my workmates came to spy on me, after warning me beforehand to play hard to get and not to succumb to any physical temptation in the early stages of the relationship. He had also told me he would easily find out whether I'd taken heed of his advice by the expression on my face next day: a roguish smile would divulge all and I would be in trouble! So it may be imagined how I felt when I saw him and his entourage sitting in the corner of the pub watching my every move. I turned tomato red and wanted to flee, but I was too embarrassed to tell my companion. The following day, when we all gathered in Naim's office to dissect the goings-on of the evening before, there were too many episodes to recount and I suspect they'd be far too naughty to repeat to gentlefolk. In a nutshell, Naim is a man who deserves great respect, who has had a wonderfully colourful life, has not been immune to his share of hard times but has always taken them in his stride with an upbeat attitude. I shall retain these happy memories and consider myself lucky to have had the pleasure to be part of his life.

*   *   *

Then there was my secretary, Lucy Wastnage. She came with me from Namara House. She was considered mysteriously attractive, with a sultry Mediterranean complexion inherited from her Italian father. In fact her father doted on her and rather spoiled her. She was the only one to be photographed with me, sitting on the floor in my new office above Garrard. I felt totally relaxed in her presence and we could not have had a better working relationship. I have to admit, however, that I did indulge her, especially when she and David Tang began courting long before their marriage some years later. The saga of Lucy's romance began when she was introduced to David Tang by Tania Foster-Brown, whose ex-husband, Guy Salter, worked for Prince Charles when David happened to be a member of the Prince's Trust. The relationship was a *coup de foudre* that sizzled with electricity. The two were phoning each other for most of the day, and then continued for the best part of the night. Calls from Hong Kong were therefore monopolizing Lucy's office telephone line and messages on a variety of topics were clogging the fax machine. Some expressed the tenderness of two people in love, others took the form of quizzes to which each party had to respond. Occasionally Lucy's sense of mischief led her to give the wrong answer deliberately – such as that Naim would make the ideal companion or was the most accomplished man she could hope to meet. It was part of her teasing technique, designed to raise David's temperature with jealousy annd exasperation at her contrariness. As the relationship grew in its intensity, David kept her awake at night by telephoning her in a roller-coaster fashion, pitting his well-known limitless energies against hers but eventually reducing her to a walking shadow through lack of sleep.

At this point my indulgence manifested itself in a number of ways. I became much more tolerant with her than usual and turned a blind eye to the flood of outside communications. I was reluctant to spoil a budding relationship that seemed more full of promise than usual; hence my decision to let her travel with David to New York, then on to Mexico, where they stayed on Jimmy Goldsmith's legendary estate. With further trips on offer, Lucy found herself facing a difficult dilemma. She was reluctant to give up a job in which she was spending some of her happiest times, while the lure of David's lifestyle and her love of his company were proving too much of a temptation to resist. She had to make a choice, for she could not pursue both paths simultaneously. Her loss was painful for us all. She had become an integral part of a team that had perfected the art of combining serious enterprise with unabashed fun. David Tang showed his appreciation to me by signing a declaration on one of his China Club brochures: 'This is to confirm that Emperor Naim Attallah is to enjoy free lunches and dinners at the China Club for life.'

Best Friends, Best Days
by Lucy Wastnage (now Tang)

They say some of the best days of your life are your school days. I would agree, because I met friends at school who are still my good friends. I would add that some of my other best days were working for Naim as his secretary. Not only did I meet some of my favourite people, I also found in Naim a great man whom I would cherish as a lifelong friend. For this I have to thank Julia Ogilvy (Rawlinson): it was through her that I got the post after I left *Harpers & Queen* working for Louis Dominguez. Heaven only knows what Naim saw in me when he took me on. I could never claim to be a very conscientious employee; but maybe he saw the loyalty in me.

When I compared my situation with other friends, who all seemed to have such mundane and boring jobs, it made me think how lucky I was. To be working with Naim was always far from boring!

Most days his driver, John, would pick me up from my home before we went on to collect Naim from his in South Street. He'd go to the hairdressers while I waited in the car. Then, in the Namara House days, it would be on to the office in Poland Street, where the building housed a wonderfully eccentric team, including Pickles and a girl named Claudia Ward with whom I sadly lost contact after we moved to 106 Regent Street. With the move the road trips to radio stations to promote Naim's books ceased, along with visits to The Women's Press.

At the new offices the atmosphere was more corporate but still always fun. Hattie Beaumont, his cook, moved with us, and she and I regularly had a giggle over what we could divert from Naim's cooked-lunch allowance for hosting important clients to scoff for ourselves in the kitchen, or even in Naim's own office while he was in the boardroom. He was always entertaining amazing people like Auberon Waugh, Richard Ingrams or Lord Stockton; or actresses, writers or journalists.

After a year of being Naim's secretary, I started my relationship with my now husband. We were introduced by Tania Foster-Brown, who also worked at Mappin & Webb (though she was someone I already knew when I started the job). Naim soon became exasperated by the fact that his personal fax number was being used by David to keep sending me faxes; or with me for blocking the telephone line. I'd be on the phone for hours, cigarette in hand, oblivious that none of Naim's important business calls were getting through to him!

At this point Naim not only put in another fax line for me, he also hired me an assistant called Sarah Winstone. When I look back I was certainly overpaid and any normal boss would have sacked me. But no, for all the girls who passed through his doors Naim was a giver. The pinnacle of his benevolence was for me when he granted me three months' paid absence to go to Hong Kong and sort out my relationship. If he had not done that, or been so generous in spirit, I might never have married the wonderful husband I'm with today.

Actually I probably came close to getting the sack from Naim a couple of times a day on average. I was always burning holes not only in my own desk-top but also in his. There were also happenings like the time I stuck a reception sign on his (the chairman's) door, then had to try to rip it off again when I heard he was about to take a rather serious meeting with John Asprey and had the whole door falling in! All these things, and more besides, set me thinking how wonderfully lucky I've been to have worked for such an amazing man.

Also, when you consider his background, his Middle Eastern origins mean he has always been a very tactile man, a bit like the Italians. To the English, who are so suspicious of people touching them or being openly friendly, I think it all comes across as rather seedy. What outsiders fail to understand is that he is only holding a hand, or giving a friendly hug, or making a slightly naughty insinuation. None of it infers anything more than a show of friend-ship or a joke. This, I have to say, is one of the reasons why I adore this man: because I know his loyalty has no boundaries as mine have none for him.

* * *

Sarah Winstone, who had been sharing Lucy's secretarial duties, was another pretty girl. She was a sweet person who became a close friend of the irrepressible Hattie, and together they got up to all sorts of tricks that brought them close to being dismissed. Ostensibly, only the intervention of the other girls and the pleading of Paul Clayman, the deputy managing director of Mappin & Webb, made me reconsider and give them another chance. If the truth be known, I would never have gone ahead with firing them. Their presence was a real joy, and the occasional misdemeanour only served to remind me of my own behaviour when I was their age. Sarah had an especially endearing side to her personality, with a smile that gave her face an added sparkle. She was an easy-going companion, as I found out when she came with me on one of my trips to the Dordogne. She invariably charmed those around her and uplifted everyone's spirits.

After Lucy's departure, Sarah was assigned to both Tania Foster-Brown and Jenny Aeron-Thomas in public relations and advertising respectively. Her place was filled by Mariella Lindemann, a school friend of Lucy's. Mariella's German father had bequeathed her an Aryan look, fresh and expressive but rather solemn. I suspected her sense of humour of being of the continental type, more restrained than its English counterpart. While she mixed well with the other girls, her temperament was different. She was not as malleable and was inclined to take herself more seriously than her youth warranted. There were signs that she had a problem relaxing in an office environment such as ours, where informality and spontaneity combined to break down conventional barriers. I felt she never got the measure of me and that it was a struggle for her to cope with the many facets of my character, while on my side I found her hard to read. Nevertheless she was highly efficient and we both acknowledged the disparities that separated us. However, there were fleeting moments when Mariella revealed her true self. On these occasions I was totally won over.

Emily Potter was a professional secretary who had worked for Andrew Lloyd Webber before his elevation to the House of Lords. It was not a job she much liked. She and Andrew were constantly at loggerheads and she decided to leave. I recruited her as a senior PA to take charge of my private office. As soon as she arrived on my floor and found the atmosphere so relaxed, she was astounded. No parallel existed between her previous assignment and the new one. It took her some time to adapt, and even then she was still considered by the other inhabitants of the floor, including myself, to be a bit of a battleaxe. Once she had familiarized herself with her new surroundings, she decided she ought to take full control of my life. She became over-protective and set out to rationalize my general behaviour. Like a dragon at the gate of a treasure house, she guarded my private office and made sure no casual visitor could burst in without a proper appointment. She also did her utmost to ensure my focus remained on the job, away from the distractions the other girls were likely to introduce. Her efforts on this front failed miserably, I am glad to say. When she first arrived, her office attire was low-key and conventional, though her style loosened up with the passage of time. In sharp contrast, her evening outfits were glamorous to the point of being *risqués*. Emily was certainly a sobering influence, whose loyalty and dedication were unquestionable. Although she resisted, in the end even she succumbed to the contagious environment; she became one of us and enjoyed being more laid back.

Jenny Aeron-Thomas was, at twenty-six, the oldest of the girls. She was tall and slender with fabulous legs, blonde hair and a gorgeous bosom. In her work she was rather serious and methodical and slightly more reserved than her colleagues. Flippancy did not feature in her nature, though she was not averse to having some orderly fun. Shy and easily embarrassed, she kept more to herself than the others. Once I caused her some confusion when I inadvertently walked into her office as she was changing into her bicycling outfit. She came from a rather different background from most of the other girls on the floor, but managed to have a harmonious relationship with them. The world of Sloanes was not her stamping ground, but they all shared a common purpose transcending disparities in upbringing and culture. It was a team made up of a motley of pretty young hopefuls determined to make their mark in life. My relationship with Jenny was close but somewhat formal. We worked well together and she was always very much on the ball. There was never any need to emphasize a point when briefing her. I remember her fondly.

Tania Foster-Brown was a highly gifted young lady whose sheer impudence made her the life and soul of the party. She was eager to learn, unafraid to take risks, supremely self-confident and a born leader. Recognizing her multitude of capabilities from the outset, I immediately took her under my wing in a PR role. She became one of the favourites and played a crucial part in glamorizing the image of Mappin & Webb.

One of the things that marked Tania out from the pack was the way she combined femininity with a tomboyish disposition and a general strength of character. As a brown-eyed brunette with a gamine appearance, she was direct and disarming in the way she dealt with others and was always ready to startle with an improvised piece of mischief. It was presumably her way of neutralizing the dazzling effect she created, especially on discerning men. Her keen observation of a situation often triggered a wit that was spontaneous and *point-device*. She had a rare talent for transforming the ordinary into something droll; a gift for peppering a story with funny comments to heighten its entertainment value. To any event she could give operatic dimensions. She never professed to have any acting skills and always denied there was anything special in the way she could recreate a real-life drama and imitate the characters taking part for the benefit of those not privileged to have been there. Tania would accompany me on a mission or to a particular function where I would be delivering a lecture and then return to the girls-only office at 106 Regent Street (it was guarded by a buzzer to restrict casual access) to report the proceedings verbatim. Taking centre stage, she would mimic me down to the last nuance. (Patrick Ryecart as a professional actor could also do a 'Naim', but his was not as good as hers.) She could retain most of the phrases from my speech and deliver them in an authentic manner, gesticulating to emphasize a point and taking a bow at the end to the tumultuous acclaim and merriment of her colleagues. It was as if the world was her stage and she could conjure drama out of sheer mundane reality. Once, when I was in my office recording *Thought for the Day* for BBC Radio 4, she clambered perilously up on the scaffolding outside so she could watch through the window before reporting back to the girls.

Tania's promotional talents took a variety of forms; she even became a model in photo shoots for advertisements that were to appear in the glossies. Once she had to go to John Swannell's studio to be photographed wearing a silver motor-cyclist's helmet. The only problem was that as soon as she put on the helmet she could no longer hear a word of his instructions. Nevertheless the pictures came out beautifully. The poise of her body language was ideally suited to the genre. Her face became synonymous with the new direction Mappin & Webb was taking. People in the industry were surprised by Tania's sudden rise to prominence from being a junior. Jennifer Sharpe of *Harpers & Queen* said to her, 'I can't believe Naim has got a totty like you in charge of PR!' This tongue-in-cheek remark was not so uncalled-for as it might have seemed: from the start it was my avowed policy to discover and nurture new talent and give it scope to develop and succeed. Tania was one of many who were to prove that my faith in them had not been misplaced.

I had always been interested in watches. It was one of my foibles. Tania visited watch factories with me while I combined serious business with my hobby. Journeys in Switzerland could become fraught as I tried to stay in contact with my London office by mobile but had every conversation cut off as the car sped in and out of the long road tunnels. She often travelled with me on buying trips, to Geneva, Florence, Milan, Paris; and throughout the UK when we were promoting products or holding exhibitions. Her companionship was always pleasurable and our journeys were full of funny incidents and mad escapades. We simply found a common ground where the gulf between employer and employee did not exist, without ever jeopardizing our work or undermining respect for authority when it once more became appropriate.

Ours was a most unusual and warm relationship, rich in its rewards. She was able to exert a positive influence through her unrestricted access to me, often interceding on behalf of others, but never allowing this special intimacy to go to her head. There were a few occasions, however, when I would instruct my secretary, 'Foster-Brown – barred!' Such extreme measures were prompted by a rare misdemeanour or a trifle too far. But neither of us could resist a quick resolution to such an unhappy state of affairs and the making up more than compensated for the original falling out.

I was always certain Tania would go places. Since those days she has, with dedication and hard work, scaled the ladder of success on her own account. As her early mentor I can feel both a comforting pride and a sense of gratification.

Creativity from Within
by Tania Foster-Brown

How am I going to write something new about Naim, who's had so much written about him already? We all know that he's a larger-than-life character who inspires affection and love in those who come into close contact with him.

For those of us who worked with him closely, his combination of benevolent dictator and concerned father figure was quite unique. He recognized talent, even in the young and unworldly-wise, and gave it air to breathe. He loved having fun and the office buzzed with ideas and possibilities.

At times he could be impossible, with obsessive passions on particular projects – but his enthusiasm was so contagious you found yourself agreeing to his suggestions and sharing his totally genuine delight when things you planned worked out well. He never took personal credit for anything – but shared it round 'his girls'. He did not believe in consultants or external agencies. 'Creativity comes from within,' he would exclaim to senior advertising executives trying to work on our business!

Naim has a wicked sense of humour and conventional formalities were often pushed to one side. He had an urge to shock out of a sense of devilment, and I would occasionally sit aghast as he repeated some mischievous anecdote to a journalist lunch guest. On that note he was punctilious in his punctuality and it wasn't unknown for a guest to miss the first course if they arrived late. I have never arrived before him at any rendezvous since I have known him!

This heightened sense of needing to be on time could become stressful, especially when sitting next to Naim on an aeroplane that was delayed for take-off!

He was hard and uncompromising when he needed to be, but also sentimental. He was horrified that I cycled to work throughout my first pregnancy, and when during my second pregnancy I had a slight accident on the bike it was too much for him to bear. His chauffeur appeared outside my house the next day and drove me to and from work from then onwards. No matter how much I made protestations about this special treatment, he would have it no other way. There were many other similar instances that set him apart from other chief executives.

Above all, we had great fun, and he gave me the chance to learn to do a job that I had no formal qualifications for – by teaching and trusting and guiding. All the girls loved working with him – it often didn't even feel like work – and we all knew that once we were part of his family, then his loyalty was there for ever for each of us.

I certainly credit working with him as being the most important factor in making me who I am today – mostly in work ways but also in personal development.

*　　*　　*

Henrietta Garnett was a perfect jewel, petite in build with expressive eyes and the delicate features of an English rose. I first caught a glimpse of her when she strolled into a Park Lane banquet escorted by Stephen Quinn, the publishing director of *Vogue*. It was a charity event to which my wife and I had been invited. Henrietta sparkled in a black evening dress elegantly emphasizing the contours of her shapely figure and I could not wait to be introduced. I wound my way quickly to where she stood with Stephen and made the necessary social prelude to the more structured conversation that followed. She worked for Condé Nast and I made a conscious decision that as soon as it was opportune she should join the bevy of intelligent young women who graced the fourth floor of my Regent Street offices. I got my way soon after this first encounter and Henrietta became part of that enlarged family. She was assigned special projects in direct collaboration with myself. Her autonomy was absolute. Affectionately I called her 'Poulet', reflecting in some small measure her soft lines and gentle manner. She was my cherished muse, whose presence was a sheer joy. *Soignée* and well-bred, she never failed to charm and I loved her dearly.

Pip Gill was an attractively dizzy blonde with a difference. She combined a hectic lifestyle with cooking flair: a real treat on a good day and shambolic on a bad one. Her saving grace was a finely tuned ability to overcome her darker side by a charm offensive that came to her naturally. Outrageously expressive in words and action, she seldom caused real irritation even when her behaviour was quite over the top. One accepted such infringements with tacit resignation, rather than make life difficult. She was employed as a cook to oversee my private dining-room at 106 Regent Street, having taken over from Hayley Lindsay, a former model who was tall, blonde and pretty. Pip managed in no time to make the transition feel painless and soon stamped her own mark on everything she did inside and outside her area of responsibility. She brought to the kitchen a manic exuberance that in spite of the chronic disorder resulting from her colourful workstyle strangely

[491]

never failed to achieve its objective. Her strength was knowing how to please. When guilty of a lapse of discipline, she would wriggle herself out of it through sheer ingenuity. My anger, when it came (by no means infrequently) was always dispelled quickly through her unfailing knack of winning me over.

Pip could be hysterically funny, given that taboos were never a restraining factor. If, for example, a request for a week's holiday was turned down by me for some reason or other, she would barge into my office, disregarding the sanctity of the place, and lift her blouse to her face to reveal a naked breast; and then, taking advantage of the impact of this unexpected revelation, would repeat the request with a meek smile that was too captivating to resist. Stunned, I would accede to her wishes without a murmur. Such were the perils of life with Pip that nothing but the totally unfeasible was ever denied her. She remained with me long after I retired from Asprey, with more rather than fewer madcap episodes to come.

*

In the spring of 1991, I took a real interest in Crown Confectionary, as *Private Eye* reported on 10 May.

> An urgent press release informs me that Crown confectionary, a firm making up-market chocolates, has 'embarked on a major expansion programme under the guidance of their new chairman, Mr Naim Attallah'. Crown, it reveals, was first brought to the attention of Mr Attallah when launching his famous book *Women*. He asked one of his secretaries to find a company who could produce some personalized luxury chocolates as a present for his guests at the launch. The Palestinian tycoon was so taken by the bonbons that he bought the company. (Pass the sick bag, Alice, or rather Camilla/Sophie/Emma etc.)
>
> 'A man of Attallah's talents can only spell success,' the press release adds. 'Attallah's name is synonymous with quality.'
>
> Presumably this is a reference to his vulgar perfumes 'Avant l'Amour' and 'Après l'Amour', and to the many pornographic books published by his imprint Quartet, such as *Naked London* (pictures of Camilla/Sophie/Emma etc. with no clothes on.)

The diversification proved less than successful in the long term as a result of stiff high-street competition and the little time I was able to devote to overseeing the management of the new company. This latest acquisition was done on a whim, as was often the case. Although the experience was costly in financial terms, it did broaden my knowledge while providing the Namara

Group with an excellent base for promotional activities of a different kind. We often used a variety of the chocolates we produced to embellish important social events and provide novel themes for our parties. We started creating a number of objects made of chocolate that were conceptually brilliant. The discerning market we were targeting was, however, much too small to make an impact. It was as hopeless as trying to get an arthouse film put out on general release.

Strangely enough, we accidentally uncovered a bizarre niche never exploited before. Out of the blue an order came for chocolate penises of all shapes and sizes and the market in these products suddenly took off. We could hardly keep up with supply. Who bought these penises and for what purpose? Whatever the explanation, the line kept the chocolate factory going for over ten years, which only went to prove that the combination of sex and chocolate has for some an irresistible appeal. Kinkiness was certainly a force to be reckoned with.

Forty-one

In early June 1991 a lunch took place at the *Observer* newspaper with Donald Trelford, the editor, at which I was one of the guests. Its after-effect was an international political row that soured Britain's relationship with France. I had known Donald for a number of years, particularly during the period when the *Observer* was owned by Tiny Rowland. Our paths crossed periodically in a number of ways, socially and otherwise. When we met we would discuss general topics of the day, including his own remarkable *entente* with Tiny, who was hard to handle and rather unpredictable in his choice of friends and business associates.

At the time Donald had a television slot on BBC2 in which he appeared in conversation with political leaders. He was contemplating an interview with Edith Cresson, who had recently been appointed prime minister of France by President Mitterand. *En passant* Donald asked me whether, in my diverse activities, I had ever met her, faintly hoping I might contribute to his research process. As it happened, I had met her, before there was any talk of her becoming prime minister. Some four years earlier I had interviewed her for my book *Elles* – the French edition of *Women* – but had never been able to use the interview as I had missed the deadline for its inclusion. The interview had been in French and remained unseen by anyone, having subsequently lain dormant in one of my files. Donald asked whether he could see it, notwithstanding the fact that it was conducted in French. He would have it translated, he said, and return it to me as soon as he had had the chance to read it.

Three days later an excited Donald came on the telephone. The interview, he reckoned, was sensational, and with my permission he proposed to publish it in a world exclusive as the cover story for the 'Review' section of the newspaper the following Sunday. At the same time he would negotiate worldwide syndication rights, for which I would receive half the total benefits in addition to a substantial fee for its UK publication. I said yes without hesitation.

The interview had all the impact Donald anticipated and more. The majority of people were appalled by the ill-considered statements Madame Cresson made about Anglo-Saxon men. She tossed statistics into the air without their having the least basis in fact. In my opinion, she had shown herself to be vain, arrogant and full of her own importance. She kept looking at her watch all the time we were talking, warning me my time was up, but then carrying on with her pontifications regardless. Everything to do with her was studied, and she failed to convince of any sincerity. What was beyond doubt was that she came over as an attractive woman in her prime who was highly intelligent and confident. Her movements and gestures were all part of her repertoire. There was no doubt that without much effort she beguiled Mitterand, who was not at all immune to feminine wiles.

Edith Cresson's sex appeal was of the sort that men would fall for then try to master and subdue. I felt it as I was talking to her. Her delusions of superiority stirred one's animal instincts sexually, though I would have been far too embarrassed to admit it. In different circumstances I could see myself falling prey to this egocentric woman were it not for her contrived haughtiness, which overrode and negated every other consideration. But before analysing the furore that followed the publication of the interview and making a considered judgement, it is essential to quote the passage that triggered off the whole controversy. I asked her why most men preferred the company of men in Anglo-Saxon countries.

Yes, but the majority of these men are homosexuals – perhaps not the majority – but in the USA there are already 25 per cent of them, and in England and Germany it is much the same. You cannot imagine it in the history of France. Traditionally the image of Frenchmen has been heterosexual, an image given to them by men of power, by the kings, etc. Frenchmen are much more interested in women; Anglo-Saxon men are not interested in women, and this is a problem that needs analysis. I don't know whether it is cultural or biological but there is something there that isn't working – that's obvious. Moreover, I remember from strolling about in London, and girls are making the same observation, that men in the streets don't look at you. When you do this in Paris, the men look at you; a workman or indeed any man looks at passing women. The Anglo-Saxons are not interested in women as women; for a woman arriving in an Anglo-Saxon country it is astonishing. She says to herself, 'What is the matter?' It is a problem of education and I consider it something of a weakness. A man who isn't interested in women is in some way a little maimed.

The *Observer* of 16 June summarized the interview under a front-page heading: 'French PM: One-in-four Englishmen gay':

Continental people have sex, it was once written: the English have hot-water bottles. As if to prove the point, France's first woman prime minister, Edith Cresson, has bared her soul in a remarkably candid and controversial interview on the subject of men, sex, power, discrimination – and the supposed amorous failings of the Anglo-Saxon male.

The fall-out was immediate and it went round the world. On Monday morning the *Daily Telegraph* reported:

A certain *froideur* has befallen Anglo-French relations after a decidedly undiplomatic attack on British manhood by Mme Edith Cresson, the French prime minister.

The fifty-seven-year-old mother of two, whose quick temper and sharp tongue are renowned in Paris, has suggested that the Anglo-Saxon male at best lacks the passion of his Gallic counterpart, and in one in four cases is homosexual.

The remarks were made four years ago to the publisher Naim Attallah, but surfaced in yesterday's *Observer* to ripple what might be left of any *Entente Cordiale* . . .

Not since one of Mme Cresson's predecesors, M. Jacques Chirac, dismissed Mrs Thatcher's remarks as *couillons* during a European summit has a French prime minister been quite so disparaging about the British.

But as diplomatic rows go it was perhaps somewhat short of the lamb wars or a single European currency. 'I don't think we have a position on this one,' the Foreign Office confessed yesterday.

The *Telegraph* also included a few ill-informed assumptions of its own, stating that the book *Women* had 'featured conversations with more than 150 unsuspecting women, frequently over lunch, and containing remarks they would never have made had they known they were on record'. These women had been furious, alleged the *Telegraph*, 'but none more so that Mme Cresson, who was apparently too boring to make the book'. The next day the *Telegraph* printed an unequivocal apology:

Mr Naim Attallah assures us, and we entirely accept, that all the 289 women he interviewed for his bestselling book *Women* were aware that their remarks were being tape-recorded for inclusion in his book.

Therefore the statement in yesterday's *Daily Telegraph* that they were 'unsupecting' and said things they would not have said if they had known they were on the record is without foundation.

We also accept his assurance that, contrary to our statement, none complained to him, orally or in writing.

In particular the interview with Mme Edith Cresson, now the French prime minister, was conducted only for the French, not the British, edition and did not appear in the French edition because of the publisher's schedule. Therefore our statement that she was 'too boring to make the book' is unfounded.

We apologize sincerely to Mr Attallah for the misrepresentations in our news story and for those reflected in our leading article.

When I met Max Hastings, the editor of the *Daily Telegraph*, at a Downing Street reception, he greeted me with the words, 'You are a gentleman. I shall be writing to you a personal letter of appreciation.' And he did.

For Edith Cresson the whole *affaire* came to the fore as another diplomatic contretemps was brewing over the campaign of remarks she had been making against the Japanese from the moment she became prime minister a month earlier. These were aimed at Japan's export policies, despite the fact that one of France's great success stories in recent years had been its luxury-goods export trade to Japan. Among her accusations were that Japan wanted to conquer the world, and had already taken over the world's photographic industry, forced its own people to pay high prices at home to finance cheap exports and sealed off the domestic market to foreign competition. According to her, the Japanese were too busy plotting against the American and European economies to be able to sleep at night. They were 'ants . . . little yellow men who sit up all night thinking how to screw us'. Japan was the 'aggressor', she claimed on television, and 'lived in a universe different from ours, a universe of domination'. In reaction to her pronouncements, far-right groups in Japan were already organizing protests outside the French embassy in Tokyo, but she was showing no sign of backing down. Later in July, on a visit to America, she gave an interview on the ABC network repeating that the Japanese 'work like ants, live in little flats and take two hours to commute to work'. On 14 July, Bastille Day, the demonstrators in Tokyo guillotined her in effigy.

Her immediate reaction to the publication of the interview was to say she had no recollection of ever meeting me, let alone of being interviewed. An aide denied, moreover, that she had ever made the 'gay' remark. This inflamed the situation even further. When the media sought my reaction to the denial, I was able to produce the evidence by exhibiting the tape. The French authorities, having been given 'not only the date – Wednesday, 27 September 1987 – not only the place – at her then office in the Boulevard St Germain – but also the time of the interview – 11.30 a.m., sought to establish that she had been misrepresented, allegations which did not survive the briefest study of the tape transcript', as John Sweeney wrote for the *Observer* from Paris on 23 June. He gave a graphic description of their official disgust:

As slowly and stately as Montgolfier's gondola, the left eyebrow laboured heavenwards: 'Disgusting.' The right eyebrow the same. 'Evil. *Stupide*.' His hair, cut *en brosse*, bristled with distaste. His stomach, an overwrought shrine to the magnificence of French cuisine, shuddered in pain like a Sumo wrestler with tummy ache.

The eyebrows climbed ever more upwards and now the lips were brought into play, squeezing together until opening to create a small explosion of compressed air, exactly mimicking the Paris Métro hiss. 'We would never do a thing like this.'

He paused to work the gondola eyebrows, sumo tummy and Métro door some more. 'This rubbish. Trash. Garbage. It is always the English that play these games. Always Great Britain.'

He pronounced 'Great Britain' as if it were not a country but a particularly nasty form of sheep apoplexy.

Jean-Philippe Atger is the French Bernard Ingham, the man charged with handling press relations for the new French prime minister, Madame Edith Cresson.

With delicate disdain, he held a photocopy of a *Sun* story between finger and thumb; its headline, slotted on page three to the right of a pair of breasts, screamed: BRITS BLAST POOFTER JIBE FROM MRS FROG.

It was all the *Observer*'s fault.

Last week Atger was breathing garlicky bunkum and balderdash at your hapless reporter after our paper brought Anglo-French relations to a new low by disclosing that 'MRS FROG', er, Mme Cresson, believes that one in four Englishmen is gay and, more, they lack all interest in women.

Madame Cresson's fall-back position had subsequently become that the *Observer* story was not in the tradition of *le fair play*. 'If this conversation took place,' she told the listeners to a French radio programme, 'I was not only not prime minister, I was not even in the government.' She claimed she did not remember meeting me, but, 'Maybe I had a conversation with an English journalist because I had a lot of conversations with English journalists. All I know is that if the conversation took place, and if he found the things I said interesting, he would no doubt have included them in his book. I have nothing to add to this interview that has been taken out of a drawer.' When pressed about her allegation that a quarter of Englishmen were homosexual, she simply stirred the pot again, saying, 'It's difficult to produce a statistic.' The inference was that she remained unrepentant.

The tabloids, with the *Sun* in the vanguard, certainly spotted in the story a green light to let fly with a few blasts of chauvinism. Under the headline 'Britanny Fairies' the *Sun* said:

Edith Cresson, France's first woman PM, claims one in four Englishmen is homosexual. That's a bit rich coming from the leader of a nation where most men carry handbags and kiss each other in public. They don't call Paris Gay Paree for nothing, you know.

Julie Burchill in the *Mail on Sunday*, sharpening up her gift for delivering a provocative insult, asked how it was that, if France was so straight, it had an 'AIDS rate higher than in most African countries and higher than any Western country apart from the USA (which is really a Third World country anyway)?' She found Mme Cresson's claim that British men did not look at women in the street 'incredible'.

Because back here in dear old Blighty, the problem that personable women have to face is not too little male attention but too much. . . . men who not only look at you in passing but indeed look at you as if they were trying to pick you out of an identity parade of suspects who might have done in their dear old mother . . .

In fact how very pleasant to be as plain and past it as Mme Cresson – an honorary man, no less! And if it is true, as she claims, that Frenchmen still ogle her – well, is it worse for a quarter of men to be homosexuals, or for the majority to be shameless, perverted gerontophiles?

Mr David Jones of Bolton, Greater Manchester, suggested in a letter to the *Observer* that for Mme Cresson's next state visit to Britain he could envisage a 'guard of honour of scaffolders at Heathrow, ready to receive the premier by ceremoniously intoning, "Cor, I bet she does the business." '

Marjorie Proops, in her column in the *Daily Mirror*, turned the theme into a case for exhortation:

Maybe it's not a bad idea to keep your heads up, lads, and take a keener and closer look at the passing talent. Somehow we've got to go on breeding good, strong, silent Britons – and it can't be done without your cooperation.

There was also the inevitable facetious question raised in the House of Commons, which brought a welcome interruption to the business of serious politics and reduced the chamber to hilarity. The Conservative MP Tony Marlow said that, in view of Mrs Cresson having 'sought to insult the virility of the British male because the last time she was in London she did not get enough admiring glances', he wished to put down a motion saying: 'This House does not fancy elderly Frenchwomen' – but was ruled out of order by the Speaker.

With Mme Cresson's remarks rebounding in various directions on other matters besides these, it began to seem to many commentators that Mitterand's judgement in appointing her as prime minister might soon be seriously called into question. Julian Nandy in the *Independent* on 20 July commented on how her predecessor, Michel Rocard, had been criticized for his reluctance to speak out on current issues during his three years in office, but there had been no such problem for Edith Cresson in the two months she had been in the job.

> She talks, what she says gets into print and, more often than not, it boomerangs. It has become known as *parler cru*, or talking raw. In the meantime her popularity rating has zigzagged, while President François Mitterand – who appointed her – has publicly backed her bluntness . . .
>
> Last week, however, her popularity, after falling 16 per cent in seven weeks, began to rise. In the weekly *L'Express* a poll showed that she had picked up seven points . . . The poll was published just as Mrs Cresson made unfashionably frank comments on illegal immigrants, stressing that laws requiring their expulsion should be applied more strictly.

An assessment by Robert Cottrell in the *Independent on Sunday* of 21 July put more detail on the situation:

> But to question Mrs Cresson's wisdom is, in effect, to question that of Mr Mitterand. He put her there. So had he since come to think, as he was asked during his annual 14 July television interview, that this was *une fausse bonne idée?*
>
> Mr Miterrand insisted not. 'After fifteen years of technocratic language,' he said, 'I find it healthy to have a prime minister who speaks clearly.' The people of France, he said, 'have a living language. Mrs Cresson has a living language . . . It is true that Mrs Cresson upsets people. Well, some people are against her. I am for her. She is rather charming, don't you think?'
>
> Since you cannot say 'No' to the president of France on live television, the question was left hanging.

Edith Cresson failed to serve a full year as prime minister, though this gave her time to plumb new depths of unpopularity before she resigned after a poor showing by the Socialists in the elections. I have sometimes since wondered whether, in some indirect way, I contributed to her demise as prime minister. The aftermath of the interview showed her, I thought, in a silly light and made it clear she was quite incapable of reining in her loose tongue. There were even persistent rumours that she had formerly been Mitterand's mistress, leading her to feel the presidential backing she received was his way of appreciating the favours she had bestowed on him over the years; and, this being so, that her vulnerability was well protected.

Under Mitterand's patronage, she went on to be the European Commissioner for Education, Research and Sciences in Brussels. One of her first actions was to appoint her own dental surgeon, René Berthelot, as her personal adviser on HIV/AIDS, a subject of which he knew little. After two years – though eighty-five thousand pounds the richer – Berthelot had produced a total of twenty-four pages of notes later deemed to be unqualified and grossly deficient. Another project she generated, known as the Leonardo da Vinci Vocational Training Scheme, which she claimed was the best-administered programme in Brussels, became implicated in massive fraud, and the company she had chosen to run it was stripped of its five-hundred-million-pound contract. Investigations uncovered a whole nest of falsified contracts, forged handwriting and embezzled funds, leading to the resignation of the entire Santer Commission in 1999. Allegations that she had personally gained from any wrongdoing remained unproven, though the commission inquiry said she had 'failed to act in response to known, serious and continuing irregularities over several years'. Though the Advocate General of the European Court of Justice recommended that she be stripped of half her forty-seven-thousand-euro pension, she was allowed to escape the imposition of any financial penalty. 'Maybe I was a little careless,' was the extent of her public admission.

Forty-two

Ken Perkins, as a professional soldier, had spent thirty-eight years in the British army, the first two in the ranks and the final eight as a general. His speciality was counter-revolutionary warfare, and he was described as 'having more medals on his chest than any other soldier of his generation'. In July 1991 Quartet published *Khalida*, his first work of fiction. Its story begins in Aden in the 1960s, when a young British soldier, Corporal Kelly, is seduced by an Arab woman in a desperate ploy to divert his attention from a cache of explosives. Unbeknown to Corporal Kelly, he fathers a daughter, Khalida, giving birth to whom the Arab woman dies. This leaves the girl in the care of her guerrilla uncle guardian, Salim, who later becomes her lover. Two decades later, Salim has apparently renounced his revolutionary past to become a respectable ambassador in London, where Kelly is now operating as a smooth arms dealer, unaware of the presence of his daughter, who has grown up with the fantasy of avenging her mother's death.

The publication of the book saw the Churchill clan assembled in force for its launch, Ken Perkins being one of its newest recruits, as 'Peterborough' wrote in the *Daily Telegraph*, with Lady Soames in the lead of a dozen relations by marriage:

> Major-General Perkins, who is married to Winnie's granddaughter, Celia Sandys, has written a thriller incorporating material from his colourful military career which fell victim to the Official Secrets Act when he attempted to include it in his memoirs. But as his in-laws fell upon one another yesterday, Perkins seemed a little lost. 'We don't get together very often,' explained Lady Soames. 'But we all run to each other in times of triumph – and disaster.'
>
> There was one outsider. The actor Robert Hardy, almost an honorary Churchill, chatted to Lady Duncan-Sandys and her daughter Laura. The gregarious publisher Naim Attallah explained that it was Laura who had provided him with his initial *entrée* to the clan when he furnished her with a job.

At the same time word was circulating about a new magazine to be called the *Oldie* and launched the following year. Richard Ingrams and Alexander Chancellor, who had already secured my financial backing for the project, were actively engaged in producing a dummy. The target circulation was for two hundred thousand copies – in retrospect rather an ambitious figure – and the aim of its editorial policy would be to combine intelligence with irrelevance. Ingrams, the former editor of *Private Eye*, was to edit the *Oldie* with the support of Chancellor, who was then editing the *Independent*'s Saturday magazine. My role was to be chairman of the board, which would consist of Richard Ingrams, Auberon Waugh, Alexander Chancellor, Steven Glover, John McEwen and Patrick Marnham. I was also to contribute an interview column to the journal.

The founders promised a magazine that would not patronize its readers, drawing a comparison with the US market leader, *Modern Maturity*. 'It is very fashionable to be old nowadays, but one can feel quite culturally isolated,' said Chancellor, aged fifty-one. 'The *Oldie* will be an amusing magazine and it will be cheering to talk about things that people of a certain age talk about.' It was Richard, however, who soon became the moving force behind the magazine, while Chancellor's role was to diminish during the few months following its launch. Richard assumed total editorial control and moulded the contents to suit his own perception of what it should be as a new organ. As an organ player himself in his home life, he was deft at the fine tuning it needed to produce the melodies that charmed his ears. The atmosphere of *bonhomie* at the outset helped him achieve his ambition without the least resistance from the board. The euphoria following the launch indirectly gave him the mandate to link the magazine with himself so that he and it became an indivisible entity.

In September 1991 I attended a party at the Queen Anne Orangery in Kensington Gardens to celebrate the publication of the memoirs of a very dear friend, Quentin Crewe. The title he gave them was *Well, I Forget the Rest*. This remarkable sixty-four-year-old writer had been for more than half his life confined to a wheelchair, from which he greeted the friends and former wives who turned up to salute him. The *Evening Standard* covered the event as follows:

Naim Attallah, something of an authority on these matters, confessed his unbridled admiration for Crewe's romantic endeavours. 'He is the greatest seducer,' he said. 'I don't know how he does it. There's no way I could have achieved any of the things he has if I had those disabilities.'

Lord Snowdon, who invented Crewe's first electric wheelchair, disclaimed any part in such goings on. 'I don't think it has anything to do with my chair,' he told me. 'And if it has, it's a peripheral thing. It's his sheer strength and will of personality.

Quentin was a truly extraordinary man. As well as being a successful journalist and writer he was also a determined adventurer who had defied his disabilities by travelling through some of the most difficult terrain on earth. His exploits were legendary, but his powers of conquest where women were concerned remained the aspect of him I most admired. I saw it happen at first hand when his daughter Candida brought him to have lunch at Namara House. While waiting for me to come down from my office on the fourth floor he went to kill a few minutes browsing in the bookshop on the ground floor. It so happened, at the time, that a twenty-six-year-old model with stunning looks was working in the shop between modelling assignments. Before I could get down to greet him, Quentin had engaged her in conversation. Two months later she was his lover, accompanying him on a long journey through India. When I saw them together on their return, the girl was so besotted that she could not keep her hands off him. She hugged and caressed Quentin with a tenderness that belied the difference in their ages or any *impuissance* arising from his handicap.

Despite his disability, Quentin had three wives, five children and lovers aplenty, but his was no straightforward tale of triumph over adversity. When he was a boy his mother's nightly admonition was, 'Keep your hands above the sheets!' It was advice he never heeded. He continued to delve beneath the covers even after a Swiss governess had shown him a cautionary Victorian illustration of the madness and degeneration that lay in store for those who failed to take note. Using all the authority of her position, she pointed to the perpetrator of such shameful acts, explaining that the consequences of his wickedness had come about because *il joue toujours avec sa quéquette, comme toi*. Later, in view of what happened to Quentin, it was as if the governess had been a genuine Cassandra figure, a real prophet of doom, for he was struck down at an early age by muscular dystrophy, a cruel disease that had him confined to his wheelchair for the rest of his life.

When I interviewed him for *Singular Encounters*, I mentioned to him how his reputation for attracting beautiful young women was fabled. Did the secret lie in his combining being such a great raconteur with an irresistible charm, or was there some inherent sexual chemistry that attracted feminine beauty and youth? His response was typically diffident:

It gets less easy, but I think they're intrigued by something different – that is to say, somebody in a wheelchair. The only explanation I can think of is that those who seduced me wanted to discover what it was like to go to bed with somebody disabled. Or there is always the other possibility, that one is less frightening to them, that one isn't a great beast who's going to leap on top of them and beat them. Whatever it is, I've been very lucky.

His explanation seems quite plausible, especially in the light of a more recent instance where the publisher of the *Spectator* reportedly said she had slept with former home secretary David Blunkett to find out what it was like to sleep with a blind man.

Quentin was one of my heroes, and his death, like that of Auberon Waugh, has left a gap in our society that can never be filled. One hopes that these two men, who loved women with a true passion, are receiving their rewards in heaven from celestial creatures even more beautiful than those who dazzled and beguiled them in their terrestrial lives.

In August, Richard Ingrams embarked on a promotional campaign to explain the *raison d'être* for the *Oldie* prior to its launching some time in the New Year. As the financier of the project I found myself involved with the press to some degree. When asked for my reaction by the *Sunday Telegraph*, I said, 'I like anything new, out of the ordinary and nonconformist. I like the people involved. Which is why I think we are going to have an exciting adventure.' The *Oldie*, Richard emphasized, would not be a satirical magazine like *Private Eye*, or seek to rival it, for he still had 'a financial stake in *Private Eye*'.

His successor [at *Private Eye*], Mr Ian Hislop, will have no role in the *Oldie* – not simply because he is only thirty-one. 'He is keen on rock.' This merits disqualification.

The role of Alexander Chancellor as a 'supreme consultant', in Richard's words, would not be signalling any resemblance to the *Spectator*: 'I don't want anything to do with young fogeys.' Richard also made it clear that he would like to make use of the many experienced writers who had been ' "thrown on the scrapheap" by employers determined to recruit young journalists, however untalented'. Lord Deedes was highly supportive of the venture from the start, believing it might attract a big response 'if Richard establishes the right psychology'.

Each generation is left out of step with the previous generation. With this generation the gap is the widest because of the speed of change due to science and technology. We also have fashion cults moving at bewildering speed with the sense of cultural isolation for the old.

Auberon Waugh, one of the founders of the *Oldie*, the editor of the *Literary Review* and now about to become an *Oldie* columnist, told the *Sunday*

Telegraph he could offer a word of hope for Mr Hislop. 'Hislop,' he predicted, 'will mature – in thirty years' time.'

The *Oldie* sounded to the *Sunday Times* as if it would be 'like a cross between the *Spectator* and the Age Concern brochure', with a column 'lambasting the idiocy of the telly, interviews with very old people by Naim Attallah and a regular slot called "Still With Us".'

'It occurred to us that there are a lot of people we assume to be dead who are no such thing,' Ingrams explained. 'You find them by looking at the birthday lists. There was an obituary recently for a Romanian pianist who gave a recital at the age of 103. I'd never heard of her, but she would have made a good interview.'

A dashing gunmetal fifty-four, Ingrams is deeply offended by the concentration of the press on the youth market; by the way the *Independent* devotes 'two whole pages to pop music – rubbish'; by the idea that the young have more money to spend: 'All the ones I know are broke.' . . .

And who does Ingrams consider will be the *Oldie*'s natural audience? 'Oh,' he says with confidence, 'young people. Without a doubt.'

Zoë Heller, in her 'Notebook' column in the *Independent on Sunday*, said the *Oldie* would not be going the way of the American trend with advertisements showing ancient couples snogging in public places – 'trying in some embarrassing American fashion to keep up – or fake up – youthful appearances'. ' "How *disgusting*," Ingrams said, when I mentioned the decrepit snoggers.'

It will *shun* jeans; it will waggle bifocals in the face of fashion; it will be *proud* to be oldie. Moreover, it will not be seeking to fill a 'market niche'. The tyranny of market forces is precisely what it will set itself up against. And in any case it will not be directed at any particular age group. Helloey? For the benefit of confused youngies everywhere, I went to ask Ingrams more.

If the *Oldie* is not going to be for old people, what, I asked, does the term 'oldie' mean? 'Well,' said Ingrams, 'it's er, it's . . . well I suppose it's partly a description of me.' . . . 'Is an oldie like a fogey?' I asked, seeking specificity. 'Oh no.' Ingrams shook his head. 'A fogey is a Tory and a bore. I think.'

Zoë Heller persisted in pressing him on the issue till she detected 'youngie' tendencies in his replies, at which Richard exclaimed:

'Anyway, I am a grandfather. I wear glasses, I have grey hair and I'm going deaf. I don't like pop music. I don't like modern films. I hate nearly every-thing that's on television. So I *am* an oldie.'

Zoë Heller felt some misgivings that the *Oldie* management team was looking rather male dominated, but Richard hastened to reassure her with the fact that he had been 'positively bombarded' with requests from women wanting to contribute. She did not find this surprising, since most women would have claimed, in her view, 'that the business of getting older is much tougher for them [women] than it is for them [men], that while there is an aesthetic of male ageing – sexy crow's-feet, distinguished greyness and so on – they have no equivalent in which to take comfort'. Moreover, she wondered, to what extent would they be aware of how much Ingrams regarded anti-feminism as being inherent in the *Oldie* position.

'Oh yes, feminism is a malign force,' he says, 'and the terrible thing is that the Labour party and the BBC and the Church of England have all given in to it. It's the wetness of the men who are running these things. They're trying to appease the harpies.'

Ms Heller lost no time in going round to repeat some of these views to the publisher, Carmen Callil, who had been attending some of the inaugural meetings and was said to have an eye on becoming the *Oldie*'s architectural correspondent.

Callil, who founded the women's publishing house Virago, stamped her foot and said she wasn't going to put up with it. 'I only went along in the first place because Liz Calder [head of Bloomsbury Publishing] dragged me there. I told her they'd be chauvinistic and anti-homosexual. Well Ingrams is just going to have to watch his step.'
'Well actually,' I said smugly, 'Ingrams says that *you* are going to have to watch *your* step. He says you might be "interior decoration" critic if you behave yourself.'
Callil says she will be having words with Ingrams. And it is quite possible that the war of the sexes will prove fiercer than the enmity of the ages.

Right at the end of the year the *Sunday Express* magazine was asking me if the *Oldie* was all a jolly New Year jape? Or was I mad? Or had I been consumed by an overdeveloped spirit of goodwill? Nothing of the kind, I retorted.

'With the *Oldie* we've found ourselves a niche. Maybe you succeed by going against the trend. Newspapers have a preoccupation with the young, which is nonsense. They are uninfluential and have no money . . . I'm not saying that if you're thirty you must be stupid. The young are sexually more competent, eat a lot, stay up all night – but take everything so much for granted that enjoyment is limited. As an "oldie" you savour things. Instead of jumping on top of a woman, you hold her hand, send her flowers, pay her attention. Have a glass of champagne. When you're young you drink plonk.'

We were looking forward to the *Oldie* hitting the stands on 19 February 1992, and all the signs were good for it to be generating its own publicity.

Back at the end of August I had submitted myself to a questionnaire compiled by Rosanna Greenstreet for the *Guardian*. Looking at it again fifteen years later I realize how my responses encapsulated my whole life's philosophy in only a few words. If I were asked the same questions today, the same responses would still apply, for despite the march of the years I have not undergone any radical changes in character. The level of energy may have decreased, but the zest for life remains as strong as ever and my habits have hardly changed at all.

The Questionnaire
compiled by Rosanna Greenstreet

What is your idea of perfect happiness?
To relax in our house in the Dordogne in the company of our three most princely Dobermanns.
What is your greatest fear?
Drowning, since I can't swim.
With which historical figure do you most identify?
Napoleon, for his grand vision and enduring influence.
Which living person do you most admire?
The Pope for his simplicity and compassion.
What is the trait you most deplore in yourself?
Impatience in the face of mediocrity.
What is the trait you most deplore in others?
Stupidity.
What vehicles do you own?
Bentley Turbo.
What is your greatest extravagance?
Compulsive buying when it comes to clothes.
What objects do you always carry with you?
A silver heart.
What makes you most depressed?
An environment of poverty and suffering.

What do you most dislike about your appearance?
My approaching baldness.
What is your most unappealing habit?
Biting my nails when under stress.
What is your favourite smell?
A woman's body after a heavenly bath.
What is your favourite word?
Enthusiasm.
What is your favourite building?
The Hyde Park Hotel [now the Mandarin Oriental], Knightsbridge.
What is your favourite journey?
Driving through the villages near our house in the Dordogne.
What or who is the greatest love of your life?
My work in general and my wife in particular.
Which living person do you most despise?
I despise politicians who pretend they speak for the majority of the people.
What do you consider the most overrated virtue?
Celibacy.
On what occasions do you lie?
Rarely, but when I do it is only to protect others.
Which words or phrases do you most overuse?
Don't get your knickers in a twist.
When and where were you happiest?
When, at the age of fourteen, I was living with my grandmother in Nazareth.
How do you relax?
By trying not to think about women.
What single thing would improve the quality of your life?
Everlasting youth in outlook.
Which talent would you most like to have?
To play music.
What would your motto be?
Loyalty above all things.
What keeps you awake at night?
Nothing keeps me awake at night.
How would you like to die?
Peacefully among friends.
How would you like to be remembered?
As a man who nurtured and encouraged the talents of others.

*   *   *

On 13 September 1991, my most cherished friend and associate Theo Cowan died in his office at Namara House at the age of seventy-three. It happened just after lunch when, following his usual custom, he had taken a snooze for half an hour in his favourite chair opposite his long-time friend and assistant Jane Harker, with whom he shared his desk. That same morning Theo had been to see me at Regent Street to discuss various issues that were pending with regard to Namara Cowan. He was jolly, and as usual kept me *au courant* with what was happening in our show-business arm. We were then in a difficult period compounded by Theo's generosity in giving ample time to many of the famous stars he represented without receiving a commensurate return for his services. He wanted my reassurance that my support would continue till the dawn of better days, which we were likely to see soon. He left my office happy and reassured, and reported the gist of our conversation to Jane Harker before settling for his forty winks. When it was time for him to wake up, Claudia Ward shook him gently and he keeled over, quite dead. He had departed peacefully, having ended his journey discreetly, just as he would have wished.

Theo was a legend in his own lifetime, considered by many to be the doyen of Britain's show-business publicists. He was judged by his peers to be the best and, as *The Times* said, was admired by stars and scribblers alike. For more than four decades he projected or protected an élite stable of clients, including the veteran actor Joseph Cotton, Sir Richard Attenborough, Dirk Bogarde, Sir John Mills, Michael Caine, Jeremy Irons, Bob Hoskins, Jenny Agutter, Julian Lloyd Webber and, until their deaths, David Niven and Peter Sellers. In his letters to his clients, continued *The Times*, 'he would usually sign himself "Beau-nosh" – a reference to his prodigious enthusiasm for food of almost any description. "A legend in his own lunchtime," they would joke.'

The *Daily Telegraph* remarked that 'the supreme publicity agent was himself something of a mystery':

> his public persona was universally loved, his private one hardly known. His life, it appeared, was his work; and the discretion which his clients valued was never applied more rigorously than to himself. Women adored him as much as he loved them, but he never married. It was known that he had nursed a special *tendresse* for the late Margaret Lockwood, and in the actress's reclusive years he was the only man who could break into her isolation.

Dirk Bogarde added his personal tribute, addressing Theo's departed shade directly with his memories of the many years they had got through together with 'good movies, bad movies, and here and there a reasonably respectable one'. Theo had always been there on the journeys all over the country:

Red carpets and station-masters in top hats. Black ties and eternal dinners with Mayors. Day after day from one city to another. You and me. Everything planned like clockwork, ready on time, never once late, not even the train . . .

Discipline you taught; patience, humility and tact. You did amazingly well by doing not what you were engaged to do – keeping me away from the worst excesses of the popular press. Keeping me 'out of' rather than 'in' the public eye for which I will ever be grateful.

Those subtle warnings about X and Y who might look kind but couldn't be trusted with a fly-swat or a feather duster. The 'killers' of their time. How frightened we all were of them! But it was you who said: 'What they say today you'll eat your chips from tomorrow. Remember that through your tears.'

Like most of those who were well-acquainted with Theo, I can never forget him. His presence alone was a joy. At parties he knew most of the guests and his popularity was something uniquely apparent. For a number of years my wife Maria and I, accompanied by our son, went to the film festival at Cannes to be looked after by Theo, where he was king of 'The Croisette'. We attended many film premières and were treated regally by everyone we encountered for being merely in his company. Together we raided all the famous restaurants in town and the surrounding hills. It was truly a memorable experience to watch Theo as he devoured one after another of the exquisite dishes he could not resist even after being fully satisfied. I miss him often for his wise counsel, but even more for his kindness and generosity of spirit.

The memorial service for Theo was held at St Martin-in-the-Fields. It was conducted by the Reverend Albert Watson: a most moving occasion with figures from the world of entertainment there in force to pay tribute to one of the best loved publicity agents of his generation, whose popularity among the show-business fraternity was unparalleled. Readings were given at the service by Joss Ackland and Jeremy Irons, while tributes were paid by Donald Sinden, Michael Parkinson and Jenny Agutter, who also read warm appreciations from some who could not be there – Joseph Cotton, James Stewart, Lillian Gish and Barry Cryer. Ron Goodwin introduced a recording of Peter Sellers reading 'Help'; Petula Clark sang 'I'll See You Again'; and Larry Adler, accompanied by Roy Budd on piano, played the theme music from the film *Genevieve*. Other music was provided by a jazz band made up of Mr Budd with Ian Christie on clarinet, Richard Willcox of BBC Light Entertainment on trombone, Mike Wheeler of Rank Film Distributors on double bass, Bryan Jones on trumpet and Lon Sanger as vocalist. The organist was Mark Stringer and the whole congregation joined in singing 'On The Sunny Side Of The Street' and 'When You're Smiling'.

In fact it turned out to be more of a gig than a memorial service, but that was the way Theo would have liked his life celebrated, with the merriment that was his hallmark. The ceremony was a joyous interlude for remembering a man whose legacy was laced with good memories. I left the church and went out into Trafalgar Square with feelings of mixed happiness and sadness. Theo was no more, but his unobtrusive shade would always remain with those who had had the privilege of knowing him.

The autumn of 1991 saw Quartet publish a number of books by European writers, most of them in translation. A few of them are listed here to draw the reader's attention to what Quartet was aiming to achieve: to bring the imprint further international recognition to enhance an established reputation for avant-garde publishing and the pursuit of works of literary merit.

Hervé Guibert's *To the Friend Who Did Not Save My Life*, translated from the French by Linda Coverdale, was a distinctive contribution to the literature of AIDS, presenting in journal form the life of a young man who was living with the condition and soon to die from it. Based on the fate of the celebrated French philosopher Michel Foucault, it saw the process as taking place at three levels: as a social document, as an unflinching clinical examination of the illness and its treatment, and as a commemorative account of the unorthodox lifestyle of its protagonist. At the outset he intellectualized the disease: 'it was an illness in stages, a very long flight of steps that led assuredly to death, but whose every step represented a unique apprenticeship. It was a disease that gave death time to live and its victims time to die . . . '

The End of the Novel by Michael Krüger, translated from the German by Ewald Osers, was a novella, both playful and profound, about a novelist close to finishing the novel that had taken him nine years to write – and before that, nine years to research. With only a few sentences left to write, he began to reflect, but the more he reflected on his *magnum opus*, the more he found himself cutting from the text. Entire chapters were jettisoned in progressive reduction till in the end he opted out of the whole business of literature, locked the door of his house, flung the key in a lake and set off on a journey 'as if I were alone in the world'.

Body Snatcher by Juan Carlos Onetti, translated from the Spanish by Alfred Macadam, presented the work of a Uruguayan writer who was one of the precursors of Gabriel García Marquez and Carlos Fuentes. It concerned an attempt by a pimp and a widow to create the perfect brothel, an ambition doomed to failure through the petty self-righteousness of a society in which stupidity and lust overwhelmed integrity and love. The book was a tragi-comic fable of grotesque ideals and lost illusions. It had been written in 'one of the richest, least self-satisfied versions of Spanish narrative prose', wrote *El Pais*, 'and is always centred on the same tight range of relentless themes: the solitude of contemporary man, the exploration of failure [and] ill-fated lives'.

A novel from Sweden, translated by Laurie Thompson, was *Island of the Doomed* by Stig Dagerman, an author who had been, according to Michael Meyer, 'The best writer of his generation in Sweden [he only lived from 1923–54], and one of the best in Europe.' It was a haunting, powerful allegory about the state of modern man and the dark regions of the soul, finding its metaphors in a tale of a shipwreck in the Pacific. Trapped on an island where the only bush bore a deadly fruit, the survivors relived the various guilts of their lives in nightmares till one by one they succumbed to death.

Thomas Bernhard's *Histrionics* was a set of three play scripts translated by Peter Jansen and Kenneth Northcott. Bernhard had been singled out as a key figure in German literature by George Steiner and compared to Kafka by John Updike. His dark, absurdist plays had a kinship with Beckett and Pinter but possessed a wild energy all their own. 'His minimalist, repetitive prose,' wrote John Banville in the *Observer*, 'tumbles along like a shot soldier held upright by a mixture of adrenaline and terror.'

Mozart and Posterity by Gernot Gruber, translated by R. S. Furness, was a strikingly original study of the impact of Mozart's music in the two centuries following his death. It was the story of his evolution from being a forgotten composer to becoming a youth beloved of the gods. Along the way he had been romanticized, hero-worshipped, trivialized and debunked as cultural figures like Goethe, E. T. A. Hoffmann, George Bernard Shaw, Richard Strauss and Herman Hesse strove to define the elusive nature of the composer's genius and discover 'the true Mozart'.

Trial of Strength: Furtwängler and the Third Reich by Fred K. Prieberg, translated by Christopher Dolan, was acclaimed by Peter Heyworth in *The Times Literary Supplement* as providing 'the most illuminating account yet written of musical life under the Nazis'. With scrupulous research and meticulous attention to detail, the book addressed the vexatious matter of how far one of Germany's most pre-eminent figures had been able to continue working under the Nazi regime without colluding with its fundamentally immoral and loathsome activities. In his 'trial of strength', he had succeeded in helping Jewish colleagues, often against impossible odds, and had held firm to his position as a custodian of the higher ideals of German art; but in the end he had lost out to the ascendancy of von Karajan under Göring's promotion.

Finally there was David Tack's *Impressions of Spain*, for which V. S. Pritchett wrote a foreword. The launch party for this has already been described. In his black-and-white photographs Tack got under the skin of the 'real' Spain 'as opposed to its popular image of cheap plonk and red-faced Benidorm louts', said the *Independent*, having lived 'among the peasant farmers and clam fishers and, fascinated by the country's religion, visited many closed orders'. As an insider, he had managed to depict the lives of ordinary people whose way of life had remained unchanged for centuries, 'seeking the ageless spirit of a nation undergoing great change', as the *Daily Telegraph* put it. The quality and depth of his work avoided all clichés in its explorations of varied and little-known cultural traditions. *Impressions of Spain* was another collection of remarkable, unusual photographs to be proud of.

*

On 2 October Mappin & Webb, in association with the World Gold Council, held a 'Celebration of Gold' exhibition at 170 Regent Street. Exhibits included a seven-kilo nugget prospected in Brazil, a Japanese 24-carat-gold dress and a Lau Dynasty Chinese bowl. Seven jewellery designers, including myself, created unique pieces for the occasion. Among the many items I was responsible for were two centrepieces, a 22-carat-gold egg weighing four and a half kilos, priced at £66,390, and a 22-carat-gold tiger weighing in excess of two kilos and retailing at £34,950.

My jewellery ensemble for the exhibition included bracelets, rings, earrings and gold hearts; all had a discreetly erotic feel to them, the emphasis being largely on weight and a simple concept of fine lines. My *pièce de résistance*, however, was a gold wishbone choker that had matching bracelet, ring and earrings. *Tatler* described this set as having 'a bold design whose greatest virtue is a striking, contemporary simplicity'. Much credit for my personal endeavours in producing these fine pieces of jewellery and the two centrepieces must go to John Nix, the manager of the Asprey workshop, whose professionalism and tireless pursuit of excellence gave the finished products an added lustre.

The exhibition was a grand affair, and I was delighted when the choker was snapped up by a discerning client on the first night for a cool £10,860. It was beginner's luck, John Asprey teased me, when a number of the items I designed sold very quickly. The press came to the opening night in force and found themselves dazzled by the sheer glow and collective impact of the gold. Patricia Miller, in the *Evening Standard*, remarked that,

> When he was a student Naim was so poor he lived on Weetabix . . . now he has his breakfast egg out of a £2,775 golden stand he designed himself and uses a silver egg as a doorstop. (It is so heavy you could hardly lift it and it retails at £5,500.) When he shows off his golden prizes, he will have 24-carat-gold leaf sprinkled in every cup of punch. Naim traces his love of the arts to his childhood in Palestine, where his father collected paintings, miniatures and carpets. His first design [for Mappin & Webb] was a platinum heart about an inch long, set with a single diamond. He meant it for Valentine's Day and sold it for £7,950. He designed his own wedding ring, which he wears on his little finger and calls 'a bond'. 'When you love someone a ring is a bond. I never had one when I got married. I would have felt chained then.'

The most spectacular event of the evening occurred when Julia Lemigova, the beautiful 'Miss Soviet Union' (the last before the collapse of the Soviet state), the daughter of a high-ranking KGB official, aged nineteen, appeared on the scene. She was wearing the 24-carat-gold wedding dress by the Japanese designer Yumi Katsura. It was worth £180,000 and made from twenty-five metres of pure gold brocade, with a tiara, veil and long train. As Julia moved between the guests she was like a vision from a world of tsarist fable – a princess arriving for a coronation. Her wonderfully formed features were in harmony with the whole effect. It was a moment of pure theatre – and the gold was real!

I had met Julia only three weeks before the exhibition and we became friends almost immediately. She often called in at my office in that period which rather unsettled the other girls, especially since they felt she had forged a warm relationship with me without even trying. They looked on disapprovingly and Tania Foster-Brown, whose natural abilities as an actress I have already described, never lost an opportunity (a 'golden one' in this case) to send up Julia. She mimicked her every gesture and movement while cheekily poking fun at the way she used her body language to endear herself to me and fished for compliments about her well-toned figure. Tania did it to entertain and curb the resentment of the girls on my floor, who were suspicious of this interloper.

The exhibition was a great success in London. Tributes kept pouring in, but the one I most appreciated was in a letter from Sally Goldsby, the public-relations manager of the World Gold Council, who was the driving force behind the whole project. The exhibition, she wrote, 'had undoubtedly been a huge success'.

> Firstly the magazine promotion featured probably the best photographed gold jewellery ever seen in this country. Secondly the gold artefacts initiated by you are some of the most exciting ever made. Also, the displays of the shop and the overall presentation of the exhibition were of a very high standard. Your own enthusiasm and support have been second to none! We really could not have staged such a successful event without Tania's [Foster-Brown's] relentless and professional hard work. We have thoroughly enjoyed working with her and hope we can arrive at a close working relationship with Mappin & Webb.

After that glowing accolade, the exhibition moved to Mappin & Webb, Edinburgh. Sally Goldsby joined me and Tania, with of course our golden girl Julia Lemigova, who became closely associated with the exhibition. Her parading in the sumptuous gold dress caused the biggest sensation in Scotland. She was mobbed by onlookers together with an army of photographers who flashed their cameras in a frenzy of excitement. On a personal level those three days I spent in Scotland in company with Sally, Tania and Julia would have been any man's dream of a heavenly escape from the daily round. We returned to London fully reinvigorated and proud to have achieved such a remarkable feat. Julia was hailed as the beautiful Miss Russia who had brought a sparkle to grey Edinburgh. All in all it felt like a job extremely well done.

Julia, with her dark hair and brown eyes, was a quintessential Caucasian beauty and knew exactly how to present herself in every situation. It was a safe prediction that she had an international modelling career ahead of her. During her time in London she modelled the kaleidoscopic range of silk scarves I had designed for Mappin & Webb, and also my 'friendship' rings and bracelets of intertwined bands, of which John Swannell took the photographs. In the advertising for the rings, both her hands and mine appeared together in the photograph.

What no one could have foreseen for her was a darker episode when she became emotionally involved with Edward Stern, a prominent member of an eminent Jewish banking family. After Stern was shot in Geneva in 2005 by a mistress with one of his own guns – he had reasons to fear enemies, including some in the Russian mafia – Julia came forward to tell her story. She claimed Stern had been the father of her son, born in 1999, though he never fully accepted the fact. When the child was five months old she advertised for a nanny and engaged a Bulgarian woman who applied in person. Within days the baby became seriously ill and was taken to hospital, where he died. The doctors found evidence of injuries that suggested he had been shaken, but a subsequent inquiry was inconclusive and the nanny disappeared. Later Stern's mistress contacted Julia to try to prise details of their sex life out of her, and at one point, said Julia, offered to tell her 'the truth about the death of your son'. When Stern was murdered he had been wearing a latex body stocking and his mistress confessed to having shot him during an argument about money after a sado-masochistic sex session. Julia came to believe that Stern had arranged for her child to be killed and that his mistress had been trying to blackmail him over the baby's death.

I could never have imagined it possible that my sweet Julia would become embroiled in such a cycle of high international drama, where the main players were unsavoury characters out to use their wealth and power in the ruthless pursuit of illicit and immoral ends. But all of this happened many years after I last saw her, which was when I bumped into her by chance on avénue Montaigne and took her to dinner. That was a year after she had left London to live in Paris and before we finally lost touch. She opened a beauty salon in France that specialized in natural therapies and building women's confidence to live lives that matched their personalities and enhanced their well-being.

The time came when *Private Eye* was celebrating thirty years of exposés and satirical attack and John Dugdale for the *Guardian* wished to compile a set of thoughts from some of its prominent victims. Despite its relentless lampooning of me over the years, which at times had had its funny moments, I agreed to participate along with the likes of Melvyn Bragg, Lord Deedes, Roy Hattersley, Peter Jay, Nigel Dempster, Polly Toynbee and Andreas Whittam Smith. The piece I wrote went as follows:

> I first felt the brunt of Lord Gnome's organ in the early seventies when I became a target for his satirical abuse. I was genuinely wounded. More hardened victims congratulated me on my elevation to this exclusive club, explaining that the Establishment in its perversity had finally acknowledged my so-called success and I should be flattered – a bad notice is better than no notice.

Private Eye is no longer what it was: irreverent, outrageous, extremely funny, inaccurate, unpredictable, nasty. No one, friend or foe, was safe from its exacting scrutiny. It had a rich crop of talented contributors, the great majority of whom have long since left. Perhaps my favourite column was Auberon Waugh's 'Diary', with its irresistible and often absurd combination of wryness and savagery. The *Eye* was the scourge of City slickers, crooked developers and corrupt local councillors, in the best tradition of satire's exposure of vice. Law courts became backdrops for legal battles, the most protracted of which were followed avidly by the nation.

Our language has been enriched by several of Lord Gnome's more dubious phrases, originally coined to shock and provoke. Sadly, for some years his organ has been showing signs of impending impotence, and although I wish it well on its thirtieth birthday, I would rather have seen it in more robust condition.

At about the same time, Peter McKay, who was a one-time contributor to *Private Eye* and among the old guard, wrote a disparaging piece in the *Evening Standard* directed against Richard Ingrams and his forthcoming venture, the *Oldie* magazine. Under the heading 'Money for Old Dope', his words carried a dire warning on the future of the undertaking and Richard's relationship with his financial backers. He thought it sounded like the kind of project 'dreamed up by drunks and forgotten the next morning'. Why, he asked, since I was already losing money on 'other sensible magazines' like the *Literary Review* and the jazz magazine the *Wire*, had I decided to hazard more when Mr Ingrams appeared unwilling to 'risk any of his own resources'?

> Mr Ingrams has always been a smart financial operator. He raised money from friends to start *Private Eye*. He collected money from readers to pay for libel damages.
>
> Now – aged fifty-four – he extracts money from Naim Attallah to finance his lifelong obsession, gerontology. Mr Attallah, I would have thought, has more chance of seeing a return if he financed a troupe of geriatric piano accordionists working the Northern Line on Sunday evenings.

Peter McKay's prediction would prove to be not far off the mark. Richard Ingrams's character was to show its true colours as soon as his personal interests were no longer in tune with those who had supported him in the first place. By his own admission, he was someone who invariably bit the hand that fed him.

The year 1991 had been another in which achievements and conflicts ran side by side, but I remained bullish and totally immune to controversy. When, on the last day of the year, the *Daily Telegraph* asked me to give my resolutions for the year to come, I said, 'I have two. First, I shall love women more and expect less in return, and secondly, I shall resolve that nothing mundane is worth spending a sleepless night for; happiness and serenity are my goal.' Happiness was a condition I was likely to achieve, but serenity was more problematical. In the *Guardian* Cosmo Landesman took me to task over one of my New Year resolutions:

> Publisher and new-man-about-town Naim Attallah has boasted for many years that he loves women. So I was surprised by one of his New Year resolutions – 'I shall love women more and expect less.' Personally I loathe those 'I-really-love-women' type of men. Do they really love all women – Imelda Marcos, Myra Hindley and Mrs Thatcher, for instance? Placing womankind on a pedestal is just their way of putting other men down. The message is: I'm not threatened by women, unlike you, you uptight, macho misogynist!' One thing I've noticed about 'I-really-love-women' men – they never mention how much they love their wives.

Although Landesman's piece was largely satirical, it also had a provocative thrust. To any generalization there are always notable exceptions, but these do not negate the essence of the argument. He is entitled to his pet hates in the same measure as I am free to choose the gender of people to whom I find myself drawn. As for his concluding sentence, that the 'I-really-love-women' men never mention how much they love their wives, I would beg to disagree. To speak for myself, I have always mentioned my love for my wife at appropriate times and without labouring the point. Perhaps my only weakness is my reluctance to make a name for myself by being beastly to others!

Forty-three

It was surely unpresumptuous of me to believe that by the autumn of 1991 my credentials as an international publisher were safely in place. Quartet was being acknowledged on a level previously undreamed of and, along with its sister company, The Women's Press, was outstripping its most optimistic targets. Besides that, my interest in such magazines as *Apollo*, the *Literary Review*, the *Wire* and now the proposed *Oldie* were causing significant ripples in the media and I was being likened to an emerging press baron. My forays into films and the theatre were no longer considered as incidentals, a means of diversification for its own sake. My profile at Asprey was constantly being raised with the rapid expansion of our customer base through the policy of acquisitions I had devised. As a result, I was featured heavily in the press and, with such coverage, was accustomed to scrutiny. The most worrying aspect of all this of course was having to live up to expectations, some of them unreasonable, and maintain what the papers were calling 'the Midas touch'. It was a supplementary burden I carried but one largely of my own making. Those who live in the limelight are bound, somewhere along the way, to find themselves treated as fair game by a voracious media machine that loves nothing more than the chance to knock anyone with a high profile off their pedestal at the first signs of a flaw in their image.

Melanie McDonagh was assigned the task by *Who's Who Magazine* to assess my own contribution to publishing in parallel with that of my well-known adversary George Weidenfeld. Each interview was quite long and well written, appearing under the joint heading: 'Weidenfeld and Attallah: they came, they published, they conquered'. My own interview under its own heading, 'Palestinian prince of publishing', summarized my life in these words:

> Perhaps it was his over-protected but happy childhood in Nazareth that set Naim Attallah off so adventurously and effectively in so many directions: finance, publishing, films, writing, interviewing, fixing pylons despite fear of heights, designing jewellery. But if it all fell apart, he'd gladly carry your bags for you. 'I'd do it very well.'

The interviewer covered familiar ground already touched on in the pages of this book. I would, however, like to reproduce the beginning of the article and its endpiece for their insight into certain aspects of my persona.

I was with Naim Attallah for all of an hour and a half when he gave me his heart. It was only afterwards he let on that he'd given it to Auberon Waugh and Richard Ingrams as well and only later still that I found out that the ebullient Sarah Sands had one too. By now there are probably enough of us to form a club. But still, few Englishmen would be so profligately generous. 'Hold out your hand and shut your eyes,' he demanded. I did. 'Oh God,' he muttered. 'Where is it?' Then a heavy weight in my palm. I looked down on a plain little silver heart. 'I designed it for Mappin & Webb,' he said, beaming. 'We're doing it for Valentine's Day.'

It was Mr Attallah all over. The drama. The pleasure in giving presents. The enthusiasm. And the refusal to confine his activities to a manageable bracket . . .

What makes him so energetic? One theory that he suggests himself is that he was never allowed to take the smallest risk when he was a little boy. He was the pampered only son, a sickly child who was never allowed to play with other boys or to ride a bicycle. He paints a poignant picture of the little voyeur, sitting on his parents' balcony watching the road where other boys played. 'That's why I'm so adventurous now,' he says. There may be something to be said for deprived childhoods after all.

The year 1991 saw the departure of Anna Groundwater, who had been Quartet's publicist for a few years. She had previously left my private office in Namara House for a short spell before returning to the fold to join Quartet. Her appointment caused consternation among the denizens of Goodge Street as her reputation for diva-like behaviour preceded her. She was also reputed to have a fiery temperament that won her very few friends. While her period of tenure secured and sustained for Quartet a high degree of press coverage, she remained a most controversial figure. Since I was not a witness to any of the upheavals she caused in her working environment, I remained steadfast in my support and refused to hear anything disparaging about her. Blinkered as my assessment of her may have been, the bond between us remains as strong as ever. As Anna now writes her recollections, happy memories return to brighten my day.

Exciting Times
by Anna Peile (née Groundwater)

I joined Naim's organization in 1982 as his PA and then became publicity manager at Quartet – a job which I loved – through until I had children. Naim was enormously accepting of anyone providing they showed a bit of enthusiasm or attitude and I suppose we all came through routes of someone knowing someone else. When I got there I found it was a place that was already supposed to have something of a reputation for being a processing school for double-barrelleds. This may have been the case, but it was certainly not staffed by flower-arranging dimwits. It was very feisty. The first launch we had to do was for Derek Jarman's book – at the Diorama in Islington. I think, if I could remember enough about it, that it was probably the coolest party I ever went to.

Times were exciting then – everywhere – post-punk clubs – very lively. Naim asked me once who, of anyone, I would like to have in his basement dining-room for lunch. I asked for Piers Paul Read, being in a post-Read Catholic moment, and found myself unable to shine when Read appeared. At around this time, Naim's office got ransacked. Among the precious things taken was the most precious of all, the tiger-skin which lay, head intact, on the floor of his office. It was close to his heart. I played a vital role in its recovery.

I met lovely people working there, the best of whom was Jubby Ingrams. I won't forget meeting her, heart sinking as a girl in a sloaney navy coat walked in – but she could not have been more different – great great fun, we laughed our way through several years. We organized so many parties together – and appeared painted in gold with lilac silk chiffon dresses or in unbelievably tight black rubber floor-length sheathes at various book launches.

Naim and I did not always have the smoothest of relationships. After a while, there was an argument – I cannot recall what over – and I remember [here my own recollection differs from hers] tossing the keys of the office on to the desk at 9.30 in the morning and going off to have a very good breakfast at the Brasserie in South Ken with Cosima. Maybe that was why he called me the diva – that was the good thing about working there, you could pretty much be yourself. I was soon back. Naim was very indulgent, providing you were loyal – he could not bear apparent disloyalty. But he has proved the most loyal friend to me – and now godfather to my daughter. The best time he stood up for me was when Susan George had rung to complain about my lack of deference, demanding my removal from her publicity campaign – he refused. He could also be exceedingly generous, but I wouldn't embarrass him by repeating how!

*   *   *

The January 1992 edition of *Women's Journal* had an amusing feature entitled 'Who Deserves a Sainthood?' Auberon Waugh was quoted as nominating me for this supreme honour for 'my love of employing people'. He went on to expound on this statement, saying, 'his face shines with happiness in the company of those in his employment'. This was deeply gratifying.

January also saw the official opening of the Highgate Bookshop. I had acquired the freehold of the shop and leased it to Pipeline Books, which by now was running it successfully under the management of Elisabeth Cook, previously manager of the Penguin Bookshop in Covent Garden. This made Pipeline the proud owners of eight shops as they had recently taken over the Dulwich Bookshop as a going concern with all its existing staff. Auberon Waugh, described by the *Ham & High*, the local newspaper, as a class warrior, author, literary editor and Croatian champion (having been president of the British Croatian Society since 1973), reopened the Highgate Bookshop with a grand flourish:

> 'It's a wonderful thing to open a shop. I've never done it before, and I hope you have a wonderful time here. Now, about my book . . . ,' began Mr Waugh, skilfully inserting a plug for his newly published memoirs into his official duties.

> Writing an autobiography was, in Bron's view, rather like opening up your house to the paying public: 'You can't really complain if they shit on the carpet because you have invited them in and they have paid for it.'

> His own life has not been without strangers shitting on the carpet, or, rather, gobbing over the parapet. Mr Waugh shared a childhood memory of when forty-five evacuees from the slums of London came to stay in his family's house in Somerset. He recalled the 'phlitt, sput and flop' as they spat on him from the top part of the house where they were housed, occasionally scoring a silent, but deadly, direct hit.

Revenge came within Bron's grasp when the local ratcatcher called to lay down poisoned bread as bait. He went straight to his grandmother to tell her how the evacuees had started scoffing the poisoned bread.

> It was, he recalled: 'My first taste of power in the great class war. I was able to pick out as many as I chose and the poor little things were then taken away and stomach-pumped. It was my one great happy moment in childhood.'

Bron was uniquely hilarious in the way he could mix mischief with a rare descriptive perspective on events which he saw in a totally different light from everyone else. Writing six weeks earlier in his *Daily Telegraph* column, 'Way of the World', he had cleverly given a plug for the *Oldie* magazine:

> Dirk Bogarde's letter in this newspaper last week, pointing out that older people are much funnier and wiser than the young, is only part of a dawning awareness among the over-fifties that we hold nearly all the cards in life's

poker game: we own nearly all the wealth in the sense of property and savings; we have nearly all the free disposable income. We are also within a short throw of comprising the majority of adult voters.

This, as I never tire of pointing out, is the philosophy which has inspired the New Year's publishing sensation, *Oldie* magazine. It will grab our putrid and corrupt advertising industry by the throat and shake it, putting a final stop to all the pressure on editors and publishers to make their wares appeal to the young. The young, economically speaking, are rubbish, and will remain so until they are fifty, their children grown up, their mortgages paid off, and earning more than they have ever earned before.

At the first serious meeting of the *Oldie* board on Monday I will be putting my proposal for an Oldies Association, partly an irresistible pressure group, partly a magazine-distribution wheeze, partly a massive popular movement, with traces of the Italian Risorgimento (1815–16) and traces also of other, more recent historical movements.

I see gigantic parades, as in Red Square, composed of a human tide of shuffling oldies, flanked on either side by their cavalry, the wheelies, in invalid chairs. I hear speeches and cheering and massed voices singing anthems – except that where Mussolini's admirers sang of *giovinezza* and *primavera* – youth and spring – the oldies will sing of *vechiaia* and *autumno* – old age and autumn.

As a straw in the wind, I see that the EC is about to ban tobacco advertising in youth-oriented magazines. By the time we have finished, there will not be a single youth-oriented magazine left in the country. Our badge and banner, far from being a lightning flash or red star, will be the Ministry of Transport device signifying Old People Crossing. '*Hoc signo vinces*' will be our slogan, taken from Emperor Constantine.

Both December and January were notable for the large amount of publicity the *Oldie* magazine was receiving prior to its launch. Richard Ingrams's picture was plastered everywhere – playing the piano, looking sombre with his reading glasses resting on his nose, in denims, in a punkish outfit posing in the *Observer*, displaying more versatility than the most accomplished of actors in presenting the various aspects of his persona.

Toby Young, writing in the *Evening Standard* of 14 January, with the bold headline 'There's no fool like an Oldie fool', reproduced the *Observer* picture of Richard attired in street-cred leather looking exactly the type of ageing swinger he himself loathed. In his article Toby discerned a desperate man who would do anything to hype the new magazine.

In the past fortnight he has given interviews to virtually every broadsheet newspaper and even put in an appearance on *Tonight with Jonathan Ross*, a programme not noted for its large audience of retired people. 'I'll do anything for publicity,' he admits . . .

And then there's the title. It's all very well being tough-minded about the onset of old age if, like Richard Ingrams, you're only fifty-three. But genuinely old people aren't so blasé about it . . . The reason Ingrams is calling it the *Oldie* is not to attract older readers but to demonstrate his contempt for those who are obsessed with youth. 'Just look at that Freddie Mercury business,' he says. 'They were running pages of stuff on someone they'd never heard of. I'd never heard of him.'

Would there be enough people, Toby Young wondered, who shared Ingrams's hatred of middle-aged trendies, to turn the *Oldie* into a success, especially at a time when the advertising industry was in a deep phase of recession? The media buyers were unlikely to be keen to woo a magazine that gave their profession the blame 'for so many of the ills of modern Britain'. Nevertheless it was true that Richard Ingrams did have 'a considerable cult following in his own right'. 'The most realistic assessment', in Toby's view, was that the *Oldie* had 'a slim but fighting chance of success'.

> It's just possible that Richard Ingrams will tap a rich seam with his broad-side against youth-obsessed media folk, just as he did with *Private Eye*. If he pulls it off, who knows, even the hated advertisers may come round.

A marketing-company director, Peter Wallis, had given as his opinion that: 'If he can really get well-off, high-spending, disgruntled middle-aged people, and persuade media buyers that he's got them, that's the Holy Grail.'

After the first issue of the *Oldie* appeared on 19 February, Nigel Dempster, having been a long-time foe of Richard ever since parting from *Private Eye* in acrimonious circumstances, wrote a lengthy article in the *Daily Mail* in which he poured scorn on the magazine and its chances of survival. He was none too complimentary about Richard either. In his view, 'it had become apparent that "Lord Gnome" is doing little more than making an exhibition of himself. He has gone from juvenile to senile in one easy step.'

> He is now to be seen most evenings, when not at work on his proofs and headlines, surrounded by a large group of young acolytes in one of Soho's busier watering holes, the Groucho Club.
>
> His grizzled head remains smiling and, yes, gnomic, as gales of twenty-something laughter and bright-eyed chatter swirl around him. Here his troubled spirit seems to find some kind of balm. And of course – Ingrams

loves a contradiction – it was here, in a temple of youth, that the idea for the *Oldie* crystallized.

The premise did appear to Dempster to be sound: 'a magazine written by senior, but not elderly journalists, who would be able to impart their wisdom to a sophisticated market unburdened by the worst idiocies of "yoof" culture and the meretricious baggage that goes with it'. But he found the layout 'curiously lacklustre' and the advertising scant – 'in the main provided by principal backer Naim Attallah'.

> To me, the *Oldie* is the ultimate conceit and folly of Richard Ingrams. There is no need, no marketplace even, for the magazine, yet he has persuaded friends and acquaintances into funding the publication – which serves only to provide him with a position he has lacked since retiring from the *Eye*.
>
> Ingrams was a cult figure in the sixties and seventies when the *Eye* was a biting innovative publication fearing no one and losing fortunes imprudently defending libel actions brought by monsters like Robert Maxwell.
>
> But his day, as proved by this silly venture, is over. In the words of his hero Muggeridge, he clings on to the past like 'the one tune in the memory of a deaf man'.
>
> 'So,' as *Private Eye*'s adolescent poet E. J. Thribb would say, 'farewell, Richard Ingrams. And farewell, *Oldie*.'

Both Ingrams and the *Oldie* were to prove to have more staying power than Nigel predicted, but Jane Thynne in the 'Media and Marketing' section of the *Daily Telegraph* earlier reported the disillusionment of many potential readers at the choice of name for the magazine. Her opening paragraph said it all:

> 'What a ghastly name. Why not *Dignity*, *Seniority*, *Doyen*, *Maturity* or *Eldership*. But not *Oldie*!' appealed Mrs Joan Swinge from Bournemouth. The name makes marketing men, too, feel faint. The *Oldie*'s logo, the little triangular street sign of two stooped OAPs, has already been dropped by the Department of Transport because it was considered offensive.
>
> When people stopped thinking that Richard Ingrams's new venture was a hoax, and some still have not, they started advising him on how to change it . . .
>
> 'There have been complaints,' mumbles the editor, gazing out of the window. 'But they know it's hopeless to try to persuade me. I don't think Bron liked the name either. But what I like about it is it's really saying we're not all that tremendously serious.'
>
> Yet they are . . .

The magazine had already received approaches from 'companies wanting to advertise electronic stairlifts and alarms which ring when you fall over'. But, Ingrams winced, 'We're trying not to have those kind of things. Someone said they wanted to write about oldie diseases, but I thought ughh.'

The Grim Reaper, however, will get a glamorous degree of attention. 'Oh, we're not avoiding death at all. In fact, I want a death column and we may have a feature on where people want to be buried, and perhaps "A Good Way to Go" about how people would like to die.' . . .

Unsurprisingly, Ingrams's new venture has brought foreign film crews flocking. 'Canadian broadcasting were hugely delighted. They said to me, "We could never talk like you do. We couldn't even use the word old. We have to talk about mature Canadians." '

In Scotland the *Scotsman* focused on the tremendous amount of personal coverage Richard was enjoying as a result of the new magazine:

Finally the *Oldie* is out. And its editor is in. A master of advance publicity, Richard Ingrams has in recent weeks enjoyed many middle-aged double-page newspaper spreads, through which he has exhorted the world to revere wrinkles by reading his new magazine . . .

There was just one apology the magazine was making – for failing to keep a promise never to mention Madonna. A new biography of her was reviewed under the justification: 'It only goes to show how rash it is to make promises of any kind.'

It's been a while since Ingrams's slights have been reported so widely. Since his scene-stealing departure from *Private Eye* in 1986 (he announced his resignation at a farewell lunch for Auberon Waugh) he has been something of a jobbing hack . . .

The years between the *Eye* and the *Oldie* also featured a personal crisis: Ingrams's wife Mary, with whom he shares two children, Jubby and Fred, left him after almost thirty years. Another son, Arthur, was born with cerebral palsy and died, aged six, in the seventies.

Professionally, the columns and writing of recent years never quite matched up to the glory days when he ruled the establishment. In and out of court he went, sued by business tycoons and newspaper moguls, threatened frequently with imprisonment, an acerbic star in the journalistic field, always the first to relate a gossipy tale and the most merciless in his description of its protagonists.

The return to magazine editing had been prompted by the way 'hitherto respectable newspapers' were 'pandering to young readers'. It just took a pop-music feature in a serious newspaper to have him in a miff. 'He refuses to accept that his response to these rock articles is an overreaction.' In any case, being an oldie was a state of mind:

> 'There's no one age or anything like that when you become one,' he asserts. 'It's very hard to define, you know. In my own mind I always think of an oldie as someone who can't set the video.' . . .
>
> Young people, according to Ingrams, will be interested: for too long [the] marketing tyrants have said young people are only interested in rock music, sex and nothing else.

Julie Burchill, the *Mail on Sunday* columnist and founder of the *Modern Review*, a quarterly devoted to pop culture, was reported as having said she found the first issue of the *Oldie* 'disgraceful'. Her comment on Richard Ingrams and his cohorts was that they 'were once famous for being young and irreverent', but now were comporting themselves like 'babbling senile morons'. 'I think a little more growing-older-gracefully would be in order,' she said. 'They are carrying on like malcontented adolescents who don't feel at ease with the world.'

As a knock-on effect, I was also on the receiving end of much publicity through my financial backing of the project. My link with Asprey, incorporating Mappin & Webb and Garrard's, kept being mentioned to give the story a more glamorous edge. The *Women's Herald* in Glasgow provided a typical example, asking whether the *Oldie* would turn to gold for 'the man with the Midas touch' who had been 'bewitched by gold since he was a child'.

> At a Celebration of Gold exhibition in Edinburgh recently, he could not conceal his delight in the wealth of *objets d'art* and jewellery. These included the pieces he designed himself – a sensually curving suite of jewellery and a lithe panther in solid gold . . .
>
> 'Gold is a beautiful metal,' he enthuses . . . 'It shines and glitters but has constancy. Men have fought and died for it. It evokes all kinds of historic memories. Gold is revered and people of great taste appreciate its beauty.'

The reverberations of the *Oldie*'s advent reached even as far as the offices of the *New York Times*, which carried a long article to coincide with the first issue. It seemed to them to be a 'sort of *Rolling Stone* for the graying set'.

> Mixing humor and rant with serious reportage, it wants to do battle with the cult of youth. To borrow a phrase from Huey Lewis and the News, a

group few at the magazine would have heard about, the *Oldie* wants to make it hip to be square.

'I call it hip replacement – putting hip into old,' says Emma Soames, formerly the editor of *Tatler*, now deputy editor of the *Oldie* . . .

Mr Ingrams asserted that that youth culture could not even be considered genuine culture. Pop music, for instance, had 'nothing to do with art; it's just a big racket'. He would be 'reaching out to the "culturally isolated" older person, who "feels like a bit of a stranger in the modern world" '. But,

Despite the fact that he was starting a magazine during an economic recession that had well-established publications on the ropes, Mr Ingrams commissioned no market research. 'This whole youth-culture thing has come about because the media is being directed by marketing men,' he said. 'You've got to do what you think is good and then if people buy it, they buy it; if they don't, you pack up. You can't go out into the street and try to find out what people want, because they don't know until they get it.'

The magazine would feature such people as those Richard Ingrams called 'old blood', including Germaine Greer, Dame Barbara Cartland and Auberon Waugh. Germaine Greer had argued in her recent book on the menopause that 'women should spurn the Joan Collins route to artificial youthfulness'. She would, however, 'be writing quite a lot about her life in the country', Richard said. 'It will take in politics as well, but basically it will be about her garden. She has all these geese.'

The Times of London had meanwhile sent Kate Muir along to talk to Richard at the Groucho Club.

The magazine is the solution to Mr Ingrams's mid-life crisis. It fills the limbo between being too old to edit *Private Eye* and too young to die . . . [He] still peppers his conversation with the 'rathers' and 'terrifically' of the junior dorm and refers to his best friends by their surnames. By moving directly from caricaturing himself as the naughty schoolboy of *Private Eye* to the batty eccentric of the *Oldie*, he has successfully circumvented adulthood . . .

Today he is sitting at a table in the darkest corner supping his third cappuccino. Such are the trials of the teetotaller, which Mr Ingrams became many years ago when he discovered he preferred a bottle to a glass of wine at lunch. Among the sharp suits of the Groucho he sticks out like an escaped don in his corduroys and cashmere sweater which is riddled with either moth or bullet holes.

A month later the *Sunday Times* remarked that Richard Ingrams seemed to have become a permanent resident at the Groucho, saying, 'I regard it as a home from home.' This made a curious contrast to his remarks in October 1985 after it opened: 'I was privileged to be taken to lunch the other day at the Groucho Club . . . I have no desire whatsoever to join.'

'I have to eat my words as well as the pudding,' he tells me. It is the club's puddings that have caused this volte-face. 'Treacle pudding, bread-and-butter-pudding,' dribbles the old 'un, 'they appeal to oldies.'

I wondered why he did not patronize the Academy Club in Beak Street, Soho, whose *genius loci* is his friend Auberon Waugh. 'It's a bit too spartan for me,' says Ingrams. 'I've complained to Bron that it should have cushions on the seats.'

I have another theory. Ingrams (54) at the Groucho is usually surrounded by a bevy of literary lovelies. Waugh (52) at the nearby Academy is similarly placed. Could there be rivalry between these two revered oldies? Were they to patronize the same club, it would inevitably turn into a competition to see who could attract the most nubiles.

Alan Taylor in *Scotland on Sunday* wished a fond hello to the *Oldie*, as 'Richard Ingrams's latest adult comic hobbled into newsagents, its market the long in the (false) tooth, the post-menopausal and the pre-retired'.

Most disappointing, though, was the advertising, which offered no recourse for the incontinent, those abandoned by heartless offspring or the battered victims of grandchildren. The ad department ought to sort that out right away. I did, however, study the classifieds with my magnifying glass and was encouraged to ring a number that promised to infect me with 'insane laughter'. For just 36p an off-peak minute a man shrieked down the phone as if someone was tickling his oxsters before delivering a truly awful joke about the Big Bang theory. Alexander Graham Bell must be turning in his grave.

In the autumn of 1991, Selina Blow (ex-Quartet) was living in New York and making a name for herself in the world of fashion. The New Yorkers loved the architectural and horticultural inspiration that she brought to her designs, giving them a dotty English look that was perfectly in tune with her personality. An illustration for an article in *Avenue* magazine showed her one spring Saturday afternoon, walking two Austrian pugs along the upper reaches of Park Avenue, dressed

in an iridescent purple velvet jacket (modeled on one worn by her aunt in

1905), a man's simple white dress shirt, nondesigner blue jeans, and a pair of gold leather Robert Clergerie ankle boots. Around her neck was a big silver cross, à la Madonna, decorated with large faux stones. On her finger she displayed a crystal ring surrounded with water sapphires and a variety of moonstones. A large brass belt completed her colorful ensemble. Its buckle featured a brass replica of Blow's company logo: an exotic two-headed peacock, plumes spread to the wind.

In the interview Selina's passage through Quartet was covered by the following account:

> After high school, she pursued furniture restoration and interior design before settling in at Quartet Books, the publishing house run by the flamboyant Palestinian Attallah. Her job as a press officer brought her into London's fashionable circles, where she became known as one of Attallah's gaggle of well-connected young women. 'We had to go to all his parties and dress up in these plastic dresses,' Blow recalls. 'I was actually enormously fond of him. But through the eyes of others,' she adds, 'this must have seemed completely repulsive.'

In the first instance, Selina was never compelled to wear one of the plastic (actually rubber) dresses she referred to, and secondly, no one to my knowledge found these attires repulsive. On the contrary, most observers waxed lyrical about the ingenuity and dramatic effect these revolutionary outfits contributed to the merriment of the occasion. Selina's comments, as quoted, did not go down well with me at the time, but on reflection I counted her unconsidered remarks as being part of her forthright character, both amusing and artless in equal measure. Selina is adorably eccentric, with a sense of humour to match. I enjoyed her company when she was working at Quartet, and subsequently when we used to meet in New York. In those days, despite her many creative talents, she had to struggle to make a reasonably comfortable living. New York could and can be a harsh place in which to live on a limited budget. During my frequent trips to the Big Apple, we would go shopping, and, as a concession to Selina's weakness for good food and cakes, indulge ourselves in culinary pursuits – and the occasional shoe-hunting expedition.

Working at Quartet
Selina Blow

I worked for Quartet on Goodge Street from 1987 to 1988. It was a colourful and extraordinary time. Naim ran an eclectic and curious publishing house.

The main cornerstone to the firm was David Elliott, with bow tie, wild hair and a great knowledge of books. He often commented with affection and distraction, 'I don't know why I am working with all you débutantes.' Next to him in the running order was Jubby Ingrams, who was very much at the heart of Quartet – vivacious, extraordinary, witty and charismatic. Then came Olive, an accountant from Aberdeen, who sported a grey pudding-basin haircut and ruled the accounts and expenses with a heavy dry humour and an iron fist. The office cat, Saki, had been named after Mousaka, the Greek tavern on the ground floor. Following her various misadventures, including falling out of the window on to Mousaka's striped canopy, she had to wear a surgical lampshade around her head almost permanently. Things were more highbrow in the next building, where the editors were housed. I particularly remember Zelfa Hourani, who spent many arduous hours pursuing the hoped-for publication of her book on the lives of Middle Eastern women. It was remarked that she was so determined to publish it (and she did) that she was already practically doing it herself on the photocopying machine. There were many more equally delightful people making their contribution to the beat of life in this menagerie.

I was a minor in the press office, run by Anna Groundwater. In fact the job involved a lot of time in the post room sending out books. My début, and only, experience of jousting with the press was when a journalist phoned to ask me to comment on a poem written in Japanese for the actress Charlotte Rampling. I had no idea that my remarks were going to appear in the *Evening Standard* that very evening. 'It kind of rambles and I'm not sure what it says,' was the gist of my response. Naim reacted with shock and humour. 'Anna's going to kill you!' he said. After that I was returned to the post room forthwith and left press statements to Anna, who was far more capable of fielding media enquiries with punchy one-liners.

Every so often, Naim would invite Jubby and me to eat in his swish basement dining-room, where he hosted lunches with bemused but intrigued literary journalists. At these he would cajole Jubby into describing in detail the attentions of her latest admirer. I remember the cheeks of a senior literary editor slowly growing to a shade of crimson as she obliged. Then there was the famous launch of Parfums Namara, where all we girls were given rubber dresses to wear. A slightly troubled journalist asked Jubby, 'Don't you feel humiliated wearing these dresses?' 'No,' Jubby replied, 'it's great. They're free and we can take them home.'

I was also involved in the publication of Naim's massive volume of interviews with women, which created much press attention. (After the book was published, some married 'notables' who featured in its pages became concerned at what local charities they headed were going to make of their views on love, lust and life.) We took *Women* to the Frankfurt Book Fair, where the Quartet stand nestled between Hamish Hamilton and Faber. The fair involved Jubby and me walking the aisles wearing '*Literary Review*' sashes. Mysteriously a heavy book of pop-up German pornography, with machine-guns appearing out of every orifice, turned up on our desk. At a dinner with French publicists, and feeling exhausted by the atmosphere of dry air and a diet of frankfurters and apple strudel, I ordered a generous plate of steak tartare, much to Naim's amusement. Back in the UK I enjoyed travelling with Naim to promote *Women*, and ended up at a radio station in Brighton. The interviewer asked Naim, 'Why do you only employ beautiful women?' 'Noo,' he replied. 'There are ugly ones too.' Naim was never one to get tripped up by a snide comment.

With a wardrobe of rubber dresses, crushed midnight-blue velvet dresses and a lot of books I left Quartet. Naim packed me off into normal life with an Asprey knife and fork in fond memory of my steak tartare moment at Frankfurt.

Forty-four

The period 1991–2 saw the publication by Quartet of the memoirs of three women, each in her own way an outstanding figure. These were *Palace of Solitude* by the ex-Empress Soraya of Iran, *Keeper of the Gate* by Selwa 'Lucky' Roosevelt, the former President Ronald Reagan's chief of protocol for a remarkable seven years, and *The Sieve of Time* by Leni Riefenstahl, Hitler's favourite cinematographer who was among the greatest of her profession in the twentieth century. These women had one thing in common: all three had exerted great influence within their own milieu and had a direct impact on the world stage.

Palace of Solitude, an account Princess Soraya wrote many years after the events it describes, was originally published in France to great critical acclaim. *Paris Match* called it, 'A testimony of historic import, the chronicle of an unusual personal destiny'; *Figaro* described it as, 'A tale from *The Arabian Nights*'; *France-Soir* declared that, 'Princess Soraya writes with nostalgia . . . control . . . attention to detail; and *Point du Vue Images du Monde* thought it 'the definitive autobiography'. The translator for the English edition was Hubert Griggs. The book told a story that began with great promise and ended in sacrifice; of a life distinguished by love and strife and unfulfilled because of the vagaries of destiny. Soraya Esfandiary Bakhtiary was only sixteen when she married the Shah of Iran. Seven years later she had been repudiated and divorced for failing to provide the Shah with a much-needed male heir.

Her mother was German, and her father a Persian from the proud Bakhtiary tribe. Her upbringing was somewhat nomadic and she received her education in Isfahan, Berlin and Lausanne, so when she was chosen for her beauty and culture to be empress she came to the task with a sense of rootlessness. Nevertheless she displayed great strength of character in a turbulent period of Iran's history arising from the country's poverty, the exploitation of its oil by Western companies and the political threat posed by nationalism and communism. She helped the Shah to grapple with all these problems. Her misfortune – sterility – was one that could carry no personal blame, but it undermined what had begun in genuine love. The Shah was never able to reconcile the affection he felt for her with the harsh political imperative. Their divorce followed at her suggestion and she severed all ties with Iran for the good of the country.

There were two reviews in the UK which stood out above the rest. One was by Parviz Radji, the last Iranian ambassador at the Court of St James before the downfall of the Shah. The other took the form of an interview conducted by the late Lynda Lee-Potter, the well-known *Daily Mail* journalist. Parviz Radji's review was most enlightening, especially since it came from someone who had been close to the Shah and who had some intimate knowledge of events during that period. I therefore sought the author's permission to reproduce it in its entirety.

Two Loves of the Lonely Princess
by Parviz Radji
(originally printed in the *Spectator*, 4 July 1992)

Mohammad Reza Pahlavi, the late Shah of Iran, married three times. His first wife, Fawzia, sister of King Farouk of Egypt, was acknowledged to be ethereally the most beautiful. His third, Farah Diba, was without doubt the most humane, and by far the best educated. Soraya Esfandiary, his second and the authoress of the melancholically titled present volume, was incomparably the loveliest. The one and only time I saw her, the impression she made was an enduring one. Her piercing iridescent eyes were the colour of emerald. Her lily-white skin, as the Persian metaphor describes it, [was] like a marble piece under which a candle was aglow. She had been endowed by nature with an over-abundance of feline allure.

The Shah chose her from her photographs, and throughout their seven-year marriage he remained, uncharacteristically, not only faithful but uxorious. Her court life in Tehran was miserable due entirely to the endless intrigues and rivalries of the Shah's ambitious and meddlesome sisters and the machinations of his domineering mother. Despite that, her married life seems to have been happy, if curiously formal, French being the only language in which they would *tutoyer*, and there is a telling passage about the seriousness with which husband and wife viewed one another:

> I can still remember the masked ball at Princess Ashraf's house, for which Muhammad Reza had decided – royalty demanded it – to disguise himself as a lion, and I, for the same reason, as Madame de Pompadour.

She endured the political vicissitudes of her husband's confrontation with Mossadeq and credits herself with suggesting to the Shah the idea of mounting a coup against the recalcitrant prime minister. She shared his flight into temporary exile and detected in him a tendency both to despondency and indecisiveness at moments of crisis, and to vainglory and megalomania when

[535]

success seemed assured. It was her inability to provide the Pahlavi dynasty with a male heir that spelt the end of her reign as Empress.

Her separation from the Shah was with reluctance but not acrimony and led, predictably, to a crisis of identity and to two years of frenzied and aimless travel. Eventually she settled to a *dolce vita* existence in Rome and attempted to fulfil her childhood ambition of becoming a 'Scarlett O'Hara'. Her film, *The Three Faces of a Woman*, was a flop but in the process she met the director, Franco Indovina. He had a wife and children, was 'an impossible love', as she describes it, not least because to begin with, they couldn't even communicate in the same language. But her initial qualms were somehow overcome, and they shared together five years of blissful harmony, until he died in a plane crash in his native Sicily.

'*A quoi ça cert de voyager quand on ne peut jamais se quitter,*' Simone de Beauvoir would have said to her, but to no avail. After Franco, Soraya fled again, to Denmark, to the fjords of Norway and to the vapidity of Roman high life. And, again, she recovered to settle, in Paris this time, where she lives today.

Palace of Solitude is a straightforward account of Soraya's life and two loves. It is not a book of captivating literary style or enormous historic value. Moreover, for some curious reason, virtually every Persian name in the book, whether individuals or places, has suffered a degree of mutilation, many beyond the point of recognition.

As someone who has suffered perhaps more than her fair share of tragedy in life, I was pleased to read in the final chapter that Soraya is not sad. 'Will I love again?' she asks. If a personal comment is permitted, may I say I very much hope so.

*   *   *

Lynda Lee-Potter's interview began with a description of Princess Soraya walking through the foyer of the Plaza Athenée in Paris, with every head turning to follow her progress. Her hair had just been done and a make-up artist had put touches to her face. The suit she wore was in white, designed by Christian Lacroix. She could still, in her late fifties, create an impression of beauty with her wide mouth, fine bone structure and slanting green eyes. The Shah, she said, had not been someone to show what he felt, but he had wept when he announced his divorce from her over the radio, telling his subjects, 'People of Iran, I have a duty to give you a son.' In the many anguished months up to that moment he had tried to find ways of remaining married to her, even suggesting tentatively that he take a second wife. 'He was weighing every possibility for us to be together, but I am too European-minded. I told him: "We are not living in harem times." ' It had been the right decision, she said.

There are many different kinds of happiness. Some people are happy because they are free. For the Shah it was important to be powerful. When I left Iran I knew in my heart I wouldn't come back. Officially I was going on vacation to St Moritz. The Shah escorted me on to the plane, as he always did. We said goodbye in front of many people, and I never saw him again.

Two months later the divorce was finalized and for a year the Shah made a desperate search for a fertile young consort, finding in the end Farah Diba, who became the new empress and fulfilled the promise of providing an heir, though history decreed he would never succeed to the throne. When Farah was in exile with the Shah in Cairo, she was said to have confided that Soraya 'remained the Shah's true love'. But Soraya was clear about the reality:

The most important thing for the Shah was his country and his people. He would never have abandoned his people for me. He would not have been happy if he had. His country was more important to him than any woman even if he loved her deeply, and I accepted that . . .

We got divorced so he could have children, it was the decision of both of us. Maybe I am wise but not strong. I have done much weeping but I was happy when his son was born. I cut off the life I had before in my country. Looking back, everything was destiny. My life was meant to be like this . . .

The Shah insisted when they were divorced that she should have the title of princess and he ensured that she was financially secure.

The death of Franco Indovina brought to an end a period of happiness in which they had lived together in Rome in a house she described as, 'Warm, full of sunlight with wide picture windows looking out on a garden filled with flowers and trees.' With Franco she had learnt to be carefree after previously learning how to be an empress. But Franco's wife and two daughters were the leading mourners at his funeral and there was no place in the ceremony for Soraya. Bereavement could, she felt, be worse than divorce: 'To deaden my sorrows, I returned to my worldly pleasures. Parties where I talked too much, dances where the music had no importance.' Through grief she had come to a tranquillity:

It would be terrible for people to think my life has been bad. I look back on my life as a good one.

I have seen much unhappiness but one nice day of spring makes me happy, an animal gives me joy. I am all right with myself . . . I would love to be in love but it is not a thing you can command to your body or your heart. You can only wait and if it is meant to be it will come.

It was a source of regret for Quartet that Princess Soraya opted not to come to London for the launch of her book. I had already planned down to the last detail a royal party for her that would have received massive coverage in the press and helped to sell the book to a far wider readership than it actually reached. Perhaps she felt the glare of publicity that such an event was likely to attract would put her ill at ease. I could think of no other explanation for why she should decline to promote her life story to an interested world. It was undoubtedly a disappointment to all those who had worked on her book this side of the English Channel as well as to the British media, which would have welcomed her warmly but were deprived of the privilege. From a public-relations point of view, her decision to stay away was a bit of a disaster.

In stark contrast with Princess Soraya, 'Lucky' Roosevelt proved to be skilled in the art of the charm offensive. She promoted *Keeper of the Gate* with such gusto as to make us all feel like novices. This book of memoirs was truly fascinating and attracted a great deal of attention. Her many friends were spread around the world and her popularity was so strong as to be virtually unassailable. She was chief of protocol to the US State Department and the White House during the Reagan years, a key insider and the most famous of the 'power brokers'. Her task was to promote America on the international scene and help its leaders and spokesmen to avoid the sort of gaffes and disasters that could provide fodder for the front pages of the daily papers and television news. In this she reported directly to Ronald Reagan, George Bush Snr and George Schultz with tremendous style and verve. She had arrived at this position from being the Tennessee-born daughter of Lebanese immigrants who had won a scholarship to Vassar and rejected the arranged marriage to a suitor she called 'the sheikh' her family had planned for her. Instead she married Archibald Roosevelt, the grandson of President Theodore Roosevelt, a prominent CIA operative and a director of the Chase Manhattan Bank. Her career took her from being a reporter and journalist, CIA wife and world traveller, to the position she occupied at the heart of the world's most powerful government.

Her tenure of seven years in the post of chief of protocol was quite unprecedented. It was unusual for anyone to stay in that position for more than two years. She presided over state visits, including those of Mikhail Gorbachev and Queen Elizabeth II; she travelled to summits, oversaw the diplomatic corps and accompanied presidents and potentates, prime ministers and princes when they visited the USA. From her viewpoint she observed the world's high and mighty at their best and worst. She witnessed the friction between Nancy Reagan and Raisa Gorbachev, the warm friendship between the Schultzes and the Shevardnadzes and the inside battles between members of the White House staff.

The party to launch *Keeper of the Gate* was held in Regent Street at Garrard. It was attended by a host of politicians, writers, diplomats and journalists along with many personal friends of the author, who flocked to pay her tribute. Reporting the party for the *Daily Express*, Alice Freeman remarked that during her seven years as chief of protocol, she had supervised 'some 30,000 diplomats along the way', which meant that 'a throng of champagne-sipping party-goers were no match for her well-honed skills'. While the rest of us indulged in chit-chat, 'Mrs Roosevelt was relaxed enough to muse on gambling', saying, 'That's how I got my nickname. I was always lucky at poker – and, of course, no one could pronounce my first name.' Despite this she had never played cards at the White House. 'Not once in all those years. I don't think I even asked Nancy whether she played bridge – but of course I never had a day off.' As everyone minded their etiquette,

Lady Menuhin opted to play a different tune – introducing her husband, legendary violinist Sir Yehudi, with the memorable line: 'Have you met my old fiddler?' Sir Yehudi was unabashed. 'Everywhere I go, I am the oldest person,' he confessed. 'In fact I even once met President Roosevelt.'

The book was hailed as a great success in the UK, receiving favourable reviews from leading newspapers and periodicals, many of which touched on her warm-heartedness and good humour – as well as her resourcefulness. Dean Godson in the *Spectator* singled out her remark that her job was 'rather like being the mayor of a small town with an incredibly demanding constituency'.

Predictably, representatives of Third World dictatorships turned out to be the most demanding of the lot. Thus, the Zaireans in President Mobutu's entourage complained that the breasts of Roosevelt's junior protocol officers were too small, and chastised their hosts for not providing call girls (they declared that such matters were much better handled on their trips to France).

King Hassan of Morocco also created his share of problems by dispatching some unconventional advance men – namely, the royal teamakers. To the consternation of the Secret Service, they arrived at the White House dressed in pantaloons, red fezzes and pointy slippers, carrying silver teapots, bunsen burners and picnic hampers; to the even greater horror of the White House curator, they proceeded to settle down on the red-carpeted floor of the main hall, portable stoves ablaze. Only the timely intervention of the protocol office averted a major diplomatic incident.

Bricks were just as likely to be dropped on the American side, though it was disappointing to discover that a story about Yitzhak Shamir being served spinach sprinkled with bacon was apocryphal. It was true, however, that the US Air Forces' Singing Sergeants serenaded the Israeli prime minister with, 'Soon I'll be done with the troubles of the world, I want to meet my Jesus.' Dean Godson felt Lucky might have said more about the more unfortunate and perplexing side-effects that could follow at times from over-enthusiastic diplomacy, as in the case of Nicolae Ceauşescu, who 'used his public receptions in the West to legitimize his rule in the eyes of ordinary Romanians'. There were also hundreds of American pronouncements, including a speech of praise by Mrs Roosevelt herself to President Li Peng, that 'emboldened the Chinese regime to launch its brutal crackdown at Tienanmen Square'; but then, 'as she observed in the middle of a flap over a dinner menu, "apple pie is much more complex than arms control" '.

Paul Johnson in the *Sunday Telegraph* felt her memoirs gave 'an unvarnished picture of White House infighting', and that she was 'particularly good on the destruction of General "Al" Haig'. Sue Crewe in the *Literary Review* considered that

> Her relationship with the First Lady [Nancy Reagan] throughout the Reagan presidency is one of the more intriguing threads of the memoir. In an effort to be fair, the author bends over backwards so far that one fears for her lumbar muscles, but she doesn't manage to disguise the fact that she loathed Nancy and despised her philistinism and insensitivity. 'Lucky' was particularly incensed when Mrs Reagan insulted the serious and literary President Alfonsin of Argentina by putting athletes and popular entertainers at his table. The chief of protocol felt obliged to apologize to his ambassador, concluding sourly, 'I did not add that Mrs Reagan had forbidden her staff to show the seating to anyone until immediately before the dinner.'

The seating at official banquets was one of Lucky's constant worries, she told Andrew Stephen in an interview for the *Observer* magazine:

> 'You'd be *amazed* at the kind of things that heads of state get ruffled about. Have I made a mistake? Do these two people have a language in common? Did so-and-so get the food they wanted because they're allergic to the thing they're serving. There's a million little details to be preoccupied with. Once

one of these events began, you sort of held your breath and hoped it would go off flawlessly.

Getting flags and national anthems right was another pitfall, especially at the time of the break-up of the old Soviet Union. Giving gifts to Arabs that depicted owls was forbidden, since they are regarded as birds of ill-omen in the Middle East; and blue and white had to be avoided for more pragmatic reasons when Arabs were in town, those being the colours of the Israeli national flag. Prince Philip once took umbrage at being asked to turn off a light in his car for security reasons, since he was making himself into a better target, and slammed the door in Lucky's face in a fury.

But he later apologized. 'There are few men in the world more attractive than Prince Philip,' she now says diplomatically. And 'the Queen is far lovelier than her photos'. She cannot speak too highly of that other heroine to Americans, Margaret Hilda Thatcher, either: 'It was a pleasure working with her. She was a joy – no fuss, very unfussy, very undemanding. Very appreciative of everything. She has more humour than I think she's given credit for by your press.'

In summary, as she looked back at her career, she said:

'You know, it's interesting. Looking back, you see things before they actually become apparent to the public – and that's one of the great joys of the job. You have insights into what's coming. I realized that with the visit of the first Hungarian into Washington just at the end of the Reagan administration: already he was talking about capitalism, a market economy, freedom of speech. And all of a sudden, I thought: "My God! What am I hearing?" And then I realized we were moving into a New World. The whole thing was a wonderful experience.'

Douglas Fairbanks Jr said her account was, 'A generous and unique glimpse into Lucky Roosevelt's fascinating life'; while in Nicholas Cage's opinion, 'Of all the books that have come out of the Reagan administration, Lucky Roosevelt's is the most fun. [It is] by far the most fascinating behind-the-scenes view.'

Leni Riefenstahl may have been slight in build, but she was big in everything else. She was a giant of her generation, with so many talents it was hard to conceive of their all being in one person. Before the advent of the talkies, she had been a silent-film star in Germany; prior to that she had been a brilliant dancer. She then went on to become a formidable sportswoman, an amazing photographer and a film-maker of prodigious scope and ability. She always had a highly perceptive eye, was a stickler for the minutest detail and a perfectionist in whatever assignment she took on. Her single-mindedness could be both a strength and an irritation. Difficult to handle, impossible to shift from any set course, she embodied the Aryan discipline with a steely resolve to have her own way, whatever that might entail.

The first time I set eyes on her was at the Frankfurt Book Fair, in the German section. Many years before that chance encounter I had tried with no success to make contact after seeing some of her films on television. The impact of her work had completely bowled me over with its artistry and power. Tracking her down turned out to be an extremely difficult process. Eventually, through a highly reliable German source, I did secure an address for her in Munich. But though I wrote, I received no reply. This was perhaps not surprising, but when I saw her in Frankfurt and introduced myself, her eyes flashed as she casually informed me she remembered getting my letter. No explanation was forthcoming as to why she had never replied, but she was friendly and suggested I submit a written proposal for what I had in mind. With that, our cooperation began, and led in due course to the publication of her memoirs, *The Sieve of Time*, on her ninetieth birthday. It was edited and in part translated from the German by Jennie Bradshaw (now Erdal). 'My aim,' wrote Leni, 'was to tackle preconceived ideas, to clear up misunderstandings. I spent five years working on the manuscript; it was not an easy task since I was the only one who could write these memoirs. The book did not turn out to be a happy one.'

In fact, to mark her seventy-fifth birthday back in 1977, *Stern* magazine had wanted to write up her life story, but Leni Riefenstahl had refused to sanction the project in the belief that she was the only one who could do justice to her own life. Her career began on the stage in the early 1920s, working as a ballet dancer for Max Reinhardt among others. Her début as a film actress came in 1925 with *Der heiliger Berg* (*The Holy Mountain*), filmed in the Alps by Arnold Fanck, her mentor, who was the father of the vaguely pantheistic mountain cult in Weimar cinema. In the late 1920s, Riefenstahl became the high priestess of this cult, starring in, among other films, *Die weisser Hölle vom Piz Palü* (*The White Hell of Piz Palu*, 1929), directed by Fanck in collaboration with G. W. Pabst; and *Stürme über dem Montblanc* (*Storm over Mont Blanc*, 1930), directed by Fanck. Her last film with Fanck was *SOS Eisberg* (1933), but a year earlier she had laid the foundations for her own company and co-authored, directed and produced, besides playing the leading role in, *Das blaue Licht* (*The Blue Light*), which the critic David Thomson has called 'the pre-eminent work of mountain mysticism'.

Hitler admired her artistry, and despite her loathing for Joseph Goebbels and the fact she was never a party member, commissioned her to make a film record of the 1934 Nazi rallies at Nuremberg. Premièred in Berlin in 1935, *Triumph des Willens* (*Triumph of the Will* – Hitler had suggested the title) won a gold medal at the Venice Film Festival and established Riefenstahl as Germany's foremost film director. The next year she filmed the 1936 Olympic Games in Berlin. This was not a Nazi party commission, but came from the International Olympics Committee. The gala performance of *Olympia* in Berlin in April 1938 marked Hitler's forty-ninth birthday, and it took the prize for best film at Venice. The power of the imagery in these two films and the virtuosic way they were cut and assembled make them unforgettable, though, given their historic context, their aesthetics were destined never be disentangled from the political polemic of their background. In the words of David Thomson, Leni Riefenstahl became 'arguably the most talented woman ever to make a film', but was 'still neglected in an age of feminist militancy'. Jean Cocteau had hailed her with the words, 'How could I not admire you, for you are the genius of film and have raised it to heights seldom achieved?' The pioneer of the British documentary movement, John Grierson – a committed man of the left – gave it as his opinion that, 'Leni Riefenstahl is one of the great film-makers in history', likening his salute to the one Churchill gave to Rommel:

> Leni Riefenstahl was the propagandist for Germany. I was a propagandist on the other side . . . I took Leni Riefenstahl's films and cut them into strips to turn German propaganda against itself; but I never made the mistake of forgetting how great she was. Across the devastation of the war, I salute a very great captain of the cinema. There has been only one true masterpiece of the Olympiad and that is of course Leni Riefenstahl's in 1936.

On a trip to New York, I was invited to lunch by Tina Brown, who was then editor of *Vanity Fair*. During the course of our conversation, I happened to mention the proposed memoirs of Leni Riefenstahl. Sharp as ever, Tina wasted no time in extracting from me a commitment to give a *Vanity Fair* contributor, Stephen Schiff, the first exclusive coverage of the book prior to its publication in the UK, by arranging for him an interview with Leni. In my wild exuberance at the prospects of gaining a heightened profile for the book, I readily agreed but omitted to ask Tina for any kind of financial consideration. Unbeknown to me at the time, the *Sunday Times* had already interviewed Leni under the impression that their interview would be run as an exclusive prior to the book's publication. While Leni acknowledged that she gave the interview to someone she knew at the *Sunday Times*, she was adamant she had never given the newspaper the right to publish it before the *Vanity Fair* article. The *Sunday Times* then became equally entrenched in their position and a legal battle ensued that cost Quartet a great deal of money. In this Quartet found itself having to protect what were essentially the interests of *Vanity Fair*.

By the time the litigation was over, and *Vanity Fair* had published their long-awaited interview ahead of the field, Quartet found itself deeply out of pocket for having kept its word to the magazine. Yet when I applied to *Vanity Fair* for reimbursement of the legal fees incurred on their behalf, they washed their hands of the matter completely. The affair, they claimed, had not been of their making and consequently they admitted no responsibility. Given that *Vanity Fair* had not paid Quartet any fees for what were, essentially, first serial rights, I was in my view justified in feeling aggrieved. My goodwill gesture towards Tina Brown had misfired badly on this occasion, and I resolved afterwards that journalistic favours were hardly ever likely to bear fruit. In retrospect the magazine was guilty in my opinion of unethical behaviour, and I have often wondered whether Tina was aware of the turn taken by events after she had extracted my promise. I was too proud to broach the subject with her, for I have always believed in the honour of a commitment irrespective of any commercial consideration.

The launch party for the book was held appropriately at the Museum of the Moving Image on London's South Bank. A comprehensive invitation list was sent out, but very few people turned up for the occasion. Those who stayed away did so as a sign of protest, claiming that Leni had been a Nazi who collaborated with the Third Reich, and that having any truck with her would compromise their own strongly held anti-fascist convictions. They were not even prepared to be attracted by the extaordinary fact that she had just returned from diving in the Maldives to film underwater in her ninetieth year, and that her next stop would be New Guinea. 'The only dangerous animals are the journalists who turn up,' she said.

Among the guests were Auberon Waugh, who happily posed with Leni, the newscaster Gordon Honeycombe, and Claus von Bulow, who was sporting a newly grown beard. Von Bulow stalked around the museum, the *Sunday Telegraph* reported, casting a quizzical eye at the television screens that were showing clips from some of Leni's work. 'These films have extraordinary power,' he said, 'but now some of them send shivers down my spine. They make such horrible things seem so attractive.'

Notwithstanding the general boycott of the launch party, the book itself received phenomenal review coverage, Celina Sippy, Quartet's publicity manager, having done a fabulous job with the promotion. None of the critics could resist the urge to write about the book and Leni's picture was splashed across many a front cover, including that of *The Times Literary Supplement*. Both critics and media observers were almost unanimous in acknowledging her genius as a film-maker, but the label that claimed she had been a propagandist for Hitler and his ideology continued to stick in general. Her denials that she had simply been pursuing her artistic endeavours fell on deaf ears and failed to convince any of them. She was to remain the *bête noir* of the media until her death at the age of over a hundred.

The historian Ian Buruma was allotted the task of assessing the book for *The Times Literary Supplement*. He began by looking at some of her main claims: that she had never been a Nazi, that she had never heard of Hitler before 1932, and that she had no idea what happened to the Jews until she was told in 1945. Yet, he said, this was Hitler's greatest propagandist, who when she heard of his death 'threw herself on her bed and "wept all night" '. Perhaps she had been lying for so long that she believed 'her own fibs'. Nevertheless he was prepared overall to give her the benefit of the doubt, granting credence to a 'rich, poetic inner life'. 'But the mind that looks in, naturally sometimes fails to look out, and is bound, therefore, to miss a few things – the rise of Hitler, for example, or millions of people disappearing into cattle-trucks.'

[With] her experience of rapturous mountain films, starring pure, clean, heroic German youths seeking the sublime on moonlit nights, the step towards becoming Hitler's propagandist was not a big one. She was, one might say, exactly the right woman in the right place at the right time. Was she an opportunist? Let us say that career and faith formed a seamless whole. The reason she continues to fascinate us is that she lifted Nazi propaganda to something approaching excellence.

Buruma's feeling was that her claim that *Triumph of the Will* was not propaganda, but purely and simply a documentary, was absurd and did not bear scrutiny. She had repeated the assertion that it had 'nothing ideological in it' to Gitta Sereny in an interview in the *Independent on Sunday*, but this too was 'nonsensical'.

In speech after speech, the Nazi ideals, woolly and murderous, are extolled. If Riefenstahl missed the point of her own most famous work, her boss certainly did not . . . The film, Hitler wrote [in a preface to a book called *Hinter den Kulissen des Reichsparteitag-Films* (*Behind the Scenes of the Nuremberg Rally Film*)], was 'a totally unique and incomparable glorification of the power and beauty of our movement'.

[545]

If Riefenstahl really thinks that her film is nothing but a dispassionate chronicle, her simulation of great passion, indeed worship, is the product of a deeply cynical mind, or else she is the truest of coins, the believer in whom the faith simply is reality. Again my inclination is to give her the benefit of the doubt. *Triumph of the Will* is a work of passionate engagement. Riefenstahl is intoxicated by the sheer beauty of it all.

A fellow film-maker, Lindsay Anderson, added his comments in the *European*, saying that even more memorable than *Triumph of the Will* was *Olympia*:

Its power and poetry have never been surpassed. Riefenstahl's account of its preparations, shooting and above all editing, shows the meticulous concentration of the true film artist. It won the Grand Prix at the last Venice Festival before the war. But its identification with the Nazi myth cast a shadow over its director for the rest of her life. And it put an end to her career as a film-maker.

One cannot help feeling that this condemnation and the continual repression that went with it were largely unjustified. Riefenstahl was naïve and certainly unwise to accept Nazi patronage. But she was not the first artist to sacrifice her good name for the opportunity to practise her art.

Helena Pinkerton wrote a very level-headed notice for the *Jewish Chronicle*.

That these two films, *Triumph of the Will* and *Olympia*, were also the artistic masterworks of a huge talent might not be seen as a redeeming factor. Yet her hefty book of memoirs, timed to coincide with her ninetieth birthday, portrays a woman whose greatest sins were political *naïveté*, self-absorption and a measure of cowardice. She was never a Nazi party member. Nor, she says, did she share the Nazis' views on race and Aryan supremacy . . .

And an objective viewing of *Olympia* leads to the conclusion that its most exalted star is the black American athlete Jessie Owens.

Why, therefore, had she not left Germany when the Nazis attained power, but stayed on 'despite the repressions which she claims to have abhorred'? Here it had to be remembered that many stayed 'who could and should have left, including indeed many Jews, who had better reason that Riefenstahl did to jump ship'. These had stayed 'because they felt themselves to be, above all, Germans'. Her book was worth reading to correct the many misconceptions there had been about her, for 'hers was an independent artistic vision', though she 'did allow her art to serve an evil master, and for that she must take the rap. She was certainly not heroic. But how many were?'

During an interview for *The Times* with Christian Tyler, he suggested that, 'like Marlene Dietrich, she could have gone to America'.

> Riefenstahl corrected me. Dietrich had to go to the US for her career and denounced the Nazis from there because she had been better informed of the truth by her circle.
>
> Riefenstahl's own Jewish friends – they loyally defended her later – had initially been impressed by Hitler and had advised her not to leave Germany, she said.
>
> 'You could have followed your instinct and kept away from those men.'
> 'But it was too late.'

'Riefenstahl is a tough old bird,' concluded Philip Purser in an article in the *London Review of Books*.

> When nearly sixty she began a new career as a photographer specializing in anthropological studies, notably of the Nuba people in the Sudan. At seventy-one she qualified as a scuba diver and added underwater photography to her portfolio. She has never been short of professional admirers . . . Nor, of course does she lack detractors; the latest has been Susan Sontag, who traced a line of fascist exaltation right through the *oeuvre* . . . Obsessed by these extremes of approval or censure, Riefenstahl seems unable to look back on the things she did with any objectivity or even to recognize ordinary cause and effect.

In a review in *The Times*, Mark Almond said Riefenstahl was a film genius, but predicted that her 'overlong self-defence', as represented in the memoirs, would 'do little to lift the shadows from her reputation':

> It fits too easily into the catalogue of gifted Germans who went along with Hitler, preferring to promote their own careers and genius under his patronage and remaining wilfully ignorant of the nature of his regime until too late . . .
>
> Her films will remain her legacy, arousing ambivalent admiration.

Although she had written her memoirs 'to tackle preconceived ideas and to clear up misunderstandings', Janet Watts found in an interview conducted for the *Observer* that she was not proud of the result, admitting that she was 'not gifted in writing'. She had felt it was a necessary duty, and sure enough 'the book has already been rubbished'.

Yet many people have loved Leni Riefenstahl, too. The Nuba people of the southern Sudan, for example: and they have played a part in her survival. When she finally admitted (after many struggles) that her film career was over, she went to Africa, discovered the Nuba and – almost by accident – began a new career by photographing them . . .

In all her tribulations, Leni Riefenstahl vibrates with life. For many people she will never be able to pay for her great mistake . . .

'I am not happy. But if I have not an interview . . . if I have nothing to do with the press . . . If I see my Nuba, if I dive . . . I fight against depression. Even if it is hard, I say to the life, yes.'

Quartet was to publish two more books of Leni Riefenstahl's. One of them, *Olympia*, covered the 1936 Olympics in Berlin. The other was *Wonders of the Sea*. Both were photographic books to take the breath away. *Olympia* was all in black and white, its stunning photographs documenting the spectacular games for future generations. *Wonders of the Sea* contained photographs she had shot in beautiful colour at the age of eighty-five during spectacular dives she made in the Red Sea, the Caribbean, the Maldives and the Indian Ocean. These images of great natural beauty depicted the fantastic variety of marine life: minuscule prawns, sponges, bivalves, coral in bloom and the wonderful world of fish. The splendours of their shapes and colours were again caught on film for posterity. Leni's patient, tireless efforts had resulted in a photographic collection of outstanding beauty, each intricate composition as delicate as a painting.

With her death at the age of a hundred and one in 2003, the world said farewell not only to a remarkable woman who had made her mark on history, but also to one who had evoked in unforgettable imagery the time when Germany's colossal renewal of power was poised to inflict human misery and slaughter on an unprecedented scale. Her detractors understandably continue to argue that her work is a celebration of that power – unwittingly perhaps, but undeniably. When, however, her creative contribution is viewed through an artistic perspective, devoid of its moral equivocacy, then it seems to transcend these considerations.

There was no doubting that Leni herself continued to struggle with her inner demons till the end. She survived a helicopter crash when she was ninety-eight, on her last trip to visit the Nuba. The film-maker Ray Müller visited her in hospital and asked what in her life she regretted. There had been many, many mistakes, she said. What mistakes did she mean, he asked. 'Well . . . ,' she responded, 'I mean, this relationship with the Third Reich.' For a film he made in 1993, Müller had previously made the point bluntly to her: 'I feel this country [Germany] is still waiting for you to say publicly: "I made a mistake, I'm sorry . . . " ' Leni replied:

Being sorry isn't nearly enough, but I can't tear myself apart or destroy myself. It's so terrible. I've suffered anyway for over half a century and it will never end, until I die. It's such an incredible burden that to say sorry . . . it's inadequate, it expresses too little.

Forty-five

In April 1992, in line with the avowed policy of Asprey, I embarked on a new acquisition, this time in Scotland. The move was a popular one with the Scottish press since it aimed to ensure the long-term survival of their most respected Edinburgh-based jeweller, silversmith and clockmaker, Hamilton & Inches. Founded in 1866, and a holder of the Royal Warrant, the company had been experiencing difficulties in the recession and was under-capitalized. Deirdre Inches Carr, the joint managing director of the hundred-and-twenty-five-year-old George Street firm, described the move by Asprey as a very exciting step. Mrs Carr, great-great-granddaughter of the founder, Robert Kirk Inches, added that Hamilton & Inches would retain total autonomy after the takeover.

It was a company, Gordon Milne wrote in the *Scotsman*, that employed thirteen in its workshop and twenty-odd salespersons and administrators.

It has a distinctly upmarket image and its workshops have been responsible for a huge variety of silver, clocks and fine jewellery. Four years prior to the takeover, it was given the task of repairing the Calcutta Cup rugby trophy, badly damaged in high jinks after the dinner following the Scotland–England clash. A huge life-sized silver sculpture of an eagle owl, being completed by Hamilton & Inches and the centrepiece of its window display, has been officially marked by the Assay Office as Scotland's heaviest ever work in sterling. The 26-kg sculpture, the head of which lifts off to serve as a champagne cooler with a capacity of one magnum, is likely to sell for tens of thousands of pounds.

In a press release I emphasized that it had become part of group policy, since the acquisition of Mappin & Webb and Garrard, to keep widening our base. With competition becoming increasingly fierce and the recession hitting ever harder, we realized that we had to grow if we were to safeguard all we had achieved in the last fifteen years. Asprey was obviously looking for an opportunity which would be complementary to its group activities.

Hamilton & Inches were going to benefit from becoming part of a strong group, and while it would have a close association with Garrard, its autonomy would not be encroached upon. There was no point in merely duplicating the Mappin & Webb or Garrard outlets. Hamilton & Inches would preserve its own image and retain its clientele together with its traditional policy of exceptional service, quality and value for money. Asprey intended to give strong financial backing to the company so the business could meet the challenges of an increasingly competitive future. We also believed in the principle of competition within the group. There were no plans to change the products sold by the Scottish jeweller, but I promised that the public would see a much livelier company, once the fine tuning was completed.

The 'Observer' column in the *Financial Times* reported the news as follows:

Britain may be in the grip of its worst recession since the 1930s, but the House of Asprey, owners of the world's most expensive gift-shop, seems to be on a Ratners-style expansion binge.

First it gobbled up crown jeweller Garrard, and Paris's exclusive René Boivin, not to mention Mappin & Webb. Now it has pocketed Hamilton & Inches, Edinburgh's royal silversmiths and official repairers of the Calcutta Cup.

When Asprey began buying up the opposition just under two years ago its market capitalization was less than half the size of Gerald Ratner's family firm. Capitalized at over £200 million, the 211-year-old Asprey is now five times as big as poor old Gerald's outfit, and its appetite is not yet sated. 'We are in our prime; I am very bullish,' says Naim Attallah, the well-known publisher who doubles as Asprey's joint managing director.

Like all good jewellers he refuses to disclose how much he has paid for his 'pearl of the North'. The target was undercapitalized and feeling the recession, and Asprey could hardly turn down the chance of picking up Scotland's crown jewellers.

However, Attallah insists that his firm is not over-expanding like Ratners. For a start he has no debt and close to £20 million of cash in the bank. With Sears maintaining a protective stake Asprey seems safe enough for the moment.

Acquiring a company is one thing, but finding the right person to manage it is a much harder proposition. Whenever such an appointment had to be made, I agonized over the choice, and sometimes got it wrong. People change with authority and a greater measure of responsibility; they are often overwhelmed by the enormity of the task. Although experience is a very important consideration, I have always considered it much over-valued. Energy, creativity, discipline, hard work and a sharp observant eye matter a great deal more. Along with that, the knack of enthusing people and opening their eyes to greater perspectives is equally important. Finding all these qualities in one person is seldom easy. It often involves a calculated gamble, but it is one that occasionally comes off.

This was the course I took with Julia Ogilvy, aged twenty-seven, who was running the publicity side of Garrard. She was highly disciplined, dedicated to her work and always early at her desk. We often met in the lift in the morning when everyone else was still *en route* to the office. Since I am a stickler for time-keeping I was naturally impressed. When her husband James moved to Fife in Scotland, Julia found it hard to keep commuting to London and asked me whether we could find her an assignment in Scotland that would make her life more practical and less exhausting travel-wise. With the acquisition of Hamilton & Inches, the opportunity arose for Julia to play an important role. Indeed, my secret ambition was loftier than people expected. I dared contemplate putting her in charge of the whole operation despite her youth.

Such an appointment was certainly going to be controversial for a number of reasons. Her lack of experience in a key managerial position was one, another was whether some of the staff who had been with the company a number of years would accept her in the post. The first signs of opposition came from within the Asprey board on the grounds that Julia, though she was highly regarded, would not be able to cope with employees twenty or thirty years her senior in a Scottish environment entrenched in tradition. But once I took the decision I was not to be swayed. I even had to persuade Julia to accept the challenge, for she, too, was taken aback by my proposal. To assume the role of managing director of Hamilton & Inches had never entered her head. However, after much reflection, she grasped the opportunity to make her mark in the business community.

When her appointment was announced following the resignation of Deidre Inches Carr, the *Scotsman* profiled Julia with the opening statement, 'Deep within the hallowed halls of Edinburgh's finest jewellers and silversmiths insurgent forces are at work.'

The woman prepared to ruffle such fastidiously arranged feathers is Julia Ogilvy. Three weeks ago she became the first outsider to manage the eponymous family firm . . .

Although she does not take over till 1 August, Mrs Ogilvy, twenty-seven, who is married to Princess Alexandra's son James, is spilling over with ideas to modernize, promote and package the firm.

Marketing is Mrs Ogilvy's forte. Her post at Garrard, which she held for five years, encompassed every aspect of promoting the business. It also allowed her to indulge her love for jewellery.

'I have always been interested in jewellery and I know about antique jewellery and silverware in a small way. Half the battle is liking it. To love what you are selling is very important,' she said . . .

'I think they were quite keen to put a woman in the job because Deidre has done so well and it is good to have a woman as the figurehead in a company like this.'

Naim Attallah [is] a man often charged with promoting female staff according to the length of their legs rather than the length of their CVs . . . But Mrs Ogilvy asserts that her expertise in a specialist field won her the position.

Julia was looking to carry fresh stock from new designers and was keen to coax younger people away from costume jewellery to the real thing. The expense was not as prohibitive as some might think. There were numerous things to choose from for ten pounds upwards, she said.

Julia proved to be more than equal to the challenge. Her first priority, without any prompting from me, was to gain the confidence and respect of the staff and convince them that some of the old ways needed updating to meet the fierce competition in the marketplace. She achieved both these goals in a short time and it was plain to see that the atmosphere at Hamilton & Inches was reflecting a fresh approach and a more focused objective. The displays in the shop improved and an inspired style of management based on consultation and the full cooperation of staff was introduced. The showrooms took on a grand appearance with the hallmark of elegance stamped in every corner. A revitalized energy began to sweep through the entire premises, and Julia was like a beacon of light illuminating her domain with her ineffable charm. Her dress style became less prudish, after some whispers from me, with skirts shorter and tops lower to bring a dash of verve and sophistication to her new position. She became my jewel in Scotland, for I could see she was far exceeding the most optimistic expectations I had of her. Julia has made Scotland her home since then and is very keenly involved in regional affairs. She now devotes her time to cultural and charitable activities and is highly regarded for her dedication and love of Scotland.

Rising to the Challenge
by Julia Ogilvy

Naim definitely loves women. I can't believe any of his female friends would say otherwise on the whole. From the point of view of a woman, however, he does take some getting used to. I remember, from my first visit to his famous office high above Soho with its dark walls and tiger-skin rugs, the feeling of being on some kind of filmset in an X-rated movie. On the other hand, the aspect that struck me immediately was his boyish enthusiasm for everything, augmented by the speed at which he spoke, his arms waving in the air. It was clear he had a short attention span and didn't suffer fools gladly. That suited me fine. Hearing good news made him happy and he always liked it if you agreed with his ideas, however outlandish they might seem. If you were lucky, he might forget about them later. It soon became obvious that life around Naim was always going to be entertaining, and often hilarious, and that when it came to women you didn't need to have any worries about being politically correct. He is an incredibly tactile and warm-hearted man and was often in need of a hug to cheer him along.

My days of working as PR manager at Garrard are a period I remember with great affection. Generally we coincided in the lift at around 7.30 a.m. It seemed to make sense to get on with the day as soon as possible if, like me, you had a husband working in the City and functioned better early on. (Even now it quite irritates me if I can't reach people in their office at 8 a.m.) Naim was obviously impressed by my timekeeping, though it never occurred to me that this might be a key reason for later promotion. I only knew it was a great chance to catch up with him and get some fast decisions. On other occasions I would be summoned to his spacious office at Regent Street (somewhat toned down in comparison with his Soho space) to discuss some new project. An even rarer piece of luck was to be invited to one of his fabulous lunches. It was always stimulating and fun to catch up on any gossip. You could rely on Naim to know what was going on. He always had gorgeous girls working for him, though it was a mistake for anyone to assume that he just liked women pretty. I certainly never met one in the entourage who wasn't brainy as well. He loved the challenge.

Among several hilarious memories I have of those times was the occasion when Naim bought one of his assistants a set of very sexy lingerie and immediately insisted she must try it on to show him. Unfortunately she forgot that the corridor from the ladies' loo to his office was monitored by security cameras. It took the security guards a long time to get over that one. I was fortunate enough to receive the occasional present, such as one of the tiny silver hearts he gave to all his visitors, but thankfully I don't think he would have dared to try me on the lingerie. He was always a little more circumspect where I was concerned, perhaps because I gave an impression of being fearsomely organized and bossy. It was still strangely flattering to be asked to sign a photo of me for his office: a rather sultry shot taken for *Harpers & Queen* by a smooth Italian photographer.

Soon after this I came to a major turning point in my life – a time in which

Naim played a very significant role. My husband and I had rather rashly fallen in love with a house in Scotland and I had begun commuting from Fife to London every week. Just as I was summoning up the courage to tell Naim I would have to leave him (he hated anyone leaving) to work in Scotland, he announced that Asprey was buying the well-known, traditional but by now near-bankrupt Edinburgh jewellers, Hamilton & Inches. His first thought was that I could work there and run the marketing side, but before long he'd decided I would make the perfect managing director. He was not at all put off by the fact that I was only twenty-seven and was restricted to a background in marketing. He had the agreement of my immediate boss, Richard Jarvis, but I knew he would have huge trouble in persuading the Asprey board, let alone me! The idea amazed me, and, overwhelmed by the prospect, I soon refused him. This was clearly not part of his plan. He introduced a diversionary tactic by saying I had to be a director and he needed me to come to the lawyer's office in St James's to countersign the acquisition papers for Hamilton & Inches. I arrived to find a room full of people and a set of papers with 'Managing Director' beside my name! Fortunately, with the support of my family, I had come round to the idea and was ready to go. The decision led to some of the best years of my working life.

Naim had known I could rise to the challenge, and he was right. I became convinced, too, that a woman was right for the role. Good 'people skills' were essential in those early days to remotivate the team, and ultimately marketing was probably the most relevant skill I could have had. Naim remained constantly in the background, encouraging me and so obviously proud of my achievements. Some years later, after Naim had left the Asprey group, I had the chance to lead a management buyout and had his full support all the way. Today I lead a different life, having left that period behind to found a charity, Project Scotland, providing full-time volunteering opportunities to young Scots, transforming their lives and those of their communities. I am proud to sit on the board of Lloyds TSB Scotland, to be a trustee of Columba 1400 and an Alpha leader. I can still look back on those earlier days and say that much of what I do now has only come about because of the faith, confidence and pride Naim had in me. I owe him a lot.

*   *   *

The month of June 1992 was a important milestone in the annals of Asprey's expansion into big-time acquisitions. We had been talking with Ratners, the struggling jewellery business, with a view to purchasing the Watches of Switzerland chain of shops. It took us weeks of round-the-clock negotiations to close a cash deal worth twenty-three point two million pounds. Watches of

Switzerland, which operated as an upmarket autonomous business within the Ratners portfolio, was experiencing difficult trading conditions. They had seen their profits dive from two point six nine million to eight hundred and eighty-seven thousand pounds on a turnover of twenty-one point seven million in the past year. The last available figures showed net assets standing at nineteen point two million pounds. The chain, which had twenty-five stores throughout the United Kingdom, would certainly help us to achieve our strategy of widening Asprey's geographical coverage. Jim McAdam, Ratners' chairman, with whom I developed a warm relationship during our extended negotiations, told the *Financial Times* that he had achieved a 'fair price' for the chain – although it was believed in some quarters to have been less than the company was originally seeking.

The *Daily Mail* wrote that:

Asprey's colourful deputy chairman Naim Attallah was cock-a-hoop. He first made an offer for Watches of Switzerland before Christmas. 'It was a higher offer, but I can't say how much. We want to keep good relations,' he said.

Last year, the newspaper believed, Ratners had been understood to be looking for something nearer fifty million pounds. *Retail Weekly* reported how:

Asprey's acquisition from Ratners has given a significant boost to its representation outside of London. The acquisition will also bring some economies of scale since Asprey already generates annual sales of £23 million in luxury watches, the amount paid for Watches of Switzerland. Although the business will be run as an autonomous unit, Asprey's deputy chairman, Naim Attallah, says there will be rationalizations and cost-cutting. Watches of Switzerland is represented outside of London in locations such as Leeds, Bournemouth, Newcastle-upon-Tyne, Sheffield, Cardiff and Jersey. Asprey is also to add two stores to the eleven-strong Mappin & Webb chain this year. In Paris, Asprey is to open a second René Boivin jewellery shop.

The *Independent*, announcing the acquisition, said:

Asprey, apart from its flagship store in Bond Street, London, has outlets in New York and Paris and owns Mappin & Webb and Garrard. Watches of Switzerland's upmarket positioning will fit in with the profile. The group last year reported profits of £25 million on sales of £100 million.

The Times drew a comparison between Asprey and Watches of Switzerland:

While the new acquisition is a comparatively prestigious operation, with prices starting at about £45 and ranging up to £9,000 or so for a gold Rolex Oyster, Asprey frequently scales new heights of luxury. Three years ago, it sold a fountain made of crystal, gold and semi-precious stones for more than £500,000. A diamond and emerald jewellery set is currently on offer at £2.25 million. The purchase from Ratners – for the equivalent of about 24.2 million Marks & Spencer prawn sandwiches – may be seen as poetic justice.

Activities at Asprey were now taking a new direction as a result of its various acquisitions. The structural reorganization of the whole group was going ahead in earnest. By 10 August the boardroom shake-up at Asprey had taken place, the first commentator to report on it being Michael Foster in the *Evening Standard*, who saw it as consolidating 'the power of publisher Naim Attallah as group chief executive, while giving more freedom to subsidiaries'.

It involves Asprey recognizing that its board of directors should shrink – and get more involved with strategic decisions – while giving more management headroom to the growing collection of subsidiaries.

John Asprey remains chairman and Naim Attallah gains the title group chief executive, while also taking on the role of managing director of Watches of Switzerland, Mappin & Webb and Asprey in Geneva.

A new subsidiary, Asprey (Bond Street), will take over Asprey's central showroom business based in Bond Street.

Four members of Asprey's board of directors will resign to take new positions on the board of Asprey (Bond Street).

The next day the rest of the British press followed suit, each paper reporting the news in its own fashion. John Thornhill in the *Financial Times* hit a more laconic note than usual, and was less sensational than some of the others, with 'Asprey alters structure following acquisitions', explaining it as 'turning the parent company into a holding company, and devolving most operational responsibilities to five separate business units'.

The move is designed to enhance the operation of the individual companies and allow group management to focus more on supervisory and strategic issues.

The Asprey board will be slimmed down to six members, with four executive directors resigning to concentrate on running the new subsidiary, Asprey (Bond Street) . . .

The Garrard, Mappin & Webb and Watches of Switzerland chain will also be run as separate businesses, with the rest of Asprey's companies, including international businesses and the Hamilton & Inches store in Edinburgh, being operated as part of another division.

Today was more creative with its headline, 'Purrfect Timing', above a photograph of me with the head of Kaiser, my tiger skin:

Naim Attallah, publisher, partygoer and self-publicist, has bagged more than a tiger-skin rug at posh gifts group Asprey. Next month, he takes over as chief executive of Asprey's main board. He also takes control of Watches of Switzerland, which becomes one of the group's four main subsidiaries. The others are Asprey (Bond Street), Garrard and Mappin & Webb.

The Times, with 'Attallah sparkles in Asprey reorganization', was more specific and filled in with more background information:

Mr Attallah's promotion comes as part of a corporate restructuring of Asprey, which in recent years has expanded far beyond its landmark Bond Street shop . . .

From September, the Bond Street shop will be run by a new subsidiary, Asprey (Bond Street), which, alongside the group's other trading companies, will be owned by and report to the Asprey holding company for the whole group. John Asprey will continue as executive chairman of the holding company, and will also chair Asprey (Bond Street), with Mr Attallah as his deputy.

After the reorganization, four main board directors, including Edward Asprey, the chairman's cousin, will resign from the company. But all four will immediately be appointed to the board of Asprey (Bond Street).

Mr Attallah is also to become managing director of Watches of Switzerland, a role he already fills at Mappin & Webb. Yesterday he explained his plan for Asprey's most recent acquisition. Mappin & Webb had lost its way a little under Sears ownership. 'We revitalized it. Now we plan to do the same with Watches of Switzerland . . . [which] has a magnificent name. It does not take away business from other parts of the group at all. If it is run properly it could expand everywhere.'

The *Daily Telegraph* carried the story with more panache, showing a picture of me holding some of the luxurious items from the Bond Street stock above the heading 'Attallah takes title in Asprey shake-up':

Mr Attallah, who joined Asprey in 1973, has effectively been chief executive under chairman John Asprey for the past two years, but the latest move formalizes the arrangement, he said yesterday.

From next month, Asprey . . . [is] splitting its holding company and trading functions by creating a new subsidiary, Asprey (Bond Street), to take over the activities of the Bond Street showrooms.

Four directors will resign from the holding company board to join the Bond Street board. The Bond Street base accounts for more than half of group profits.

Mr Attallah, who will be deputy chairman of Asprey (Bond Street), said the changes were part of a desire to keep each of its businesses autonomous within the group.

Asprey said the separation of functions would allow the central board to concentrate on management issues and 'adopt a more strategic focus', leaving trading details to the Bond Street board. The moves are also designed to clarify the respective roles of Mr Asprey and Mr Attallah.

The *Independent* shed more light on the board shake-up. John Asprey had removed his cousin Edward Asprey from the board, it reported, as well as three other directors 'from the main board'. The 'slimmed-down board' was 'part of a shake-up' that saw 'the promotion of Naim Attallah, the publisher, from joint managing director to joint chief executive'.

Executive directors Edward Asprey, Tom Craig, Edward Green and Robert Philpot are all to resign from the Asprey board on 31 August. They will join the board of the newly created company Asprey (Bond Street) – one of the five operating subsidiaries under Asprey plc.

Edward Asprey, who joined the main board in January 1991, is a cousin to John Asprey, the chairman and 51-per-cent shareholder. Edward has a small shareholding and runs the Asprey Gun Room in Albermarle Street.

He stressed yesterday that the shake-up simply reflected the new holding company's structure. 'I'm remaining on the board of the main trading element of the group.'

In the mid 1970s the company was riven by a family row, which pitted John Asprey and his father Eric against another branch of the family.

Asprey, which has close trading ties with the royal family, has started to feel the impact of the recession.

In March it closed a store in the City of London. In June it reported a 21-per-cent fall in annual pre-tax profits to £19.3 million despite a much-enlarged business.

Mr Attallah said the changes were necessary to cope with the rapid expansion of Asprey. Over the past two years it has purchased Mappin & Webb, Garrard & Co. and René Boivin in Paris.

Most recently it paid the struggling Ratners group £23 million for Watches of Switzerland. Advised by Hambro Magan, it is looking for more high-quality acquisitions.

The changes leave the Asprey board with three executive directors and three non-executives, including Geoffrey Maitland-Smith, chairman of Sears, which controls 25 per cent of Asprey.

From 1 September Asprey will be a holding company only. The divisions under it are: Asprey (Bond Street); Garrard & Co.; Mappin & Webb; Watches of Switzerland; and Other Businesses, which includes Hamilton & Inches of Edinburgh.

The company said: 'The new structure will allow the principal businesses to operate autonomously under central management guidance.'

The holding company board would 'concentrate on group management issues and adopt a more strategic focus', it said.

Even the *Bookseller* reported the changes at Asprey because of my links with the book trade and publishing:

Publisher and author Naim Attallah has been appointed group chief executive of Asprey, the luxury-goods retailer. Best known in the book trade as chairman of The Women's Press and of Quartet, he joined Asprey in 1973 and has effectively acted as chief executive under chairman John Asprey for the past two years. The latest move formalizes the arrangement, he told the *Daily Telegraph*.

Mr Attallah has also assumed the role of managing director of Watches of Switzerland and remains managing director of Mappin & Webb and Asprey SA Geneva. His third book, *Of a Certain Age* (Quartet), based on interviews for the *Oldie*, is published on 12 November.

The *Sunday Telegraph*, under 'City and Business', included a profile of me by Jim Levi headed 'Colourful character in the Queen's gift shop', for which he came to interview me at Regent Street.

The order from Naim Attallah to his personal assistant comes out deadpan as if it were for a gin and tonic: 'Mariella, bring me two women and two singular encounters.'

For a brief moment photographer Nick Rogers and I take the request literally and grin broadly in expectation. After all, this man seems to have the charm to conjure up anything he wants.

Of course, what we receive are two copies of the paperbacks Attallah has written: *Women* . . . and its companion male equivalent, *Singular Encounters*, a slimmer volume he produced three years later . . .

He can be hard to take seriously. For our interview he sports an excessively loud tie with a matching jacket lining which even a circus clown might eschew. 'I just love colourful things,' he says.

Yet last week Attallah became chief executive of Asprey, the jeweller whose Bond Street store is often called the Queen's gift shop.

Since Asprey went public in 1988 Attallah has been the guiding light behind a rush of acquisitions . . .

In Levi's view, I seemed as a Palestinian immigrant an unlikely partner for John Asprey and his late father, Eric, in a business that went back to the age of Victoria. Having first befriended the family when I began as a customer 'buying and selling carriage clocks in the Bond Street shop in the early 1970s', I soon had John Asprey plugged into my Middle Eastern connections and became 'the only non-family member on the board'.

'We are a good team,' Attallah says. 'We were pioneers in arranging exhibitions for Asprey all round the world. Today John and I are almost indivisible: he is the salesman and I am the administration and takeover guy.'

Not all family members took to the presence of the exotic interloper. But after a bust-up in 1980 Geoffrey Maitland-Smith of Sears moved in as peacemaker. Sears bought out the rebel family investors and [gained] Attallah.

One business colleague says: 'He never seems to relax. Although he has this reputation as a party-goer, he is a hard-working businessman who knows how to cut costs.' . . .

Originally, I had wanted to be a journalist, producing my own primitive newspaper in Arabic as a boy in Haifa during the war, but later a career in banking succeeded in defining my future.

Richard Ingrams, who used to poke fun at Attallah in *Private Eye*, has him as a backer of his new organ, the *Oldie*. . . . 'He is a good man to do business with,' says Ingrams. 'He has a good instinct for what will work and gives quick decisions.'

And in the columns of the *Oldie* Attallah has at last found a regular journalistic slot. Ingrams says: 'He is a good interviewer who does his homework thoroughly.'

Attallah is working on a third book of interviews – this time of what he calls 'real oldies'. 'These are people in their eighties and nineties, such as Enoch Powell, Lord Soper and Lord Shawcross,' he says. He interviewed Hardy Amies last week.

Attallah has managed to blend his elegant lifestyle surrounded by beautiful things and beautiful people with a puritanical, punishing work schedule. 'I am always up at 5.30 every morning and I am like a fiend at that time,' he says. 'An almost supernatural force seems to tell me there are so many things to be done and so much excitement to have.' . . .

Indeed, he still hankers for the simple life he led as a teenager when his parents sent him to live with his grandmother in Nazareth away from the civil war in Haifa.

'I remember that period with much more affection than anything else,' he says. 'We lived like people at the time of Christ, getting up with the Morning Star to feed the hens and going to sleep on the floor when the sun set.'

With the acquisition of the famous jewellery house of René Boivin in Paris in the spring of 1991, the Asprey group had incorporated a company that had achieved international fame and recognition for its innovative and breathtakingly beautiful jewellery. The pioneering work done by René Boivin was abruptly curtailed by his death in 1917. His wife Jeanne then took the courageous decision to continue her husband's work. To assist her in the task she created the 'Women's Workshop' by taking on Suzanne Belperron, Juliette Moutard and, later, her own daughter, Germaine Boivin. Masquerading as a male concern, they went on to create some of the masterpieces of twentieth-century jewellery making.

Jeanne had a less stereotypical image of women than other jewellers of the time: 'neither doll-like nor masculine, but more natural and relaxed', and the individualistic taste of the Boivin clientele, which came to include the Duchess of Windsor, Lady Diana Cooper and a whole host of actresses, also influenced the designs. Jacques Bernard, the proprietor since 1970 and at the time of the takeover, continued to uphold the inimitable Boivin style while designing new pieces for modern women.

I conducted the negotiations for the purchase of René Boivin, which were swift and conclusive. Jacques Bernard and I seemed to get on well from the outset and we were both excited about future prospects for the firm as part of the burgeoning Asprey group. We needed a foothold in Paris, and what better vehicle for this could there be than the House of Boivin, whose second-hand pieces of jewellery always fetched a great deal of money at auction. We were confirmed in having the *crème de la crème* and were truly on our way to dazzling the market with our varied products. Asprey's portfolio of companies encompassed the best names in the luxury-goods market and became the envy of our competitors. The Asprey name had taken on an international dimension and was poised to break new ground on many fronts. Our customer base had widened beyond recognition, leaving us in a less perilous position.

But the temptation to concentrate on a very few high-flyers among the customers was to remain strong. The market demands quick turnover and exists in the here and now. Hence the dilemma. Planning for the future is a long and arduous process which entails curtailing short-term benefits in favour of long-term gains. To get the balance right is an art in itself, requiring a speculative golden touch which few of us possess. Asprey's great success over a span of two decades was to prove its undoing in the years that followed.

Forty-six

Despite my attaining high executive office, I had lost none of my zest for living and my readiness to be completely open about myself had not changed over the years. I have always believed in being honest irrespective of the consequences. An amusing challenge to my confidence came in a free supplement to *New Woman* in the April of 1992 which, under the heading 'Seduction Styles', solicited a number of men in the public eye, 'from well-known Casanovas to men in the street', to divulge their secrets. Their general finding was that most men avoided trying to impress a woman with any ostentation or lavish spending on a first date. Most were also on rather shaky ground over what to cook as the 'food of love', and then there was the dilemma of expectations about where the evening would end. I replied to their set of six key questions with concise directness.

1. *When you meet an attractive woman, what do you say/do to try to impress her?*
   Be myself, neither more not less. Pretence rarely achieves its ends.
2. *If you wanted to woo her with your charm where would you take her?*
   I would invite her to lunch at my private dining-room and pay her all the attention commensurate with her beauty and intellect.
3. *How much would you spend on your first night out with her?*
   Money wouldn't matter. She would be my princess for the night.
4. *What sort of clothes would you wear to impress her?*
   I would wear my usual attire which is invariably colourful.
5. *If you were to cook a meal for her, what would it be?*
   Since I am a gourmet and a good cook, I would try to satisfy her every wish. A partridge with truffles would be a strong contender.
6. *On your first date . . . how would the evening end?*
   I would let things take their natural course. If the gods were smiling on me, I might just have to relinquish some self-control.

While my ascendancy at Asprey continued to hit the headlines, rumours became rife around town of a possible merger between the *Literary Review* and the *Oldie*. The *Evening Standard*, known for its benevolence in reporting my various activities, penned the following concerns in its issue of 18 August:

I worry for the future of my two favourite publications now that Naim

Attallah has further increased his already considerable workload by becoming chief executive of Asprey, the trinket people.

Is he still going to be able to find time to keep an eye on the *Literary Review* and the *Oldie*, the two publications that he benevolently supports for his friends Auberon Waugh and Richard Ingrams? Both are splendid organs, but, as neither sets the heather alight saleswise, they both benefit, as indeed do their incumbent stewards, from being kept under a beady eye and a tight rein.

The kindly Mr Attallah is a wealthy man. But he did not become wealthy through stupidity. He is an astute dealer. I believe, therefore, that there just might well be some truth in the rumour currently doing the rounds that he is considering merging the two magazines.

The *Literary Review* loses in the region of £120,000 per year. Indeed, only last June Mr Waugh said: 'When Naim decides that he wants to take matters easy he may feel that he does not want to continue fully subsidizing the magazine.'

The operative word here is 'fully'. There is no question of him deserting it completely. So a merger would make sense.

Mr Attallah tells me that this rumour has passed by his ear, but, as he is an honourable man, I wouldn't expect him to have said anything different. If he does decide to cut his losses – and who would blame him? – and amalgamate the two magazines, his editors will, quite rightly, be the first to know.

What chances the *Old Review*, coedited by Messrs Waugh and Ingrams, on the stands by Christmas?

I appreciated the sentiment, but stood robust in my resolution that the *Literary Review* under the editorship of my close friend Auberon Waugh should never be deprived of its separate identity, notwithstanding the amount of losses it incurred. As the most important things in my life were not the pursuit of wealth or the acquisition of power, these were secondary considerations. Wealth and power could be useful, however, in supporting worthy enterprises in the field of learning and the arts.

In June 1992 I celebrated the publication of a book by another friend. This was *A Trade of Charms* by David Elliott. It was published by Bellew, a small imprint for which David acted as a consultant. The *Bookseller* wrote up a description of the event at the Academy Club:

The Academy is a charming little place, cosy by comparison with, say, the Groucho, but perhaps a little too cosy on a hot summer's evening, especially when the party is crowded by such luminaries as the Academy's founder Auberon Waugh, Richard Ingrams, Philip Knightley and Anthony Sampson, not to mention Naim himself.

David has more experience than most of the book business, as bookseller, as publisher with Quartet, and, too briefly, as founder-editor of *Book Preview*. *A Trade of Charms* looks nostalgically at the past and casts a jaundiced eye on conglomerations and growth in publishing and bookselling, but ends on an upbeat note. The small and dedicated will survive, he believes: 'There will always be these raggle-taggle gypsies – strange, crazy people. For them profit is only a means that keeps the business going. Joy is what they are about. And they can recognize a naked emperor.'

D. J. Enright wrote about *A Trade of Charms* in *The Times Literary Supplement*, calling the book 'racy and picturesque', wearing 'its snippets of learning lightly' and making 'its points with force and ease, perhaps just a little too much ease'.

Though Elliott is no unspotted innocent, and has clearly had a jolly good time himself, at the end of his onslaught no one is left standing. Except Naim Attallah, to whom the book is dedicated, and Quartet Books, for whom Elliott currently works. When he says, 'I did not come across unhappy authors, some driven to madness even, until I joined Quartet,' all he means is that hitherto it was solely as a bookseller that he had met authors. He then found them courteous in general, if at times boring, and interested exclusively in how their books were selling. 'I always told them only good news, never the truth.' Obviously publishers can't resort to that expedient. He sums up resoundingly: 'Let the few remaining con-glomerates hurl their ludicrous advances, via agents, at the few remaining bestselling authors. Let the book chains cut each other's throats by discounting whatever popular silliness is grabbing attention. Let those who confuse the book trade with commerce gobble each other up.'

For myself I found *A Trade of Charms* to be highly entertaining as well as instructive. A personal chronicle that comes from someone who is addicted to the book trade, it is told with great sincerity and the mischievous sense of humour that has always been David's trademark.

While I was celebrating David's book, my friend Richard Cook, editor of the *Wire* magazine, decided to change direction in his career and take up a new challenge in the music business. He felt he had given the magazine all his energies and it was time for a new editor to come in with a fresh approach. His years at the *Wire* gave the magazine a solid business base from which it could move on and consolidate its reputation as the leading jazz organ. I leave it to Richard to recall the pioneering days of the *Wire* as he saw them.

Establishing the *Wire*
by Richard Cook

I joined the *Wire* as editor in 1985, at the request of Anthony Wood, the man who had started the magazine some three years earlier. Like most such enterprises, the magazine – dedicated to the coverage of jazz, improvised music and other associated matters – had struggled with its distribution and costs. Chrissie Murray had worked for a time as the production editor but didn't want to take on a full editorial role. In order to put the whole thing on to a more viable footing, Wood decided to find a significant backer. So he sold the controlling interest in the title to Naim Attallah and Quartet Books. Naim had an impressive list of jazz-related titles in the Quartet catalogue and the link made sense. He was also the proprietor of the distinguished book-review title the *Literary Review* so the organization was already magazine-friendly.

Wood had used me as a contributor to the *Wire* and knew that I knew my stuff. I had been working at the music paper *NME* for a number of years, but was young and hungry for more responsibility. So Wood offered me the job as editor. He would remain in a sort of managing-editor role, and was the principal link between the title and Naim.

When I started, it suddenly felt like walking into a whirlwind of problems. What Wood hadn't told me – how could he? – was that he really knew next to nothing about being a journalist or running a magazine. The small team of people who worked at the *Wire*'s stately offices in Beak Street (shared with other members of the Quartet organization) were already worn out by Wood's attempts at running the ship. Within three weeks, Wood unwisely picked a fight with me over a trip I had made to Scotland without his consent. The subtext was that he probably realized I wasn't going to be a very good second fiddle to someone like him, and that I was already undermining his authority. So he asked me to leave. I told everyone else in the office of the situation, and waited for their reaction. When they all threatened to leave too, Wood stalked out, which left me no alternative but to apprise Naim of what had come to pass.

I think the boss was surprised, but he worked an ingenious compromise. The following week, Naim held a sort of summit meeting in his office. Wood suggested that we go back to working together, and that it would all work out, but I refused. Naim asked me if I was prepared to go on with Anthony back in his old role, and I said no. After I departed from the meeting, Naim told Anthony that he should take a sabbatical for six months or so, even though he was 'the father of the *Wire*'. It was a gentle push, and after this cooling-off period he never came back.

For the next seven years and eighty-something monthly issues, I acted as editor and, eventually, publisher of the *Wire*. (Chris Parker, one of Quartet's editors, acted as publisher in the early years.) We had never had more than five full-time staff, and it was always a battle to meet our deadlines and fill our advertising pages, but it was a very happy office and we always felt we were a part of the Quartet family, the sort of publishing organization that has all but disappeared from the corporatized world which that field of business has become. Compared to some of the projects which Namara was involved in – such as Naim's celebrated books of interviews, including the spectacular *Women* project – it must have sometimes seemed that we were a peculiar and unglamorous part of the organization. But the *Wire* steadily became renowned in its own right. We initiated a series of British Jazz Awards which secured television coverage and stood out as celebrity occasions in what was otherwise a very prosaic part of the music business. We were the first to report on the British 'jazz revival' of the 1980s. Our designers Paul Elliman and Lucy Ward became award-winners in their own right. The *Wire* became a kind of cult magazine, and its reputation as a provocative and radical read went around the world.

It often only just paid its way, and I can recall such groundbreaking events as the arrival of a fax machine in the office and the wonderment of using such 'new technology'. The phenomenon of desktop publishing, which would revolutionize small magazines, was still some years in the future. Computers were not our province: even an electric typewriter was exciting. But through issue after pasted-up issue, I think we achieved something special.

Naim supported the *Wire* heroically, attending all of our special events and in his own way doing much to promote the magazine, hosting lunches with jazz celebrities and giving us all a bit of charisma. I sometimes wondered if he really felt that his money was being well spent on a magazine which always seemed destined to remain small and marginal, but he never gave up on it, or on me. But after seven years I felt it was time for a change – the magazine needed a break from me, and I had to move on too. Naim let me go with his usual grace. I don't think we exchanged a cross word in those seven years.

The *Wire* had begun to shift, in any case, away from jazz and towards a more inclusive approach to 'alternative' music, taking in all manner of other styles. Today, it is still being published, but eventually Naim let it go too, and it now exists as a cooperative venture, financially secure and still famous around the world. Without the patronage of a sympathetic place like Namara, though, it would have disappeared long ago. During those seven years, I think I did a lot of my growing up: I got married, became a property owner and learned how to edit and publish magazines. I owe much to Naim, who as far as I'm concerned is the real 'father of the *Wire*'.

*   *   *

The autumn of 1992 was a very hectic period, not only in publishing terms, but also across the Namara Group's entire range of activities. This coincided with the expansion of my duties at Asprey following my elevation to group chief executive and managing director of the main subsidiaries. The whole period was to become one of the most exciting and productive of my career. It also signalled the beginning of a more accomplished interviewing style in the wake of *Singular Encounters*. Though the book drew mixed reviews, these had been less hostile than those that had greeted *Women*. The cynics were still not convinced by my technique as an interviewer and were withholding judgement until my next endeavour, *Of a Certain Age*. When this was published it proved to be the turning point. The collection was very well received and it established an interviewing format rarely used: an interplay between the questions and answers without the obvious presence of an interlocutor. The tendency, especially on television, was for the interviewer to draw the limelight away from his subject on to himself, a growing practice that I found somewhat exasperating.

The book consisted of interviews with fourteen diverse subjects, starting, in alphabetical order, with Sir Hardy Amies, the amiable dressmaker to the Queen, who called me a closet queen when he saw the lining of my jacket and who later became my style guru. Next came Claus von Bulow, the former chief executive assistant to J. Paul Getty, who in 1985 had been acquitted in America of the charge of attempting to murder his wife. I found him eloquent and worldly, but when my interview with him was published as a double-page spread in the *Daily Mail*, he became rather angry and our newly developed friendship was to suffer a short period of *froideur*. Mollie Butler was charm itself and I liked her immensely. She was deeply touching on the subject of her marriage to Rab Butler, who was always the Conservatives' prime minister in waiting but who never made it.

Lord Dacre (the historian Hugh Trevor-Roper) was a special case who became, through the interview, a real fan and paid me tribute in various letters he wrote to me over the years. 'What a wide range of entrepreneurial activities you command!' he said in one. 'In spite of which you are by far the best – the most *professional* – of interviewers! I remember your cross-examination of me with pleasure; unlike nearly every other interviewer, you had briefed yourself so well, which was formidable, but also flattering.'

Lord Deedes, the great Fleet Street survivor, a giant among his peers, featured prominently; while Professor H. J. Eysenck, a leading critic of psychoanalysis in Britain and a psychologist who insisted that he worked with facts rather than feelings and impressions, was also included. The list continued with Reuben Falber, assistant general secretary of the British Communist party, who had recently admitted 'laundering' large sums of money from the Communist party of the Soviet Union; and Diana Mosley, still 'in denial' on questions of Hitler's personal responsibility for Nazi atrocities, who had a legendary beauty and charm that remained beguiling and who later became my good friend.

Another charmer was John Murray, the distinguished publisher, by many considered the cultural guardian of all that was best in British writing. To my question of whether he still found himself excited by the sight of a pretty woman, he responded with a gentlemanly twinkle:

> Oh, yes. I dream about them. At one stage I thought it would help me to go to sleep, but I have discovered that it doesn't. One of the reasons I love going on the Underground, the Northern Line to Hampstead, is because I'm fascinated by the different fashions. I'm particularly expert on the kind of bottoms that authors have. I'm amazed that Americans always have such big bottoms and I think bottoms can reveal almost more clearly the character of the person . . . well perhaps not more than the face, but the way people move their bottoms gives a strong indication. And of course the sexual impulse is still there. But, alas, no competence . . .

The writer, journalist and politician Conor Cruise O'Brien, who had served as representative to the UN secretary general Dag Hammarskjöld during the Congo crisis of 1961 and written his best book about it, *To Katanga and Back*, was someone with whom I felt no political rapport whatsoever, while Enoch Powell, as an elder statesman, had a profound effect on me with his knowledge and intellect. Despite his controversial pronouncements and an austere public image, he was at heart a romantic man who sent his wife love poems on every anniversary. Lord Shawcross, the Attorney-General and later president of the Board of Trade for the post-war Labour governments, had also been the chief prosecutor at the Nuremberg trials.

Barbara Skelton, author of three novels and two volumes of autobiography, had moved in London's literary and artistic circles and married the critic Cyril Connolly, and later the publisher George Weidenfeld, with whom she had a hate-fuelled relationship. And finally there was Lord Soper, Methodist minister, famous speaker on Tower Hill and a pacifist, who was still at the age of eighty-nine capable of admiring a pair of good legs on a woman.

Of a Certain Age was included by Alastair Forbes in his round-up of

Christmas books for the *Spectator*, and he was rather generous with me: 'Naim Attallah's exemplary candid interviews with Barbara Skelton and Claus von Bulow alone are worth the £15 he charges for his latest hardback.' Then he added: 'But someone should tell him there is no such person as "Lady Diana Mosley", even if brilliant novelist Nick Mosley's mum was Lady Cynthia.' I had already been rebuked for my mistake by Diana herself, and felt truly mortified. Alastair, however, made up for having chastised me *à propos* Diana's proper title by adding that: 'He deserves much credit for confiding Quartet's list to the discerning good taste of brilliant Mr Pickles, whose Encounters and Robin Clark reprints are also admirably chosen and printed.'

In *The Times* in October a lengthy profile of me by Ginny Dougary appeared in its Saturday Review and upset my equilibrium just at a time when I was settling down to a more peaceful life, far removed from speculations of a sinister nature about my personal agenda. The article gave what I felt to be the wrong impression regarding my financial resources by shrouding them in mystery; and questioned my intentions by misjudging my political motives in highlighting the plight of the Palestinians. On this score, the article rankled with me, and in an effort to avoid litigation I reached an agreement with *The Times* that I would put my own point of view in a letter, headed 'No Mystery Man', that would be published in a prominent position.

Ginny Dougary's profile of me in the Saturday Review (31 October) begs various questions which greater perspicacity might have answered. Indeed, the article goes to considerable lengths to convey the somewhat absurd aura of mystery in which I am thought to be shrouded. While this makes good copy and serves to lend almost fluorescent colour to my personality, it does so at the expense of any ultimate objectivity. I am hardly alone in having a character made up of contradictory elements, but why need this contradiction be tainted with innuendoes which so invariably damage a person's good standing?

The article places far too much emphasis on imaginary sources of my so-called wealth. The mystery exists only in the minds of the needlessly mystified. My greatest wealth is in fact my energy, since what I earn I find myself continually spending on what I consider to be good causes. I have never been a slave to Mammon, nor have I hoarded money after the fashion of some more legendary twentieth-century moguls. Quite simply, I work hard. If people worked fifteen hours a day, as I do, they would find their earning capacity increased. There should be no mystery in that.

As for the 'extravagant rumours' of an 'Arab conspiracy', these were almost certainly inspired by the fanciful notion that in publishing some books concerning the Palestinian side of the tragic situation in the Middle East, I was involved in some kind of plot. My avowed purpose has always been to redress the balance, since the other side in that dispute has never wanted for champions in its cause.

Criticism is perfectly healthy so long as it is not founded on the ubiquitous premise that success is to be envied rather than encouraged. There is also the question of tone. To write of me 'bad-mouthing' my father and 'despising' the establishment reveals a rather unnecessary penchant for the emotive. I confess to sheer stupefaction that some secret sources believe my love for women carries with it sinister overtones. Curiouser and curiouser . . . It could be that my natural way of expressing myself has been misunderstood, and in some bizarre way taken to support a number of suggestions in the article.

Having said that, I suspect my particular idiosyncratic nature will continue to invite the more imaginative kind of speculation.

The reviews of *Of a Certain Age* kept coming in. William Trevor wrote in the *Literary Review*:

> This is an enjoyable book. It is more than the views and opinions of people who have lived a longish time: the people themselves leap off the page at you, and although their personalities must be allowed some credit for this, it's the subtlety of the interrogation that ensures these portraits emerge. Making real people real at second hand isn't as easy as it seems.

Cristina Odone, the editor of the *Catholic Herald*, undertook to review it herself for her own paper:

> The men and women featured in *Of a Certain Age* (many of the interviews were first serialized in the *Oldie*) touch off echoes in any reader of history or the newspapers: as they muse on Hitler, Stalin, John Betjeman, the Zionist movement, we feel we are turning the pages of that sometimes sad, sometimes spectacular volume that comprises the twentieth century. Those who do not subscribe to Vico's theory of cyclical history will be surprised by how many of the issues that used to fascinate, perplex, obsess the likes of Conor Cruise O'Brien (Israel and the Palestinians) and Enoch Powell (the EC) are still at the forefront of our own agendas.
>
> Throughout – with the possible exception of Conor Cruise O'Brien, who, though his interviewer is a Palestinian, keeps defending the Israelis' policies in the West Bank – we sense that the interviewer is as unabashedly interested, as childishly delighted, in these walking testaments to history, as you or I would be.
>
> Though Attallah himself admits to being particularly happy with the

Lady Diana Mosley [*sic*] interview ('she is outrageous, simply outrageous!' he says, rubbing his hands with glee), some may argue that his Enoch Powell interview, where the former parliamentarian admits to writing one poem a year to his wife on their marriage anniversary; or the Barbara Skelton interview, where she accuses King Farouk of stealing her rings, might prove more entertaining.

Andro Linklater, in the *Spectator*, thought that while my '*escadron volant* of pretty assistants are clearly thorough researchers', I might just have hired 'one mouse with spectacles to check the spelling of *de rigeur* [*de rigueur* was spelt correctly] and the capitalization of Labour Party [there was a 'mouse' and she followed *The Oxford Dictionary for Writers and Editors*],' but I had made a 'good interviewer':

> indiscreet enough to ask Lord Soper about masturbation and von Bulow about rumours of murdering his mother, and above all sufficiently sensitive to let them espouse their true character. It is an indolent way of making a book, but the result is unexpectedly satisfying. I hope St Peter will study Attallah's technique when it comes to dividing the sheep from the goats; it will make Heaven a place worth getting to.

The late John Diamond wrote a piece in *The Times* in which he compared my approach with the techniques of Bernard Levin and Keith Waterhouse in their books:

> If Waterhouse and Levin have an engaging arrogance, then Naim Attallah's skill is his remarkable self-effacement.
>
> Attallah has interviewed thirteen of the great and the good (plus Diana Mosley who is neither). His technique is one that is still pretty common in America, but was last used in this country by, I think, Miriam Gross in the *Observer* some years ago, before the interviewer became the star of his own writing. Attallah's long interviews run as simple transcriptions, well-researched questions in italics, answers in roman type. There is none of the extraneous 'as we sat in his simple but comfortable home' or 'her fingers clenched nervously', no descriptions of face or clothes, no interpretation of what the interviewer thinks about what he or she did say.
>
> It is a book that demonstrates quite conclusively that what the reader wants in an interview with subjects who really have seen the world change, even helped change it, is to hear their words. No interviewer on the subject of Lord Dacre's dress sense can be as compelling as Lord Dacre is on secret-service recruitment, or his part in the Hitler Diaries farce; no interviewer need give Lady Mosley any more than the short

length of rope with which she hangs herself. Enoch Powell in his own swift-chosen, precise words says more about Powell than any newspaper biographer can, and Attallah's great, if modest, skill is that he lets him do it. It is because of this, and entirely to Attallah's credit of course, that he would make a lousy newspaper columnist.

Ulick O'Connor the Irish playwright, who is a good friend of mine, reviewed the book from an Irish viewpoint for the Irish *Sunday Independent*. Naturally he had a great deal to say about the interview with Conor Cruise O'Brien. Our meeting had been heated at times and ended with O'Brien being less than happy with the outcome. When I asked him how he reacted to the accusation made by a lot of people that he was 'a British stooge', he came back with the riposte: 'For "a lot of people" read the IRA and *their* stooges, some of whom you have clearly been talking to. Give them my regards.' Earlier I had broached a speculation among 'his opponents' that he had only obtained the job of editor-in-chief at the *Observer* through a possible connection with the British Intelligence Service. 'Are my opponents the IRA?' he had asked in return. 'I imagine they are, since nobody except the IRA has its spokesmen talk like that. I have never had any connection whatsoever with British Intelligence or any other intelligence organization.'

O'Brien had successfully repudiated 'these two suggestions with the force one would expect from him', wrote Ulick. He found him less effective, how-ever, 'when asked about his activities in the 1970s when he served as Minister for Posts and Telegraphs with responsibility for Information in the first Fine Gael/Labour Coalition'.

Naim Attallah puts it to him that Mary Holland [the distinguished journalist, notable for her fair-minded reporting on the Unionist v. Republican conflict] has described the atmosphere in RTE [Radio Telefis Eireann] in the mid 1970s as one in which people were 'quite simply frightened out of their minds . . . self-censorship had been raised to the level of an art and caution lay like a thick cloud over everything'.

O'Brien: 'I think it appeared to Mary Holland like that but it is a ridiculous portrayal. I do not think you would find anyone in Dublin to agree except Mary Holland and some Republican sympathizers.'

Poor Mary. Every time she holds an opinion different from Cruise O'Brien she is represented as a sort of thwarted shrew.

On the question of Israel, I probed O'Brien 'mercilessly . . . on his pro-Israeli stance' and asked him why did he 'not condemn Israeli terrorism'.

Cruise O'Brien: 'The degree of sympathy I have with Israel is based on the realization that Israel is the result of horrendously extreme conditions. That is why I write as I do. It's an emotional issue with me.'

Naim Attallah: 'But what about the poor Palestinians? They weren't responsible for the Nazi atrocities?'

Cruise O'Brien: 'No, they were not, and they have suffered as a result of the Nazi atrocities. But they haven't suffered quite as much as the Jews.'

Naim Attallah: 'What do you say about Israel's treatment of the Palestinians?'

Cruise O'Brien: 'The treatment of the population of the West Bank in Gaza is based on the laws, regulations and practices with which the British governed all of Palestine under the mandate. The military regulations are there; they are British ones.'

Naim Attallah: 'But you were always anti-colonial . . . '

Cruise O'Brien: 'Yes . . . All right . . . '

Ulick thought I had found in Barbara Skelton a 'truly marvellous subject' who spoke 'without inhibition on her fascination with the opposite sex'.

Why Cyril Connolly, who resembled an ulcerated gorilla, should have turned her on, God knows, but he did.

'I was very pretty, and funny and lively, and Cyril was what I wanted for a husband.'

She went at Connolly like a vacuum cleaner out of control, with the result that the poor man, determined to succeed as a writer, ran out of gas, feeling that 'sex was sapping his mental energy'. This understandably disappointed Barbara and led her to fall in love with Lord Weidenfeld just because 'I was seeking sex for satisfaction again'.

Ulick O'Connor considered that what distinguished the book from others of its kind was 'Naim Attallah's gift of selecting interviewees who can provide illuminating insights into the structure of society and . . . elicit from them material which, when viewed in the context of the whole book, can give us a valuable insight into contemporary English life', this being 'a real insight into the post-colonial period of a class which once ruled a quarter of the globe'.

Emma Soames in the *Evening Standard* used *Of a Certain Age* as a springboard to, 'Hail the heroes of old,' as she so eloquently put it. 'Now ancestor worship is everywhere,' she said, 'captains of industry, admirals of the media, musicians and even dress designers are being rehabilitated in the public eye thanks to the fact that they have survived intact and in charge into their sixth decade and beyond.' She felt that as the 'power behind such venerable institutions as Asprey, Mappin & Webb and the *Oldie*', I ought to be 'gratified to find that a book of my interviews' had 'helped launch a brand-new initiative on the style pages of national newspapers, promoting the glories of old age'. 'It must be an occasion for celebration in twilight homes throughout the land that the wisdom and wit of their inhabitants have finally been recognized and inflated to cult status in magazines they have never heard of.' Thankfully her prophecy that it could not be long 'before this country is governed by a Kremlin-style gerontocracy' has never come to pass.

Russell Davies took an innovative approach when he reviewed the book for the *Sunday Telegraph*, adopting a pastiche of the question-answer formula:

Naim Attallah has constructed another book of interviews. Did you enjoy it?

I think 'construct' is putting it a bit high. The best you can do with interviews is park them all in a row, like motor cars, and hope they amount to a decent display. Then you stand at the front and sell them, which, curiously enough, Attallah doesn't do. He offers no preamble at all, and draws no conclusions. He's a bit cagey for my taste, though he sounds amiable. Everybody gets one question he or she experiences as offensive, which is good tactics . . .

The frankness of these people is attractive, though, surely?

Yes and no. It is refreshing and even liberating, here and there, to read the words of public figures who no longer need to dissemble and fudge as people in mid-career do . . .

I would call most of the people in this book arrogant, and the worst of it is, so would they.

Russell Davies is particularly interesting on the theme of the drift to the right in later years, saying that for Conor Cruise O'Brien he felt some sympathy.

He was born on shifting ground – socially, politically, ecclesiastically – and he seems to have slid off to the side of all mainstreams he has tried to join. No doubt they will bury him in Ireland, but the homeless blue helmet of the UN will rest on his coffin.

The rightward trend was generally there with the interviewees, 'though Thatcherism inspires reservations in almost everyone'.

There is a saving decency, a distaste for ruthlessness, at work. Then again, far out to the Right throughout these people's lives, there has been Hitler, acting as a political 'Stop' sign. He's the missing interviewee in the book.

I was myself subjected to interrogation by Frances Welch, the wife of the satirist Craig Brown, for a piece she was writing for the *Sunday Telegraph* that November, headed 'A Passion for the English Rose'.

In his pocket Naim Attallah has what he calls a new toy. It is a cream plastic box, the size of a small lighter, with a tiny button on top. Some sixty seconds after he presses the button, an attractive aristocratic English blonde is at his side, awaiting instructions. 'I press it, she hears and she comes.' . . .

After the blonde has gone, he leans across his shining black boardroom table at Mappin & Webb. 'If you ask me which nationality of girls I prefer I would always say English. You ask an American woman, would she like to go to the opera, and she is analysing: "Is he going to hold my hand; is he going to make a pass?"

'An English girl is more confident and easy-going,' he says. 'She says, "Yes, yes, yes, I'll go to the opera; I'll deal with any other situation as it arises." '

Attallah has had success with English girls, in the sense that he has persuaded a great many daughters-of-the-famous to work in his various offices.

My earlier experience of the English had not been so congenial, as when in Palestine my family had suffered mistreatment from the authorities.

'I remember being woken up at four in the morning and the soldiers dragging us out of our beds and taking us to a football ground for communal punishment. Some soldier had been shot or something.

'When I arrived [in Britain] I expected the worst and found the best. Everybody was kind and polite and said "yes sir, no thank you" and I thought where are these barbarians?' He leans over and lowers his voice: 'Unfortunately, the people who go to the colonies are . . . well, not so civilized.' . . .

There is something appealing in the ingenuous side of Attallah. Asking whether he feels he has been accepted in English society I find myself hoping – for his sake – that the answer is yes.

'I just get on with people whatever their background. I find people with "humble backgrounds" have tremendous breeding. You're born with it or you're not.'

'Were you born with it?'

'I expect to behave well,' he says, with a shrug and one of his long serious looks. 'I was never vulgar.'

Forty-seven

There were activities galore in motion on the Asprey front, and plans for future expansion were being formulated at breakneck speed. The reason for this manic haste was to take advantage of the bubble of success before it burst. We were generating healthy profits, more than anticipated, and I was determined to invest a large portion of these in broadening our field of operations still further. We needed to make ourselves less vulnerable to the whims of the luxury market, which relied in the main on exclusivity with a much narrower customer base. 'Asprey looks to Europe', announced *Retail Weekly* on 4 December 1992:

> Luxury-goods dealer Asprey plans to step up its overseas expansion next year.
>
> Chief executive Naim Attallah says: 'We are going to look at overseas expansion with a more serious eye.'
>
> Mappin & Webb, which used to have a significant presence overseas, is ready for expansion, Attallah believes. He is targeting Germany and Eastern Europe.
>
> Asprey has reported pre-tax profits for the first half of up to £11.2 million from £10.9 million.

My actual priority was to open a Mappin & Webb shop in Prague, one of the most beautiful cities in Europe. Its historic heart had been restored with care after damage caused during the Second World War. There was a new age dawning following the disintegration of the Soviet Union. I could see the potential of being first, leading the way before the invasion of other retailers.

In the meantime my investment in Julia Ogilvy in Edinburgh was confirming itself to have been a wise one. The transformation she achieved at Hamilton & Inches was eye-catching and the market acted positively as she gradually gained the respect of the industry. I felt proud of my protégée when *Retail Weekly* reported that 'Hard work pays off for Julia':

> Julia Ogilvy, managing director of Hamilton & Inches . . . was one of the honoured guests at the 1992 Women of the Year Luncheon. She was selected together with 499 other distinguished women for her outstanding work in the jewellery trade.

According to Naim Attallah: 'She works very hard, she is very committed and brings creativity to everything she does.' Mr Attallah did not know that Ms Ogilvy had been so honoured until contacted, so modesty can be added to her attributes . . .

'An invitation to the Women of the Year Luncheon is not just a recognition of my own achievements but a chance to celebrate women's many triumphs in British public life,' said Ms Ogilvy.

With the success of the Asprey group, and the Namara expansion into magazines and publishing, my own profile went on slowly climbing in the gossip columns. *Tatler*'s round-up of the 'thousand most socially significant people in 1992' included me, curiously under the heading of 'Shopkeepers', in a list that had Sir Hardy Amies at its head. Of me it stated:

> Tireless entrepreneur and publisher, owner of Quartet Books, famed for employing a harem of attractive (usually blonde) English girls. As one former employee says, 'Saying you have been a Naim girl does wonders for a flagging CV.'

When Nigella Lawson had a go at my good friend Hardy Amies in the *Evening Standard* of 11 November over remarks on Princess Diana he was quoted as having made in Australia, I have to admit I was dismayed. Nigella wrote:

> Sir Hardy Amies, the courtier-couturier, has apparently caused some consternation by a pronouncement made in Melbourne in response to the domestic troubles of the Waleses. The Princess of Wales, according to Sir Hardy, 'has ensured the succession by producing two sons. That is all we want from her.'
>
> In other words, she has served her purpose and, one can only conclude, no further consideration to her is due or desirable.
>
> Perhaps we should not be surprised to hear such a view from a man who, in Naim Attallah's recently published book, *Of a Certain Age*, claimed to despise women's minds.
>
> It was such a relief to see the boast in print, to have the evidence confirmed. For, after all, haven't his clothes, throughout the years, indicated as much?

Nigella's attack on Sir Hardy Amies lacked a real understanding of a rather complex character. During the war, he joined the Belgian section of the Special Operations Executive (the SOE) and was second-in-command to Lieutenant-Colonel Claude Knight, whom he later succeeded. He had worked with various groups of the Belgian Resistance, organizing sabotage and arranging for agents to be parachuted into the Ardennes with radio equipment. At the same time he continued working for the Board of Trade, designing clothes that conformed to the wartime clothes-rationing requirements for the domestic market. He was said to have tweaked the design of his colonel's uniform and had it made up by a civilian tailor. A note on his SOE file read: 'This officer has done very well on the course. He is far tougher both physically and mentally than his rather precious appearance would suggest.'

Hardy Amies combined bravery with a queenly mien in his private life. His perceptive eye and discerning taste gave him an inimitable chic and elegance behind which lurked a wicked sense of humour which never failed him and could be deadly. He did not despise women's minds. A more appropriate assessment would have been that he understood them less. For the uninitiated in high camp, his sharp wit was very likely to be misconstrued, but his generosity of spirit more than made up for the acerbity that characterized so many of his impromptu pronouncements. Invariably funny, with a slight sting in the tail, they bore not a thread of malice. I often found myself at the sharp end of some of these remarks, which I regarded as more banter than put-down. They were simply typical of the rich repartee with which he often enlivened an otherwise dull occasion.

My friendship with Sir Hardy Amies came about as a result of my publishing his book *The Englishman's Suit* in 1994. It sprang up over lunch in my Regent Street dining-room when he asked me whether I would be interested in looking at a manuscript he had written with a view to publishing it. He wanted a quick answer from me, unlike those other publishers, he said, who sat on manuscripts for months and then sent a curt rejection slip. I promised I would give him my answer within one week. True to my word, I did just that, and promised the book would be published within six months.

Naturally he was delighted. To show his appreciation, he dedicated the book to me, conspiring with the Quartet staff to keep this totally secret till finished copies arrived. His inscription carried a *double entendre*: 'To Naim, who took a week to say yes.' It brought the colour to my face when I saw it, coming as it did from a famous queen! It was the ultimate expression of unadulterated cheek, but in a curious sort of way it endeared him to me. It was another example of his roguish sense of humour, which I had encountered on many occasions. Once, sitting next to him upon his insistence at one of his fashion shows, I was treated to a commentary on some of his creations that was hilarious. He would nudge me and say of a particularly attractive dress in a loud voice, for he was partially deaf, 'Any old bag would look good in it!'

On another occasion, seeing me at a black-tie dinner hosted by *Vogue*, he told my wife that in my attire – which incidentally I considered to be very smart – I looked just like a waiter. When I reproached him for this remark, he remained adamant. The following week he sent me the most splendid design for a black-tie outfit, drawn in colour, which he said was being cut specially for me at that very moment. Two fittings later I found myself the proud owner of a most distinguished and exclusive dinner suit, tailored with Amies's usual flair and precise attention to detail. It marked the beginning of a new phase in our friendship; he began sending me his latest men's designs so that my tailor in the East End could copy them for my benefit. This was his response after I told him that his fashion house was far too expensive for my budget. Needless to say, I had a soft spot for him, and he beamed with joy whenever I was in his company. Very few people knew about his record as a war hero till his obituaries were published after he died on 3 March 2003.

The *Evening Standard* had included another nice example of Hardy Amies's repartee from the interview in October 1992:

> Exquisite types tend to be lured to *haute couture*, but few are finer than Sir Hardy Amies, the Queen's dressmaker since 1960. Now, at eighty-three, he has given the world a flash of his soul, disclosing an enduring obsession.
>
> 'I love flesh, I'm very tactile, very MTF – must touch flesh,' he says in *Of a Certain Age* . . .
>
> 'I'm tremendously physical but I can't say I have ever desired a woman,' adds Sir Hardy. 'I did once get engaged to a girl, but I cannot think why; it wasn't that I wanted to go to bed with her.'
>
> Asked if he has ever fallen madly in love, Amies replies: 'Oh yes . . . every week, mainly with the milkman.' Sadly he is disinclined to elaborate on this association. 'Oh dear, oh dear, I was just passing that off as a joke,' he tells me from New York. 'I hope the milkman doesn't take that seriously.'

Another bit of interesting news reported by the *Evening Standard* back in September had concerned the *Oldie*. We were beginning to experience cash-flow problems in trying to maintain it as a fortnightly magazine and another injection of capital became necessary. I persuaded Tony Lambton to increase his original holding of ten thousand pounds in the *Oldie* by a further investment of twenty thousand pounds. The story was leaked to the press – hence the headline in 'Londoner's Diary': 'Lambton revitalizes the *Oldie*':

> When, seven months ago, the *Oldie* magazine was launched to meet the needs of the emerging gerontocracy, its editor Richard Ingrams sounded a note of warning. 'It's a crazy thing to do,' he said.
>
> Subsequent events seem to show that he may have been right. The

magazine, whose circulation is estimated to be a modest 25,000, soon parted company with one of its most estimable contributors, Dame Barbara Cartland, and, in a bid to curtail expenditure, dispensed with colour.

Now, however, it has received a welcome, perhaps crucial, infusion of funds. Its benefactor is Lord Lambton, the former Tory defence minister. He has just invested £20,000 in it.

As the *Oldie*'s primary backer, I was quoted as saying, 'We have been talking about this for some time,' and described as having a philanthropic approach to the magazine.

He is adamant that the *Oldie*, launched with some £225,000, will survive, peremptorily dismissing suggestions to the contrary. 'These rumours are rubbish,' he says.

Lord Lambton . . . tells me, 'I think the *Oldie* has a lot of potential, though it could improve.' Perhaps Richard Ingrams should take note.

Towards the end of the year, Harvey Porlock in *Publishing News* announced his list of winners for the 1992 Porlock Awards to the literary world. He cited as his 'tribute of the year':

'I too suffer from chronic Naimophilia and the author is so good on the subject that I have to quote him at some length, so here we go: "The longer I worked for him the more I came to regard his qualities as special, he never went back on his word, he never complained . . . " ' *Anthony Blond (former colleague of Naim Attallah), reviewing* A Trade of Charms *by David Elliott (former employee of Naim Attallah) in the* Literary Review *(proprietor: Naim Attallah).*

The paragraph could have appeared in *Private Eye*. It came as no surprise to find myself the butt of the joke, since it had become the fashion to lambaste me with this kind of satire. But it made good copy and was harmless.

A few late reviews for *Of a Certain Age* continued to come in. Just before Christmas, Clare Colvin wrote in the *Sunday Express*: 'What a relief to read interviews where the subjects are allowed to speak for themselves.' She thought the results of the question-and-answer format were illuminating.

Attallah has chosen well-known people in diverse fields . . . This eclectic mix . . . yield their secrets to Attallah's gentle, but persistent, questioning. Nor is he afraid of offending his subjects . . . This is an immensely intriguing and satisfying book. I look forward to its promised sequel.

On the last day of the year Shaun Usher penned a piece for the *Daily Mail*:

You are hereby invited to a glorious and impossible blend of cocktail party, university high table and debate concerning what really matters in life.

Fellow guests are male and female achievers of all kinds, old enough to have valuable experience and displaying that frankness based on cool indifference to what anyone thinks of them.

Publisher and master interviewer Naim Attallah hosts such a dream occasion, drawing out more than a dozen heavy-hitters in politics, journalism, the arts and commerce. A Brains Trust distilling the essence of struggle, love, triumph and defeat . . . what a salon.

All in all, December had been a hectic month. I seemed to have featured in the press more than usual as a result of increased activities on all fronts, especially where Asprey and Quartet were concerned. Both companies had a high profile for different reasons. In Asprey's case it was because of its many international clients and the nature of its business; the elements of family feud had also, over its turbulent recent history, made it a prime target for the gossip columnists. All these factors, compounded by the meteoric success the company had achieved during the previous fifteen years, attracted a con-tinuous stream of publicity. In Quartet's case it was because its eclectic list and experimental stance gained friends as well as enemies and was always the subject of controversy of some kind or another. It did not publish books merely for their commercial viability. The crusading campaigns in favour of oppressed minorities, including the Palestinians, were never popular issues with right-wing elements, nor were they commercially profitable. But Quartet continued to survive because of the dedication of its staff and its innovative approach to publishing, casting aside many of the old languid habits and replacing them with a more focused determination to turn books around in the shortest possible time. It was its unpredictability that kept the imprint in the news.

Asprey became the subject of speculation in connection with a possible bid to take over Mallett, the Bond Street antiques dealer, which began its life in Bath a hundred and twenty-five years earlier but moved to Bond Street in 1908. The City was so rife with rumour that the entire press covered the story extensively. I had been keeping an eye on Mallett for some while and I was simply testing the waters. It was also an exercise in brinkmanship to see where the weakest link in the chain was located should Asprey decide to mount a proper bid. The strategic investment I made of six point eight per cent was time-biding and it hit the headlines, the *Daily Telegraph* announcing on 23 December: 'Asprey has eyes on Mallett':

The luxury-goods retailer Asprey appears poised to bid for troubled antique dealer Mallett after building up a 6.8-per-cent share. Mallett's share price leapt 19p to 73p yesterday after it announced it had 'received an approach which may or may not lead to an offer for the whole of the issued share capital'.

Asprey chief executive Naim Attallah confirmed the company had bought 6.8 per cent of Mallett in the last two days, but 'purely for investment purposes'.

Michael Baws in the *Daily Mail* detected a double mystery, asking:

Who sold the 6.8-per-cent stake that Asprey has just bought in loss-making West End antiques dealer Mallett. Is [Attallah] behind the mystery bid approach that Mallett announced yesterday?

Attallah played a straight bat to both questions. 'I don't know. They were bought through my brokers in various parcels,' he said to the first. As to the second: 'We have only bought for investment purposes.'

The *Independent* said that Peter Dixon, Mallett's finance director, had declined to confirm Asprey's involvement or to say 'whether the approach was considered friendly or hostile' but thought the move looked likely to be in line with Asprey's recent history of 'spending freely on acquisitions'. The *Financial Times* predicted boldly that the two companies were taking a 'first step towards [a] merger'.

Negotiations are in a very early stage but Mallett does not seem opposed to a full bid. 'We look favourably on people who are going to improve our share value,' said the company yesterday . . .

Along with Partridge, its Bond Street neighbour, Mallett is regarded as the leading dealer in antique furniture in the UK. Both Asprey and Mallett are stressing that negotiations have barely started but Mallett would certainly fit neatly into Mr Attallah's programme of luxury acquisitions.

At the same time as Asprey was in the news because of the strategic investment in Mallett, I was busy in Manchester with Tania Foster-Brown promoting Mappin & Webb. The occasion was a silver exhibition by Mappin & Webb worth a million pounds. Among the exhibits were a thirty-kilo bar of silver the size of a phone book, a baby's bath that was worth thirty thousand pounds and a silver spoon three feet long that was worth two thousand five hundred. Tania arrived wearing a crash helmet of gleaming silver that was priced at nine thousand pounds. *Lancashire Life* reported that I lived up to my reputation for ties with 'a bright floral number' as I 'reflected on silver, plus the success of his new book of interviews with people *Of a Certain Age*, including celebrities in the silver-haired set'. 'As he put us at our ease with champagne and canapés he confided the secret of his success with celebrated interviewees: "I put them at their ease," he said. "They know I am not trying to catch them out." '

Despite all these activities at home, I never stopped travelling, mainly to Geneva, where Asprey had a trading Swiss subsidiary and its investment portfolio held with Pictet et Cie, one of the most prestigious private banks in Switzerland. New York was another place I visited regularly to oversee our shop in the Trump Tower on Fifth Avenue, a stone's throw from Tiffany. New York was then full of energy and dynamism, with an unparalleled social ambience. The hordes who negotiated their way through the traffic on foot were in sharp contrast to the rest of the United States, where people were addicted to their cars and walked very little. New Yorkers are a breed apart, distinctive in their habits, motivated by big money and great benefactors of the arts. Every time I made the trip I felt rejuvenated, but always ended up exhausted back in London. Each stay in New York had a specific purpose, such as that reported in *Women's Wear Daily* for 20 November. The Fifth Avenue store had been transformed into a dining-room for forty or so guests for the unveiling of a new Chrysallis watch.

The watches, ensconced in leather sample cases, were brought around to the tables so that everyone could get a close look. There were no take-home samples, however; the watches start at $20,000 retail.

The watches have two lives, as a subtle daytime look or a bejeweled evening number. They feature a unique design that incorporates sliding gold panels on the bezel. When the panels are pushed back, a setting of diamonds, rubies or emeralds is revealed. It was designed by Jacques Bernard, chairman of the French jeweler René Boivin, which is owned by Asprey.

Back in London the business reports regarding Asprey were mainly positive against the background of the continuing recession. 'Asprey glitters in the gloom,' said the *Evening Standard*, while the *Financial Times* recorded that pretax profits had risen to eleven point two million from ten point nine million pounds. Group turnover had risen similarly. We had anticipated that Watches of Switzerland would be a drain on resources, but were 'servicing the loan taken out for the acquisition, and making a profit'. The interim dividend was being maintained at one point one pence. In Edinburgh, as I had predicted, Julia Ogilvy was receiving a great deal of publicity in her new post as managing director of Hamilton & Inches. Avril Groom in the *Scotsman* wrote a lengthy article referring to Julia as my 'secret weapon', as indeed she was. For a total revamp of the store, completed that November, she had called in one of Britain's best-known luxury-shop designers, Christopher Vane Percy, to refurbish the 'unloved' Edwardian interior, the point being, said Julia, 'to maintain Hamilton & Inches' uniqueness'.

The restoration involved pale marbling of the stucco ceiling, replacing the functional sixties' shelves and lighting with panelled-timber display cabinets and brass, glass-shaded lamps, making a feature of the grand fireplace with great vases of fresh flowers (one of Julia's hallmarks at Garrard), and displaying small items on round tables with heavy cloths that you might find in an Edwardian drawing-room.

'No shop – even one like this selling expensive merchandise – should be intimidating,' she says. 'I want to create a warm, friendly, buzzy atmosphere, where women will feel happy shopping alone – as many do here – without feeling they need a man to guide them through the protocol.'

Besides following her plan to place relatively inexpensive gifts alongside those of high quality, she had 'upgraded the top end, to include the only stock of Patek Philippe watches in Scotland and diamond jewellery worth up to £90,000'.

I want to prove there is no need to go to London for good jewellery. The same applies to repairs. I've read stories of people flying to London clutching their antique silver teapots, yet we have three floors of excellent workshops for repairs, and we make all our own silver . . . Next year we intend to introduce a house tartan.

*

Quartet also ended 1992 on a high note. We had published an amazing number of books that year, which makes it extremely difficult to select for mention any in preference over others. Under the direction of Stephen Pickles, our literary output was phenomenal, though not always profitable. Nevertheless he managed to give Quartet an intellectual edge rarely found in commercial publishing. Here are a few examples:

All the World's Mornings by Pascal Quignard had been translated from the French by James Kirkup. It was a novel based on the romantic and tragic story of the real-life Sainte Colombe, a composer of genius and player of the bass viol in the France of Louis XIV. Disquiet was introduced into his life and those of his two daughters through his gifted, ambitious young protégé Marin Marais. In the same year the book became a notable film, Tout les matins du monde, starring Gérard Depardieu.

Richard Wagner's Visit to Rossini and *An Evening at Rossini's in Beau-Sejour* by Edmond Michotte were a pair of short memoirs translated by Herbert Weinstock and reprinted together to mark the bicentenary of Rossini's birth. Michotte had effected and been present at a meeting between Wagner and Rossini in Paris. He made notes on this, as well as on a later evening with Rossini when the composer expounded his views on singers and *bel canto*.

Maria Callas by Jürgen Kesting was translated by John Hunt. It was a major biography that took the focus away from the drama of Callas's life to concentrate on her art. As the *Luzerner Tagesblatt* had written, Kesting was primarily interested in 'her place in the tradition of operatic singing' and her ability 'to transform suffering, love, hate, in short the entire gamut of human emotions, into sound and vocal shape'.

Saracen Chronicles: A Selection of Literary Essays by Juan Goytisolo, translated by Helen Lane, joined the two volumes of memoirs by this important Spanish writer of the anti-Franco intelligentsia that were already in the Quartet list, *Forbidden Territory* and *Realms of Strife*. It consisted of twelve essays that linked Goytisolo's own thought in a masterly sweep with the themes that ran through Spanish and Latin American literature as revealed in the work of such writers as Octavio Paz, Vargas Llosa and Carlos Fuentes.

Living with Beelzebub by Gael Elton Mayo was the second volume of memoirs by this author to be published by Quartet, the first being *The Mad Mosaic*, which we had kept in print since 1983. Both were books of a very special character. 'What a life! But above all . . . what courage!' David Niven had declared spontaneously of *Living with Beelzebub*, just before his own battle with motor neuron disease made it impossible for him to read any more. Alastair Forbes defined its quality in his review in the *Spectator* on 24 October, saying that Gael Mayo had 'well named her carcinoma-wielding spook Beelzebub'.

True valour [he wrote] lies in enduring fear, in living with fear and in overcoming it enough to go on living one's life. On her very first page, surely right in not sparing her readers, Gael Mayo takes us into the Royal Marsden (curious postwar euphemism) Hospital and writes, 'entering the hallway I think, everyone in here has cancer . . . ', and upstairs, in the Head and Neck Ward (as she mercifully discovered when Beelzebub's invading metastases finally sent her back there to take her last breath just a week ago), continues: 'Unless you can be of help don't visit. What solace can be given to someone who has lost an ear, an eye, half their face? . . . Cancer is not an enemy that can be confronted face to face, it is a sneak that comes up from behind . . . For twenty years I have lived with a spook, at some times closer to me than others; right now he is close.'

It was a heroic tale, into which 'her indomitable cheerfulness could not be kept from breaking'. It was also the sort of book that gave Quartet its heart and soul. The link with Gael Elton Mayo also happily brought her daughter, Georgia de Chamberet, to work for Quartet for many years. In the brief memoir that follows, Georgia affords an insight into her mother's relationship with Alastair Forbes, originally given at his memorial service in 2005, followed by her recollections of life in Goodge Street.

Alastair Forbes, man about town and book reviewer, and my mother, the writer and painter Gael Elton Mayo, were lifelong friends. A strong presence, Ali was an uncle figure to me, who periodically bawled me out for being 'a silly girl', but was also loving and funny. At the end of the *Daily Telegraph*'s obituary of my mother, in 1992, he wrote:

> It was in the company of Evelyn Waugh's Ukrainian-speaking brother-in-law, Auberon Herbert, that one summer afternoon in Strasbourg some forty-five years ago I first met Gael. With her freckled sun-tanned shoulders held in a white *faille* dress (a speckled Moran hen's egg in a white cup, I teasingly told her she resembled) it was impossible not to fall in love with her on the spot. So in no time we set off, like the Owl and the Pussy Cat in my happily not pea-green car, on many a memorable journey, in which the originality of her painter's eye and natural writer's observation of all we came across contagiously awakened in me a fresh appreciation of life and people that I have never since lost. Yet, when in due course all occasions combined to inform against our 'love affair' (as such relationships were still referred to in those days), it was miraculously to be replaced by what I can only call a more than two-score-year-long 'affair of Love' that was to last until our last Goodnight a few hours before she died. By then we had become not just the dearest of dear friends but what Goethe in a very different situation called *Wahlverwandschaft* – Kindred by Choice – allowing me to treasure no less my love of her three children and my memories of happy times with all of them on both sides of the Channel and the Atlantic.

In her autobiography, *The Mad Mosaic*, published in 1983, Gael refers to Ali as 'the professor' who 'gives lessons about life'. She writes:

It was a peculiar affection we shared. Was he just a rather special friend to me? What on earth was I to him, since I did not belong to the group who ran the world, and it was the world's affairs that interested him most? Was it an *amitié-amoureuse*? He loved other women and attended all the balls or parties that were given, and spent much time talking with politicians for the writing of his weekly slasher – I say slasher because he had incisive vision and could cross-section events or show them in a new light. In any case we shared a friendship that for some reason made various people cross or jealous, probably because they could not fathom it, but neither could we, so what did it matter? I also led my own other life in a different world. But sometimes we would go off together – once it was on the road to Spain – he was at a loose end perhaps when he suggested it – no matter why – but we made one memorable trip to what Rose Macaulay then called the Fabled Shore; we saw the coast long before the concrete blocks sprang up. In Benidorm there was one *fonda* (with bed bugs) and the most curious shells on its deserted beach. I remember one lurid conch like a red mouth; the creature that had lived inside had come out like a wet smile in the surrealist sunset.

At one point, when Gael was living in New York, Ali arrived to cover the Eisenhower–Stevenson campaign, and she accompanied him to the election meetings. Ali lost his job over Suez, when, according to Gael,

> he labelled Anthony Eden as a fool. What was the point of a political column if not to tell the truth, he asked (much later)? His fear then must already have been a premonition – yet his column was the only one not to follow a line or take orders. He was accused of 'blatancy' but this was its value . . . The professor held definite views and had high standards about language and ways of expression. He could be a martinet and ticker-off with the best intentions, but to know him was educational.

The 'public' Ali may have been a larger-than-life, witty man of letters notorious for his name-dropping and feuds, but the 'private' Ali could be a warm and kind friend. During the last twenty years of my mother's life when she courageously fought off cancer of the face and neck, he sent her amusing postcards and letters, and was comforting. I remember him arriving once for lunch with an armful of roses from his garden under the Sussex downs. After my mother died, Ali drove me to Chelsea Town Hall to register her death, and was a tremendous support. Later, whenever he was in my neighbourhood, he'd come by for tea and talk. I will miss that voice booming down the telephone line his endearing expressions like,

'Minute, Papillon,' and his encyclopedic knowledge. Wherever he was, Ali kept alive plenty of 'laughter and the love of friends' – the two things which he lived by.

The Quartet Years
by Georgia de Chamberet

My mother, Gael Elton Mayo, novelist, painter and 'Girl Friday' for Robert Capa, Henri Cartier-Bresson and David Seymour at Magnum Photographers in its early years, was introduced to Naim Attallah by Patrick Seale. Quartet Books published her autobiography, *The Mad Mosaic*, which sold unexpectedly well and was reprinted, leading to the later publication of her account of her illness, *Living with Beelzebub*. Quartet was avant-garde, innovative and independent, rather like Canongate today. I was going nowhere fast after leaving university, so was sent by my mother to see Naim Attallah in his plush Poland Street offices. He hired me to work with Quartet's production director, Gary Grant.

So one autumn day in 1987 I turned up at 27 Goodge Street, a Dickensian building in London' s West End. I was greeted at the head of the stairs by an intriguing and enigmatic individual, who disappeared into a small office piled high with books and manuscripts, making a remark as he did so about the bars on his office window and the Birdman of Alcatraz. This was Quartet's editorial director, Stephen Pickles. His office on the first floor was at the back of the building, next to Gary's, and mine was at the front, overlooking Goodge Street. Quartet had a good reputation for publishing lavish, high-quality art and photography books and Gary was an expert at overseeing such projects, when not in the pub across the road. Production was not really my thing, so I began to do occasional odd jobs for Pickles, which rather annoyed Gary. Initially I made telephone calls to Charlotte Rampling, Lothar Schirmer and Joanna Richardson.

Editors in the building at the time were Linda Brandon, Zelfa Hourani (responsible for the Middle East and Africa list) and Alethea Savile on the top floor; with Chris Parker (whose passion was jazz) and Julian Bourne (the son of the notoriously eccentric Eton classics professor, who had retired), alongside copy-editor Rosemary Graham on the second floor. Zina Sabbagh and Eliza Pakenham were to join Quartet's editorial department later.

When I changed jobs, Pickles became my boss. He was a tough but inspirational teacher, and a perfectionist when it came to editing. I will never forget the brilliant blue-pencil job he did in just a few hours one afternoon on the manuscript of George Hayim's memoirs. He had a phenomenal, internationalist vision of where he wanted to take the Quartet list. Over the years we worked to develop the Quartet Encounters paperback series of twentieth-century European classics – publishing Aharon Appelfeld, Giorgio Bassani, Hermann Broch, E. M. Cioran, Stig Dagerman, Heimito von Doderer, Julien Green, Pierre Klossowski, Ismaïl Kadaré, Miroslav Krleža, Arnošt Lustig, Osip Mandelstam, Pier Paolo Pasolini, Fernando Pessoa, Fyodor Sologub, Abram Tertz, Boris Vian – which brought great intellectual kudos to the company. Pickles also championed the publication of translations of works by important authors largely unknown to the English-reading public – notably Thomas Bernhard, Per Olov Enquist, Tahar Ben Jelloun, Annie Ernaux, Ernst Jünger, Eduardo Galeano, Hervé Guibert, Juan Goytisolo, Witold Gombrowicz, Antonio Muñoz Molina, Manuel Vazquez Montalban, Yves Navarre, Juan Carlos Onetti, Giorgio and Nicola Pressburger, Pascal Quignard – which attracted the attention and the praise of leading British and American critics of the day. A connoisseur of opera and classical music, Pickles also published biographies of grandiose figures such as Maria Callas, Herbert von Karajan and Wilhelm Furtwängler. I was particularly involved with translations from French as I am bilingual. In 1992, James Kirkup's translation of Jean Baptiste-Niel's *Painted Shadows* won the Scott Moncrieff Prize, and that year also we won the *Independent* Award for Foreign Fiction with *The Death of Napoleon* by Simon Leys.

Pickles was divinely charming and witty – and fiercely protective of his privacy. His wickedly funny book, *Queens*, published in 1984 by Quartet, featured a photo of him on the cover as a wildly handsome young man. I remember a bleak period when Pickles lost friends to AIDS. Derek Jarman came to visit once or twice; he had incredibly clear, almost electric-blue eyes, and was beautiful and gaunt like an effigy on a tomb. Pickles was a Soho man and a regular at the Coach and Horses pub, immortalized in the play *Jeffrey Bernard is Unwell*.

Those of us in No. 27 Goodge Street were teased as being 'serious' by those in No. 29 next door, where it was Party Central. David Elliott was the Main Man when it came to sales and marketing, and Jubby Ingrams his Queen Bee. Mischievous and sexy, she had a *gamine* quality, and most of the men at Quartet worshipped her (the cockney musician, Louis Vause, in particular). Invariably the weekend would kick off on Friday afternoons with gossip and hilarity in sales and marketing. Various PR ladies sashayed in and out of No. 29 Goodge Street over the years – tough cookie Anna Groundhog [Groundwater] (envied by all for getting hold of the company's gold credit card!), socialites Lucy Blackburn, Anna Pasternak and Nina Train who dreamed of marrying dukes, clever Daisy Waugh, sultry Emily Berens, eccentric Selina

Blow, gorgeous Tamara von Schenk, babelicious Susie Craigie Halkett – I do not remember all of them. Olive, an older and rather formidable, straight-talking Scottish woman in charge of accounts, kept a sharp eye on everyone from her second-floor vantage point, accompanied by her terrifying Rottweiler called Jake.

Quartet's book launches have become legendary for their glamour and star quality, attracting media razzmatazz and column inches of gossip. Different worlds collided, affording a unique and glitzy contrast to the usual, pre-dictable crowd that pitched up at regular publishing-industry launches, that were drab affairs done on the cheap at which the best on offer was peanuts and a glass of acidulated, lukewarm white wine.

Towards the end of my time at Quartet, I became managing and com-missioning editor of an English-language paperback list, Robin Clark. We reprinted Lesley Blanch, Steven Berkoff, Alethea Hayter, Robert Hichens, W. W. Jacobs (a new collection of his stories, selected and introduced by Peter Ford), Emanuel Litvinoff and W. M. Thackeray's *Book of Snobs*. I also began to find success with authors like Daniel Pennac, and a young black British writer S. I. Martin, published in Quartet's general list; and with Peter Bush's anthology of Cuban stories, *The Voice of the Turtle* (later published in the US by Grove Press). At this time Anthony Blond, a once great publisher down on his luck, joined the company to establish his own imprint under the Quartet umbrella. I helped out on certain titles, and with his own book, *Blond's Roman Emperors*. He was shambolic and fun, and boozy lunches in Soho became a feature. Being at Frankfurt Book Fair with Blond was quite an experience.

Although Blond and Pickles got on well together on one level, there was an underlying undercurrent of competitive, bitchy tension. This was fuelled by the vicious, almost feudal, nature of Quartet's office politics, with the various head-honchos scurrying and vying for favour with Big Boss, Naim Attallah. Pretty much from the beginning of my time at Quartet, I decided to keep out of the way and out of the firing line, which worked well for me until the knives of change came out in Goodge Street – of which I was naïvely unaware until too late, by which time Blond was long gone, Pickles had been dispatched, and I was next. In-house accusations, and an article in the *Bookseller* implying that the editorial director's policy of publishing translations was the cause of *all* the company's growing financial problems, rankled.

Naim Attallah gave a great many people that crucial first break. During my time at Quartet both my parents died, and I will always remember his kindness. He showed positivity and encouragement when, in February 1997, I founded my own 'small is beautiful' company, BookBlast Ltd.

Forty-eight

In February 1993 Asprey and Mallett ended their talks of a merger. There were many issues on which we failed to reach agreement, but the most basic one concerned the price. It also became obvious during negotiations that our business methods differed vastly. Theirs were perhaps more steeped in tradition, which meant they sometimes overlooked the market changes, whereas ours, though similarly based, were more disposed to move with the times. There were factors that could suddenly boost their sales, such as a falling pound, and this gave them pause for further reflection. Suddenly they changed tack and became more bullish as to the future prospects of the company in its independent state.

I was disappointed that the merger failed to materialize, though breathed a deep sigh of relief none the less. As it turned out, the two companies were better off remaining apart. I could sense a management incompatibility with Mallett that would certainly have given Asprey more problems than I would have cared to cope with. A clash of personalities looked inevitable and would not have augured well for the future of the enlarged group. The press covered the story of the failure of talks and launched at once into speculating on our next move. Three weeks later the *Evening Standard* reported that next on Asprey's shopping list was likely to be the luxury interior design company, Colefax & Fowler.

Just before Christmas [Naim Attallah] snapped up a 6.8-per-cent stake in Bond Street antiques dealer Mallett and immediately entered bid negotiations.

They broke down on price, with the Fayed brothers, who are 30-per-cent shareholders, refusing to take a loss on their holding.

Some of Asprey management have been taking a look at Colefax & Fowler in Brook Street and Fulham Road. But chief executive David Green, who controls 23 per cent of the shares, refuses to comment.

In the year ending March 1990, Colefax made £4 million, but profits fell to £700,000 last year and the company has slipped into the red to the tune of £200,000 in the interim stage of the current year. Colefax is capitalized at £10 million but has a turnover of £30 million.

Against a current share price of 54p, Asprey is unlikely to secure its target at under 100p a share. Asprey is capitalized at £234 million and, despite its recent spending spree, has no debt.

The truth was that we never seriously considered the acquisition of Colefax. Our plate was already full and we needed a period of consolidation before we embarked on any new venture.

Such, however, was not the case with the Namara Group. If an opportunity for diversification was there, I could never resist it. I was always seeking a fresh challenge in areas where I had no prior expertise, in which I could learn and then put that learning to the test. Being always afraid of stagnation I needed the incentive of new goals to pursue, and whatever the pressure on my time, I always managed to talk to the press about current issues. My friend Cristina Odone, the editor of the *Catholic Herald*, asked me in an interview about the challenges of bringing Christian ethics to business. I was delighted to be asked, for it was a subject that concerned me. The interview began and Cristina soon introduced its main theme:

> To achieve financial success, the Yuppies under Maggie had resolutely over-looked ethics, side-stepped morals, and waved goodbye to scruples. Not so Attallah, who has managed somehow to make a fortune and become successful without leaving a string of corpses in his wake . . .
>
> 'I try to help people whenever I can,' the 'angel' behind everything from West End plays to the *Literary Review*, says modestly. 'I think you can be successful without losing sight of your Christian upbringing. That, at least, has been my endeavour.' . . .
>
> He was born in Palestine of Greek Catholic parents [that is, members of the Greek Catholic church], the only son after three girls ('I was considered a miracle'). Brought up in a protective, close-knit middle-class environment, young Naim suffered a shock when he alighted on English shores at eighteen. 'I felt completely alien, an outsider in a strange land – which went on for years, as I would meet the products of a public-school education, men and women who truly "belonged" in a way I never could, to the Establishment – [but it] must have been one of the spurs behind my desire to succeed.'
>
> Determination coupled with hard work and an unfailing sense of PR brought him swiftly to prominence . . . His own energy level would leave a marathon runner out of breath: a flurry of constant activity, he wakes before dawn and often attends evening social functions. Monday may find him at the Frankfurt Book Fair and Tuesday at a publishers' conference in Brighton. On the way, he may fit in a visit to a church, where he just likes to light a candle and pray for the loved ones in his life . . .

'The key to being a Christian businessman is never to see money as your ultimate goal. Always keep your priorities – love, peace of mind and the family above all – firmly in place. That keeps you from yielding to hedonism, envy and the kind of cut-throat competition that is all too often at the root of so much in the money-making world . . .

He emphasizes the need for brotherhood in the competitive dog-eat-dog world of business: 'I don't think I ever wittingly hurt anyone. If at the end of the day you know that to clinch a deal or strike a bargain [means] you hurt someone, how can you go to sleep?'

In his own sunset years, Attallah predicts he will retire to the Dordogne, where he already has a house. The area reminds him of his home in Palestine. 'When I am sitting in France I look at the full moon in the sky. I think of the moon coming behind the hill in Nazareth. My grandmother would be holding me in her arms, and together we would look up at the moon . . . Spiritually, I yearn for those days to come back.'

*

In March 1993 I wrote an article for the *Sunday Express* comparing a trip I made to China that January with one to the Soviet Union in 1991. The Russian trip had been an eye-opener. I could never have imagined the poverty endured by the people and the lack of any basic amenities to make their lives tolerable. The average salary of a young person was the equivalent of twenty dollars a month and their accommodation was atrocious. People had to queue for the most meagre rations. Milk was in very short supply and you could hardly find a slice of lemon to put in your tea. However, their resilience was something to admire; they proved it in resisting both Napoleon and Hitler. But I could not help feeling that the population at large accepted their serfdom. Their living conditions had scarcely improved since the Revolution, with the gap between rich and poor remaining the same, the only noticeable difference being that members of the Politburo had replaced the old aristocracy.

I had always dreamed of visiting Russia and China, but my experience of Russia meant that I approached my trip to China with some apprehension. First impressions of a country tend to begin at the airport, and although I had to fill in the same bureaucratic forms giving details of personal items and foreign currency on arrival at Beijing, the welcoming efficiency and smiling faces contrasted sharply with the stiff formality of the Russians, whose faces had been like expressionless masks. My hotels turned out to be luxurious, again in sharp contrast with Russia, where food was scarce or lacking in variety at even the best hotels. The populace looked more cheerful and there was no sign of food shortages in the big cities. The hustle and bustle there indicated a new epoch in the making. Progress was well and truly underway and the signs spoke volumes for what was to come.

My impressions as a traveller in China began with Beijing, whose tourist landmarks were stunning, not just for their physical dimensions but also because of an overwhelming awareness of the past rubbing shoulders with the present. At the city's heart lay Tiananmen Square, which five years before had been the scene of a violent crackdown by the nervous authorities on peaceful dissident demonstrators. The name of the square comes from the imposing gate and tower at its north end, which gives access to the Forbidden City. In imperial times edicts had been flung from its parapet to humble officials below for dissemination throughout the empire. In all, twenty-four emperors had ruled from the Forbidden City during about five centuries, and it was a truly amazing architectural feat, with its magnificent complex of palaces, halls and pavilions.

The scale of everything we visited impressed, especially that of the Great Wall of China, the most massive construction ever undertaken by man, which twisted and turned like a giant headless dragon – a chilling memorial to the half-million conscripted labourers who died building it. In the present the focus of endeavour for the authorities was the task of keeping a population of one point two billion free from starvation and disease. Beijing was a city of cyclists. Men and women, old and young, clogged the roads like an army of ants on the move, all streaming somewhere with a purpose. Weather conditions were freezing when I was there, but far from being hampered by the elements, people seemed to be invigorated by them. Therein surely lay evidence of the extreme hardiness of the Chinese.

From Beijing I went to Shanghai, the country's main commercial centre since the nineteenth century, with its history of gaiety, decadence and violence. Life centred on the Bund, the old European name for the road that runs alongside Huangpu Park, on which I stayed at the Cathay Hotel (renamed the Peace Hotel) that had once been the most palatial in the Orient under its green pyramid roof. Now, it seemed, there were crowds flocking to it from all over the world to hear the resident Chinese band play 'When The Saints Go Marching In' – a New Orleans renaissance in a most unlikely land. The hotel had been built in the 1930s by one of the Sassoon family and I was given the suite in which Noël Coward wrote *Private Lives*. From my window I had a clear view of the Huangpu River, a wide stretch of brown water teeming with craft ranging from ocean-going vessels to single-oared sampans. The sirens and horns of the boats hooted across the water day and night, giving voice to the energy of the city and keeping sleep at bay. At dawn a blare of music from speakers began along the promenades as the Chinese, young and old alike, did their morning *taiji quan* exercises, played instruments or sang. It was an uplifting spectacle, almost scary.

Our own day began with a determined walk along Nanjing Road, a long tree-lined boulevard containing some forty thousand shops. Most of these stayed open from 9 a.m. to 11 p.m., seven days a week. The street bustled with thousands of shoppers creating an alarming congestion of human bodies. The traffic was interlaced with legions of bikes, though by its ability to keep moving it displayed an orderly chaos, more miraculous than anarchic. During my four days in Shanghai I witnessed neither an accident nor an angry word.

The shops were stacked with merchandise, some of excellent quality. Most notable were the exquisite silks and cashmere garments. A metre of the finest silk cost about four pounds fifty and a cashmere sweater about ninety pounds. Food was plentiful and richly varied. It was all a sign of the great commercial resurgence already going on in China. The growth rate stood at around twenty per cent and looked likely to remain steady. Whatever the Communist leaders decided to do on the political front, the commercial revolution was clearly irreversible. The Chinese have always been entrepreneurial by nature, working hard and able to divorce political ideology from commercial expediency. There was no sense of the sort of repressive atmosphere associated with authoritarian regimes or any sign of resentment towards the foreigner. As a British official in Shanghai told me, the Chinese didn't have any need for outsiders – they simply allowed us to come in.

'Call me a cow, call me a horse' went an old Chinese saying. Roughly interpreted it means that the Chinese remain unperturbed by either praise or criticism. They just get on with things, quietly, confidently. Since it is said you can discover the essence of a country through its proverbs, armed with *Selected Chinese Sayings* by T. C. Laai I set out to put the truth of this to the test. Unfortunately, apart from fairly obvious words of wisdom, such as, 'What I lost in the saltfish I gained in the red herring,' an Oriental equivalent of swings and roundabouts, most seemed enigmatic to the point of impenetrability. What were we to understand by the admonition, 'Do not lace your boots in a melon field, nor adjust your hat under a plum tree'? One proverb that did make sense, however, was, 'A person without a smiling face should not open a shop.' China appeared to be a sea of smiling faces and their shop was now open to the world.

Before boarding the plane home I had to change back all my Chinese currency. The girl in the exchange booth asked me for a foreign coin for her collection. I searched my pockets, but without success. I could not bear the disappointment on her face, so I asked around my colleagues and managed to secure a one-pound coin. It made her day; it also made mine, for she smiled.

Shanghai was the city that I liked the most, perhaps because of its European connections. I was seriously considering an outlet in China for the Asprey group, but felt the time was not yet quite right for such a move. It would have meant a larger investment than usual, with too few customers immediately on stream. The boom in personal spending had not yet arrived, though the signs of its coming were clear to see. It would have been too great a gamble to take at that juncture as we could not afford to bide our time in expectation of future returns.

*

On 1 May 1993, Count Paolo Filo della Torre, an Italian aristocrat who lived in London and was established on the social scene, wrote a dispatch for the Italian newspaper *Panorama* in celebration of my birthday. It was headed 'King Midas on the Banks of the Thames'. 'Remember King Midas,' he asked, 'the mythological king who transformed everything he touched into gold? He is reincarnated today in the guise of Naim Attallah, an extraordinary cross between a pasha of the Ottoman Empire, from which his Palestinian family descend, and an exponent of the British aristocracy.'

> Attallah . . . sees gold and silver in abundance as chief group executive of Asprey plc, jewellers to the Queen and purveyor of luxury goods. But his major success derives from his association with beautiful and intelligent women . . . Women appreciate his warmth and strength of spirit and often confide in him. 'Can you imagine a terrestrial paradise without Eve? In fact without a host of Eves?' he asks with a twinkle in his eye. And in fact Naim is invariably surrounded by young, elegant and beautiful girls of blue-blooded stock and noble names. He has devoted his book *Women* to them . . .
>
> In her long review of the book in the *International Herald Tribune*, Suzanne Lowry recalls how Sigmund Freud, despite his fame, had not managed to discover what women really wanted in life. Naim Attallah is well on the way to discovery in his belief that they search for someone who can be the custodian of their innermost thoughts. He has certainly emerged as an unbeatable *confidant* . . . His various books are published by his own company, Quartet, and include the much-acclaimed *Of a Certain Age* . . .
>
> Many people attribute all Naim's successes to his enthusiasm and his energy. However, he confesses: 'At night I don't sleep for more than five hours.' Somehow one suspects he lives these as intensely as his waking hours.

Although the *Literary Review* was doing well as a prestigious and highly readable literary magazine, it had continued to cause a serious drain on my resources. Auberon Waugh, well aware of my accumulated losses, which by that stage had topped the two-million-pound mark, was very concerned that I should have to carry on single-handedly shouldering the magazine without the help of some other benefactors to ease the burden by sharing some of these losses through annual contributions. He fired off the first shot in his campaign to gain support in his *Spectator* column, the truth of the matter being, he said, that 'the country is swimming in corporate money'.

This brings me to a rather delicate point. For fourteen years Britain's liveliest and most worthwhile literary magazine has been entirely paid for by one man, the great and noble philanthropist Naim Attallah. He not only houses it free of charge, encourages the various enterprises he is associated with to advertise in it, but has also been picking up the losses – currently about £120,000 a year.

Naim is a model proprietor who never interferes, never complains, but I do not think it is reasonable to expect him to go on paying this enormous sum out of his own income indefinitely. Is there any company or individual who will join in? Tiny Rowland, perhaps? The *Literary Review* is much cheaper than the £6 million a year the *Observer* was losing and I feel sure we could work in ways of encouraging African industry. I think I may have found one new benefactor; he talks of putting up £30,000 a year if two or three others will do the same. If any philanthropist is remotely interested, I would be most grateful if he would get in touch with me; I promise to protect his or her confidence with my life.

Thinking back, there was an irony in the way I was accused by Anne Smith of stealing the magazine from her, and then by her supporters, who kept on reviving the falsehood over a number of years. The *Literary Review* was never going to be a commercial proposition. I became involved in it because Anne Smith had shown great courage in founding it and I could not bear to see her efforts thrown away. Her subsequent behaviour did not deter me from backing the magazine, especially as it became so important to Bron, with his entire life revolving around it. For him it was a labour of love that was to endure in its intensity until his untimely death.

He rang me ten days before he died, his voice quavering with weakness as he apologized profusely for his illness, which had prevented him from continuing to edit the magazine. He felt he had let me down. I was close to tears. This colossus of a man maintained his nobility to the very end. There was certainly no one else remotely like him.

*

In April I interviewed the Duke of Devonshire at his London home in Chesterfield Street, Mayfair, for the *Oldie*. I found him to be congenial, a true English gentleman with a disarming honesty. I did not want the interview to end, for I enjoyed being in his presence and was struck by his down-to-earth view of the world. He had none of the patrician arrogance of his class. On the contrary, he showed the kind of humility normally associated with great sages as they delve into the incomprehensible. The following vignette appeared in the *Daily Telegraph* under the heading 'Peerless':

> It seems there are occasional bleak moments at Chatsworth, seat of the Duke of Devonshire. Interviewed by Naim Attallah in the *Oldie* magazine, he announces he could rub along quite well without a handle.
>
> Devonshire, asked about the future of the House of Lords, says he would be sorry to see it go, 'although I wouldn't in the least mind losing my title and being called Andrew Cavendish. I'd mind very much if my possessions were taken away, but my title, no.' Attallah proceeded to ask Devonshire if he gets on well with his son. 'I get on very well with my son . . . He also gets on well with his mother and stands up to her too, more than I do.' Is the Duchess 'a strong character'? Devonshire replied: 'That would be an understatement.'
>
> The Duke seems to have been on good form. At one point he told Attallah that 'when I was young I used to like casinos, fast women and God knows what. Now my idea of heaven . . . is to sit in the hall at Brooks's having China tea.'

There was no question he refused to answer. His honesty came to the fore when I suggested that his image had been rather tarnished a few years earlier when he revealed, in the Old Bailey witness box, a side of his private life that at the time many people would have considered rather disreputable. He replied that being in the witness box and speaking on oath was a salutary experience, 'and it was very painful for my family. The only consolation was that I didn't attempt to lie. My private life isn't all it might be, but it would only make it worse to lie about it.' At this point I asked him if he ever repented. Again he was forthright: 'I find repentance very difficult, particularly if you are aware that you may do the same thing again . . . one has to be very careful of repentance.'

Years later his wife, the formidable Debo, told me that the interview I conducted with the Duke was the best he ever gave. I was flattered and surprised, for I thought she might have minded my intrusive questions about his private life. In fact she seemed relaxed about it. She rose even higher in my estimation and we occasionally corresponded. With her sister Diana and her other Mitford siblings, she belonged to an aristocratic family that has become something of a legend.

On 19 May 1993, the *Daily Mail* reported that I had been accorded an honour by the University of Surrey:

> Publisher and chief executive Naim Attallah was slightly mystified to find himself being fêted by the University of Surrey. First they asked him for an interview for their graduate magazine, then the chancellor approached him about accepting an honorary master's degree.
>
> Explains the former penniless Palestinian: 'Years ago I was an engineering student at Battersea College, and it turns out the college was closed down in the sixties and became part of the University of Surrey. Apparently that is the connection.'
>
> However tenuous the link, Naim, sixty-two, is more than flattered to receive the degree. 'At the time, I wasn't able to graduate from Battersea because I didn't have enough money to finish the course.'

The honorary degree was greatly appreciated. Curiously it filled an important gap in my life, at least where my mother was concerned. As I progressed in my career and attained a certain measure of success, my mother was naturally proud of the achievements of her only son. She always had one reservation, however. As she told well-wishers, her single regret in life was that I had never gained a university degree she could speak of with pride, as the parents of other sons did, among friends and relations. With this honorary degree her life's ambition was fulfilled. Her son had been accorded one with even more pomp than usual. What more could she ask? It made an old lady happy, for the significance of the award mattered to her greatly.

Craig Brown was never a great admirer of mine. He lambasted me in the *Mail on Sunday* on the publication of *Women* by penning the most scathing review of the lot. Subsequently he and Bron had lunch with me in Beak Street. It was meant to be a kind of *rapprochement*, though that was not quite how it worked out by my reading of the situation. Craig was in the same mould as Bron. Both of them felt passionately about things, and particularly about people. Once they had taken against someone, it would be extremely hard to divert them from their target. Bron's avowed enemy at the time was Lord Gowrie, and he never missed an opportunity to attack him. The reason, as I discovered later, was that Grey had enchanted Bron's girlfriend away from him when they were at university. Bron had lashed out at him ever since with vitriolic spleen. It took me months to persuade Bron to let bygones be bygones and allow me bring the two of them together. Thereafter their friendship revived, and Bron became very supportive of Grey and would not tolerate a word of criticism against him.

Craig's coolness towards me was something I found strange in so far as I could not decipher it. I was a supporter of literature and the arts, spending most of my money bolstering endeavours closely related to them, so even if Craig did feel some kind of antipathy towards me, I could not see why that should stop him being more appreciative. Perhaps I misread where he was coming from and misjudged him unfairly. It did not surprise me to see myself featured in his *Evening Standard* column of 28 June 1993, written with his usual blend of satire.

> Every now and then a conspiracy book is published which reveals a bizarre new secret dynasty, stretching from either Christ or Napoleon or Hereward the Wake. The authors invariably claim that each member of these secret dynasties is particularly gifted in business, or in fortune-telling, or in the arts.
>
> Shock! Horror! I think I have just spotted another such dynasty. Over the past few years, three men and one woman have come under the media spotlight for their penchant for the high life, and their inability to say: 'I've had more than enough, thank you.'
>
> From France, Jacques Attali. From Palestine, Naim Attallah. From England, Roy Hattersley. And from the world of fiction, Lady Chatterley. Spooky, eh?
>
> And where do they all spring from? Many centuries ago, Attila the Hun was also censured for taking rather more than his fair share of the pickings, and for improper personal extravagance.
>
> Attila, Attali, Attallah, Hattersley, Chatterley. Are they by any chance related?

In the autumn of 1993, the painter and portraitist Emma Sergeant was interviewed by Celia Lyttleton, the art critic, for an article Jane Procter, the editor of *Tatler*, had commissioned. The subject was society's promising young painters. The feature had to be accompanied by a good example of the work of each artist by means of a coloured transparency of their choice. Emma's preference – a large portrait of me which she had painted in 1991 – was sent to Celia, who in turn presented it to Jane Procter. The latter saw red and refused point blank to entertain its inclusion. Emma telephoned me to enquire whether I knew what lay behind her opposition. Naturally I was taken aback and at the same time perplexed. Although the reason for this bizarre turn of events was never given, informed sources attributed Jane's intemperate behaviour to my having made her husband, Tom Goldstaub, redundant following Asprey's acquisition of Mappin & Webb, where he had been the head of marketing.

As it happened, my relationship with Jane's husband could not have been better. Now, as managing director of Fintex, the fine-cloth merchants in Golden Square, he was always perfectly accommodating and I subsequently became one of his most regular customers. I therefore felt at a loss to understand his wife's action, given the importance of the Asprey group in the luxury-goods market and its close association with Condé Nast, principally as advertisers. Jane's throwing down the gauntlet, I could only conclude, was a deliberate attempt to humiliate me and one to which I had to respond. My reaction was swift. I suspended all advertising contracts for the Asprey group with Condé Nast until such time as the incident had been properly investigated by Jane's employers and a satisfactory explanation produced.

A few weeks later, when tempers had cooled, a conciliatory top-level meeting took place at Condé Nast, chaired by their managing director, Nicholas Coleridge. Present at the meeting was myself accompanied by Tania Foster-Brown, who had once worked at Vogue House but was there this time acting as a peace broker. A weepy Jane Procter was summoned to the meeting and tried to bluff her way through with some cock-and-bull story that made little sense. A suggestion that Emma Sergeant was stirring the pot went down badly with me and almost brought the meeting to an abrupt halt. At this point Procter changed her tactics, becoming apologetic and managing to placate her employer as well as myself with the claim that she was possibly the victim of circumstance. A few months later the whole truth had come out and Procter and *Tatler* had parted company.

After meeting for the first time in 1982, Emma Sergeant and I got on so well that our encounter led to a friendship that remained close over the years that followed. Her first portrait of me was done in charcoal the year of our meeting and hangs today in our house in the Dordogne. It is a moody picture, strongly expressive of character and conveying a lean and hungry look. Emma must have captured me at a phase in my life when those characteristics were dominant. It was also the time when Rupert Birley and I, having met at Emma's, took to meeting up regularly at her place for coffee in the early mornings. These were gatherings that I sorely missed after Rupert's tragic disappearance on a beach off West Africa. He was undoubtedly the embodiment of that cliché 'the heart-throb of his generation', whose good looks, poise, charm and outstanding intellect combined to set him apart from his peers. All those who knew him well and grew to love him – among whom I count myself – were shattered by his loss, which happened when he was at the zenith of his youth with a life full of promise ahead of him.

In January 1994, I wrote a foreword to mark an exhibition of Emma's work at Agnew's. It took the form of a tribute which best encapsulates our friendship and gives an insight into her background and her work as an artist. For that reason, I reproduce it in full.

Orpheus and the Underworld
Emma Sergeant, 1994

I first met Emma Sergeant twelve years ago at a Quartet Books party. Emma was then in her early twenties and exuded an energy and zest for life which sent out shock waves to those around her. Her youthful beauty was untarnished by the levy of life and when she moved about the room, eyes followed her.

In those days it was often alleged that I employed only beautiful and desirable young women who graced the London social scene and attended my publishing parties: if Emma had possessed mere beauty alone, she might easily have merged into the general glamour of the occasion. But she had other qualities: a sublime smile, a musical resonance in her laughter, an impish elegance and a light in her eyes which one sensed was linked to her vision of the world. All this, and much more, made her stand head and shoulders above the rest.

As I came to know Emma Sergeant I discovered that her artistic talent was outstanding. From the outset she had been determined to succeed and had worked very hard to ensure a steady progression in her *oeuvre*, at an early age demonstrating the boldness required to push back the boundaries of modern art. As a result the evolution of her work is truly remarkable. There is nothing preordained about it; it does not follow a set pattern; it possesses enormous power and the ability to surprise, even to shock.

She studied for two years at Camberwell and then at the Slade, graduating in 1983. In 1981 she won the Imperial Tobacco Portrait Award for her painting of Lord David Cecil. This resulted in commissions to paint Lord Olivier among others.

In 1986, an exhibition of her paintings and drawings of Afghanistan was held at Agnew's to raise money for UNICEF to help Afghan refugees. In 1988 she exhibited 'Faces from Four Continents', again at Agnew's. She has had many commissions to paint portraits, which include Imran Khan, Lord Carrington, the Earl of Verulam and Roani, Chief of the Kayapo Indians.

*   *   *

While on the subject of young portrait painters, happy memories come streaming back. It was the year 1985 when I met Marie-Claire Black, now

Kerr, at a cocktail party. I cannot recall the venue or the exact nature of the occasion. All I can remember is talking to her with a greater degree of animation than usual. I was captivated by her. She had large expressive eyes set in a symmetrical face marked with a hardly noticeable scar from a recent car accident. She was very conscious of her scar, though it simply added to her air of mystery. The encounter that evening led to a short and intense relationship that culminated in her painting me one long weekend when my wife was on a visit to New York.

She captured me on canvas, perhaps a shade more youthful than I was, but with a haunting look that expressed more of my inner self than I knew existed. On the same occasion, I, in turn, captured her, brush in hand, with her piercing eyes trying to translate her vision of her subject into a tangible form. My medium was simply a camera and the resulting picture stands in my office until this day. I remember our whirlwind friendship as being magical. It lasted a few precious weeks in which we saw a lot of each other, oblivious of the disparity between our ages and our backgrounds.

Forty-nine

Asprey was again hitting the headlines. There are two things the press likes: success and failure. At that time we fell within the first category. The Midas touch seemed still to be ours. There was another acquisition. 'Asprey expands further with £11m Swiss deal,' announced the *Financial Times* of an agreement reached with Les Ambassadeurs, a specialist retailer of high-quality watches and jewellery.

> The consideration of £10.8 m will be funded by a seven-year Swiss franc loan fully underwritten by Lloyds Bank.
>
> Les Ambassadeurs, an affiliate of Siber Hegner Holdings, is among the most upmarket watch and jewellery chains in Switzerland . . .
>
> Mr Naim Attallah, Asprey's chief executive, said Credit Suisse had suggested the acquisition, knowing that Asprey was keen to broaden its customer base and expand in Europe . . .
>
> The acquisition is conditional upon the Swiss authorities approving the transfer of leases over certain lengths.

The *Daily Telegraph* headline read: 'Asprey in £10m Swiss watch buy': 'In the year to December 31, [Les Ambassadeurs] had sales of £13.8m and made profit before interest and tax of £440,000.' 'Swiss gem for Asprey,' said the *Evening Standard*.

As the Asprey group grew in prominence so did my public profile. I was well aware that publicity and over-exposure carried both advantages and great risks, but I was willing to take the chance. The alternative would have been more damaging in the long term. The myth I could not dispel, however, was the speculation about my wealth. Most of the media considered me rich, or made that assumption. In actual fact I was not. I juggled my finances in a way that gave rise to the speculation. My income from Asprey and from the Namara Group was constantly being supplemented by large overdrafts from the banks. The reality had more to do with my lifestyle and my willingness to back projects for the simple reason that I found them interesting or felt they addressed a cause seeking to rectify an injustice, whether social or political. The display of my wealth, if that happened at all, was never knowingly overt.

Dominic Lawson hit the nail on the head in the *Financial Times* when he wrote that wealth is more a matter of appearance than reality.

In the old days it was not so. A man was wealthy if he had land, thousands of acres of it. It was probably inherited. At any rate it was not borrowed. If anything it was lent to tenants and others less fortunate.

But now anyone with vigour, by careful wooing of the banks with a strange urge to gamble, can acquire almost overnight the trappings of old money. Of course the bankers know that those Landseers, those grouse moors, are theirs. But the public sees the borrower as the source of wealth and it is in the banks' interest not to shatter the image

Few would have given much, he said, for my chances of attaining wealth and influence when I first arrived in Britain as a penniless Palestinian, but with a few pounds I had hired a Rolls-Royce to take me around the City of London. 'People were impressed. A Palestinian driving a Rolls-Royce was clearly a man of substance.' I could not have succeeded by surface charm alone, he said. I had, by all accounts, 'a brilliant head for figures, the sort of man who can make a killing on the foreign exchanges without recourse to a calculator'. But as J. Paul Getty had understood, even for the genuinely rich it was fatuous to try to express their wealth in a single figure. When he was told *Fortune* magazine had listed him as the richest man in the world, he remarked to his brother-in-law, 'I don't know how much money I have. If I don't know, how would they know?' 'Money,' commented Lawson, 'is only a measurement of value, and value is akin to mercury, an elusive, volatile substance which makes us look foolish when we try to capture it. It measures us, rather than the other way round.'

July 1993 was a defining month for Asprey. Events came so thick and fast that there was no time for us to take stock of the exciting new situation. Sears, who up to then had held a twenty-five-per-cent stake in Asprey, decided to sell their holding, thus paving the way for us to get a full stock-market listing. This meant we were less constrained than ever before and could see even greater things on the horizon. As the *Evening Standard* announced on the 6th: 'Sears sells to clear Asprey's way'.

> The sale of the 20.3 million shares, via brokers Smith New Court, will widen Asprey's share base sufficiently to meet the Stock Exchange require-ments for the company to move up from the unlisted securities market.
>
> Asprey revealed profits of £21.6 million in the year ending March, up from £19.3 million. The final dividend has been lifted to 4p from 3.75p, making a total of 5.1p from 4.85p.
>
> Trading is ahead of expectations in the current year, says vice-chairman Naim Attallah. He intends to increase his stake by buying up to 250,000 of the shares sold to Smith New Court.

The next day all the main London papers picked up the news of the sale of Sears's holding as their lead story. Asprey had not been central to Sears's strategy, said the *Financial Times*, nor was Sears able 'to exercise control over its investment'. Mr John Asprey and family trusts, it added, had 'increased their stake to nearly 52 per cent through the purchase of 1.1m additional shares yesterday, securing the group from takeover'. Shirley Skeel in the *Daily Telegraph* said:

> Asprey chief executive Naim Attallah, whose reputation as a writer and publisher is as colourful as the Asprey family's own feud-filled history, said he was 'very excited' about the greater public exposure. 'We will be more internationally known and the pressure will be on us to perform better. The prospect is riveting because we love hard work.'

'Pearly king sees the world as his oyster' read the headline to a summary of past events below the article:

> In the past two years, Asprey has been on an acquisition spree, twice sweeping up companies from under the nose of Gerald Ratner.
>   Unabated indulgence by the rich has seen the Bond Street shop continue to prosper, and a new outlet is now open in Prague, with Shanghai next on the list.

The Prague Mappin & Webb outlet was not due to open till the new year, and the Shanghai project, as we have seen, remained a pipe dream. In the *Independent*'s assessment I was quoted as saying: 'Rich people have become more selective. If they spent £20,000 last year they will spend £10,000 this year.' Meanwhile, said the *Guardian*, the sale of the Asprey stake virtually completed 'Sears's campaign to prune its sprawling empire', a retailing combine that stretched from Selfridges and Richards to Olympus Sports and Freemans mail order. *Today* came straight to the point with its headline: 'Sears flogs Asprey gems stake for £92m'. Liam Strong, chief executive of Sears, was quoted in *The Times* as saying 'the investment in Asprey had not been central to Sears's strategy, which was to concentrate on mass-market retail and home-shopping businesses'. Following the announcement of Asprey's pre-tax profits results, commented the *Retail Jeweller*, 'Asprey has received extensive coverage in national newspapers which are fascinated that a luxury-goods retailer can fare so well in a recession.'

The *Scotsman* was a day behind the rest with its main assessment, but featured an expansive interview with me by William Cook, who called me 'a man who juggles his jewels with a prolific career in publishing'. After telling the story of my business career, the article shifted to focus on my work as a publisher and magazine proprietor and my newer vocation as an interviewer, suggesting there might be collisions between my different functions.

'Naim Attallah: Man or God' read the humorous headline above the *Literary Review*'s assessment of his most recent tome, *Of a Certain Age*. Attallah's defence is typically robust: 'One of the most successful books that Quartet has published is *Women*. Is that vanity publishing? Would I have been more clever to give it to a competitor? None of the books of mine that Quartet has published has lost money.' . . .

He denies his *Women* is an intrinsically sexist exercise, designed to lump half the human race together. 'The very feminists who accuse me of doing that use my book as a reference . . .

'I find we [men and women] do have certain things that are complementary. Certain things women can do better than men. They love more detail than men. Men like to think of the thing as a whole. In certain things, women are much more patient, and women in general find it very difficult to divorce love from sex, whereas men find it easier.' Sexist? Perhaps not, but it is hard to imagine a successful woman making such sweeping statements about men.

In his favour, Attallah maintains a strict neutrality in his Q&A format, if not his choice of guests, and the result is a string of interviews which are always revealing, though often spectacularly uncritical. Subjects are allowed to say the most outrageous things. One can only hope Attallah's silence on such occasions does not equal deference.

Finally he asked me my views on the role of interviewer. 'Today the interviewer is a bigger star than the person he is interviewing,' I said, 'but I don't want you to learn about me.'

'People tell me things they don't tell anybody else, because they feel comfortable in my presence. They feel they are the stars, and that I am only some kind of a catalyst.'

And that's probably the best definition of Naim Attallah – an agent who helps bring about all manner of reactions, without suffering any sort of change.

On Friday, 9 July, in the *Daily Telegraph*, E. Jane Dickson set out to analyse how it was that in 'recession-blasted Bond Street, where some of London's most expensive shops are sprouting SALE signs . . . Asprey, purveyors of gifts to the gentry, remains an untoppled monument to senseless spending'.

The reasons for Asprey's soaring profits are simple. 'In a recession, the very rich will be less affected than the rest of us,' says Jill Bousoulengas, editor of *Retail Jewellery*. 'Also, with interest rates slipping, investment jewellery can be more valuable than money in the bank. Trade at the top end of the market is fairly buoyant.' Watches in particular have seen a massive upturn in recent years . . . Asprey's talent for diversification is one of its strongest suits.' . . .

John Chataway, stores analyst at stockbrokers Carr, Kitcat and Aitken, attributes Asprey's success wholly to the hedonism of the super-rich. The 'recession investment' argument is in his opinion a red herring. 'Everybody who buys that kind of jewellery recognizes that it is going to depreciate. The unique strength of Asprey is the extraordinary international clout of its name.'

There you have it. Just as housewives continue to pay a few pennies more for Heinz beans, playboys and princelings will pay astronomical sums for an *objet d'Asprey* simply because it is from Asprey. Making out the cheque is half the fun. It may not make much sense to you or me, but then, the rich are different.

At the weekend the *Observer* also featured an interview with me by Lindsay Vincent in the paper's 'Mammon' column. Previously, she felt, I had a 'curiosity value' for my propensity to give parties at which my staff 'dressed up in minority garb – perhaps something of an irrelevance in the great scheme of things'.

Asprey, to some minds the Queen's gift shop, [had] long been regarded by Square Mile fee merchants as a closed party, not least because it was controlled by the Asprey family and Sears, the retailing group whose interests range from Selfridges to Saxone shoes.

From tomorrow, however, Attallah becomes something in the City . . . Suddenly, in investment terms, the chief executive of Asprey matters.

'These institutions snapped up our shares in one hour. In one hour,' Attallah repeats. 'These people believe in us and our management. These people . . . I will never disappoint.'

On 6 July 1993, at the London Hilton, the first ever UK Jewellery Awards were handed out with ceremony, and were being referred to in the trade as the 'Jewellery Oscars'. The award for Retail Personality of the Year was sponsored by Swatch and was given to me. The commendation read:

Since [Naim Attallah] became chief executive of the Asprey group last year, the group has embarked on a strategy designed to secure their long-term prosperity. On the acquisitions side the company has been very active . . . While believing that the company's success is never attributable to one person alone, Naim believes that his own role in the company has been to inject energy and enthusiasm at all levels of business operations and has made a point of never losing touch with the various companies within the group.

'It's been a busy old time for Naim Attallah,' declared Horace Bent in the *Bookseller* a week or two later. 'A flurry of articles about him in the national press a fortnight ago followed the announcement that Asprey, the jewellery business of which he is chief executive, was seeking a listing on the London Stock Exchange.' In the same week I had been voted Retail Personality of the Year and then it was the 'turn of academe to pay its respects' with my master's degree from the University of Surrey. 'What next?' asked Mr Bent. 'President of the Publishers Association? Guardian of the Net Book Agreement? The sky's clearly the limit.'

Meanwhile Bron, writing 'From the Pulpit' in the *Literary Review*, reiterated the need for rich benefactors to come forth and commit some funds to lighten my financial burden in supporting the magazine. It was a follow-up to his *Spectator* piece, but was perhaps more passionately expressed. Any idea of approaching the Arts Council, he wrote, was out of the question.

> Much against my wishes, an approach was made to the Arts Council last year for help to launch a circulation drive. The response of that worthless, idle body was to send dozens of pages of forms with instructions on how to fill them in, taking endless hours to complete, and then to refuse to help in any way.

While the losses stood at about a hundred and twenty thousand pounds a year, there had never been a literary magazine that failed to lose money.

> To those who ask why we do not then obey the laws of the market and disappear, leaving only a faint fragrance behind, my answer is that it is not quite as simple as that. Naim does not threaten us with instant closure when he asks if I can come up with three new sponsors at £30,000 each. The point is that after fourteen years he is beginning to feel lonely, and it is to relieve his feelings of loneliness as much as to secure the magazine's future that I launch this appeal.
>
> In fact, I launched it a few weeks ago in the *Spectator*, reckoning that their readers might be richer than ours. It produced various helpful suggestions of people to whom I might apply, but no offers of help . . . But the truth is that although these are hard times for some, the country is still swimming in corporate money . . .

The *Literary Review* is a lovely little corner of our contemporary scene, but it can't survive without help.

In August, as if urged on by the heat of the summer, I snapped up another little gem for Asprey, the whiz-kid fashion designer Tomasz Starzewski. The bug of fashion had never left me ever since the departure of Arabella Pollen from the Namara camp. I often thought back to those early days when Arabella and I took on the fashion world and became the talk of the town. We even made an impression in New York, thanks to Arabella's youthful zest and irresistible charm.

When the news broke in May that Arabella had fallen from grace with Courtaulds, I felt disheartened. The talent she demonstrated was unquestionable and represented the epitome of Englishness, pure and simple. The *Independent* of 23 May, under its heading 'From riches to rags in designer fashion', summarized the exact situation. After building up an eighty-five-per-cent shareholding in her company, Courtaulds had decided to pull the plug. Their action sent shock waves through the fashion community. 'This will put the development of a strong British fashion industry back by years,' said the *Independent*, who described Arabella rightly as 'one of the brightest names in British fashion'.

Now, with Tomasz Starzewski, I was to recreate my previous role of backer, but this time through the multiple resources of the Asprey group. The news of the acquisition was well documented in the press. 'Does Naim Attallah have a better eye for clothes than Martin Taylor, Courtaulds Textiles' outgoing chief executive?' asked 'Observer' in the *Financial Times*. Mr Taylor's image had been given a 'rare knock' by the corporate decision over Arabella Pollen, he commented. 'Now it is the turn of one of the very few other youngish British designers, thirty-two-year-old Tomasz Starzewski, who has weathered the recession to see Attallah's luxury-goods group buy up a controlling share' – my eye having alighted on this 'first-generation Polish immigrant who took his first step up the ladder from above a Fulham fish and chip shop in which he sewed and slept'. The *Daily Telegraph* described me as finding the acquisition 'incredibly exciting', there being 'so much scope'. 'About 80 per cent of our clientele are young people. The mere fact that he is part of that group . . . can only mean giving us access to those customers.' It would also, I hoped, make Asprey appear trendier, as quoted by 'Pembroke' in the *Independent*: ' "Tomasz appeals to the young. He will add some glamour and show that we are not just traditional but as chic as anybody else," says the wild-of-tie Mr Attallah.'

In an article for the *Sunday Times Magazine*, 'Frocks and Rocks', Annabel

Heseltine wrote how Starzewski had 'dressed some of the richest ladies of the land and scaled the heights of British style'. With a glittering seal of approval from Asprey, he was *en route* for fame and fortune. Among his 'lunching ladies', whom he saw at his Pont Street salon in Knightsbridge, were the Princess of Wales, the Duchess of York, Princess Chantel of Hanover, Shakira Caine, Nicole Hambro, Cosima von Bulow and Vivien Duffield. 'His greatest achievement in recent times must be to have managed to make the flamboyant Ivana Trump, famed for her tiny skirts and big hair, look chic. His order book is full.' Asprey had singled him out in a year that had seen the departure of couture designers Victor Edelstein and the House of Norman Hartnell and 'top of ready-to-wear stylist' Arabella Pollen, though it seemed 'a strange move for a company whose name is synonymous with tooled wallets, shooting-sticks and tradition'.

[Asprey] is not, however, synonymous with diamante buttons the size of oysters, diaphanous gold coats and baby-pink fur collars. Yet the luxury-goods companies love to go shopping for names . . . 'If I didn't think Tomasz had the potential we wouldn't be sitting here today,' said Naim Attallah. 'He also has great enthusiasm and warmth. I see no reason why, with our backing, we shouldn't realize that potential. Tomasz is complementary to us and will help us broaden our base to a selective younger client. And we can show off our jewellery to best advantage whenever the occasion arises.' . . .

For Starzewski the new deal means freedom. He will have his nose to the drawing-board most of the time, of course, but there will be infinite back-up from Asprey when it comes to staging expensive shows, paying for supermodels and spreading the Starzewski name. 'I will be allowed to design for the first time without having to worry too much about the bills or how I am going to survive for the next six months, as I have been doing for the last ten years.

'I would like to think that I am very much part of the future of British fashion. It has gone through a very sad time where many designers have disappeared and London has lost its kudos as an inspirational centre, and as a venue to attract the international fashion world to come and look. This marriage between Asprey and myself will give confidence to British fashion because it will show the international market that serious money is prepared to invest in British talent.'

In an interpretation of events offered by *The Times*, they saw me as the 'irresistible chief executive of Asprey . . . trying to shake off the clocks-to-jewellery image once and for all'. The teaming up with Tomasz Starzewski was part of a drive 'to convince the younger, more hip generation that there is more to Garrard, Mappin & Webb, and other parts of the group than old clocks and dusty silver ornaments'.

> 'Tomasz's clients are politicians, royalty, the younger generation, the Sloane Rangers,' he enthuses. 'They don't come into Asprey. Tomasz will broaden our customer base.' Regular Starzewski clients such as the Princess of Wales and Mrs Thatcher may not be quite what Attallah has in mind, but he is on the right track. Asprey has injected about £120,000 into the designer's company in return for a 76-per-cent stake. On more traditional ground, it is buying Ronald A. Lee Fine Arts, a Mayfair antique-clock and -furniture retailer. Attallah flies off to France tomorrow to recover from the excitement.

This second Asprey acquisition, which took place at the same time as Tomasz Starzewski, involved purchasing the entire issued share capital of Ronald A. Lee, thus adding an even wider dimension to the antiques portfolio. The deal also involved an injection of loan capital of three hundred thousand pounds to cover all existing liabilities. Tony Keniston in the *Antiques Trade Gazette* asked whether this was part of the beginning of a trend for 'personal businesses in the antiques world to become part of large companies' when 'large financial institutions are not best suited to running well-established independent businesses'. The chairman, Ronald Lee, though eighty, was to continue with the company, as was his son, Charles. The autonomy of the business would continue in line with group policy. 'My father,' said Charles Lee, 'thinks Naim Attallah is an extremely interesting fellow, and I have been great friends with John Asprey for years. The marriage is based on the right principles.' Charles went on:

> It was inevitable, really . . . Families, however rich they are, cannot cope with the present international situation . . . You have to face up to the brave new world . . . I have always worked in Mayfair, it's my patch. So joining up with Asprey could be an extremely fruitful relationship.

Mr Keniston remained sceptical, wondering how many antiques dealers would really want to become part of a large company. 'Very few, I suspect. Indeed, numerous dealers have entered the antiques trade specifically to get away from such an environment.' But as was evident to everyone, 'financial considerations can all too easily take the fun out of dealing. Unfortunately, few need reminding.'

Meanwhile people in the jewellery trade were increasingly to be heard complaining about the recession. They found that customers were becoming more choosy and demanding good value for money. The days were truly over when prices were so firmly fixed that no one contemplated a haggling battle before a purchase. Even the very rich – probably the worst culprits when it came to wanting a bargain – never expected to pay the full retail price of an important item. It was taken for granted that some sort of discount would be given if asked for. Against this background, in September 1993, *Diamond Insight* in New York printed a statement I had made:

Change is in the air in the sense that customers worldwide are purchasing more selectively and expecting good value for money. The bonus of recent years which made retailing easy is unlikely to recur in the same manner. Standards of craftsmanship and service have to be maintained at the top end of the market if prosperity is to be sustained.

The Asprey group has a huge potential and would like to develop its different strengths in the new millennium. Their first priority is to broaden the customer base in order to lessen vulnerability to political and economic change. We also have to aim to complement our present activities by further diversification in those areas in which our expertise and experience already stand us in good stead. Finally, we want to encourage and nurture creativity within the group to enable us to remain leaders in our field.

While I could scarcely keep up with the work load I had punitively imposed on myself with the flurry of Asprey acquisitions, and prided myself on my hands-on approach with regard to every company within the group, I still managed to create time to carry on with my interviewing. This meant extensive travel within the United Kingdom and abroad. There was one particularly difficult assignment that faced me. It entailed driving through the Swiss Alps from Italy to meet that elusive and very private writer, Patricia Highsmith, famous mainly for psychological thrillers such as *Strangers on a Train* or her *Ripley* series, featuring unsettling psychopathic characters. On this trip I had the help of Ros Milani-Gallieni, who was working for Garrard on special projects.

Apart from her driving ability, Ros's company was a sheer delight. We flew to Milan, where we hired a car and proceeded towards Lugano, the nearest town to Patricia Highsmith's hideaway, where we spent the night before negotiating the Alps in search of her. She had given us directions to a small village, where she said she would be waiting. She was there when we arrived, looking dishevelled and rather strange. She asked Ros to stay behind and invited me into her car. We drove up a mountainous road for about twenty minutes before reaching our destination. The house stood in a semi-wilderness and its interior was sparse, its décor rather grim. It struck me as an unhappy environment in which she must have led a kind of monastic existence. She offered me an alcoholic drink as we entered, but I declined. I needed to have my wits about me for this potentially difficult encounter.

The interview was full of drama, as I suspected it might be. Twice during the course of my questioning Miss Highsmith stood up furiously and refused to proceed. As I tried to placate her with apologies for any intrusion into her private life, she poured herself a large whisky and gradually became less tense and more amenable. Her hostility finally disappeared when I referred to her book *People Who Knock on the Door*, which she had dedicated to 'The courage of the Palestinian people and their leaders in their struggle to regain a part of their homeland'. Her face then became animated and I realized how committed she was to the Palestinian cause. From then on the interview became less of a burden and I felt I had achieved my goal. Any unpleasantness had been avoided, partly because of my Palestinian origins. Her initial anger somehow turned to sympathy. She drove me back to where Ros was waiting and the parting was more congenial than the reception had been. Ros drove us down to Milan airport, handed in the car and we flew back to London. For a short trip, it had had more than its share of melodramatic moments.

Ros and I often travelled together to Milan and Paris and seemed to work well together. Her grasp of languages was an added bonus, especially in Italy. I once met her parents and we spent an operatic evening at La Scala, Milan. I particularly remember the visit since we stayed at the Excelsior Hotel Gallia in the so-called Madonna Suite, named after the pop singer, who must have used it on several occasions. It happened to be the only accommodation available at the time. We had searched elsewhere without any luck, so we figured why not live it up for the night and follow in the footsteps of Madonna? Such extravagance is something I have always been partial to. In Paris we stayed at either the Plaza Athénée or Hôtel de Crillon, or even L'Hôtel, where Oscar Wilde was said to have lived his last days and finally died. Ros's task in Paris was to coordinate the marketing and publicity of René Boivin there with its boutique within the Garrard showrooms in London. She also played a major role with her counterpart in Paris, who was in charge of René Boivin's new flagship shop at 49 avenue Montaigne together with the boutique in rue de la Paix. The new shop's inauguration party was a sumptuous affair. Among the guests were Antoine Gridel and the Duchesse Sophie de Würtemberg, Princess Jeanne-Marie de Broglie, Cheryl Shaker and the Princesse Woussoun, Mmes Pierre Schlumberger and Hélène de Ludwighauzen, Princess Anne de Bourbon and Josephus Melchior Thimister, and M. and Mme K. Scheuffle of Chopard. Jacques Bernard, the president of Boivin, and his wife greeted the guests, while John Asprey and myself with our respective wives were visibly beaming with joy and pride. Our dream of having a highly prestigious shop on avenue Montaigne had become a reality at last.

In all of these activities Ros was a key figure. I met her when she was introduced to me by my wife Maria. Poised and elegant, she had perfect manners, and combined in her face the freshness of a Nordic complexion with a faint hint of the Mediterranean. She was attractive, with a mysterious air of restraint that was hard to define. My first impression was one of a young lady totally in control who would seldom allow herself to be distracted by emotional demands likely to disrupt her structured life. I was fascinated by the intriguing mix of messages she seemed to send out to the world. She was certainly someone out of the common run who had hidden depths worth exploring. Little did I know that this short encounter would lead to a working relationship destined to develop into a close and long-standing friendship that would weather the rocky patches that were to lie in its path and come through unscathed.

Over time I was to discover that beneath what seemed a cool exterior Ros was a woman who was passionate about her work and passionate about people but kept her feelings in separate compartments. The phrase 'a woman for all seasons' was one that might have been used to describe her.

A Working Life with Naim
by Ros Milani-Gallieni

Naim – a four-letter word – requires no introduction. The contacts and net-work flooded all around him whenever he called with a quest from his desk at Asprey plc. During my years beside him, in his role as group chief executive of Asprey, the luxury-goods consortium encompassing Mappin & Webb, Tomasz Starzewski, Asprey Bond Street, Asprey New York, René Boivin, Sangorski & Sutcliffe and the wonderfully distinguished Garrard the Crown Jewellers, my tasks took on the true meaning of multi-tasking – which I am still slave to today. In creating and running the most exclusive events for him, where aspiration turned into reality, he transmitted to me a wealth of enthusiasm and energy. This in turn opened out into an expansive vision of opportunities and developments for the benefit of the group.

My first interview at Asprey, shortly after a three-year stint with Anouska Hempel Couture – and three years before that with Mr Armani at Giorgio Armani in Milan – was a relaxed and welcoming affair. Naim offered me the opportunity to use and develop links with Europe and the five languages I had at my fingertips. It was an inspired chance. Work centred round the fourth floor at 106 Regent Street, which was the inner sanctum, buzzing with pretty girls, all of them much younger and more dynamic than I was. Security looked on approvingly as new arrivals and good-lookers asked to be shown their way to the fourth floor. As you opened a door you would invariably be met by an aroma of fresh-brewed coffee, or at mid morning the fragrances of fresh herbs and fish dishes being grilled or steamed for Naim's punctual lunch at 12.30 p.m. Press, buyers, bankers, lawyers, writers, designers must all look back on colourful memories of those times with him, and sometimes 'one of us gals' would be invited to spice up the table, though the calibre of the guests daunted us!

The settings were carefully prepared, and it was always a greatly animated table, with lively stories shared over large goblets of Cloudy Bay white wine, and a good strong coffee to end. Then a discreet bleeper, custom-made in black croc, would summon a 'gertie' to clear us all out of the boardroom and back to our duties. Naim would then leave the room, leading his friends out and enjoying compliments about the flamboyantly colourful silk linings of his newly tailored navy-blue cashmere suit, or about an unusual stone he had set in a handsome bold signet ring – a cabochon emerald.

Among the major jewellery exhibitions I set up and oversaw was the complete rebuild of the new René Boivin store after the move from L'Opéra to avenue Montaigne with Jacques Bernard at the helm of the famous Parisian signature. The prestigious Boivin collection was inaugurated with the grand opening of the Paris store in May 1993, celebrating over a hundred years of history and treasures – a collection I now have in a book to revive the dream from time to time. The French house of *haute joaillerie* had been brought into the Asprey group in April 1991 and boasted an exclusively designed showroom within Garrard the Crown Jewellers. Then in October 1993 there was Vienna, the venue chosen for the celebration of Garrard's 150th anniversary as Crown Jewellers to the British monarch. The British Embassy opened its doors to this spectacular one-off royal gala and exhibition, held within the rooms of the ambassador's home – quintessentially British territory in Austria. It was magnificence all round.

The pieces had been selected from the Regent Street store a month in advance with stealth-like secrecy. Antique clocks, Queen Adelaide's restored crown, silver wine coolers, each the size of a small bath, ultra-fine jewellery set with the most sought-after stones, watches and more left the West End with a code word for their destination. Long preparations had gone into emphasizing the significance of this grand opening for the exhibition, with the inauguration being marked by our most elegant and striking Princess Alexandra. She was escorted and introduced to selected guests by David

Thomas, the Crown Jeweller, alongside Naim and John Asprey. A complex exhibition of this size and value was a highly intricate affair requiring many preparatory journeys to Vienna to ensure a seamless outcome for the occasion. The presentation also ran along a carefully planned series of media events, with the sexy Elizabeth Hirnigel in control, gathering all the great and good of Vienna to flock to Naim, our visionary chief executive. Elizabeth was one of that special breed of high-powered public-relations women who combine fantastic professional standards with a very impressive list of social contacts.

With Boivin the creations designed in the firm's more recent times by Jeanne Poiret, the widow of Jules René Boivin (1893–1917), are undoubtedly unique, though the life and spirit of its exquisitely created collection today lie in the dark, locked away since Boivin closed its doors. Pieces of intricacy rarely beheld – in the forms of animals, birds, flowers or fruit, each piece articulated, *tremblant*, sliding, pivoting – linger in vaults, a project that sadly never got to where it should have been: on the most beautiful girls and women of all ages, perceptive enough to understand its immense beauty.

The sadness of Boivin's current fate has its reflection in the dejection surrounding the latter days of Naim's and my projects – a friendship that at that time got locked away too when a then irreconcilable difference cut us apart. There followed a deep and complex silence, a troubled understanding of notions, of misled emotions, misguided aspirations. It all spiralled out of control and spun into free orbit. Naim was suddenly unapproachable and disappeared off to France for an entire month. How had I managed to alienate a man of such strength and emotional courage? To safeguard his well-being and allow me time to consider my work priorities, which had all along been my biggest challenge, he had set an end. I began to realize there was a gulf between us that had to be negotiated if our relationship were to survive. He wanted me to be emotionally driven in everything I did, with no defined boundaries. 'It was,' he said quite stoically, 'the quest for an intellectual climax that was missing.' Its absence was for the most part the cause of it all. I now know that this meeting of minds was to him far more potent than anything else, and certainly immeasurably more gratifying.

Fortunately, over time, we completed our journeys, our characters did grow further and stronger and more secure. The void between us became a subject we gradually started reapproaching and exploring with the confidence of reflection and thought. Through laughter and anger we came to a full circle, and are now, in these pages of Naim's third book of memoirs, within a rich tapestry of people's thoughts and feelings concerning an exceptionally driven and inspiring man and his journey through life. What I feel today about my learnings with Naim is that his style, enthusiasm, passion, spontaneity and completely sincere affection – which is still a part of our relationship – have made me understand the person he saw in me more than ten years ago through his nurturing and care; and this has also enabled me to see the person others see in me.

This person has now come into its own space with precisely the foresight he so clearly envisaged: 'When she was a girl, she was a place. Now she's a woman, she's an entire world.' A completion of the circle seems to have come about, a notion so well put by one of my dearest friends, who once wrote: 'Happiness is not about doing everything you want to do, but in *wanting* to do everything you do.'

Fifty

The publication in September 1993 of my latest book of interviews, *More of a Certain Age*, made it another busy month. The notices were favourable. This new style of interviewing seemed to be striking an appreciative chord with the majority of reviewers, who now saw some merit in the question-and-answer format. An abridged version of my interview with Sir Laurens van der Post was published in the *Daily Telegraph* to the anger of at least one reader. Mr Michael Loewe of Cambridge fired off a letter to the paper to make his strong views known:

> I write to protest against the offensive terms in which Naim Attallah conducted his interview with Sir Laurens van der Post. Is Mr Attallah quite incapable of recognizing wisdom, greatness or nobility when he meets it?

If Mr Loewe had ever got round to reading the full version as it appears in the book, he would have been more incensed. Before conducting the interview I had been well briefed by the late Anthony Sampson, the writer and political commentator, who knew a great deal about the activities of van der Post through his extensive South African connections. I was therefore well prepared for my encounter with him. Unsurprisingly, I found him not to be the saintly figure his admirers portrayed. There was a definite flaw in the character of a man whose frequent exaggerations were in fact a litany of untruths. His intellectual arrogance suggested he had come to believe the myth about himself that he himself had perpetuated. The interview turned out to be the most exhausting I ever undertook. He lost his composure more than once and became angry enough to want to throw me out. It was only his ego, his need to be in control of the situation, that stopped him from actually doing it. Then he unexpectedly changed tack by insisting on a second session at a later date to attempt to repair the damage of the first session, but while I agreed to this, I refused to rise to the bait. At the outset I really wanted to form a better impression of a man considered by so many to be a sort of guru, touched by divine wisdom. In this ambition I failed miserably. Van der Post was my second failure, the first having been Conor Cruise O'Brien, with whom I had a similar but infinitely less charged experience.

Fortunately there were many others in the book who yielded more rewarding results. In the case of Lord Amery, the former Conservative MP and son of Leo Amery, Churchill's political colleague, I had been warned that the subject of his brother John, who had been pro-German during the war and was hanged as a traitor in 1945, was still too sensitive to bring up. Nevertheless it seemed important to my enquiry and I moved the questioning round to face it, suggesting how difficult it was to imagine the depths of disappointment, shame and anger that must have been there for the family at the time. I wondered if the subject had been suppressed within the family and whether his father had ever come to terms with what had happened. He replied with a matter-of-fact directness:

> It wasn't suppressed. My father offered his resignation and I offered mine; we were both quite clear that it was the right thing to do, but we were both refused. He came with me to say goodbye to my brother in prison and indeed he wrote a short verse in the taxi which took us there, and I think it sums up his feelings:
>
> > At end of wayward days
> > You found a cause
> > If not your country's.
> > Who shall say whether that betrayal of our ancient laws
> > Was treason or foreknowledge?
> > He rests well.

This led me on to my next question on the change of his own feelings from wanting to kill his brother with his bare hands to compassion when he saw him in prison. After all, blood was thicker than water. That was about true, he agreed.

> Also, if I had seen him during the fighting he would have been with Hitler and I would have been fighting against Hitler, but when I saw him in prison the war was over and the Russians were dominating half of Europe.

To my probing as to whether his brother's plea of guilty had come as a shock after everything that had been done to try and help him, Lord Amery replied, 'No, I think it was a logical act.' The public hangman, Albert Pierrepoint, had said of John Amery that he was the bravest man he ever executed, and I wanted to know if that had made the pain of it all harder to bear. 'No,' said Lord Amery, 'I think it was appropriate. He was an Amery.'

Winston Churchill's daughter, Lady Soames, was someone for whom I had unbounded admiration. She had met General de Gaulle once, and said that whatever differences and quarrels there may have been between him and Churchill, she felt he had still represented the soul of France for her father.

The only time I had a conversation with him was at luncheon in the Elysée, when I sat next to him shaking with nerves. He was not an easily approachable person and we had an extraordinary conversation. He asked me, 'Que faite-vous à Paris, madame?' and so I panicked and I said, 'Je promène mes chiens, monsieur le président.' Instead of putting me down for giving an absolutely asinine answer to his question, he became very interested. He wanted to know what dogs I had and where I walked them, and then suggested I take them to the Île de Cygnes, which is a little island in the middle of the Seine. He drew it for me on the menu, and thereafter I always used to walk my dogs on the Île de Cygnes with grateful thoughts of the general.

She felt, despite his stern image, that de Gaulle was a man it would be possible to warm to:

He was very fond of my mother, ever since the time when she flew at him for making a very anti-British remark. My father had missed it because he was at the other end of the table, and anyhow papa's French wasn't very good, but when the general insulted the British Fleet, mama retaliated in perfect French. The next day there arrived the most enormous arrangement of flowers, and thereafter he respected and liked her very much. For years after my father died he sent my mother a personal letter on the anniversary of his death.

Some generous accolades came my way as a result of my efforts, Marjorie Proops, the famous 'agony aunt' of the *Daily Mirror*, writing to me to say:

You were an extremely kind, considerate and sensitive interviewer, while at the same time a probing and analytical one. I imagine that many people feel bruised when they read pieces about themselves. I didn't feel the least bit bruised when I read yours, only delighted that it was the first opportunity I had had to meet you.

The novelist Elizabeth Jane Howard, whom I had interviewed for the *Oldie*, sent back a card after being given a complimentary copy of *More of a Certain Age*: 'Thank you for sending me a copy of Naim Attallah's book. It is full of people whom I want to read about, not least because I thought Mr Attallah the best interviewer I've ever had.'

My correspondence with Lord Dacre had continued during the year since the publication of my interview with him in *Of a Certain Age*. 'You are the best interrogator who has ever interrogated me,' he wrote on one occasion. When I sent him a copy of my interview with Lord Goodman, he wrote back to say:

I love and venerate Arnold G. but I enjoyed your account, as I enjoy all your accounts of interviews. Unlike most interviewers, you do the necessary homework. Gibbon wrote of Poisson's review of his great work that his praise is tempered 'by a decent admixture of acid' (I quote from memory). He relished that *decent* admixture. So do I. It gives flavour to the praise. You mix it very decently.

For the new book Bron approached him to try to persuade him to do a notice for the *Literary Review*. 'How can I possibly resist so civil a request?' he responded.

Quite frankly I would have preferred not be asked – simply because I am so overburdened at present, and doubt if I would do it well (would I know the persons interviewed?). But I respect Naim Attallah as an interviewer and I am sure that the book deserves a good review. So between my respect for him and the irresistible courtesy of your letter, I would do my best – if you can't find, as I rather hope you can, a more suitable reviewer.

The result outstripped all expectations and is reprinted in full below. Its inclusion reveals more about the book than I could have done, since his prose is unsurpassable for its elegance and clarity.

Who Is This Subtle Man Who Asks the Questions?
by Hugh Trevor-Roper

If you are to be interviewed by Mr Naim Attallah, do not suppose that you will get off with easy answers, for he comes well briefed and will press you hard. 'You are very searching in your questions,' exclaims the poetess Kathleen Raine. 'You are going too deeply into my life,' protests the Duke of Devonshire; and Sir Laurens van der Post draws the line when pressed to discuss his relations with the Prince of Wales and Lady Thatcher. But on the whole the patients submit to this tactful psychoanalyst. Indeed, they are stimulated. 'This has been such a good interview that it's made me think very deeply,' says John Mortimer, who has had to face the unresolved contradictions of his own psyche. 'It's terribly interesting being interviewed by you,' says Tony Benn, who is so happily constituted that every question merely confirms his own solid convictions.

Mr Benn does bang on a bit, on his 'stiletto principle' (the stiletto being the heel on the floor, not the knife in the back). 'If you really do press very hard on something, you can win, just as a woman with a high-heeled shoe can go through a parquet floor.' Socialism – real socialism, not the 'milk-and-water liberalism' of the Social Democrats – comes to him straight from 'the Book of Genesis and the New Testament'. So it is absolute Truth, just as Thatcherism is 'absolute Evil'. After this uncompromising homily, the amiable epicureanism of the Duke of Devonshire comes as rather a relief. Having genially allowed that the 99 per cent of the public who regard dukes as freaks are probably right, and that his own political career was due to 'gross nepotism', he admits that his idea of heaven, now that he has passed the stage of 'casinos, fast women, and God knows what', apart from being at Chatsworth, is to sit in the hall of Brooks's 'having China tea'.

To meet Mr Benn on his own terms we must look for more forceful characters. Lord Amery, an equally unbending, though less ideological opponent, does not give much away – indeed he thinks we have already given away too much; we could and should have kept the old empire going – and here is Lord Hartwell, who also does not give an inch, though he gave away the *Daily Telegraph* in a fit of absence of mind. His tones are clipped, his judgements summary. Why does he think that Sir Peregrine Worsthorne 'couldn't edit a school magazine, let alone a national newspaper'? 'My experience of him,' he replies. 'I use my judgement.' And what of Rupert Murdoch? 'He's become purely a financier. He's very good at tabloids . . . '

These patients are all much of an age – a high age – and so the war and, to those who knew him, Churchill loom large in their memories and rationalizations. Particularly of course to Churchill's daughter, Lady Soames. Others had brief but memorable contact with the great man. Sir Bernard Lovell, afterwards Astronomer Royal, was ordered by Churchill to develop the new device H2S, thanks to which bomber pilots could see what lay below them, even in the dark and through cloud, and so detect submarines surfacing at night. Now Sir Bernard looks back on the experience 'almost as if disembodied', so remote it seems, and faces the moral questions which linger on. It was chilling, he says, to see the havoc wreaked on Hamburg and other German cities by that device, and yet did not that same device, by defeating the submarine menace, turn the tide of war? It 'saved us from starvation' and made the landings in Normandy possible. So narrow was the margin of victory, so thin the dividing line between good and evil in science.

Sir Bernard is a thinking scientist. He ranges over the social and moral problems raised by science: the social conditions of research, the moral problems of its results. To me, this is the most impressive of all these interviews. The most moving is that of Dame Cicely Saunders, the founder of the hospice movement, which enables the terminally ill not merely, she insists, to die with dignity, but to live with dignity till they die: a saint with the engaging human quality of always falling in love with Poles. Why so? asks Mr

Attallah. 'I haven't the faintest idea,' she replies. 'It just happens.' This endears her to me. I love Poles.

There are also men – or more often women – of letters: here is Lady Longford, brimful of good sense. I am sorry that she has changed her view that Father D'Arcy was Mephistopheles and thinks that Koo Stark would have made a much better Duchess of York than Fergie. Marjorie Proops, doyenne of agony aunts, refused to believe any ill of Robert Maxwell, who made her a director of the *Daily Mirror* and got her to sign sheaves of papers unseen. She insists that she was in good company: everyone she knew agreed. She must have lived exclusively among bankers. John Mortimer is always exhilarating, P. D. James sensible. All these bare their souls to so perceptive and sympathetic an inquisitor.

But Patricia Highsmith stands firm. As an earlier interviewer wrote, 'Her manner precludes intrusive questioning.' Mr Attallah fares no better. Does she regret being an only child? 'No, I never missed having brothers and sisters.' Has she ever wanted children? 'No. Absolutely no.' Has she ever regretted not marrying? 'No.' Is she unhappy? Not at all. 'When I get up in the morning, I first of all make the coffee and then I say to my cat, "We're going to have a great day." '

Lord Amery, Lord Hartwell and Miss Highsmith adopt variants of the Maginot line of defence. Lord Wyatt prefers the counter-attack. The subject is his most popular pronouncements in the *News of the World*, delivered as 'The Voice of Reason'. Is not that title, in the circumstances, rather presumptuous? 'Not at all,' replies the oracular voice. 'Do you read my column?' 'Sometimes,' answers the questioner, their roles suddenly reversed. 'Well, you obviously don't read it enough, so you don't know what you're talking about. I think very much as ordinary people do.' QED.

In the end, one of the most interesting persons in these discussions is Mr Attallah. Someone (preferably a little more subtle than Lord Wyatt) should interview him.

*   *   *

Among the other reviewers of *More of a Certain Age* was Clare Colvin, who had separate notices in the *Sunday Express* and the *Daily Express*. In the first she wondered why people tolerated an interviewer asking questions to which they'd give a brisk, 'Mind your own business,' if they came from a passing acquaintance. Was there a 'deep-seated need for a confessional, an urge for exposure?' or was the interviewee lulled into forgetting 'the interview is destined for a wider public?' The key to a successful interview, she thought, was the questioner, and it was clear that 'Naim Attallah . . . has the gift of drawing more from his subjects than they may have at first intended . . . His courteous persistence is a lesson to other interviewers.' The poet Kathleen Raine had been drawn into finally remarking of the confusion in her relationships, including that with the homosexual Gavin Maxwell: 'You are very searching in your questions . . . it's what we have done to harm others that embitters old age, it's the pain we've caused that catches up with us.' Clare Colvin also picked up on intriguing similarities in the childhoods of those in similar fields.

Both P. D. James and Patricia Highsmith are noted writers of psycho-logical crime novels. Both suffered from being children of warring parents.
P. D. James observes: 'It was a time of trauma. It is good for a creative artist to have this, but I'm not so sure it's good for a human being. Perhaps that is why some creative artists aren't very easy people.'

In her second notice she focused on John Mortimer and his tempestuous marriage to Penelope Mortimer, plagued by his infidelities which were causing her heartbreak. Despite the marriage being so stormy, Mortimer admitted he had been able to enjoy himself while working flat out as a barrister and writer.

'I must have had enormous stamina.
'The funny thing is that I would often leave the house in the morning battered after some long argument and angry scene, and go down to my chambers and give advice to elderly company directors on exactly how they should conduct their married lives.
'Everybody else's life was absolutely easy to put right.'
Does this make the creator of Rumpole a heartless beast?

W. F. Deedes provided a review for the *Weekend Telegraph*, declaring that, 'This is the age of the interview, and most newspapers employ journalists practised at baring the soul of a personality in the news.' It was therefore dis-concerting to 'come across someone who excels at baring souls and is not properly a journalist at all'. All of us have feelings 'too deep for expression, thoughts we are reluctant to share even with those we love, let alone strangers'.

This is where the interview takes the character of safe-breaking with skeleton keys.
Naim Attallah is a dab hand with skeleton keys. He is the smartest burglar in the business. Click, click, one by one the tumblers go down and the safe door swings open.

Out of context the questions might sound 'abrupt and impertinent', but they follow a long, stealthy approach from someone who has done his homework. When, in the first series of interviews, Attallah netted me, I was mildly alarmed by what he had already found out.

Having pressed the Duke of Devonshire into saying that, 'The essential ingredient of marriage is tolerance, but I really can't go further than that,'

Attallah asks if he thinks that men are not naturally monogamous, and too much significance is given to one or other partner straying from the path. The duke replies, 'Those marriages where neither partner has been unfaithful are relatively few and astonishingly lucky.' Full marks.

There can be two opinions about all this. One, towards which I occasionally incline, might be that there is altogether too much inquisitiveness about private lives nowadays, mainly for the purposes of selling newspapers . . . The second is that, in proper hands, revelations about other people's lives may guide us in our own. Read no history, read biography, someone said, and there is something in it . . .

A few of Attallah's exchanges make you ponder on a higher plane than some of us dwell. We are a degree better off for sharing the valuables he has dragged out of the safe.

Peter McKay started off his review in the *Mail on Sunday* by quoting Tony Benn on Margaret Thatcher: 'She was a strong, principled woman who defended her class with absolute commitment.'

To whom does the left-wing Mr Benn confide this extraordinary sentiment? Why, to Mr Naim Attallah, the idiosyncratic publisher and interviewer, who has the knack of asking interesting questions and getting unusual answers . . .

After skirting round her spinster status, Attallah pounces on the novelist Patricia Highsmith: 'Have you been a lesbian?' Highsmith: 'Yes.'

Rather comically, he leaves it at that . . .

He gently taunts the astronomer Sir Bernard Lovell on the fabulous literary success of Stephen Hawking, the disabled scientist who has become rich via his books about cosmology. What does Sir Bernard think of Hawking? 'I don't think I am going to answer that.' Why is that? 'Hawking's terrible physical state places great inhibition on any criticism.' We get the picture.

In a recent book Marjorie Proops had told about an affair she had with the office lawyer at the *Daily Mirror*, which led me to ask her: 'You were very much a symbol of respectability at the *Mirror*. Did you ever think it was hypocritical to trade on that image given your own personal circumstances?' 'No,' replied Marje. 'The phrasing of the question is the point,' commented McKay, 'not Marje's answer.'

Woodrow Wyatt is chided about leaving two of his wives out of his *Who's Who* entry, to which he replies, 'I left them out because they're excess baggage.' So I suppose is Attallah's book in a literary sense. But you'll be glad you brought it along.

Diana Mosley in the *Evening Standard* found *More of a Certain Age* less satisfactory than its predecessors, even though the interviewer had 'not lost his cunning'. For her the book lacked the element of surprise.

For example, all of us know that Lady Soames and Lady Longford are perfect ornaments to their sex and adored by everybody. If Naim Attallah could have detected a flaw it would have been thrilling. But it is naturally not his fault; he found none because there were none.

She was quite bowled over by 'the delightfully naïve vanity of Sir Laurens van der Post', which made him the ideal subject for a frank interview. 'Until I read it I knew nothing about him, but now I am his fan for life.' Then, to illustrate the irony of how the very thing that people 'most abhor' can return to haunt them, she cited the story, as told by Lady Soames, of how Clementine Churchill destroyed the Graham Sutherland portrait that Sir Winston had so disliked. Yet Sutherland's pre-portrait study of the painting had come to adorn, 'as dust jacket, the best post-war book about Churchill'.

Thus instead of being consumed by the flames it has bobbed up again as if by magic to be seen by however many thousand people acquire the book. Had the portrait not been burnt, in all probability a photograph of Churchill and his cigar would have been used.

She ended on a critical political note:

This volume could have been entitled *Of a Certain Smugness*. In politics, the further Left you are, the more smug you become. It is rather endearing, for it illustrates the unconquerable optimism of mankind. Faced with the desert [that] Communism has made in any part of the earth it touched, it is nevertheless still quite fashionable to boast of having been a Communist at school or at Oxford, as several of these interviews bear witness.

Georgia Metcalf in the *Daily Mail* found there was one great enigma at the heart of 'this substantial book':

Naim Attallah, the flamboyant Palestinian entrepreneur who whirls around London in scarlet and orange socks and hand-made suits lined in peacock-blue silk, has snapped up practically every swanky shop in Bond Street, employs the brightest and most aristocratic girls in London and dresses them in rubber sheaths and diaphanous togas . . . why, I wonder, has such an exotic figure chosen to interview so many elderly, crumbly British National Monuments with an average age of at least seventy?

They had 'grown into appropriate septuagenarian virtues – dignity, serenity and faith', which had 'transformed them from ambitious mavericks to pillars of the English Establishment'.

Distinguished and admirable they may be, glamorous and indiscreet they're not.

But Attallah has two secret weapons up his silk-lined sleeve to tackle the permafrost of his subjects' English reserve: meticulous background research and a completely un-English lack of embarrassment about emotional matters . . .

The best bits are when Attallah chisels away enough of the façade of these national treasures to expose some raw bricks, like Lord Forte's simmering feud with his rival at the Savoy Group.

'Hugh Wontner had Claridges as his private house . . . and he didn't even have a bloody share . . . he also had a string of call girls – that's how he ran the great Savoy, and yet he looked down on me because we had Little Chefs on the motorways.'

'The one thing that must sweeten the bitter pill of old age for the Great and the Good,' said the *Catholic Herald*, 'is the prospect of Naim Attallah coming to interview them.'

Who could ask for a more thoughtful recorder of a lifetime's achievement? Unlike most other practitioners of the science of interviewing, Attallah does not approach his subjects as victims. His scalpel probes, he tests, he measures – but not in order to expose feet of clay: rather, to diagnose why these men and women stand head and shoulders above the rest as icons today . . .

Attallah's skill is two-fold: a wide-ranging line of questioning and an ability to listen . . . [The] Catholic Attallah seems to have taken a cue from the rule of St Benedict, whose first tenet is, 'Listen': even the most wary feel lulled into self-revelation by that most irresistible of tributes – a keen and sympathetic listener.

My second collection of interviews with 'oldsters', said Francis Wheen in *The Times Literary Supplement*, had been 'published by Quartet, which he owns, and many of the interviews first appeared in the *Oldie*, which he also owns'.

The phrase 'vanity publishing' springs to mind – only to spring out again as soon as one starts to read. For no interviewer could be less vain than Attallah . . . [One] learns almost nothing of his own tastes or opinions. He is courteous, diffident and, above all, curious; he genuinely wants to listen rather than sit in judgement . . .

It is, I feel sure, not Attallah's intention to provoke his subjects into thus revealing the nastier or more touchy side of their character, but some people need no provocation. In *More of a Certain Age*, the Duke of Devonshire speaks of his 'great admiration' for his Hitler-worshipping sister-in-law, Unity Mitford: 'Rightly or wrongly she had a strong feeling for Nazi Germany . . . ' Rightly or wrongly! Most interviewers would seize on such a jaw-dropping inanity and press home their advantage. Attallah allows it to hang in the air, unmentioned but hideously conspicuous.

There is more guile in Attallah's technique than he lets on. He is not shy of venturing into forbidden zones, but he does so with catlike stealth.

'And still they talk,' said the *Observer*. 'As a guide to the un-divine comedy of modern manners the persistent Attallah is unbeatable'; but in the *Spectator*, Lucy Hughes-Hallett took a more objective view of the overall effect. While the elderly made good subjects, 'having seen and done more than the rest of us', and tended to be 'less cagey in their responses and less conventional in their self-images than the up-and-coming', it did not follow that they had necessarily come by the 'kind of maturity one likes to hope might be the compensation for physical decay . . . none of those interviewed, brilliant though they are, are truly sage'. She saw considerable drawbacks in the lack of editorial commentary as well as lost opportunities for coherent narrative.

The medium virtually obliges the subjects to boast – this volume is raucous with the sound of self-blown trumpets – and it gives them far too much space to indulge in self-important pronouncements . . .

What an interview of this kind does give us, and it's a benefit which outweighs all the awkwardness of the form, is the subject's voice. Nearly everyone in this book has already written an autobiography, but future historians may well find these interviews, variously circumspect, bad-tempered or self-glorifying as they are, more directly revealing . . .

There is a wicked pleasure to be had from reading Patricia Highsmith's staunch refusal to tell Attallah anything of any interest . . .

Laurens van der Post loses his temper. 'I shouldn't even have to respond to these remarks.' Abruptly the timeless man of wisdom begins to look like a man pathetically dependent on his disciples' flattery: 'I don't know anyone who's ever called me a charlatan, certainly no one who knows me would ever call me that . . . Who are these idiots? I can't cope with this . . . '

This is good knockabout stuff. But the haunting and memorable revelations are those that are made willingly: Hartwell's admission that, though he loved his wife, he is actually glad that she died before he lost the *Telegraph*, 'She would have been shocked'; Lady Longford describing the sadness of writing her own memoirs and feeling with sudden acuteness that 'these happy times really were past'. These tiny, vivid glimpses of a person's real nature and experience make up for the windiness of much of the text.

One or two of those who escaped being interviewed for the book made copy for the gossip columns, like Lord Tebbit, who, *The Times* reported, had turned me down, 'because, says Attallah, "He said he was too young." Attallah . . . reluctantly admits that at a mere sixty-two Tebbit may have a point. "I was running out of oldies," he explained.' A problem of a different kind arose with Barbara Skelton, who had 'carved her exotic path through the café society of the 1940s and 1950s', taking in many lovers along the way, and who told Daniel Farson for his *Evening Standard* column that when I went to interview her for the *Oldie* in Paris I had 'displeased her by arriving in his Rolls-Royce without inviting her out for dinner or a drink'. My umbrage at this remark was given an airing in the *Standard*'s 'Londoner's Diary' a few days later:

> 'I turned up in a beaten-up old car belonging to one of my staff in Paris,' says Attallah . . . 'I found her very charming but she didn't give the impression that she wanted any hospitality. And to cap it all, Richard Ingrams didn't print the interview in the *Oldie* because there was too much sex.'

*   *   *

While I had been basking in the critical acclaim *More of a Certain Age* had been earning, there were black clouds gathering on the horizon that threatened to spoil my little triumph. The *Oldie* magazine was in trouble. The circulation had not been improving and the original capital had evaporated, leaving the magazine in a serious financial state. I was unwilling to sink further funds into it since I could see no prospects for its survival as a fortnightly publication. It was going to need much greater resources and more sustained backing for many years if it was to stay afloat. The press got a whiff of the crisis and various headlines began to appear, 'Wrinkly Organ Seeks a Partner' being a sample. There was a view in the press that Richard Ingrams was presiding as editor over a doomed publication, the readership for which was literally dying off. Among those who initially subscribed, some had been prevented from renewing because of an unavoidable appointment with their maker. Auberon Waugh was quoted as admitting, 'The *Oldie* is in trouble.' A solution being floated was that the *Oldie* should merge with *Punch*, Bron saying that the title would have to be bought first from Lord Stevens, who had been approached and was brooding over it. 'There are too many publications for the younger market,' said Bron, 'so it is a shame. The *Oldie* never had enough wind behind it.' Wind, ran one comment, was all that poor old *Punch* did have, and in the end they 'couldn't even give it away'. A less moribund merger was required.

As was my wont, I continued in the role of knight in shining armour and rode to the rescue. To save the *Oldie* I borrowed a further sum of three hundred thousand pounds from my personal bank. I must have been mad. There was no way, however, I could sit back and see it fail, despite my better judgement; I just could not bear to see our past efforts wasted. As an optimist by nature and a fighter by instinct, I frequently ignored the voice of reason. I also considered the value of the original capital at par with the new shares allotted to me, which had the effect of reducing my own shareholding so as to maintain some value for the old shares. That is to say, instead of becoming owner of a hundred per cent of the *Oldie* by injecting three hundred thousand pounds, I opted for seventy-five-per-cent ownership by giving the founders value for their shares. On 22 September the *Evening Standard* reported this injection of capital without knowing the source, saying that the magazine 'claimed to have averted closure today, winning the support of new backers at an emergency board meeting'.

Publisher Naim Attallah, who precipitated the crisis when he announced that he wanted to reduce his 51 per cent stake, said: 'There is now no question of closure. We have considered a few approaches and believe they will give sufficient backing to help the magazine continue with the same energy as before.' He said the magazine, which sells 20,000 copies, needed an injection of £300,000 to survive, but declined to identify the source of the new funds.

Mr Attallah, who is also involved in the loss-making *Literary Review*, said his new commitments as chief executive of Asprey meant he could no longer bankroll the *Oldie*.

The sniping from the journalists who had worked in close collaboration with *Private Eye* in earlier times had erupted afresh with the advent of the *Oldie* and Richard Ingrams's high level of exposure in the media. He seemed to be everywhere and attracted publicity, both good and bad. Peter McKay, a veteran of the old *Private Eye*, and Nigel Dempster could never resist having the occasional dig at Richard. On 10 October McKay recalled in the *Sunday Times* how Ingrams used to say, back in the seventies, how he hated Jimmy Goldsmith because 'he was power mad, kept mistresses and sued papers which offended him. And that he was mad enough to start his own magazine.'

Now! But what has happened since? Ingrams kept control of his pension, *Private Eye*, by appointing a protégé, Ian Hislop. He took a mistress. He forced the *Guardian* to apologize to him for saying he was anti-Semitic – a fantastic notion, it is true, but one which appears in the official history of *Private Eye*. And he started a loony magazine for 'oldies' and got Naim Attallah to put up the money for it.

Perhaps the time had come, suggested McKay, for Ingrams, scouting for new suckers, to approach Sir James with a 'better understanding of the man he professed to loathe'. Three days later, in the *Daily Mail*, Dempster suggested I should have an early recommendation for a knighthood in the New Year's Honours for investing to keep afloat 'the eighteen-month-old magazine which is edited by ageing hypocrite and adulterer Richard Ingrams and employs other deadbeats'.

Says a loyal Naim: 'It's losing about £180,000 a year and I have refinanced it. I am determined it should be given a proper chance to survive, with good husbandry. I'm not rich, but I've always been loyal to my friends.'

The 'Mr Pepys' column in the *Evening Standard* of 12 November described me as 'a general good egg . . . always made to sound hugely rich, but I hear he has an overdraft like the rest of us'.

However, he has managed to borrow hundreds of thousands of pounds over the past five years to keep two of our native wits, Auberon Waugh and Richard Ingrams, in regular employment.

Waugh, who edits the Attallah-owned *Literary Review*, honourably, if fulsomely, repays this kindness by writing frequently about Naim's 'saintliness'.

Ingrams, editor of another Attallah loss-maker, the *Oldie*, isn't so generous. Now he is taking six months off from the *Oldie* after Naim went to the trouble of pumping another £300,000 into the magazine.

But he is generous in one regard. He says in the *Oldie Annual* – on the front of which he egotistically plasters his name as 'editor' – that the magazine sells 25,000 copies. The figure of 17,000 is more realistic.

I suggested here some time ago that Naim might cut his losses and merge the *Literary Review* and the *Oldie*, making Waugh editor of the resultant *Old Review* . . . surely this idea's time has now come.

A note in the *Daily Express* 'Diary' said that while I may have been pouring thousands into an ailing magazine, happily I had

enough wealth still to finance a lurid new sartorial image. He is lining his suits in bright, multi-coloured material by leading designer Gianni Versace, with ties and handkerchiefs (in suit pocket) to match. I came across him unveiling the new look in the West End. The startling effect in pinks, greens and white was not unlike that of certain curtain material, but he assures me proudly: 'They are by Versace. It is my new look.'

*

The Irish playwright Kieran Tunney, for whom my earlier attempts to promote a staging of his play *Aurora* had been unsuccessful, was now relatively destitute. Despite his unenviable situation, he was a proud man with grandiose ideas, tending to overstate his talent, which was nevertheless above the ordinary. He found it hard to cope with the diminishing attention he was receiving in his twilight years. It left him inclined to keep harking back to his early days of promise when he had been considered a heart-throb by many of his contemporaries, and was indeed much in demand for his debonair looks and convivial personality. In New York, where he lived at that period, he mixed with the cultural élite, but great literary success always eluded him. He remained on the periphery, being photographed by Cecil Beaton and acquainted with Greta Garbo, Somerset Maugham and Noël Coward, but never gaining for himself true celebrity status.

The various conversations I had with him made it clear to me that he could neither understand nor deal with this failure, rejecting implications he could not reconcile himself with. As Stan Gebler Davies said in an article in the *Mail on Sunday*, 'his luck ran out at about the age of twenty, the year he wrote his masterpiece, *Aurora*, and when Coward pinched Gertrude Lawrence, the leading lady, so he could re-stage a play of his own'. Subsequently Maugham commended it to Peter Daubeny, the pioneering impresario of the 'World Theatre' seasons at the Aldwych, who wanted to produce it if he could get Tallulah Bankhead to play the lead. When she turned the part down, Daubeny passed the rights on to C. B. Cochran, who set his sights on Vivien Leigh. As Davies wrote:

Leigh rang Tunney. 'Kieran, you clever thing – this is Vivien. Darling, I'm insane about *Aurora*, and of course I'll do it for Cochran. In about a year's time.'

Of course, it was not to be. 'Vivien would have been so good at playing it,' he muses. 'She was schizophrenic, but she was divine. It was the illness which plagued her all her life which prevented her from doing it.'

The play has so far been optioned twenty times but appears to be no nearer production than it was in 1947 . . . But it is still finding admirers. The latest enthusiast [has been] the ebullient Naim Attallah, who published the script in 1989 along with Tunney's unfinished autobiography.

There it rests, the most widely admired unperformed play of the century.

Perhaps his work had ceased to be greatly appreciated because it belonged to an era long gone, while he himself had been replaced by a new breed of playwright. At the time, Tunney certainly could not match the subtlety of Noël Coward or the sharp wit of Oscar Wilde, and apart from *Aurora*, the rest of his writing was not of great substance. Kieran naturally believed otherwise. He had the crazy idea, apparently suggested to him by the late Lord Olivier, of selling the rights to his entire literary output for large sums of money and was looking for potential buyers. The objective was to allow him to escape from his small flat in Dolphin Square and move to a better climate than London's for the sake of his health. It was the fantasy of a desperate man, who refused to live in the real world and could only survive through the dream of a brighter future. I felt very frustrated at not having been able to help him.

Then a story appeared in the *Sunday Times* in October, to be followed by another in the *Observer* a couple of weeks later. Tunney had placed an anonymous notice in the 'Business Opportunities' section of the *Financial Times*, under the heading 'Wanted Billionaire Art-Lover', offering the rights to all his dramatic works, past, present and future, for five hundred thousand pounds, intriguing the theatre world and precipitating widespread speculation as to who this mysterious figure could be. The names of John Osborne, Michael Frayn and Peter Shaffer were bandied about, so it came as rather an anti-climax to discover it was 'a dramatist who once occupied centre stage but now lives in penury'. Rebecca Fowler, the *Sunday Times* arts correspondent, continued:

He is Kieran Tunney, who claims to have been the protégé of George Bernard Shaw and an intimate of Tallulah Bankhead, the actress. He holds on to the memory of former glories and dreams of seeing his work live again.

Despite suffering from emphysema, the wasting lung disease, he believes the plays that once took him across the world are ready for a revival. If he moves from his modest Pimlico flat in west London to a sunny Californian climate, Tunney says his talent will have a final chance to flourish.

A spokesman for the theatrical profession confirmed he'd been a leading figure in his youth: 'He moved in that very chic circle and was part of the Noël Coward era. He really is from a different time.' While there had been little sign of a stampede to snap him up, Tunney lived in hope and claimed to have had two serious enquiries. By the time the *Observer* piece was printed, he said he had received 'dozens of replies' and believed 'Larry's ruse' was going to put him in the big time.

He refuses to name the interested parties, but at present they are reading his extensive collection of plays, which include *A Priest in the Family*, the *Observer*'s 'play of the season' in 1951, and *Aurora* . . .

'It was Larry's idea to sell the rights,' said Tunney . . . 'He wanted me to get *Moon on the Run* staged, a play I wrote about him and the National Theatre, which he called a "marvellous surreal portrait of theatre in the Sixties".' Olivier told him to ask for £750,000, 'but in times of recession I decided on half a million'.

Tunney added that his plays were being produced around the world, but he could not be specific where. 'I know nothing at all about money except how to spend it,' he said. By then Kieran was very ill, and he suddenly disappeared without a word. He died five years later in 1998. One of the books by which he set great store for his posthumous reputation was *Tallulah, Darling of the Gods*, his biography of Tallulah Bankhead which he claimed was a personal account of his relationship with the actress and told of their meetings 'in their own words'. The conversations were entertaining and judged to sound like Tallulah, but when the book was published her attorney put out a statement to assert that Tunney was not a close friend but someone who had annoyed her constantly by asking for money.

The whole episode had been a sad tale of a fall from fame into total obscurity. I had not been able to produce Tunney's play, but it is doubtful if anyone could have saved him from himself.

Fifty-one

As Asprey continued to make the news, a newspaper report under the heading 'Spinning Web' kept the public *au courant* with our progress, commenting that either I must be off my rocker or there was still wealth 'amid the ravaged countries of Eastern Europe'. The moves towards opening a Mappin & Webb branch in Prague were seen as daring, though some observers thought there was 'probably more demand for expensive jewellery in China'. I was still toying with the idea of opening another outlet in Shanghai.

Women's Wear Daily gave Asprey full coverage for the opening of our newly expanded accessories collection at the store on Fifth Avenue with a reception for select customers. 'Sunflower' was the name of the collection and it was an innovation in that it included, besides jewellery, 'handbags, belts, small leather goods and home accessories in silver, all with sunflower ornaments trimmed in gold vermeil'. We were hoping to reach new customers with this collection and to make the company less intimidating to the general public. 'There are many people who aren't familiar with what we do,' I told the journal, 'or only think of us as bookbinders or silversmiths. This is a way to expose them to Asprey through a well-known theme – the sunflower.' We also knew we had to 'de-emphasize our Englishness' to a certain extent and Philip Warner, vice-president of Asprey New York, announced a mailing of the catalogue to ten thousand American Express platinum-card holders. By the day after the reception more than fifty pieces had been sold, including '18-karat-gold sunflower earrings retailing at between $1,850 and $2,500, brooches from $1,575 to $5,250 and toursade necklaces of either citrine or peridot beads with sunflower clasps for $7,650 and $11,000'.

As a piece of trade chat, *Retail Jeweller* picked up on my appearance on a late-late TV show, *Crystal Rose*, to talk about beautiful women, providing a 'laterally-minded glimpse of the jewellery trade' for 'nighthawks and insomniacs'.

> Surrounded by a bevy of beauty queens, ex-James Bond girls, hostesses and women who'd had plastic surgery to improve themselves, he had the audience whooping with approval as he explained that for him beauty comes from within. It's all to do with energy, personality and intelligence, said Mr Attallah, who apart from being chief executive of the Asprey group is also author of a book on beautiful women.

Not all the other guests were convinced. He took a bit of stick in very good part. As far as viewers were concerned he veritably sparkled.

Back in London there was coverage too for the party given at Garrard in Regent Street to mark the start of the new partnership with Tomasz Starzewski, with many of the elegant guests opting to wear their favourite Starzewski outfit. Among those who were there to wish the venture every success were Hardy Amies, Princess Katarina of Yugoslavia, Issy von Randwyck, Jennifer d'Abo, Vivien Duffield, Leonora Lichfield and David Frost. Tomasz was photographed in animated conversation with his compatriot, the actress Rula Lenska.

In November 1993, the *Financial Times* selected what they described as five of the leading lights in the high-profile world of luxury goods. I was one of the them. The others, summarized in alphabetical order, were as follows:

Bernard Arnault, the chairman of LVMH, a 'company behind a string of prestigious products from Hennessy cognac and Christian Dior cosmetics to Christian Lacroix couture'. In the early days, he had been known for his ruthlessness in fighting and winning the battle for control of the company. His publicists had tried to mellow his image by revealing that what he had *really* always wanted to be was a concert pianist. 'But the ruthlessness is still there.' When his rivals Yves Saint-Laurent set out to name a new fragrance 'Champagne', they ran into a raft of lawsuits from the champagne industry. 'And who runs the biggest champagne business in France? Arnault.'

Jean-Louis Dumas, chairman of Hermès, a great-grandchild of Émile Hermès, the tanner founder. Little sign remained of his youth, when he and his young wife had taken off in the 1960s in a battered Citroën 2CV 'to hit the hippy trail to Katmandu'. After serving an apprenticeship at Bloomingdales in New York, he eventually returned to Paris to mastermind the transformation of Hermès from 'its original base, as a Paris leather-goods maker, into one of the world's most successful luxury-goods groups'. He had 'expanded Hermès without compromising its reputation for quality' and the firm had 'weathered the recession better than most of its competitors'.

Joe Kanoui, chairman of a newcomer, the Vendôme luxury-goods group. It had been formed only that August 'by putting together the luxury-goods interests of Richemont, the Swiss holding company based on the South African Rupert family's Rothmans tobacco fortune'. Its main components were Cartier jewellery, which Kanoui had himself been instrumental in rebuilding, and the Dunhill tobacco and leather-products company. He had raised Cartier's round-the-world retail network from ten to a hundred owned shops, with sales topping seven hundred million pounds. He had evolved a philosophical theory for luxury goods, expressed in such pronouncements as: 'If you make something for all, it no longer has luxury. Above all, you must avoid thinking that expensive things are necessarily luxurious. Caviare, for example, is not a luxury good, merely an expensive consumable.'

Alain Wertheimer, sole owner of Chanel. He ran the company with super-secrecy and ensured as little was known about himself as possible. When he took over the company in 1974, 'its only real asset was Chanel No. 5, which had been one of the world's best-selling perfumes ever since its launch in 1924, when Pierre Wertheimer, Alain's grandfather and one of Coco's admirers, bought the rights'. The saying was coined that Chanel had 'one foot in the grave and another on a banana peel'. Alain Wertheimer was inspired to appoint the German Karl Lagerfeld as Chanel's chief designer, the theory being that 'Lagerfeld's designs would bring back Chanel's *élan* and generate pages of free publicity'. The calculation paid off and Chanel became a company with sales of around three hundred and thirty-one million pounds a year.

What man does not dream of making the grade and in the process being acknowledged by his peers and the public at large? I was no exception and was flattered to be included in such illustrious company. I was cited as someone who 'still prefers to see himself as a patron of the arts, rather than a businessman, but seems to revel in his role at Asprey'.

His new responsibilities seem to have done nothing to diminish his enthusiastic manner, nor to cramp his style. He still appears at his office each morning in his customary uniform of odd socks, knuckle-dusting rings, a (very expensive) watch on each wrist and a psychedelic silk tie.
A quick glance at Asprey's accounts justifies his *joie de vivre* . . .
Asprey have been sheltered from the problems that have beset his competitors for years and Naim Attallah, reluctant businessman though he may be, has done deal after deal to take it into yet more areas of the luxury-goods business.

The Asprey group swept from strength to strength, experiencing an upward trend in profits. This was notwithstanding the reduction in profit margins as a result of increased competitiveness. We were showing a healthier trading pattern, but while the future looked encouraging, we had to be alert to changing market conditions. It was inevitable that the bubble would burst one day, due to economic and political factors beyond our control. My concern had always been to keep liquidity high to guard against a bad period of trading should it ever occur. Back in 1978 I had succumbed to pressures from the main Asprey board, which felt that my accumulation of large cash balances was not giving the company the kind of return to be expected from a managed portfolio. All along my argument had been that, as a trading company, we were not in the business of investing in the stock market. We needed quick access to money to bolster our trading activities without risking a loss by having to convert an investment at the wrong time.

Instead of sticking to my guns, I gave way – with disastrous consequences. In a matter of only nine months we lost a third of our investment in common with others worldwide following the crash of the stock markets during that period. We were never to recover the substantial loss we incurred. While we were having to lick our wounds in grave silence, I reverted to my original policy of maintaining our surplus in cash. Quite apart from that, it was becoming more difficult to strike a proper balance between the desire to have a greater variety of merchandise and the need to exercise stricter control to avoid over-stocking. Despite all this, our trading results spoke volumes about our success, now widely acknowledged by the City and the media.

'All-round growth lifts Asprey £1m' said a headline in the *Financial Times* on 9 December, reporting the level of our increase in pre-tax profits to twelve point two million pounds in the half-year to 30 September. Sales for the group had risen forty-five per cent, but 'margins were under pressure'.

Mr Naim Attallah, chief executive, said that now 'the richer the person is the more he wants value for money'. Valued, high-spending customers were asking for and getting bigger discounts.

Sales at Asprey rose by more than 30 per cent, at Garrard by 18 per cent and Mappin & Webb by 24 per cent.

The group benefited from a full six months' contribution from Watches of Switzerland, acquired in June 1992, and three months from Les Ambassadeurs, the Swiss chain, bought on July 1. Mr Attallah said losses at Asprey's New York were lower . . .

Earnings per share rose by 15 per cent to 8.04p (6.97p), and the interim dividend is lifted by 14 per cent from 1.1p to 1.25p.

'Asprey spreads to £12.2m' stated the headline in the *Independent*, though I was quoted as admitting that the strategy was cutting margins:

The strategy is to broaden the customer base. We must be less vulnerable to the whims of a few people. Once that strategy is in place, margins are bound to drop. If you broaden your customer base, you have to compete with others who are targeting the same people.

We had not yet broadened our base enough and were still looking for acquisitions, 'but not big ones'. Higher promotional activity had also partly contributed to reduced margins. Work was continuing on improving performance at Garrard and Mappin & Webb, and the house broker, Smith New Court, was forecasting twenty-five million pounds in group pre-tax profits for the full year, up from twenty-one point six million the last time. 'Pembroke' in the *Independent* dropped a hint that well-heeled travellers at Heathrow might find it worth making the trek to Terminal 3, which, I had revealed, was where the bargains were for Mappin & Webb luxury items.

The sharper bargaining powers of those passing through the terminal – a large proportion of whom come from Asia, where haggling is normal – means that they pay about 2.5 per cent less than shoppers in the Mappin & Webb outlet in Terminal 4, dominated by European travellers.
Not that Mappin & Webb does anything as vulgar as discounting. It is more a case of giving the store manager that extra bit of discretion.

Asprey had 'added some sparkle to the high street' with the report of its rise in interim profits, said the *Daily Telegraph*, while the *Daily Express* took up a story from Sheffield, where the Watches of Switzerland outlet had been slow to show a profit. 'At home in an office featuring exotica like tiger-skin-draped sofas, Attallah has changed the name, the merchandise and the image.' Now the newly born Zeus was 'set to be the first of a new chain of shops' and a 'roaring trade' was hoped for. In Edinburgh, reported the *Scotsman*, a small loss for Hamilton & Inches the previous year had been turned into a 'good' profit – a fine performance in recession. *Retail Jeweller* on 16 December quoted me as summing up the situation: 'Despite the present economic climate we are encouraged by our progress and anticipate a satisfactory outcome for the remainder of the [financial] year.'
The *Daily Mail* stood alone in giving the whole situation a negative spin with its headline of 9 December: 'The stingy rich hammer profit margins at Asprey'.

Millionaires are like the rest of us – only meaner. The breed of man who buys his Christmas pressies at Asprey of Bond Street does not worry about the bill, you might think. Wrong. He haggles, complains, says he can get it cheaper down the road, and hopes to cut the price by 25 per cent.

Hence yesterday's odd-looking half-time profit figures from Asprey . . . 'It's the rich who are stingy these days,' moans Asprey's chief executive, Naim Attallah.

I made 'Sayings of the Week' columns twice in December, first in the *Daily Telegraph* on 11 December, on haggling by the super-rich: 'If you're spending £750,000 and pay cash down, then everybody will give you a discount.' The second was on the following day, in the *Independent on Sunday*, with my remark: 'The richer the person is, the more he wants value for money.' On the same day the *Sunday Telegraph*, in its 'Spirits of the Age' column, expanded my assessment of the haggling trend: 'Naim Attallah . . . says the recession has not bitten the very rich too hard but has altered their habits. Haggling over prices has now "become practically a way of life" for his well-heeled customers.' 'Even the big punters at Asprey ask for discounts these days,' said *Investors Chronicle*.

But chief executive Naim Attallah has the right philosophy for running prestige businesses. Against the prevailing trend, he believes in de-centralization, and the success of Mappin & Webb and Watches of Switzerland has proved him right. Store managers are left to merchandise and run their shops for their local client base, whether at Mappin & Webb in Prague, due to open in April, or Watches of Switzerland in Sheffield, which was the only store bought from Ratners which failed to reach profitability. Renamed (Zeus) and moved downmarket, it promises to be a great success.

With all of this happening Asprey were ending 1993 on a high note. Not only were we enjoying great prosperity, but we also seemed to have accomplished feats beyond our wildest expectations. Garrard had celebrated its hundred and fifty years as Crown Jewellers by producing special merchandise to commemorate the event and by staging in October the magnificent exhibition at the British Embassy in Vienna, in the organization of which Ros Milani-Gallieni played a key role, as she has already described. Garrard's finest works of art and craft were shown off to marvellous effect in the setting of Britain's Viennese embassy, with its polished floors, dripping chandeliers and expansive mirrors. It provided the perfect backdrop to the meticulously prepared collection of treasures. For three months Ros and I had exercised ourselves over all the relevant arrangements. We visited Vienna twice to ensure that nothing would go wrong on the night; in fact everything went according to plan.

The evening was hailed as a triumph, 'Bystander' of *Tatler* reporting the event under the heading 'Viennese Whirl'. The throng of guests included, besides Britain's Princess Alexandra, many of Europe's most distinguished families, including the Thurn und Taxises, the Windish-Graetzes, the Schonburg-Hartensteins and the Auerspergs, Princess Marie Christine of Bourbon-Parma and Count and Countess Karl Draskovich. The occasion owed much to the British ambassador and his wife, Mr and Mrs Terence White, while their eleven-year-old golden retriever, Jasper, showed himself to be an expert scene stealer. As 'Bystander' wrote, he was a 'true party lover', 'particularly fond of pretty ladies, upon whom he lavishes attention; sometimes even bringing them a present from his soft-toy collection'.

Many of my pretty assistants were there to entertain the guests and attend to their needs. It was a soirée where beautiful art intermingled with beautiful people. The combination was irresistibly captivating, with the music of *Tales from the Vienna Woods* seeming to resonate in the large reception hall without actually being heard. The whole occasion was fairytale-like in concept and execution and worthy of the Crown Jewellers of Britain.

The Asprey Christmas party of 1993, which I helped to organize, was another more sumptuous affair than usual. The accumulation of a unique portfolio of prestigious brand names to add to the group had put us very much in vogue. The idea now was to take much of the dread out of Christmas shopping and make it positively enjoyable by laying on a candle-lit cocktail party for selected clients, complete with champagne and a jazz band. The list of guests was much enhanced by virtue of our more diverse activities and reflected the esteem in which we were held. It included the Viscount and Viscountess Portman, Lord and Lady Somerleyton, the Paul Spicers, the Christopher Gilmours, the Simon Parker Bowleses, the Enoch Powells and the Sholto Douglas-Homeses among other couples, alongside Judith, Countess Bathurst, Countess Sondes, Sir Clive Sinclair, Claus von Bulow, Auberon Waugh and the doyenne of the fashion world, Jean Muir. To add to the fizz of the occasion, a group of young ladies who worked for the Asprey group, and were mainly attached to my office – Sophie Hedley, Mariella Lindemann and Hayley Lindsay – acted as hostesses. They all looked extremely winsome in black evening gowns specially designed for the occasion by Tomasz Starzewski and set off by brooches from the Sunflower collection.

With the cream of London society there to enjoy the event, the Asprey girls did us proud. They had no problem enchanting the captive throng of distinguished guests. It was without doubt the group's most ambitious evening, planned with meticulous care and a discerning eye for detail. *Tatler* reported the evening in their April issue of 1994, devoting two pages mainly to photographs taken on the night. 'Bystander' described the party in only a few words, leaving the photographs to speak for themselves.

The final event of the year to which I made a contribution was the auction of celebrity ties in aid of Crisis at Christmas, the charity for London's homeless, which was held at Leadenhall Market in the City by Jeeves of Belgravia, the London dry cleaners. The actress, Jenny Seagrove, hosted the occasion. Along with Sir John Harvey-Jones, Ralph Steadman and John Cleese, among others, I chipped in with a donation: a pair of ties, one of them, 'For Love', bought for Valentine's Day and covered with hearts. They raised a hundred pounds.

*

Meanwhile, on the publishing front, Alastair Forbes had listed as his choices for the 'Books of the Year' round-up in the *Spectator* three books from Quartet: *The Honour of the Tribe* by Rachid Mimouni, *Women of Sand and Myrrh* by Hanan al-Shaykh and *My Golden Road to Samarkand* by Jascha Golowanjuk, a Samarkand-born Swede. 'I don't, alas, get as many new books coming my way as I should like,' he wrote, 'but I am grateful to Mr Naim Attallah's adventurous publishing house, Quartet, for sending me such worthwhile volumes . . . all of which I have read with interest and horizon-bending enjoyment.'

During 1993 a new recruit had begun to grace the offices of the *Literary Review*. Her name was Jo Craven. She was a delightful young lady with heavenly looks, who enlivened the atmosphere and became one of Bron's favourites. Her recollections of the time she spent there give a further insight into what Bron was like, both at home and in the office. The piece that follows illustrates yet again the reason why Bron was loved and revered, especially by the young.

Saved from Spiritual Death
by Jo Craven

When I first walked through the door of the *Literary Review*'s Beak Street office, in 1993, straight from university and fresh off the train from Yorkshire, I was amazed to be greeted like a long-lost friend by a beaming Bron Waugh, whose first words were, 'How long can you stay?' Never one to miss an opportunity, I dived in with, 'As long as you like.' 'Good,' he said in a very pleased way, looking around the room at the other two staring members of staff for confirmation. It would be some time before I would witness him wave vaguely at his own daughters and mistake many another stranger for an old friend. But it would never occur to him to go back on his word and I stayed for the next five years.

Within weeks Bron had invited me to stay in his Brook Green flat, taking pity on my penniless state and constant flat-hopping. At that point I was working for free as 'a slave'. I couldn't have been luckier and quite enjoyed my friend's taunts about our 'special relationship'. My part of the deal was to make sure there was always plenty of loo roll and Bran Flakes, and occasionally arrange a party with food from Lidgates. Bron's son and girl-friend would also move in, his daughter for a period, and then my boyfriend, and then the deputy editor. It was open-house for the impoverished.

In the overcrowded office I would package up books, type in copy, eventually commission reviewers and generally be in the same room, at the same lunch table as Bron, his other editors and some of the most fascinating figures in British literature. I've never been so drunk in all my life. I loved sharing a couple of bottles of wine over lunch – Bron always paid from his own pocket – and often in the afternoon, over a game of bridge, I could never remember the rules, probably because of the port we'd sip, and maybe thanks to lunch. Then there'd be more boozing after 6 p.m., downstairs in the Academy Club, from where I'd stagger back to the flat; and late at night in Brook Green, Bron would often suggest a nightcap of sweet gin, half gin and half red Martini. It was revolting, but I'd do anything to please this kind generous man for saving me from spiritual death in an ordinary office. By the following morning, I honestly thought no one noticed as I sat at my computer, nestling a can of Coke to cure the worst of my hangover.

I always knew I was lucky to be part of this wonderfully ramshackle universe, so removed from the regular working world. I was one of the last in a long tradition of girls who either worked at Quartet Books, waitressed in the Academy Club or slaved on the magazine. Most had already gone off to find fame. Of course one day it would come to an end: the rickety buildings heated by plug-in radiators, doing everything by hand, paying only £25 for reviews – many writers framed the beautifully handwritten cheques rather than cash them – and top writers being paid with wine from Bron's cellar. It couldn't last. Every few months reality would come knocking. Naim Attallah, the endlessly benevolent owner, would apologetically announce that he just couldn't keep supplementing us while we failed to make any money. Bron would go into a spin. He most of all didn't want anything to change and was always the first to say how much we had to be grateful to Naim for. Naim in turn was hugely fond of Bron and was only doing what any rational person would when the debts kept coming. Selfishly the rest of us found it hard to understand that twenty-first-century accounting had a part in our lives. We were used to being paid terribly and producing a brilliant magazine, and having so much fun that we didn't want anything to change. For me, the moment of departure came when I finally gave up on the notion that someone would headhunt me as a brilliant literary editor, and decided £7,000 a year could be improved on. Two years later Bron died, but the *Literary Review* lives on with its present proprietor, Nancy Sladek, who keeps Bron's flame burning and the spirit of Naim's commitment.

Fifty-two

The year 1994 began with an attempt on my part to bring about a reconciliation. I engineered a meeting between old foes Nigel Dempster and Richard Ingrams by inviting them to lunch. To my great surprise the general atmosphere during the meal turned out to be more congenial than expected. The after-effects were not so promising, however. Hardly a week had passed before the two combatants were returning to the fray. The bitterness between them had penetrated far too deeply to be reversed. From Nigel there was always talk of an alleged betrayal on Richard's part. By contrast, Richard was not only secretive but firmly dismissive as to the causes of the split and was not to be drawn on the subject. Each used his powerful press organ to berate the other whenever an opportunity presented itself. No let-up in the feud was likely as it had become something of an institution. Peter McKay, another one-time contributor to *Private Eye* who had also fallen out with Richard, was less vitriolic. He mostly stood on the sidelines, taking the occasional dig at Richard to keep his hand in and never failing to report in his column in the *Evening Standard* the latest twist in the saga involving the two protagonists. On 5 January he wrote a short piece entitled 'The Richard and Nigel Show' on hearing of my intervention to try to promote peace in the long-running hostilities. He had taken luncheon with Nigel Dempster and found him in a pensive mood, uninterested in discussing the current scandals of high society. Instead he was preoccupied with having had lunch with Ingrams, 'a sworn enemy he has often said he loathes', at the instigation of 'Mr Naim Attallah, the Palestinian former steeplejack, who is . . . Mr Ingrams's benefactor in the no-hope *Oldie* magazine'.

> How did he find Mr Ingrams? 'Very fat – a great big paunch,' the perennially slim Mr Dempster avers.
> Otherwise, he is worryingly non-committal about his old enemy.
> Might he be about to sign up for the *Oldie*, perhaps composing a series about high society between the wars? It is a worrying thought . . .
> The years swirl on, allegiances shift, old enemies are sometimes reprieved and new ones take their place. An unsettling time.

Early in February my very good friend Cristina Odone, the editor of the *Catholic Herald*, asked me among other Catholics, such as Auberon Waugh,

Lord Longford and Peter McKay, 'to pen their heart's desire for Valentine's Day'. She stressed that 'Catholic lonely hearts, of course, wanted more than just flowers and champagne from potential suitors'. For my response to this light-hearted appeal, I wrote two versions. One, not intended for publication, was addressed teasingly to Cristina, as I thought the world of her, just to solicit a cheeky reaction. Before the intended piece for the *Catholic Herald* could be published on 11 February, 'Londoner's Diary' in the *Evening Standard* ran a lead story with the sensational heading, 'Naim and his Catholic Tastes in Love', clearly having had a sight of the private version addressed to Cristina.

> It was inevitable that Cristina Odone, the angelic, sympathetically constructed thirty-two-year-old editor of the *Catholic Herald* would at some time attract the attention of Naim Attallah, sixty-two, the publisher celebrated for sauntering across the metropolis dispensing solid silver hearts to maidens who arouse his fancy.
>
> Regrettably, however, the couple's eventual collision has not, I hear, given Attallah the satisfaction he might have hoped for. He has just departed on business to Italy, nursing a bruised ego.

Their conclusion was that I had 'replied with relish' to Cristina's request, and 'in the heat of [my] ardour apparently misinterpreted [it]'. My submission, 'written in vividly candid prose, required complete revision'.

> 'Mature man of parts,' it read when sanitized, 'with distinctly catholic taste for the unusual, seeks enduring relationship with energetic and enterprising woman.'
>
> The emphasis, reflects Odone coolly, was supposed to be on 'faith and integrity' as opposed to 'curvy with black hair'. But perhaps they will meet again.

I was furious when I saw the piece, and feared Cristina herself must have been responsible for the leak. Some while later I discovered it was a series of well-intentioned accidents that led to the rumpus, but at the time I telephoned the *Evening Standard* to protest, as reported by 'Londoner's Diary':

> I have received a charming telephone call from *Literary Review* publisher Naim Attallah, following my story yesterday that he had sent an inappropriate Valentine's message to *Catholic Herald* editor Cristina Odone. 'It was a joke,' Attallah tells me. 'We are the best of friends. I adore her.' His message may be judged by readers for themselves when it appears in Miss Odone's paper this week.

The full text of the piece, as intended for publication among the *Catholic Herald*'s lonely-hearts pastiches, went as follows:

Mature man of parts with distinctive catholic taste for the unusual seeks enduring relationship with energetic and enterprising woman. He offers extensive experience in the realm of human endeavour and steadfastness in reliability and friendship. He values unpredictability and a degree of coquetry in women. He is an ardent explorer of emotional landscapes and a strong navigator and crusader in a perilous world.

Four years later I referred to the event in an article written for the *Daily Express*:

Greatly enjoyed Monday evening when I was invited to the Ivy for cocktails. The occasion marked the publication of Cristina Odone's second novel, *A Perfect Wife*, which promises to be a polished successor to *The Shrine*.

Her first novel was full of passion, dealing intelligently with sex and religion, the sacred and the profane – a combination which has proved irresistible to many writers. Cristina Odone is well placed to write with conviction and authority on the theme. As a Roman Catholic with a strict convent education behind her, she struggles to live a disciplined life. But she is the first to admit that lust can exert a fearsome power, even on the devout. (The men who fall at her feet find it quite powerful too.)

From her Swedish mother and Italian father she has inherited that tantalizing mix of northern poise and Mediterranean ardour. It is the southern heat which prevails, however. She exudes a deep sensuality and flirtatiousness, and has always said that she would be a very bad girl were it not for her faith. Just the sort of statement which is guaranteed to feed a man's fantasies. Her vocabulary is enchantingly biblical – sin, temptation, evil, grace, are all regulars.

I have always felt a natural sympathy with Cristina Odone. We are both Catholics, highly volatile, both conscious of the challenge of the faith. I also attended a convent where one learnt the seductive power of religion. Indeed there's nothing quite like being taught by nuns to put the hormones into overdrive. There is such emphasis on the sinfulness of everyone, the carnality of the world.

Until she resigned last year, Cristina edited the *Catholic Herald*, a previously moribund organ which she transformed into a smart read. During her reign she fanned the flames of fundamentalist fury against trendy liberals in the Catholic church.

Three years ago we had a serious tiff. For St Valentine's Day . . . [and here I repeated the story of the spoof that misfired].

Some might say that Cristina gives Catholicism a bad name. Not me; I think she is its very lifeblood. At thirty-seven, she is still searching for the man of her dreams. The lucky devil who marries her will gain a wonderful wife and excellent breeding potential.

Only after this appeared in print did it emerge that it was not Cristina who told Peter McKay about the private version I had penned for her, but Melanie McDonagh, the writer and journalist, who happened to be at Cristina's as she was preparing a Valentine's card to send to me in response. Then Peter McKay simply passed the information on to 'Londoner's Diary'. It had all been no more than a storm in a teacup, and I regretted the period of alienation between me and Cristina that followed the appearance of the story in the *Evening Standard*.

Another 'Valentine's Day' story had drawn the attention of the papers shortly afterwards; this time it was my new personal assistant, Henrietta Garnett, who attracted the spotlight. I had given myself 'an admirable present for St Valentine's Day – a new PA', *The Times* 'Diary' declared on 14 February 1994.

Attallah has lured the personable Henrietta Garnett away from her longstanding boss Alexandra Shulman, editor of *Vogue*. But relations between Asprey's . . . and *Vogue* remain cordial according to Attallah. 'Henrietta will work as personal assistant to me, and Alexandra is being very sweet. She agreed Henrietta would have a different scope because we do everything here.'

Two days later, the 'Diary' column was able to round off the story on an even happier note, after it had turned out to be 'a very bountiful Valentine's Day' for Alexandra, when she started off her evening at a party to launch a new range of perfumes from Elizabeth Taylor. There she won the raffle, 'to her great surprise'. The prize consisted of a ruby and diamond pendant 'valued for insurance at £3,850'.

Yesterday Shulman was still in a happy state of shock.

'I am so amazed at having won anything that I have not had time to think what I'll do with it. I'm just staring at it with delight.'

At the start of February, in anticipation of St Valentine's Day, Victoria Hinton of the *Daily Express* had made a visit to Aphrodisia, my wife's shop in Shepherd Market, and written a comprehensive description of the premises and its contents. She had spoken at length to my wife Maria, who extolled the romantic nature of her merchandise and detailed some of the benefits likely to be derived from it. Victoria Hinton started off her article by describing the tiny dimensions of the shop and its devotion to romance rather than sex or libido. Eerie music pervaded the atmosphere – 'New Age whale-mating calls, dolphins singing, that kind of thing'. 'This, the owner Maria Attallah says, is to get you in the mood for romance, but then – according to her – just about anything gets you in the mood for affairs of the heart.' So far as Victoria Hinton could see, it was all pretty innocent stuff. Where was the rhino horn, the Spanish fly, tiger bones, deer antlers 'and all manner of grisly things taken from (usually endangered) animals and ground up to perk up flagging sexual urges'?

> Mrs Attallah has no truck with them. 'I remember seeing a stall in Tangiers with hedgehog skins and bats. I thought: "Yuck, this is more death potions than love potions. If this is love, I'll join a nunnery."
>
> 'What's an aphrodisiac? Something that unwinds you and relaxes you. You know what it is? It's up here,' she says, tapping her head. Yet, if it is all in the mind, why go to a shop called Aphrodisia to buy things to make you feel romantic? 'You don't need a lot of money. You can give someone just one flower. It's using your imagination. . . .
>
> 'What is sexiness? It's a visual awareness, it's conversing, it's a relaxed sense of humour. An ugly person can be sexy.'

Yet wasn't there anything, Ms Hinton wanted to know, 'which has a sort of, mmm, physical effect'?

> Maria Attallah has a way of fixing you with her piercing eyes which makes you understand why, when dodgy types do walk in expecting heavy-duty aphrodisiacs, they head for the door pretty smartly. Ginger, she concedes, ginseng, and chocolate which contains phenylethyamine, which our bodies produce when we are in love, may act as a love tonic.
>
> For thirty-five years Maria has been married to Naim Attallah . . . This is a lengthy relationship among the high-profile London society circle they inhabit, so they must be doing something right. From her beautifully shaded hair, elegantly manicured hands and soft, touchable wool clothes, this is a woman who looks after herself. Yes, she still lights scented candles when he comes home, and puts on atmospheric music.
>
> 'He is thoughtful. He has his (professional) territory and I have mine – I think it's important.'
>
> Risk further probing about the Attallah relationship and you get a charming, slightly accented: 'That's rather personal,' and that's that.

Maria had to admit that the British were not terribly good at romance, though it was not because they didn't have feelings, because, 'Everyone has feelings. If they are cut, they will bleed. It's just that our upbringing has taught us not to show it.' Any customers to the shop, with its tasteful decoration in 'rich greens and dark wood', could rely on being treated with discretion, though they would not be encouraged to expose their emotional lives in too much depth. 'We want to keep it light, it's too much if someone comes with big problems.'

You may not be able to scientifically quantify the effects of Maria Attallah's 'gifts of love and charm', but there is a strong chance that if you go there before St Valentine's Day, whatever you buy may warm the cockles of your loved one's heart.

One tip. Gold is a particularly effective aphrodisiac.

*

In mid March, John Asprey and I were in Hong Kong on one of our regular visits there to oversee the activities in our office, opened the year before. It was managed by a well-connected French lady, Elizabeth Cassegrain-Thomas, who had previously been in charge of Garrard's marketing, covering the Far East but based in Hong Kong. Elizabeth was a popular figure in the region, noted for her business acumen and social contacts. Her hard work and dedication had my full appreciation and we considered ourselves lucky to have secured her services.

Hong Kong was then still a British dependency and the press continued with the colonial tradition of printing the biographical details of visitors of note and so gave John Asprey and myself the treatment. The *South China Morning Post* for 17 March was highly impressed with the invitation they received to a champagne reception at the Mandarin Oriental Hotel to meet us. Seeing its gold embossing and royal coat of arms, they said, 'we positively stiffened at the possibility that it might be a summons from Buckingham Palace to higher things'.

But the scrolled writing bore a call from the lovely Elizabeth Cassegrain-Thomas, Asprey's representative in the Far East, to meet her chairman, John Asprey, and the company's chief executive, Naim Attallah, who merits as many column centimetres in the business pages of British newspapers as he does in the gossip columns.

As jewellers by appointment to the Queen, they felt Asprey had done well in bringing on board someone whose name was Elizabeth, 'with all its regal connotations'. When they contacted her, they found her in a great fluster, saying, 'I'm running around like a chicken without a head.' She appeared perfectly normal, they assured her, and felt sure she'd be looking perfectly composed – 'Elizabethan even' – by the time of the reception.

Earlier, on 5 March, the *Hongkong Standard* had heralded our imminent arrival. John Asprey, they wrote, possessed 'impeccable credentials, and obviously went to all the right schools', having been educated at Stowe before studying at the Sorbonne in Paris and then doing service in the Scots Guards. He had taken 'his rightful place as head of the family firm' after studying watchmaking with Patek Philippe in Geneva. 'On the other hand,' they continued, 'Naim Ibrahim Attallah has done all sorts of interesting things.'

> His biographical data lists him as publisher of The Women's Press, the launcher of an Arab perfume and the producer of a play with the novel title of *The Beastly Beatitudes of Balthazar B*.
>
> He has also co-produced films with David Frost and produced and presented television documentaries. His published books include *Women*, *Of a Certain Age* and *Singular Encounters*.
>
> We have a feeling Mr Attallah is a lot more fun than Mr Asprey.

Hong Kong was not an easy place in which to do business, even with our extensive range of merchandise. All the famous brands of watches had their own agents there, and jewellers from all over the world competed in a market noted for its surfeit of product from every corner of the globe. Our calculation was that only specialist items made in our own workshop in London, with a unique pedigree of craftsmanship, were likely to sell; and then only to the high élite, who seek the best that money can buy as long as exclusivity is guaranteed. Even though it was a highly competitive market, Asprey could not for reasons of exposure remain on the periphery. It was necessary to be seen, as a public-relations exercise that would eventually have the effect of attracting new customers to the outlets in London and New York, even if these did not come directly through the Hong Kong office. With the international rich communities growing to be so mobile, it was always hard to pinpoint an original source that had triggered a particular sale, no matter where it happened in the world. In this way, global publicity had become an integral part of a merchandizing policy aiming to maintain and bolster an international status capable of competing at a level commensurate with the quality of the products.

I had always believed in spreading the word through careful targeting and by being on the spot, even when tangible results were not always immediately forthcoming. The key to opening doors is perseverance, and a readiness to sacrifice time with the aim of achieving the ultimate objective. The stony road to success can be hard to negotiate. I had vivid memories of our pioneering days in the Arabian Gulf, when Asprey, with a turnover of only eight hundred thousand pounds worldwide, set out to promote itself in Abu Dhabi and Dubai, starting off with a number of exhibitions. These were aimed basically at selling in order to increase our turnover and make some profit. It was a hopeless exercise at the beginning, with sales so low as hardly to cover the cost of freight, let alone the overheads. Eventually perseverance did yield the results we were looking for, but they took a number of years to achieve, and they came about not so much locally as through people coming to London and heading for our showrooms in Bond Street. These customers had originally become acquainted with our products through seeing them at various exhibitions held in their countries of origin.

Hong Kong, of course, was the gateway to China. The possibilities of establishing some sort of trade link there had me bursting with personal enthusiasm. The potential was immense, and I could see the giant of a nation that was mainland China, which had lain dormant so long, capturing world markets and becoming a superpower during my own lifetime. To my lasting regret, it was an opportunity that eluded us for a variety of complex reasons, one of which was that the rapid expansion of the group had left us without the financial muscle to grow further. A fresh injection of capital could have been the answer, but it would inevitably have depleted the Asprey family shareholding – a move that would never have found favour with members of the family who were at that period intent on maintaining a controlling interest in the group. Had I been in their place, I would have welcomed a reorganization of the capital structure. It would have propelled the group into a different league of companies and a new sort of ball game, increasing the worth of the company to rank with some of the conglomerates of the present day. They were, however, too afraid of losing control – fears that became a reality some years later when, panic stricken at the first signs of a difficult period in trading, the family caved in and sold out rather than weather the storm.

It was a tragedy of momentous proportions to see our hard-won achievements disappear overnight along with a business that had survived two hundred years – and all because the close advisers who suddenly mushroomed out of nowhere, claiming to know how to lead the family on to more fertile ground, pressurized them into opting for money in lieu of the business. Had Eric Asprey been alive, none of that would have happened. He had constantly lectured me about the need to maintain the family business at all costs.

Unfortunately his legacy passed into other hands, and although I had no part in the selling of the business, I felt I had let him down in being unable to stop it. The sadness has remained throughout the years – but more of this later.

April was a mixed bag of a month. My losses on the *Literary Review* and the *Oldie* continued to be highlighted in the press. I was unsure whether this was out of sympathy for me or simply because the media get as excited about a loss and its adverse implications as they do about a success. Perhaps there was more in it of the former than the latter. The *Evening Standard*, in its 'Mr Pepys' column, became unusually cheeky in providing me (once again the 'Palestinian former steeplejack') with a suggested solution, taking a swipe in the process at Richard Ingrams and Auberon Waugh. 'Mr Pepys' said he had been taken to one side by me at Daphne's, the fine Chelsea restaurant. 'Normally an upbeat, cheerful man, I can see his mind is troubled. Why so?' The losses on the two magazines were evidently the cause.

> What is to be done? Both Waugh and Ingrams make good money elsewhere. Both have failed to make their organs successful. The solution is simple. Sack both of them. Appoint young men without outside incomes who have to make the magazines succeed. Mr Attallah looks thoughtful, but I doubt if he'll take my advice. He's a kind man, addicted to bailing out middle-class, middle-aged English ponces he admires.

Writing in the same paper, my friend John Wells displayed in his column his usual whimsical humour, as one would have expected of him.

> There was a joke going round recently at the expense of the one West End theatre manager, renowned for his apparently bottomless coffers when it comes to putting on new shows, being surprised by a rival having a drink in a flat in Maida Vale with his mystery backer. It was Yasser Arafat.
> It was only Yasser's persistence in backing shows in London's West End, the joke continued, that had brought the PLO financially to its knees and forced Mr Arafat to the negotiating table.
> The joke, I am sorry to say, has resurfaced.
> This time it is my old friend, the publisher Naim Attallah, whose name has been linked with the swarthy embracer of his fellow men.
> Fellow-journalists chuckle no end at the idea of Auberon Waugh's *Literary Review* and Richard Ingrams's *Oldie*, both subsidized to a considerable degree by Naim's generosity, contributing to the Middle East peace process.
> I would like to nail this silly story once and for all, like the other equally ridiculous suggestion that taking out a life subscription to Mr Waugh's

Academy Club is an absolute guarantee against any further public attacks by Mr Waugh, the noted acerbic columnist.

With the *Oldie* magazine trailing behind its original expectations, Richard Ingrams asked Hugh Cudlipp, who was highly sympathetic to the concept of the magazine, to write him a report of how he saw its future, incorporating any recommendations that he might be able to come up with. Hugh wrote to Richard on 16 May 1994, under the heading 'Some Thoughts about the *Oldie*'. The report was fifteen pages long and very constructive. Under a sub-heading on page 11, 'Final thoughts, some philosophical, some practical', he said the following:

> In a way too elusive to define, Naim Attallah's interviews with their probing, persistent, disturbingly informed but never hostile or brutish interrogation, their gentle exhumation of past horrors and personal crises as well as glories, reassembling the bones at the end and deftly replacing the tombstone, are psychologically perfect for *Oldie* readers. I urge the Editor to put him under a long contract so there is no danger of him being purloined by the *Literary Review*. Watch Waugh.

I was extremely flattered to be praised by someone as legendary in the press world as Hugh Cudlipp and felt that perhaps I had arrived.

At Asprey worrying events were taking place. I was particularly concerned about a deteriorating relationship between John Asprey and Ronald Lee, of R. A. Lee (Fine Arts) Ltd, which had been precarious at the best of times. John, who was a marvellous salesman, with a charm to match, could nevertheless show a regrettable lack of deference when aroused. He also displayed an impatience with people whose methods of working differed from his own. As a result, he tended to leave behind him a trail of disaffected individuals. Impulsiveness can have its merits, but a pause for reflection may sometimes make a better alternative.

Ronald Lee, who was eighty-one, found John very difficult to deal with and there were many occasions when I had to intervene to lower the temperature. They were like chalk and cheese and a parting of the ways seemed likely to occur sooner rather than later. The *Antiques Trade Gazette* reported the incident that broke the camel's back on 16 April. It concerned a failed attempt to purchase two historic panel paintings from the thirteenth century for the British Museum. They had come up for sale at the Bristol Auction Rooms, and Ronald was acting as underbidder on the museum's behalf. To his astonishment, he saw them being 'knocked down to Asprey (bidding on behalf of an anonymous British-based collector) for £120,000'.

The long-established Lee family business was taken over last summer by Naim Attallah's Asprey Group. Son Charles continued as a director and Ronald was retained on a consultancy basis.

Asprey maintain that, so far as they were concerned, Mr Lee was bidding in a private capacity and managing director Timothy Cooper described the incident as 'an unfortunate misunderstanding'.

However, Ronald Lee described his position as 'untenable', and the eighty-one-year-old dealer added: 'I call it "quietly retiring", but it is a resignation.'

The old boy retired amid some bitterness. I tried to defuse the atmosphere as best I could, but John was beginning to show signs of petulance, another development that caused me unease. Our relationship was the key to the success of the Asprey group. We were different but complementary. Lord Rothermere (Vere), who was my friend, and even a member of the Academy Club, set an example as a very astute operator. A true press baron, well aware of his own limitations, he appointed David English to run his empire. It was a wise move that paid dividends. The secret of their success was that each adhered to his own area of responsibility without encroaching on the territory of the other. The fruits of this cooperation came with the emergence of the Daily Mail and General Trust as one of the most profitable press conglomerates in the United Kingdom. The same principle had so far applied to the Asprey group, John being chairman and the salesman *par excellence* while I was group chief executive.

This pairing worked extremely well until the group grew in size and stature; then cracks began to appear in the fabric of our relationship. At the instigation of his friends, and a number of members of his family, he began to interfere in areas where his competence was perhaps not up to the mark. He started issuing instructions to other sectors of the group, and while these were seldom fully implemented, they set off ripples of discord. None of this went down well with the senior management in the group, who invariably reported John's aberrations to me with a degree of apprehension. John would then in most cases deny the incidents concerned and matters would stabilize for a while. But these were danger signs portending a more serious situation ahead.

To move the focus from Asprey's internal problems to fashion, Tomasz Starzewski had been actively preparing for British Fashion Week, under the auspices of the Asprey group, as reported in *OK* magazine, with Baroness Izzy van Ranwyck as one of his patrons. His creations were displayed at the Natural History Museum in the British Fashion Council Tent. 'Tomasz's brand-new collection is fashionable, stylish and fun and his show was appreciated by a discerning audience.'

My relationship with Tomasz was also great fun. Within the Asprey group he was directly responsible to me, and we had a close working partnership as a result of this proximity. It was certainly not bereft of its lighter moments. We both, as *bon viveurs*, liked to escape on occasion from the pressures placed upon us by our different roles. Our sexual orientation might not have been exactly the same, but we both loved women for a variety of reasons. In that domain the disparity worked in ways that were quite complementary and consolidated the relationship further. We undertook a few promotional trips abroad, accompanied by a small entourage of exquisite young ladies, who not only carried out their assignments with immaculate precision, but also brought colour and glamour to the proceedings. Life at the top end was undoubtedly good and we were determined to savour the delights while they lasted.

The Asprey Era
by Tomasz Starzewski

I had reached a point in my career when I needed to be part of a large parent company. A friend of mine mentioned Naim. I remember saying to him, 'I think I'm the wrong sex,' because Naim had always been known for supporting and encouraging quite a lot of my women friends over the years. But my friend said, 'He could still be the one, you ought to meet him.' I can't remember exactly how the interview was instigated, and unbeknown to me Naim was married to a Polish woman. I think that was a lucky connection and a good omen at that. From Naim's point of view, another advantage was the innocence of my ways, my unbounded enthusiasm plus an extraordinary clientele, which he reckoned would be a great asset to Asprey.

He made it very clear from the outset that we were not going to get old-fashioned management. It became as though we lived in a crazy, spontaneous though not reckless arena of activity; but each of us in the team knew that as far as the group was concerned the question was how Naim had managed to do something so impossible as set us up in this unique situation. We also knew that the way to get to him was through his PA, whoever the PA happened to be at the time. It was important for us to find out his mood and his thoughts, or whether we needed to orchestrate a campaign to win him round. I also knew he had fundamentally banned men from his floor. However, I was quick to work out that my worth would be greatly enhanced by tantalizing him with the latest acquisition of tender young staff with good credentials. Dealing with Naim was an education in itself.

Early in our association I told Naim I needed a managing director to look after the commercial aspects of the business and to keep a tight purse. One day I asked him if he remembered a pop/folk duo called Nina & Frederik. 'Well, their daughter is coming to see me,' I said. She had been working in Rome for Valentino and had moved to England because she wanted to be near her current beau, the ex-husband of a great friend of Naim's. I then met this incredibly beautiful, chic girl, Anna Maria van Pallandt, who looked just like her mother, Nina, used to look, but who was also relatively icy and distant. Naim interviewed her as well to see if she'd make part of the team, though it never occurred to me she might be material for a managing director. I may therefore have said something out of order when Naim announced, 'This is your new managing director.' Against all expectations, she turned out to be highly efficient and sensible. She took in her stride the responsibility of seeing that money kept coming in. My main concern at that point was to design clothes to sell and not to bother myself with accounts.

Eventually my team was headed by this beautiful Dutch girl, Anna Maria. My press attaché was Sophie Hedley and Fiona Sleeman looked after the customers admirably. They were all great girls. With Anna Maria it took time to earn her friendship as she was very reserved. She came from a colourful upbringing, her parents having been very much part of that swinging seventies mad calypso crowd, gravitating between Lisbon and Ibiza on their yacht, the *Sir Leonard Lord*. Yet their offspring was a very focused and serious young woman, protective and sensible.

Soon after the wonderful Sophie Hedley was promoted by Naim to be the new PR of the company, I found a crazy French assistant designer who produced incredibly spectacular illustrations and had learnt English through watching television. It was a time of constant laughter. We were always in fits as we tried to work out how to sneak into Naim's office to get what we deserved – or thought we deserved. The process would be me saying, 'I do need a new watch,' or Sophie saying, 'I quite like that ring,' knowing full well Naim's unbelievable generosity. This always provoked the complete annoyance of the rest of the group, bar Tania Foster-Brown, who was then Naim's head of marketing and had that same wicked sense of humour. She was the one who taught me the works, because the other young woman belonging to Naim's inner sanctum at the time was Julia Ogilvy, whom I found completely terrifying.

It was a heady period. When I look back at it, I appreciate Naim's acquisition of Tomasz Starzewski even more than I did at the time. It was quite a controversial decision for Asprey. I remember sitting at a dinner party with some great friends of mine, and my hostess taking me aside and saying,

'I've placed you next to this person, because I think you ought to know there are some members of the Asprey family who deeply disapprove of you being part of the group.' And I remember being sat next to this unbelievably frosty Frenchwoman, who stuck her nose up at me and just said, 'Who are you?' then ignored me.

Naim showed great courage in bringing me into the fold, which at that point was really about jewellery and applied art, whether watches or pictures. It may be thought that fashion can be a logical extension of all that, but in fact it is quite a distinct sort of proposition. I don't think we ever realized how protected we were from Bond Street by Naim in Regent Street, who ensured the non-interference of the hierarchy. In the end it seemed the little group of us all working together somehow managed to charm its way through. Ultimately we were able to pacify the parent company, though of course we continued to shock. There was a very concentrated, sexy period when everything seemed to get bigger and greater than it probably was, but it was also a period of immense calm – though that, of course, was only a transient moment in one's life to be appreciated much later. Then Asprey was sold and the magical group of people who had all been working together disappeared and went elsewhere – but it had been an exhilarating experience.

I know there's a preconceived idea about fashion designers not needing to work hard, but that was never the case with me. I think I gave even slightly more than expected, though my curiosity was not just about what was happening with us in our sector, but what Naim was up to in publishing. Some of it consisted of the most exciting books of the day. I was fortunate to be able to lay my hands very quickly on a copy of anything that took my interest. Naim would send one round straight away. Another thing that made it a very exciting period was flying to New York to do a recce with a view to consolidating and enhancing our international reputation; or, on two or three occasions, travelling with Naim to Milan and to Paris, along with Anna Maria and Sophie, when a great time was had by all.

The best way for me to summarize that part of my life is to say it was an indelible era of spontaneity and mischief, though also very naïve and innocent. I'm not sure it could exist in today's context, because we probably thought we were being naughty and wicked when in fact it was underpinned by good intention and had a rather beautiful quality about it. I consider that says a lot about the people involved. And in a way we were never shaken up or brought to heel. I can recall Naim losing his temper only once, and it wasn't anything to do with work. We hadn't actually done anything wrong in the office – it may have been something we never told him. We were given unbelievable trust and that was truly magical. That's really it.

Fifty-three

At Quartet the emphasis of the previous fifteen months had been on publishing works of fiction and non-fiction by foreign writers, a number of them from the Middle East. The following examples are again taken at random.

A Witkiewicz Reader, edited, translated and with an introduction by Daniel Gerould. Stanislaw Ignacy Witkiewicz, who wrote under the pen name Witkacy, had come to be regarded as the outstanding dramatist of modern Polish theatre. He committed suicide after the Russian invasion of Poland in 1939 and his work was in eclipse till the liberalization of the Communist regime in 1956. Then it was rediscovered and played a leading part in freeing the arts from 'socialist realism'. Professor Gerould's anthology gave the first overview of his work in English, including play texts, extracts from novels, philosophical and aesthetic essays, together with reproductions of his drawings and paintings.

The Compassion Protocol by Hervé Guibert, translated by James Kirkup. Guibert had died in 1991 from an AIDS-related illness, the suffering of which found its way into his novels, a series of three that began with *To the Friend Who Did Not Save My Life* and ended with *The Man in the Red Hat*. *The Compassion Protocol* (the second in the sequence) told, he wrote, 'of my astonishment, my rage and the grief of a man of thirty-five on whom is grafted the body of an old man. But the happiness of remission makes an inroad into the unhappiness.' Quartet published the complete trilogy.

Worlds of Difference by Georges-Arthur Goldschmidt, translated by James Kirkup, with an introduction by Peter Handke. This novel, called 'an undeserved present to German literature' by the *Frankfurter Allgemeine Zeitung*, told a story of a small Jewish boy taken out of Nazi Germany to be hidden in a remote orphanage in the French Alps. As he grows he is conscious of his exclusion as a Jew and his isolation as a German, finding the French language a struggle and suffering torment and persecution from the other boys. His salvation lies in developing an ability to distance himself from physical pain, achieving a transference into a 'secret realm' where his innermost thoughts are freed.

The Book of Hrabal by Péter Esterházy, translated by Judith Sollosy. Conceived as a tribute to the great Czech writer Bohumil Hrabal (author of *Closely Observed Trains*), this fantastical novel has two angels in the background, who shadow the household of the author and his wife Anna in the guise of secret policemen. The angels communicate with God by walkie-talkie, their mission being to prevent the abortion of Anna's fourth child. Anna – a blues-singing housewife – addresses the story of all that comes about to Hrabal himself.

The Man Who Came to a Village by Héctor Tizón, translated by Miriam Frank. In a tale told with biblical simplicity, an escaped convict fleeing into the Argentine mountains arrives at a remote village where the inhabitants greet him as their long-awaited priest and saviour. His protestations are ignored and he finds himself installed as their chosen leader, engaging in philosophical discussions but disturbed by his own ambiguous identity. The scenario unexpectedly shifts with the arrival of a group to oversee the villagers in building a road to connect them with the outside world, heralding a total change in their traditions. This was the first of Tizón's novels to be translated into English.

Diary, Volume III: 1961–1966 by Witold Gombrowicz, edited by Jan Kott, translated by Lillian Vallee. This completed the ambition of Quartet to publish all three volumes of Gombrowicz's *Diary*, widely considered to be a masterpiece of Polish and European literature, standing even above his novels and plays. Through the *Diary*, wrote Czesław Miłosz in the *New York Times*, could be discovered 'a great writer whose complex and multilayered thought belongs to the heart of our labyrinthine century'. *Kirkus Reviews* called it his 'great unscrolling of spleen, playfulness, opposition, brilliance and subversion'.

The Island of Animals by Denys Johnson-Davies, illustrated by Sabiha Khemir. A fable by a foremost Arabic scholar, adapted from a tenth-century text from Basra, to expound on man's responsibilities towards his fellow creatures, man having been chosen by God as the sole creature answerable at death for his actions in life. The Islamic teaching is that man has been created by God to share with every other creature the bounties of the earth. As a verse in the Qur'an stated: 'And there is no animal in the earth nor bird that flies with its two wings which are not of communities like yourselves.'

The First Century after Beatrice by Amin Maalouf, translated by Dorothy S. Blair. Another fable, in the form a novel, that looked apprehensively beyond the end of the twentieth century to the growing divide between North and South. It centred on an investigation by a French entomologist and a journalist companion into the disturbing fact that female births were becoming increasingly rare for no apparent reason.

Girls of Alexandria by Edwar al-Kharrat, translated by Frances Liardet. Doris Lessing called the writing of Edwar al-Kharrat, a Coptic Christian by birth, more 'Proust than Durrell'. His evocation of Alexandria in the 1930s and 1940s, through the stories of nine girls in nine chapters, placed them at the centre of a vibrant mosaic of family, schooldays, adolescence, wartime. The writing created captivating impressions of the streets and shorelines, the loves and scandals, of those who lived in the old city. Only through language, said the author, through the jumbled word-images thrown together in the bottomless rag-bag of your mind, could you travel to Alexandria.

Prince of Shadows by Antonio Muñoz Molina, translated by Peter Bush. Some twenty years after the end of the Spanish Civil War, a republican exile is ordered to return to Madrid to seek out and liquidate a man suspected of colluding with the police in betraying members of the anti-Franco resistance. With his victim in hiding, a theme of *déjà vu* begins to spread around him like a net as he hunts him down, reprising events from a similar killing years before, till it seems his control over his destiny is passing out of his own hands into those of a mysterious police inspector, the 'prince of shadows'.

Fire in Casabindo by Héctor Tizón, translated by Miriam Frank. After a battle in 1875 on the *puna*, the tableland of the High Andes of Argentina, a mortally wounded one-eyed combatant sets out on a quest to track down his assailant and kill him so his own soul may be freed and find peace. With the story told in powerful, economical prose, the hero wanders in search, flashbacks mingling with present encounters and moments of delirium in a vividly realized book. Tizón was not of the magic-realist school but he wrote from the heart of the Latin American tradition.

My Golden Road from Samarkand by Jascha Golowanjuk, translated by Henning Koch. In Samarkand the childhood of a ten-year-old boy from a bourgeois background comes to an end as the Bolshevik terror spreads across Russia from Moscow. His family have to flee in disguise to try to reach the Caspian Sea, plagued by treacherous guides, predatory bandits and Bolshevik double agents ready to betray them. Golowanjuk had settled in Sweden in 1929 and become a popular author known affectionately as the 'foreign bird of Swedish literature'.

Oedipus on the Road by Henry Bachau, translated by Anne-Marie Glasheen. A mythic and lyrical prose poem by a leading Belgian poet, novelist and playwright that tells the story of the blinded King Oedipus as he takes the road from Thebes to Colonus. His companions are his fourteen-year-old daughter Antigone and Clios, the shepherd bandit who joins them. Their adventures through a beautiful, ancient land set many trials for them in their journey towards self-knowledge, in which they are called on to become, by turn, beggars, singers, labourers, storytellers and sculptors. It was a profoundly realized imaginative treatment of themes that have fascinated over centuries.

The Fallen by Juan Marsé, translated by Helen Lane. In the aftermath of the Spanish Civil War, a gang of street children gathers in a disused air-raid shelter in Barcelona, a city still suffering for its anti-fascist past. Between them they swap and embroider stories that build up into a Goyaesque fresco of corrupted lives. Using the children's half-imagined, half-real scenarios, telling of secret sexual and political tortures, renegades and assassination attempts, Marsé recreates the sordid, violent world of Barcelona in the wake of General Franco's victory.

Mazurka for Two Dead Men by Camilo José Cela, translated by Patricia Haugaard. A novel by the Nobel Prize winner that was claimed to be a culmination of his literary art. It takes place in a backward Galician village community during 1936 to 1939, the years of the Spanish Civil War, starting with an abduction and killing and ending with the vengeance of the dead man's brother. In between are woven several narrative voices, including that of the dead man's widow. Varying themes and moods, touching on the comic and the grotesque, build like a musical composition. The music of a blind accordion player from the local brothel sounds at the start of the action and again at the end.

The Chrysalis by Aïcha Lemsine, translated by Dorothy S. Blair. The 'chrysalis' of the title is the set of rigid traditions and attitudes binding family and married life in the Maghreb, where the principle of male dominance is fiercely defended by the tribal matriarchs. The story, by an Algerian prize-winning author, traces the story of two generations of Algerian women, a barren wife and her stepdaughter, and the long fight to win through to social independence.

The Ogre's Embrace by Rachid Mimouni, translated by Shirley Eber. The *Nouvel Observateur* had called Mimouni, 'The Voltaire of Algiers . . . one of the great discoveries of French-Algerian literature of recent years.' *Figaro* said he was 'one of the best Algerian contemporary writers . . . comparable to Kafka and Camus'. The book consisted of seven texts telling of the impact the absurd bureaucracies of the country had on the lives of some of its individual public servants and citizens, from a postal worker to a park keeper to a station master, for instance. There was no escape from those in power for anyone. Mimouni observed it all with a witty eye and a laconic response.

A Marriage Out of Time: My Life with and without Emile Bustani by Laura Bustani, with a preface by John Freeman and a foreword by Moham-med Heikal. This told the remarkable story of a Lebanese woman who, after her husband died in an air accident, took over his extensive business interests in the Middle East and guided them through the subsequent years of civil war and invasion. It was also a tribute to the partnership of their marriage before the tragedy. Emile, a Maronite Christian, had been a man of rare integrity, refusing to employ people in his companies on any sectarian basis. To mark the book's publication there was a party in the ballroom of the Hyde Park Hotel, though, alas, I was not at my best, as the 'Londoner's Diary' in the *Evening Standard* quickly deduced.

'I'm only half the man I usually am,' he announced, propping himself up on a black-and-gold cane. 'I had some surgery on my teeth earlier in the day and I injured my back three days ago. It's not a very manly injury, I'm afraid.'

One of my main objectives in becoming a publisher was to publish books of Middle Eastern interest, covering not only the Palestinian conflict and the suffering of the Palestinian people – which we did comprehensively – but also to promote Arab culture that had been so long ignored in the West. Historically the Arabs of ancient times contributed to the fields of science, medicine, mathematics and the arts. The eclipse of their contribution was largely due to the colonizing powers, which for centuries suppressed knowledge of their cultural evolution and almost destroyed the resulting heritage. Tribal strife was another key factor, impeding progress and diverting attention to more mundane pursuits which stifled learning and higher ideals. There remained, however, a rich crop of emerging writers whose work deserved recognition in the West, and especially in the English-speaking world.

[666]

I was determined to do my part in having the output translated into English to stand alongside Quartet's international list, which was made up of sometimes obscure or newly discovered talent together with established writers. Although, from the commercial perspective, it was unrealistic to expect good financial returns in the short term, the inclusion of books emanating from or relating to the Middle East enabled Quartet to extend its frontiers to a readership in areas hitherto unknown to it. Leaving politics on one side, our Arab contribution in fiction was substantial. While Zelfa Hourani took charge of the Arab fiction list and developed it to great effect, I remained in direct control of what we published under the headings of non-fiction and politics.

A title of particular importance was Najib Alamuddin's *The Flying Sheikh*, published in 1987, which chronicled the whole story of the founding and establishment of Middle East Airlines, of which he was chairman and president for twenty-five years. Sheikh Najib, who came from an eminent Druze family in Lebanon and became known as 'The Flying Sheikh', had a more detailed understanding than most of the complexities of Lebanese politics. He steered the airline through the stormy passages of Arab–Israeli conflict and sectarian strife in Lebanon, and ultimately ensured its survival in the face of formidable intrigues that had both internal and international origins. In 1993, Quartet went on to publish *Turmoil: The Druzes, Lebanon and the Arab–Israeli Conflict*, in which, with a vivid sense of history, Sheikh Najib traced the origins of the Druzes, of their relationships with other Islamic and Christian groups and of their position in Lebanon's modern times of strife. He had many insights on the influence of the oil wars and the disastrous effects of the international arms trade in the region as a whole.

Dina Abdel Hamid told a more personal story in *Duet for Freedom*, published in 1988, with an introduction by John Le Carré. As a member of the Hashemite dynasty, Princess Dina had been briefly married to King Hussein of Jordan, but her book gave an epic account of events following the capture of her second husband, Salah Ta'amari, a spokesman for the PLO, during the 1982 Israeli invasion of Lebanon. By an extraordinary chance, her attempts to contact Salah and free him from the hidden labyrinth of the notorious prison camp of Ansar, opened up the chance of negotiating with the Israelis for the release of thousands of Palestinians and Lebanese in exchange for six captured Israeli soldiers. *Duet for Freedom* was a true love story with many wider implications. Princess Dina is honorary godmother to our son Ramsay – honorary because of our religious differences, she being of Islamic descent while we belong to the Greek Catholic church.

In 1993 Quartet published Pamela Cooper's lively and readable memoir, *A Cloud of Forgetting*. Pamela's first husband was Patrick Hore-Ruthven, the son of the first Earl of Gowrie, who died on a commando mission in the Western Desert during the Second World War. She was the mother of Grey Gowrie and the Islamic scholar Malise Ruthven and had a long-standing connection with the Middle East from the time when she worked with Freya Stark in Cairo on her Brotherhood of Freedom project, designed to promote ideas of democracy among influential Arabs. With her second husband, Major Derek Cooper, she became active in the post-war years in humanitarian relief work. They were instrumental in founding the charity Medical Aid for Palestinians (MAP) and in 1976 dramatically got themselves expelled from Israel for their outspoken expressions of indignation at the treatment they saw being meted out to Palestinians in the country. For six weeks in 1982 they were trapped in Beirut during the Israeli siege and bombardment in the events leading up to the massacres of Palestinians in Sabra and Chatila. Derek's side of the story of their adventurous life together was told in a biography by John Baynes, *For Love or Justice: The Life of a Quixotic Soldier*, which Quartet also published three years later.

It was a sign of the mark being made by Quartet that in 1994 Peter Lewis made us the focus of an article in a double issue of a prestigious literary journal, *Panurge*, entitled 'Quartet & Arab Women'. He selected four Quartet titles: Djura's *The Veil of Silence*, Aïcha Lemsine's *The Chrysalis*, Sabiha Khemir's *Waiting in the Future for the Past to Come* and Hanan al-Shaykh's *Women of Sand and Myrrh*; but first he assessed the situation in British publishing for translations intended for the domestic market. The situation in general, he concluded, was dire, John Calder's departure in despair for Paris having said much about the 'closed, reactionary intellectual climate in Britain'. Calder and Marion Boyars had previously made great efforts, together and under their separate imprints, to introduce into Britain new writing from abroad, but now silver linings were hard to find. Quartet Books, on the other hand, had 'been pursuing what may be called the Calder–Boyars enterprise with considerable imagination'.

In 1993, for example, Quartet published fiction and non-fiction titles translated from a number of European languages, including Romanian and Swedish as well as French, Spanish and Russian. In spite of having high reputations in their own countries, most of these authors are unknown in Britain, although the list does include Julien Green, translations of whose fiction first appeared decades ago.

Even more unusual and enterprising, however, has been Quartet's commitment to what it calls the 'Middle East', but which includes most of the Arab world.

The evidence indicated that writing in such countries as Morocco and Algeria was 'flourishing as never before'. The French 'colonial connection and its francophone legacy' meant there was a significantly better situation in France for the publishing of this new literature, but recognition in Britain was still 'barely perceptible'. The common thread in the four books he had under consideration was that their authors' primary purpose was to 'explore and give voice to the experience of women in their cultures', though none of them could be said to be writing feminist polemics. The lack of educational opportunities would have made such attempts at writing impossible for even the preceding generation. Djura, in telling the story of the violence against herself encountered within her own family in *The Veil of Silence* (translated by Dorothy S. Blair), was speaking for all those women 'who keep silent out of fear, who seek a decent life while they are forbidden even to exist'. Yet she still tried to hold on to those positive elements in her heritage that she could identify with, her song troupe, Djurdjura, having the aim of singing 'out loud what their mothers would only murmur under their breath'.

In *The Chrysalis*, Aïcha Lemsine gave a historic sweep to these cultural changes in Algerian society over two generations, where a young woman who has broken free to become a doctor is sucked back into and almost destroyed by the old ways, the situation only being redeemed by her stepmother's defiance of convention and show of womanly solidarity. Sabiha Khemir's *Waiting in the Future for the Past to Come* was unusual in that it was written in English in the first place. It reached out for a more mythic, storytelling way of giving an account of the changes in women's experiences and expectations in post-independence Tunisia. The collision between tradition and modernity was there, but with 'a sense of new life emerging from the old without a radical severing of connections with the past'.

Hanan al-Shaykh's *Women of Sand and Myrrh* was a follow-up to her first translated novel, *The Story of Zahra*, that Quartet published with success in 1986. *Women of Sand and Myrrh* (translated by Catherine Cobham) inter-wove the stories of four women living in an unnamed Arab country in the Arabian Gulf. Two of them belong to the country itself, the other two are Lebanese and American respectively. Al-Shaykh, said Lewis, 'is primarily a psychological novelist, exploring the inner lives of her main characters as they try to define themselves through their relationships with women and men . . . in a social context that inhibits their potential for development and fulfilment'.

In Lewis's view, only one of the four books he had listed would have been available in Britain had there not been a publisher in London committed to issuing 'a substantial number of books in translation'. On the continent most countries – including a large one like Germany with no shortage of writers of its own – had an abundant supply of books translated from English.

The reverse is not true. To its credit, Quartet has been doing a great deal to rectify this state of affairs, and its advocacy of writers from the Arab world is particularly to be applauded. Very little normally reaches us from these countries, and this is most regrettable when literary activity there is flourishing as never before. Perhaps the next time an Arab writer is awarded the Nobel Prize for Literature, Brits will not look totally mystified and resort to snideries about positive discrimination being exercised in favour of unheard-of second-raters from the Third World.

The following summaries of other selected fiction that we published in this area will help to give the reader a flavour of what was certainly expanding into a major list worthy of close attention. *My Grandmother's Cactus: Stories by Egyptian Women* (translated and introduced by Marilyn Booth) was an anthology of stories by the latest generation of women writers in Egypt. Like some of the others already mentioned, they often featured experiments with new narrative patterns that drew on legend and myth. *Beneath a Sky of Porphyry* (translated by Dorothy S. Blair) was a second novel from Aïcha Lemsine, this one being set at the time of Algeria's war of liberation from the French, telling of the effects of the conflict on the lives of a group of villagers. In much the same vein was *Fantasia: An Algerian Cavalcade* by Assia Djebar (translated by Dorothy S. Blair), which set the life of a young girl against the same background of conflict, based in part on eyewitness accounts of ruthless acts of barbarism by the French colonial forces. *Return to Jerusalem* by Hassan Jamal Husseini, a leading Palestinian diplomat and businessman, was a novel (written in English) that told the story of a Palestinian journalist arrested in Kafkaesque circumstances in Jerusalem by the Israeli security forces and absorbed into Israel's prison system to suffer the authorities' interrogation techniques alternating between brutality and cajolery.

The genre of historical novel was also represented, including an international bestseller, *Leo the African* by Amin Maalouf (translated by Peter Sluglett), based on the colourful life of the sixteenth-century geographer and traveller Leo Africanus, author of the renowned *Description of Africa*, written in Italy after he had been captured by a Sicilian pirate. *Elissa* by a Tunisian author, Fawzi Mellah (translated by Howard Curtis), was set between the eighth century BC and the present, and concerns a scholar who purports to be translating a letter from a collection of Punic tablets that tells of Elissa's fabulous voyage after fleeing Tyre, which leads to her becoming Queen of

Carthage (aka Dido); though he loses track of what he has translated and what he has invented.

Another novel set in Alexandria by Edwar al-Kharrat, *City of Saffron* (translated by Frances Liardet), centred on the growing up of a boy who slowly gains an awareness of the nature of the lives of the adult men and women around him. *Behind Closed Doors: Tales of Tunisian Women* by Monia Hejaiej described the importance of oral storytelling in the lives of three women of Tunis, their views competing and contradictory, in preserving a conservative, moralistic attitude to set against the rebellious and subversive. From Libya there came a distinguished trilogy, *Gardens of the Night* by Ahmed Faqih (translated by Russell Harris, Amin al-'Ayouti and Suraya 'Allam), published in one volume. It began with *I Shall Present You with Another City*, where the narrator is in Edinburgh as a student, writing a thesis on sex and violence in the *Arabian Nights*; the second title in the sequence, *These Are the Borders of My Kingdom*, found him back in Libya in a loveless marriage, suffering a breakdown which brings on trances that make him think he is a prince in the *Arabian Nights*, falling in love with a beautiful princess; and the third was *A Tunnel Lit by One Woman*, in which a female colleague seems to embody the princess of his visions, though the reality gradually evolves towards disillusion.

The theme of North African migrant workers in France was the subject of *Solitaire* by a Moroccan author living in France, Tahar Ben Jelloun. Ben Jelloun had a powerful imagination, as *Solitaire* (translated by Gareth Stanton and Nick Hindley) showed. His twenty-six-year-old central character is condemned by emigration and exile to be trapped in both internal and outward isolation – his own thoughts and the hatred and racism on the streets. Another novel by Ben Jelloun, *The Sand Child*, was the story of a family where the father can produce only daughters, and when the eighth arrives vows that she must be brought up as a boy; with the result that her/his future is marked by the deceptions and hypocrisies that dissect Arab society. The sequel to this, *The Sacred Night* (translated by Alan Sheridan), took up the story of the boy becoming a woman after the father's death, struggling to be reborn in a corrupt, enslaving society through suffering and mutilation. *The Sacred Night* was winner of the 1987 Prix Goncourt.

The input of Jennifer Bradshaw (now Erdal) meanwhile steadily built up a list of Russian titles reflecting aspects of Soviet and post-Soviet history and Russian culture in general. One of the earliest was Vladimir Kornilov's *Girls to the Front*, the first of this writer's books to appear in English and one which gave an unromanticized portrayal of women conscripted to dig trenches outside Moscow as the Germans advanced on the city in 1941. *Novy Mir* had accepted it for publication back in 1971 until it was decreed that its description of events in the Great Patriotic War were 'incorrect'. *The Women's Decameron* by Julia Voznesenskaya presented in fictional form the voices of women telling of their experiences under Soviet Communism, using the device of a maternity ward placed under quarantine to bring them together to exchange their stories. Other titles by Voznesenskaya followed. *The Star Chernobyl* (translated by Alan Myers) told a story of three sisters, one of whom, Anna, hears about the disaster at the nuclear plant from abroad and tries to ascertain its extent through her second sister, Anastasia. Both are concerned for the third sister, Aneka, who worked at the power station; Anastasia's search in the 'Dead Zone' leads her into a labyrinth that is a devastating condemnation of official incompetence and deception. *Letters of Love: Women Political Prisoners in Exile and the Camps* was Voznesenskaya's compilation of authentic letters from women prisoners in the Gulag. It prompted Mary Kenny to say in the *Sunday Telegraph* that 'Voznesenskaya could be another Solzhenitsyn'.

Edward Kusnetsov's *Russian Novel* (translated by Jennifer Bradshaw herself, as was Leonid Borodin's *The Year of Miracle and Grief*) used a 'novel within a novel' technique to illustrate the dangers of non-conformity in an authoritarian conformist society, as one character writes a novel about a friend whose hopes of happiness have been dashed after he has been framed for a crime of which he is innocent. 'The twin faces of Life and Literature grimace from the book like theatre masks,' said the *London Review of Books*. Victor Nekrasov's *Postscripts* (translated by Michael Falchikov and Dennis Ward) was a collection of short stories that welded fact, fiction and memory into elegiac accounts of Russian life from the Great Patriotic War onwards. *Galina Brezhnev and Her Gypsy Lover* by Stanley Laudan was a documentary account of the bizarre relationship between Brezhnev's daughter and the gypsy playboy, thief and con artist Boris Buryata, who used her protection to run spectacular rings round the KGB, till they finally managed to put a stop to his career.

Three relatively little-known novellas by Leo Tolstoy (translated and introduced by Kyril and April Fitzlyon) were published together in one volume: *A Landowner's Morning, Family Happiness* and *The Devil*. They were all largely autobiographical and written at different points in his career. Fyodor Dostoevsky was represented by *Winter Notes on Summer Impressions* (translated by Kyril Fitzlyon), the first English translation of impressions he gathered from a journey he made to Western Europe – and to Britain – in 1862. There was a major new translation of *The Brothers Karamazov* (by Richard Pevear and Larissa Volokhonsky, who also included annotations), Sidney Monas, of the University of Texas, thinking it, 'Far and away the best translation of Dostoevsky into English that I have seen . . . Faithful to the original text, and it is, like the original, extremely readable – and a gripping novel.' *Summer in Baden-Baden: From the Life of Dostoevsky* was written as a biographical novel by Leonid Tsypkin (translated by Roger and Angela Keys) and had 'a fantastic realism that burlesques Dostoevsky's own . . . a crazily marvellous book', thought Victoria Glendinning in the *London Daily News*, while Nikolai Tolstoy said in the *Sunday Times* that, 'Though a novel, it reproduces real life . . . persuasively.' Real life was also emphatically there with Dostoevsky's *A Writer's Diary, Volume I: 1873–76* (translated and annotated by Kenneth Lantz and introduced by Gary Saul Morson), which packed over eight hundred pages with an intensive flow of writing that embraced everything from humorous anecdotes to trial reports, autobiography, philosophy, polemics and original stories. Besides writing it, the author had made the time to edit and issue it as a monthly publication.

In parallel with these other developments, the Quartet Encounters list, presided over by Stephen Pickles, continued to grow prodigiously. It kept to its literary focus in the main, though widened its scope to bring in other items of international cultural interest. Lou Andreas-Salomé's *The Freud Journal* (translated by Stanley W. Leavy and introduced by Mary-Kay Wilmers) was a personal view of Freud's studies and relations with colleagues against the background of a literary coterie that included the poet Rilke; Rilke himself was represented by *Rodin and Other Prose Pieces*, he having at one time been secretary to the great sculptor (translated by G. Craig Huston and introduced by William Tucker), *Early Prose*, which included memories as well short fiction pieces, and his *Selected Letters 1902–1926* (translated by R. F. C. Hull and introduced by John Bayley). Gaston Bachelard's *The Psychoanalysis of Fire* (translated by Alan M. C. Ross and introduced by Northrop Frye) was an idiosyncratic exploration of ideas concerning fire in human evolution and their symbolic and subconscious connotations. Bruno Walter's *Gustav Mahler* (translated by Lotte Walter Lindt and introduced by Michael Tanner) was an indispensable source book for any study of the composer, coming from the foremost interpreter of his music, who had been deeply and personally involved in realizing much of it in performance.

With over a score of other titles to choose from, the following list can only be highly selective, but will show the consistency of quality achieved by Pickles.

Hermann Broch, the son of a Jewish textile manufacturer in Vienna, was an industrialist, mathematician and philosopher who came to literature reluctantly as the only way of expressing his thoughts and feelings. *The Guiltless* (translated by Ralph Manheim with an afterword by the author) was a book he called 'a novel in eleven stories'; it portrayed a group of eleven lives in the pre-Hitler period. *The Sleepwalkers*, one of his major achievements (translated by Willa and Edwin Muir and introduced by Michael Tanner), was a trilogy that traced from the 1880s the social erosion and dissolution that culminated in the Nazi era. Another Viennese novelist of stature was Heimito von Doderer, who was an active Nazi up to 1938. His vast trilogy, *The Demons* (translated by Willa and Edwin Muir and introduced by Michael Hamburger), explored every strand of life possible in Vienna, both comic and tragic, where the 'demons' concerned arose from people's minds in the tumultuous years between the two world wars. Thomas Bernhard was born in Holland but grew up in Austria and wrote in German, becoming, George Steiner considered, 'one of the masters of contemporary European fiction' in the post-war years. *Concrete* (translated by Martin McLintock and introduced by Martin Chalmers) was a story in his 'black idyll' style about a writer who goes away to start a project but finds himself obsessively following an altogether different line of inquiry set off by a tragic memory. *On the Mountain* (translated by Russell Stockman with an afterword by Sophie Wilkins) showed him working in parallel with themes to be found in Kafka and Beckett in a novel written as one sentence.

E. M. Cioran had been born in Romania in 1911, but had won a scholarship in Paris and subsequently made the decision to live in France and write in French, though he said he had no nationality – 'the best possible status for an intellectual'. He was regarded as a foremost contemporary European thinker, the heir of Kierkegaard, Nietzsche and Wittgenstein, who wrote incomparable, elegantly styled essays on the state of man in the modern world. Five of his collections found a place on the list (four of them being translated by Richard Howard): *Anathemas and Admirations* (introduced by Tom McGonigle), in which incisive estimates of literary figures were interspersed with caustic aphorisms; *A Short History of Decay* (introduced by Michael Tanner), whose theme was the 'philosophical viruses' of the twentieth century; *The Temptation to Exist* (introduced by Susan Sontag), a 'dance of ideas and debates' on 'impossible states of being'; and *The Trouble with Being Born* (introduced by Benjamin Ivry), which started out with the proposition that the disaster of life begins with the fact of birth, 'that laughable accident'. The fifth title (translated and introduced by Ilinca Zarifopol-Johnston) was *On the Heights of Despair*, a youthful work, written in Romania, which showed him to be already a 'theoretician of despair'.

Representing Swedish literature was, first, Stig Dagerman, whom Michael Meyer thought to be 'the best writer of his generation in Sweden and one of the best in Europe'. *A Burnt Child* (translated by Alan Blair and introduced by Laurie Thompson) was set in Stockholm in a family where the mother has died, the drama being played out between the husband and son and, respectively, the father's ageing mistress and the son's timid fiancée. *German Autumn* (translated and introduced by Robin Fulton) gave a documentary portrait of the Germans in defeat immediately after the fall of the Third Reich which courageously saw them as suffering individuals. *The Games of Night* (translated by Naomi Walford and introduced by Michael Meyer) was a collection of stories showing his versatility. *The Snake* (translated by Laurie Thompson) was a *tour de force* where the threads of disparate stories, arising from a conscript army camp, are brought together in a denouement. Then came Sweden's Nobel Prize-winning Pär Lagerkvist who had two titles in the list: *The Dwarf* (translated by Alexandra Dick and introduced by Quentin Crewe), a dark historical tale of a Machiavellian dwarf at the court of a Renaissance prince; and *Guest of Reality* (translated and introduced by Robin Fulton), a set of three stories linking the growing of a boy into a young man. A major novel of social concern from Sweden was Per Olov Enquist's *The March of the Musicians* (translated by Joan Tate), which told about the political uprising of the workers in a remote northern part of the country against their exploitation by sawmill owners and browbeating by hellfire preachers on Sundays; the author's profound empathy with his characters gave this small episode in Sweden's labour history a universal resonance.

Gabriele D'Annunzio was a leading writer of the so-called Decadent school. *The Flame* (translated and introduced by Susan Bassnett) was his scandalous novel about a passionate affair between a young writer and a great actress, in which they battle for supremacy in love and art; it was scandalous because based on his own relationship with Eleanora Duse. *Nocturne and Five Tales of Love and Death* (translated and introduced by Raymond Rosenthal) was a selection of his prose fiction demonstrating what a formidable pioneer D'Annunzio had been as a writer. Equally pioneering was his compatriot and contemporary Luigi Pirandello, known mainly for his experimental plays, though his short stories were also among the greatest in literature. Those selected for *Short Stories* (translated and introduced by Frederick May) showed his concern with the masks people use socially and their interplay with the reality behind them. Elio Vittorini was a writer from Sicily who aimed for 'neo-realism' in his work and produced an undisputed masterpiece in *Conversations in Sicily* (translated by Wilfrid David and introduced by Stephen Spender): first published in 1939, the censorship it was constrained by gave it an underlying power in the story of a young man's journey back to Sicily to console his mother after his father had deserted her. From the next generation, Pier Paolo Pasolini was seen primarily as a film-maker of originality in Britain, though in his native Italy he was regarded rather more as a poet, critic and novelist. Helping to rectify our view were *A Dream of Something* (translated and introduced by Stuart Hood), a story about three friends from northern Italy whose search for money takes them abroad, though they return home to political violence and an end to their carefree roistering; *Theorem* (translated and introduced by Stuart Hood), which was written in tandem with the making of a film of the same title, in which Terence Stamp played the young man gaining a sexual, emotional and intellectual hold over a rich bourgeois family; and *Roman Nights and Other Stories* (translated by John Shepley and introduced by Jonathan Keates), a selection of five stories from Pasolini's miscellaneous writings that reflected the cultural changes taking place in post-war Italian society.

Yevgeny Zamyatin chose exile from Soviet Russia in 1931, foreseeing the clash between writers and the state that lay ahead. *A Soviet Heretic* (translated by Mirra Ginsburg and introduced by Alex M. Shane) was a collection of his writings on fellow writers and the condition of literature in the Soviet Union, as well as his letter to Stalin, seeking voluntary exile, and his letter of resignation from the Soviet Writers' Union. The status of Osip Mandelstam as the pre-eminent Russian poet of the twentieth century gave him no protection from murderous NKVD brutality. *The Noise of Time and Other Prose Piece*s (collected, translated and introduced by Clarence Brown) was a selection from the range of his writing, including a work of invective and outrage against the state's official campaign against him. Yury Tynyanov's *Lieutenant Kijé & Young Vitushishnikov* (translated and introduced by Mirra Ginsburg) were two glittering novellas by a Russian master satirist about abuses in the eighteenth and nineteenth centuries which allowed him to be obliquely critical of those of the Soviet regime. Abram Tertz, the *nom de plume* for Andrei Synyavsky in his *samisdat* publications (that won him hard labour and exile), wrote *Little Jinx* (translated by Larry P. Joseph and Rachel May and introduced by Edward J. Brown) as a black farce containing the line: 'Were we not guilty, neither Hitler nor Stalin could have surfaced among us.' *The Fatal Eggs & Other Soviet Satire* (translated, edited and introduced by Mirra Ginsburg) was a famous subversive anthology by seventeen boldly comic writers, including Mikhail Bulgakov, Ilf and Petrov and Zamyatin.

There were also the stories of Aharon Appelfeld, with their subtle and profound recreations of life in Europe's Jewish communities as they moved into the gathering shadows of the Holocaust; and Giorgio Bassani's artistic account of the impact on a Jewish family in Italy as Mussolini's fascism geared up the anti-Semitic component in its laws under pressure from Nazi Germany. Those titles have been given earlier, with the list of Jewish authors published by Quartet. Another important aspect of the Quartet Encounters list was the way it demonstrated the importance of literature in delineating the dimensions of human experience and suffering within the history of the twentieth century's traumatic events. While this summary of the list has not by any means been comprehensive, it is enough to show there was a spirit of adventure at work in Goodge Street for which it would have been hard to find an equivalent elsewhere in British publishing at the time.

Fifty-four

The Asprey success story continued without signs of slowing down. The press was hard put to it to find superlatives to describe the company's achievement over a relatively short period. Since I was the architect of the expansionist policy – and not the City's ideal image of a chief executive of a public company – the media, and the gossip columnists in particular, were keen to cover every aspect of my activities. This blitzkrieg of personal exposure was now causing me some concern as it provoked resentment in the Asprey family circle which might become a source of conflict. I had to tread carefully to maintain solidarity with John, aware there were ominous signs that our relationship was already under threat. In the main, we were still close, but not as close as we had been.

Our working relationship had so far been free of family interference but a concern was John's susceptibility to outside influence. Whereas no problems arose from this when we operated at close proximity, out of sight John was not easily containable. He would be guided by some notion that had little basis in reality. As the conglomerate grew, the division between our tasks grew wider. It prevented us from spending so much time together. This was a worry in itself. I was no longer able to exercise the kind of restraint that John needed to function at his best. He would get carried away in buying stock, eager to prove to the trade that he was in control of his family's destiny. In this way he earned himself the title of 'Mr Big' at the Basel Fair. On the basis of his excellent track record, he began to harbour a belief in his own infallibility as a salesman. It was all done impetuously, but the side-effects were beginning to bring about an imbalance in the ratio of sales to the stock being purchased or held. It was a disparity which had the potential to become serious if left unchecked, and we could not afford to ignore it. But on the surface at least, and in the midst of the euphoria of success, such matters appeared inconsequential as no one with responsibility wanted to cause a fracture in the relationship between John and myself; the belief was that having worked so well up to this point it was bound to return to its proper level.

Against this background, Asprey announced more acquisitions and further expansions. In a deal worth one point eight million pounds (which also included one freehold house), the group bought four shops in the Channel Islands from the Signet Group – three in Jersey and one in Guernsey. They were purchased in the name of Watches of Switzerland, though it was not planned that they would trade under that title. As the *Retail Jeweller* reported:

> In Jersey, two shops, both former H. Samuel stores, will trade as a Jewellers and Silversmiths Co. and a Zeus store.
>
> The third heralds another diversification for the group – Time Jewellers will cease trading in jewellery to become a confectioners under the banner The Chocolate Shop.
>
> In Guernsey the acquired property will continue trading as Jewellers and Silversmiths. Mr Attallah said all thirty-three staff in the new venture are being retained.

Excluding in-store concessions, this brought the total of group shops outside mainland Britain to about fifteen. The four premises concerned were our first outlets in the Channel Islands. In the same week, our watch distributor, J. W. Benson, was opening a Zeus store in the duty-free zone at Waterloo Station to serve passengers using the Channel Tunnel. Zeus was a new trading name, launched in the previous financial year, to target a younger client base through offering a lower price range than Watches of Switzerland. Counting the UK shops and the Mappin & Webb branch in Prague, we now had more than fifty outlets overall. 'Mr Attallah told *Retail Jeweller* that his company was always looking for new opportunities and more purchases were likely.'

The various acquisitions and incentives had already helped to raise the group's pre-tax profits by close on eighteen per cent to twenty-five point four million pounds in the twelve months to 31 March. As the *Financial Times* recorded:

> Although the Asprey business continued to contribute more than 75 per cent of sales, acquisitions made during the past two years contributed £18.6 million to turnover, helping to push the total up by almost 30 per cent from £144.7 million to £187.6 million.
>
> On a year-by-year basis sales rose by 16.8 per cent . . .
>
> A final dividend of 4.8p is recommended, making a total of 6.05p (5.1p) for the year.
>
> Earnings per share jumped to 21.12p (14.44p), after an 'abnormally low tax charge' due to an overprovision last time.

The strategy of enlarging the customer base to counteract the severity of future recessions was being accounted a success in a market in which recovery was still awaited. 'Naim Attallah, Asprey's Action Man' was the heading in *Women's Wear Daily* in the United States: 'Via a series of acquisitions, he has elevated Asprey from the two-store, $12 million firm it was less than five years ago to a mini-empire of European fine-jewellery retailers and design houses.'

What's significant about the line-up, Attallah pointed out, is that each division addresses a slightly different consumer need. Garrard, for instance, is for the customer who's looking for the absolutely one-of-a-kind piece, such as a very special wedding ring. Mappin & Webb, on the other hand, is the traditional shop for gifts or self purchases. For the person who wants the highly unusual piece – a jewelled octopus ring with moving parts, for example – there is René Boivin's line.

It was also a question, while expanding organically, of making the group 'less vulnerable to the whims of the very rich who have become much more selective in their buying', as I told the *Evening Standard*. We had 'responded to the change in trading patterns in jewellery retailing', I said to *The Times*. 'While wealthy customers are now spending less, middle-market customers are spending more than ever,' though it inevitably meant lower margins. 'Asprey remains a sparkler,' proclaimed the *Daily Telegraph*, but,

'The wealthy will still pay a premium to adorn themselves,' sighs Naim Attallah, the colour-coordinated chief executive of Asprey, 'but they will no longer accept prices that are out of this world.'
That explains why margins have fallen in the jewellery group . . .

'Sharper than a serpent's tooth,' said the *Daily Telegraph* 'City Diary' in the same issue:

Naim Attallah, philogynist, publisher of the *Literary Review* and chief executive of Asprey – which revealed its results yesterday – is a sensitive soul. 'I love nature and the sense of total freedom enjoyed by animals that we have lost,' he waffles, explaining why his office is littered with paintings and sculptures of lions and tigers, and a tiger skin.
The man named Attullah-Disgusting by *Private Eye* also goes on to tell me how, rather like the Queen's experience with her corgis, he was bitten on the neck and hand by two of his Dobermann pinschers recently, when he tried to stop them fighting.

The Asprey shop in Bond Street was still making the lion's share of the profits in the group as a whole, as I told the *Birmingham Post*, it having accounted for 'three quarters of last year's £25.4 million group profit'.

But profits from the Asprey showroom can depend heavily on the activities of a handful of big spenders – though Mr Attallah will not confirm that the

Sultan of Brunei's legendary spending spree in London last autumn was a factor in the year to March . . .

'There are a few people who go round and feed the big jewellery houses of the world,' Mr Attallah said. 'But you cannot rely on their trade for ever. You cannot build a business on the assumption that they will be there for ever, or that someone will replace them.

'Look at what is happening in the Middle East. Asia is the biggest market in the world now.'

Nevil Boyd Maunsell in his 'City View' column in the *Birmingham Post* commented separately that I was developing 'a view of the world as a place where the distribution of people who are not only rich but inclined to spend their wealth is constantly shifting'.

Five years ago who would have thought Saudi Arabia was about to become a debtor nation or that the luckless Kuwaitis could be reduced to spending their oil revenues on such serious things as reconstruction and tanks?

Nor indeed that Mr Attallah would be pinpointing Glasgow and Prague as the two centres to open up with new Mappin & Webb shops this year?

After escaping the worst of the recession have the Scots really abandoned their canny financial customs? Or just the Glaswegians?

And Prague? Mr Attallah is convinced there is a lot of spending power there. Russian spending power, much of it. Even two years ago unthinkable.

For whatever reason, Prague has become a commercial honey-pot where the small flat hired for Asprey's manager will cost 6,000 German marks a month, say £2,400.

We may have been hesitating over the Shanghai initiative, but, regarding the Prague venture, Dominic Prince in the 'Money' column in the *Sunday Express* found me 'very bullish indeed': 'Prague has more tourists than anywhere else,' I told him. 'In my view it will become the economic capital of eastern Europe.'

And in the UK things are expanding rapidly too. Attallah, aware of the reliance on operations like Asprey and Watches of Switzerland for profits, is intent on expanding the Zeus operation.

Zeus started life in Sheffield as a Watches of Switzerland outlet but soon changed into, as Attallah puts it: 'A more affordable outlet for young people. You get a well-crafted watch, even if you pay less for it.'

Appropriately for a man with such interest in the timepiece business, Attallah himself always wears two watches.

'I love them,' he says. 'I'm always racing against time. It gives me the variety if I can look in different directions.'

A recent additional competitive factor in the luxury-goods market was the new role the auction houses were suddenly taking upon themselves. They were assuming the function of a retailer with the preposterous claim that it was cheaper to acquire jewellery and *objets d'art* through them than from an established retailer. An article by Anthony Thorncroft appeared in *Country Life* to give credence to this theory. I felt very strongly that its text was biased in favour of the auction houses and fired off a letter to the editor to present a counter-balance to the argument:

> In the section on jewellery in the article 'Speculate to Accumulate', Anthony Thorncroft advises your readers to purchase their jewellery direct from the auction houses in order to 'buy a good investment and save the retailer's profit'. As if to emphasize the point, a Sotheby's photograph displaying jewellery recently sold at their auction rooms is featured on the page opposite.
>
> In the past few years, auction houses have encroached on the retailing sector more and more, arguably to the disadvantage of both. I should like to take issue with Mr Thorncroft and his advice.
>
> Mr Thorncroft has not mentioned that an item purchased at auction within the financial constraints of the purchaser does not necessarily ensure a good investment. The buyer may not have the required expertise to evaluate the item or to judge its authenticity. It is not unknown for items purchased to fail to match their descriptions in catalogues.
>
> Besides, one of the most important factors in retailing is the after-sales service – not a feature of the auction houses. It is also worth remembering that the commission added by the saleroom to the purchases is not inconsiderable.

*

By July 1994 the *Oldie* magazine was in crisis again. The money ran out and the entire capital of the company, which stood at seven hundred and twenty thousand pounds (five hundred and forty thousand of this being my own contribution) had been extinguished. I was no longer willing to sink further funds into a project that looked unlikely ever to succeed in the form it had taken. The magazine was costing twenty thousand pounds a month, and a much larger investment was needed for such a burden to be sustained. A total rethink and restructuring was also imperative if the magazine was to have any prospects of survival. Where we had all gone wrong was in our inability to contain the overheads, which were clearly engulfing the initial modest revenues, while relying in part on a short-term upturn in advertising and circulation. In the real world, such a degree of optimism is nothing if not foolhardy.

Once the news broke that all was not well with the *Oldie*, the media coverage became incessant, fired up to some degree by Richard Ingrams's high profile and my own involvement with Asprey. The newspapers had a field day, spreading doom and gloom about the situation as if the demise of the *Oldie* would be a national catastrophe. The headlines varied, but the message was clear, the presumption being that the *Oldie* was already dead and buried; that despite all the publicity, any hopes of a revival had been abandoned and not a single investor could be found willing to come to its rescue. Abundant messages of sympathy poured in, but when it came to hard cash the commodity was unavailable. The reaction of the public to the closure was muted in some quarters while in others a tacit silence provided no consolation. It was only the existing readers of the magazine who put on any display of real emotion and wrote many letters of support to the *Oldie*, pleading with its directors not to let it fold and to reconsider their decision.

From this point on, every minute twist and turn in the drama was given wider publicity than could ever have been expected. Richard's face was to be seen peering out from every broadsheet on the news-stands as he tried to drum up extra backing from the media by extolling the virtues of keeping the magazine alive. Running the campaign to shore up public endorsement of the magazine was a task Richard performed extremely well. As a result, some positive noises began to be heard from potential investors, though they fizzled out as quickly as they came. But then, for no logical reason, a new wave of optimism suddenly rose to a crescendo as suggestions poured in from employees and well-wishers. The founders, despite the hopelessness of the situation, began to be carried away by the regenerated zeal arising from within and spilling out to enthuse many who had never heard of the *Oldie* before. While even I was beginning to soften my stance, I remained convinced that unless there was a major rejigging of the way the magazine operated its chances of survival were remote.

The press meanwhile continued with its speculation unabated. There were those who took a sympathetic, regretful line, while others saw the magazine as an Aunt Sally ripe for some knockabout fun. 'The *Oldie* limps to an early grave,' announced Alexandra Frean in *The Times* on 19 July, with falling sales forcing the closure of this magazine for the over fifty-fives, 'which was widely believed to be a hoax when it was launched two years ago'. Richard Ingrams had conceded that 'his crusade against the "cultural isolation" of the older citizen had failed and the fortnightly magazine was simply not selling well enough to justify its continued existence. Its last issue will be published on 5 August.'

Auberon Waugh in the *Daily Telegraph* the next day saw it as a symptom of the advertising industry's misplaced belief in the youth market: 'Advertisers refused to support anything which failed to set its sights at the young despite the generous and loyal support of its proprietor, my friend Mr Naim Attallah, who deserves a statue in the hall of modern British heroes.'

It had been a bad week for Mr Ingrams, declared 'Mr Pepys' in the *Evening Standard* on the 22nd, the 'sad, if inevitable demise of the *Oldie* magazine' having seemed 'to be greeted by the majority of London's literati with crudely disguised glee'.

> This is a shame. Huge unsold piles of the magazine were occasionally a nuisance to pedestrians but, all in all, it was nothing if not an amusing addition to the news-stands. Now, though, unless new funding can be found it will be gone for good. We are told that Naim Attallah, a wholly decent man, who invested some £580,000 in the venture, has had enough and is not willing to continue stumping up £20,000 a month to keep it going.

Mary Kenny, in the *Sunday Telegraph* of 24 July, assumed the *Oldie* was dead and gone for sure:

> Sad that the *Oldie* magazine is no more. But it was a brilliant try, and something like it will one day appear again. Naim Attallah, its major financier, is a great hero.

The *Sunday Times* made the same assumption and asked, 'Should we mourn it?' *Oldie* readers who 'felt cast adrift on a sea of yoof' only needed to turn to the previous Monday's *Daily Telegraph* to find the eighty-one-year-old William Deedes reporting in brilliant prose from a Rwandan refugee camp.

> Thus [wrote Mary Kenny], though I am sorry for Richard Ingrams personally, I am quite glad his experiment in oldie separatism has failed. The day may come when our old need their own magazine, but the fact that it has not come yet is generally to be applauded.

On another page of the *Sunday Times*, Joanna Pitman interviewed Richard Ingrams and extracted some of the lighter stories he had to tell.

> On a budget that would barely have fed a family of sparrows, he managed to produce a magazine stuffed with irreverent cartoons and columns that

poked gentle fun at the problems and the joys of the doddery. There were also regular contributions, many unsolicited, from the punters themselves. The 'Still With Us' column, which amounted to a series of premature obituaries, was written about 'people we thought were already dead'.

'Hugh Cudlipp (the former Mirror Group chairman) wrote in one day. I had always thought he was dead, so I invited him to write a "Still With Us" column and he produced a marvellous piece about his prostate problems.

'We had Germaine Greer as a regular and Barbara Cartland for a few weeks at the beginning. I had to sack her, though, because she kept on plugging those pills in her columns – some miracle cure that she had discovered for arthritis or something . . . Every time she mentioned these wretched things we used to get hundreds of people ringing up wanting to buy them.'

In *The Times*, on 27 July, Roy Greenslade lamented 'the likely loss of an oldish friend', but although it was possibly on its deathbed, it was refusing to go quietly.

Its loyal staff of eight have decided to work without pay in the hope of finding a new benefactor.

Their enthusiasm flies in the face of advice from those anxious young men in suits, known as accountants, who are convinced there is no prospect of the magazine breaking even . . .

Hark now to the I-told-you-sos. They will say it was flawed from the start, always a maverick publication, a whim, a vanity. It was a joke magazine, a self-indulgence for its founder and editor, Richard Ingrams, something amusing for the former *Private Eye* chief to pass his time.

All correct up to a point, Lord Copper. But so what? For a couple of years the *Oldie* has brightened the hours of all who have chanced to read it, whether strapped into their nursing-home chairs, shaking in a dentist's waiting room or, like my mother, happily at home.

The *Oldie*, thought Mr Greenslade, was a 'little gem', a 'zimmer frame for the mind'. It wasn't the *Modern Review*, 'deconstructing and deriding', while politics of the *Spectator* or the *New Statesman* variety were 'blissfully absent', like the heavy-handed humour of the 'defunct *Punch*'.

The *Oldie* is a gentle, idiosyncratic magazine, easy on the eye, making a virtue of reminiscence without indulging in sentimentality. It has treated elderly people as grown-ups, not as has-beens in their dotage, venerating old age as a period of wisdom rather than as an excuse for the saccharin of nostalgia.

Toby Young, the editor of the *Modern Review*, gave his consideration to 'the short and undistinguished history of the *Oldie*' in the weekend *Financial Times* for 6/7 August. The announcement did not come as much of a shock, he said, for had it not been 'known in the media as the *Foldie* from virtually its first week of publication'? There were fairly obvious reasons for the *Oldie* and the *Modern Review* to have been seen as rivals: 'Our staff are bright, dynamic and forward-looking, theirs were befuddled, gouty and backward; we're young and well-dressed, they had bits of egg encrusted on their cardigans; we're fresh and talented, they smell of camphor.' The *Oldie* was 'never really intended for the elderly. Rather, it was for disgruntled, irascible, middle-aged people who felt sidelined by what they perceived as the media's obsession with "youth".' The magazine was 'poorly designed' and the writing was 'often tired and self-indulgent, showing few signs of being edited'. In Young's view, these 'low editorial standards' had been 'particularly disastrous' in a magazine relying on retail sales for its survival. 'The longest piece in the latest issue is a four-page interview with someone called [*sic*] Rumer Godden by, you guessed it, Naim Attallah.'

> In one sense, the *Oldie* can be judged a heroic failure. Like Eddie the Eagle, it deliberately ignored conventional wisdom and professional advice and, as a result, came crashing down to earth. No doubt its failure will confirm its contributors' dim view of the modern world . . .
>
> Perhaps you'll think it ungracious of me to crow at the *Oldie*'s failure, but, believe me, if the position were reversed they'd do the same . . .
>
> So farewell then, the *Oldie*. Keith's gran thought you were crap.

Mr Young suspected that by the time his readers got to read his piece the *Oldie* could well have folded already. In fact his assumptions were already out of date. With the pressure mounting to try and save the *Oldie*, and in the absence of anyone coming forward to help in its rescue, I had begun to think in terms of the inconceivable. How many times, I kept asking myself, will I need to be stung financially before I wake up and call it a day? Sentiment has always played a crucial role in my life. As the eternal sentimentalist, I have often acted against my better judgement. A drug addict may resolve to kick the habit but he needs the inner strength to do it. Whereas I have the strength, I lack the hardness of spirit which is a vital ingredient in the harsh world of business, where a ruthless disregard for sentiment is one of the most important prerequisites.

Provided there would be a major restructuring of the *Oldie* – slashing its overheads dramatically, reducing its staff and turning it into a monthly – I agreed I would continue with my backing for the magazine. In my heart of hearts, I knew this was a decision I would live to regret. Meanwhile the press in general welcomed the news, though there were still many who had their reservations. '*Oldie* resuscitated,' said *The Times* of 29 July, while the *Guardian* reported, 'It had one foot in the grave last week, but yesterday it took on a new lease of life.'

> Richard Ingrams, editor of the magazine aimed at the fifty-plus age group, said: 'It is very good news. I am reasonably hopeful about its survival.' . . . The full-time staff of nine will be reduced to two and it will move offices. Losses described last week as insurmountable, running at £20,000 a month, are likely to be reduced to under £4,000.

Richard Ingrams announced 'there would be a subscription drive and an attempt to capitalize on the publicity surrounding the magazine's premature obituaries' and 'denied the closure announcement had been a publicity gesture'.

Richard himself wrote in his column in the *Observer* of 31 July that it had been good to be able to report the reprieve of the *Oldie* at the end of that week, 'albeit as a monthly magazine and with a greatly reduced staff'. From all the letters he had received, he deduced there was 'a very loyal readership out there, whose tastes are not catered from by alternative organs'. The battle on behalf of the older v. the young was by no means won, however. Only that week he had 'received a polite letter from the BBC' telling him that his 'services on the Radio 4 *News Quiz* would no longer be required on a regular basis. The men in suits, it seemed, had decreed that "new voices" would be the order of the day.'

From the point of view of the staff of the *Oldie*, it was also pointed out, the rescue had been only partial. Most of them had to go and it fell to James Pembroke, at twenty-seven and a half the business manager, to have to tell them. According to one story in circulation, he then took himself into an office, closed the door and sat down before addressing himself in the empty room: 'Sorry, Pembroke, old chap, but we have to let you go too.'

Auberon Waugh had not been uncritical of the old *Oldie*, but he agreed to have a column in the new monthly version, despite having previously suggested it should be renamed the *Goldie* if it was ever refloated, this being a better title 'in the age of hormone replacement therapy, where the over-fifties own 70 per cent of the wealth and nearly 50 per cent of the free, disposable income'. The appointment provoked Hunter Davies into having a go at Bron in *You* magazine over his claims to genteel poverty. Accepting that his wage for editing the *Literary Review* must be modest, he nevertheless totted up his other sources of income speculatively – Bron's earnings from books, from book reviews for the *Daily Telegraph*, from his columns in the *Spectator* and now the *Oldie*, and his unearned income from the estate of his late father – and estimated that he must be raking in 'about £150,000 per annum'. 'Right, Bron,' he challenged, 'lie your way out of that.'

Meanwhile there was a report that the latest issue of the *Modern Review* was out, complete with an article crowing over the *Oldie*'s death.

*

With the crisis at the *Oldie* having been dealt with, and everyone involved in the drama resuming their usual activities, I was able to give some attention to what was happening at Quartet, particularly as I was due to host a party at the Groucho Club for Shirin Devrim's autobiography, *A Turkish Tapestry: The Shakirs of Istanbul*. *The Times* reported the occasion on 29 July and found Shirin there, 'a blue-blooded Turk . . . surrounded by royalty'.

> On my first glance around the room I took in Princess Esra Bereket Jah, wife of the Maharaja of Hyderabad and the author's niece; Princess Sumaya, daughter of the Crown Prince of Jordan; HRH the Crown Prince Alexander of Yugoslavia; and the Jordanian Ambassador.

Devrim's family tree had been highly distinguished, featuring a great-uncle who had been grand vizier of the Ottoman Empire, and a stepfather, Prince Zeid of Jordan, who had fought in the Arab Revolt alongside Lawrence of Arabia and become Iraq's first ambassador to Britain. Given such a background, asked *The Times*, 'wasn't a Soho drinking club a bit of a comedown?' Devrim admitted she had a few doubts, but said although it looked so scruffy, 'they assure me it's the place for the media'.

Shirin Devrim was herself more than all of this implied, coming from a family that was supremely artistic. Her father and mother were a writer and a renowned artist respectively. An uncle, known as 'The Fisherman of Halicarnassus', was considered a Turkish Hemingway. An aunt was an acclaimed etcher, her brother also a respected artist and a cousin one of Turkey's leading ceramicists. She was a national institution as a leading actress in Turkish theatre and the first woman director of the six city theatres in Istanbul. She had originally studied in America and become professor of drama at three American universities. Her book was as much the story of her family as of her own life.

Quartet's relentless pursuit of European authors continued:

> *Himmelfarb* by Michael Krüger, translated by Leslie Willson, was a bitter and often very funny comedy on the vanities of self-delusion.

Its protagonist, an anthropologist, receives a letter from someone he thought long dead, whom he had known in Brazil in 1942 when he was researching native customs. This was his former guide, Leo Himmelfarb, an expatriate German Jew whose intellectual vigour and curiosity had shown up his own inadequacies. He awaits this daunting reunion in trepidation, preparing to dismantle the life he has built for himself. Quartet had previously published two other novels by Krüger: *The End of the Novel* and *The Man in the Tower*.

The Green Elephant by Giorgio and Nicola Pressburger, translated by Piers Spence, was a parable set in the Jewish quarter of Budapest in the dying days of the Austro-Hungarian Empire and concerned the dream of a sausage-maker of being visited by a green elephant. An important rabbi interprets it as meaning destiny has great things in store for him, and from then on he can only think of the future, not the present. The years go by and he becomes bitter and disillusioned at the lack of any fulfilment, hoping only that his son might benefit from the promised change of luck. Through the son the prophesy eventually comes true in a way no one could have predicted. The authors were twins, who wrote two books together before Nicola's death in 1985.

The Innocents: Three Tales of Rome by Marco Lodoli, translated by Roma Keys, was a trilogy of urban stories about various marginalized characters caught between drifting and hoping, reality and dreams, on the sometimes violent streets of Rome. Through their restless desires they seek fulfilment or the achievement of fantastic deeds.

No Man's Land by Juan Carlos Onetti, translated by Peter Bush, was an early novel by the leading writer of his generation from Uruguay. He lived and worked in the city of Buenos Aires for many years until imprisoned by the military regime in Argentina; after his release he moved to Spain. It is about the lives of those whose parents came from Europe, hoping to build a better life in Argentina, but as Martin Seymour-Smith has said, the book's 'hero' is the city, which is seen 'as a disrupting force in the lives of people: as the malevolent power that prevents communication'; so to that extent he was an existentialist who anticipated rather then followed Sartre. Other Onetti titles published by Quartet were *Farewells & A Grave with No Name*, *The Pit & Tonight* and *Body Snatcher*.

Memory of Fire by Eduardo Galeano, translated by Cedric Belfrage, was another masterpiece of Latin-American literature from a Uruguayan writer, originally published in three volumes. It was a book of extra-ordinary scale, starting from the Indian creation myths and sweeping through history by way of the Spanish Conquest, the campaigns of Simón Bolívar and Pancho Villa to the Peróns and Pinochet, taking in other references from the North American continent to Thomas Jefferson, Billy the Kid, the Kennedys and Elvis Presley. The *Sunday Telegraph* thought it 'a work of dazzling originality . . . an intriguing and richly absorbing book, put together like pieces of a mosaic to reflect a grand and tragic picture'.

And then there was *Olympia* by Leni Riefenstahl, with an introduction by the eminent historian of film Kevin Brownlow. The collection of photographs was Leni Riefenstahl's tribute to the athletes of the 1936 Olympic Games, whose efforts she had filmed for posterity to make what many considered to be her cinematic masterpiece. The com-bination of stark realism and visual genius was revealed majestically in the full beauty of the duotone black-and-white reproductions. In capturing and presenting the divers, swimmers, sprinters, jumpers and others as the ultimate practitioners of their art form, she reached the pinnacle of her own art. The aesthetic of her lens gave a view of the epitome of the beauty of athleticism, the excitement of competition and the pressure of the political atmosphere.

For me, of course, to have published Leni Riefenstahl's *Olympia* was in keeping with Quartet's established tradition of publishing photo-graphic books of high distinction in our bid to rank supreme in this artistic medium. Not only were the photographs of the highest quality, but their impact was overwhelming. The historical relevance of the book was equally important. It was bound to remain a source of immense interest to academics and researchers into the Nazi era in Germany.

Fifty-five

For the financial press, Asprey was to remain a topic for discussion and scrutiny, its strategy a constant subject for analysis. In its dash for growth, said Caroline Southey in the *Financial Times*, Asprey was not yet 'reaching for the main market'. It remained to be seen whether the group could manage to hold on to 'its exclusivity and simultaneously achieve significant increases in sales volumes with better margins'. The aim, she reported, was to cut Asprey's contribution to profits to thirty-five per cent from seventy-five per cent, and so reduce the group's reliance on the Asprey business to a less vulnerable position with the wider customer base that was the company's constant pre-occupation. The additions had already made their presence felt and some notable improvements had been achieved, but

> Asprey's management still has a long way to go to improve the performance of the acquisitions. Many of the businesses were in bad shape and it has had to develop a corporate structure more compatible with a diversified group . . .
>
> Mr Attallah concedes the group will not achieve maximum growth through expansion alone. Of equal importance will be its ability to drive down costs.
>
> Although the group's jewellery-and gift-manufacturing capacity has been enhanced through the acquisitions, Mr Attallah believes little headway has been made in rationalizing and integrating production facilities.
>
> Asprey produces only 12 per cent of what it sells, far too little in Mr Attallah's view. He has set the group a target of 35 per cent by the end of the year.

The City analyst Peter Temple produced a lengthy six-page company profile on Asprey. He was rather positive about the future and considered the shares' rating as looking too low. The policy of expansion by acquisition to broaden the customer base should, he thought, increasingly bear fruit in terms of enhanced profits growth. Meanwhile the group's fortunes were tied to some degree to the economic cycle in the United Kingdom, though an increasing proportion of sales was being generated abroad. After summarizing the rationale behind the acquisitions programme, he concluded it had been 'an attempt to broaden its operations away from the traditional Bond Street clientele to include a broader cross-section of the world's affluent'. The investment made in the acquired companies was 'probably as much about acquiring customer information as about acquiring the actual "brands" themselves'. Alongside a certain complementarity, the opportunity 'of marketing to a wider customer base' was also present.

He confirmed the company had come close 'to losing its independence in the 1970s when a family feud led to Dunhill (now part of the Vendome luxury-products combine) acquiring a substantial stake in the company', which had been used as a base from which to launch an eleven-milion-pound hostile bid that valued the company at some fourteen million pounds.

> Dunhill's opportunism and its identification of the company as an under-valued property was borne out when, through the rest of the 1980s, the group's profitability increased steadily . . .
>
> However, the structure of the group in its present form really dates back only to August 1991, when the group acquired Garrard and Mappin & Webb . . .

The string of further acquisitions had then followed steadily, and there was little doubt 'that similar acquisitions' would happen in due course, given that the group was 'anxious both to spread the scope of its retailing activities and to gain access to a broader customer base than has traditionally been the case'. Decent sales increases had been achieved in the group's main businesses in the previous year in spite of the lingering impact of the recession.

After a detailed breakdown of the current situation within each of the group's component companies, Mr Temple went on to give my own role a full assessment.

> Any consideration of Asprey from an investment standpoint can hardly fail to take into account the role of Naim Attallah within the company's development over more than twenty years . . .
>
> Attallah joined the Board of Asprey in 1974 and was a key figure in the battle for control of the company around the time of the Dunhill bid. Since then his charismatic presence has been a feature of the group and has undoubtedly contributed to its considerable success. Attallah's role within the group is to concentrate on the administration and the company's strategic expansion, while the Chairman, John Asprey, functions as salesman and design supremo.
>
> This partnership has been a fruitful one with Attallah's particular strength said to rest in his uncanny anticipation of the global shifts that

have occurred through the 1970s, 1980s and 1990s. Interestingly enough, this has led the company to look increasingly towards Eastern Europe and the newly emerging markets in the Far East . . .

The problem from an investment standpoint is that the long-standing influence which the flamboyant Attallah has exercised over the group's affairs clearly has an effect on investor perceptions. What happens as and when Attallah ceases to have a management role in the company is uncertain, since there are no obvious succession plans.

Peter Temple felt, however, that investors did not need to have undue worries on this score about the shorter term preoccupation of the market, and could feel secure in the knowledge that control of the group was locked up in family hands.

When it came to the cash-flow summary, there was a strongly cash negative pattern in each of the past two years, though this could mainly be put down to a large increase in stocks, attributable in turn to the acquisitions. 'The ratio of stock to sales remained constant through the year', but the management would be advised to look carefully 'at all aspects of the group's stock position with a view to keeping future increases in inventory levels to a minimum'. The stock position was understandable, and 'in contrast to other retailers, the type of merchandise sold by the company is not of the sort to rapidly go out of fashion'. The return on capital was fourteen per cent and could arguably be higher.

The current low level of interest rates could also produce benefits, especially where the affluent lifestyles of Asprey customers were built on credit.

Much of management's attention, however, rightly appears devoted to the search for new outlets for its products and keeping hold of old customers while developing new ones. When the products that a retailer sells are as expensive and profitable as Asprey's, then customer service has to be on a different plane to that of a normal retailer.

There is every sign that management has been good at anticipating where the next fruitful source of new customers will be.

The new acquisitions appeared to have some scope for squeezing more profitability out of them.

For the moment, Asprey has the luxury of its Bond Street shop as a dominant and seemingly unstoppable profit contributor. But if the aim of the acquisition strategy was to broaden the base of the business away from the source of profits then attention will have to be paid to making the newer assets in the group earn their keep.

In fact, economic conditions are on the company's side in this respect.

Taking the overview, there was in the City near-unanimity that the group 'could make a pre-tax profit of £30 million in the current year', and the estimates looked 'well founded'. Earnings per share were likely to be only slightly up, from 21.1p to 22p per share, because of the rise in the tax charge. 'Profits of this order put the stock on a multiple of around fifteen times earnings for the year to March 1995', but this was clearly cheap in view of the company's ten-year track record.

> Part of the reason for the discount inherent in the rating is the market's lack of detailed knowledge of the idiosyncrasies of ultra-high-priced retailing, and the perception that management is dominated by one individual. The solid family control position also virtually rules out any bid premium on the shares.
>
> Yet, over the period from 1984 to 1994, Asprey has produced compound sales growth in the region of 20 per cent per annum and compound growth in pre-tax profits of about 15 per cent per annum with only one 'down' year. Consistency of this sort merits a higher rating.

On 10 September 1994, Vincent Boland in the *Financial Times* reported that the Mappin & Webb store in Prague had finally opened the day before to the 'Czech Republic's new rich', who were already no strangers to 'German cars, French perfumes, Italian clothes, Japanese electronics and American computers'. But, he wondered, were they yet ready for 'a hand-made diamond-studded, £45,566 René Boivin wrist watch'?

> One man who thinks they are is Mr Naim Attallah [who said] he believed Mappin & Webb's £2.5 million investment in the new store, located on the main tourist route through the centre of Prague's Old Town, would show immediate results. He said he expected turnover of £2 million in the first year and profits of about £150,000.
>
> [But] the store's main target is not, he insisted, the thousands of tourists who pass its front door every summer as they traverse Prague's famous Royal Route.
>
> 'We are opening for Czech business,' he said.

'Asprey set to become jewel in Prague's crown' said a headline in the *European* of 30 September, but unfortunately other news headlines of the 10th had announced another message: 'Sparkle fades at Asprey by £89m' in *The Times*; 'Asprey shares plunge 40pc after warning' in the *Daily Telegraph*; and 'Asprey loses shine as big spenders stay away' in the *Daily Express*, to cite some examples. Inevitably this adverse publicity, arising from a profits warning Asprey had announced earlier in the week, partially marred the

Prague opening. Rather than be dispirited by this sudden turn in events, however, I resolved to ignore what I hoped would be only a passing cloud and get on with celebrating the occasion with our usual verve. The distinguished guests, carefully chosen from among the élite of Czech society, had turned up in great numbers, unconcerned by the bad publicity hovering in London, and graced the opening with their unmistakable enthusiasm. They were impressed by the range of merchandise on display, and by the sheer elegance of the shop. The evening was a triumph; the difficulties being encountered by Asprey at the time were not allowed to cast their shadow over the proceedings in Prague.

In any case, John Asprey and I were in need of a break and, in company with our wives, we spent two days in the beautiful city, discovering its many treasures and marvelling at some of its architectural masterpieces. We were not going to let a temporary setback, as we viewed it then, darken the horizon when our unflagging energy continued to be our greatest asset. We returned to London refreshed, only to be faced with a flood of speculation about Asprey that seemed to have been swamping the financial market. Our success over the years, with not a single setback worthy of note, was forgotten, as it seemed, overnight and I had to brace myself for a confrontation with members of the press and City analysts who up till then had backed the company but who now had their knives out. The hero of yesterday was suddenly the fall guy of today, and the fact that, in a time of recession, everyone was feeling the draught was not a mitigating factor. From the moment the warning was made public, journalists began searching for the phrases that would put the most pessimistic spin on the implications. The group statement said the shortfall could be put down to the unexpectedly low level of high-value sales in the current year, though full-year profits would depend on the Christmas period. 'However, in the absence of any signs of improvement in the Asprey business, it is likely that sales and profits for the full year will fall well below current market expectations.' My own remarks made it clear that I thought it was too early to comment on the dividend, for either the interim or half-year results, but the disappointing performance from Asprey vindicated the group's strategy for broadening its base. It was too soon for the acquisitions to be already reducing the volatility of the Asprey results, especially since we had been acquiring them with a view to their future potential rather than because they were thriving businesses.

The negative headlines continued to pile up. 'Cold wind of economic recession takes sparkle and glamour from Britain's most exclusive shopping street,' said the *Guardian*, which went on to announce that in Bond Street several 'shop fronts were empty; others were offering goods at 75 per cent discount in closing-down sales'. 'Asprey balance sheet loses sparkle,' it said in its business columns. 'Asprey nosedive after warning,' was how the *Evening*

Standard expressed it. Another headline, 'Queen's jeweller on the rocks', went on to make the irrelevant point that the 'Asprey group owns Garrard which made engagement rings for three ill-fated royal couples'. The *Daily Mirror* took a slightly different slant. 'Stoned again,' it said:

> After the controversy over the cost of the Royal Household, the Queen is now hit by news that her jeweller lost £45 million in a day.
>
> It never reigns but it pours.

'Even the shares are expensive at Asprey' ran the headline to a piece in the *Daily Mail* by Michael Walters, who was struck by my confidence:

> Utterly unstoppable, completely unabashed and absolutely bullish. That was the mood yesterday afternoon of Naim Attallah, part-time publisher and all-time chief executive of Asprey . . .
>
> Not bad that. Especially considering he had just warned the Stock Exchange that the group was likely to be only marginally profitable at best in the half-year to 30 September . . .
>
> Perhaps you get a touch blasé in such a refined business.

To illustrate his point, he recounted the story of a gold-plated full-size juke-box priced at four hundred and twenty thousand pounds in the Bond Street store, which a group of stockbrokers thought represented a misjudging of the market. Their suspicions were confirmed when they found it still in stock some months later, but a fortnight after that, 'some rock star had spotted it and bought it – ordering another for his second home'.

A mere five weeks before the profits warning, 'the slump that is now in focus had not become apparent'.

> Until yesterday morning [9 September], brokers were hoping for first-half profits of perhaps £1.3 million. Suddenly, there may be none.
>
> What a tricky business satisfying the seriously rich must be. When something does not sell at Asprey, the rumour goes, it must be too cheap. The secret is to mark the price up. Somehow that does not look right for Asprey shares. As investors discovered yesterday, you need to be very rich indeed to be able to hold them happily.

As *Today* reported, the dive in the value of Asprey shares by a hundred and ten pence to two hundred pence was against an international situation where 'interest rate jitters hit the stock market with a vengeance . . . sending shares plunging'. The fall had been sparked by 'an unsettling rise in America's key-prices index which prompted fears of a US rates rise'. Asprey therefore became a focus for deepening the gloom occasioned by 'depressing company news in Britain'.

In the context of everything else that was happening, a high court ruling against Asprey involving one of its two established, up-market pawnbroking companies might have seemed a relatively minor affair. The companies were E. A. Barker and T. M. Sutton, Sutton having come into the group as part of the Mappin & Webb purchase deal from Sears four years before. The plaintiff was a Mr Mathew, who had pledged silver jewellery with Sutton but never redeemed it. Its sale by auction produced a surplus that was owed to Mr Mathew but not paid to him for some time. When he did receive it, he claimed he was still owed interest and disputed the rate offered – a lower rate than when he had been the debtor. The judge agreed with the plaintiff that the rates should be the same, a ruling that had implications for the whole pawnbroking industry.

Rumours then began circulating in the City that Asprey was in further financial trouble because of a bad debt of thirty million pounds, and that the group was planning to write off forty million pounds' worth of stock. The share price dropped eleven per cent, even though there was no basis in the rumours whatsoever. I told *Retail Jeweller* that we did not know where the story originated: 'Malicious people will always spread rumours if they believe you are down but we are going to prove them wrong.' It was essential to deny the gossip and I made a decisive statement on 11 October: 'During its entire history as a public company, Asprey has never experienced a material bad debt and the board considers that the level of provision is unlikely to be increased significantly in the foreseeable future.' For the *Daily Mail*, this was one of the 'surprising statements' from me that investors 'were becoming used to'; and they thought I was only adding to the confusion by saying that trading in the second half of September had been encouraging.

The *Financial Mail on Sunday* of 23 October then latched on to an alleged remark by John Asprey that the overseas customers who seemed to have disappeared 'were back', using it as an attempt to launch an insidious smear in my direction:

> He is uncertain as to why they vanished . . . But Mr Asprey must regret that chief executive Naim Attallah warned the stock market of Asprey's lack of trade just before the upturn. The profits warning, which sent the share price plummeting to 135p, came only six weeks after Attallah had sold nearly 35,000 shares at 310p. The buyer was John Asprey.
>
> Remarkably he claims nothing but goodwill towards his chief executive, whereas the less-forgiving souls in the City are asking questions about Attallah's running of the business.

In the midst of the Asprey upheaval, I also needed to contend with the results of a big story by Chris Blackhurst that the *Observer* ran on 18 September. It concerned a preposterous legal action that was being waged by the heirs of Yusif Bedas, the Lebanese banker and founder of Intra Bank, for whose estate I had been co-trustee with Antoine Best, a financial consultant in Geneva, now deceased. Their claim was that we had misused our role as trustees to cede to Intra Bank shares that belonged to them as beneficiaries. It was a trumped-up accusation that was baseless, but they hoped that by establishing the case in Lebanon they could open the way to mounting a legal action in Europe. Some years later the courts in Lebanon dismissed their claim.

The article by Mr Blackhurst, who could not resist saying how my star was on the wane, was headed 'Attallah faces family's ire over $7m will' and leaned heavily on inaccurate statements from the Bedas family. My lawyers considered it to be libellous and proceedings were instituted against the *Observer* newspaper. In due course the case was settled out of court with an appropriate apology:

> This [article] has been understood to allege that Mr Attallah . . . had misused his position as executor of the estate of Yusif Bedas, a Middle East businessman who died in 1968, in order to enrich himself.
>
> It was not, in fact, our intention to make any such suggestion. We accept that any such allegation would be totally without foundation. We apologize to Mr Attallah for any embarrassment or distress that has been caused to him by our article.
>
> We have paid a sum to a charity nominated by Mr Attallah and have paid his legal costs.

The Bedas family have never stopped making more outrageous assertions, namely that they were the victims of a conspiracy perpetrated by the trustees, who, on the contrary, under the most complex and perilous circumstances, salvaged some of the estate that would otherwise have been searched out and seized by the Lebanese authorities.

Despite all these tribulations, my good spirits never deserted me. I even managed to find time to extol the virtues of good-looking young ladies and do my bit to help banish the stereotype of the dumb blonde. The *Telegraph Weekend Magazine* asked me whether I went along with the assumption that any pretty girl was bound to be a dimwit, when the British were currently producing 'intelligent beauties who are making their mark in every area'. I was asked my opinion as someone who swore by the policy of employing desirable, clever young women. 'In publishing particularly, a combination of intelligence and beauty is an unbeatable commodity. These women make the best ambassadors,' I said, unworried at any suggestion of 'political incorrectness'. 'They are the fuel that drives and exhausts us at the same time. Without them our lives would be devoid of colour and moments of bliss.'

This brings me to the very subject, with two new additions to the Quartet powerhouse of talent, Tamara von Schenk and Susie Craigie Halkett. They were already firmly established in Quartet and, like all the other girls before them, were showing a single-minded determination to make their mark. Sheer impulsiveness accounted for my meeting with Tamara von Schenk at a cocktail party. I must have sensed I would be on the same wavelength as Tamara, a striking blonde of German stock, for I homed in to speak to her without waiting for an introduction. Why overlook such an opportunity, I reasoned, when I was fortunate enough to be caught in her magnetic field? I found myself talking to an elfin-like creature who was elegant without being sensational, sultry without being threatening, and who possessed an aristocratic look that was apparent even if you knew nothing of her background.

Tamara was every inch an aristocrat, with the sort of complexion and comportment men dream about. She cast a light, unobtrusive shadow for one with such a rich, distinctive aura. I felt comfortable in her presence. It was nothing like a first-time encounter but felt as if our paths had crossed many times before. Each responded to the other with the sort of ease that usually develops after many years of acquaintance. I firmly believe in the concept of our destiny preordaining every step we take and that it is pointless to fight it, but I am equally convinced that we can help it along in our chosen direction. This may sound like a paradox, but the undeniable truth of it emerges as the years pass. Tamara's life took on a new dimension after our first meeting. I offered her a job at Quartet. She was not trained for it, but proved equal to the challenge. She accompanied me to Cologne for a chocolate fair to act as my translator, and later performed a similar role at the Frankfurt Book Fair. In the piece that follows, Tamara gives her recollections of her time with Quartet and the friendship that developed between us.

Dealing with Variety
by Tamara von Schenk

It wasn't too difficult to establish who the infamous Naim was the evening I met him in 1993. One man alone managed to dominate a large group of charmed women. His body language, enthusiastic and energetic, coupled with colour flashes from his vibrant suit lining, matching tie and large ring adorning his left hand, singled him out as some exotic species among the rest of the grey and drab business-suited men. I decided to take a closer look and forty minutes later walked away, slightly stunned, as I had just been hired, having had no experience, as publicity manager for Quartet. I tried to dismiss his reputation as a serial womanizer and the fact that I was a slightly overweight blonde in heels and put the whole thing down to utter madness. It was only later that I understood that this was part of an extremely generous, if somewhat obsessive, and spontaneous nature which made up the complex persona of Naim Attallah.

The glamorous reputation of the Attallah posse of well-bred, rich, partying girls had worn off by the time I joined Quartet in May 1994. From day one my friendships with Georgia de Chamberet, Pickles and especially Susie Craigie Halkett were sealed. I felt lucky to be working with three such strong individuals in one of the last remaining independent publishing houses that still adhered to the original ideas of publishing. The variety of material that came through our doors ranged from the avant-garde to more traditional material covering the latest in photography, gay literature and a mixture of undiscovered gems from Europe. Naim's roots were important to him, and this was strongly reflected in the extensive Middle Eastern list, which was quite a novelty at the time.

A week-long trip to Cuba to compile an anthology of young Cuban writers was an unforgettable privilege. The days were spent collecting a wide breadth of material from a stream of struggling and often highly talented writers, desperate to smuggle out what they had written to bypass the harsh restrictions of the Castro regime. Those we met came from all walks of life and our journey was a tremendously humbling and thought-provoking experience and definitely a sharp contrast to the madness and predictability of the Frankfurt Book Fair, which came a few months later.

Of the many books that passed through my hands, the one I worked on in my last few months at Quartet was the most memorable. It involved a close association with the author herself, Elizabeth Wurtzel, whose work and private life fused together with her hugely successful book, *Prozac Nation*, which besides being my last was also my most challenging project. I went beyond the call of duty as publicity manager when I invited Elizabeth, depressed, paranoid, self-obsessed and highly complicated, into my home, where she stayed far longer than expected. I chaperoned her day and night during her publicity tour – an interesting experience to say the least. This title was the first personal account of a life of depression eased by the wonder drug Prozac, and as such both marked a turning-point in Quartet's history and an end to my time there.

To this day I have the valued friendship of Naim, a fiercely loyal man who in return expects no less from those close to him. Being the colourful character he is, he has so often been misunderstood and surrounded by rumours. Those who know him well are aware of his extreme vulnerability. In difficult times, he has maintained his dignity and the high standards he sets for himself. I can truly say that I am happy to have met such a man.

* * *

Susie Craigie Halkett, who hailed from Scotland, was disarmingly engaging, with a smile that blended sophistication with natural diffidence. She went about her work responsibly and with diligence. Her low-key approach to things endeared her not only to the Quartet enclave but also to those on the outside she had to deal with in discharging her duties. Her unassuming presence was charmingly unencroaching and that was in essence the secret of her popularity. Looking back, I remember being struck by the way she conducted herself and glided through life, seemingly unflappable. I wanted to discover more about her. It was not simply her beauty that aroused my interest but an instinct that told me there was more to her than was visible to the casual eye: there was an intriguing depth to her that I was determined to plumb. In pursuit of this aim, I arranged for her to accompany me to New York on two occasions, and once to Frankfurt to attend the book fair. On all of these trips she stayed with me and I found her company both stimulating and relaxing. The differences in our characters produced from time to time some innocuous ripples but these never lingered on to have any destabilizing effect on our working relationship. Her time at Quartet as editorial assistant and publicist was remembered with great affection. I retain fond memories of our travels and am certain Scotland could not have sent forth a better child to enchant and capture the English.

Meanwhile, at my Regent Street office, a new light appeared in the form of Jess Collett, a young, attractive blonde who could have dazzled the socks off any red-blooded youthful male, let alone a man of my age. Her presence enlivened the atmosphere, and in her own words she sums up that time with a stylish cheekiness.

Getting Away with Murder
by Jess Collett

When I walked into the marketing department of Mappin & Webb in 1995 as office skivvy, the only thing I knew about Naim was that he and my dad used the same hairdresser – and still do, what class! I was surrounded by nubile young ladies accredited with brains, looks and charm. The only man to be seen in the office, apart from Naim himself, was the postman!

I seemed to fall into position of youngest (who gets away with murder) with extreme ease, and was soon known affectionately as 'Blondie'. On Naim's bad days I hopped on to his knee to cheer him up, and on his good days I did the same. After a month, I was presented with a beautiful watch for my services. I might have left at this point, pawned the watch and got the money I needed for going to Mexico. But I didn't.

Instead I had the most exciting, amusing and of course instructive six months. I met some lovely people, posed in a very short pvc skirt, modelled thousands of pounds' worth of jewellery and watches up my arm, sat at the wheel of a couple of Ferraris in Bond Street, drank fine champagne in Winston Churchill's underground cabinet war rooms and stuffed A LOT of envelopes.

So, as my only experience of working in an office (I am now a milliner), I would say it was a very good advertisement.

Fifty-six

In September 1994, Anna Pasternak hit the news big time with her fictional account of the romantic involvement of Princess Diana with Captain Hewitt. The book, *Princess in Love*, caused a terrific rumpus and made Anna the target of some vicious personal attacks followed by an orchestrated hate campaign that went far beyond the normal levels of acceptable criticism. Although Quartet were not the publishers of her book, they nevertheless found themselves engulfed in telephone calls from the media seeking to winkle out some gossipy stories about Anna from the time when she worked at Goodge Street as a publicist. I kept as clear as possible from the fray to avoid being misquoted, given the high degree of sensitivity of the subject matter and my own relationship with Anna. Irrespective of how I felt about the book, discretion and loyalty *vis-à-vis* an old employee who was also a friend would have precluded me from airing an uninformed opinion. For this reason I declined to take sides in what turned out to be an explosive issue solely because of Diana's iconic status at the time. Public indignation was exaggerated by the media and Anna became the scapegoat in what should have been a storm in a teacup.

Meanwhile our creative endeavours on behalf of the Asprey group were continuing with unabated drive and enthusiasm, despite the rough time we were having with the press. 'Garrard roars in with gold-plated motorcycle,' declared the *Yorkshire Post* of 22 September, referring to the centrepiece of a Garrard touring exhibition that was arriving in Harrogate – a gold-plated Ducati Monster 900 with an asking price of ninety-five thousand pounds. The picture in the paper also featured one of my assistants, Tania Foster-Brown, looking glamorous and sexy beside the fabulous machine, wearing a smile that signified she had found the answer to every girl's dream of what a luxurious and decadent toy should be: the ultimate sex object. The idea for it originated with Bill Foreman, the workshop manager at Garrard, who came to see me one morning saying he'd had a dream showing in great detail a Ducati motorcycle gold plated. He suggested that as Ducati had just won the world championship and was at the forefront in the world of motorcycling, were we to purchase a superbike model, gold plate the metal and respray it in 'Garrard blue', it would provide a 'people magnet' for our outside shows.

In the end, we used nearly a kilo of pure gold in the plating solution and plated not only the most visible parts but also some sections hidden under the engine covers. The fuel tank and the front and rear mudguards were stripped and professionally stove-enamelled in the house colour, and then, to give it a finishing touch, the dual seat was recovered in leather of Garrard blue. Adrian Lawrence, one of our diamond mounters, who was a keen motorcyclist himself, supervised the work on the bike over a period of five months. The dismantling and rebuilding of the machine, which took place on the fifth floor at Garrard – the difficulties of transporting such a large and powerful bike up five floors when there was not enough space for it in the lift may be imagined – were carried out by two Ducati-trained engineers. The finished article attracted much attention, from both the media and prospective purchasers. Several security men achieved their fifteen minutes of fame by accompanying the bike on various television shows during its travels at home and abroad. Eventually it was sold to the Sultan of Brunei as a Christmas present for his son.

As far as our troubles at Asprey were concerned, we could not afford to let the rumours in the marketplace go unchecked since the danger was always present that they would have a destabilizing effect on morale within the group. Every day brought a new twist to the situation. Our efforts to reverse the downward trend in current trading became more difficult as a result. Valuable time was spent trying to placate the market and dispose of wildly inaccurate rumours when we should have been boosting our selling activities and redressing the trading balance. In the mixed bag of press coverage, the factual was outweighed by the speculative, which did nothing to help an already jittery market, and especially not the luxury-goods market, which included jewellery. The *Investors Chronicle* on 28 October reported that shares in Asprey had been continuing to slide and quoted my claim that the fall was the result of malicious rumours about the state of the company finances. The company was getting stronger by the day, I said, and 'when the results are announced the Asprey family will use the low price to boost their shareholdings'. With shares at a hundred and thirty-five pence, the advice of the *Investors Chronicle* was to hold on.

The *Independent on Sunday* backed a less gloomy view by giving us a platform on 23 October to express our unshaken confidence that in time trading would improve and that the current decline in profits was nothing mortal. The *Mail on Sunday*, in sharp contrast, came forward on 13 November with the rumour that Asprey had lost the support of its bankers, based on an unsigned 'secret' memorandum from within the Bank of Scotland, purportedly written on 28 October, that made the stark statement: 'Asprey the jewellers and luxury-goods group is in potential default on a £20 million loan facility and may face receivership.' It concerned a loan facility of twenty million pounds that had been signed on 29 June and went on to say that, at the time, Asprey's directors may not have been 'wholly open with us . . . with regard to the achievement of the budgeted level of profit'. Since then, it said,

> Our perception of risk inherent in the group's business has altered fundamentally. However, any action we take now to enhance the safety of this lending will damage this relationship, and Naim Attallah, the chief executive, is not a man to shy away from publicity, and he could damage the bank's reputation if he were to make any of our actions a public matter . . .
>
> Whilst we have experienced a rapid and severe shock, we do not believe the position is terminal, but nevertheless we must take action now to improve the safety of our lending.

The Bank of Scotland in fact stepped in quickly, as the *Guardian* confirmed on the 18th:

> The bank confirmed that a document cited in a Sunday newspaper had originated from the Bank of Scotland. But it said the document had been prepared at the end of September, before discussion had taken place with Asprey about a profit warning, and not at the end of October, after the bank had been reassured about the company's financial position.
>
> 'In the course of October,' the statement said, 'the bank received further information from the company. In the light of that information the bank was and remains satisfied that no event of default has existed at any time during the currency of the [loan] facility and the management of the company has not misled or sought to mislead the bank.'
>
> The bank confirmed it has full confidence in Asprey and its management, and that the loan facility remains fully available to the company.

Meanwhile no amount of denial was able to prevent such headlines as the *Evening Standard*'s for 14 November, 'Asprey on brink of £20m crisis', or 'Paper's claims knock Asprey' in *The Times* the next day, or 'City rumours tarnish Asprey' in the *Sunday Times* on the 20th. In his article under the latter headline, Randeep Ramesh wrote:

> While Attallah has tried to limit the damage done by last weekend's press report, many investors believe there is no smoke without fire. The story was based on an internal memo prepared by Richard Ramsey, Bank of Scotland's director of structured finance. However, when it emerged that

the date on the memo had been altered from 28 September to 28 October pundits began openly speculating on a bear raid.

The bank, in the words of one insider, 'flipped', and launched an inquiry to see how the unsigned, draft memo was obtained. It existed as a file on the computer of Ramsey, who had originally negotiated the loan with Asprey.

According to an unnamed source, the loan had been Ramsey's 'big deal' after the Edinburgh-based bank offered better terms in June than Asprey's usual bankers.

'When the profit warning came, Ramsey suddenly became very worried and wrote the memo to put himself in the clear. He wanted to make sure his judgement was not called into question. But it was revised later when the other directors saw it. That memo did not have a wide circulation.'

I was then quoted as protesting that I was tired of dealing with things that took up my time and my lawyer's time. 'Handling these stories is not what I am paid to do.' At that stage I had not ruled out calling in a private detective to find out the source of the damaging rumours. In any case, I insisted, the *Mail on Sunday* story was flawed on at least two counts. For one thing, the company remained in profit and it could only break its banking covenants if it went into the red. For another, the bank could not call in receivers anyway since the loan was unsecured.

That the family were prepared to buy back Asprey from public ownership out of disillusion with the stock market was confirmed by John Asprey, speaking from Oman and quoted in the *Daily Telegraph* (19 November):

'If this nonsense continues, then one's feelings towards the City are not as warm as they should be,' he said. 'What the City doesn't understand is that we can't orchestrate our clients. In a fantastic year, we do extremely well.'

The Times reported on 24 November that Asprey had

yesterday sought to reassure investors about its financial health by maintaining its interim dividend despite a sharp slump in profits . . .

Naim Attallah, Asprey's chief executive, said the decision to hold the interim dividend at 1.25p demonstrated the board's confidence.

Concern about Asprey's financial position intensified earlier this month when a Sunday newspaper alleged the group was under pressure from its bankers. Yesterday, Mr Attallah again dismissed the story and said the group had issued a writ against the newspaper earlier in the week.

It is hardly surprising that I should have been increasingly quoted as asserting a belief that there was a plot to smear Asprey in certain quarters of the City and the press. Typical of my reported comments were:

'We are not in trouble. OK, we have had a downturn in profits, but our balance sheet is solid. We are launching a new marketing initiative and our efforts to broaden our customer base have been going to plan.'

Yet no matter how often we insisted that Asprey was not in trouble over any bad debt or mythical showrooms full of unwanted stock, the inaccurate inferences continued to be kept in circulation in one form or another in column after column. 'Angry Asprey boss fights back' was the headline in the *Daily Mail* of 24 November:

Naim Attallah complains he has been spending more time fighting off 'completely scurrilous' rumours than running Asprey, the jeweller to the Queen . . .

'I have thirty branches of Watches of Switzerland. Where is the stock problem there? At Asprey, what stock are they referring to? It's all fanciful.

'As for big customers, anybody who is somebody in the world has bought at some point at Asprey, from Haile Selassie to all the kings and ex-kings in the world . . . '

Attallah has just opened 'the most beautiful shop in Prague' and last week a new branch of Mappin & Webb in Kingston-upon-Thames.

'I don't know where it is. I spent last week fighting off the rumours so I haven't been able to see it,' he regrets.

As good an objective summing-up as any of the real situation with which we were having to work was provided in the autumn issue of *Fine Art Auctioneers and Dealers*:

The good recovery which Asprey had achieved since their 1991/2 profit setback came to a dramatic halt in the past few months.

This was mainly due to a fall in the volume of turnover in the core Asprey Bond Street part of the business which for the past couple of years had been contributing over 75 per cent of total profits. Sales of high value items to certain customers in the export market are unusually low so far this year, 'with no current signs of an upturn'. This will pull down the Asprey profits significantly in the first half. Garrard is suffering too from a reduction in export sales – throughout as severe as Asprey's – which will eliminate its contribution to group profits. Mappin & Webb is trading better than last year, but at Watches of Switzerland the increase in overheads, due partly to the expansion of the brand's network, has exceeded growth in sales. Its contribution to profits will be down compared with last year. The net result of all this is that the Asprey group will be only marginally profitable at best.

It remained to be seen how trading in the Christmas period would go, but even if it went well, the elimination of profit in the first half-year would remain a serious setback. 'New management strategies at the recently acquired companies, including reviewing costs and a continued determined drive to improve exports, could eventually bring a return to earlier levels of profitability.' In the light of the situation, their advice to investors remained not to take any action but to await further trading news.

In all my thinking, I continued to take the longer view, as I made clear in the speech I contributed that year to the annual *Financial Times* conference in London. My opening point was that Asprey's most pressing challenge in the 1990s was to persuade the customer that spending is a pleasurable activity. During the previous two decades, improved standards of living had created a culture to spend and spend again, to reap the benefits of hard work. This had led to a complacency among retailers, who had failed to predict a change in economic markets. Now they were being forced to reassess their business.

> The recession does of course destroy, but it also cleanses. It highlights weaknesses and imposes change. It demands increased effort and encourages flair and improvisation, which ought to be prerequisites for survival.
>
> In our own sector of retailing, which is at the top end of the market, things have changed dramatically. The world of luxury goods has its own culture. Setting aside those who have inherited wealth, you are dealing with people who are normally at the top of their profession and are often singular in their views and tastes.
>
> They lack time, they are accustomed to excellence, and they require care and attention bordering on homage. Contrary to popular belief, the very rich are not easy targets: they are not short of suitors, so they can afford to be choosy and highly discriminating.

Then there were those, at the other end of the spectrum, who were still making their way up the ladder. Their resources were not as great, but they expected the same attention and respect in the way they were treated. It was almost a symbolic act for them to visit a luxury store, keen to enter into a world of opulence, but they needed to be courted – even seduced – into making a purchase. In any case, the good retailer ought to treat all customers with equal devotion. Then those who buy will return and those who do not are more likely to come back and buy next time.

Retailers in our sector can no longer expect the important customers to pay them a visit as a matter of course; they have to go out in search of them.

The proper way forward is to grow through expansion of the customer base. The upper reaches of the luxury-goods market are particularly vulnerable to fluctuating fortunes. The rich and powerful account for a large proportion of business, but they form an unpredictable enclave.

Millions of pounds can change hands at the very top of the market or not, as the case may be. In order to combat this phenomenon one has to be less dependent on the moneyed minority. The volume of customers has to be increased in order to protect against the vagaries of turnover and profit.

From this it followed that there should be a geographical expansion into such potentially profitable markets as Eastern Europe, the South of France, South-East Asia and South America. To ignore the potential in the worldwide changes in trading patterns would be to risk fading into the mists of time. You had to be ready to advance wherever there was the glimpse of an opening. A survival instinct, an eye for potential crises and safety nets were all important, but the result of never taking a chance, exploring an opportunity, backing a hunch or embracing the element of adventure must ultimately be death by dullness.

The rich have become more careful with their money and are no longer easy punters; the middle classes, who are increasing in numbers, expect good value for their money; and taste is a matter for the individual and not to be imposed by the retailer.

But above all courtesy and service to the customer must be considered paramount.

A line of a sort was drawn under our contention with the *Mail on Sunday* on 5 February 1995, when its City editor, Clive Wolman, recorded in his 'Comment' column:

Last week I visited the ornate office of a former adversary, Naim Attallah, chief executive of the Asprey luxury-goods chain, to smoke a peace pipe together.

Readers may recall that, back in November, we published a leaked internal draft memorandum from the Bank of Scotland . . . suggesting that Asprey was in more financial trouble than had been made public.

Asprey and the bank responded by saying that, prior to its publication, a series of meetings between the two of them had resulted in the bank taking a much more sanguine view of its customer.

Where the profit warning was concerned, Asprey had 'wanted to err on the side of caution', and it had been rather pessimistic, provoking a general over-reaction.

But Attallah says: 'Despite difficult trading conditions, our financial situation is fully under control. Our philosophy since I joined Asprey more than twenty years ago has always been to follow the money.' . . .

One reason the stock market may have reacted so severely to September's profit warning is that Attallah sold Asprey shares in July and August.

However, in late November chairman John Asprey bought 170,000 Asprey shares at 143p (after buying 370,000 in August) and Attallah has bought 77,500 shares (at 136–138p) in several tranches since mid December.

They would clearly like the investors to follow their philosophy of following the money.

That November Gillian Glover came to interview me in my Regent Street office for the *Scotsman*. Under the headline 'Cat Who Got the Cream', she drew a colourful picture, saying the first thing to be noticed were the cats: four tigers straining at and pawing their four separate gilt frames.

Their eyes burn as bright as a Blake bequest, and the jungle blurs around their flanks . . . Beneath these painted pacings sits another cat. A cat with an added dimension, Naim Attallah.

He bounds forward from his grand desk and claims immediate control; but the gesture is benevolent, protective. The world is already at bay in this silken, sound-proofed domain, high above London's Regent Street . . .

It was not the 'fluctuating appeal of emeralds and diamonds' that had brought Gillian Glover to interview me, but the fact that my fifth collection of interviews, *Speaking for the Oldie: The Last Unabridged Interviews*, was due to be published on the following Monday, the 21st. One was therefore facing, she wrote, 'a man who has sought out and cored nearly 1,000 of the twentieth century's most influential personalities'.

This constitutes much more than the recreational interest of a diversely talented businessman. This reeks of passion . . .

'You have to keep pushing at the boundaries of life,' he declares, 'or you don't exist any more.'

For another interviewer I was 'The man who really pulled his socks up', the socks being as usual of two different colours – for why, I asked him, shouldn't a person be as colourful as he pleases? The question was then raised as to how many other chief executives of public companies have been interviewers? I refused to fit into the pattern in any other respects either, claiming personally 'to have no ambition to be wealthy'.

'The money I earn I put into literature and art,' he says. 'I can live comfortably without holding a lot of money. I thank the Lord for every day I rise. No one can take that away from you . . .

'When I retire I don't want caviare. I want fresh air and the time to read a book.'

It was a relief to get away for a time from the unwanted limelight of the Asprey situation and give attention to *Speaking for the Oldie*, a collection of interviews I had originally conducted for the *Oldie*. They had been presented in abbreviated form for the magazine, but now were given at full length. Yet again, the media were generous in their praise, the sole exception being an anonymous dismissive paragraph in the *Sunday Times*:

We are told on the dustjacket that Attallah has a 'growing reputation as a master interviewer who has a special gift for drawing out confidences'. I am sure the blurb writer was not influenced by the fact that Attallah owns the company which published the book . . . I found most of it tepid stuff.

Katie Campbell in the *Evening Standard* said the question-and-answer formula allowed 'for no fudging, rewriting or quoting out of context', the 'resulting candour' being 'often riveting'. The book overall represented 'vanity publishing at its best'. She found the subjects 'well-chosen and balanced'. Sister Wendy Beckett, for example, 'the popular nun cum art-historian', argued for the 'ordination of women and homosexuals', while the former Bishop of London, Dr Graham Leonard, explained how it was just such arguments that had 'led him to Rome'. One of the 'Birmingham Six', Hugh Callaghan, described how it felt to be an Irishman convicted in an English court, while Judge Stephen Tumin 'praises the British judicial system'. Peter Jay had been put on the defensive by the subjects of TV-am, Washington and Robert Maxwell; he replied, when asked whether he had not found it faintly bizarre to be going to work at the *Daily Mirror* for a 'bully with a tarnished reputation', that he had received the thumbs-up from the Foreign Office, the Bank of England and some 'very senior ex-Labour cabinet ministers'. Wilfred Thesiger came across as 'radiantly naïve, if not absurd' in blaming the West, 'notably its cars and aeroplanes, for the current catastrophes in Africa', while defending 'Haile Selassie's rule in Abyssinia as one of tolerance and clemency'. Quentin Crisp presented a 'profoundly sad' figure, hated by his father, ostracized by his siblings and taunted at school, who was left 'feeling an outsider, compelled to use exhibitionism as a means to gain attention'.

Robert Kee agreed to write a notice for the *Literary Review*, starting it off by observing that if you were watching a brilliant conjurer it was the trick you noticed rather than the man's personality, wondering only afterwards how the trick was done. 'So it is with Naim Attallah, a magician interviewer of the highest order who publishes the *Literary Review* on the side.' This produced an incentive to be particularly hard on the book, but it proved to be uphill work.

> Only an interviewer of quality could get, as Attallah does, a nun, a con- secrated virgin as the technical term goes, to say: 'I don't actually believe the state of the hymen has very much to do with the holiness of the person; it's just a fact like whether you have all your teeth,' or bring someone once described as the cleverest man in the world to say: 'I do not believe in the unconscious.' . . .
>
> Attallah has a guileless way of asking questions. Seldom for him 'with due respect', etc. Asking the nun about her attitude to television fees (for yes, it is she, Sister Wendy Beckett), he begins, 'I don't want to sound dis- agreeable but . . . ', and on getting only a rather inadequate answer, does not delay but moves on to obtain an admirable amount of sense on other matters.

Robert Kee found the interview with Hugh Callaghan the simplest but also the most moving, for 'Callaghan has already told of his dreadful experience in an impressive book, yet Attallah draws it from him again as if he had never spoken of it before. Familiarity with the story is immaterial here.' The longest interview was with Lord Healey, who had been inter- viewed many times before and was known as an 'old bruiser'. Even here the charge of overfamiliarity was avoided by the interviewer's

> freshness of approach, his use not just of intelligence, knowledge and energy, but his ability to make people actually enjoy answering his questions, [which] leads to an agreeable surprise or two. Lord Healey . . . is happy to proclaim in one breath the interesting news that he has more and more in common with Wordsworth and in the next denounce himself as a 'clapped-out old fart'. He has never seemed less clapped-out.

The point, Kee thought, was that the interviewees were all brought 'to feel at their intelligent ease, a state in which clever people do occasionally say odd things', but always remained 'intellectually stimulating and engaging'. The

'[E. H.] Gombrich interview, which is one of the best in the book, contains the admission that he finds some bits of Michelangelo's work "repulsive".'

The contemporary standard of interviewing for profiles, a prominent feature of today's press and on the whole welcome as such, is a high one. But it is a different trick from that performed by the true interviewer. The profile requires a discreet awareness of the interviewer's personality; the subject is, in the light of it, exposed in the photographic sense. The true interviewer lets the subject's mind expose itself.

Robert Kee's review gave my spirits an uplift at a time when the Asprey saga was showing no signs of receding. Although it had been published in the *Literary Review* – a connection which was likely to stir up the critics – I was grateful for his appreciation of my efforts as an interviewer. His opinion was one I respected.

Someone else I respected was an old friend, William MacQuitty, whose autobiography, *A Life to Remember*, with a foreword by Arthur C. Clarke, we had first published in 1991. After he had written his manuscript, he wondered what to do with it, and his wife Betty had suggested, 'Take it to Naim Attallah.' At the end of the book, he described climbing the stairs to my office, where

Naim rose from behind a large black desk, arms outstretched, and embraced me warmly. It was nearly twenty years since we first met, but he was quite unchanged by his huge success.

'I'll publish your book,' he said. 'You are my friend.'

When Quartet took the book on, by happy chance it brought MacQuitty back into partnership with Peter Ford as editor to guide it through the press. More than twenty years earlier, Peter had worked with him at Thomas Nelson on his beautifully illustrated book on *Buddha*, for which the Dalai Lama wrote a foreword. Of *A Life to Remember*, the *Daily Mail* said it was 'a gripping auto-biography . . . Author, photographer, conservationist and mordant wit, MacQuitty spills a multitude of beans in these revealing, ironic memoirs.' Like myself, he had started out as a banker, but in very different circumstances – with the Chartered Bank in India in the days of the British Raj. Like myself, he was an encourager of teamwork in others, marshalling their talents to great effect. The high point of his days as a film producer at Pinewood Studios had been the making of *A Night to Remember*, still unrivalled as the definitive account of the sinking of the *Titanic*, the ill-fated liner whose launch he had witnessed in Belfast at the age of six. Later he was instrumental in founding Ulster Television.

It pleased me that, at the same time as I brought out *Speaking for the Oldie*, we reissued *A Life to Remember* in a quality paperback edition. As Arthur C. Clarke said, it 'had shouted to be written' and 'shouts to be read'. Bill MacQuitty seemed to be unstoppable. A year or two later Quartet published his informal handbook, *Survival Kit: How to Reach Ninety and Make the Most of It*, which prompted Yehudi Menuhin to comment, 'Everything he says is everything I believe in.' He was an old friend who stood by me when others hesitated. I shall always remember him with great affection.

Fifty-seven

The year 1995 signalled more trouble at Asprey. Rumours in the press continued to fuel wild speculation about trading difficulties as well as a struggle to meet financial commitments. As if that was not bad enough, serious cracks in the management structure had begun to appear. John took to meddling in matters where I felt he had little competence because of his lack of business qualifications. Someone put it into his head that he should from now on exercise more authority as both chairman and majority shareholder. Furthermore the same voices, whose identities were well known, instilled in him the belief that the problems facing the company stemmed from my expansionist strategy, while my style of management was hardly one to give the City analysts the comfort they were expecting. Although he never came out with it plainly, insisting throughout that his support for me was beyond question, his manoeuvring behind the scenes diluted the so-called assurances he was making.

Though I was fully aware of the situation, I was always conscious of my promise to John's father that I would stand by his son whatever the circumstances. Eric had insisted that, come what may, the business should remain in family hands, and I had assured him I would always strive to make sure it did. Eventually his wishes were thwarted when, at the final crunch, John opted to seek the advice of others. His character had always been highly suggestible. He leant his ear to whoever came to see him and took advice from the most unlikely sources, being swayed by the last thing someone had said to him. With the advent of the company's phenomenal success, achieved through our very close association in which neither of us encroached on the territory of the other, he had undergone a radical change towards me as a result of the constant hammering he received from his family circle, which had widened to encompass a distant relation through marriage who lived in Australia and happened to be a law practitioner. As was clear from the history of the firm, intrigue had always been endemic in the genes of the Asprey family. I was not at all surprised that it should recur. I had seen it at first hand when I joined Asprey and saw how members of the family fought among themselves and stopped at nothing to discredit each other. It had never occurred to me, however, that John would shift sides so easily. In hindsight, it is possible to understand his predicament, landed in the firing line in a situation with which he found it hard to cope. His weakness in the face of the onslaught from within became the defining factor in the loss of the business. He cast friendship aside without realizing it and chose division rather than solidarity, a choice that would ultimately set the seal on the company's fate.

Perhaps unwittingly, John went along with those of his friends – and there were many of them – whose purpose seemed to me to be to oust me and so leave the field clear for their manipulation of him. Yet the plot had some distance to go yet. It was going to need some careful orchestration. John began taking executive decisions behind my back whenever I was away. He took the opportunity to undermine my authority, invariably at the instigation of others since he was never in my opinion his own man. When confronted by an accusation, he would either deny it or put the blame elsewhere, feigning innocence and dismissing the episode as irrelevant or trivial. Our working relationship came close to breaking point when he took to disregarding memos I issued in my capacity as chief executive, especially those concerned with keeping within budget when buying new stock, since this was an issue at the very heart of our difficulties. To the outside world he projected an image of unity, but in reality he sang a different tune, depending on who was listening.

Matters were coming to a head far sooner than I had anticipated, but I refused to be rattled. I had enough to do already, coping with all kinds of pressure and pretending everything was well in the Asprey camp when this was not the case. I was determined nothing was going to prevent me from pursuing my duties with the same scrupulous attention I always gave them. John's occasional petulance seemed to be containable, and I was more concerned to win time, hoping the tide would once again turn in our favour and dispel the current uncertainties.

But beware the Ides of March. I was on a trip to Paris with Tania Foster-Brown when, in my absence, the next instalment of the plot was being hatched and John was rallying support from members of the board with a view to getting rid of me. As I was to find out later – in fact from John himself – the family pressures had been mounting to such an extent that John could no longer resist demands for my dismissal. He used an additional argument that it was the outside discontent that eventually convinced him the only way of saving the day was to accede to the wishes of his new inner circle and send me packing. The most hurtful aspect of the whole affair was that he was able to persuade Tim Cooper and Nick Harrington to go along with him. Tim had always been my close ally, one of the trio, consisting of John, himself and me, at the heart of the institution, and our indivisibility over a span of two decades had brought prosperity and wealth to both the Asprey family and many friends and shareholders. We had grown together with the job, and a comradeship of the kind that only exists between special friends had strengthened with the years.

Tim's involvement in the plot was something I could not believe, any more than I could comprehend what the real reasons were behind it. As an army officer, he must have realized the gravity of the move in which he was being asked to participate. Whatever would make him take part in what amounted to an act of betrayal? All the answers were to surface in time and sadly none of them made good reading. The involvement of Nick Harrington, whom I regarded as my protégé and whom I had fought hard to elevate to the Asprey main board, was even more puzzling. As chief accountant, Nick had very little to do with John, enjoyed a good working relationship with Tim and had been until recently my most trusted lieutenant. He had access to me on a daily basis, was a good man, highly principled and a practising Catholic. I could not imagine what circumstances would have driven him to abandon his strong principles of loyalty and lend his support to the conspirators.

The first I heard about the plot was through a telephone call from Tim, who informed me that a decision had been taken by some members of the board to relieve me of my duties and that John had suggested I refrain from attending the next board meeting, which was scheduled for after the Easter break. My response was simple: I had no wish to shoot the monkey; let the organ grinder tell me himself. As I anticipated, a nervous John soon phoned and, in an attempt to defuse the situation, agreed to a meeting that same afternoon at my home in Mayfair. It was an encounter I shall never forget. Before me stood the man I considered to be more than a brother, and he was telling me of his own predicament, of how he was having to repel the forces ranged against us both, admitting, near to tears, that the decision had not been his. I knew that to be true: John was not the instigator, simply the executioner. Naturally he was full of regret and put the blame on others for what he described as their intemperate decision. He was offering to make immediate amends and recommended I get rid of Tim and Nick, since he believed that, with the loss of trust, a clean start would be preferable. I was taken aback by this outrageous suggestion and said I would think about it, though in reality I never contemplated such a move for a moment. More details concerning the plot emerged later. George Magan, the independent board director, had been totally against it and informed John of his uncompromising opposition. He said it was a move that would spell disaster both through repercussions in the stock market and a deterioration in morale throughout the company, making the present difficulties far worse.

As soon as I was back in my office after Easter I spoke to Tim and Nick about my meeting with John and told them all that had transpired. And, on this rare occasion, I managed to set aside my emotions in favour of a more measured approach. I said they were still an integral part of my team and I was willing to overlook their unfortunate lapse of judgement. As to the sensitive matter of loyalty, it was something they would have to square with their own consciences. Tim tried to explain how John had been utterly unrelenting in his daily bombardment about what his friends and family expected him to do to relieve the present situation, until, out of sheer desperation, he unwisely agreed to give his support. In retrospect he felt only contrition and offered to put his fate at my disposal, having resigned himself to the consequences of his actions. For his part, Nick was too shattered by the whole experience to speak up in his own defence, indeed he was so deeply affected that his life at the office would never be the same afterwards. It was apparent he had listened to John and paid a heavy penalty. Seeing him in this state of profound self-reproach, I could understand how agonizing the inner conflict had been for such a religious man who possessed a great deal of integrity. The perspective suddenly shifted: it was not I but Nick who was the victim of the plot. The destructive results of attempting to rule by dividing loyalties were plain for all to see.

Deep suspicions continued to be voiced in the press reports, and inevitably the spotlight was on me as shares dropped another twenty per cent. 'The crown slips at royal jeweller,' the *Daily Telegraph* reported on 17 March:

> The problem with Asprey is that while the chief executive says gold, the share price says plate, or worse. For all Naim Attallah's reassuring comments yesterday, the market does not believe him, and it fears that something deeply tarnished is about to tumble out of the stockroom.
>
> Perhaps there is a clue in the royal jeweller's back room. Last September, it admitted that stocks had risen to £147 million, a huge sum for a company that turned over £188 million in the year to last March. In its statement yesterday, made at the behest of the Stock Exchange, the company said it had fallen somewhat. However, this is not a reassuring ratio. The last audited profits were £25.5 million, and for the year about to end, Asprey now suggests a figure of £6 million, 'before provisions'.

It was hardly surprising the markets were nervous, the paper added, when only a five-per-cent overstatement on those stocks would be needed to wipe out profits for 1994–5. In *The Times* of 18 April, Melvyn Marcus started a lengthy analysis of 'How Asprey's shares lost their shine' by saying:

> Once upon a time the Asprey family, who sell baubles wrapped in purple paper to the easy come, easy go fraternity, feuded with each other. This

was a harmless enough habit that conjured up images of flying jade and the swish of bejewelled daggers. But that, as they say, was then. John Asprey, chairman of Asprey, long ago decided to bet the family's fortune on Naim Attallah, Asprey's chief executive. Attallah is an author, publisher and socialite who hails from Palestine. He is reputed to wear (intentionally) bright socks that do not match. He is also reputed to wear two watches: a trait he would presumably like to encourage.

Although the plot to remove me had failed, its repercussions continued to be felt throughout the group. The news was being leaked by the perpetrators in ways to undermine my authority. Despite the denials issued by the company, no one was convinced. Gossip and rumour were rife. The most damaging aspect of it all was the effect it had on the staff. The atmosphere became depressingly tense and morale throughout the group sank like the shares on the stock market. Gone was the impetus that had driven us on to achieve the successes of previous years. Instead the power struggle, simmering on beneath the surface, was destabilizing the company and making it seriously vulnerable to outside influences.

John's actions meanwhile became increasingly erratic, while his occasional statements did little to repair confidence. He was no longer focused and it seemed clear to me that he was acting only as the moment required. He held court constantly to a string of advisers who struck me as mediocre and whose sole purpose, it appeared, was to fill the vacuum and further their own ambitions by gaining some sort of foothold in the company. On his home ground he was in the doghouse, having aborted a carefully planned coup to see the back of me and return power to the family camp. Within a couple of months he was at it again, though this time with a more subtle strategy. The suggestion was that another independent director should be added to the two existing ones, on the grounds that this would please the City analysts and somehow curb the powers of the group chief executive. In another, parallel, move, I was given to understand that the time had come for me to appoint a deputy to help me run the conglomerate so as to ensure an orderly transition on my retirement. The message was clear: my ascendancy at Asprey was slowly coming to its end.

John had grandiose ideas of ruling supreme, surrounded by a new *équipe* of achievers of his own ilk with the blessing of the City. In my view he had lost his bearings. He could not see that his tactics, formulated by the others, were bound to bring about not only the end of the present era but also the loss of a company that his forebears had nurtured for over two hundred years. In myself I felt extremely hurt, but I went along with the masquerade since the fire in my belly was by now all but extinguished. The plan pulled no wool over the eyes of the press, who saw through it, as they made plain in the coverage they gave to Asprey events.

On 4 May, three days after my birthday, the newspapers were full of news of my retirement and the appointment of a new independent director. A cartoon in the *Independent*, however, put it more crudely, showing me being peremptorily kicked out of an Asprey cuckoo clock by a boot on a spring. The *Guardian* announced that

> A new executive director is being recruited to run the group's multiple retailing operations and Howard Dyer, chairman of Hamleys, has been appointed as a non-executive director. Chief executive Naim Attallah, who will be sixty-five on 1 May 1996, has indicated his desire to retire by December 1996.

The summary in the *Independent* quoted dealers as attributing a rise in Asprey shares by five pence to 'Mr Dyer's reputation as a tough negotiator with a good relationship with the banks'.

> Asprey also announced the closure of seven shops, including one of the five Les Ambassadeurs stores bought two years ago.
>
> Some analysts regarded the closure as evidence of a strategy to spread the group's revenue stream away from the core Bond Street shop by diversifying the high-street chains.
>
> Most analysts felt that it was evidence the company was winding up recent acquisition-activity.
>
> 'We applaud signs that they are getting to grips with troublesome subsidiaries,' said one shareholder.

The paper went on to quote an unnamed institutional shareholder as saying:

> 'The company is approaching its considerable problem in a most diffident manner. Waiting eighteen months for the appointment of a new face after hearing the old face no longer fits is not very encouraging. We want someone with City credibility who can put the worst type of rumours to bed.'

'Mr Attallah,' the paper concluded, 'will head the search for his replacement' in the lead-up to the boardroom changes due to take place in December 1996.

The Times detailed the stores to be affected by closure as the Mappin & Webb store in Birmingham; five Watches of Switzerland stores in respectively Oxford, Newcastle, Edinburgh, Upper Regent Street and Meadowhail; and the Les Ambassadeurs outlet in Lucerne. These Asprey had described as 'underperforming assets' (*Daily Mail*). There would be some redundancies among forty-six employees involved, but also some relocations. 'Attallah closing the book on Asprey,' said the *Daily Telegraph*. The *Financial Times* remembered that, 'In the past Mr Attallah has claimed that "elements" had tried to destabilize the company.' Who were those who conspired to change the order of things at Asprey and what was their true motive? They were not a single entity, although they were allied in a common cause. They regarded me as a threat to their own ambitions, and since I possessed a strong, dominating personality, they did not face an easy task. They knew that a head-on challenge was not the way to go, for they stood no chance of winning. Their only plausible tactic was to split the partnership between John and myself after it had been rock solid over almost two decades. The pact had endured and fought off a number of assaults in the past, but times had changed. The partnership was under stress.

It was natural that, as Asprey grew, the close collaboration between me and John should have suffered. Our different roles in a vastly enlarged company kept us physically apart and the lines of communication between us inevitably became more formal and less frequently used. We each had our own entourage, with the result that in practice two camps came into existence, though in theory, and especially to the outside world, we continued to present a united front. When John and I were together, no one dared to intrude into the relationship. All the antagonists could do was complain that John was under my spell, and until that was broken there was no way any efforts on their part could yield the results they hoped for. Their thrust clearly became diverted into a new kind of warfare: to discredit me as much as possible while boosting John's confidence by attributing most of the company's success to his endeavours and leadership. Massaging his ego was one weapon in their armory, but another, even more potent, was the continual drawing of his attention to the amount of press coverage I was receiving. The implication, they suggested, was that the Asprey profile was being used to further my own personal ambitions.

This was already something that John's wife, Victoria, was rumoured to be incensed by. She had never approved of the close working relationship I had with her husband and by no stretch of the imagination could she be counted among my supporters. She was not an easy person to get on with at the best of times. On marrying John, she became far too grand to fraternize with employees of Asprey, even on special occasions. A case in point had been her refusal to go out to a celebratory dinner after the illustrious Vienna reception held at the British Embassy to mark Garrard's 150th anniversary as Crown Jewellers. John and I had suggested it might be an appropriate sign of appreciation to invite the three main hostesses from the Asprey group who had made the evening such a resounding success. The incident was particularly embarrassing since we had to tell the girls to go out and eat on their own and they must have guessed that Victoria was the cause of what amounted to a snub. It went directly against the company ethos of giving credit where it was due and fostering the spirit of solidarity between staff and management so important in maintaining morale. In any case, the girls concerned came from impeccable family backgrounds. I could only think it had escaped her memory that she herself was working in the handbag department at Asprey's Bond Street showrooms during the time she was courting John.

The way Victoria began to assume airs and graces therefore seemed quite ironic. A fiery redhead with tight, thin lips that spelt danger, she expected John to be constantly at her beck and call. He could hardly leave her side during a reception as his attention had to be focused her way and certainly not on any other attractive female who happened to be in the vicinity. Invariably she surrounded herself with people she considered compatible with her position as wife of the chairman of Asprey, and exerted great influence over her husband. She had her pet hates, notably among people of whom she did not approve. Top of the list came myself, because of my position within the group and my close relationship with John. George Magan ran me a close second: he was far too talented and resourceful for her liking. Then sharing third place was Tomasz Starzewski, for no apparent reason, and Steve Eaves, an executive of Asprey whose choice of merchandise she made no secret of loathing.

My lifestyle was certainly not to her liking and the influence I had over John – in terms of both our business cooperation and social mix – caused her more resentment than anything. She was, it seemed to me, a woman of many tantrums who essentially lacked a sense of humour and wanted to mould the world according to her whims. Words, in her company, had to be carefully selected to conform with a high moral tone if one hoped to curry favour with her. But for many, and especially for those who had known her well prior to her marriage to John, the attitude she assumed was much too transparent to carry any credibility. Nevertheless she became the fulcrum of discontent and so provided those who were conspiring to unseat me with the moral backing they needed. As a result they gained heart and became bolder.

Most notable among the conspirators – though not for his administrative qualities or business acumen but rather more for his mediocrity – was Tom Craig, a former director of Christie's. He had passed his sell-by date long before John recruited him to be his adviser on public-relations matters. When the idea was first floated I had warned John against it, but his heart was set on making the appointment. I only relented in the end and gave approval because of the strength of the arguments being put forward that his connections in the Far East would be of benefit to Asprey. For the first few weeks Tom's aura held John in thrall. They were often to be seen together in deep conversation in the chairman's office, presumably planning for Asprey great things in which Tom would play a crucial part, becoming the new force behind the Asprey legacy.

The initial trip that John and Tom made together took them to India. The expedition was hailed as a big success, not so much on the grounds of the sales it achieved as on the purchases made of old jewellery and other objects of *vertu* from a maharaja friend of Tom's. They spent in excess of a million US dollars on this merchandise, which when closely assessed turned out to be a bad investment. Quite aside from the question of value, the disposal of the pieces then proved to be difficult. As an opening foray, it did not augur well for their future collaboration. Tom in fact became, in my estimation, the most pronounced liability within the group. Needless to say, it was not a story that could have a happy ending. What led to his downfall is mentioned at the end of the piece that follows by Elizabeth Souissi, who worked for the Namara Group for many years and played a key role in its public-relations division.

Elizabeth was a woman with endless energy and remarkable versatility who possessed an endearing personality, theatrically luminous with an engaging sense of humour. Her recollection of the period reminded me of an incident I had completely forgotten about – as if the shock of it had obliterated it from my mind. Perhaps it was this protective mechanism that had all these years spared me the painful memory of what had been a heinous act. Although she does not mention in her piece the name of the Asprey director concerned, she had revealed his identity to me at the time. It was Tom Craig. Who was behind him was never a matter of conjecture. This was much too close to the bone. But as a company embroiled in one scandal after another, we could not risk being entangled yet again. As a precautionary measure I opted to isolate Craig by stripping him of any meaningful task until such time as this shameful affair simmered down and a severance packet could be arranged so that we could see the back of him. This all happened a few months later.

'Cow Grams' and Dissemblers
by Elizabeth Souissi

I came to work at Namara indirectly because of 'cow grams'. At the beginning of my career I worked for many years in the theatre, and sadly during my time as a thespian never received one. A 'cow gram' was a special telegram dispatched to a performer on the occasion of a first night or a première – always very funny, always treasured, and sent by the legendary public-relations man, Theo Cowan.

Now, in the late 1980s, my career had evolved to PR, and I was an account director for an established agency in Sloane Street. By chance, through a financial journalist friend, I then finally, to my delight, met Theo over afternoon tea – me talking about the changing politics of PR and he telling amusing stories and eating cake. Out of the blue, two weeks later, I got an extraordinary call saying I had to come and meet his company chairman, Naim Attallah. One of his co-directors, Janie, was off to help launch TV-am and he thought I might be right to fill the vacancy. Arriving at the given time at Namara House, a five-storey building in Poland Street, I climbed to the top floor.

A beautiful assistant with long blonde hair was curled up in a leather arm-chair at one side while Naim sat at the end of the office, which was mostly made of glass, behind a huge desk with rubies adorning his lapels and fingers. The rooftops of Soho were all around, a tiger rug complete with head was on the floor, and expensive accessories and books were scattered around. 'Tell me about yourself,' he said. After ten minutes he said, 'OK.' This, I quickly learnt, was his way of showing approval and moving on.

As I left the office, Sonamara, the golden goddess, said, 'We are giving a party tonight in honour of the new deputy editor of the *Sunday Telegraph*. Naim would like you to be there.' And what a party: a bevy of beautiful girls dressed in black with 'I love Richard Addis' printed on their dresses, managing to pour everyone drinks from endless jeroboams of champagne from Naim's private cellars. And so began seven years of working with an extraordinary, eccentric and hugely talented set of people who made up the Namara Group.

My position bridged the corporate clients and in-house side of our business (Namara owned three magazines and had interests in many ventures). This meant I worked on and off with everybody: Theo and his team, who handled the big stars; Laurie Bellew, a fastidious craftsman, Theo's long-term partner (though they rarely spoke), who looked after the light-entertainment side; and finally, to complete the diversity, Bertie Rope and Bob Wright and their department, which specialized in the top end of property development.

Our clients ranged from actors to directors, bookbinders, TV channels and solicitors, from top chefs and restaurants to architects and banks. We mixed and matched all under the guidance of Naim, who encouraged, directed and often mediated between us – not forgetting the stoic company secretary, Tim, who meticulously kept the books balanced and our feet on the ground. For the reality was that Naim, being as canny and foresighted as always, often subsidized the business – one venture with another. Entertainment is a notorious loss leader.

The media was filled with our clients and activities, and this in turn opened many doors for his other serious business adventures. One small example was that Naim and Bron Waugh opened an exclusive members' club in Beak Street. Above the club were the offices of their magazine, the *Literary Review*. But beneath, hidden behind a heavy grey door with just a small brass nameplate, was the Academy Club. This was a haven for quiet meetings over toasted sandwiches and fine wine. I remember one such meeting – a first meet with the then ex-minister David Mellor, who had just days before finally resigned as Culture Secretary. I was able to reassure him of the only rule of the club (he was nervous of everything and everybody at the time), that 'anything said there may not be repeated outside', to which he immediately responded by asking me whether it were true that women did not find him very attractive.

Our lives bobbled on, the ideas, the interaction, the events. Naim moved his offices to above Garrard on Regent Street, to continue consolidating more closely with Asprey, and I was told to move my team up to his old offices on the fourth floor. My account executive then was Claudia Ward, who was the second of the actor/writer Simon Ward's beautiful trilogy of daughters. I felt the move was good for Claudia's concentration as it wasn't just once that I tipped a bucket of water out of the first-floor window on to some fawning inamorato trying to attract her attention in the street below.

I had not long been installed behind that huge desk when Sophie McEwen from downstairs called me: 'We can't wake Theo from his nap.' Four flights down he was slumped at his desk – his pulse was weak and I immediately started to administer resuscitation, while Bertie called the emergency service. The ambulance took thirty-five minutes in the West End rush hour and after a while I felt Theo slip away. Bertie called Naim, but Laurie simply packed his briefcase, changed out of his work clothes, which was his nightly routine, and said he was off on a week's holiday, which was his way of dealing with the shock. He knew Theo had died at his desk.

Dirk Bogarde, a life-long client and friend of Theo's, wrote a definitive obituary for the broadsheets entitled 'Dear Thumper'. Laurie returned after a week and arranged a wonderful memorial service at St Martin-in-the-Fields. Standing with Naim and Michael Sellers, I watched as Petula Clark sang, Jeremy Irons read poetry and Michael Caine gave the eulogy.

Some time later I was at a reception at Claridge's where I met four old school friends. It seemed we also had business connections in the form of husbands (theirs) and employees (mine). Shortly after this get-together, I was called by an acquaintance of this group, a seasoned director of Asprey, asking me to lunch. He was an acknowledged fine-arts specialist, with an international reputation, and I was flattered. When I arrived at his club, however, I found I had to enter by the tradesmen's entrance and was seated in an annex for lunch. Women were not allowed in the main dining-room. We were off to a bad start – my boss was Arab and my husband was Arab, and never in my life had I been treated in this way.

Towards the end of the lunch, during which we had simply chatted about the general state of the arts, he dropped in that he had heard I had taken over Naim's old offices, and also understood that Naim's private telephone and fax lines were still connected. Were his old personal papers still there? He began to insinuate that it was odd how Naim had made his fortune and wondered if there were any skeletons in the cupboard – or even whether unusual or untoward dealings were still ongoing. So this was it. If there was anything that came in on Naim's fax or phone, however innocuous, would I let him know? – just a number or two might even be useful to understand Naim's activities.

As I walked back to the office, I knew it had been presumed I was 'old school'. I had been asked to spy on Naim, who was not one of them. But to me 'old school' meant honesty and loyalty, not running with a pack of wolves.

I went to Bertie, who told me I must go to Naim. How does one tell a man who had been the dynamics behind the fortune reversal of Asprey – now such a major world player in the luxury market – that some kind of coup against him was in the making? Naim listened with surprise, and then, always one for action, set up a meeting with the managing director of Asprey and the head of security. Between them, they decided to set up a sting, bugging the director's office, so all conversations could be recorded – and setting up a casual meeting between myself and the director. Somehow I knew that Naim had trusted too many people and I sensed there were other undercurrents.

During the aforesaid sting, I mentioned the director's request for information from Naim's old office. I was met with a full-on quiet smile:

'I'm sorry, I don't know what you could possibly be referring to.' I was not surprised but neither was he.

I went back to Poland Street with a real sense of loss. Theo had gone, Laurie had also moved on and talent hunters were at the door. Some of the group was being sold off. Naim – the indomitable, dynamic Naim – was under siege. The seven years' good luck I had spent at Namara House were at an end.

*   *   *

Meanwhile the 'other bunch' of malcontents were the so-called 'City friends' of John and Victoria, mainly of the latter. Their criticism of me was unrelenting. I was not one of them and had not been to public school. I therefore had no access to the old-school-tie privileged connections of their circle. They could not see me as typical chief-executive material, while I was at pains to steer clear of City analysts who wielded greater power than is usually acknowledged. I refused to be intimidated by them when being questioned and treated the occasional show of arrogance (when the gentlemanly mask slipped) with the disdain it deserved. My tough speaking up won me no friends in the City, while my ability to argue a point did little to add to my popularity. These were typical of the people encouraged by the tacit approval of Victoria, and John found it hard to keep them under control when the going got tough. They went on badgering John to take action, recognizing that his readiness to bow to pressure and his tendency to swerve between one opinion and another must ultimately make him give way to their demands.

The non-executive directors, with the honourable exception of George Magan, played politics to try to enhance their influence within the company. John made an easy target for them. My own view of their function was perfectly clear. I saw their task as being to give the executive branch of the company advice as independent observers and basically to ensure that the interests of all the shareholders were being properly looked after. In the case of Asprey it was an odd situation that required careful handling. How were we to reconcile the interests of a family that owned fifty-two per cent of the shares with those of the minority shareholders? As group chief executive my responsibilities were towards all the shareholders in equal measure and not just those with the controlling interest.

In the end it was a conflict that was to prove intractable. There was many a measure that I attempted to implement which could not be enforced because John refused to abide by it. If I complained to the board, the only response I got was that the reins of power were technically held by the Asprey family and I would somehow have to work the problem out with John. The

[727]

situation was potentially fatal since our financial decline was largely due to the gigantic mountain of stock that John had been accumulating at a time when the recession was biting and our sales were suffering as a result.

David Young, a former senior partner of Spicer & Oppenheim and deputy chairman of Touche Ross, who was also chairman of the Lombard Insurance Group, was perfectly suited to be an independent director. He was highly recommended by our merchant bank, Hambro Magan, who considered his presence on the board would inspire greater confidence. He turned out to be level-headed and he and I formed an excellent working relationship in no time at all. Our modes of operation were different and our views did not always coincide, but we seemed to be complementary in many ways. His conservatism, a typical trait of his profession, frequently gave me pause for reflection in a way that often worked to the advantage of the company. On the other hand, despite his support for me as group chief executive, I had the feeling that his ultimate loyalty would, if tested, veer towards the majority shareholder. I was sure he would not move to defend my corner, regardless of its merits, if it meant jeopardizing his own position on the board. Indeed, why should he have done so? Within the constraints mentioned, he would undoubtedly have acted honourably. My assessment of him was spot on. In due course, he was to play a major role in brokering my retirement package, and was quite prepared to serve the future administration.

Howard Dyer, the most recently appointed non-executive director, was again recommended by Hambro Magan. Besides being chairman of Hamleys, he was also chairman and chief executive of Ascot Holdings, the group's property and hotels company. I welcomed his appointment, believing it would add strength to the board and that, in his capacity as a retailer, he would show a better understanding of our business than most. John Asprey was ecstatic at having a board member of his calibre and in no time at all had pronounced him the new messiah who would guide the company back to more fertile pastures. It was typical of John's mercurial character to go over the top in this way, and embrace someone who hitherto had been a total stranger. This premature burst of enthusiasm led to his becoming John's latest guru for a short period of time and unfortunately gave Howard the wrong signals. The division within the company thereupon took a turn for the worse. The board's disarray was of Babylonian proportions and events ushered in the most destructive period of my entire tenure at Asprey, bringing my health and morale to their lowest ebb.

George Magan, the original non-executive director, who had joined us from Morgan Grenfell, rose above it all. He had no axe to grind with anyone and remained composed and constructive, as he had through all the years I worked with him. He was a unifying factor who never strayed from his goal of raising the profile of Asprey to international status. He genuinely believed that the strength of Asprey lay in the working partnership of John and myself and always maintained in private that the demise of this special relationship would gravely affect the future of the company. The result he foretold came to pass less than a decade later. His own contribution behind the scenes to Asprey's success was substantial. Not only did he help the Asprey family to amass its great fortune, but he also assisted me in turning the company into a conglomerate of the finest purveyors of luxury goods and objects of rare beauty and craftsmanship. Our portfolio of famous brands was the envy of many of our competitors.

Odile Griffith, one of George's senior executives at Hambro Magan, was assigned to work with me on all major acquisitions and proved more than equal to the task. We found common ground from the outset and our cooperation became a byword for quick resolution and efficiency. Looking back, I can only pay her tribute for her dedication and unswerving support.

The clique of schemers included a number of disgruntled employees who had once held senior positions within the company but had never been at the nerve centre. They enjoyed a lifestyle above their station and could not reconcile themselves to the loss of it. One glaring example was Robin Raw, who had first been employed by Asprey in Bond Street a few months before I joined as a consultant in the early 1970s. He had been brought in by the family in the role of general manager as a compromise candidate to avoid plunging the company even deeper into a power struggle between the two family factions who were vying for control. Maurice Asprey and his cousin John had both been contenders for the post that was given to Robin, who on the face of it had all the qualifications necessary for the job. Unfortunately, however, he lacked diplomacy and flexibility. He was too set in his ways, and once embarked upon a certain path, was not to be diverted from it. Not long after my arrival, a real crisis developed involving Robin; discontent among the staff reached a level that threatened serious disruption. A campaign to oust him gained momentum and gave Maurice Asprey a welcome pretext to call for his immediate departure, though he and his father Philip had been responsible for bringing him in in the first place. Now they were clamouring to get rid of him, no matter what it took. John was less affected by Robin's unpopularity, and though he voiced some concern about the whole situation, he did not go so far as to want to throw him out. Eventually the family took the view that internal unrest was too high a price to pay for not getting rid of him.

I was then delegated to negotiate a severance agreement with Robin, which I concluded to the satisfaction of all. A few years later, in the early 1980s, when a vacancy to run Asprey in New York came up, both John Asprey and Tim Cooper, the latter being a friend of Robin's, proposed him to me as the ideal candidate to fill the position. My immediate reaction was to baulk at the suggestion, for I had seen at first hand how he functioned. The many deficiencies he had were for me enough to preclude him from being a potential candidate, but John and Tim were of a different opinion. He had, they maintained, changed a lot since his early days at Asprey and was now much improved. They claimed the concerns I was expressing were no longer relevant, and at once went to work on me to get me to reconsider.

They arranged for me to see Robin, and I had to admit that I found him more relaxed and, on the face of it, more flexible. He had, no doubt, been briefed to play it cool in order to secure my endorsement. I was won round to the extent where I admitted he might be a great asset as 'our man in New York', given his Englishness and his *savoir faire*. We were all to be proved mistaken. His tenure in the New York store, over more than ten years, obstinately failed to yield the results we were expecting. The New York branch lost money consistently, and we felt we could no longer carry the burden of having to subsidize it. Trading in the city was admittedly extremely competitive, but the feeling gained ground that Robin's approach was much too complacent ever to achieve the breakthrough we were looking for.

At Garrard, in London, I was meanwhile tussling with a parallel problem. After appointing Richard Jarvis to replace Edward Green, I was desperate to find a suitable position for Edward, who was now monitoring Garrard's interests in Japan. It seemed to me that the infiltration of Edward into the New York set would be likely to boost sales and turn stagnation into a flurry of fresh activity. He had a background in a distinguished Jewish family and vast connections within the international Jewish community. The recall of Robin Raw therefore looked timely, and I was proposing that he should take over the helm of the newly acquired Watches of Switzerland. By virtue of Tim Cooper's friendship with Robin, I sent him to New York to offer him what I thought he would see as a most fulfilling new challenge. But Robin and his ambitious wife Jane were, on the contrary, very reluctant to move from New York. During Robin's presidency of Asprey New York they had established themselves on the social circuit, where their mode of living and the comforts they enjoyed suited them very well. In the end, however, they bowed to the inevitable and resigned themselves to returning to England.

Everything seemed to have simmered down until Robin, on his arrival, came to see me to discuss the terms of his new appointment. He was expecting to be given the same facilities that he had enjoyed while abroad.

This was out of the question. It would seriously have compromised the position of more senior people within the company to have elevated Robin to a status he had done nothing to deserve. The whole system of salaries and benefits would have to have been reviewed to accommodate his demands. Finding himself in a corner, and well aware that I was adamant, he grudgingly accepted slightly improved terms on those already offered. But then, rather than settle down to his new job, he set about plotting a way to send shock waves throughout the conglomerate.

Early in 1992, Robin went to see the two Asprey directors who were then representing Sears Holdings, Geoffrey Maitland-Smith and Harold Perlin, with serious allegations against John Asprey, Tim Cooper and myself. The gravity of these accusations led the two directors concerned to refer the matter, without our knowledge, to the company's auditors, Ernst & Young. John Asprey and I were furious that Geoffrey had chosen this route without talking to us first. It became a sore point and could have wrecked the excellent relationship we had formed and maintained throughout the years of our association. It led to our formulating, as a precautionary measure, and on the advice of the auditors, a procedure for dealing with such matters that would avoid a recurrence of the unsatisfactory way in which the affair was handled. In the meantime, we instituted a full-scale investigation to be carried out by the auditors to remove any remaining doubts left by the allegations. When all the aspersions were found to be baseless, Robin was immediately suspended and eventually dismissed. I could only think the motive behind his actions was that he was simply trying to derail us.

What the whole exercise made alarmingly clear was the amount of intrigue that was bedevilling the company even at its very heart. Every detail of the accusations had been leaked to the press by someone who had access to internal information. The *Observer* gave the facts a dubious spin with its headline of 20 November 1994, 'Asprey Trio Faced Probe', going on to say that three Asprey directors had been investigated by the company's auditor, whose accountant 'launched the inquiry after allegations were made' against John Asprey, myself and Tim Cooper.

It coincided with preparation of the company's annual audit. All three directors were cleared by Ernst & Young, according to an Asprey spokesman . . .

The firm prepared a report, dated 16 July 1992, and presented it to the Asprey board a day later. In what may be part of a continuing attempt by an unknown source to damage Asprey, part of the minutes of that board meeting have been leaked to the *Observer*.

Such was the seriousness of the subject under discussion that as well as Richard Murray, the Ernst & Young partner in charge of Asprey, two solicitors from Macfarlanes, the company's City lawyer, were also present.

Richard Murray had said that 'his firm, when faced with suggestions or questions, which together clearly amounted to allegations, found themselves in an appalling situation'. While they were mindful of the vital importance of fulfilling their duty to the shareholders, they were also aware of the damage that could be done to the shareholders through any mishandling of the situation.

Whoever supplied the portion of the minutes to the *Observer* did not send any details of the allegations themselves, though the paper was able through 'inquiries' to say they were believed to relate to a 'sale of items of jewellery to customers in the Middle East and the performance of subsidiaries, notably in Switzerland'. These insinuations were surfacing only a week after the leaking of the Bank of Scotland's draft memorandum concerning the twenty-million-pound loan facility, which made it look as if there may have been a calculated attempt

> to harm further the company which has not recovered from a shock profits warning in September. Increasingly, the company appears to be the target of a concerted campaign of rumours and leaks . . .
>
> An Asprey spokesman said: 'Ernst & Young looked into these allegations and found no truth in them whatsoever.' He added: 'We're talking about something that happened two and a half years ago. We have to ask ourselves, why are people bringing up these allegations now?'

Asprey had also shown the *Observer* a letter from Macfarlanes confirming the conclusion of the auditors that the allegations had been baseless.

Robin Raw had meanwhile been to an industrial tribunal to claim wrongful dismissal, the outcome of the case being a settlement out of court, as the *Daily Telegraph* reported the following week, on 27 November 1994. His solicitor, Peter Carter-Ruck, described him as being 'very pleased' with the settlement and I confirmed it as being 'satisfactory to all parties'. Raw had been sacked in 1992, the *Sunday Telegraph* explained, when he

> complained to at least one big investor about the alleged activities of Asprey's Geneva subsidiary. His concerns included its over-reliance on a few rich Middle Eastern clients and the role played by Attallah's private companies, Namara and Al Manara, which he alleged received commissions on Asprey's Middle Eastern business . . .
>
> When Raw was sacked, director Timothy Cooper said his allegations

about the policies pursued by Attallah and chairman John Asprey had destroyed 'the relationship of trust and confidence' between him and the board . . . Raw [also] criticized Asprey's acquisitions, including Watches of Switzerland.

We only agreed to settle his claim out of court for two reasons. The first was to demonstrate that, by not retaliating in the same vein, we were above sinking to Raw's level. The second was our reluctance to be seen washing our dirty linen in public. Asprey had already suffered more than its share of unwanted publicity and needed no more tinder to reignite the pyre. I had no wish to be vindictive, though I could not say the same about Robin. He seemed to have shown a degree of ruthlessness that defied comprehension. He had betrayed the three people who had offered him a unique opportunity to redeem himself after he had botched his first job with Asprey. Where else would he have have received the same consideration?

The final person to mention as flirting with conspiracy was Edward Asprey, whose father, Algernon, had plotted to wrench control of the company from us after we had brought him in from the wilderness and rehabilitated him. We were aware that the son was another whose strategy for survival seemed to be to engage in subversive activities. He was nevertheless perceived as a lightweight, with no particular influence, except that he carried the Asprey name, which gave him some kind of cachet. His telephone conversations, especially those with Tom Craig, had been monitored and recorded by security after they became concerned about the constant internal leaks of information and the damage these represented to the company. Having gathered the relevant tapes as part of their job, they then handed them over to me and I kept them as evidence of pathetic fumbling attempts to spread rumours and innuendoes, all of them of a divisive nature. On many occasions I saved Edward's skin when both John and Tim became exasperated by his bungling and were thinking of sacking him. Yet he considered me to be his greatest foe and never lost an opportunity of disparaging me on the outside. I could easily have shown him the door, but I opted to ignore it and treat his intrigues with the contempt they deserved.

*

Despite the turmoil at Asprey, which had been incessant since late 1994, I managed to maintain a level-headed approach to most things. I made a point of never allowing a crisis to take over my life. My optimism remained unassailable and my purchase of some Asprey shares reflected my confidence in the future of the company. On the philosophical side, I had given the

Independent Magazine in December my fantasy for the Christmas presents I *really* wanted:

> There is nothing of a material nature I would like for Christmas since I have been blessed with worldly goods beyond expectations. However, in an ideal world, I would wish to sustain the energy I have at present complemented by the love of life and the hunger for knowledge which I have had since childhood.

I was also able to crystallize my thoughts further on the importance of women in life and the workplace for an issue of *Options* magazine:

> Women are motivated by being an integral part of a project. They like to work in an atmosphere which is friendly, varied and which acknowledges achievement. Power-wise, they may be less ambitious than men, but they are equally eager to succeed. And they bring a healthy, complementary tension between the sexes, creating vitality at work. I prefer to work with women because they energize me and I find them more flexible and adaptable to change.

In the same column, Auberon Waugh contributed his own views, which differed from mine only in the detail:

> Women bring cheerfulness, glamour, kindness, sympathy and generosity of nature. Some women may be as ambitious as men, but not in my office, thank God. Women's motivation is totally different from men's – an extension of the nest-making syndrome. At the *Literary Review*, it's a bit like producing a baby a month.

Some of the subjects for the interviews I was continuing to conduct for the *Oldie* held views that attracted comment, like James Lees-Milne's contentious prejudice against Bangladeshis. He had already called them 'ghastly people' who 'ought not to exist' in his published diaries, and added to this, in conversation with me, that 'until they can be stopped breeding I really do think the future is very bleak indeed'. 'Heaven knows,' wondered the *Evening Standard*, 'why this queeny old fool, a sort of Alf Garnett in spats, is regularly hailed by critics as "supremely civilized", possessed of a "dry wit" and so on. The fault must lie in the translation.'

Spike Milligan, thought the *Daily Express*, must have spiked 'his guns for a knighthood' after telling me he did not consider the Queen 'a very charismatic woman. I've never been moved by one of her speeches, because she's got such a cold voice. And she likes hunting and shooting, which is just murder.' This, of course, was what Spike really felt, but it came hot on the heels of his much-publicized piece of anarchic humour when he called his friend, the Prince of Wales, a 'little grovelling bastard', following this up with an apology saying he supposed a knighthood was now out of the question.

The troubled times continued at Asprey, where, wrote Nils Pratley in the *Daily Telegraph* on 6 May, 'it is Mr Attallah's craggy Palestinian features that have become the public face of the company'.

> Asprey has undergone unprecedented scrutiny in the past year as the share price has collapsed after a couple of dreadful trading statements and persistent rumours that worse was lurking,
>
> There is not much Mr Attallah could do about the trading. The past year has been tough for retailers of luxury goods . . .
>
> More worrying has been what Mr Attallah calls 'the orchestrated campaign to discredit us'. The tales have certainly been persistent . . .
>
> In twenty years he has taken the company from virtually no profit to £25 million at the peak and maintains that the underlying strength is still there . . . 'I hope when I leave, Asprey will be perceived as a very strong company with great potential for the future.' . . .
>
> Mr Attallah's last months could still provide plenty of excitement.

The recession, however, was still with us and sales were lower across the entire spectrum, from Garrard to Mappin & Webb and Watches of Switzerland. The stock held at Asprey was much above the budgeted target, with John still refusing to be reined in despite my pleas. The imbalance was causing us a grave shortage of liquidity. John found it hard to adapt to changing circumstances and fell back on the argument that the wealth of stock generates sales, and that unless we had plenty of it, the chances of overcoming the current difficulties would stay remote. His most important customer over the years had failed to make any substantial contribution to our turnover during the previous twelve months. John was hoping that this abstinence from spending would be short-lived. The same thing had happened in the past and been rectified at a later date. John's optimism would have been well placed had the time factor been irrelevant. But the pressure on us could not be tolerated and a major breakthrough needed to happen as soon as possible.

The problem of stock had come to the surface as a result of its slow-moving performance and it had to be addressed. Measures to remedy the situation were already overdue since the stock had reached an unprecedented level of a hundred and forty-seven million pounds against the preferred level of a hundred and twenty-five million. The shortage of liquidity stemmed from this stock excess of twenty-two million pounds. These difficulties were compounded by virulent internal division. John chose to countermand many of my instructions, at the cost of his own credibility. Senior management of the group continued to report to me in my capacity as chief executive and seemingly took little notice of anything John had to say. What some of us could only see as his silly behaviour was shrugged off by those who witnessed it as another display of petulance. He was certainly not doing himself any favours, nor was he advancing the interests of the company. He appeared to be suffering from the delusion, fostered by his so-called friends, that he was the lifeblood of the institution; that it was solely thanks to his salesmanship that Asprey had scaled the heights of success in the previous two decades; and that I was the black devil who led him astray. Not that this was the official version: the semblance of unity was well rehearsed and stage-managed. The might of the City was directed against me, with shareholders now openly clamouring for my resignation. In a show of solidarity, the board of Asprey refused to heed their call and a battle for my removal was postponed until the next AGM, when, by rotation, I had to submit myself for re-election. This rallying behind me was more a matter of expediency than a genuine show of support, as future events would show.

When I look back on my relationship with John, it is obvious that it had many facets. Until the early 1990s, our working partnership had proved ideal. Our complementarity held it together and preserved it in the outside world. It was to endure a number of setbacks, but none of these ever affected its solidity. John, being conscious of his own vulnerability, kept some of his connections close to his chest and avoided sharing them with me. A prime example among these was the Sultan of Oman, with whom John had developed a special relationship. My many attempts to persuade John to let me meet the Sultan fell on deaf ears. He maintained that I would not be welcomed by the tightly knit cabal of English advisers who surrounded the Sultan, including Tim Landon, the most prominent member of the group. Apparently Landon, who had helped the Sultan usurp power from his father, had intimated to John that my presence in Oman would not be favourably received. Apart from one short trip, I was never allowed to go to the sultanate in case my presence upset the equilibrium of current arrangements.

I had mixed feelings about the reasons for my exclusion. Basically John was not keen to introduce me to the Sultan lest it undermine the exclusivity of his dealings with him; in other words, my sudden bursting on to the scene might dilute his own influence. The Tim Landon story was credible, but it did not represent an insurmountable barrier. It served John's purposes to use it as an excuse. Had I ever met the Sultan, who knows what the encounter might have produced. As it was, I was never to know.

After the early 1990s, when our success was at its zenith, John's character underwent some palpable changes. By this time he was a wealthy man and the warmth that naturally ties associates together during their years of struggle seemed gradually to ebb away. Our relationship was going through a period of adjustment to take into account the disparity in our wealth and John's new entourage. We were no longer able to travel together on a regular basis as we had previously, enjoying those lighter moments of fun that had characterized our close link over the years. John was moving in a circle of friends who extolled his success to gain patronage and win for themselves the kind of influence that could secure for them an important role in the destiny of Asprey. Their advice followed the usual theme: that John should exercise his power not only as chairman and majority shareholder but also indirectly as executive supremo.

Fifty-eight

It made a welcome change when the newspapers covered a story not connected with Asprey. There was a relief in thinking that life still existed beyond the confines of the embattled company. Every morning for the past few months I would start the day by having to deal with the latest episode of the Asprey saga. The constant harping on the same subject made matters worse as well as tedious. The story the *Daily Express* ran on 21 February 1995 concerned the late Sir Nicholas Fairbairn and his unpublished manuscript. On his deathbed, it seemed, the flamboyant MP for Kinross and West Perthshire, known as a politician, advocate, wit and raconteur, had enquired anxiously about when his second volume of autobiography would be published. It was to be entitled *A Life Is Far Too Short*, its predecessor having been called *A Life Is Too Short*. A family friend was quoted as saying, 'It annoyed him that he had no firm publication date. It covered the most interesting part of his life as a parliamentarian.' Had he lived, he was evidently planning to write a third volume to make it a trilogy.

The first volume, published in 1987, had sold moderately well for Quartet, and naturally did best in the author's native Scotland. It told the story of his childhood and youth through to the early stages of his political career. In his career in the law, he had become one of the most brilliant advocates of his generation, and the account included reconstructions of some of his most challenging cases. His interest in the arts also featured, especially in the spheres of theatre and architecture. The original commission had been for a one-volume autobiography, but the text ended with his election to Parliament in 1974. Nicholas Fairbairn then undertook to write and deliver a second and concluding volume. The two editors at Quartet who would be looking after the book were Piers Blofeld and Jeremy Beale. As time went by, Jeremy got the impression that Sir Nicholas was finding the second volume very difficult to write. His political and personal life had been going through a chequered phase. A former mistress had tried to hang herself outside his London flat and a serious drink problem was showing signs of undermining his health.

In February 1988 Sir Nicholas had written to say the manuscript would be ready that autumn; and in April 1993 he promised the writing would be finished that summer. Finally, in February 1995, shortly before his death the same month, he delivered a mass of manuscript that in Jeremy's view would be 'best described as incoherent', consisting of 'a selection of anecdotes and rants, including some unattractive score-settling (notably with Michael Mates), none of which added up to anything like a concluding volume of autobiography'. Nevertheless Quartet tried to see what might be salvaged to make a publishable and saleable book that would reflect favourably on its late author. The idea had the blessing of Lady Fairbairn, but unfortunately the solicitors to the executors of the will insisted they must have total editorial control. Letters to the solicitors then went unanswered and suggested drafts were never returned. Fairbairn gradually became an increasingly peripheral figure, remembered more for his drinking and for disinheriting his daughters than for any of his better qualities. Eventually it was decided that the project was unlikely to yield any significant result and work on it was terminated. Through circumstances it ended sadly as a book idea that remained just that.

On a subject nearer to home, on 30 May, the *Evening Standard* published a scathing review by Ed Marriott of *A Timeless Passion*, the first novel to carry my name as author. 'Lurid sex, but little else' ran the headline. The synopsis had sounded promising, wrote Mr Marriott, outlining the story of Carlo, who returns from London to Italy for his mother's funeral and rediscovers passion through an adulterous affair; but 'as a work of fiction' the book 'fails lamentably'.

The characters are cut-outs, vehicles only for Attallah's peculiarly trite philosophies . . .

Then there are the sex scenes, described in a lurid Technicolor reminiscent of the worst romantic fiction. This is a world where nipples 'burgeon like hyacinth buds' and male ejaculation causes whole hillsides to 'sing in chorus'.

But most astonishing is Attallah's attempt to liken Carlo's mental journey to Jesus' crucifixion . . .

In Mr Marriott's judgement:

Attallah has written a book that is heavy on metaphor, homily and home-spun analysis, but light on the stuff that brings novels alive: rounded characters, credible conversation, explicable motive.

All of this was to help stoke the flames of a literary onslaught on myself instigated almost ten years later by the publication of Jennie Erdal's memoirs, *Ghosting*. In these she proclaimed how I had taken credit for writing the novel when the real author had been herself. The second novel to appear under my name, *Tara and Claire*, was also her work, she said. Although the themes for the two titles were my inventions, I would never dispute the fact that the finished books were realized through her writing. The part with which I find myself at odds concerns the reasons behind the arrangement. Her version of how the collaboration came about is so heavily laden with shortcomings in memory that it can only suggest a large measure of ill-will towards me, in spite of the many years of our friendship and close working relationship. The true motivation behind the writing of the two novels was not as she claims and had nothing to do with my ego. There were other, more mundane considerations that she omitted to mention, but I have no wish to expound on this issue. It would give me no comfort to breach the only remaining ethical aspect of our long-standing collaboration.

However, if restitution is what she is after, she need not worry. The spoils are truly hers. She is welcome to *A Timeless Passion* and *Tara and Claire* as her own imaginative property. I have omitted them from my list of literary works and the unsold stock bearing my name has been pulped. Another small book, *A Woman a Week*, where I now consider her contribution to have been too close for comfort, has similarly been omitted from my authorship list and any remaining stock destroyed. A vow had been broken, and this in my view completes my intellectual liberation from what regrettably turned out to be an ungodly alliance

With the question of authorship disposed of, it can be said that reviews of *A Timeless Passion* in fact turned out to be a mixed bag and there were those who took it seriously. Albert Read in *The Times Literary Supplement*, after deciding that its downfall as a novel was due to the fact that, 'as it progresses, the characters and the narrative possibilities are pushed around and moulded by the ideas expressed', concluded on a positive note by saying it had 'a charming simplicity and clarity to it, and what emerges is a work that is elegant, thoughtful, romantic and unassuming'. The *Daily Express* neatly encapsulated the story, calling it

a moving novel in which sedately married Carlo, a London ad executive, returns to Italy to bury his mother and has an ecstatic love-at-first-sight affair with unhappily married Petra. The calm, wifely lovemaking and the wildness of the affair with Petra are ingeniously contrasted.

Ulick O'Connor in the *Oldie* thought it 'an original first venture', though it 'could well have dispensed with some of the descriptive passages of love-making that occur'; Simon Ward in the *Literary Review* said it was

hardly the typical English novel, although its language is fine and resonant. It is rather the French novel of ideas and contemplation. Its structure, with Carlo's journey a mirror held up to the Stations of the Cross, possibly daunting in a longer work, succeeds in giving shape to what is basically a philosophical argument on *la condition humaine* first between Carlo and Carlo and then between Carlo and Petra.

The overwhelming nature of their suddenly discovered love forces them both to question the paradoxes that lie behind such passion: the betrayal of others, the necessary duplicity balanced against their own experience of the purity and inevitability of love.

Cristina Odone in the *Catholic Herald* saw the love story as providing

a sensual leitmotif to Attallah's cerebral and spiritual preoccupation with Everyman's burden: our ability to make sense of an existence which places our infinite spirit in a finite world . . .

By the end, the hero discovers that in every choice lies a renunciation and finds his faith waging war against his love: it is from this dilemma that the novel draws its timeless passion.

In the wake of the press coverage for the book, *ES* magazine made an assessment of who was making the grade up or down on the party circuit that June, with the convivial character actor Christopher Biggins holding top place; though he was being closely pressed by Lord and Lady Linley, Salman Rushdie (who had not been hindered by the fatwa from 'schmoozing with all and sundry') and Bob Geldof. On the way down, however, was 'financier and publisher Naim Attallah, whose currency has devalued since no one can look him in the eye after reading the lurid sex scenes in his new novel'.

Also still sliding downwards was Asprey's share value as the worsening of the group's crisis had become common knowledge by the end of June. The newspaper coverage had continued to do nothing to help matters. Over the previous few months, the constant highlighting of the difficulties facing the group had brought about a dramatic fall in share price from three hundred and fifty pence to fifty-nine pence. An article in the *Evening Standard* by James Bartholomew on 8 June had been without doubt the most damaging. Given great prominence in a double-page spread, it chronicled accusations that had been shown to be false long since; and while it referred to these as falsehoods, the mere repetition of them was enough to keep doubts alive in people's minds. There were also insinuations of share dealings by myself and other directors, done prior to the announcement, the previous September, warning that results were going to be only 'marginally profitable'. The implications of wrongdoing, added to the leaked memo from the Bank of Scotland and other allegations hinting at incestuous dealings between Asprey and my own company, Namara, were perhaps the last straw in a losing battle with the media. From that point on, everything seemed to be going downhill.

The 25 June headline to an article by Jeff Randall, City editor of the *Sunday Times*, read: 'Queen's jeweller crashes into loss: Asprey's stock revaluation wipes out profits'. There were to be write-downs on unsold stock of about ten million pounds as well as a charge of about five million relating to store closures and redundancies. By now Nick Harrington had announced his resignation from the board as financial director for 'personal reasons'.

The City has long suspected that Asprey's troubles run deeper than the group has been prepared to admit. But the extent of this week's exceptional losses are likely to shock even its sternest critics.

In 1993–94, Asprey made £25 million pre-tax. But since then, the group has been hard hit by collapsing margins, management problems, and persistent rumours that at least one heavyweight Middle East client had ordered millions of pounds of custom-built jewellery and then changed his mind . . .

According to one City observer: 'Asprey is still a wonderful name. But the company is in dire need of a finance director; the chief executive has got to be changed; and I'm not sure that John Asprey is the right man to be chairman.'

Mr Randall pressed home his attack in the 'Agenda' column of the same paper, quoting a remark I had made that, 'It is good for Asprey to have new blood.'

Too right. It needs a new finance director and a replacement for Attallah pronto . . . The trick, however, is finding the right leader. If the appropriate man, or woman, comes along, Attallah ought to quit early.

The chairman, John Asprey, may also consider his position. He owns 50 per cent plus of the group, so what he says goes. But his time in the chair cannot be described as a success, and in order to rebuild the value in his shareholding he could do worse than make way for an outsider.

John was again a focus for hostile comment in the *Sunday Times* on 2 July, when Kirstie Hamilton quoted a former adviser describing him as 'a brilliant man to sell a diamond bracelet but completely unsuited to being chairman of a public company'.

In the financial columns of the press there were now numerous if unoriginal headlines referring to the 'tarnishing' of the royal jewellers, to the 'sparkle' and the 'shine' being lost. On 11 August we finally came to the Asprey group AGM, held at the Meridien Hotel, when I needed to stand for re-election to the board if I was to work out my notice of retirement. As the

Independent commented next day, it was a 'feisty and occasionally disorganized meeting at which the Asprey board were peppered with questions from angry shareholders demanding explanations for the company's recent dire performance'. The investors, said *The Times*, accused the management 'of having no control over the troubled business and of being complacent about its future'. Shareholder George Williams was quoted as saying: 'One can have no faith in any of you gentlemen sitting there. This business is not in your control. I have lost faith in you.' A particular focus of investor criticism was 'a £1.4 million diamond-studded egg', illustrated in Asprey's annual report, which was set with 220 carats of princess-cut diamonds in white gold and contained a pair of diamond and platinum earrings. Why did this 'foible and bauble', one shareholder who was critical of the high stock levels wished to know, have three and a half years expended on it? Had it been just to show 'how clever we were'? John Asprey explained that when the princess egg was started three and a half years earlier, 'the market looked particularly buoyant', but by the time it was finished no one would buy it.

A question fired in my direction by someone mindful of my literary career said: 'You have to have a chief executive who is twenty-four hours on the job and you haven't.' This, said the *Independent*, 'appeared to anger Mr Attallah', who responded: 'I work longer hours than anyone else in the company. I get into the office at 7.30 a.m. and I never have any holidays.' The expansion programme was also inevitably heavily criticized.

> In response, Mr Asprey said that the company had a 'wonderful basket of names', but that the recession, the Gulf War, and problems at the Lloyd's insurance market had reduced the spending power of wealthy customers. Mr Attallah added: 'If we hadn't taken these steps we would be in an even worse position today.'

As it came to the vote, those shareholders who wished to see me gone had their chance to make their feelings known with a show of hands. In the event,

> more shareholders voted against Mr Attallah's reappointment than in favour. The chairman, John Asprey, then ordered a poll in which the proxy votes cast by institutional shareholders carried the vote in Mr Attallah's favour.
>
> The poll results showed that shareholders present at the meeting voted against Mr Attallah's appointment by a ratio of four to one. But the total vote including proxies saw Mr Attallah win 51.8 million votes with only 1.2 million against.

Thus, said *The Times*, 'Mr Attallah was assured of his seat on the board until he retires next year'. Meanwhile it was confirmed that Lloyds Bank had 'obtained security over Asprey's four principle outlets', while also receiving 'a fixed charge over the shares in the group's subsidiary companies'. The net result of this, in simple terms, was that all the assets and buildings of the group were mortgaged to Lloyds Bank.

On the same day as the AGM, the first public airing of a fresh and unrelated problem heading in my direction came with a piece in 'Londoner's Diary' in the *Evening Standard* referring to a biography entitled *The Man from Nowhere: The Mysterious Life of Naim Attallah*. The authors were two investigative journalists, Frank Dobson and Ken Parish, who were dropping hints about my lack of cooperation, implying I might have something to conceal. 'I'm trying to produce an objective biography,' Mr Dobson claimed. 'Naim is a very fascinating and complex man, whose origins are shrouded in mystery.' The publishers were Blake Publishing, who had already run an advertisement in *Publishing News* on 14 July, announcing a publication date of 10 October (though this was later revised to the following spring) and asking, 'But where did this enigmatic and exotic figure, and his money, come from?' Mr Dobson was guaranteeing to have all the answers. *Private Eye* was quick to take its cue from this at the end of August:

Naim Attallah-Disgusting has a new dirty book to plug – his own *Timeless Passion* – but the world of letters is more interested in a forthcoming dirty book *about* him.

While the awaited biography promises to reveal secrets from Attallah's murky past, his present is none too chipper.

There was more to Mr Dobson's 'objectivity' than was immediately evident. The fact was that he had initially been approached by the family of the late Yusif Bedas, who were looking for material to bolster their allegations that, as an executor of the Bedas estate, I had cheated them out of a portion of what was due to them. They were willing to resort to the underhand tactic of commissioning Dobson to investigate my dealings not only in the Gulf but worldwide. The brief they gave him was simply to dish any dirt he could find by whatever means possible, hoping this would lend plausibility to their vicious campaign to discredit me. The manuscript Dobson produced was calculated to insinuate that my so-called wealth must have been derived from their purloined inheritance. Despite the lack of any supporting evidence, they were determined to sully my name by using concoction and innuendo. While Dobson did his best to imply a lack of candour on my part, my solicitors, Biddle & Co., were quite unable to obtain a glimpse of what the authors' text contained.

I finally got to see the manuscript at the Frankfurt Book Fair that autumn when the proprietor of Blake Publishing, John Blake – a former editor of the *People* – agreed to give me sight of a copy. I was able to tell him almost at once that the text contained a lot of inaccuracies, and that if it was published in its present form I would have no alternative but to sue for damages and prevent its distribution. John Blake said he certainly had no wish to fall out with me. The suggestion he made was that I pay him the advance he had laid out to the authors and take over the rights and the manuscript. The sum involved was not large, and in the meantime Mr Parish had judiciously dropped out of the collaboration and left Mr Dobson to finish the book on his own.

Mr Dobson was unaware of the negotiations that then ensued between Blake Publishing and Quartet. He was naturally livid when he received a letter from John Blake in February 1996 confirming that the 'contract signed between yourselves and Blake Publishing on 3 May 1995' had been transferred to 'another publisher', adding that: 'Your new publisher will be Jeremy Beale, Quartet Books.' He put his side of the story in a piece which appeared in the *Observer Review* on 25 February called 'Passage of rights – the strange case of Naim Attallah, the man who bought his own biography'. I did not deny that Mr Dobson had sent me a list of fifty-seven questions some time before, and that I had refused to cooperate with these because of their scurrilous nature. So now, Peter Hillmore of the *Observer* wanted to know, would I sue Quartet if they published the book? 'Maybe,' I said, 'but look, the copyright belongs to the author and at the end of the day the rights will revert to him.' 'Mr Attallah has been putting difficulties in my path,' protested Mr Dobson, 'advising people not to talk to me, ever since he heard about the book. This is just one more difficulty.' Other publishers and agents were evidently in agreement that they had never heard of another case like it.

'Attallah has last word on biography', was Chris Blackhurst's headline in the *Independent* on 22 February:

What was billed in this spring's *Bookseller* lists as *The Man from Nowhere* now shows every sign of becoming the biography that goes nowhere . . .

Mr Beale, of Quartet, said yesterday his firm intended to publish the book 'subject to editorial and legal requirements'. He had not read the manuscript before buying it, he admitted.

Quartet, he said, operated independently of Mr Attallah. 'We pride ourselves on editorial freedom and we publish books independently of Mr Attallah's taste,' he said.

Mr Dobson was then quoted as saying: 'I am not interested in a publishing deal with Quartet because it would not be the book I've written. This is a blatant and rather stupid attempt to suppress a story I believe should be told.' He had already instructed his lawyers to seek return of the photographs and manuscript he submitted to Blake Publishing. Mr Dobson ended up with a manuscript that was unpublishable since no responsible publisher would have touched it with a bargepole.

After the turbulent Asprey AGM of August 1995 I felt a desperate need for a break. I decided to spend a few days at our house in the Dordogne, simply to unwind and recharge my batteries. Getting away from it all for a short period would also, I considered, give me the opportunity to reflect on my future in the calm of the countryside. The decision taken a few months before to retire from Asprey when I reached the age of sixty-five had not been entirely voluntary. I was not the retiring kind in that sense. As I write this eleven years further on, I am still hard at work, rising at five-thirty and putting in a full day at the office. The reason for my decision to quit Asprey at that time and call it a day was the realization that the bond between John Asprey and myself was broken and pretending it wasn't was wearing me down.

John oscillated from one extreme to the other, showing solidarity one day but being caught out in intrigue the next. It was no longer possible for me to know where I stood or to be confident of his support. On the contrary, I was convinced that he aimed to get rid of me as soon as the right opportunity presented itself, though he never had the courage to admit it openly. It therefore came as no surprise to find, when I returned from the Dordogne, that a chief executive designate had been hired during my absence. John did not have the guts to face me personally with this news, but delegated David Young, a member of the Asprey board, to convey it to me. David was given an unenviable task, but did his best to be as diplomatic as possible. He suggested that I should meet the new man, and if I liked him, to go ahead and conclude his employment contract. It was a farcical state of affairs, since I knew full well that my approval was a formality when his employment had already been agreed upon by the company, my endorsement being merely a public-relations exercise. The humiliation for me was crushing, and John, as usual, wriggled out of this unpleasant situation by placing the blame on others who, he alleged, had pressurized him into going along with the appointment. I never dreamt I would ever suffer such a loss of dignity and the psychological scars I am left with will never fade. There is no plastic surgery possible to remove them and I carry them as a badge of honour to remind me that in the end decency triumphs over mendacity.

Later John was to be subjected to worse humiliation than that he perhaps unwittingly inflicted on me by the man he engineered to replace me. But that is another story for another time. My replacement, Ian Dahl, then aged fifty, came from a marketing background that began with ten years at Marks & Spencer before a period in Australia as general manager of the department store Myer Melbourne. He had then been divisional manager of House of Fraser back in England before returning to Australia to head the fashion retailer Sportsgirl and turn it from loss to profit. Currently he was working as a retail consultant in the UK while representing an overseas venture-capital company. He was, said the *Independent* of 31 August, something of an unknown quantity in UK retailing. My own high profile with the press helped to ensure substantial newspaper coverage for my successor. The *Independent* described us thus:

> Sitting next to each other yesterday, the pair appeared chalk and cheese. While Mr Attallah was wearing a pink silk shirt, designer tie, odd socks and jewellery, Mr Dahl preferred the merchant-banker look with pinstripes, white shirt and more low-key neckwear.

The *Daily Telegraph* wrote:

> Mr Dahl, dressed in a blue pinstripe suit, white shirt and sober paisley tie, contrasted sharply yesterday with Mr Attallah's purple and coral coloured socks, salmon-pink silk shirt, two gold watches and pistachio-green patterned tie.
>
> 'We have very different personalities clearly, but there is a meeting of minds,' Mr Dahl said. 'I don't see my task as a personality sales executive.'

All the papers were unanimous that there would be a change in management style at the Asprey group – from my more entrepreneurial approach to Ian Dahl's focus on retailing. 'Businesses like this tend to go through an entrepreneurial stage,' said Mr Dahl, 'but we need a period of consolidation and a return to norms of retailing. That means strong financial management, customer service, focus on shrinkage and other costs.' He saw himself as 'very much a hands-on retailer' and a logical choice to follow 'the commercial skills of Mr Attallah'.

I was generally quoted as saying I would be turning my attention back to the arts: 'I need a new dimension and there's a lot of kick left in me.' Unbeknown to me, Dahl must have been discreetly told that my remaining period as group chief executive would be much shorter than previously indicated. The transition of power was to be swift once he had familiarized himself with his new surroundings and felt he had been adequately briefed. I suspected as much when Dahl showed signs of wanting to take over almost immediately to avoid, as he put it, any ambiguity of where the power was now vested. Again John Asprey was behind the machinations, personally or as the tool of his advisers and his wife Victoria, who I was told could not wait to see the back of me.

My three months with Dahl, however, were conducted with great professionalism. He never over-stepped the mark, showing me respect to the very end. He said he was going to find me a hard act to follow, being very aware of the role I had played over twenty-one years in building the little empire he was about to inherit. Speculations about the possibility of my early leaving continued to be rife in the press. They were being fed by leaks of material from within the company that was only available to John and his entourage. *The Times* reported on 5 October:

> Speculation is mounting that Naim Attallah, the controversial chief of Asprey, the ailing Bond Street jewellers, will shortly bow out . . .
>
> [But] no handover period was specified. John Asprey, chairman and principle shareholder in the company, refused to comment on rumours that Mr Attallah will leave before the end of the year. He said: 'I am sure Mr Attallah will retire at an appropriate moment.' Asked if Mr Attallah would remain a director, Mr Asprey said the matter had not been discussed.

I had every reason to believe that these leaks were being orchestrated to make my position untenable and precipitate my exit. In the end they succeeded. The mere thought of remaining much longer in that web of poisonous intrigue made me feel ill. I became determined to shake myself free to avoid any possible lowering of my own standards of behaviour. For this reason I acceeded to their plan and left with my head high and at a time of my choosing. On 29 October 1995 the *Sunday Express* announced I would be stepping down a month later, having eased Mr Dahl into the company and myself out.

> Part of that process has involved an unwinding of [Mr Attallah's] complex and longstanding business relationship with Asprey's chairman, John Asprey . . .
>
> John Asprey was the 49-per-cent minority shareholder in Namara, Mr Attallah's master company, until he resigned as director on 25 April.

Fifty-nine

Back in the literary world, sales of the *Oldie* had come round to making a small profit but the *Literary Review* was once more the subject of speculation in the press as to its chances of survival. By this stage, its accumulated losses over the years were topping two million pounds. This was the extent of my cash losses, though the figure did not take into account some facilities enjoyed by the magazine as a member of the Namara Group. Bron cared deeply about the financial burden I was carrying and came up with the idea of forming a trust where like-minded people could join forces in allocating a yearly donation to the review, simply to spread the load of future losses. He started a campaign in the press to help him achieve this goal. The first fruits of this were reported in the *Daily Express* of 24 July: we were to be spared the misery of watching the magazine wither and die.

Anonymous benefactors, I can reveal, have come to the rescue . . .

'Bron has been buttonholing millionaires and firing off letters in all directions,' says my man with the quill pen in Beak Street. 'Now it has paid off.'

Bron tells me: 'There is no one millionaire . . . But five or six people have given us cash and it should be enough to keep us going for the next two years.'

By October Bron was able to announce 'From the Pulpit' in the *Literary Review* that the Charity Commissioners were considering an application to turn the trust into a charity. 'It is easy,' he wrote, 'to show that the magazine is a non-profit-making organization, and one which has no remote prospect of making a profit.' By November it became public knowledge that two of the world's richest men were among those who had rallied to the cause: John Paul Getty II and Lord Hanson. They had joined a distinguished list that already included Sir Tim Rice and the Duke of Devonshire. 'It may seem a little bizarre,' said Lord Hanson of his pledge of twenty-five thousand pounds, 'but the *Literary Review* is well worth supporting. It is the good-quality work that counts with me.' We were not yet out of the wood, since the cover price of two pounds, with sales of fifteen thousand copies, was never going to cover production costs. The magazine was to stay on in its offices at 'what Mr Waugh calls Château Attallah, in Soho', said *The Times*, but was likely to have to pay for the privilege. Hitherto it had been there free of rates or rent. ' "Naim has been an absolute angel," Mr Waugh said yesterday. "He has never got any advantage from owning the *Literary Review*." '

The appeal to the Charity Commissioners was a non-starter, but I remained the proprietor of the *Literary Review* for many years and sold it only after Bron's untimely death. The purchaser was Christopher Ondaatje in partnership with Nancy Sladek, who had been with the magazine a long time before assuming the editorship eighteen months before Bron died. Mr Ondaatje had made his fortune in Canada and struck me as trying to infiltrate the higher echelons of British society. Unfortunately he turned out to be someone who took a cheese-paring approach and fussed about trifles in a way that I found dispiriting. As I feared, he proved the antithesis of what a good proprietor should be, lacking sympathetic qualities and being hard to get on with. To resort to more mundane phraseology, I would describe him as a most unpleasant character. Eventually Nancy managed to buy him out and has continued happily as sole proprietor, successfully running the magazine to which she has dedicated so much attention, and maintaining its character with high consistency.

While the situation at Asprey during 1995 had occupied a large chunk of my time, mostly spent in fending off media pressure and trying to contain and neutralize the intrigue it was mired in, the year had also presented me with a multitude of other problems. Companies in the Namara Group were feeling the draft as well, and Quartet was no exception. The departure of Stephen Pickles marked in many ways the end of an era. The book trade was undergoing a recession of its own, with wholesalers and retailers demanding increasingly large discounts from publishers. We were also having to live with the new economic margins of the public libraries, whose budgets had originally been cut with savage brutality by the Thatcher government and had remained at the same ludicrous level ever since.

The difficulty at Quartet stemmed from its having placed too great an emphasis on world literature, especially with the expansion of the Encounters series. Admirable as this might have been, it reached the stage where the size of the investment was widely disproportionate to the level of sales. The more praise we received for the series, the more hopeful we became that the day would come when the sales would rise dramatically and justify the losses we had incurred. However, this was wishful thinking from a commercial point of view: time and again in publishing, experience had shown that literary endeavours were unlikely to bolster one's finances. Despite the losses, I never wavered in my belief that the venture would help consolidate Quartet's reputation as an innovative company, willing to take risks to add to the intellectual wealth of the nation. The reality remained, however, that in the year to the end of June 1994 Quartet had made what Christopher Gasson in the *Bookseller* of 10 November called 'a staggering loss of £217,000, on sales of £464,000'.

'If there was ever a publisher that needed Prozac,' commented Mr Gasson, 'it was Quartet, the literary house known for its rarefied translations of European and Middle Eastern literature in the Quartet Encounters series.' He was making a reference to Elizabeth Wurtzel's best-selling memoir, *Prozac Nation: Young and Depressed in America*, which also represented a success for Stella Kane, our publishing director, who acquired the manuscript at the Frankfurt Book Fair in October 1994. Within less than a year it had sold twenty-two thousand copies. Representing a whole new style of publishing that was youth-oriented and popular, it told the story of Elizabeth Wurtzel's progression from the age of ten through breakdowns, suicide attempts and hospitalizations, till given Prozac in combination with other psychoactive drugs – all of which worked sporadically as Elizabeth's spirits rose and fell 'like the lines of a sad ballad', as the blurb described it.

Jeremy Beale, who had been appointed managing director in the spring to succeed Stephen Pickles, made a statement to the *Bookseller* saying:

An imaginative and ambitious publishing policy has obviously been a failure, but what we are trying to do is to continue to be ambitious and to make it work, partly by doing it more effectively and partly by publishing more popular titles. We are now doing more commercial books, which will bring up the profile of the list. We are publishing books which will appeal to a younger generation of readers, like *Prozac Nation* and *Bongwater*. *Bongwater* is a grunge novel by Courtney Love's ex-lover Michael Hornburg. It features a character called Courtney and has proved a huge success among grunge fans.

Another development area is music. In the 1970s we had a very fine jazz list, but that went into decline. We have now started to find substantial books on rock and pop which will be complementary.

Among the titles that chimed with this new concept was a biography by Ben Watson called *Frank Zappa: The Negative Dialectics of Poodle Play*. It was a pioneering title, representing a post-modernist breakdown of the barriers between high and low culture and a growing intellectual interest in rock and pop. *Confusion is Next: The Sonic Youth Story* by Alec Foege, with its account of an influential experimentalist band that had survived through a decade of change and development, came into the same category. Stella was also finding a fresh line in American writing for a young market with Scott Frank's

Tales from Geronimo, a memoir of heroin addiction in the Arizona desert, and a novelization of the life of Elizabeth Bathory, the sixteenth-century Hungarian countess who bathed in the blood of young virgins, *The Blood Countess*. Alongside these were still some literary translations, like Konstantin Paustovsky's *Rainy Dawn* and Ulfat Idilbi's *Sabriya*. Pearl Abraham's classic novel of a young woman growing up as the eldest daughter of a rabbi in a Hasidic New York community, *The Romance Reader*, also belongs to this period.

The measures taken had begun to show some signs of success by the autumn. Overheads had been cut by twelve per cent through a staff reduction from ten to six and moving out of one of the two Goodge Street premises to consolidate activities in the one remaining. Sales were up by eighteen per cent. 'The year has been very important for Quartet,' Jeremy Beale told the *Bookseller*.

> We have published almost all our list very successfully, which has meant that we were very careful about purchasing. The list had to contract, but now that we are finding our feet again we are hoping to expand it.

*

On 4 November 1995 an announcement was made of the purchase of Asprey by Prince Jefri Bolkiah, the brother of the Sultan of Brunei. 'The prince of Brunei,' said the *Wall Street Journal*, 'likes the jewellery from Asprey plc so much that he's buying the company.' The news travelled like wildfire and everybody – with the notable exception of myself – got down to predicting a brave resurgence for the Asprey group. The amount of the purchase price varied slightly as given in different newspaper reports, but the actual figure was two hundred and forty-three million pounds. The agreement sent the Asprey share price soaring by twenty-four per cent from a hundred and ninety-nine pence to two hundred and forty-six pence, and the professional analysts thought Prince Jefri could well have picked up a bargain. They based their judgement on the calculated value of the stock (three hundred and twenty pence a share) and the highly valuable assets represented by the brand names within the group. In making their announcement, Asprey said that Ian Dahl had now become chief executive, having been hired as my heir apparent in the summer; while 'Mr Attallah, who had been with Asprey for twenty-one years and had become chief executive in 1990 [would] leave the company immediately'.

The *Wall Street Journal*'s assessment of events during my years of tenure was generally accurate from an outsider's point of view:

Asprey, whose name is synonymous in Britain with wealth and luxury, did especially well in the ostentatious 1980s, winning a Queen's Award for Export in 1986. In 1990 it embarked on what turned out to be an overambitious expansion plan, snapping up the queen's jewellers Garrard & Co. for £75 million, Watches of Switzerland for £33 million and three smaller jewellery chains across Europe for another £15.3 million. The purchases stretched the management to its limits and all have performed poorly, analysts said.

Asprey's problems stem largely from a slump in demand, say analysts. According to the Economist Intelligence Unit, jewellers in the UK experienced a 9 per cent fall in sales between 1990 and 1993. Moreover, the company relied too much on orders for custom-made items from a few wealthy clients, and were left stranded when these dried up.

The new Russian rich were very keen to buy at the end of 1994, but had soon disappeared. New political pressures in the Middle East, including the first Gulf War, had made that area no longer certain as an easy source of income. These factors illustrated how fickle the market had become and how little it was possible to do about it. The hope of the company was that Mr Dahl would be able to combine Asprey's strong brand name with modern marketing methods. In the opinion of analysts, there was no reason why the company could not succeed again provided it became a 'proper retail company'. They had taken note of a former comment by Mr Dahl that, 'The gospel of St Michael is very much about disciplined management.'

The *International Herald Tribune* remarked that Jefri Bolkiah was finance minister of Brunei and his brother, the country's ruler, was thought to control a fortune of about twenty-four point seven billion pounds. Prince Jefri, said the *Financial Times*, was known for his extravagant lifestyle. He had recently bought the former Playboy Club in Park Lane for fifty-five million pounds, 'to convert into a private residence' at a cost, some said, of a hundred million pounds (though others put it at fifty-five million) and was 'converting another house in Hampstead in north London into his private gymnasium'. The *Sunday Telegraph* reported that the prince planned to use the Asprey group as 'a springboard to amass a global portfolio of luxury brand names', having picked up on the favourable view being taken by the stockmarkets in New York and Milan of such luxury groups as Gucci and the jewellers Bulgari. Before making his bid, he had needed to seek the approval of Buckingham Palace.

John Asprey was quoted in the press as saying: 'My family and I have known Prince Jefri and his family for many years. His ownership of Asprey will enhance the style and status of the group and the Asprey family is delighted to play an important role in its future.' But, it was also pointed out, back in 1980, when Dunhill came so close to acquiring the company, he had vowed he would never lose control of the business, saying, 'I expect it will go on in the family for ever.' The opinion of some unnamed insiders was that the surrender of the business was something that would distress John deeply, one of them saying, 'He will put a brave face on it. But it must hurt him. I just never thought John would do it. To be the one who sells the family business after all this time must be very difficult.' A spokeswoman told the *Guardian* of 4 November that the takeover was the result of 'an off-the-cuff conversation a long time ago'.

According to the *Sunday Times*, negotiations to complete the deal had been far from easy, reaching fever pitch about ten days before the announcement. The main sticking point between the prince's team and Hambro Magan acting for Asprey had been the price. The difficulty in valuing the company lay in the discrepancy between the then depressed value of the shares, because of Asprey's operational difficulties, and the 'strength and potential of the brand names'. In the view of 'Lex' in the *Financial Times*, the group was certainly going to need 'time and substantial investment to regain its lustre', but it did not follow that the prince's acquisition 'was a rich man's folly'. He was 'collecting some of the most glittering brands in the business', while 'the continued involvement of the Asprey family should help to safeguard the special character of the business'.

> Whatever it lacked in execution, the expansion strategy pursued by Mr Naim Attallah, who now steps down as chief executive, was logical. As a stand-alone business, Asprey was unpredictable because it operates only in the realm of the super-rich. Effectively managed, the current portfolio . . . could be a desirable financial asset. Precious jewels like Asprey are at their best in the setting of a larger group, or in patient private hands.

Tim Cooper, talking to the *Daily Telegraph* as managing director of the Bond Street store, attributed Asprey's problem to there having been, for about two hundred years, 'almost a belief that if the merchandise is good enough it will sell', and unfortunately this was no longer the case. The deal was to involve a 'major cash injection' to cancel out much of Asprey's current borrowing of forty million pounds and fund new ventures in Eastern Europe, America and the Far East. Meanwhile, for the headline in the *Daily Express*, I was 'The man who lost his touch of Midas', but Rosemary Carpenter wrote in the article which followed it: 'Don't think for a moment that just because Naim Attallah yesterday stepped down from being chief executive of Asprey we have heard the last of him.'

[That] flamboyant dynamo of a man will already have half a dozen other projects in hand and be set to burst like a shower of firework sparks all over London again . . .

'I'm alert all the time,' he told me when I last interviewed him. 'I don't think money is that important. It gives you comfort and confidence but money has a lot of negative aspects. You're scared to do anything to lose it. If you stop being enterprising you might as well be dead.

'When I get up at 5.30, I spring out of bed. I'm happy to do what I'm doing.'

His appetite for work is legendary. He rarely takes holidays and thinks lying on a beach is a boring waste of time. 'Nobody got where they are without hard work and determination.' . . .

With prescience he said to me: 'If people don't like what I do, that's fine. If people don't like what I do, I say, "Goodbye. Thank you very much." '

Maurice Weaver went along to Asprey for the *Daily Telegraph* to sound out the atmosphere at the Bond Street store following news of the buy-out. The staff had 'long had that insecure feeling familiar to workers everywhere when financial pillars crumble'. 'Porcelain vowels' were hiding 'worries about what changes – and possible redundancies' would come with the new ownership. The female assistants were keeping their composure, 'redolent of a good schooling', while the men had 'the sombre air of displaced corporate executives'. Nadia Homer, the store's public-relations officer, explained: 'These are people who enjoy working in elegant surroundings, where old traditions of craftsmanship are valued.' Mr Weaver found two regular customers to talk to, one a charitable-trust administrator from Hampshire who had just spent forty-eight pounds on bridge accessories and had them gift-wrapped without charge.

'That's the wonderful thing about the place,' he said. 'That and the fact no one suggests I have a nice day. It's very straightforward and, you know, honestly English. Nothing synthetic. Mind you, I have been coming here for years and I think the staff need to sharpen up a bit and I imagine a few people will be sent off on management courses.'

The other customer he spoke to was a doctor from New York, who indicated a window display in a lady couturier's close by.

He said: 'I guess you just have to say it's 1995. Look, I've just seen a window display over there showing two nude men fondling a half-undressed woman. See what I mean? We live in a changing world. Traditions and the old ways pass. You may regret it, but that's the way it is.'

Sixty

The dreaded day of my physical departure from Asprey was emotionally charged. The girls attached to my office on the fourth floor of Garrard's in Regent Street were openly in tears as my hour of leaving the premises for the last time rapidly approached. We exchanged hugs and kisses, pretending to be strong and trying only to remember the happy times spent together in that most congenial and remarkable of atmospheres. Everyone was aware of what had gone on behind the scenes, though the subject was never broached. The girls were far too sensitive and distinguished to intrude into the reasons for this unholy conspiracy. It was beyond them to fathom the betrayal or come to terms with it. The looks of despondency on their innocent faces told the whole story. The moral support they showed me was unique and unstinting. Without it I would have felt forlorn and deserted.

There was no trace of my comrade of twenty years. No doubt he was far too preoccupied with his new alliance with the royals of Brunei; or was he too nervous to face me? In the early 1970s, when I first joined Asprey, the Inland Revenue had valued the company at one point four million pounds, indicating a value of three pounds fifty a share. Over two decades the value of the company, including all the acquisitions, had risen to two hundred and forty-three million pounds. John Asprey had become rich beyond his wildest dreams, but he had paid a price in pride and status that I could never have accepted. But before we look more closely at that, we need to try and define where and why it went wrong.

The simplest and most plausible answer is 'success'. Too much success too soon can often have a devastating effect. People change entirely when good fortune engulfs them and they begin to believe in their own invincibility and the flattery of others. In the time I knew him, John had changed. Even through to the last days, however, there were still moments when we were together that the old spark in our relationship would come alive again. Momentarily the friendship would seem to have survived, as if the disturbing events of the past few months had hardly made a dent in it. But the reality was different. As soon as John was once more surrounded by his personal clique the intrigue resumed. He could not shake off the family trait. Even the saintly Eric, John's father, whom I held in the highest esteem, was pathologically distrustful, though there was never an ounce of malice attached to his watchfulness. His benevolence was its redeeming factor and one accepted it as an endearing side of his character.

In the early days of our association, John and I travelled regularly together and bought stock for the showrooms in Bond Street and for special customers. We were adventurous in our selection of merchandise and our joint efforts over the years laid the foundations for the successes that followed. The turnover of the company grew and our lines of stock increased in diversity. It was bonanza time, when our discerning eyes rarely let us down. As he basked in this new-found prosperity, John became bolder and started to be much more speculative, especially when he was operating on his own without my company. His confidence had soared with the growth of the company, but alongside it an element of erratic behaviour began to creep in. I have already described how he started to buy large quantities of stock which was far out of our range and had very limited market appeal. It became increasingly likely that the company was going to find itself carrying a lot of items it could not dispose of.

Another problem staring us in the face was the way the bulk of our turnover rested in a small number of customers whose purchasing power was immense but who, as often as not, acted on a whim. This meant there was always the underlying fear that sooner or later their custom would vanish in favour of one of our competitors, or that they would simply cease purchasing luxury goods in large quantities. In these circumstances, success could become self-defeating through not being sustained – hence my concern that our period of sensational growth might come to a halt and our overheads, by now substantial, might start to devour the profits of the past few years. Our competitors were more securely placed than ourselves, with large numbers of retail outlets internationally and less reliance on a handful of customers. We were going to remain vulnerable to the vagaries of fortune unless we could continue with our forward thrust and expand our client base. Meanwhile our competitors had the advantage of such brand names as Cartier and Tiffany, acknowledged and recognizable worldwide.

Asprey was synonymous with quality and the Bond Street emporium was without doubt the most luxurious gift shop in the world. Its special commissions had an élitist edge about them and were highly prized. But Asprey's reputation had more to do with its after-sales services and the craftsmanship of its leather goods produced on the premises. These were on a par with, or even better than, those of Hermès. I was in a hurry to broaden our customer base, feeling we had no time to waste while we had the money to implement it and little dreaming that the solidarity that was our strongest weapon would, as a result, give way to division and dissension. Had John remained steadfast and acted with greater responsibility, refusing to be deflected from our resolve, none of the things that subsequently happened would have been remotely conceivable. At the Basle fair, he would determinedly buy a whole range of stock on display without any regard for its value and in total disregard of my instructions as chief executive. No previously formulated budgets, it seemed, were applicable to him, on the grounds of his being majority shareholder. This was a preposterous idea in itself, but unfortunately it found sympathy with a number of board members. Any complaints that I made about it were dismissed as an occupational hazard that I had no choice but to accept.

Besides all this, the recession of the mid 1990s was biting and our major customer, for reasons never explained, reduced his purchases dramatically in the crisis year up to 1995. The repercussions were felt immediately throughout the group. We had no money to order saleable fresh stock and we were struggling to keep our heads above water. The City was meanwhile placing the blame on me for the state in which we found ourselves. The outcry that had become a regular daily feature was something that I had to respond to and try to face down while John was shielded from the onslaught of criticism. My dilemma centred on whether sacrificing my relationship with John was a viable alternative. Should I have fought much harder than I did to restrain him, even if this had meant my dismissal earlier rather than later? Or did I have no choice but to do as I did, and feign solidarity, hoping for the best?

All the clever financial pundits attributed the difficulties being experienced to my expansionist policy. Had they been privy to the true facts, their assessment would certainly have been different. My tenure at Asprey through twenty-one years brought untold wealth to the family. Then the poor results of one year, because of excess stock provision, showed a balance-sheet loss of ten million pounds. It was no more than a blip in the career of a company that had scaled heights it had never envisaged. As the saying goes, 'Après moi le deluge,' and that seems in a peculiar way to sum up the outcome of my achievement. None of my successors – and they were many – managed to make their mark. In fact, to this day, as I write eleven years later, the old Asprey remains a pathetic shadow of its original self, the subject of much more low-key controversy, having lost most of its original assets and squandered millions of pounds on grandiose ideas that proved as risible as they were tragic. The glory days of Asprey sadly came to an end with my departure. To my chagrin, my legacy failed to survive the chaos that followed.

And what of John Asprey? His dreams of forging an alliance with the royal house of Brunei came to nothing. His powers were stripped by Ian Dahl, the man he brought in to replace me. He was side-lined and became isolated in the company that bears his name, and eventually he left of his own volition. His dreams of ruling supreme, egged on by his so-called friends, lay shattered. I imagine that his one consolation in the twilight years of his life must be his wealth, but alongside it is there the nagging feeling that it was perhaps achieved partly at the expense of others?

As for myself, refusing to be put out to grass I found new pastures awaiting me. The chronic sadness of the last few months at Asprey was consigned to oblivion. The stifling atmosphere within the company soon seemed a distant memory. I felt released and invigorated, ready to take on the world again whatever the cost. One role was to be replaced by another that was possibly even more challenging, but this time my destiny was clear and distinct: the freedom to operate without the constraints of others. I set sail to explore fresh seas and my journeys of discovery were to uplift my spirits and lead me intellectually to more fertile landfalls.

Epilogue

When I was a student taking an exam, some of the answers I could not conjure up in the time allocated would spring to mind the minute I left the hall. I felt the same on completion of this volume of memoirs. The enormous task of chronicling that twenty-year period when I was at the height of my success was a daunting undertaking by any standards. I could not have done it without recourse to my archives, but where the subject matter was not in the public domain or covered by the press, I had to rely on memory. It is only now, when I feel free from the congestion of assembled events, incidents and thoughts, that additional happenings involving other people and issues begin to come to my mind. But mostly I am aware of the many names I have failed to mention; those who, at some time during that period, played a part in the success of our ventures, Asprey excluded.

Among the many:

May Ayas	Jan Diakow	Stephen Parker
Georgina Asprey	Louisa Ferdinando	Kristen Rae
Georgina Balfour	Claudia Fitzherbert	Gill Rose
Caroline Bernard	Jon Forss	Zina Sabbagh
Lola Bubbosh	Sophia Fraser	Tony Silcox
Lindy Burleigh	Leonie Frieda	Charlotte Smith
Trudi Butler	Ariel Gottlieb	Stephanie Stewart
Robert Carter	Jane Harker	Pippa Stone
J. J. Caruth	Polly Hayward	Anita Sumner
Tim Cochrane	Debbie Holmes	Roy Trevelion
Susannah Constantine	Caroline Jefford	Sue Trevelyan
Andrew Corbett	Dima Khayyat	Sarah Wasley
Camille Davies	Anna Therese Lowe	John Watson
E. J. Davies	Sarah Lutyens	Daisy Waugh
Judy Davies	Prudence Murdoch	

Anna Therese Lowe, mentioned above, worked at Quartet. She was a bright young thing, rather slim and pretty, with a gift for words. When my wife Maria opened her shop Aphrodisia in Shepherd Market, Anna penned a description of the shop and the philosophy behind its exclusive merchandise that was lyrical in its composition and showed a flair for sensitive and romantic writing. I was very fond of her and rather spoiling. I took her to stay in our house in the Dordogne and she blended with the countryside like a budding flower undulating in a gentle breeze. A year later she had a serious riding accident when she fell from her horse head first. Luckily she recovered, but only after a long period of rest and recuperation.

A loss painful to record was that of Jubby Ingrams. Her death at such an early age from a heroin overdose had a shattering effect, not only on her family but on all those who knew her. She and I were great buddies and I saw her grow from a bubbly girl into womanhood without ever losing the impish zest of youth or the determination to live life to its fullest degree. Always entertaining, she was the soul of any party and had a magical aura that captivated everyone who had the good fortune to know her. Her funeral service was as sombre as it was touching, with everyone close to tears as the various tributes came from people of widely diverse backgrounds. Jubby was loved by all and for them her death was a tragedy of incalculable proportions. The mere mention of her name still brings a lump to the throat.

Another sad break with the past came as the manuscript reached completion at the end of 2006, the event being the death of Tony Lambton at the age of eighty-four in his home at Villa Citenale near Siena. In the mid 1980s I and my wife had stayed there and been given a guest bedroom that he claimed was haunted. It was typical of Tony to try to unnerve his guests while playing the perfect host. The ghosts must have been hibernating when we were there as they never made their presence felt. Any discomfort we experienced was of a less ethereal kind, for the old-fashioned bed had a sinking mattress that made sleep virtually impossible. During the night we were forced to lift it off its base and deposit it on the floor to give it a flat, stable surface on which we tried to get a night's repose. Tony's response was to be rather amused when he realized his guests had spent the night on the floor in preference to making the most of an imposing bed that had no doubt been witness to many an indiscretion, perhaps even of an ecclesiastical nature. The villa had been the family home of Fabio Chigi, who became Pope Alexander VII in 1655 and rebuilt the house for his nephew, Cardinal Flavio Chigi.

Tony's life could have been described as having much the same flavour as that of a dissolute monarch of a bygone age, but in his case his wicked sense of humour redeemed his less orthodox indulgences. There was also a counterbalance in his notorious frugality. Once, when there were several people expected for lunch at Villa Citenale, he suggested we should have as a starter a tomato salad. He then led the way into the gardens where there was a vegetable patch he tended, of which he was very proud. Dozens of tomatoes were flourishing in the Italian sun, but I had only picked a few before he commanded, 'Don't pick any more.' I tried to say there wouldn't be enough for everyone, but he was adamant: 'I can't stand wasting food!' Another time I took my wife and Lambton's live-in companion Claire Ward into Florence for a sumptuous meal. When we got back, Tony was furious at what he called our wasteful pursuit of gluttony. He had his eccentricities, but was a great friend and, to some, a much feared enemy. His departure made our world a duller place.

The world suffered a tragic and irreparable loss with the death of Auberon Waugh five years ago. His memory is for me as sharp today as it ever was. His uniqueness as a person, one who combined wit with a sardonic sense of humour and whose eloquence drew on the music of words, stood supreme and unassailable. The years we worked together were the happiest I can remember. Soho is, as a result of his death, no longer a place where I hanker to be. The void his departure created is too painful to bear, especially for those members of the Academy Club who, as I did, saw him in his element on almost a daily basis. It is only England that can produce the likes of Bron to enrich future generations.

While going through some research, I came across a vignette by Sam Leith, today the literary editor of the *Daily Telegraph*, describing how Bron took him on as the unpaid 'slave' in the *Literary Review* office. Sam had written to a number of newspapers and magazines, looking for openings as a gap-year student. The only reply he received was from Bron, who told him, 'We would love to have you here as long as you are available. Unfortunately we have no money of any description. Would you be prepared to work as a slave for no wages?' Bron, Sam remembered, may have been sharp in print but was an exceptionally nice person. Having arranged to lodge rent-free with relatives in London, he then spent 'eight extremely happy months slaving at the *LR*'.

This involved reading proofs, helping with commissioning, running errands (one important duty was to scamper to Fortnum's to buy fruit cake when the Academy Club ran out), playing bridge in the office on Wednesday afternoons and, when he decided to treat the staff, going out for lunch with Bron.

I returned from one such lunch with my eighteen-year-old brain soused with claret and port and my eyes visibly rotating. The then deputy editor, Lola Bubbosh, directed me to a sofa to sleep it off. Bron himself slept off lunch in his own chair, his snoring rising in crescendo until it became unbearably loud – at which point he'd wake with a start and look round crossly to see who had disturbed him. My eventual leaving present to him was a pillow, stencilled with the magazine's logo.

Bron's genius was to charm big-name writers into contributing for peanuts; but he had to pay Julian Barnes in wine from his own cellar. There was visible pain on his face as he'd lift the telephone with the words: 'All right, Barnes. We're talking some serious claret . . . '

This to my mind is vintage Bron. On an even lighter note, life can be full of surprises, some of them bizarre to say the least. I recall the day when one of my pretty personal assistants, who shall be nameless, burst into my office requesting a private audience. She said she had a favour to ask, and plucked up the courage to blurt it out. 'I would like you to fuck my mother. I'm having problems with her at home and it's all down to her not getting enough sex. She needs a good bonk to lift her spirits.' She then proceeded to describe the physical attributes of her mother as voluptuous, curvaceous and full of Eastern promise. I could hardly believe my ears but managed to retain my composure and explain that, should we embark on such a course, complications were bound to ensue – the temporary relief of her mother's sexual frustrations would most likely end in an even worse situation. It would also be totally inappropriate since it would compromise all three of us. The magical cure she was advocating would inevitably be counter-productive. As an alternative, I suggested that a flirtatious lunch at my office could perhaps ameliorate her mother's present unhappy state and bestow some benefits if not the ultimate relief she was seeking. The compromise worked admirably well and the mother was appreciably transformed after tucking into some good food served with wine and a sexual *frisson* all round. She left the premises with a cheeky swagger in her step.

Another surprise awaited me some six months ago when the last thing I was expecting while boarding a No. 38 bus at Green Park was to get a friendly wave from the woman driver. It was Mary Hemming, the ex-joint managing director of The Women's Press. What a transformation: from a rabid feminist to a paragon of public service!

To conclude I would seek the indulgence of those whose lives have crossed with mine but whom I have failed to acknowledge. It is simply because the years play havoc with one's memory and erase vital data indiscriminately.

'Tout passe, tout casse, tout lasse,' as the French say.

1 March 2007

The worldly hope men set their hearts upon
Turns ashes – or it prospers; and anon,
Like snow upon the desert's dusty face
Lighting a little hour or two – is gone.

from *The Rubáiyát of Omar Khayyám*
translated by Edward Fitzgerald

Index

Heine, Heinrich 295
Hejaiej, Monia 671
Heller, Zoë 439, 506–7
Hellman, Lillian 22, 86, 179
Helvin, Marie 234, 409
Hemingway, Ernest 238, 688
Hemingway, Margaux 238, 285, 299, 373
Hemming, Mary 465, 466, 467, 470, 471, 472, 473, 763
Hennessy, Val 51, 52, 314, 316
Hennigan, Alison 465
Hentoff, Nat 180–1
Hepburn, Audrey 230
Herbert, Auberon 588
Hermès, Émile 639
Herzl, Dr Theodor 62
Herzog, Chaim 195
Heseltine, Annabel 267, 612–13
Hesketh, Colonel Roger 339
Hesketh, Laura 339
Hess, Rudolf 383
Hesse, Herman 513
Hewitt, James Captain 703
Hewkin, Andrew 321
Heyworth, Peter 513
Hichens, Robert 592
Hickey, William 146, 177–8, 254
Hicks, Sophie 111, 145, 270
Hift, Fred 30
Highsmith, Patricia 615–16, 626, 627, 628, 632
Hill, Derek 78, 347–9
Hill, Graham 385
Hillier, Bevis 89
Hillmore, Peter 177, 184, 208, 281, 283, 284, 745
Hindemith, Paul 419
Hindley, Myra 519
Hindley, Nick 671
Hinton, Victoria 651–2
Hirnigel, Elizabeth 619
Hirst, Damien 466

Hirst, Jonathan 135
Hislop, Ian 282, 309, 505, 506
Hitchens, Christopher 60–1, 206, 226, 307
Hitler, Adolf 92, 337, 349, 383, 404, 408, 423, 439, 534, 543, 545, 547, 570, 572, 573, 595, 631, 676
Ho Chi Minh 103, 137
Hobbs, May 22
Hobson, Harold 84
Hockney, David 142
Hodson, Gillian 84
Hoffmann, E. T. A. 513
Hogarth, William 385
Holden, Anthony 184
Holland, Jools 107, 409
Holland, Mary 574
Holland, Stuart 23
Holmes, Debbie 760
Holmes, Richard 22
Holt, Rodney 162
Homer, Nadia 755
Honeycombe, Gordon 458, 544
Hood, Jim 161, 162
Hood, Sir Tom 161
Hood, Stuart 676
Hope, Emma 270
Hordern, Michael 11
Hore-Ruthven, Patrick 667
Hornburg, Michael 751
Horne, Camilla 184
Hoskins, Bob 510
Hourani, Zelfa 532, 590, 667
Houston, Morven 467
Hoving, Walter 230
Howard, Anthony 184, 436
Howard, Elizabeth Jane 623
Howard, Richard 674
Howarth, David 35, 91
Howe, Earl 385
Howe, Irving 41
Howell, Veronica 313
Howorth, Jeny 311

Kleinman, Philip 176, 177
Klijn, Gerard 35
Klossowski, Pierre 591
Knight, Lieutenant-Colonel Claude 579
Knight, Renee 127
Knightley, Philip 86, 566
Koch, Henning 664
Kornilov, Vladimir 671
Kott, Jan 663
Krleža, Miroslav 591
Krüger, Michael 512, 688
Krzowski, Sue 391
Kuenzler-Alamuddin, Ida 103
Kurtz, Irma 250
Kusnetsov, Edward 672

La Valle, Suomi 78, 233, 273
Laai, T. C. 597
Lacroix, Christian 536
Lagerfeld, Karl 640
Lagerkvist, Pär 675
Lahr, John 307
Lamb, Ron 216
Lambrichs, Louise 189
Lambton, Christabel (née McEwen) 193
Lambton, Lord, Antony (Tony) 174,
    191, 192, 193, 197–8, 247, 248, 267,
    288, 295, 367, 413, 451, 456, 581,
    582, 761–2
Lambton, Lady Belinda (Bindy) 193, 247
Lancaster, Emma 232, 245, 277
Land, Pat 391
Landesman, Cosmo 308, 372, 519
Landon, Tim 736
Lane, Cleo 400
Lane, Helen 587, 665
Lanerolle, Ros de 40, 390, 392, 464–72
    passim
Langan, Peter 142, 143
Lantz, Kenneth 673
Lantz, Robert 401
Laski, Marghanita 363
Lasky, Melvin J. 251

Lasson, Sally-Ann 342
Laudan, Stanley 672
Laurence, William 137
Law, Janet (now Parker) 80, 127, 250
Lawrence, Adrian 704
Lawrence, D. H. 295
Lawrence, Gertrude 635
Lawrence of Arabia 150, 688
Lawson, Dominic 606–7
Lawson, Horatia 79
Lawson, Nigella 79, 111, 158, 194,
    197, 202, 203, 214, 215, 229, 238,
    239, 241, 243, 246, 248, 250, 263,
    277, 278, 371, 579
Lean, David 92
Leavy, Stanley W. 673
Le Carré, John 667
Ledger, Catherine 215
Ledrum, Wendy 270
Leduc, Violette 438
Lee, Charles 614, 658
Lee, Jack 326, 327
Lee, Laurie 55
Lee, Ronald 614, 657, 658
Lee-Potter, Lynda 535, 536
Lees-Milne, James 55, 734
LeFanu, Sarah 40, 391, 465, 467
Lehman, Evelyn 297
Leigh, Mike 98, 100
Leigh, Vivien 169, 635–6
Leith, Sam 762–3
Le Marr, Barbara 185
Lemigova, Julia 515–17
Lemsine, Aïcha 665, 669, 670
Lenska, Rula 639
Leonard, Dr Graham 711
LeRoy, Catherine 172
Leslie, Ann 363, 364
Leslie, Tanya 439
Lessing, Doris 125, 128, 358, 373, 665
Lester, Howard 156
Lester, Richard 322
Leveson-Gower, Marcia 212

Levi, Jim 560–1
Levin, Bernard 282, 573
Levy, Paul 148, 228
Lewis, Huey 528–9
Lewis, Peter 103, 668–70
Lewis, Raymond 381, 382
Lewis, Ronald 327
Lewis, Russell 383–4
Leys, Simon 591
Liardet, Frances 664, 671
Lichfield, Leonora 639
Lichfield, Patrick 169
Lindemann, Mariella 487, 644
Lindsay, Hayley 491, 644
Linklater, Andro 573
Linley, Lord 458; and Lady Linley 741
Li Peng, Chairman of the Chinese
    National People's Congress 540
Lipman, Maureen 363
Litchfield, David 375
Little Beaver 147
Littlewood, Joan 240
Litvinoff, Emanuel 189, 592
Liveright, Horace 388
Llewellyn, Dai 267, 342, 344
Llewellyn, Roddy 118
Llewellyn, Vanessa 267
Lloyd Webber, Andrew 401, 487
Lloyd Webber, Julian 510
Lloyd, John 162
Lock, Graham 404
Lockwood, Margaret 11, 97, 510
Lockwood, Victoria 207, 271
Lodoli, Marco 689
Loewe, Michael 621
Logue, Christopher 228
Loncraine, Richard 119
Longfellow, Henry Wadsworth 460
Longford, Elizabeth Pakenham, Lady
    626, 629, 632
Longford, Frank Pakenham, Lord 55,
    243, 475, 649
Lord, Graham 360, 361, 474

Louis XIV 387, 586
Love, Courtney 751
Lovell, Sir Bernard 625, 628
Lowe, Anna Therese 760–1
Lowe, Jacques 167, 168
Lowry, Suzanne 214, 281, 374, 598
Lucan, Lord 371, 385
Luckham, Claire 155, 156
Ludwighauzen, Hélène de 616
Lunghi, Cheri 458
Lustig, Arnošt 190, 591
Lutyens, Sarah 760
Luxembourg, Princess Charlotte of 435
Lymington, Viscountess 247
Lyons, Stuart 13
Lyster, Amanda 248, 253, 267
Lyttelton, Humphrey 405
Lyttleton, Celia 602

Maalouf, Amin 663, 670
Macadam, Alfred 513
McAdam, Jim 556
MacArthur, General 136, 137, 193
McBean, Angus 78, 169–70, 178
MacCabe, Colin 307
MacCarthy, Fiona 448
McConnell, Valery 366
MacCorkindale, Simon 321
McCullin, Donald 57, 59, 60, 61, 161,
    264
McDermid, Val 40
McDonagh, Melanie 520
McDonald, Penny 270
MacDonogh, Giles 439–40
McEwen, John 503
McEwen, Sophie 725
McGonigle, Tom 674
McKay, Peter 117–18, 269, 518, 628–9,
    634, 648, 649, 651
McKenna, Virginia 326
Mackenzie, Suzie 265
Mackie, Philip 24
Mackintosh, Cameron 401

Rowland, Tiny 108, 494, 599
Rowlatt, James 78
Rowse, A. L. 307
Rubinstein, Michael 22, 50, 148, 173, 196, 226
Rudd, Melissa 218
Ruddock, Joan MP 358
Rufus-Isaacs, Jackie 117–18
Rumens, Carol 177, 185–8, 288
Rupert, Anthony Edward (family of) 639
Rushdie, Salman 384, 409, 741
Rushton, Willie 211, 399, 409, 456
Russell, Ross 23, 403
Ruthven, Malise 668
Ryan, Ned 113
Ryan, Susan 248
Ryecart, Marsha 109
Ryecart, Patrick 109, 110, 458, 489
Ryle, John 184

Saatchi, Charles 466
Sabbagh, Zina 590, 760
Sabu 147
Sackville-West, Sophia 252, 277, 278, 285, 393, 394–5, 430
Sackville-West, Victoria 285
Sackville-West, Vita 55, 252
Sadoff, Melissa, Countess Andrassy (Lady Stevens of Ludgate) 317–19
Sagan, Françoise 439
Sage, Lorna 370
Said, Edward 59
Sainsbury, Barry 396
Sainsbury, Paul 396
Sainsbury, Sonamara 395, 396–7, 453, 724
St Albans, Duchess of 89
St Aubin de Terán, Lisa 358
St George, Sarah 271
Sale, Jonathan 461
Salisbury, Harrison E. 137
Salman bin Abdul-Aziz, Prince of Saudi Arabia 94

Salter, Guy 484
Salvoni, Elena 436
Sampson, Anthony 566, 621
Sandford, Roc 248
Sands, Julian 342
Sands, Sarah 521
Sandys, Celia 502
Sandys, Edwina 208
Sandys, Laura 109, 170, 502
Sandys, Lord 110
Sanger, Lon 512
Sangster, Robert 385
Sansom, Polly 454
Sarton, May 40
Sartre, Jean-Paul 428, 439, 689
Saunders, Dame Cicely 358, 625
Saunders, Kate 459–60
Savile, Alethea 590
Savile, Lord 252
Scales, Prunella 436
Scargill, Arthur 214
Schenk, Tamara von 592, 699–701
Scheuffle, M. and Mme K., of Chopard 616
Schiff, Stephen 543
Schirmer, Lothar 590
Schlesinger, Alexandra 463
Schlesinger, Arthur 453, 463
Schlumberger, Mme Pierre 616
Schmidt, Michael 128
Schonburg-Hartensteins, the 644
Schouvaloff, Alexander 106
Schubert, Franz 231
Schultz, George 538; and his wife 539
Schwarzwäller, Wulf 383
Scott, Camilla 267
Scott, Debra 232
Scott, Jock 427, 428, 429
Scott, Minnie 192
Scott, Selina 121, 478
Scriabin, Alexander 254
Seabrook, Jeremy 179
Seagrove, Jenny 645